METROPOLITAN LANDSCAPE ARCHITECTURE

RESEARCH CONTRIBUTIONS AND DRAWINGS

Michiel Pouderoijen

Stephanie Holtappels

Fabiana Toni

Danielle Wijnen

Bastiaan Kwast

Hans Stotijn

Eelco Dekker

Clemens Steenbergen | Wouter Reh

METROPOLITAN LANDSCAPE ARCHITECTURE

URBAN PARKS AND LANDSCAPES

THOTH Publishers Bussum

Contents

Acknowledgements – 6

Foreword – 8

LANDSCAPE AND THE CITY – 14

The landscape architectonic exploration of the city – 15 /

The classic city and the landscape – 17 /

The modern city and the landscape – 20 /

Analysis and design experimentation – 23

1 STAGING URBAN SPACE AS LANDSCAPE – 25

HORTI FARNESIANI, ROME 1556 – 27

An urban balcony – 28 / The Seven Hills – 32 / A keystone in the villa landscape – 36 / The genius loci of the Palatine – 42 / The rise and decline of the Horti – 48 / A manneristic diorama – 52 / The integrazione scenica of time and space – 60

JARDIN DES TUILERIES, PARIS 1664 – 65

The spatial axis – 66 / The Paris Basin and the Seine – 70 / The residential landscape and the city – 74 / The Jardin des Tuileries – 80 / The urban transformation of the spatial axis – 86 / The representation of the horizon – 94

REGENT'S PARK, LONDON 1811 – 105

The landscape scenography of the city – 106 / The landscape of the Thames – 110 / The urban transformation of country life – 114 / The integration of the landscape into the urban pattern – 116 / The Grand Design – 120 / Regent's Park – 124 / New Street – 134 / The capstone on the Thames – 138 / The continuity of city and landscape – 140

THE GARTENREICH OF POTSDAM, BERLIN 1826 – 145

The landscape theatre – 146 / The post-glacial landscape – 150 / The system of axes and avenues – 154 Charlottenhof as a transformation model – 158 / The great water theatre – 164 / The Gartenreich of Potsdam – 172 / The limits of the garden realm – 178

2 THE LANDSCAPE IN THE URBAN NETWORK – 183

CENTRAL PARK, NEW YORK 1857 – 185

Nature in the urban grid – 186 / A rocky peninsula – 190 / Birkenhead Park as model – 194 / The growth of the urban grid – 196 / The public planning process – 202 / The pastoral landscape as guide – 210 / The perfection of the park as urban spatial type – 222

EIXAMPLE, BARCELONA 1859 – 231

The topographic grid – 232 / Coastal plain and river delta – 234 / The topographic map as plan drawing – 238 / The urban building kit – 242 / The interplay between grid and topography – 246 / The landscape architecture of the urban grid – 252

VONDELPARK, AMSTERDAM 1865 – 257

The agricultural landscape as an urban pattern – 258 / The polder landscape – 262 / The urban transformation of the peat polder – 266 / Three phases of the 'free extension' into the peat polder – 270 / The omphalos of the peat polder city   274 / The modulation of the peat parcel – 278 / The polder park – 284

EMERALD NECKLACE, BOSTON 1876 – 289

The landscape as urban framework – 290 / The estuary of the Charles River – 294 / Boston Common as the starting point – 298 / A municipal or a metropolitan park system? – 302 / The water chain – 306 / The parks in the hills – 314 / The tail piece on the ocean, and the parkway – 318 / The first urban park system – 322

3 LANDSCAPE FORM AND URBAN PROGRAMME – 327

STADTPARK, HAMBURG 1902 – 329

Monumentalising the practical landscape – 330 / The Elbe in the North German Plain – 334 / Toward a functional design for urban space – 338 / The debate over functional form – 342 / An urban recreational landscape – 346 / The Volkspark – 350

THE NIDDA VALLEY, FRANKFURT 1925 – 355

A productive urban paradise – 356 / Rhine, Main and Nidda – 360 / Folding the edge of the city inward – 364 / The Siedlung as an architectonic settlement form – 372 / The settlement park – 376

THE GRÜNGÜRTEL, COLOGNE 1925 – 381

Green structure as an artificial landscape form – 382 / The Lower Rhine 384 / The first green belt as a boulevard – 388 / The second green belt and the spatial articulation of the city – 392 / The third green belt and the functional zoning of the green – 396 / A green matrix – 400 / The park form dissolves – 402 / Urban green space as a generic landscape   408

METROPOLITAN LANDSCAPE ARCHITECTURE – 412

The landscape architectonic conquest of the city – 413 / Keys to the design of metropolitan landscape – 422 / Landscape architecture for the metropolis – 428

Indexes (Concepts, Places and Persons) – 432
Literature and Digital Sources – 442
Map and Digital Geographic Data – 444
About the Authors – 446

Acknowledgements

The history of this book really began as far back as the 1980s, under the professorship of Frans Maas and Wim Boer's lectureship in Urban Green. The design exercise 'A city as garden', led by Clemens Steenbergen, sought out the similarities between the design of a city and of a garden. With *Het montagelandschap* (The montage landscape) from 1991, and the study *The Park: Recent trends in Park Design* from 1992, the subject of the urban landscape assumed a place in landscape architectonic research under the professorship of Clemens Steenbergen, with Wouter Reh as senior lecturer.

The opportunity for a systematic study of experimental design in urban landscape architecture presented itself in mid-2005, when Mark Veldman, as a recently graduated architect, prepared a set of analytic maps of Tokyo in its surrounding landscape. This example led to the formulation of a 'Starting Document for Urban Landscapes', in collaboration with Mark Veldman and Eelco Dekker. This document, essentially a set of 'standing orders' for future research, began with a list of twenty metropolises and an indication of the various scales at which these should be drawn. The aspects and layers to be drawn were prescribed and stipulated in a standard legend. Basic technical conditions also prescribed the format of the drawings, the method for drawing, and the map materials to be used.

On the basis of this example, several staff members worked on the research in a similar manner over a period of time. By 2007 this led to a first working document in the form of an atlas with an overview of the chosen sites. Most of the drawings were made by Stephanie Holtappels, who during several years prepared map studies of Berlin, Hamburg, Frankfurt, Cologne, Duisburg and the Randstad in North and South Holland. In addition she also supervised and collected the work of other researchers and draughtsmen, including maps of London drawn by Lonneke van den Elshout, trial drawings of New York and Central Park by Cindy Wouters, and trial drawings of Barcelona and the Park El Miro by Susanne Hoekstra. There were also several drawings used which had already been in existence for some time, from the archives of the department, by Bert van den Heuvel, Arnold Homan, Dirk Peters, Petrouschka Thumann, Tom Voorsluijs and Auke van der Weide.

The advantages and disadvantages of the method followed emerged from this first survey. The advantage was the clear organisation and comparability of the examples; the primary disadvantage was however that many of the drawings were too general in character. It appeared

to be a vain hope to be able to effectively and efficiently investigate all of the cities at one time with one general drawing programme. In addition to the more general need, there also appeared to be a need for a specific approach, focused on what was unique to the place and the moment – something which could only be uncovered by searching and delving more deeply into the place.

Beginning in 2007 supplementary studies were performed with the material which had already been collected as their starting point, focused on bringing specific aspects of the urban landscape in the different cities and metropolises to light. Stephanie Holtappels made more in-depth studies of several German cities. Bastiaan Kwast did a comprehensive study of the Vondelpark in Amsterdam. Eelco Dekker made a study of the land reclamation process in Boston in the 19th century and its relationship with the Boston Park System. Hans Stotijn delved into the confrontation between the 17th century formal system of Paris and its present infrastructure and green structure. Fabiana Toni performed studies into the specific historic character of the urban landscape of Rome and the Horti Farnesiani. She also investigated the interplay between the urban grid in Barcelona and the topography of the landscape present, with the Parque del Clot as the example elaborated. Danielle Wijnen investigated the relation between the layout of Central Park in New York and the increasing density of the urban grid in Manhattan. In addition she prepared an in-depth analysis of the park's composition. In his own unique manner, Bastiaan Kwast made clear spatial models of most of the examples in the book.

The pace of the study picked up in mid-2009. A list with significant examples took shape. These were re-examined critically, subjected to renewed landscape architectonic investigation, and described thematically. Out of this came a whole new arrangement, in which the typological relationships between the chosen examples and the development of the urban landscape as an experimental design process both came into sharper focus, supported by a wealth of accompanying illustrations.

The tireless effort, energy and analytical precision of Michiel Pouderoijen has played a crucial role in this process. He was involved in it since 2005 as a walking encyclopaedia, as coordinator in collecting the basic material and maps, and in drawing and redrawing maps – including all the metropolitan maps. In a later phase he traced, collected and processed all the picture material used. It is in part thanks to his work that the study could be presented to the publisher on time in the form of a preliminary production version, and could be laid before possible sources for funding. He also closely supervised the technical production of the book.

In addition, we owe a debt of thanks to the many persons who made material for the study available to us. The list is too long to include it here in full; we are forced to limit ourselves to but a few names. Our basic materials for the production of the maps was provided by geographical and topographic institutes in The Netherlands, Italy, France, England, Germany, Spain, the United States and Japan.

For the pictures and illustrations we received cooperation from scores of individuals, institutes and agencies. Regine Boy, Bettina Koch, Federica De Sanctis and Axel Schubert of the Stadtvermessungsamt Frankfurt am Main provided the aerial photograph of Frankfurt am Main. Jo Dansie, Auste Mickunaite, Carlos Garcia-Minguillan and Sandra Powlette of the British Library supplied us with the 1677 Ogilby & Morgan map of Moorfields in London, Grimm's 1793 print and the Panoramic View round the Regent's Park. Matthias Forster and Sibylle Michel of the Stiftung Preußische Schlösser und Gärten Berlin-Brandenburg provided the drawings and prints of Potsdam. Susanna Pelle of the Biblioteca Nazionale Centrale Firenze supplied us with two illustrations from the *Trattato d'architettura* by Antonio Filarete. Irene Pintado Casas, of the Real Academia de Bellas Artes de San Fernando, Archivo-Biblioteca, provided Cerdà's 1859 plan. Kirsten Sturm, of the Staatsarchiv Hamburg, sent us maps and drawings of the Parkfriedhof Ohlsdorf and the Stadtpark Hamburg in Winterhude, by Lichtwark, from 1905. François Wyn of the Bibliothèque Nationale de France made the drawing of the Parc des Buttes Chaumont available to us.

Elvira Allocati and David Galley of SCALA Archives looked up the profiles of Central Park for us at the The Metropolitan Museum of Art. Christina Benson and Jonathan Kuhn of the NYC Department of Parks and Recreation Photo Archive provided us with the Greensward Plan for Central Park and the image of the Ocean Parkway. Michael Dosch of the Olmsted National Historic Site supplied us with a large number of drawings and plans by Frederick Law Olmsted. Joseph Garver and Yuhua Li of the Harvard College Library, Harvard Map Collection, sought out and located for us the 1777 Pelham map, the Copeland map of 1872, and the 1876 map by the Park Commissioners. Ronald E. Grim and Catherine T. Wood of the Boston Public Library's Norman B. Leventhal Map Center provided Charles Eliot's 1893 map of the Metropolitan Park System. Martha Neri of the Buffalo Olmsted Parks Conservancy searched for a reproducible version of Olmsted's sketch map of Buffalo for us; the Grosvenor Room of the Buffalo and Erie County Public Library provided us with a reproduction of this map. David Rumsey of the David Rumsey Map Collection supplied the 1844 B.R. Davies map of London and the 1865 map of New York by Egbert Viele.

Henco Huibregtsen, Melle de Winter and Trudy Treling of the TU Delft Library provided us with diverse illustrations from book in the library. Addie Ritter of the TU Delft Library Map Room helped us with a facsimile of the Nolli map. Peter Rothengatter of the Foto Atelier helped us with photographs of material from the Tresor. Marietje Ruijgrok and Paul Suijker of the TU Delft Library Tresor collected various illustrations for us.

Our thanks also to all those within the Chair and Faculty who cooperated in the realisation of this book: Margo van der Helm and the secretariat of the Urbanism Department for outstanding service and for the production of the many texts, Hans Schouten and Addie Ritter for assistance in scanning illustrations and slides, Amber Leeuwenburg, Astrid Roos and the financial administrators for assistance in navigating the international payment system.

And finally, a special word of thanks to Kees van den Hoek of THOTH Publishers, with whom we have built up a relationship of mutual trust over the years. He believed in this project from the outset and gave it his strongest support, enabling an English edition to appear simultaneously with the Dutch. Over the years Wim Platvoet has become familiar with our professional jargon, and once again corrected the text and indices in a critical and professional manner. Donald Mader carefully translated the original Dutch text. Hans Lemmens made the whole into a beautiful book.

A generous contribution from the Netherlands Architecture Fund made the Dutch edition, together with an English edition, financially possible. We are both pleased and thankful that we have had the opportunity to close our university careers at Delft with this wide-ranging study. We hope that with this book we have rendered a service to our colleagues, the profession of landscape architecture, other design disciplines, devotees of architecture and nature, and particularly future students.

Clemens Steenbergen, Wouter Reh

Foreword

Up until now it has been our custom to ask someone from the academic side of our discipline to write a foreword for each of our publications in book form that would place the study in a broader perspective. This practice has produced several particularly fine and penetrating essays. The publication of this book however is an opportunity for us, as the authors, to look back over our university teaching and research, and in our own words set out how we ourselves interpreted and experienced it – not only because this is our last large-scale study, but also because landscape architecture has undergone a process of emancipation and, in March, 2010, becoming a major degree subject of its own in the Faculty of Architecture.

The Trias Architectonica

We see this study of urban landscape architecture as the keystone in what we among ourselves refer to as the *Trias Architectonica*, the three crucial fields of knowledge in landscape architecture, within which the design research at Delft developed. These have been discussed in the following books:

Architecture and Landscape explores the development of the basic set of design instruments for Western landscape architecture. It clarifies the ways in which landscape architectonic design differs from architectonic design, and uncovers the genesis of specific landscape architectonic spatial forms and types, as well as the way in which they developed and were differentiated from one another under the influence of different cultural and topographic conditions. It provides an understanding of the concept of *genius loci* in the terms of a landscape architectonic operations and develops composition analysis and transformation as the basic skills in experimental landscape architectonic design, oriented toward new spatial discoveries.

Sea of Land and the *Polder Atlas of The Netherlands* deal with the formal development of the Dutch lowlands. Unlike *Architecture and Landscape,* in these studies it is not the explicit architectonic treatment of the landscape which is central, but the implicit or latent architectonic form of the man-made, agricultural landscape. The Dutch polders, which arose from a continuous process of settlement, water management and agricultural technology, are a unique chapter in the development of landscape architectonic design. They provide a lesson in the command of the elementary technique of spatial design, in which it is not from aesthetics, but rather from the logic of the design and the rationality of

the realisation which here play the central role, that the beauty of the landscape arises as a matter of course.

Metropolitan Landscape Architecture delves more deeply into the concept of 'urban landscape architecture' and examines the specific instruments employed there. It surveys the most important steps by which the spatial relationship between the city and the landscape has acquired an architectonic form and expression. It reveals what the city does with the landscape, and also what influence the landscape has on the form of the city and the metropolis. The urban landscape is the most complex field in which landscape architecture is applied, where everything comes together: the set of basic instruments employed in the discipline, knowledge of how and why the the forms in the natural and agricultural landscape developed; and a knowledge and understanding of the development of the urban pattern. Although the subject presented itself at about the same time as that of *Architecture and Landscape*, because of its complexity we hesitated for a long time about launching into this study in a systematic manner. In the course of the years numerous studies dealing with various individual parks and cities were accomplished, but systematic design research was still something beyond our reach. One could also say that it was not until now that we acquired the knowledge and insight to investigate and elucidate the subject from our discipline.

As we survey this *Trias Architectonica* in retrospect, we also have to acknowledge that the insight into the various domains and instruments of our discipline being acquired was gradually shaping it. The studies covered a coherent field of study in which the potential and dynamics of landscape architectonic thought are to be found. They indicate both the universal range of the discipline and the specific character of the Dutch landscape and Dutch landscape architecture.

At the same time they point to the necessary unity of the field, which is important not only for its communicative function, but particularly because the design questions in the different problem areas are substantively related to each other. Without the elementary knowledge of landscape architectonic instruments, the agricultural landscape can not be defined as a landscape architectonic problem area or understood as a landscape architectonic task, let alone producing a plan. The knowledge of both the basic set of instruments of landscape architecture and the development of the form of the agricultural landscape is in turn necessary to be able to understand the urban landscape as a landscape architectonic task. Without this interconnected knowledge, the shaping of the urban landscape will be restricted to urban planning, technical, sociological and ecological questions.

Moreover, as a result of the all-encompassing process of urbanisation, the design issues in the various problem areas increasingly overlap with one another. For instance, that the agricultural landscape is now both a productive space and public space means that – just as in the the case of the city – its four-dimensional form must be shaped by professional instruments. In any case, that is not – as it once was – inherent in an all-embracing process of settlement. In a deeper sense the shaping of the landscape, seen as the creation of architectonic quality everywhere – in buildings, in the city and in the landscape alike – is now a design task. The *Trias Architectonica* reveal that the strength of the discipline in this lies precisely in the fact that it speaks one language but nevertheless is able to interpret and process the problem areas, and the design tasks connected with them, in all their breadth and coherence. This language is based on the grammar of landscape architectonic design, which creates spatial quality and produces a spatial dynamic across all levels of scale.

In the development of the discipline, a fundamental distinction must be made among landscape theory, land organisation, landscape planning and landscape architecture. Landscape theory comprises the knowledge of the basic elements and the material structure of the landscape, such as geology, soil science, the water system and planting in relation to use. Land organisation utilises this knowledge in the organisation of the land in the planning and development of the agricultural landscape, taking into account the various other potential functions, and has developed its own system to this end. Landscape planning comprises the systematic development of the landscape in a wide social context, as a strategic process that takes economics, ecology and urbanisation into account. These three branches of the discipline are important building blocks for the content and form of the landscape. It is however the task of landscape architecture to integrate them into a spatial form with an intrinsic coherence, dynamic and eloquence. This can only come about by means of landscape architectonic design. It is for that reason that design is a central object of knowledge and research in landscape architecture. It is for this reason – in addition to the teaching of the sciences mentioned above

as basic material and technical knowledge – that being embedded in a faculty of architecture is of such vital importance for the academic development of the profession. It is only there that landscape architectonic design can be problematised as a core discipline, explored in depth and developed as an independent thought process alongside architecture and urban planning.

Like architecture, landscape architecture needs theoretical development and criticism in order to recognise and interpret the task in a timely fashion, and bring it within the sphere of landscape architectonic design. Critical reflection on the design and form is only possible from an up-to-date knowledge of the instruments peculiar to the field. We have therefore tried to present and specify the essential design instruments as the body of knowledge, the corpus of the discipline. A reinterpretation and reassessment of the grammar and instruments of the discipline is the only way to bring about a new intellectual and artistic flowering which will transcend the diversity of individual expressions.

Stalemate

As long as architecture was the all-embracing discipline within which urban planning and landscape architectonic tasks were dealt with, the grammar of design was central to the discussion. However, modern architecture broke with the classic architectonic model of space and the design instruments and spatial typology connected with it. Form was derived directly from function, without the mediation of historical experience. In part buttressed by social science research and general planning theory, the discipline of urban planning split off from architecture and became an autonomous design field, oriented toward the programmatic and structural relationships of urban components in a larger context.

Landscape architecture separated itself from both garden design and architecture, and initially had no satisfactory answer to the claim made by urban planning that it was the appropriate design discipline for large scale tasks and the spatial structural problems which play a role there. Within town and country planning, landscape architecture was allocated the design of urban green space as its task. In The Netherlands town and country planners began to determine the arrangement of new landscapes, such as the Zuiderzee polders, in which landscape architecture was assigned the role of designing the planting for the farmsteads and along the roads – essentially just 'dressing' the landscape.

After the Second World War, new forms of landscape research developed within the framework of town and country planning, but in general these were not focused on design and formal studies as their central activity. While the relationship between architecture and landscape had been based on a centuries-old tradition of theoretical development and critique from design, that was almost entirely absent from modern landscape architecture. The design itself was hardly ever the subject of study and theoretical reflection. Because of this estrangement, landscape architecture slowly but surely lost its core and ended up in a stalemate. This process had a long history, in which, in retrospect, various important points can be identified. For instance, there was the disintegration of the Arcadian model of the agricultural villa midway through the 19th century, with the separation of the farm as a production unit and the villa as a country seat for the enjoyment of nature. This was symptomatic of what happened in landscape design as a whole, as it was reduced to a question of organising land for agricultural development. Or there was the change that took place in the urban landscape after 1900, from park to 'green space', from the specific to the generic, in which the form was neutralised and generalised into a repeatable pattern. Or there was the shift that took place in the last IJsselmeer polder, Flevoland, after 1950, from a plan based on the organisation of three-dimensional space to a purely functional zoning in which almost nothing had a spatial form any more.

The abandonment of spatial form as a framework for the integration of the different and sometimes contradictory design problems was accompanied by incursions into landscape architecture by neighbouring disciplines such as town and country planning, ecology and the behavioural sciences. Form as a framework for integration was replaced by a planning matrix, fostered by standards and vision of landscape as a 'process' derived from systems theory. This development is often seen within the discipline as a 'scientificalization' of landscape architecture, but that is in fact inaccurate. In any case, the deeper understanding here was being sought in adjacent disciplines, rather than in the clarification and testing of landscape architectonic design itself. The rise of Landscape Urbanism appeared to mark a new step in this process, in which landscape architecture, as a designing discipline, threatened to disappear from the stage altogether, and the urban landscape become a purely programmatic and procedural assignment, based on systems theory and landscape-ecological insights. On the other hand, it was our conviction that what was necessary was precisely subjecting landscape

architectonic design itself, and the genesis of the form, to scientific rigour, and that this was the essence of the scientific development of the field.

Back to the source

To rediscover the landscape architectonic grammar which would be capable of creating unity in the complex and fragmented problem fields and approaches, we had to return to the sources of the discipline's practice. Much earlier in the development of the discipline it had become clear that these lay in the classic architectonic models of the garden, the city and the landscape. The body of knowledge in landscape architecture can be renewed time and again as necessary by intensively interrogating these classic models with regard to their significance today, rediscovering the design instruments used, and opening them up for discussion in the light of current design challenges.

This landscape architectonic design research must not be confused with historical research. Although they can both enrich and enhance our understanding, each has its own content and significance. As a derivative of art history, the history of the landscape and of landscape architecture primarily comprises critical source verification, iconographic investigation and perception research. These focus on historical description, style development and periodisation, as reflected in chronological surveys and in the interpretation of culture-historical connections. On the other hand, landscape architectonic design research is oriented toward exposing and developing the basic concepts, instruments, typologies and strategies of landscape architecture.

From the very beginning we were occupied with this search for the core of the discipline and the instruments and design logic peculiar to landscape architecture. In 'the workshop in Delft' (as Sébastien Marot characterised our working collective) we sought to liberate the corpus of landscape architectural terminology from art-historical classifications and the jargon of urban planning, which obstructed the perspective on the specific quality of landscape architectonic design, with its unique combination of nature, technology and art. In order to accomplish our objective, it was necessary to have the architectonic form of the landscape re-emerge as the central object of scientific research in landscape architecture.

Everything in the visible world has a form; no substance whatever can exist without form. The landscape has a form from nature, yet uncultivated, not yet situated in human patterns of thought and cultural experience. In contrast to what many people apparently think, form is not a hobby of designers and aestheticians, but an essential part of the world as we live in it and conceive it. It is not only an evolutionary and technical concept, but also a central concept in our communication and the transmission of our culture. It is the way in which we understand space. Form reflects the balance and the patterns behind a spatial constellation. From the form of the landscape we read how it came into existence and 'how it works', and whether we find that agreeable or not. The form of the landscape is therefore a cultural heritage, which our forefathers have passed on to us. It is not the physical space as such, not the nature, but the *construct*, the creative meaning and potential of something that came into being through the efforts of man in cooperation with nature, as a product of both the hand and mind, that determines the quality of a landscape. Conceptual development and formal development have created this, as it were; the formal typology reflects the wealth that arises from this.

In our view, the heart of landscape architectonic research is therefore the analysis of the architectonic form, or in other terms, composition analysis. The design process includes not only a critical investigation of the programme, or just the collection of relevant data regarding the place; knowledge of design history and of the specific instruments of the field also play a role. In the process of uncovering the composition and the instruments used in it, the 'inner nature' of the landscape architectonic design, in which its expressiveness is implicit, is opened up for discussion and becomes subject to critique.

Drawing as a critical research instrument

The architectonic form of the design is, in turn, inherent in the design sketches and the images and concepts they call up. It appears to be a real art to extract that form through the process of once again drawing them, and not to bury it with the document itself. The meticulousness that is necessary to accomplish this develops only gradually. We have invested a great amount in research by drawing. By sketching to analyse and interpret interesting designs, and in that process repeatedly preparing new drawings in order to single out important aspects of them, we gradually came nearer to the concept of landscape architectonic form and the creative moment as the essence of design. Using this procedure, many of the designs that have played a crucial role in the development of the discipline were laid on the dissecting table and, as it were, redesigned as a model with contemporary significance.

The drawing and the map are critical research instruments because they are – unlike the words and concepts that are derived from other disciplines – completely native to landscape architecture and three-dimensional design. If something can not be drawn, in the deepest

sense it can not be accounted as landscape architectonic design. To draw something again, critically, is therefore the only way to analyse an existing design as a composition and make it accessible for design criticism. An important advantage of this strict limitation of the research methodology is that stylistic investigations, behavioural research, landscape appreciation, or any other classification whatsoever, can have no influence or get any hold on it. It is about the technique and the content of the landscape architectonic design, and nothing else.

In this form of research, the combination of research and teaching is particularly productive. In their projects the students can experiment to their heart's content with their most personal intuitions and convictions. As a result, the interaction between student and instructor can lead to efficient and sometimes profound design research. The students' curiosity and thirst for experimentation often produces surprising new perspectives. An important motivation for our work was the quest for answers to the questions posed by our students. What precisely is landscape architecture? What is designing, and how is it done? What is landscape architectonic research? The students' contribution to university level research outwardly appears small, but without their enthusiasm and willingness to work out seemingly unimportant details, and without their intelligence and inspiration, these studies would never have come into being.

The final balance

The answers to new problems were always found in the reinterpretation and transformation of the set of landscape architectonic design instruments. A good example of this is the *Horti Farnesiani*, described in this book, where a range of instruments which had long existed were transformed to explore the new questions of the growing city and bring them within the scope of the discipline. Transformation is a creative process that can be comprehended theoretically in an educational project or research project and realised in a controlled fashion.

Initially the pillars of our educational programme were two design exercises in which the individual position of a dwelling in the landscape and the landscape in the city, respectively, were central. The method that we developed with it anticipated and guided the research at the chair in landscape architecture. The students selected a favourite example that they analysed, then projected the design scheme from it, along with the composition elements, onto a new situation, in doing so transforming it step by step. It was with the aid of this that the new reality of the landscape and the nature of the the task had to be explored, understood and worked out.

The most important role of the university workplace lay in the identification, critical selection and experimental application of the components of the profession's body of knowledge in various research domains. The scientific research had the task of initiating, interpreting and clarifying this process, so that it might be of service in the development of the profession. Moreover, it is here that a further social significance was potentially to be found, because the set of instruments applied and the experimental models are transparent. This promotes probing communication regarding the quality of the design and form, rather than everything remaining a question of taste.

The experimental landscape architectonic design research, with material in the *Trias Architectonica* as its starting point, was elaborated in the masters programme of the major in landscape architecture at Delft, and acquired a further theoretical basis in the doctoral research, including that of six staff members. By discovering and working out their own subject, the researchers, with the cooperation of the students, develop new scientific pillars, which lead to a clearer view with greater coherence and depth, broaden the relation with social questions, and whet the curiosity of future researchers.

A primary aim of the new masters programme and the doctoral research is to further investigate the current interaction between architecture and landscape, and particularly what influence the concept of landscape has on contemporary architecture, in the knowledge that this provides a point of departure for a new design culture and for productive collaboration within the department, and beyond it. Contemporary architecture is deeply influenced by the landscape as both a spatial reference and a temporospatial concept. Many innovative architectonic designs explore the concept of landscape in its significance for architectonic composition. The development of new technologies for drawing and representation with advanced software also plays a role in this.

The significance of landscape architectonic design for the current problematic of the Dutch landscape is being further explored and worked out in the masters programme and doctoral research. Designs that are aimed at conservation of the landscape can be an option for only a small part of the agricultural landscape. The vast majority will have to be rearranged and adapted to new requirements, simply because the landscape is a vital and dynamic system, the quality of which can only be maintained by continual redesign. The renewal of the water system as a support for the structure of the landscape plays a large role in this. The question is how it can be transformed, not only technically and functionally, but also architectonically, and moreover can be integrated with the urban landscape.

A second focus in the new masters programme in landscape architecture and the doctoral research is on tracing, understanding and manipulating the generative processes, structures and formal elements that define the urban landscape. Here too the landscape is increasingly seen as a temporospatial frame of reference; more and more, the city changes, transforms and grows like a landscape. At the same time landscape architecture is also playing an ever more important role in the conceptualisation of public space. The generic city needs the landscape, if only to reflect itself and keep in touch with the source from which it sprang.

The publication of the research can be seen as an important test. A critical relationship with a publisher can lead to a quality product, which not only facilitates education at the school but also at other institutions, and reaches as wide an audience as possible. Publishing in book form means that the results will remain accessible on a lasting basis, and moreover is good for the international reputation of the field and the educational programme.

For exposure to practice, externally financed research (i.e., with 'third stream' funding, in which the chair carries out research assignments for parties outside the school) is of great importance, providing that this is done selectively. The question from practice must be of a fundamental nature, and there must be sufficient space and freedom to be able to approach the problem critically. In this way, it is possible to test both the questions which are current in practice and the applicability of the scientific knowledge which has been built up.

From the perspective of the university, a chair in landscape architecture with its own position and line of thought, and a specific form of research and teaching, is indispensable for a broadly based, well-functioning architecture school. The students have more options, and the instructors can also learn from one another in collaborations based on specific professional knowledge. In this way, the school has more to offer than merely the sum of its parts.

Ultimately, the most important seedbed for future creativity lies in the development of the unique qualities of the staff and the students. Like the plants in a garden and in the landscape, everyone must be able to grow in his or her role and develop, in order to flourish. It is therefore a particular privilege to be able to initiate others into the discipline of landscape architectonic design. You gradually also come to better understand the way in which, in the past, your own teachers handed down the inspiration of the profession to you.

Virgil tells how Aeneas, after being instructed regarding the future
Rome, leaves the underworld through the Gate of Imagination. That is
the poet's way of telling us that although knowledge is indispensable,
it is not enough by itself, and must be brought to life by imagination.
Thus: the knowledge of form opens the Gate of Imagination of design.
We hope that with this line of thought we have laid the foundation
for a new experimental cycle, a new round in university-level research
and design, which will open up a wonderful future for landscape
architecture.

Clemens Steenbergen, Wouter Reh

LANDSCAPE AND THE CITY

The landscape architectonic exploration of the city
The relationship between city and landscape
The urban landscape as a design field

The classic city and the landscape
Sforzinda
The Dutch ideal city

The modern city and the landscape
Une Cité Industrielle
Broadacre City

Analysis and design experimentation

The relationship between the city and landscape has always had a dynamic quality. This has been expressed in the constant appearance of new patterns. Over the course of the centuries, the classic, autonomous city was transformed into an open system without architectonic form, characterised by a chaotic relation between urban fragments and fragments of landscape.

Throughout the course of this process, the anchorage that the urban system had in the topography of the landscape has always been a task for experimental design. As a consequence, the way in which the form of the landscape resonates in the contemporary metropolis increasingly takes on the character of a landscape architectonic question.

The landscape architectonic exploration of the city

The city was discovered as a landscape architectonic question when the classic set of design instruments employed by landscape architecture were confronted with the dynamics of the growing city. The basic set of instruments was in principle complete, but could be transformed to solve urban problems. As a part of this process experiments were made involving shifts in meaning, changes in scale, additions and combinations, resulting in the creation of new spatial constructions.

The relationship between the landscape and the city altered with cultural and social developments which expressed themselves in new spatial patterns. All around the world, in the last century the more or less autonomous, self-contained city form, the composition of which was supported by the solidity of the urban ground plan and its anchorage in the topography of the landscape, changed to become an open, sometimes chaotic relation between urban fragments and fragments of the former countryside. As a consequence, the manner in which the landscape echoed in the form of the contemporary metropolis took on ever greater significance as a landscape architectonic question.

The examples selected for this book reveal the landscape architectonic exploration and conquest of the city to have been a continuing design process. Although they reflect the different places and diverse circumstances from which they arose, the cases discussed can be analysed and compared with one another. They demonstrate how, in the ever-changing interplay between the city and the landscape, landscape architecture constantly produced new design instruments and spatial forms and how these could be developed further.

The relationship between city and landscape

No city without a landscape, no landscape without the city. The two suppose each other, and are necessary to make the human habitat complete. Sébastien Marot wrote the following with respect to this, on the occasion of an exhibition regarding the importance of an inventive image of the landscape in the face of the challenge of the growing city: "In order to grasp the extent to which the idea of this balance between town and country has become ingrained in our imagination, and the degree of it remoteness from the reality of the present time, let us consider two of the most celebrated 'landscapes' by Nicolas Poussin, i.e., those he painted in Rome in 1648 to illustrate the obsequies of the Athenian general Phocion and the gathering-up of his ashes by his widow. The two towns of Athens and Megara are shown in the

background of the paintings, viewed from the open space of their respective rural outskirts. In these two ideal paintings, the overall composition of each of which matches the other point by point, the *harmonious balance* between the town and the setting of its rustic environs is reinforced. A road winding its way between the reliefs and the various elements of these environs links in each case the city and the countryside which the façades of the city's temples and monuments seem to be contemplating. The distinction between the two worlds is clear-cut and nevertheless progressive. While the thronged world of the town, dominated by the accumulation of architectural structures, stands out from the open world of the surrounding countryside, which derives its definition more from its soil and vegetation, the vestiges of old foundations show through in this rural setting, and the foliage spreads out among the urban buildings. The balance between the two worlds is enhanced still further by the nature of the site, which seems to assign each of them its place (the heights in the case of the town) and the boundary between them (a sheet of water). While putting them both into perspective, the human activities are dispersed naturally in this palette of the countryside, thus revealing, in harmony with the time of day, the various facets of the symbiosis of the two worlds. What differentiates the two paintings from this standpoint is perhaps only the moment which separates the end of the day from the beginning of the evening… In mutual contemplation, town and country, architecture and nature are captured here at the exact moment at which they *blend together*."

Here the city and the landscape are in a symbiotic relationship that perhaps never existed, except in the imagination of artists and architects. Nevertheless, the spatial relationship with the landscape has always played an important role, both conceptually and practically, in the design of the city, not only in the classic city but also in today's metropolis. This relationship stands or falls with its Arcadian inspiration, which when seeking new, intermediate forms wishes to place the concept of urbanality against the background of the landscape and nature. How is this changing relation between city and landscape conceived and designed in different constellations?

The urban landscape as a design field

The term urban landscape is of rather recent coinage and is used in various ways, for instance by photographers as a picture, by ecologists as a system, and by geographers as a territory. Seen from the perspective of landscape architecture, the term refers to the spatial relationship between two different systems, namely on one hand that of nature and the agricultural landscape each with its own topography,

Nicolas Poussin, landscape, with the funeral of Phocion in the foreground and the city of Athens in the background (Oakly Park, Earl of Plymouth Coll., © 2010, Photo Scala, Florence)

Nicolas Poussin, landscape, with the gathering of the ashes of Phocion by his widow in the foreground and the city of Megara in the background (Prescott, Earl of Derby Coll., © 2010, Photo Scala, Florence)

spatial form and visual structure, over against the spatial system of the city, which in turn has its own structure and morphology. Their interaction, and points where they penetrate each other, lead to various intermediate spatial forms.

The urban landscape can be characterised as a system that is constantly being transformed under the influence of three generative formal systems that are related to geogenesis, settlement and, finally, with the urbanisation of space in the landscape. Through the spatial distribution of rock, sand, clay and soil, nature produces an organic landscape form. Human settlement in nature, and bringing the land into cultivation creates a technical landscape form, oriented toward the production of food. Urbanisation weaves a functional pattern across the landscape, comprised of cooperative urban elements, connected by a transportation network. The dynamic patterns that arise from this are roughly to be designated as the natural landscape, the man-made landscape and the urban system. They are components inherent in the creation of the urban landscape.

As a consequence of these layers in the the urban landscape there are also three different definitions of place which can be distinguished, which each have their own significance. The *topos* is the place in the natural landscape, the *locus* is the place in the matrix of the cultivated landscape, and the *nodus* is the place in the topology of the urban system. Moreover, the different formal systems contain implicit or latent visual and formal elements and explicit architectonic definitions in the form of lines, points and planes, spaces and sightlines. These characteristics are the points of departure for landscape architectonic operations.

In this study we will only speak of an urban landscape if the interplay between the city and the landscape is conceived in landscape architectonic terms and has been given a spatial form. For convenience sake the way in which this happens can be called 'urban landscape architecture', as a way of indicating a field of endeavour and application with its own concepts, design instruments, typologies and strategies.

The classic city and the landscape

The perception of the city as a spatial entity was traditionally determined in part by the way in which it distinguished itself from its surroundings as an ideal, a construction of the human spirit. That presupposed a different world outside the city, onto which this ideal image could be projected. The classic city was in principle a clearly defined space in an undefined and unbounded natural landscape. As a human construction it was distinguished from nature and at the same time conceptually included within it. That is expressed in the classic urban typology in various ways. Aristotle defined the *polis* or city as a civil community, regulated by laws and conventions. The city was a *Res Publica*, or 'public thing', which created and perpetuated social and cultural goals and associations. These were reflected spatially in the public domain of the city, culminating in the *agora*, the central site for gatherings and administration. In the Roman city, the *urbs*, there was a change in the polar relation between the city and nature, which coincided with the systematic development of the natural landscape around the city. It is true that as an autonomous symbol the *urbs* stood outside and above the landscape, but it was at the same time the centre from which the land surrounding it was settled.

During the Renaissance the relation between the city and its environs changed again, not so much in a technical as in a conceptual sense. For the first time this relation was problematised in architecture. This can hardly be illustrated better than by two design studies which were never realised but nonetheless had far-reaching influence. In the case of Sforzinda the issue was the architectonic relation with the natural landscape, in the case of the ideal city conceived by Stevin, with the agricultural landscape.

Sforzinda
Around 1464, at the beginning of the Italian Renaissance, the architectural theoretician Antonio di Pietro Averlino (1400-1469), better known as Antonio Filarete (which in Greek means 'friend of virtue') completed his *Trattato di architettura*, an standard work in 25 books. The most famous part of this treatise is the second book, with his design for Sforzinda, named after Francesco Sforza, the Duke of Milan. In this design Filarete investigated the architectonic conditions for coherence between the city and the landscape.

In his tract *De Architectura* Vitruvius (± 85-20 BCE) had earlier used a square circumscribed by a circle to represent the human figure as the ideal basic form with harmonious proportions. Sforzinda is also

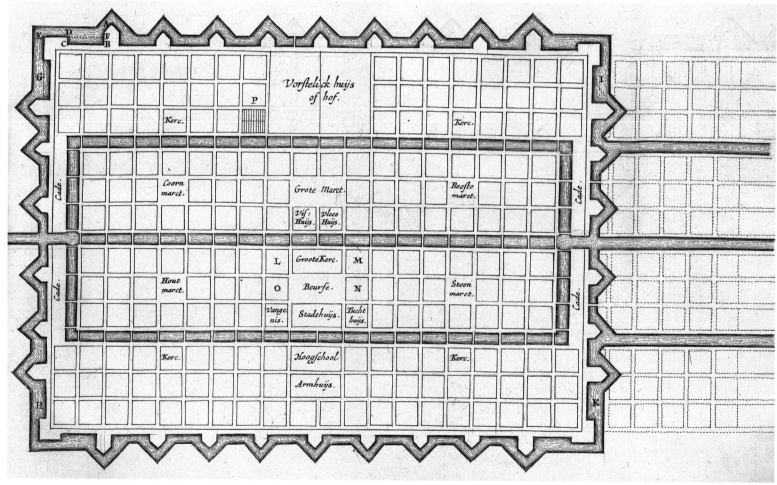

Antonio Filarete: model of the city of Sforzinda as a geometric figure in a landscape drawn in perspective (from Filarete, Antonio, *Trattato d'architettura, XV century.* Biblioteca Nazionale Centrale Firenze, Fondo Nazionale II.I.140, f. 11v)

Simon Stevin: model of an ideal city (from *Materiae politicae; burgherlicke stoffen; vervanghende ghedachtenissen der oeffeninghen des Doorluchtichsten Prince Maurits van Orangie, etc.; (...); en uyt sijn naegelate hantschriften by een gestelt door sijn soon Hendrick Stevin, (...).* Leyden 1649. Library, TU Delft, Tresor, TR 527121) constructed from squares in a circle. Following Vitruvius, Filarete's city reflects the human figure and ratio as an ideal form, which in turn reflect the perfect image of the Creator. The form of the city thereby takes on a cosmographic significance, as a geometric diagram in which the hidden order in nature is made visible by architecture.

Sforzinda was projected in a river valley surrounded by hills, drawn in perspective. Because the shape of the city in the drawing was two-dimensional, and not distorted according to the laws of perspective, it took on the character of a 'stamp' or *templum* in the landscape. The position of the city was determined by the meandering form of the Inda River, which suggests the continuance of the landscape outside the illustration. In the next bend of the river Filarete drew yet another circle, formed from trees, a place where the material and plastic representation of nature resided. This was conceived as idealised nature, a counterpoise to the subjugation and colonisation of nature by the city; here, set over against the abstraction and rationality of the city, the sensory enjoyment of nature played the primary role, as in a mythic Olympus. The two propinquent circles in Filarete's drawing represent the domain of the city in the landscape as two complementary spheres, in which the contest between the architectonic order of the city and the expressive representation of nature could be played out. This indicated that the relationship between the city and the landscape was the essential landscape architectonic point of departure.

The Dutch ideal city

In *(Onderscheyt) Vande Oirdening der Steden*, written about 1600 and included in *Materiae Politicae*, the 1649 collection of his works published posthumously by his son Hendrik, Simon Stevin (1548-1620) developed the earliest Dutch theory on urban planning. His model city was in part based on a rational structure of the system of government, and in a deeper sense on the order of the world and the cosmos. In it Stevin elaborated on the fortifications for the ideal Renaissance city proposed by the Venetian historian and surveyor Daniele Barbaro (1514-1570), and on other Italian theoreticians, who were important for the development of architecture in the Netherlands. He reconciled the demands of military engineering, which had meanwhile utterly changed, with those of commerce, administration and the polder system. In Stevin's ideal city the ground plan was not star-shaped but rectangular, so that it could be efficiently embedded in the polder parcellation of the low lands.

He designed a functional urban pattern with straight streets and canals, subterranean arched sewers and comfortably canopied pavements, in which every citizen lived close to a market. The urban grid was entirely in keeping with the texture of the reclamation of land reclamation in the north of the province of Holland. The topography and hydraulic engineering in the polder land was reflected in the composition through a system of canals, in which a harbour and quays were also included. Just as was the case for a lake-bed reclamation, a ring canal on the outside formed the boundary with the surrounding open land. The canals were part of the water management system for the adjacent polders, and further connected the city with its environs. There is also, as in the 17th century North Holland lake-bed polder, a main axis, created by a chain of city-centre functions, and a transverse axis, in the form of a water axis. In the city plan one can even recognise polder parcels drawn from the main axis, as the basis for the urban parcellation into blocks for building.

In his model Stevin transformed the parcellation of the agricultural landscape into an urban ground plan, while retaining the architectonic characteristics of the Renaissance model of the 'ideal city'. Conceptually, in this design he achieves a complete synthesis of the urban ground plan and the landscape pattern, of urban geometry and polder geometry.

The modern city and the landscape

The antithesis of the idea of a city with a delimited territory is the concept of a metropolis. As a compound of *metron* (a standard, full measure, limit or metrum) and *polis*, the word *metropolis* is a designation for a city which in magnitude has reached fullness or its limit, an all-encompassing, normative city. In this sense, the Greeks were already calling the mother city from which new colonies were founded a metropolis. New lands were discovered, explored and colonised from the metropolis, to become urban territory.

The modern city is not demarcated from its environs, but in principle is an expanding network, positioned in a limitless urban force field. This field has fundamentally nullified the distinction between city and non-city, thus creating an important condition for the rise of the modern metropolis and the metropolitan landscape. Not only does the growing city literally overrun the surrounding landscape; in a deeper sense the functioning of the whole man-made landscape and nature itself are subject to the urban force field and the organisation of the urban system. That in turn places the spatial relationship between the city and the landscape under stress. What this implies was succinctly pictured by two studies, which mark the extremes of a wide range of theoretical possibilities. The design of *Une Cité Industrielle* postulated a large-scale, planned zoning of the urban landscape. In contrast, as a model *Broadacre City* was based on a free, individual settlement of the landscape, proceeding from the house as the elementary building block of the city.

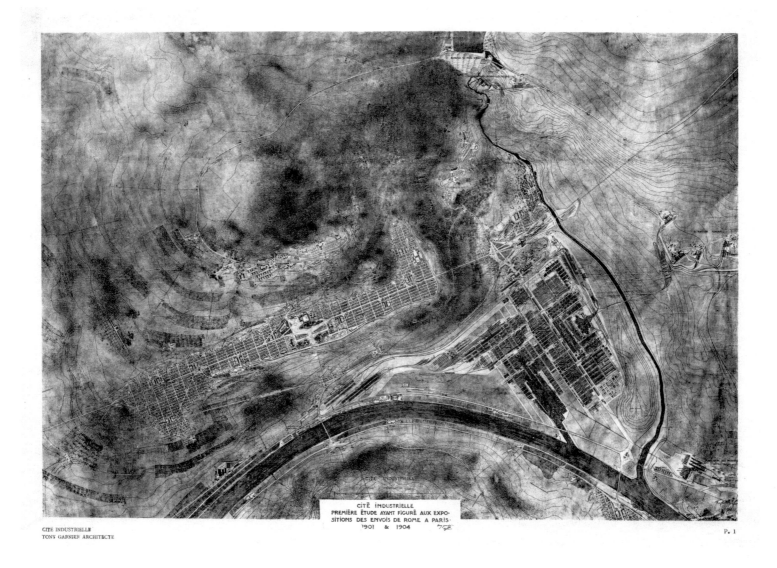

Tony Garnier: Une Cité Industrielle (from Tony Garnier, *Une cité industrielle; étude pour la construction des villes*. Vol. 1. Paris 1917. Library, TU Delft, Trésor TRG 9411 T 04)

Une Cité Industrielle

In 1918 Tony Garnier (1869-1948), the municipal architect of Lyon, in a portfolio of more than 160 drawings published a model of a new industrial city, based on the rationalised utopia of state socialism. The design is in the Beaux-Arts tradition, but informal in nature. It was strongly influenced by the thought of Emile Zola, and is at the same time visionary and extremely detailed in the organisation and rendering of the different parts of the city.

Garnier drew a city of about 35,000 residents, lying in a landscape of rolling hills in the south-east of France. The city was situated on a plateau, with a lake to the north and a river to the south. The 'old town' lay near the station for the convenience of tourists and travellers. The 'origin' of the city in the landscape lay higher up in a side valley, with a dam and a hydroelectric generating station. The urban system was constructed from various autonomous, rationally organised zones, such as a residential area, an industrial area, a public area and an agricultural area, each of which was given its own place in the landscape. Functional considerations were determinative for their position in the topography. The different zones, linked by a system of roads and pedestrian paths, had no formal boundaries and were simple to expand. The industrial area lay by the river and the harbour dug from it, close to the natural sources of energy and transportation facilities. The residential area, composed of a grid with single-family dwellings, was fitted into the topography on a plateau along the river, to the north-west of the industrial area. Here the dwellings had the optimal benefit from the sun and wind, and had no problems with air pollution. Out beyond that lay the agricultural land. Between them the original physical-geographic structure of the area was left undeveloped, as a counterpoise and open space. Garnier dramatised this unlimited, open landscape architectonically through a gigantic, tree-lined boulevard with a retaining wall on the boundary between the plateau and the river valley. Though the city was divided into different zones, this monumental balcony, also accessible for pedestrian traffic, united it into one visual spectacle.

Broadacre City

Frank Lloyd Wright (1867-1959) drew up his vision of the American city of the future for an exhibition in New York in 1934, based on an idea that he had previously developed in his 1932 book *The Disappearing City*. Wright's idea was in almost every respect the opposite of Garnier's industrial city and the idea of the rationally planned city further developed by Le Corbusier in 1922 in *La Ville Contemporaine*, but it was no less radical. His was not a design for a large-scale, zoned urban structure based on collective public transit, but an urban settlement landscape, a completely decentralised 'republican colony' for motorised man.

Broadacre City took the suburban concept as its starting point, analogous to the earlier garden city, as designed by Frederick Law Olmsted and Ebenezer Howard. But in Wright's design the suburb was transformed from a consuming to a generative urban landscape system. With this, it was a revolutionary concept in both a social-political sense and in his perspective on town and country planning.

The model was based on a freely extendable grid of 'acres', small properties of about 0.4 hectare, to be distributed to every American family from land held by the federal government, to build the ideal American city from the ground up. Each parcel offered space for a free-standing dwelling with a yard, garden, field for crops, pasture and woods. As each family would choose different combinations of these elements, this would create an infinite variety of spatial forms. Every four square miles of the grid made up a complete community, with all the accompanying facilities. Frank Lloyd Wright saw his plan as a way to restore the original relation between living and landscape, between house and place. He also saw it as a way to activate spatial relations and interactions between the urban pattern and the landscape, in a manner that is not possible in the density of the high-rise city or in the isolation of rural living. In the transitions between interior and exterior, private and public, built-up and undeveloped, the suburban landscape could be worked out into the spatial diversity of a metropolis.

In principle, the models provided by Filarete, Stevin, Garnier and Wright span the whole range of the classic and contemporary city, and reveal the points of application for landscape architectonic design. Filarete's and Stevin's models mark the classic architectonic starting point of the urban landscape, and Garnier's and Wright's models mark the transition to the metropolitan landscape. But, on further examination, they display essential similarities. The spatial zoning of the urban landscape that was worked out in Garnier's plan was was already present in Sforzinda in a rudimentary form, just as the suburban fusion of city and landscape in Wright's design is already recognisable in Stevin's ideal polder city. All things considered, the seeds of the most important spatial characteristics of the metropolitan landscape, such as boundlessness, genericity and recursiveness, were already present in the first landscape architectonic models of the city. In that sense, the urban landscape had a metropolitan dimension from the very beginning.

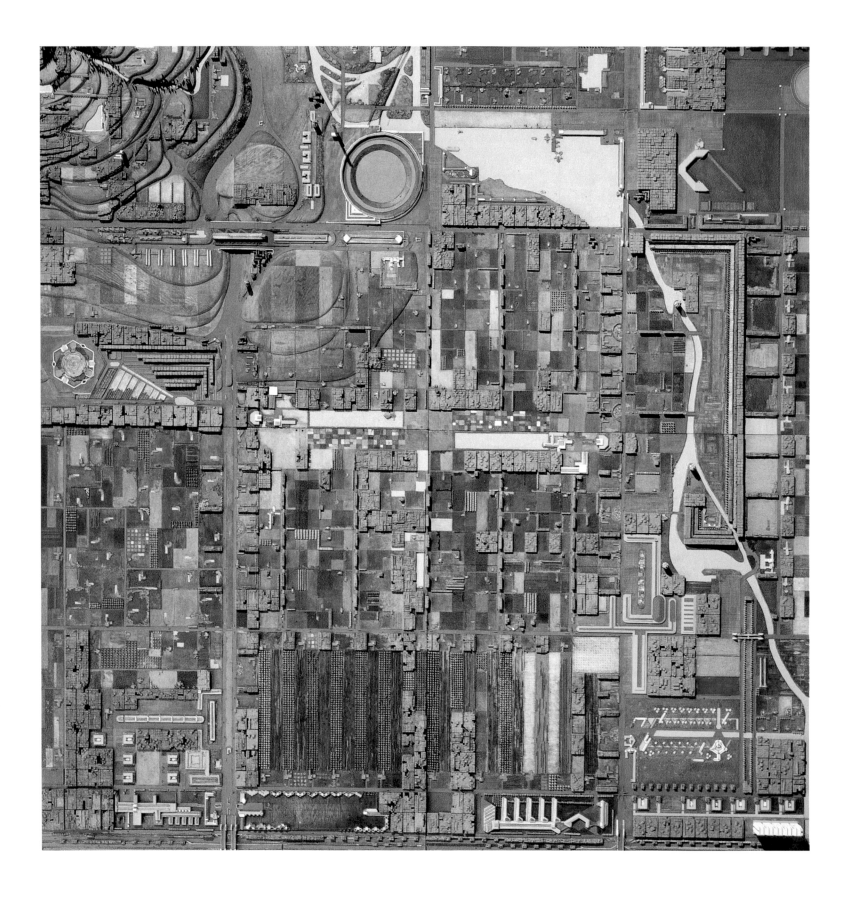

Frank Lloyd Wright, model of Broadacre City, 1934-35 (Scottsdale (AZ), The Frank Lloyd
Wright Foundation. Inv.: 3402.0089.- photo: Skot Weidemann. © 2010, The Frank Lloyd
Wright Fdn, AZ / Art Resource, NY / Scala, Florence)

Analysis and design experimentation

Historical reality is more stubborn, but in many respects more multiform and also more surprising. The real history of landscape architectonic design, with all its shortcomings and triumphs, unfolds in the examples in this book. With the thought that 'the rules of landscape architecture are only to be found and applied in landscape architecture itself', the examples are investigated at a design-technical level. They are redesigned from a contemporary perspective, as it were. Along with the history and topography, it is particularly the landscape architectonic composition in the changing urban context that is analysed with the instrumental and theoretical knowledge of landscape architecture today. The goal is to expose the design aspects and the formal schemes used, in their relation to the situation and the social and cultural context, and to interpret them in their contemporary significance.

In order to be able to analyse the urban landscape as a landscape architectonic composition, use is made of a theoretical model that was previously developed in *Architectuur en Landschap* (2003). In this model the landscape architectonic composition is analysed in terms of various notional processes: the basic form, the spatial form, the visual form and the programmatic form. Through this systematic approach the examples in this book are opened up for comparison with one another, design critique and new transformations – thereby making them relevant to contemporary design questions.

Moreover, the significance of each design must be comprehended in both its general and its unique aspects. The form of one design will sometimes appear to be similar to that of another in a number of aspects. In that sense there is a typological relationship between the examples, in which 'type' is to be understood as a scheme derived from an historical series of designed which are clearly analogous to one another, formally and functionally. General conceptions or pictures – and implicitly with that, also their ideological significance and content – were often the point of departure for producing a new design. Giulio Carlo Argan (1909-1992) therefore hypothesized a continuity in the design process between the 'typological moment' (tradition, convention) and the 'inventive moment' (breaking through the tradition). Notwithstanding typological similarities, the urban landscapes discussed here are however unique in many other respects. It is precisely that which makes them so interesting as examples. They are perhaps not to be directly related to a new design task, but inherent in them are concepts and design instruments that are still useful, providing that they are revealed in the right way as original, experimental inventions.

With this in mind, there is no pretence here of providing a complete historical overview, or a classification of the elements of the landscape architectonic building kit for the city. Rather, the intention is to distinguish the essential conceptual steps in the thought process of urban landscape architecture and the design instruments that have played a role in it. In this approach, analysis of, and experimental design of the metropolitan landscape coincide. Against this background one can also read this book as a continuing experimental design process, in which the reader also plays a part.

**The idealised city. In the square, surrounded by a labyrinth, the landscape is drawn as
a circular map of the known world, with a sacred city in the middle**
(Antonio di Pietro Averlino Filarete, *Trattato del architettura*, 1461-1464. Biblioteca
Nazionale Centrale Firenze, Fondo Nazionale II.I.140, f. 121)

1 STAGING URBAN SPACE AS LANDSCAPE

When the interplay between architecture and landscape was introduced into the city's sphere of influence, the repertoire of villa architecture, oriented to 'individual' spatial expression, had to be converted into instruments for shaping collective spatial forms in the city.

Rome was the starting point for this process, with the urban transformation of the Renaissance villa. As the most important element of the composition, the terrace was transformed into an urban balcony from which the city and landscape were united into one panorama. In Paris, the project at hand was the urban transformation of the architectonic system of the formal garden. The spatial axis evolved into the support for a formal network that embraced the city and countryside. In London the pictural scheme of the landscape garden was transformed into a landscape scenography of urban spaces and routes, with the public park as the new point of crystallisation. New urban landscapes were 'invented' in each of these cities, which were going to belong to the classic repertoire of urban landscape architecture, and are still significant as concepts today.

These different urban transformations of landscape architectonic composition elements came together and exercised influence on one another in Lenné's *Verschönerung* of Berlin, and were employed in the orchestration of a great landscape theatre embracing the city and landscape, uniting them in an urban Arcadia.

HORTI FARNESIANI
ROME 1556

An urban balcony
The Farnese family
Giacomo Barozzi da Vignola
Genius loci and panorama

The Seven Hills

A keystone in the villa landscape
The ancient city
The renovatio imperii
The villeggiatura

The genius loci of the Palatine
The Piazza del Campidoglio as a link
The mythological origin
The imperial palaces

The rise and decline of the Horti
The first phase
Expansion
Decline

A manneristic diorama
Playing with the classical matrix
The axial spatial series
The ascending architectonic route
The descending architectonic route

The integrazione scenica of time and space
Rome as space in time

The Horti Farnesiani, Rome (aerial photo: P. van Bolhuis / Pandion)

An urban balcony

The Horti Farnesiani in Rome is one of the first examples of a public urban garden. It lies on the Palatine, the hill that is regarded as the cradle of Roman civilisation. It was not called a 'villa', but a 'horti', indicating that it was a garden complex without any real residential function. That meant that it was actually a city park, in the modern sense of the term. At the beginning of the 16th century the Palatine was a labyrinth of ruins, interspersed with vineyards where people dug in search of ancient statues and frescos. Various noble Roman families owned vineyards and gardens there. At the foot of the hill lay the Campo Vaccino, the ruined Forum Romanum which had become buried under a layer of debris and soil several metres thick, where cows grazed.

The Farnese family

The noble Farnese family had played an important role in Italian politics, and had produced many cardinals. and even a pope. The family rose to great prominence in 1534 when Alessandro (Alexander) Farnese the Elder (1467-1549) became Pope Paul III. His grandsons Alessandro Farnese (1520-1589) and Ranuccio Farnese (1530-1565) both became cardinals. During the Renaissance, it was the conviction of the popes and cardinals that one of the tasks of the Church was to take a leading role in promoting culture. In their positions, the Farneses were patrons and clients for architects and artists, and also closely involved in the development of Rome.

Between 1539 and 1579 Alessandro Farnese, together with his brother Ranuccio, who like him was deeply interested in Rome's classical history, bought land on the Palatine, overlooking the Campo Vaccino. The location on the Palatine was chosen very deliberately, and underscored the position and eminence of the Farnese family. Despite its present dereliction, the hill was indisputably the centre of Roman civilisation, and many kings and emperors had built their palaces there in the past. When Alessandro became a cardinal, he turned over the management of the land to his younger brother Ranuccio, who had gardens laid out there. After the early death of Ranuccio in 1565 the area reverted to Alessandro's ownership. Under his supervision the slope above the ruined Forum Romanum was transformed into a complex architectonic entrance and stairs. The design for this is usually attributed to Vignola.

Giacomo Barozzi da Vignola

Giacomo (or Jacopo) Barozzi da Vignola, also known as 'Il Vignola' (1507-1573), was one of the most influential mannerist architects of the 16th century. Two of his masters, Antonio da Sangallo and Baldassare Peruzzi, had worked from 1532 to 1536 on a design for the Palazzo Farnese in Caprarola. After the work had been suspended for twenty years, in 1556 Vignola received the commission to finish the palazzo. In addition, since 1550 Vignola had already been working on a design for the Villa Giulia in Rome, and after 1560 he worked on a design for the Villa Lante in Bagnaia.

In his treatise Le due regole della prospettiva pratica (composed around 1545 and published posthumously in Bologna in 1583) Vignola had investigated the way in which architecture could play with the constructions of perspective. The central point was the creation of tension between perspective and motion. For Vignola, the architectonic construction was defined by a perspectival visual axis, but the route from the one space to the other always diverged from this. This playful, manneristic effect is characteristic of his work.

Vignola died in 1573, and the Horti Farnesiani was only completed after 1576. Thus he can not be the only architect involved with this

The Horti Farnesiani, as seen from the Forum Romanum

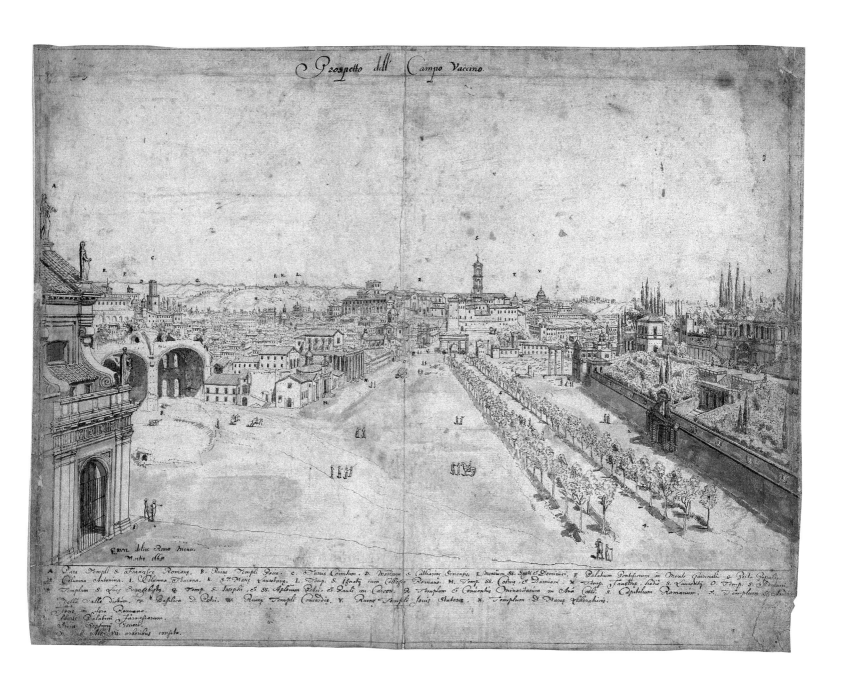

The Campo Vaccino with the Via Triumphalis, and the Horti Farnesiani to the right.
The image is apparently reversed (Lievin Cruyl (ca. 1640-ca. 1720), *Achttien aanzichten van Rome: De Campo Vaccino (Het Forum Romanum)*, 1665 Pen, sepia and brush and ink wash, and pencil; framed in sepia, 38.8 × 50.7 cm. © The Cleveland Museum of Art. Dudley P. Allen Fund 1943.270)

project. The architect of the plan as a whole was perhaps Giacomo del Duca (1520-1601), who worked for the Farnese princes after 1565, and only returned to his birthplace in Sicily in 1588.

Genius loci and panorama

After the death of Cardinal Alessandro Farnese in 1589, work on the complex was probably interrupted for several years. It was only completed in the 17th century, when the two *volières* designed by Girolamo Rainaldi (1570-1655) were added on the instruction of Cardinal Odoardo Farnese, who had lived in Rome since 1593. These *volières* were the crown and the frame for the prospect from the top of the Palatine. With them the 'urban balcony', in which the panorama of the city was opened up and at the same time connected with the *genius loci* of the classical world, was now complete.

The ingenious spatial composition against the slope of the hill is presently seriously compromised, not only by physical deterioration but also by 19th century excavations on the Palatine itself and in the Forum Romanum, which lay hidden under the Campo Vaccino. The lowest section of the stairs of the Horti Farnesiani has disappeared. The inventive architectonic route can no longer be followed in its entirety. Nevertheless, the remaining parts of the composition testify to the audacity with which in 16th century Rome the *genius loci* of the city and the landscape was manipulated, from the panorama down to the smallest detail.

Topography

airport

subway station
subway line
railway line
•   railway station
motorway
tunnel
consular road
important road

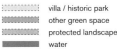

urban pattern

villa / historic park
other green space
protected landscape
water

villas
1   Villa Ada e Monte Antenne
2   Villa Aldobrandini
3   Villa Borghese
4   Villa Carpegna
5   Villa Celimontana
6   Villa Giulia
7   Horti Farnesiani
8   Villa Madama
9   Villa Pamphili
10   Villa Quirinale
11   Villa Sciarra

parks and nature reserves
12   Park EUR
13   Parco degli Acquedotti
14   Parco del Pineto
15   Parco dell' Appia Antica
16   Parco della Caffarella
17   Parco di Aguzzano
18   Parco di Vejo
19   Riserva del Litorale Romano
20   Riserva dell' Insugherata
21   Riserva della Marcigliana
22   Riserva della Tenuta dei Massimi
23   Riserva della Tenuta dell' Acqua Fredda
24   Riserva della Valle dei Casali
25   Riserva della valle dell' Aniene
26   Riserva di Decima Malafede
27   Riserva di Monte Mario
28   Riserva Laurentino - Acqua Acetosa

water
29   Tiber
30   Aniene
31   Lago Albano

places
32   Albano Laziale
33   Castel Gandolfo
34   Frascati
35   Forum Romanum

streets
36   Via Appia Antica

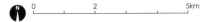

0   2   5km

The Seven Hills

Rome lies at the foot of the Sabine hills, where they open out to the south-west onto a coastal plain along the Tyrrhenian Sea. The Tiber and the Aniene, which flows down from the Campagna Romana (the Abruzzo), merge here into an extensive, swampy river floodplain. To the north-west this is bordered by the hills of Viterbo, with the mountain lakes Lago di Vico and Lago di Bracciano. To the south-east lie the hills and mountain lakes of Tivoli, Frascati and Albano. Right at the mouth of the Tiber lies Ostia.

Locally on the west the Tiber is bounded by the steep slopes of Monte Janiculum, which forms a strategic headland extending into the Tiber valley from the north, and Monte Sant'Egidio, on which the Vatican enclave lies. Once past the deep side valley to the north of this tongue of land, the river makes its way along the steep ridge of Monte Mario. The difference in elevation between the Tiber valley and the western hills is about fifty meters. On the eastern bank the topography is less pronounced. Here we find no steep inclines, but a hilly landscape which slopes down to the river, with the proverbial Seven Hills of the Septimontium, on which the classical city was built, respectively the Palatine, the Aventine, the Capitoline or the Capitol, the Caelian, the Esquiline, the Quirinal and the Viminal. The successive hill crests stand more or less at an oblique angle to the winding main valley of the Tiber. The differences in elevation here fluctuate, but are around twenty-five meters. The Janiculum is not accounted as being one of the seven hills, but had a similar significance.

Rome's origins lie on Monte Palatino, where the Tiber curves sharply and an island in this bend makes it easy to cross the river. Thus, in broad lines, the topography of the old city, as it was bounded by the Aurelian wall, is comprised of the low-lying, asymmetrical valley of the Tiber, which broadens out into a sort of bowl at the point where the city lies, and the hills that bound this valley. Together they make up a natural bowl, the morphology of which formed the conditions for its spatial coherence. Within this, the Palatine was the most centrally located hill. As a result, both nature and history joined to assure that the Horti Farnesiani occupied a key position in the proto-urban domain of the Seven Hills.

The Seven Hills and ancient gardens (from Leonardo Benevolo, *The history of the city*, London, 1980)

→ **Geomorphology and the urban domain**

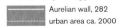 Aurelian wall, 282

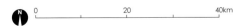 urban area ca. 2000

0   20   40km

Geomorphology, urban pattern and parks

Elevation (metres)

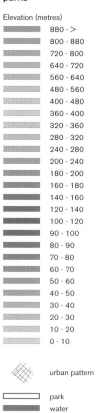

	880 - >
	800 - 880
	720 - 800
	640 - 720
	560 - 640
	480 - 560
	400 - 480
	360 - 400
	320 - 360
	280 - 320
	240 - 280
	200 - 240
	180 - 200
	160 - 180
	140 - 160
	120 - 140
	100 - 120
	90 - 100
	80 - 90
	70 - 80
	60 - 70
	50 - 60
	40 - 50
	30 - 40
	20 - 30
	10 - 20
	0 - 10

urban pattern

park

water

The hills to the south-east of Rome, near Frascati. In the centre, right, Villa Aldobrandini (aerial photo: Peter van Bolhuis, Pandion)

N   0   2   5km

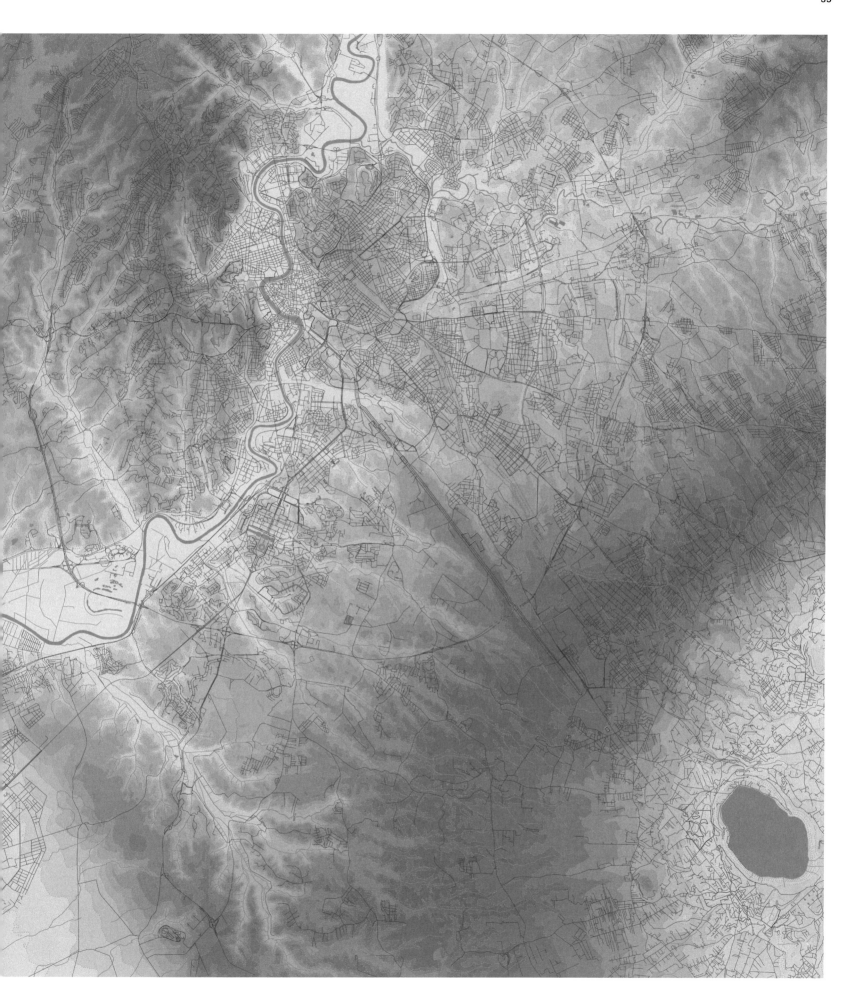

A keystone in the villa landscape

The ancient city

The first permanent residents on the hills were Latins, who celebrated an annual feast of the Septimontium (seven hills). Their settlements initially lay on the hills; later the villages expanded down the slopes into the areas between them, one of these becoming the later Forum Romanum. The oldest traces of habitation on the Palatine apparently date from the 9th century BCE, when king Evander founded the village of Pallante. According to the *Aeneid*, the mythical epic written by Virgil in the first century CE, after the fall of Troy the Trojan Aeneas landed in the region of Latinum, while Evander was still alive. Romulus and Remus, born of a surreptitious union between the god Mars and Rhea Silvia, a Vestal Virgin and daughter of king Numitor and descendent of Aeneas, founded a city on the Palatine in 735 BCE, which after Romulus's murder of Remus would bear the name Rome. Romulus secured the city on the south-western tip of the hill by marking out the moat of Roma Quadrata, a union of two villages on the Palatine, with a plough. Around 600 BCE, under the influence of the Etruscans, the first elements of urban structures and culture made their appearance in Latium.

In 2007, at a depth of 16 metres under the remains of the palace of Augustus Caesar, on the side of the Palatine that adjoins the Circus Maximus, a partially natural, partially artificial grotto was found, a circular, vaulted space about 9 meters high and 7.5 meters in diameter, decorated with figurative mosaics with tesserae of coloured marble and rows of white shells. According to archaeologists this is almost certainly the Lupercal, the cave in which Remus and Romulus were suckled by a she-wolf (*Lupa Capitolina*), after they were thrown into the Tiber by king Amulius and were washed ashore again.

Somewhat higher on the hill, near the site of what was called the 'cabin of Romulus', the Roman aristocracy later lived in a spaciously laid out complex of palaces and temples, which contrasted sharply with the busy Forum Romanum below. From the hill one also had a good view out over the games in the Circus Maximus on the south. The area where later the Horti Farnesiani would be built was occupied by the Domus Tiberiana, and still closer to the edge along the Forum Romanum by the Domus Flavia and the palace of emperor Caligula.

The decline and depopulation of Rome began when the emperor Constantine (312-327) moved the capital of the Roman Empire to Constantinople. Thickly populated districts still lay among the ruins of the imperial city, particularly in the bend of the Tiber valley opposite the Vatican enclave. The palaces on the Palatine were however abandoned.

Parts of the ruins of the imperial city were reused as building material. For instance, the Palazzo Venezia, the Cancelleria and the Palazzo Farnese were built principally from stone from the Colosseum.

The renovatio imperii

At the end of the Middle Ages Rome was a chaotic city. During the Renaissance popes and cardinals played a central role in the rebirth of its political and cultural life. Especially Giuliano della Rovere ('Il Terrible'), as Pope Julius II (1503-1513), desired to make Rome the centre of civilisation. More particularly he made it his goal to restore the ecclesiastical state, which had come close to ruin under his Borgia predecessor Alexander VI. He supported this effort by a building programme oriented to a *renovatio imperii*, a revival of imperial Rome. As part of the ecclesiastical building programme projects were also realised which focused on the architecture of the city. From 1558-1589 the 119 meter high dome of St. Peter's was under construction. Pope Sixtus V (1558-1590) had the seven votive churches of Rome, from the time of the emperor Constantine the Great, connected with one another by straight avenues. His architect Domenico Fontana (1543-1607) described these new links as streets, straight as a ruler, which cut through the undulating topography of the hill district, with fine views, terminating visually with obelisks and fountains.

The villeggiatura

The *villeggiatura* of the prelates of the Church were also an important factor in public cultural life. They built country homes in the hills on the periphery and in the cities on the edges of the Campagna Romana. During the Renaissance the ruins of imperial villas, like the Villa Hadriana at Tivoli and the villas near the old Tusculum (now Frascati), which in the Middle Ages were still the visual remains of an antique myth, took on a new, inspirational significance as an Arcadian backdrop. In Rome itself, after about 1485 villas were built on the western bank of the Tiber. In the period after the Council of Trent villas were also built in the hilly eastern district of the city. At the end of the 16th century and in the early 17th century the cardinals vied with one another to build ever larger villas on the outskirts of the city. The greatest of these are the Villa Borghese (1608) and the Villa Doria Pamphili (1630), both just outside the Aurelian city wall.

Three structures from the ancient city joined together in defining the location of the villas. First and foremost were the consular roads, the great arterial highways of classical Rome. In the hill district these are chiefly the Via Pia and the Via Appia, which like dead-straight lines

1	Servian wall	6	Baths of Caracalla
2	Circus Flaminius	7	Colosseum
3	Imperial fora	8	Baths of Diocletian
4	Circus Maximus	9	Castra Praetoria
5	Baths of Trajan	10	Aurelian wall

The imperial city

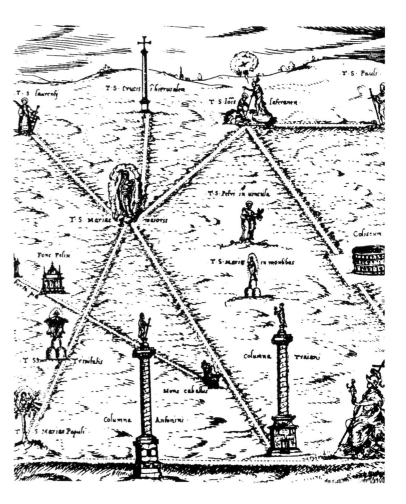

G.F. Bordino, map of Rome, in which the streets of Sixtus V are drawn as straight lines connecting the churches and obelisks, 1588 (from Edmund Bacon, *Design of cities*, London 1978)

running for kilometres connect the city with the streams, hills and mountain lakes of Frascati. In the north is the Via Flaminia, following the Tiber, while the Via Aurelia in the west cuts through the Tiber valley. Second there was the Aurelian city wall. Because during the Middle Ages these walls had become much too large for the shrunken city, there was a wide zone of pastures and vineyards both inside and outside the wall. During the period when the villas were being laid out the wall was both demolished and breached at various points. Finally, the water supply was an important infrastructure. The abandoned hill district only became habitable through the restoration of old aqueducts and the construction of new ones by the popes, among them the Aqua Vergine by Sixtus IV, the Aqua Felice by Sixtus V and the Aqua Paola by Paul V. These aqueducts were indispensable for the waterworks of the villas; the Aqua Vergine supplied the Villa Medici and the Aqua Felice the Villa Montalto. The construction of new roads and aqueducts in the 16th century served to open up the hilly eastern district of the city for the *villeggiatura*.

In both the western and eastern districts of the city visually strategic sites were occupied by villas. Lying within the bowl two to three kilometres in diameter formed by the geomorphology, the city became the stage set for the villas that nestled on the balconies of this gigantic open-air theatre. The villa's residents could look down onto the ecclesiastical and political centre of the world. Moreover, elevated above the low-lying city, the villas were within sight of one another. In the middle of the 16th century there were villas with gardens on almost all the hills of Rome. Only the Palatine was still wild, covered with pastures, vineyards and ruins.

The construction of the Horti Farnesiani on this hill was a crucial step in the completion of the villa landscape. On the north side the Horti Farnesiani is connected with the Villa Quirinale, the Villa Colonna and the Villa Aldobrandini by views. On the west side it is visually linked with the Villa Lante, the Villa Aurelia and the Villa dei Cavalieri di Malta. These villas are in turn visually connected with one another, and with still other villas. The Horti Farnesiani, in the heart of the Seven Hills, and at the same time in the centre of the classical city, formed the final piece in this series for the time being. The view over the Forum Romanum, the Basilica of Maxentius, the Colosseum, the Capitol, the city and the Roman Campagna as far as the Alban hills completed the visual unity of the urban and scenic panorama, and linked this with the history of the Eternal City.

The *Nuova Carta di Roma*, drawn by G.B. Nolli in 1768, presents an idyllic image of this. The low-lying city is characterised by many

The visual relations among the villas

The villas identified with an Arabic number still exist; the villas identified with a Roman numeral have disappeared.

villas before 1655
1   V. Medici, Madama (ca. 1517-27)
2   Casino di Pio IV, Borromeo (16th cen,)
3   V. Giulia (1550-54)
4   V. Medici (mid-16th cen.)
5   Giardini del Quirinale (16th - 18th cen.)
6   Orti Farnesiani (16th - 17th cen.)
7   V. dei Cavalieri di malta (16th - 18th cen.)
8   V. Sciarra (reconstruction)
9   V. Chigi, la Farnesina (1509-11)
10   V. Turini, Lante (1518-31)
11   Cortile del Belvedere (15th - 17th cen.)
12   V. Vaticana (15th - 17th cen.)
13   V. Borghese (1608-25; 1770-93; 1822-31)
14   V. Colonna (17th cen.)
15   Casino dell'Aurora en Giardino Rospigliosi (early 17th cen.)
16   V. Aldobrandini (late 16th - early 17th cen.)
17   V. Giustiniani, Massimo (late 16th - 17th cen.)
18   V. Altieri (17th cen.)
19   V. Mattei (second half 16th, 19th centuries)
20   V. Il Vascello (17th cen.)
21   V. Pamphili, Doria Pamphili (1644-52)
22   V. Vecchia Pamphili (ca. 1630)
I   Casino dell'Aurora, Ludovisi (16th - 17th cen.)
II   V. Altieri
III   V. Verospi
IV   V. Peretti, Montalto
V   V. Barberini

villas 1655-1768
23   V. Astalli (second half 17th cen.)
24   V. Farnese, Aurelia (17th - 19th cen.)
25   V. Corsini (16th - 18th cen.)
26   V. Paniatowski (16th - late 18th cen.)
27   Palazzina Vagnuzzi (16th cen. and 1825-1844)
28   V. Albani, Torlonia (ca. 1746-64)
29   V. Paolina (18th - 19th cen.)
30   V. Abamelek (18th - 20th cen.)
31   V. Piccolomini (18th cen.)
32   V. del Bosco Parrasio (first half 18th cen.)
VI   V. Campana
VII   V. Casali
VIII V. Corsini ai Quattro Venti
IX   V. Patrizi
X   V. Sacripanti

monuments
A   Basilica of St. Peter
B   Castel Sant'Angelo
C   Colosseum
D   San Giovanni in Laterano
E   Campidoglio
F   Pantheon
G   Mausoleum of Augustus
H   Baths of Caracalla
J   Baths of Diocletian

aqueducts
a   Aqua Marcia, Tepula, Julia (144-130, 125, 33 BCE)
b   Aqua Claudia (38-52)
c   Aqua Traiana (109)
d   Aqua Marcia Antoniana or Alessandrina (226)
e   Aqua Paola

urban axis 1748
aqueduct 1748
Aurelian wall (282)
walls of Paul III / Urban VII (1534-1644)

sight lines between villas until 1655
sight lines between villas from 1655-1748

villa
water

Elevation (metres)
120 - 140
100 - 120
90 - 100
80 - 90
70 - 80
60 - 70
50 - 60
40 - 50
30 - 40
20 - 30
10 - 20

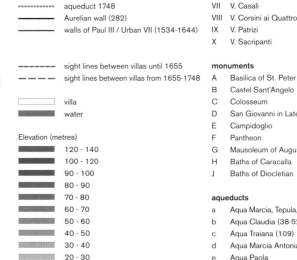

0   500   1000m

courtyards and gardens. The higher-lying parts of the city are open, with villas in a landscape of gardens, vineyards and fields. Between them lies the Horti Farnesiani, on the boundary of the ancient, medieval and Renaissance city, like a advanced pawn in the resettlement of the eastern hill district.

The urban landscape in 1748
(after G.B. Nolli, 1748)

The villas identified with an Arabic number still exist; the villas identified with a Roman numeral have disappeared.

villas before 1655

1 V. Medici, Madama (ca. 1517-27)
2 Casino di Pio IV, Borromeo (16th cen.)
3 V. Giulia (1550-54)
4 V. Medici (mid-16th cen.)
5 Giardini del Quirinale (16th - 18th cen.)
6 Orti Farnesiani (16th - 17th cen.)
7 V. dei Cavalieri di malta (16th - 18th cen.)
8 V. Sciarra (reconstruction)
9 V. Chigi, la Farnesina (1509-11)
10 V. Turini, Lante (1518-31)
11 Cortile del Belvedere (15th - 17th cen.)
12 V. Vaticana (15th - 17th cen.)
13 V. Borghese (1608-25; 1770-93; 1822-31)
14 V. Colonna (17th cen.)
15 Casino dell'Aurora and Giardino Rospigliosi (early 17th cen.)
16 V. Aldobrandini (late 16th – early 17th cen.)
17 V. Giustiniani, Massimo (late 16th - 17th cen.)
18 V. Altieri (17th cen.)
19 V. Mattei (second half 16th, 19th centuries)
20 V. Il Vascello (17th cen.)
21 V. Pamphili, Doria Pamphili (1644-52)
22 V. Vecchia Pamphili (ca. 1630)
I Casino dell'Aurora, Ludovisi (16th - 17th cen.)
II V. Altieri
III V. Verospi
IV V. Peretti, Montalto
V V. Barberini

villas 1655-1768

23 V. Astalli (second half 17th cen.)
24 V. Farnese, Aurelia (17th - 19th cen.)
25 V. Corsini (16th - 18th cen.)
26 V. Paniatowski (16th - late 18th cen.)
27 Palazzina Vagnuzzi (16th cen. and 1825-1844)
28 V. Albani, Torlonia (ca. 1746-64)
29 V. Paolina (18th - 19th cen.)
30 V. Abamelek (18th - 20th cen.)
31 V. Piccolomini (18th cen.)
32 V. del Bosco Parrasio (first half 18th cen.)
VI V. Campana
VII V. Casali
VIII V. Corsini ai Quattro Venti
IX V. Patrizi
X V. Sacripanti

monuments

A Basilica of St. Peter
B Castel Sant'Angelo
C Colosseum
D San Giovanni in Laterano
E Campidoglio
F Pantheon
G Mausoleum of Augustus
H Baths of Caracalla
J Baths of Diocletian

aqueducts

a Aqua Marcia, Tepula, Julia (144-130, 125, 33 BCE)
b Aqua Claudia (38-52)
c Aqua Traiana (109)
d Aqua Marcia Antoniana or Alessandrina (226)
e Aqua Paola

———————— urban pattern 1748
------------ aqueduct in 1748
———————— Aurelian wall (282)
———————— Walls of Paul III and Urban VII (1534-1644)

villa
garden
vineyard
vegetable garden
pasture
water

0   500   1000m

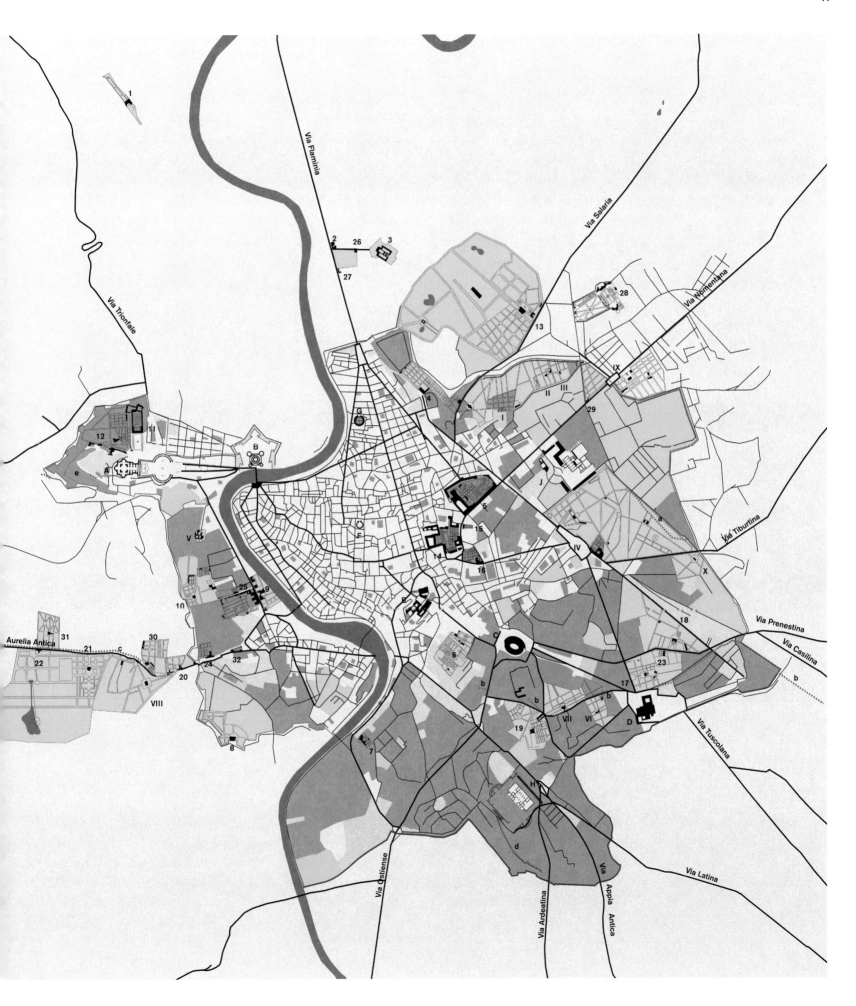

Via Flaminia

Via Salaria

Via Nomentana

Via Trionfale

Via Tiburtina

Via Prenestina

Via Casilina

Aurelia Antica

Via Tuscolana

VIII

Via Ostiense

Via Ardeatina

Via Appia Antica

Via Latina

The genius loci of the Palatine

The 16th century Campo Vaccino – earlier the Forum Romanum – lay on the north side of the Horti Farnesiani. In 1536, when Charles V returned from the conquest of Tunisia to meet Pope Paul III (Alessandro Farnese), the Campo Vaccino was revamped. The ancient Via Sacra, between the Arch of Septimius Severus and the Arch of Titus (which was incorporated in the cloister of St. Maria Nova – now St. Francesca Romana – and only in 1822 would be returned to its original state by Giuseppe Valadier) was transformed into a *via triumphalis*, a route that the emperors used for their entry to the city after a victory. This route was extended past the arch of Septimius Severus with a monumental set of stairs that led to the Piazza del Campidoglio (a square on the Capitol).

The Piazza del Campidoglio as a link
Furthermore, Paul III had a new street laid out on the north-west side of the Capitol, from the existing papal street by the Piazza del Gesu, through the plaza of SS. Venanzio e Ansovino to the foot of the Capitol, and as an extension of this street had it linked with the Piazza del Campidoglio by a stair. In this way the Capitol, which in classical times was only to be reached from the Forum Romanum, turned its 'face' to the mediaeval city. As a result, the Forum Romanum, the Palatine and the Horti Farnesiani came to lie at the back, as a part of the city's edge. Seen from the Palatine hill, the city and St. Peter's lay to the north and west; looking to the south and east one still saw an open landscape inside the city wall.

It was only a century later that the Piazza del Campidoglio itself took shape. Carlo Rainaldi completed the Palazzo Nuovo according to drawings by Michelangelo (1654). The façade of the Palazzo dei Conservatori was completed by Giacomo della Porta in 1568, three years after the construction of the Horti Farnesiani began. Furthermore, Michelangelo designed the pedestal for the equestrian statue of Marcus Aurelius, in the centre of the oval space of the piazza. The pavement with the convex geometric twelve-pointed star motif was only laid in 1940.

In 1558 Cardinal Alessandro Farnese received permission from Pope Sixtus V to obtain water for the fountains and the nymphaea of the Horti via the 'condotta dell'Acqua Felice' (named after Pope Sixtus V, whose personal name was Felice Peretti). This *condotta* was the first aqueduct of modern times, begun by Gregory III in 1583 and completed by Sixtus V between 1585 and 1587. It reused the Aqua Alexandrina to supply the Esquiline, the Viminal, the Quirinal – and also his own Villa Montalto – with water.

The mythological origin
The Scalae Caci are the oldest approach to the Palatine. According to Virgil Aeneas and king Evander ascended these stairs when they had decided to enter into an alliance. This is where the traces of the cabin of Romulus were found, and on the west side of the Scalae there are still three cabins from the 8th century BCE identifiable. At the end of the Clivius Palatinum, on the east side of the hill, lies the foundation of a temple, devoted to the dispute between Romulus and Remus, connected with the founding of Rome. According to legend, this is where Remus fell after he had jumped over the sacred boundary of the rampart. Behind the cabins of Romulus rises the base of the temple of Magna Mater. Construction of the temple began in 204 BCE and it was dedicated on 10 April, 191 BCE. After that date, the annual Ludi Megalenses was held on the platform in front of the entrance to the temple (the *pronaos*), which is still visible. Recent excavations brought the presence of a still older temple to light, probably the Temple of Victory, built in 294 BCE. The smaller building between the two temples is recognised as the Auguratorium, where diviners (*augures*) made predictions on the basis of the flight of the birds.

The imperial palaces
Because of its history and mythology, during the era of the Republic the Palatine was already a desirable place for Rome's upper class to live. The hill was almost entirely covered with prestigious residences when Augustus decided to purchase the property of the *hortator* Hortensius on the top of the Cermalus, close to the sacred spot where Rome was founded, and began the construction of his own house, the Domus Augustana, there around 44 BCE. In this same period the Domus Livia, the House of Livia, Augustus's wife, was also built. Alongside it lay an ovoid basin, probably a fish pond, which still exists. The temple of Apollo, two libraries and a portico, which provided access to the Circus Maximus, were attached to the Domus Augustana. The house served as a model for palaces that were built later, such as the Domus Tiberiana, constructed in the first half of the first century CE by Tiberius, Augustus's successor. After the fire of 80 CE Caligula extended this palace as far as the Forum.

Under the emperor Nero (54-68) the Palatine was entirely rebuilt. His Domus Transitoria was only the beginning of a very ambitious project, called the Domus Aurea because of its size, which was to stretch as far as the Esquiline, but was only partially realised. Nero's *cryptoporticus*, preserved to this day, 130 meters long and provided with windows, was intended to connect the Domus Aurea to the older imperial palaces on the Palatine. Nero planned to alter the topography and orientation

Circus Maximus   Domus Tiberiana   Basilica of Maxentius   Colosseum

**Reconstruction of the ancient city, with the Palatine in the upper centre, between the
Circus Maximus and the Colosseum** (P. Bigot, *Rome antique au 4me siècle ap. J. C.,*
Paris 1942, TUDL BK K.VII.T 2.Rom. 8 folio)

of the north-western side of the hill with the Porticus Margaritaria, a magnificent gateway provided with columns, which was to serve as a new entrance to the Domus Aurea further up.

Still more radical transformations took place under emperor Domitian (81-96), who built the Domus Flavia and the Domus Palatium (or Stadium Palatinum). He also rebuilt the north façade of the Domus Tiberiana. The Domus Flavia was in part built on the foundations of earlier buildings, such as the Domus Transitoria, the House of the Griffins and the Aula Isiaca. The House of the Griffons (heraldic animals, compounded of an eagle and a lion) was the oldest house from the Roman Republic. The Aula Isiaca was a large rectangular room, the remnant of a sumptuous republican house. In this same period the Aqua Claudia aqueduct was extended from the Mons Caelius, and an arch was built on the right side of the Clivius Victoriae. One of the pillars is still to be seen today; the other lies buried under the Via di San Bonaventura.

After Trajan and Hadrian, the emperor Septimius Severus (193-211) built the great baths, with next to them, in the extreme south-eastern corner of the Palatine, the Septizodium, a monumental façade intended to impress visitors entering Rome via the Via Appia. After that there were no further important buildings constructed on the Palatine, which was almost entirely covered.

Through its recomposition of the ruins of the classical imperial residences as a public garden, the building of the Horti Farnesiani meant a new intervention into the history of the Palatine.

The ancient landscape on the Palatine

The urban context around the middle of the 17th century

    Horti Farnesiani
    agrarian landscape
    city
    historic monuments

ancient Rome

1   Ruins of the Curia Ostillia (570-550 CE)
2   Temple of Ercole Vincitore (2nd cen. CE)
3   Temple of Fortuna Virile (1st cen. CE)
4   Theater of Marcellus (1st cen. CE)
5   Domus Augustana (1st cen. CE)
6   Aqueduct of Claudius (38-52)
7   Colosseum (70-80)
8   Arch of Titus (81)
9   Temple of Venus (121-141)
10   Meta Sudans (140)
11   Temple of Antonius and Faustina (141)
12   Domus Severiana (2nd cen.)
13   Baths of Maxentius (2nd - 4th cen.)
14   Septizodium (203)
15   Arch of Septimius Severus (203-273)
16   Santa Anastasia (3rd cen.)
17   Arch of Constantine (312)
18   Temple of Romulus (300-327)
19   Basilica of Maxentius (4th cen.)
20   Arch of Janus (4th cen.)
21   St. Alessio (4th cen.)
22   SS. Giovanni e Paolo (4th cen.)
23   St. Sabina (5th cen.)

mediaeval

24   St. Maria in Cosmedin (6th cen.)
25   SS. Cosma e Damiano (6th cen.)
26   St. Teodoro (6th cen.)
27   St. Maria in Aracoeli (6th cen.)
28   SS. Quirico e Guilietta (6th cen.)
29   St. Gregory the Great (6th cen.)
30   St. Nicolas in Carcere (6th cen.)
31   St. Giorgio al Velabro (7th cen.)
32   St. Maria Nova, now St. Francesca Romana (9th cen.)
33   Palazzo Senatorio (12th cen.)
34   St. Maria liberatrice (13th cen.)
35   Palazzo dei conservatori (14th cen.)
36   Torre Cartularia (mediaeval)
37   St. Eligius

Renaissance

38   St. Maria della Consolazione (1470)
39   Palazzo Venezia (1455-1467)
40   Palazzo Savelli-Orsini (16th cen.)

between Renaissance and baroque

41   Palazzo Caffarelli (1538-1680)
42   Horti Farnesiani (1556-1635)
43   Madonna dei Monti (1580)
44   Palazzo Nuovo (1654)

N   0   100   200m

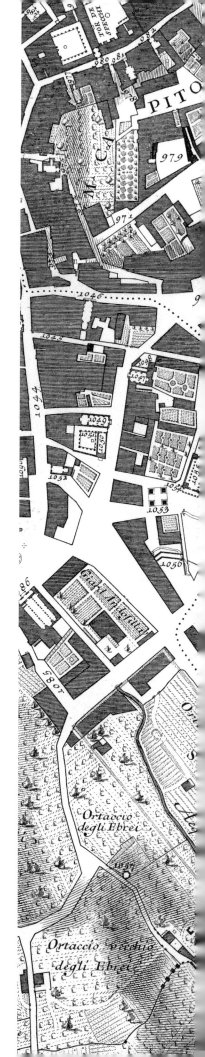

View of the Colosseum from the terrace next to the *volières*

→ **Detail of the Monte Palatino on Nolli's map** (*La pianta di Roma di Giambattista Nolli del 1748 riprodotta da una copia Vaticana con introduzione di Francesco Ehrle S.I.* Citta del Vaticano, 1932. TUDL BK KK ADB132)

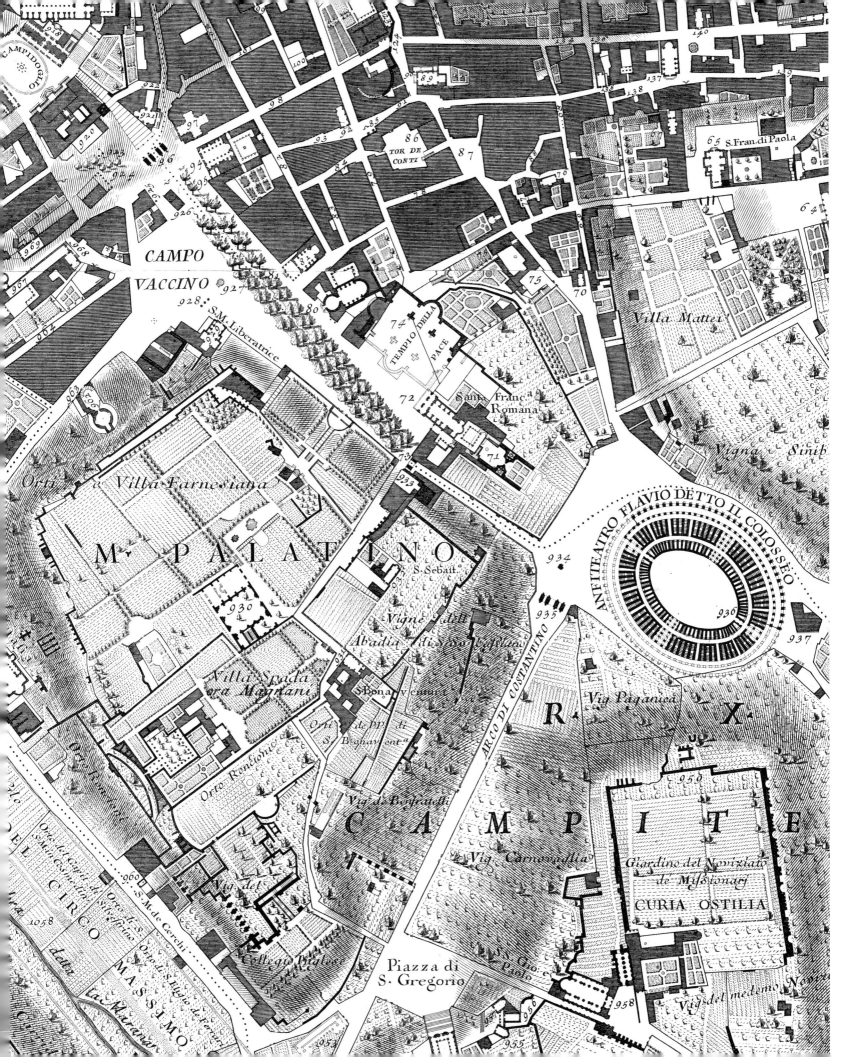

The rise and decline of the Horti

Between 1556 and 1565 Ranuccio Farnese oversaw the first transformations on the hill. Until then the planting found there consisted primarily of vegetable gardens, orchards, thickets of elm and laurel, magnolias and citrus trees. Leonardo Bufalini's orthogonal design from 1551 was adorned with *treillages* in the form of domes, pergolas, and stairs above the promenades between the flowerbeds.

The first phase

The most important transformation began between 1565 and 1589, after Ranuccio's death. The retaining wall with corner pavilions was constructed along the Campo Vaccino, together with the gate and the entrance theatre behind it, the easy stair (*gradonata* or *cordonata*) to the first storey and the *cryptoporticus* of Nero, cut into the hill. The garden, enclosed on all four sides, which initially almost entirely followed the outlines of the Domus Tiberiana, its sides straightened out and a regular arrangement imposed on the whole, was at the top of the hill. Paths were laid out corresponding to the classical foundations, or connected with architectonic elements such as the Palazzina, the Casino del Belvedere, the side gates, the Bastione Farnesiano, and the Ninfeo degli Specchi, which is sometimes attributed to Pirro Ligorio.

The Palazzina was the only residential structure in the Horti Farnesiani, with bedrooms, a parlour, a kitchen and a loggia that looked out over the Clivius Victoriae and the great arcades of the Domus Tiberiana. The building was the pivot between the lower garden along the Via Nova and the upper garden that followed the orientation of the Domus Tiberiana. What is more, its internal stairway, invisible from the exterior, connected the two levels of the garden with one another. The Casino del Belvedere, in the south-east, is a two-storey building, the ground floor of which comprised an extraordinary square room with an open loggia with a travertine balustrade, from which one could look out over the ruins of ancient Rome. The Ninfeo degli Specchi, not far from it on the same side, previously consisted of an *exedra* with side niches from which water flowed. The whole was enclosed by a vault. The Bastione Farnesiano, on the contrary, lay on the west side of the Palatine, looking out over a *velabrum*, a garden with a terrace surrounded by strong bastions. In the 16th century it was ornamented with vase plants, and in the 17th century was planted with cypresses.

Expansion

After the death of Alessandro Farnese in 1589, his nephew Odoardo Farnese (1573-1626), who was then only 16 years of age, inherited the site. Work on the garden was only resumed after 1600-1601. The Ninfeo della Pioggia was built into the north slope, initially as a summer dining room or *triclinium*. Between 1612 and 1626 this was altered into its present form. One storey higher, the Teatro del Fontanone was inserted into the monumental Domus Tiberiana. The Teatro is attributed to Girolamo Rainaldi, who continued the work of Vignola and Del Duca. On top of this stood a structure that was called the *uccelliera vecchia*, or old *volière*, a remnant of the former gardens and vineyards from the 16th century.

The path that led from the Fontanone to the Palazzina flanked the high arcades of the classical Domus Tiberiana. The Torretta, which was demolished at the end of the 19th century, rose along this path. It was comprised of a cylindrical volume containing a spiral stair, roofed with a dome.

The last transformation of the garden took place between 1627 and 1635, when Odoardo Farnese, son of Ranuccio I Farnese (1612-1646), had a second *volière* constructed to the west of the one already existing, according to the original design by Vignola. This new *volière* restored the symmetry of the design, particularly that of the monumental

The Arch of Septimius Severus and the Horti Farnesiani from the Capitoline

The entrance to the Horti Farnesiani from the Campo Vaccino (from P. Letarouilly,
*Édifices de Rome moderne, ou recueil des palais, maisons, églises, couvents, et autres
monuments publics et particuliers les plus remarquables de la ville de Rome.* T. 3. Liège :
Avanzo, 1853. TUDL TRK 9810205)

axis oriented to the Basilica of Maxentius. The two *volières* were each crowned by metal tracery in an oriental style, which made them visible from the Campo Vaccino. Two formal stairways, turning in mid-ascent, connected the Teatro del Fontanone with the *volières*, lifting the whole composition, as it were, to the level of the upper garden on the former Domus Tiberiana. After a zone with evergreens to the right and the Giardino della Palma to the left, behind the *volières* a geometric garden opened, the paths of which, fringed by hedges, mirrored the orthogonal pattern of the Domus Tiberiana lying below it. The coppice of evergreens was comprised of ilex, cypresses and laurel. On the west it extended as far as the corner of the former palace of Tiberius, from which vantage point one could survey the Forum. The flowerbeds of the Giardino della Palma extended almost to the eastern wall, accented in the middle by a fountain encircled by citrus trees. Via a stair one could descend to the *cryptoporticus* of Nero, which lay on the same level as the Ninfeo degli Specchi. On the terrace above it stood the Fontana dei Platani, with fourteen plane trees around it; this has vanished entirely today. The water splashed down through the *nymphaeum*, and was collected in the basins (fish ponds) which lay in front of it. To the south of this, on the ruins of the Domus Flavia, grew a *bosco*, comprised of natural and semi-natural overgrowth. The garden ran almost to the Circus Maximus, where the ruins of the emperors' palaces were overgrown with luxuriant scrub. Near the Casino del Belvedere lay a *giardino segreto* or 'secret garden', whose surrounding wall stood on classical foundations. It could be entered by a semi-circular stair and an arched gate, flanked by alcoves. Above the entrance lay a long, narrow terrace that led directly onto the open loggia.

Decline

In the 17th century the Horti Farnesiani was renowned among Rome's botanical gardens for the rarities in its collection of plants, which had often been brought back from India by the Jesuits. The Accademia degli Arcadi was located in the Horti Farnesiani from 1693 to 1725, when it moved to the Bosco Parrasio on the Janiculum. After that, the gardens on the Palatine fell into neglect. The Filipini family and the Bourbons moved much of the marble and almost all the statuary to Naples. These had originally come from the Villa Hadriana at Tivoli, of which Cardinal Alessandro Farnese had been the governor.

Already during the period of Napoleonic rule in the first decades of the 19th century French investigators had begun excavations on the Campo Vaccino. Around 1860 archaeological excavations also began on the Palatine, under the aegis of Napoleon III, who had purchased

the site; by around 1882 the French abandoned the complex, largely in a ravaged state. Several years later he conveyed the hill to the new government of the united Italy.

After 1870 there followed a general excavation of the Forum Romanum, right down to the ground level of the 4th and 5th century. Beginning in 1898 the Italian archaeologist Giacomo Boni went even a step further and dug the soil away to the ground level in the time of Augustus. The bottom part of the stairs to the Horti, which connected it with the ground level of that day, were removed in the course of these excavations. The outermost *gradonatas* for the descent and the *giardino segreto* were also eliminated; as a result, the ingenious construction of the architectonic route can no longer be followed in its entirety. The excavations also did violence to the layers of history the site had possessed, and broke the chain of Rome's architectonic past. Nevertheless, what of the perspectives and views that still exist bear witness to the playful mind of one of the most important representatives of mannerism in the 16th century villa architecture of Rome.

The Via Nova. Left, the remains of the entrance stair

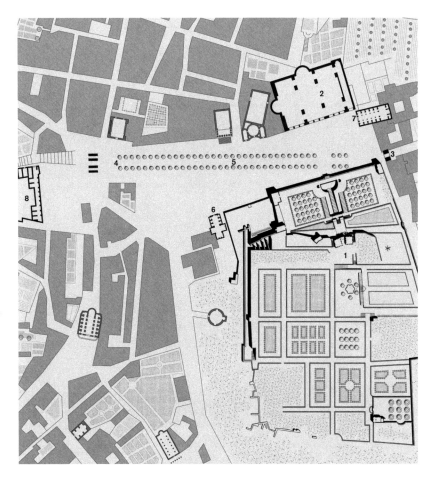

The Horti Farnesiani on the Campo Vaccino

1 Horti Farnesiani
2 Basilica of Maxentius
3 Arch of Titus
4 Arch of Septimius Severus
5 Via Triumphalis (Campo Vaccino)
6 St. Maria Liberatrice
7 St. Maria Nova (now St. Francesca Romana)
8 Palazzo Senatorio

0   50   100m

The Horti Farnesiani, projected onto the ancient city

▬▬▬ Horti Farnesiani, situation ca. 1650

▬▬▬ the ancient city

1 Via Sacra
2 Atrium Vestae
3 Porticus Margaritaria
4 Via Nova
5 Clivius Victoriae
6 Clivius Palatinum
7 Domus Tiberiana
8 Cryptoporticus of Nero
9 Basin
10 House of Livia
11 House of Augustus
12 Temple of the Magna Mater
13 Auguratorium
14 Temple of Victory
15 Scalae Caci
16 Cabin of Romulus
17 Temple of Apollo
18 Baths of Livia
19 Domus Flavia
20 Aula Isiaca
21 House of the Griffins

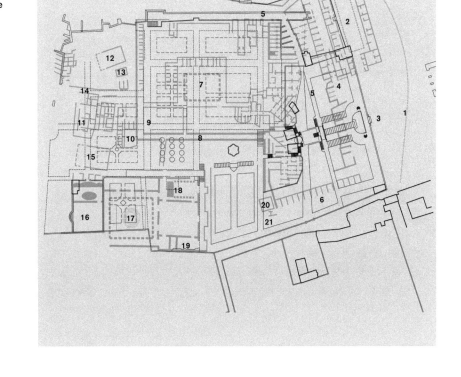
0   40   80m

A manneristic diorama

The spatial design of the Horti Farnesiani is characterised by a carefully weighed exercise using the classic topography. In this, the control of movement and the view, as well as the management of perspective, played a prime role.

Playing with the classical matrix

The most important alignments that defined the design of the Horti Farnesiani are those with the Colosseum, the immediate visual relation with the Basilica of Maxentius, and the presence of the remains of the Domus Tiberiana in the soil. These were in turn determined by the morphology of the landscape.

When Vignola designed the entrance to the Horti Farnesiani, the remains of the Domus Tiberiana were not visible, but he was certainly conscious of their presence. Not only was the garden complex, like the former palace, given an axis of symmetry oriented to the Basilica of Maxentius, but the alignments and axes of the ground plan of the palace formed the basis for the composition of the garden.

Moreover, the outer limits of the Horti Farnesiani are closely connected with the matrices of the classical city, the topography, the earlier buildings, and the urban pattern. Two roads came together at the Arch of Titus, the Via Sacra, which came from the Forum, and the Via Nova, which ran about parallel to it, but somewhat higher up on the hill. On the north-west side ran the Clivius Victoriae, first following the direction of the Domus Tiberiana and thereafter parallel to the Via Nova, but still a bit higher. The Clivius Palatinum, a paved road that climbs the hill, formed the eastern boundary of the garden. On the other side the Clivius Victoriae formed the western limit. The Via Nova and the Clivius Palatinum were shopping streets in classical Rome. The south side of the garden had no obvious boundary. Here the regular ground plan of the garden passed over into wild thickets and old ruins, which were oriented to the Circus Maximus. As can be seen on a 1676 map by G.B. Falda, this was completely overgrown in that day.

The front section of the garden, that was turned toward the Campo Vaccino, with the main gate that was later moved to the Via di San Bonaventura, also had a relation with the Colosseum. There is an urban axis which can be distinguished running from the Colosseum, between the Meta Sudans and the Arch of Titus. The wall is, as it were, a continuation of this orientation. Another important axis links the Arch of Titus with that of Septimius Severus; this was formerly materialised as an avenue with trees. Albeit to a lesser degree, the Capitol, like the

The entrance stair to the cryptoporticus, with behind it the Ninfeo della Pioggia

Overview of the composition

1   Main entrance
2   Corner pavilions
3   Entrance theatre
4   Stair *(cordonata)*
5   Cryptoporticus
6   Ninfeo della Pioggia
7   Promenade
8   Spiral stair
9   Stair
10 Terrace above the cryptoporticus
11 Palazzina
12 Gate
13 Teatro del Fontanone
14 *Volières*
15 Cryptoporticus of Nero
16 Ninfeo degli Specchhi
17 Fontana dei Platani
18 Fish ponds
19 Bastione Farnesiano
20 Casino del belvedere
21 Ilex groves
22 Evergreen coppice
23 Giardino della Palma
24 Bosco
25 Giardino Segreto
26 Arch of Titus
27 Via Sacra
28 Clivius Palatinum

0   40   80m

Basilica of Maxentius, formed an urban reference point. The terrace with the Teatro del Fontanone points directly to the Capitol along the great arches of the Domus Tiberiana.

One aim of the design of the Horti Farnesiani was the integration of the historically important buildings and ruins of ancient Rome. The visual integration of the Basilica of Maxentius was the most important motif in this. The axis of the entrance deviates somewhat from the axis of symmetry of the basilica itself, but points to the middle of it, the central point in the design matrix of the basilica. Thanks to this, the differing orientations are reconciled with one another. Since the time of the Republic, the Clivius Victoriae mediated between the directions of the Domus Tiberiana and the Via Nova. In the design this was translated into the triangular terrace between the two *volières* and the set of stairs, which made the difference between these directions visible. The eastern *volière* follows (with a deviation of four degrees) the orientation of the Domus Tiberiana and lies parallel with the highest terrace, with the Teatro del Fontanone. The western *volière*, designed later, together with the extended ramp, restored the symmetry with respect to the Basilica of Maxentius. There is also a minimal deviation between the axes of symmetry of the *volières* and that of the central stairway. The fact is that the direction of the stair is not only determined by that of the ruins under the *volières*, but also by that of a former shop premises along the Via Nova. The stair mediates between the orientation of the Domus Tiberiana and the axis of symmetry of the Basilica of Maxentius.

The axial spatial series

The face of the complex on the Campo Vaccino was formed by a massive wall with bastions. Visually, its guise as a fortification referred symbolically to Romulus's archaic Roma Quadrata. The far ends of the wall were marked by two corner pavilions. The monumental gate was centred on the wall, on the site of the former Horrea Margaritaria (a large store or emporium from the imperial age). The lower section of this gate is attributed to Vignola, while the upper section, with the caryatids and ten windows looking out over the Campo Vaccino, and the Farnese family emblem, the lily and the lion, to Giacomo del Duca. The emblem symbolised the family having taken possession of the hill. The gate is still in good condition, but has been moved to another location. It was disassembled at the end of the 19th century and and reconstructed in 1957 along the Via di San Gregorio, presently the Via di San Bonaventura. It now serves as the main entrance to the archaeological park on the Palatine. Beyond the gate the semi-circular entrance, also called the Ovato dell'Androne or Teatro di Bussi, referred

to the hill's dark and secret caves. Niches, in which stood sculptures from the Farnese collection, were cut in the *exedra*. To the left and right of the main gate were two hidden spiral stairs. From the entrance theatre the visitor ascended a stair to the terrace which lay above, with the Ninfeo della Pioggia and in front of it a *cryptoporticus*, both cut out of the hill. The Ninfeo della Pioggia has been fully restored and again, as of old, forms one of the important elements of the garden. It consists of a rectangular room with a fountain in the centre. The *cryptoporticus* has also been preserved. It has five openings, three with an arch and two between them with an architrave. The central arch connects to the stair. The two arches next to it provide entrance to a terrace above the entrance. This was partially overgrown, and in turn connected to a higher terrace for strolling along the boundary wall.

Ascending from the terrace above the entrance, two further stairs, rising parallel to the main stair from up the entrance, conveyed one to the level above the *cryptoporticus*. Beside these stairs, on a gentle slope, lay two ilex thickets. There is also a link between the first and second terrace in the *cryptoporticus*. Between the *cryptoporticus* and the *nymphaeum* two stairs to the left and right led to the level above. The right-hand stair was originally oriented toward the Palazzina further up, the left-hand stair to the Arch of Titus. From the second terrace above the *cryptoporticus* one could ascend a central stair, continuing the direction of the main stair below, to arrive on the third terrace. On this terrace above the Ninfeo della Pioggia lay the Teatro del Fontanone, the back of which lay within the Domus Tiberiana. It originally was comprised of a number of basins, from which the water was conveyed to a central pool on the terrace. From this, in turn, the water ran down

The Ninfeo della Pioggia

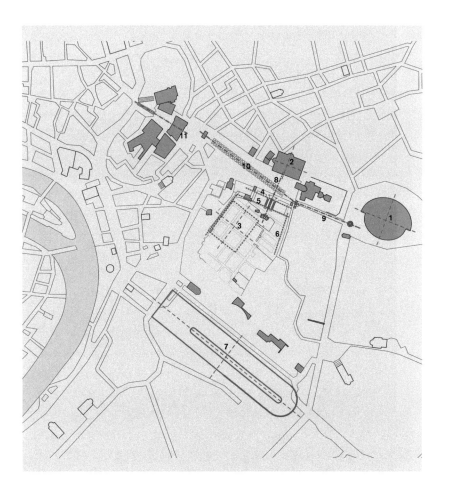

The geometric scheme

— — — axis of buildings

1 Colosseum
2 Basilica of Maxentius
3 Domus Tiberiana

·········· Roman matrix

3 Domus Tiberiana
4 Via Nova
5 Clivius Victoriae
6 Clivius Palatinum
7 Circus Maximus

·—·—·— urban axis

8 Horti Farnesiani – Basilica of Maxentius
9 Meta Sudans – Arch of Titus
10 Arch of Titus – Arch of Septimius Severus
11 Piazza del Campidoglio

N 0 100 200m

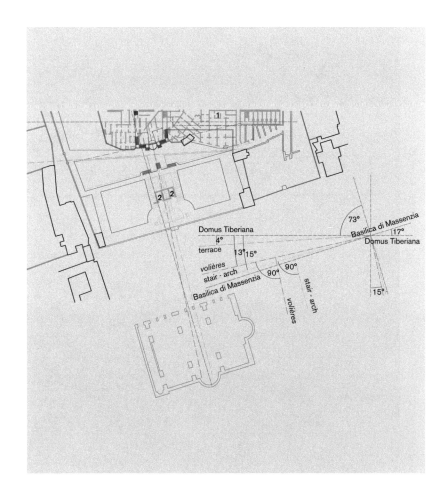

The architectonic axes and orientations

▓▓▓ The ancient foundation

1 Domus Tiberiana
2 Shops along the Via Nova

N 0 40 80m

into the *nymphaeum*. From the Teatro del Fontanone one could ascend two sharply angled stairs to reach the *volières* on the highest level. The oblique placement of these appears to be derived directly from a drawing that Pirro Ligorio made of Varro's *volières*. Together, the arches, niches and terraces made up an an axially arranged series, which could be surveyed entirely or in part in changing perspectives, the various elements connecting visually with each other and fitting with one another. The stairs and inclines played with and nuanced the axial order, and dynamised the relation between movement and perception.

The ascending architectonic route

The main entrance was through a double gate, crowned by two *hermai* and the inscription 'Horti Palatini Farnesiorum'. This inscription makes it clear that this does not involve a villa in the usual sense of the word, but more a *hortus*, a pleasure garden, a park with an engrossing architectonic route and the visual attractions connected with it.

As one ascended, the terraces on the various levels afforded an ever more complete picture of the surroundings. On the first level one could see the secondary gates along the Via della Polveriera, on the second level the Colosseum and the Palazzo Senatorio on the Quirinal, the highest of the seven hills of Rome. On the highest terrace one overlooked all of Rome and its surroundings.

The entrance scheme, designed by Vignola, is comprised of a series of architectonic compositional elements which succeed one another in an architectonic route building toward a crescendo, a passage toward the light and the panorama, from the Campo Vaccino to the top of the Palatine. Once through the main gate, on the lowest storey the visitor came into the dark, subterranean Teatro dell'Androne. From here one could just see the *volières* that form the crown of the architectonic route. They act as a visual stimulus, urging the visitor to move forward. From there, along the axis, a gentle stair which could be ascended both on foot or on horseback (a *cordonata*, in Italian, *gradonata*) invited one to climb to the terrace on the second level of the composition. In its place, however, via a *cryptoporticus* one arrived entirely unexpectedly in a cool, dark grotto. Behind it lay a *nymphaeum*, the Ninfeo della Pioggia.

Two stairs between the *cryptoporticus* and the *nymphaeum*, breaking the central axis as they ascend to the right and left, then brought the visitor to the terrace on the second level. A further stair lying on the axis brings him onward to the terrace on the third level, with the Teatro del Fontanone, which lay above the *nymphaeum*. Here an unexpected vista unfolded before his eyes. The *volières* turn out to be part of a much more complex architectonic tableau, which until now has remained

hidden. To reach the highest level one must once again depart from the main axis. Two flanking, sharply angled formal stairs at last bring the visitor to the terrace on the fourth and highest level of the composition. Here the two *volières*, combined with the panorama, form the climax of the composition. Only upon arriving on the balcony on the highest level can the visitor survey the whole architectonic composition, and at the same time the terrace above the ceremonial entrance route, a *giardino segreto*, revealed itself, which until that moment had remained hidden. Here the interplay between the axiality and the architectonic route is surpassed by the overwhelming panorama, intensified by the physical divergence of the *volières*. The Palatine hill has been transformed into a formal balcony, from which the urban panorama of Rome at the time, as far as the Alban hills could be surveyed, over the silhouette of the Basilica of Maxentius. The architecture of ancient Rome was transfigured. The *volières* were the climax of an ascent, which led from the darkness of the entrance theatre, through the underground *nymphaeum*, to the light of these airy pavilions.

The descending architectonic route

For the descent, the visitor is led along a different route. This ran from the top of the Palatine down to the Campo Vaccino entirely in the open air, with splendid views from each level. From the *volières* the visitor descends the sharply angled formal stairs to the terrace above the *nymphaeum*. From this terrace directly opposite the Basilica of Maxentius one can see the Colosseum and the Arch of Titus in the distance on the right and the Capitol on the left. A small stair (which one can also use for the ascent) on the axis of the Basilica forms the connection with the transverse terrace above the *cryptoporticus*. From this terrace the stairs to the Ninfeo della Pioggia running off to the side are hidden behind half-length walls, and the two *gradonatas* running sideways invite the visitor to descend again, to the level of the *cryptoporticus* and the *giardino segreto*. Through ten small windows in the wall along the Campo Vaccino one can see out from the *giardino segreto*, catching views of the Campo Vaccino below. The benches in the wall were turned inwards, and reinforce the introverted character of the garden. The *giardino segreto* could only be left by two narrow spiral stairs which were concealed in the wall of the semi-circular entrance theatre and that, when one was entering the gardens, had been hidden behind the two alcoves. They now brought the visitor back to the entrance theatre and the gate.

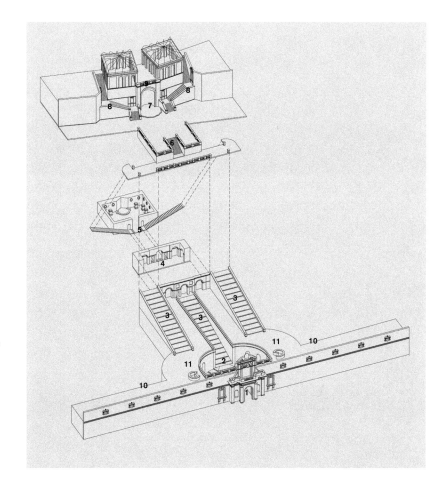

The elements of the entrance

1   Main entrance and wall along the Campo Vaccino
2   Entrance theatre
3   Stair
4   Cryptoporticus
5   Ninfeo della Pioggia and stairs
6   Stair and terrace
7   Teatro del Fontanone
8   Stair to the *volières*
9   *Volières*
10 Raised promenade
11 Spiral stair

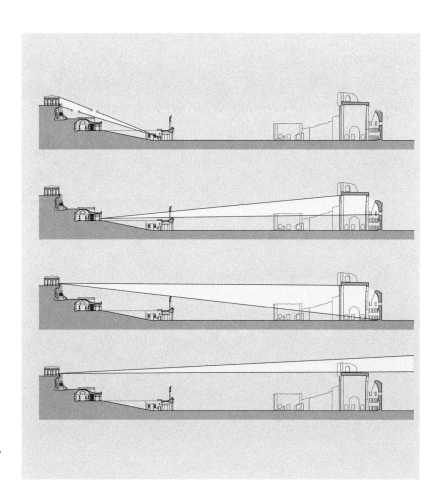

Cross-sections with views over the Campo Vaccino, toward the Basilica of Maxentius

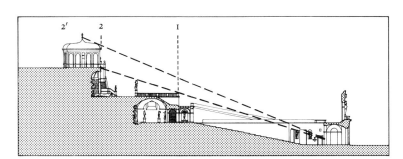

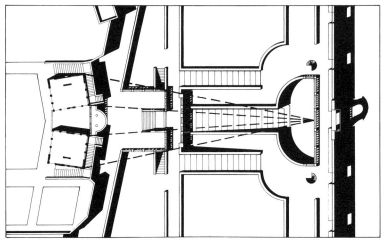

↑ ↗ **Views from the entrance theatre** (from Paul v.d. Ree, Gerrit Smienk & Clemens Steenbergen, *Italian Villas and Gardens*, Amsterdam 1992)

The Teatro del Fontanone (left) and view between the two *volières* over the Forum Romanum (right)

→ **The ascending (left) and descending (right) routes. Above: general plan. The routes are shown stage by stage, from left to right and from above to below.**

The integrazione scenica of time and space

The Horti Farnesiani is the first urban garden open to the public with a spatial system that was designed architectonically. Vignola's design magically transformed the Palatine from a deserted, wild landscape with vineyards and pastures into the first public park of the Renaissance. As a consequence, the oldest site in Rome, the spot where the city originated, became accessible to the public, not only physically, but also as a concept. An ordered space was created, from which one could look out at the everyday hustle and bustle of the city below from an historical perspective. This garden was therefore a park, in the contemporary significance of the term.

The experience of time and space is here coupled to an architectonic route through a landscape, which reveals the secrets of the place step by step, like an ascent from the darkness of ignorance to the light of knowledge and insight. Ascending along the main axis, it seems that the design intends that you will penetrate into a mountain, between revetments and through the *nymphaeum* behind the *cryptoporticus*. At the same time the visual interplay between axiality and movement provides a constant impetus to move higher up and thus conquer the massiveness of the mountain and escape from the city. Descending, it steers you along either side of the axis, via the terraces with views, the *giardino segreto* and the windows in the retaining wall, and finally down a hidden spiral stair, back to the ground floor, with your feet once again on the earth, and after these moments of clarity you are again immersed in the labyrinthine space of the city.

The park on the hilltop brings the viewer directly into contact with the history of the classical city, the palaces of the Roman emperors, and even the cabins of Romulus and the ruins of the houses and temple from the genesis of the city. The ground plan precisely follows the design matrix of the palaces of Tiberius and Nero, so that park and edifice seem interchangeable. Is one in a palace or in a park? It is this ambiguity, or better, polysemy, that gives this park a significance that transcends that of an ordinary park on a height. Here, as it were, you are in touch with the depth of things, while you stand on the top of a hill.

Here the history of the city takes on an architectonic form in the landscape, not only through the different terraces with their views, but especially through the manner in which you climb and descend the Palatine. With a refined composition of staircases, gentle stairs, retaining walls and screens the ascending and descending routes are separated, differentiated spatially and, at the same time, integrated architecturally.

The main gate of the Horti Farnesiani, where it has been moved to the Via di San Bonaventura (photo: P. v.d. Ree)

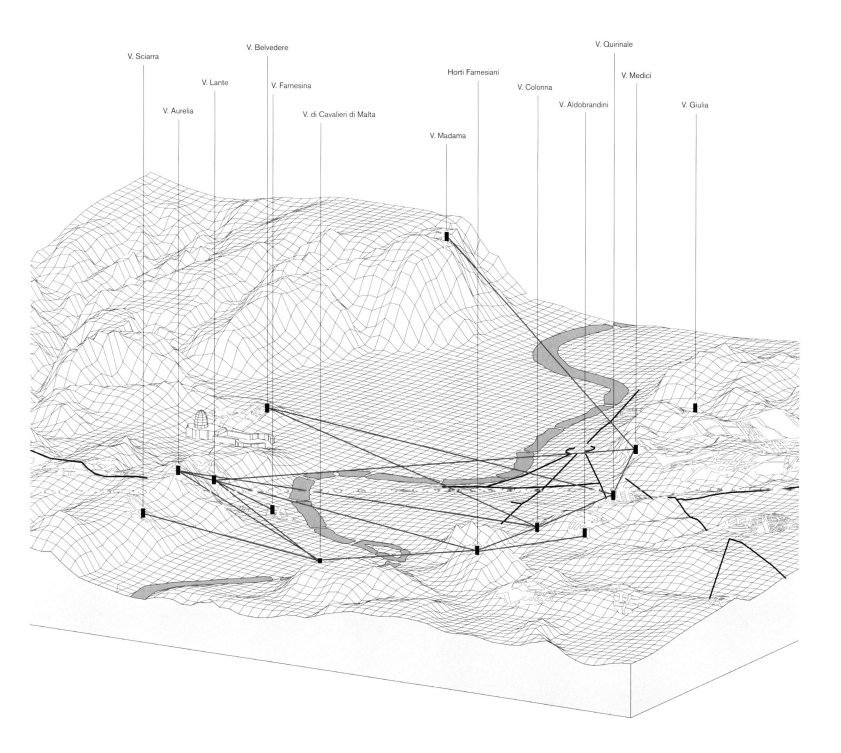

V. Sciarra

V. Belvedere

V. Quirinale

V. Lante

V. Farnesina

Horti Farnesiani

V. Medici

V. Aurelia

V. Colonna

V. Giulia

V. di Cavalieri di Malta

V. Aldobrandini

V. Madama

The Horti Farnesiani in the visual network over the Tiber

Rome as space in time

The Horti Farnesiani is an early example of urban landscape architecture. The history of the urban landscape is here captured expressively in one scheme. The multiple layers of the city's history are absorbed in a startling scenography that opens up the visual range of the urban domain, from *locus* to *panorama*.

The audacity in the handling of formidable historical material and the assimilation of earlier monumentality into a shocking garden design brought about a new balance between the blossoming and decay of the city, and restored the broken threads of history, to create a new fabric.

The Horti Farnesiani is a keystone in a network of visual relations that link the outstanding places in the urban landscape of Rome with one another. With it, the city was connected with the topography of the Seven Hills, in which the *genius loci* of Rome lies hidden, in a new, landscape architectonic manner.

Moreover, through the Horti Farnesiani this visual network was connected with the classical history of the city, and obtained not only a spatial, but also a temporal dimension, as the traversing of a space-in-time in which 2000 years of the history of the city was recapitulated and transformed in a landscape architectonic design. As a result, seen from a contemporary perspective, the urban landscape of Rome became a time machine for the Western world.

The historic layers of the urban landscape

▨ villas

1   V. Medici, Madama
2   V. Mellini
3   V. Glori
4   V. Ada
5   Bioparco, V. Borgese, Museo Nazionale di V. Giulia, V. Medici
6   V. Albani, Torlonia
7   V. Torlonia
8   Giardini del Quirinale
9   Giardini del Vaticano
10 V. Carpegna
11 Parco Giannicolese
12 V. Pamphili, Doria Pamphili
13 V. Sciarra
14 Parco di Colle Oppio
15 V. Celimontana
16 Parco S. Sebastiano e Parco degli Scipioni
17 V. Aldobrandini, V. Torlonia
18 V. Tuscolana
19 V. Falconieri
20 V. Parisi
21 V. Mondragone
22 Barco Borghese
23 V. Sora
24 V. Sciarra
25 V. Grazioli
26 V. Rasponi
27 V. Pontificia, V.S. Catarina, V. Albani, V. Cybo, V. dei Gesuiti
28 V. Barberini
29 V. Doria Pamphili, V. Altieri
30 V. Ferraioli
31 V. Corsini, V. Venosa-Boncompagni
32 V. Chigi
33 Casal di Decima

▨ present urban pattern

▨ urban pattern ca. 1748

── Aurelian wall (282)
── walls of Paul III / Urban VIII (1534-1644)

── consular roads

▨ green spaces
▬ water

········· aqueducts

a   Acquedotto Traiano/Paolo
b   Aqua Virgo
c   Aqua Claudia, condotto dell'Anio Novus
d   Acquedotto Anio Vetus
e   Acquedotto Felice
f   Aqua Alexandriana
g   Acquedotto Aqua Antoniniana
h   Aqua Marcia
i   Aqua Tepula
j   Acquedotto dei Quintili
k   Acquedotto e Villa dei Centroni
l   Aqua Claudia
m   Anio Novus

─── Via Appia Antica
─ ─ ─ view from the city
─ ─ ─ view toward the city

▨ archaeological zones

I   Baths of Diocletian
II   Parco Archeologico centrale: Fori Romani, Campidoglio, Orti Farnesiani, Colosseo, Circo Massimo
III   Domus Aurea, Terme di Traiano
IV   Baths of Caracalla
V   Via Appia
VI   Cimitero di Marco, Marcelliano e Basileo
VII   Circo e Villa di Massenzio
VIII Tombe Latine
IX   Villa dei Gordiani
X   Villa dei Quintili
XI   Tuscolo Abitato
XII   Abitato antico 'Gabii'

N   0   2   5km

Via Flaminia

Via Salaria

Via Trionfale

Via Flaminia

Via Nomentana

Via Tiburtina

Aurelia Antica

Via Prenestina

XII

Via Latina

Via Tuscolana

Via Casilina

Via Portuense

Via Appia Antica

Via Ostiense

Via Appia Nuova

Via Laurentina

A

JARDIN DES TUILERIES PARIS 1664

The spatial axis
André le Nôtre
The formal ideal city

The Paris Basin and the Seine
The Seine valley

The residential landscape and the city
In the topographic intersection
The nucleus on the Seine
The regionalisation of court culture
Versailles as the new hub
The new relation of the regional system with the city

The Jardin des Tuileries
The geometry of the Seine
Breaking the garden open
The illusionistic order of nature
The urban stage
The scenic identity of Paris

The urban transformation of the spatial axis
Nailing down the point of view
Framing the view
Dismantling the mirror image
The disappearance of the horizon
The materialisation of the vanishing point

The representation of the horizon
The horizon in the technical universe
The formal and the urban network

The Louvre axis, Paris (aerial photo: P. van Bolhuis / Pandion)

The spatial axis

In the 17th century a regional system of country estates, connected with one another by axes and avenues, arose to the south-west of Paris. The Jardin des Tuileries was one of the most important places where this new, axial relationship between the city and the landscape was worked out in landscape architectonic terms. The formal spatial design was based on an abstract concept of nature and space. In addition to the arts, such as music by Jean Baptiste Lully and theatre by Molière, in the 17th century sciences like astronomy, geography, cartography, physics and mathematics developed. In abstract thinking mathematics began to overstep the boundaries of conceivable reality. French savants such as René Descartes (1596-1650) played a large role in this.

   The pushing back of frontiers in the arts and sciences, like the concurrent economic and military expansion, was based on a centralisation of political power. As the Sun King, Louis XIV (1638-1715) was the new embodiment of Roman imperial rule. Paris was the new Rome, which in the second half of the 17th century grew into the centre of an absolutist empire. This also had repercussions for the development of a new urban landscape. In Paris, the city and countryside were united into one coherent formal system, with the axial organisation of space as its basic foundation.

André le Nôtre

The most important designer of this system was the landscape architect André le Nôtre (1613-1700). André was born into a line of horticulturalists. As a gardener, his grandfather Pierre had oversight of the gardens of the Tuileries. His father Jean le Nôtre initially worked under the landscape architect Claude Mollet and was later *Premier Jardinier des Tuileries*, the chief gardener of the Tuileries under Louis XIII. Jean initiated his son into the discipline, in which the young André, in accordance with the practice of the time, deepened his knowledge under the tutelage of painters, architects and theoreticians. Jacques Boyceau, the *Intendant des Jardins du Roy*, regarded a knowledge of architecture, drawing, painting and geometry as essential for training in landscape architecture. In 1637 André, who until then had been in the service of the Duke of Orléans, the brother of the king, succeeded his father as the chief gardener of the Tuileries. In 1643 he was appointed 'designer of plants and terraces' for the queen-mother Anne of Austria, after which, from 1645 to 1646, he worked on modernising the gardens of the Château de Fontainbleau. Later he was appointed supervisor of all the royal gardens of France, and in 1657 he even became chief inspector of royal buildings.

   André le Nôtre was primarily known for his work for Nicolas Fouquet (1615-1680), who in 1653 was appointed *Surintendant des Finances* (comparable to the Chancellor of the Exchequer) for Louis XIV. Between 1656 and 1661 Fouquet commissioned the building of Vaux-le-Vicomte, the first in a series of large new Paris country estates. Le Nôtre's design for the park of Vaux-le-Vicomte corresponded to the new ideas which expressed the political aspirations of the ruling class. In this sense it was an important model, that gave French garden art a formal identity all of its own.

The formal ideal city

An early French example in which the city and the landscape were united in a single spatial composition was the ideal town of Richelieu, in Touraine. Here, in his birthplace, with the permission of the monarch, in 1631 the Cardinal and First Minister Richelieu began building a new town according to a scheme drawn up by Jacques Lemercier. The town was included in the plans for the garden and park around the Château de Richelieu, which was erected next to it. The Mable River, which in the park was transformed into a canal that bounded the town as a rectangular moat, anchored the plan in the topography. The château, park, landscape and town each had their own place and scale, but were united by two axes which crossed one another in front of the château. The axis through the château linked the building, park and landscape with one another. The other axis, through the town, remained within the boundaries of the estate and linked the town with the spatial axis of the residence. The town's spatial relation with the landscape existed by the grace of the axis of the château.

   The axis of the Jardin des Tuileries, and that of Versailles, played a comparable role. There too the city and landscape were united in one axial spatial series. Over the course of centuries the spatial axis of the Jardin des Tuileries grew to become the Grande Axe of Paris. In this process, the axis was transformed into a city-centre space. The horizon in the landscape changed to become an urban skyline. The regional system of axes and avenues became enclosed by the expansion of the city. But the anchorage of the system in the morphology of the landscape, and the manner in which it represented nature, lent it an autonomous authority in the urban pattern. This fact continues to define the specific character of the urban landscape of Paris to this day.

The Grande Arche in La Défense

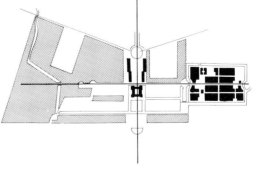

Model of Richelieu

Topography

⣿⣿⣿⣿⣿	17th century country estates
A	Clagny
B	Grand Trianon
C	Luxembourg
D	Marly
E	Meudon
F	Saint-Cloud
G	Saint-Germain-en-Laye
H	Sceaux
I	Tuileries
J	Versailles

⣿⣿⣿⣿⣿	other parks and urban green spaces
1	Belleville
2	Bois de Boulogne
3	Bois de la Cave
4	Bois de Monteclin
5	Bois de Vincennes
6	Bois des Gonards
7	Bois du Loup Pendu
8	Bois du Pont Colbert
9	Butte Montmartre
10	Champ de Mars
11	Cité Internationale Universitaire
12	Esplanade des Invalides
13	Forêt Domaniale de Fausses Reposes
14	Forêt Domaniale de la Malmaison
15	Forêt Domaniale de la Marly-Le roi
16	Forêt Domaniale de Louveciennes
17	Forêt Domaniale de Meudon
18	Forêt Domaniale de Saint-Germain-en-Laye
19	Forêt Domaniale de Verrières
20	Forêt Domaniale de Versailles
21	Forêt Domaniale des Buttes du Parisis
22	Forêt Régionale de la Butte Pinson
23	Fort d'Aubervilliers
24	Fort d'Ivry
25	Fort de Bicêtre
26	Fort de Charenton
27	Fort de l'Est
28	Fort de Vanves
29	Fort du Mont Valérien
30	Forum des Halles
31	Jardin d'Acclimatation
32	Jardin du Trocadero
33	Jardin des Plantes
34	Jardin du Ranelagh
35	Les Batignolles
36	Palais Royal
37	Parc André Citroën
38	Parc de Bagatelle
39	Parc de Bercy
40	Parc des Buttes Chaumont
41	Parc de la Villette
42	Parc de Loisirs
43	Parc de Loisirs
44	Parc de Maisons-Laffitte
45	Parc de Monceau
46	Parc de Saint-Cloud
47	Parc Départemental
48	Parc Departemental de la Courneuve
49	Parc des Beaumonts
50	Parc des Guilands
51	Parc Edmond de Rothschild
52	Parc Henri Sellier
53	Parc Jean Moulin
54	Parc Montsouris
55	Square de Choisy
56	Square Georges Brassens

airport

subway station
subway line
railway line
•   railway station

⎯⎯⎯   motorway
⎯⎯⎯   important road
▬ ▬ ▬   spatial axis

urban pattern

water

★   Eiffel Tower

The spatial axis of Versailles

0   2   5km

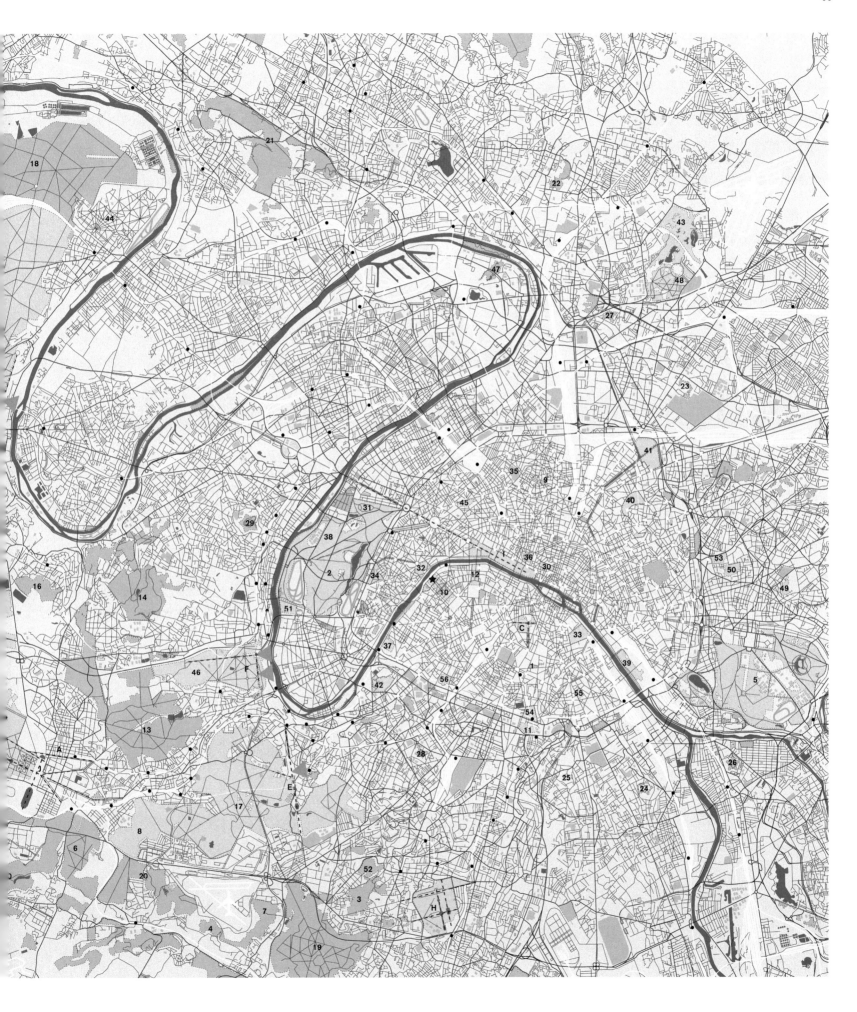

The Paris Basin and the Seine

The Basin of Paris is a large, dish-shaped geological basin in the north-east of France, named after the city of Paris, which, in geographic terms, lies almost in its centre. It is about five times the size of The Netherlands, more or less concentric in form, and is bounded on various sides by massifs: on the west by Normandy and Brittany, on the north-east by the London-Brabant Massif and the Ardennes, on the east by the Vosges and on the south by the Massif Central. Beginning in the Permian period subsidence took place in this region, as a result of which the centre of the area of subsidence moved progressively to the west over the course of time.

During the Mesozoic era the north-west side of the Paris Basin was open to the sea. This created a shallow inland sea as a consequence of marine transgression. At the end of the Oligocene epoch the sea retreated permanently from the basin. In the middle of the Lutetian age, a stage in the Eocene epoch, the connection with the North Sea was broken, after which the Basin became a lake which slowly dried up. From the Permian until into the Tertiary period the basin was filled in with calcareous Mesozoic and Tertiary sediments. First Triassic, then Jurassic, then Cretacous, and finally Tertiary rocks crop out from the edge toward the centre. The youngest rocks date from the Pliocene epoch.

In the Neogene period the regions bordering the northern, eastern and southern edges rose, so that the formations of harder and softer rock were tipped upward by tectonic forces, and then eroded partially. In these regions one finds what are called cuestas, asymmetrical hills with a steep scarp slope and a gentle back slope. They were created from folded layers of hard rock lying on top of softer layers of rock, which erode in different directions at an unequal rate. The basin itself is characterised by a succession of rock outcrops running more or less concentrically, the youngest rocks of which are to be found in the centre of the basin in the vicinity of Paris, among them sandstone and the Montmartre gypsum that one encounters in the catacombs of Paris. The landscape is undulating, with the wooded ridges of the cuestas in the east. The limestone layers of the basin reach the coast at the Channel and form the sheer chalk cliffs or *falaises* there.

The Seine valley

The name of the Seine is perhaps derived from the Latin name *Sequana*, which in turn could have been derived from the Celtic *Sicauna*. The river rises on the Langres Plateau to the north of Dijon, running via Troyes and Melun to Paris, and then meandering through Normandy in great loops via Rouen and flowing into the sea through an estuary between Le Havre and Honfleur. The area drained by the Seine largely coincides with the Paris Basin, but is smaller in size. It is asymmetric, because the watershed lies much further away in the north than in the south. The main stream angles across the basin and has many tributaries, the most important of which are the Yonne, Marne and Oise.

The Seine is the most heavily navigated river in France. Before locks were constructed in the course of the 19th century to raise the water level, the river in the city was much shallower, and often impeded by sandbanks. The whole length of the Seine through Paris is now lined with quays. The river has a low flow rate, and is artificially kept at the necessary level with the aid of reservoirs. The Pont Neuf is the oldest bridge over the river.

Geomorphology and urban domain

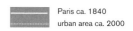

Paris ca. 1840
urban area ca. 2000

0   20   40km

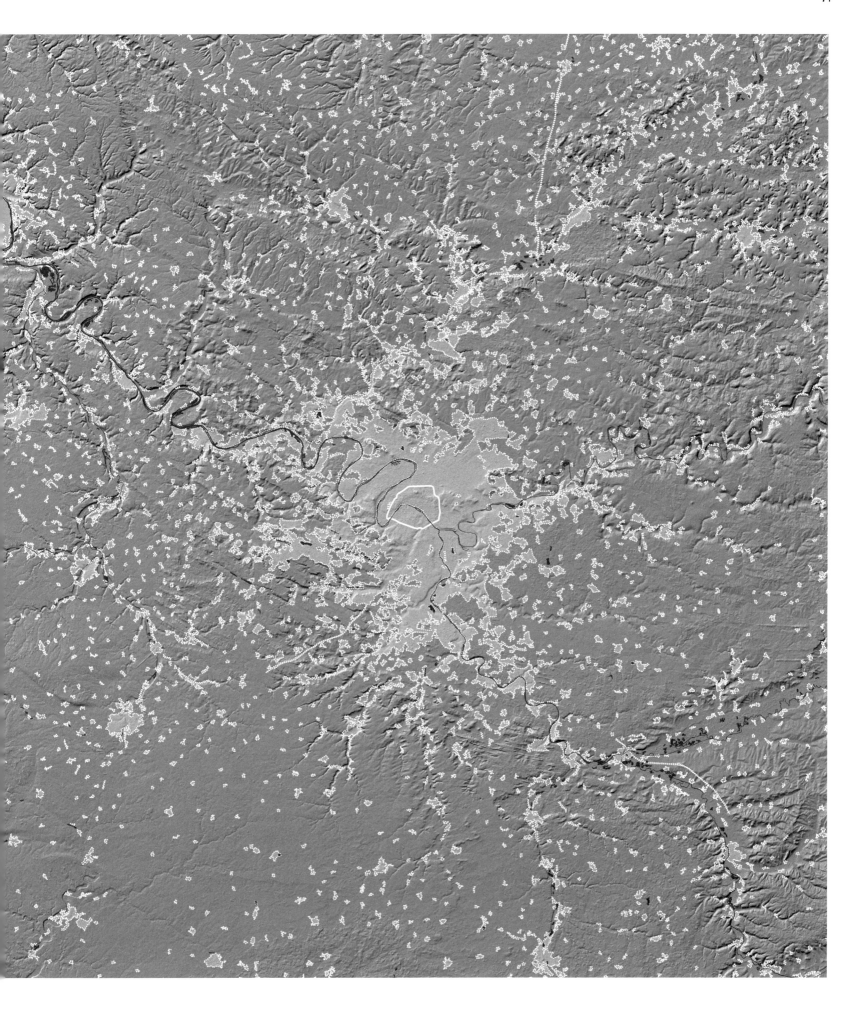

The axis of Marly, in the direction of the Seine valley

Geomorphology, urban pattern and parks

Elevation (metres)

	180 - 200
	160 - 180
	140 - 160
	120 - 140
	100 - 120
	90 - 100
	80 - 90
	70 - 80
	60 - 70
	50 - 60
	40 - 50
	30 - 40
	20 - 30
	10 - 20

	urban pattern
	park
	water

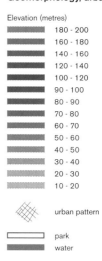

0   2   5km

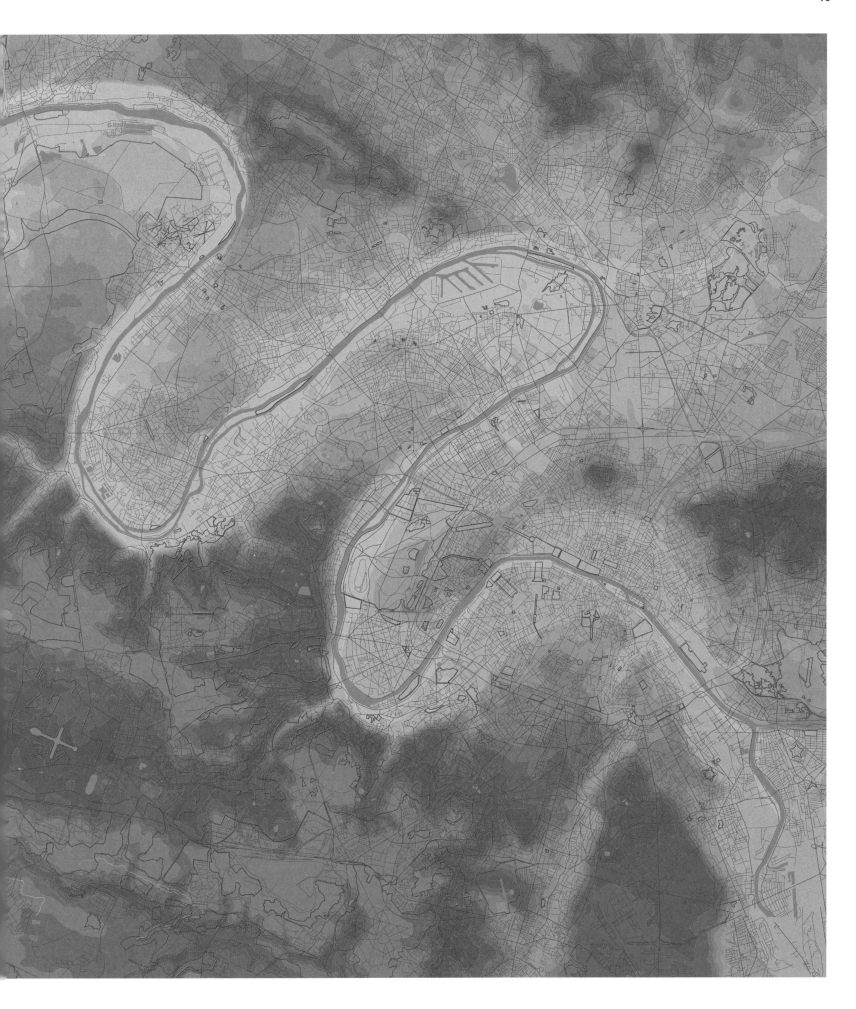

The residential landscape and the city

In all likelihood the region where Paris lies today was already occupied during the whole Neolithic period. The city arose on a spot where the Seine was easy to ford, thanks to two small islands (Île St Louis and Île de la Cité). The Celtic Parisii tribe settled there around 100 BCE on the easily defensible Île de la Cité.

In the topographic intersection

In 52 BCE the Romans under Julius Caesar captured the stronghold of the Parisii, to which they then gave the name Lutetia Parisiorum. This was a strategically important spot because of the trade routes passing through it. In the first century a new Roman city was built on the left bank of the Seine, based on the typical Roman square grid. The point where the two axes in the ground plan, one north-south and one east-west, crossed formed the topographic intersection that defined the shape of the city. The square Gallo-Roman city was not yet walled. At that time Lutetia had five to six thousand inhabitants and was thus no more than a medium-sized Gallic city, in contrast to, for instance, Lugdunum (today's Lyon), which was much larger.

With the decline of the Roman Empire Lutetia was overrun by the Germanic Migration. Around 360 Lutetia was captured by the Germans. From that date the city was called Paris. With the rise of the Frankish Kingdom under Clovis Christianity spread, and Paris became the seat of a bishop. Abbeys were founded on the left and right banks of the Seine. With the death of Clovis the city was left to its fate. After the raids by the Normans – the city was not captured – the Capetian dynasty established itself in Paris. They made it the real capital of the kingdom.

Around 1180 Philippe August had the section of the city north of the Seine walled. This was the first of a long series of circumvallations. The city expanded in a more or less concentric manner in the Seine river valley. Successive new city walls were built to surround the medieval city around 1210, 1370 and in 1549. In the 13th century the right bank of the Seine, which until then had been swampy, was drained. Areas like the present-day Quartier de Marais, which had functioned as a vegetable garden for the city, came to lie inside the walls. The Louvre, originally a fort along the Seine, and Notre Dame, the cathedral on the Île de la Cité, were built in the 13th century. The Louvre was the starting point for the most important east-west axis of the city, and determined the strategic position of the later Jardin des Tuileries at the intersection of the urban topography.

**The formal landscape (ca. 1770),
projected onto the geomorphology**

– – – – –   spatial axis

....   contour lines

   system of axes and avenues

▬▬▬   Seine

A   Clagny
B   Grand Trianon
C   Luxembourg
D   Marly
E   Meudon
F   Saint Cloud
G   Saint-Germain-en-Laye
H   Sceaux
I   Tuileries
J   Versailles

0   2   5km

The nucleus on the Seine

In the period preceding a general pacification of the country, the French kings had sought refuge in fortified castles in the Loire valley. After around the middle of the 16th century there were also châteaux being built in the valley of the Seine near Paris. In these châteaux the representative character of the building was more important than the defensive capabilities. An Italian influence played an important role in this, in part because the Italian De' Medici (or Dei Medici) family (in French, De Médicis) had become allied with the French royal house by marriage.

One of the first Paris châteaux was Meudon, the construction of which began in 1520. It lay high on the southern wall of the Seine valley, with a view out over the landscape and the city of Paris. At St. Cloud (begun 1557) and at the Château-Neuf of St. Germain-en-Laye (begun 1597) there were also grand panoramas over the Seine valley and Paris. In 1615 Maria de Médicis had the Palais du Luxembourg, modelled on the Palazzo Pitti in Florence, built on the southern edge of the city. Because of the minor difference in elevation, there was no panorama here. In the case of the Jardin des Tuileries, which she had built beginning in 1563 on what was then the western edge of the city, there were again no views, because of the low, flat location along the river and the city walls. But the site, on the long, right bank of the Seine, was however a natural point of convergence in the topography.

The 16th and early 17th century châteaux in and around Paris were, like those in Italy, still 'domestic' and of local scale. The geometric plan of the garden was of limited size, and served as a foreground. The medieval agrarian structure of the landscape was hardly affected by these occasional 'villa' projects, but they did occupy the visually strategic points in the Seine valley, with the Jardin des Tuileries in the centre.

The regionalisation of court culture

A radical change set in during the reign of Louis XIV, in the second half of the 17th century. The king moved his court and government from Paris to Versailles. Between 1590 and 1637 the population of Paris doubled to more than 400,000 inhabitants. Wars and failed harvests caused famines. Because of backward agricultural practices, there was a structural shortage of food. Farmers were forced to sell their land to cover taxes and debts.

The deterioration of agriculture resulted in a diminution in the autonomy of rural communities and a decline in the acreage under cultivation. The mediaeval agrarian landscape became subject to the free play of economic forces. The bourgeoisie, aristocrats and financiers drew profits from the situation by acquiring as much land as possible. The new landowners' prime concern was not the enjoyment of the rural life, with, for instance, views over fields and vineyards. For them agriculture was relegated to the background. The agricultural land acquired was used for an expansion of the court culture, and that required that the agrarian landscape be excluded from sight.

The king and the members of the royal household and the government, such as princes and magistrates, and the urban aristocracy sought to maximise the size of their estates by concentrating parcels of land. They wished to demonstrate their might by the control of such 'immeasurable' domains. The form of economic exploitation which fit best with these estates was primarily large-scale forestry. Woods therefore became the ceremonial backdrop for the residences which were built in the second half of the 17th century. Together with the surrounding region, Paris was transformed into one great artificial landscape of residential estates.

Versailles as the new hub

After 1661 the old hunting lodge at Versailles was transformed into a large-scale royal residence. The existing landscape was altered by levelling whole hills. The large, swampy valley in which it lay was drained in its entirety by the Grand Canal designed for that purpose. A new town was part of the spatial composition. The landscape and town were placed opposite one another on a mirror axis, and both organised spatially with the aid of geometry, symmetry and perspective. The transformation of Versailles into a royal residence was a decisive step in the life of the court moving from the city to the landscape. The garden lay outside the visual network of the Seine valley and the city. Versailles became the new hub of a regional country estate landscape. As a consequence, the regional landscape attained an autonomous status as an urban site.

At St. Cloud (1661) Le Nôtre designed the Allée de la Balustrade, high along the Seine, for Philippe d'Orléans. At right angles to that, in a side valley of the Seine, he created a new spatial axis. This brought the upper reaches of the side valley, the château and the panorama of Paris, lying below it, into one axial relation. At St. Germain-en-Laye Le Nôtre designed two new spatial axes for Louis XIV. The Grande Terrasse, constructed in 1669, was laid out 60 meters above the Seine, its length paralleling the river. It comprised a promenade 30 meters wide and 2400 meters long. The axis was intended to connect the Château-Neuf at St. Germain with the future Château du Val. Crosswise, the

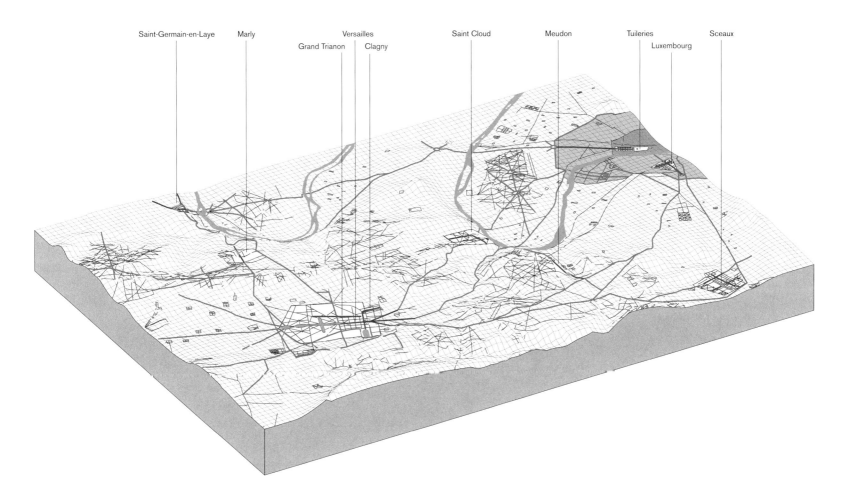

Saint-Germain-en-Laye Marly Versailles Saint Cloud Meudon Tuileries Sceaux

Grand Trianon Clagny Luxembourg

The regional system of 17th century axes and avenues

Grande Terrasse hung above the Seine valley and Paris like a gigantic balcony. In 1670 even the frugal Colbert had his 16th century château in Sceaux embellished. The Avenue de l'Octogone was laid out running north-south, across the front of the château, with a long cascade, an artificial lake and a *tapis vert*. The axis of symmetry, which ran through the château, was extended in a westerly direction. At Meudon Servien, the Finance Minister to Louis XIV, began building a massive terrace. It measured 253 x 136 meters and lay high on a hill crest at right angles to the Seine. From that terrace, which formed part of the base for the château, one could survey the city of Paris and the landscape for miles around. After 1679 the terrace was included in a spatial axis which ran for kilometres from the bend in the Seine in the north, along the length of the terrace, obliquely through a side valley with a lake, as far as the heights of the southern horizon.

Just to the north-east of Versailles, beginning in 1674 Louis XIV had the country estate of Clagny built for Mme de Montespan. It was connected with Versailles by an axis of symmetry running in a south-westerly direction across a lake, the Étang de Clagny. Marly, lying six kilometres to the north of Versailles, became a royal country estate in 1679. The house was the final element in two symmetrical rows of six guest pavilions placed along an axis. The spatial axis, oriented toward the Seine valley and St. Germain, was comprised of large terraces with promenades and sheets of water. The residences were involved with one another by means of a system of axes and avenues, water basins and aqueducts. This system was the architectonic expression of the interconnections of the regional court culture, and created a new, royal geography that was stretched over the agricultural landscape. The Jardin des Tuileries assumed a new position in this. As the counterpart to Versailles, which opened up the landscape for the city, the transformation of the Jardin des Tuileries opened up the city to the landscape.

The new relation of the regional system with the city

On the *Carte des Chasses du Roi* (1764-1773) the results of the 17th century interventions in the region to the south-west of Paris are clearly visible. The modest châteaux from the beginning of the century have been significantly enlarged and completely reorganised. These new arrangements are dominated by a system of spatial axes, the concave longitudinal profile of which fit into the geomorphology. The spatial axes were of very considerable length, always on the order of several kilometres. They extended to the horizon. Beyond the horizon the spatial axis passed from the formal garden system into an avenue, and went

from being a visual axis to being a transport axis or route. Together with the cross roads and diagonals they formed a regional system that linked the residences with one another.

When the city walls of Paris were pulled down in 1670, the boulevard around them became a ring road with numerous star-shaped, radiating avenues. This created a formal set of connections on a regional scale, in which two sorts of axiality played a role. First, there were the interconnections between the residences and between them and the city. The transport axes formed a functional infrastructure for the whole district, the ceremonial *parcours*, over which the court moved in coaches, hunting parties and parades. Aqueducts and canals were also elements in this new infrastructure. The large woods with their radiating paths on the higher plateaus formed a neutral hinterland for this system. Long tree-lined avenues ending in tremendous perspectives were joined to the important entrances to the city. In the west the most important was the Cours de Vincennes, planted with four rows of elms. In the east this was the Grand Cours, from the Jardin des Tuileries. Together they formed an artificial east-west axis, which next to the Seine itself became the most important formal support for the relation between the city and the landscape. Second, there were the 'spatial axes', the strategically situated 'carriers' of the visual system, anchored in the geomorphology and elaborated in landscape architectonic terms. These were the 'telescopes', the visual axes by which the landscape was 'brought closer' by architectonic interventions. In addition to acting as a telescope focused on the landscape over the horizon, for some of the Parisian residences the spatial axis also worked in the opposite direction, as a telescope toward the city.

All these aspects came together in the Jardin des Tuileries. It was the most important intersection in the relations between the regional system of axes and avenues and the spatial structure of the city along the Seine which was borne by the east-west axis of the garden. Moreover, because of its low-lying location, the garden afforded a splendid prospect over the river landscape.

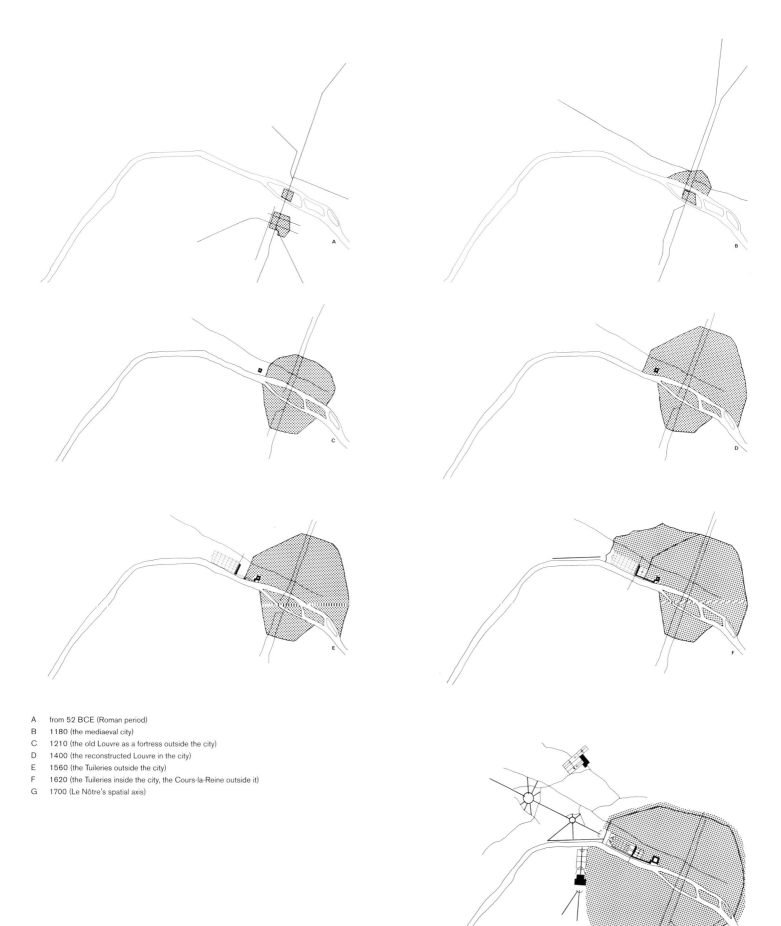

A   from 52 BCE (Roman period)

B   1180 (the mediaeval city)

C   1210 (the old Louvre as a fortress outside the city)

D   1400 (the reconstructed Louvre in the city)

E   1560 (the Tuileries outside the city)

F   1620 (the Tuileries inside the city, the Cours-la-Reine outside it)

G   1700 (Le Nôtre's spatial axis)

The Louvre and the Tuileries in the expansion of Paris

The Jardin des Tuileries

The Jardin des Tuileries lies along the Seine at a point where the swampy river bed was originally much wider. The name 'Tuileries' (or 'tile works') is a reminder of the its previous function, utilising the locally present river clay. Beginning in 1180 Philippe Auguste constructed a city wall, reinforced at the most vulnerable points at the Seine by forts. One of these forts, built outside the city, was the old Louvre. When Charles V built a new city wall at the end of the 14th century the Louvre came to lie within the city and lost its strategic importance.

After 1546 François I had a new castle built by Pierre Lescot on the square foundation of the old fort, parallel with the Seine. But the new castle was too dark and claustrophobic for Cathérine de Médicis, the wife of Henri II; she wanted views outside, to the landscape. Therefore in 1563 she began the creation of a new country residence, 500 meters from the Louvre, outside the city walls, on the site of an old tile works: the Palais des Tuileries.

The geometry of the Seine

This palace came to stand with its long side at right angles to the following stretch of the Seine. This made the gentle bend in the river visible as a break between the axes of symmetry of the Louvre and of the new plan. The Tuileries palace was connected with the Louvre by a roofed gallery along the bank of the Seine. Furthermore, a geometric garden was laid out by the new palace, parallel with the river and reaching as far as the following bend in the Seine. In the plans by Philibert Delorme, this garden covered an irregular rectangle of 70 × 270 meters. It lay west of the new palace, enclosed by walls on all four sides. The square beds of the ground plan were filled with a varied medley of ingredients in the Italian fashion. There was a *volière*, a wolf, a bear, a wild boar and a leopard. The park was a refuge, and from the start was openly accessible. Despite the spatial autonomy of the garden in respect to the palace, there was a geometric coherence between the two, as can be seen in an engraving of the original scheme by J. Androuet du Cerceau. The plan of the garden and of the palace both appear to be organised on the basis of a grid of squares.

With the erection of the next city wall under Louis XIII, in the early 17th century, the Tuileries too came to lie within the city. Now it was Maria de Médicis, the widow of Henri IV, who sought a new way of escaping from the urban straitjacket. In 1616 she commissioned a new, tree-lined promenade outside the fortifications, modelled on the Cacine, the Florentine promenade along the Arno. Called the

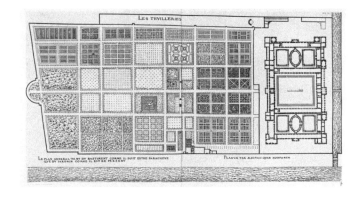

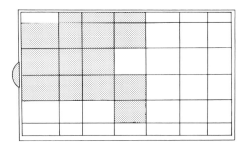

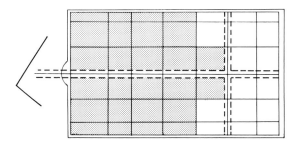

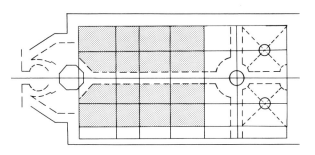

The Renaissance plan of the Tuileries and its transformation in Le Nôtre's plan (from J.A. du Cerceau, *Les plus excellents bastiments de France*. Paris 1870. TUDL TR BK Fra.N. 2 c folio vitrine).

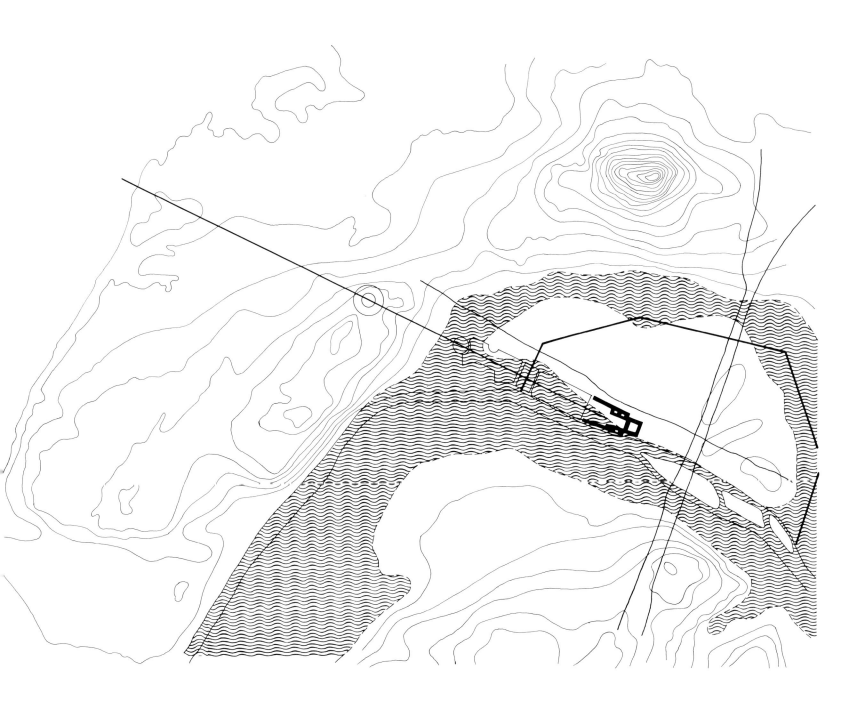

Le Nôtre's axis, with the present Louvre projected onto the relief and the original loop
of the Seine

Cours-la-Reine, it was built in a straight line along the next stretch of the river. The promenade lay in the river landscape like a classical arcade or *stoa*, and quickly became a favourite place to be seen in one's coach.

In 1664 the architect Le Vau was commissioned to draw up new plans for the Louvre and cut back the Tuileries. In his plans, the dimensions of the building were increased considerably. The garden architect Le Nôtre was called in to bring the whole into a state of balance. He retained the grid dimensions of the Renaissance garden as the basis for his new plan. The walls around the garden were demolished, and a large terrace created in front of the palace. The centre line, running east-west, which in the Renaissance framework of the garden had been only a line in the grid, equivalent to the other lines in the plan, was transformed into the central axis of symmetry in the scheme. Within the garden it was 222 metres long and 37 metres wide.

Across its width the site sloped toward the Seine by about a metre-and-a-half. Moreover, the dimensions differed on either side of the mirror axis. Le Nôtre corrected this by building an elongated side terrace along the Seine. This lay like a quay, a counterpart to the elevated terrace that was already present along the other side of the garden. The width of the Seine terrace and the adjoining parterres was however greater, so that the asymmetry of the site was balanced up by this intervention. Over its length, the perspective in the ground plan was manipulated; among the interventions, the dimensions of the water features were increased as they receded. The water landscape of the Seine was captured in an abstract formal model.

Breaking the garden open

Past the great open terrace behind the palace and the *parterres de broderie*, water basins and *parterres de gazon* which lay beyond it, the grid of the plan was filled with *bosquets*, trees and tree-lined paths. These bounded the new spatial axis, acting as coulisses. Together with the raised terraces along the sides of the garden, which as promenades opened up prospects of the Seine and the city, these coulisses ensured that the whole plan remained spatially focused on one point. This was the point where the city wall had been breached and the ends of the two side terraces came together in a *fer à cheval*, or horseshoe shape, to create a frame for a view of the landscape across the city's moat. In the Renaissance plan the axis of symmetry had ended here in an *exedra* or 'echo'. Given the situation at the time, that was all that was possible.

After the demolition of the city wall in 1670 the axis could also be continued physically beyond the limits of the garden and the city. The spatial axis was continued through the levelled landscape as a broad,

rising avenue of trees, the Grand Cours, laid out in 1667. The line where the earth touched the heavens lay on the top of the Butte de Chaillot, about three kilometres from the palace. Because of its upward slope and its great length – more than two kilometres – in relation to the foreground, the Grand Cours was clearly visible from the Tuileries.

The spatial depth of the garden was manipulated architectonically. The narrowing of the main axis created a form of accelerated perspective so that the space at the back appeared deeper. The opposite effect occured as a result of the increasing size of the water features and the length of the Grand Cours. This all created a foreshortening of the perspective and the space seemed shallower. As a result of this play with accelerated and decelerated perspective, the actual spatial depth of the axis was impossible to judge. Like a telescope, the axis maximised the visual range and brought the landscape under control visually, as far as the horizon. Beyond the horizon the avenue became part of the regional infrastructure of the residences, providing a link with Saint Germain-en-Laye and other places.

A northern diagonal axis, mirroring the Cours-la-Reine along the Seine, was projected, but never realised. For this purpose the plan called for a *patte d'oie* at the point where the city's fortifications had been breached. By framing the Grand Cours with two diverging avenues, when seen from the top of the triangle thus formed, the 'forecourt' of the city would be brought under control visually, not only in depth, but also in width.

The illusionistic order of nature

Because of the absence of statuary, the iconography of the garden was originally focused on a representation of nature as an abstract, ordered series consisting of earth, plants, water and light. In Le Nôtre's plan the relation between the ponds and parterres can be interpreted as corrections to the distortions in perspective. The correction in perspective here however has still another purpose, besides the control of the great distances involved. To the degree that the corrections to distortions in perspective approach perfection as a result of adjustments in the ground plan, the flat areas and fixtures are no longer round or square and of equal size in the real plan, but in a perspectivistic tableau. This means that the order of the plan is no longer to be found in a real geometric scheme, but in a notional, perspectivistic image. The view along the main axis is thus to be regarded as an anamorphosis constructed in the landscape. The illusion of perfect order reveals itself from the point where the observer stands. *Parterres de broderie*, *parterres de gazon* and the *tapis vert* of the Grand Cours succeed one

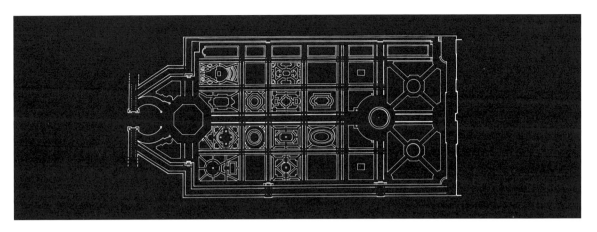

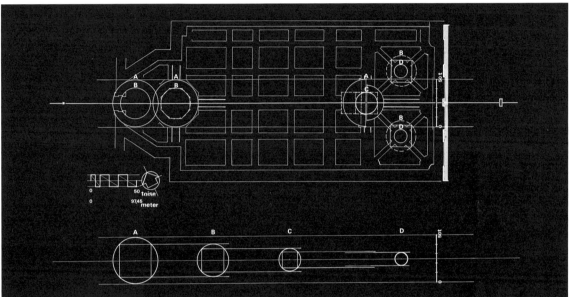

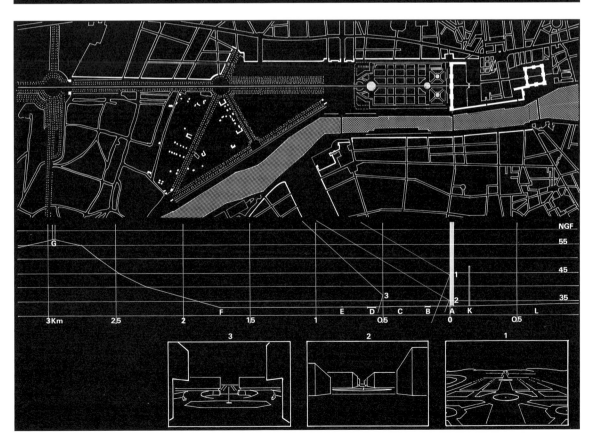

Le Nôtre's design, from his plan for the Jardin des Tuileries (top)

Increased dimensions of the more distant water basins (middle)

Plan, longitudinal profile and perspectives (1, 2, 3) of the Jardin des Tuileries and the Cours-la-Reine in the time of Le Nôtre (bottom)

another in the axial zone of the garden. Like a classification system, these suggest gradations of naturalness in the direction of the horizon.

The urban stage

From the beginning the Jardin des Tuileries was open to the public, and was the largest public space in the heart of Paris. The park as a whole formed an overwhelming spectacle. The *parterres de broderie*, *parterres de gazon* and water basins provided restful accents and details. The *bosquets*, containing intimate spaces such as a labyrinth and an open-air theatre, afforded the opportunity to escape from the larger spaces. The square plantations of trees created free spaces for play. The central *allée*, the terraces and the raised promenades along the edges offered plenty of scope for strolling and gazing out over the park, the city and the river.

With the programme, evoked by the composition itself, the garden in fact took on the character of a city park. The garden was heavily visited; there were dances, theatre performances and concerts. The park's programme was still implicit here, defined by the form of the garden. But through the grandeur of the gesture by which the landscape was placed on the stage, this garden assumed a function for the whole of the city. It connected not only the palace, but the city as a whole with the landscape. The people of the city could mount this stage themselves and identify with the magnificence of the park. The demolition of the Palais des Tuileries at the end of the 18th century served to again confirm the role of the gardens as a public, urban park.

The scenic identity of Paris

It was in this way then that the basis for the scenic identity of Paris arose in the 17th century, fixed in the system of formal avenues, gardens and country estates. The Jardin des Tuileries assumes a central place in this system because it directly connects the structure and form of the city with its *genius loci*, the landscape of the Seine. As the formal reduction of the meandering Seine valley, Le Nôtre's spatial axis connected the centre of the city visually with the landscape of the river. With it, the Jardin des Tuileries formed the formal hub of the city, with Versailles as its counterpart in the landscape outside the city. In principle, the landscape architectonic form of the city is derived from the relation between these two places.

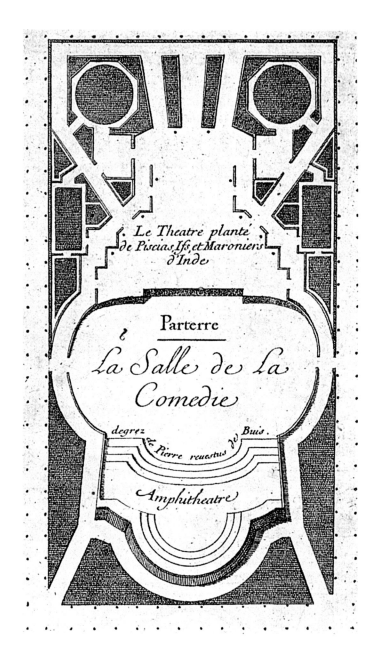

The green amphitheatre as one of the elaborated bosquets in the garden (from E. de Ganay & A., Le Nostre *André Le Nostre, 1613-1700*. Paris 1962.)

↗ **The Jardin des Tuileries and the avenue to the horizon in 1680** (Famille des Perelle, Vue du Jardin des Thuileries comme il est à présent 1680. Réunion des musées nationaux (Château de Versailles et de Trianon, Recueil de gravures grosseuvre 137, 99-023775) / Gérard Blot.)

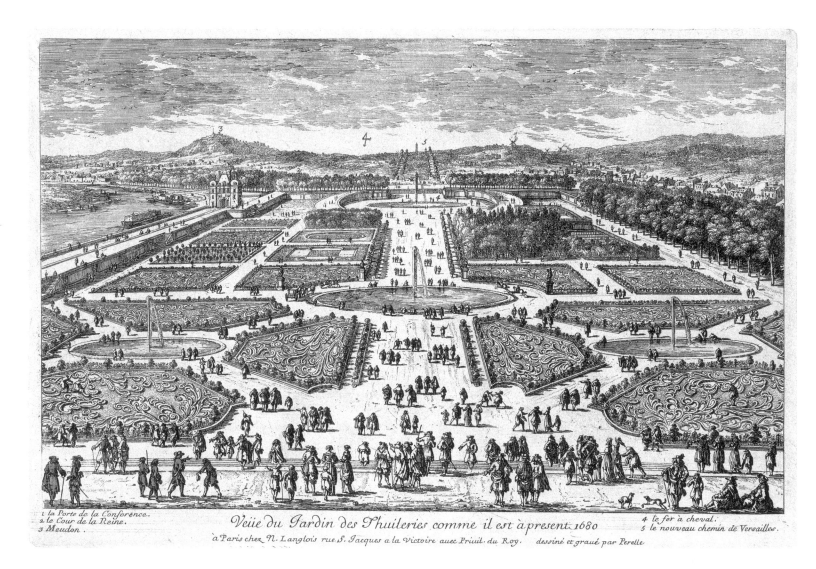

1 la Porte de la Conférence.
2 le Cour de la Reine.
3 Meudon.
4 le fer à cheval.
5 le nouveau chemin de Versailles.

Veüe du Jardin des Thuileries comme il est à present 1680

à Paris chez N. Langlois rue S. Jacques a la Victoire auec Priuil. du Roy.   dessiné et graué par Perelle.

The open space between the Louvre and the Jardin des Tuileries

The Jardin des Tuileries

The urban transformation of the spatial axis

The axis of the Jardin des Tuileries was pointed westwards on the landscape, like a viewfinder. The urban expansion of Paris took place in the same direction. As a result of this development, the landscape architectonic design and the city came to lie alongside and over each other, rather than facing one another, as at Versailles. One after another, the landscape architectonic spaces on the axis were transformed into urban space. Ultimately the whole length of the axis itself was included in the urban morphology. The urbanisation took place in a process that has lasted more than 300 years now, and is still ongoing.

Nailing down the point of view

Around 1670, during the construction of the Jardin des Tuileries, the city's defensive works along the western edge lost their strategic military importance. Louis XIV had a 36-meter wide boulevard laid out where they had stood, which encircled almost the whole city like stately, green, tree-lined promenades. Triumphal arches were erected at the intersections of this boulevard and the most important traffic arteries. These arteries themselves were straightened, and as radiating axes linked the city to the region around it, making it one formal whole.

The *patte d'oie* where the Grand Cours intersected with the boulevard became a chaotic traffic junction. The intention behind the design of the Place de la Concorde was to provide an architectonic form for the point where the boulevard and spatial axis crossed, and at the same time structure the flow of traffic. After several competitions, the design by the architect Jacques-Ange Gabriël was executed between 1755 and 1763. For the northern edge of the square he designed a view through to the Church of the Madeleine, which was framed as a backdrop between two symmetrical façades reminiscent of palaces. The dimensions and orders for the foreground and background were coordinated with one another by interventions in perspective. The execution of the design was limited to the placement of this one architectonic screen. On its south side the square remained open to the Seine, and there were no walls of buildings on the east and west sides. Some, accustomed to the walls created by the old 'Places Royales', felt the new space was too large and empty: 'it is absolutely not a square; the eye cannot define it'. The longitudinal axis of the square, with the prospect toward the Madeleine, crosses Le Nôtre's spatial axis. The rectangular plan was framed and made autonomous by a dry moat. The orthogonal form of the square cut across the triangular *patte d'oie* with the Grand Cours, and Le Nôtre's

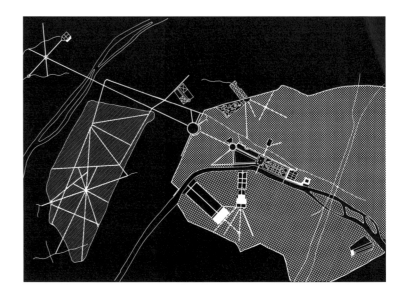

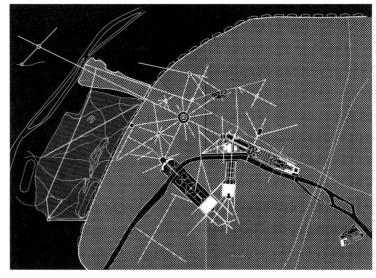

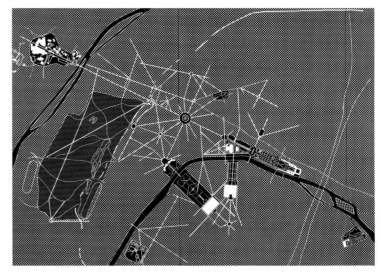

The urban transformation of the spatial axis (around 1800, 1900 and 2000, respectively)

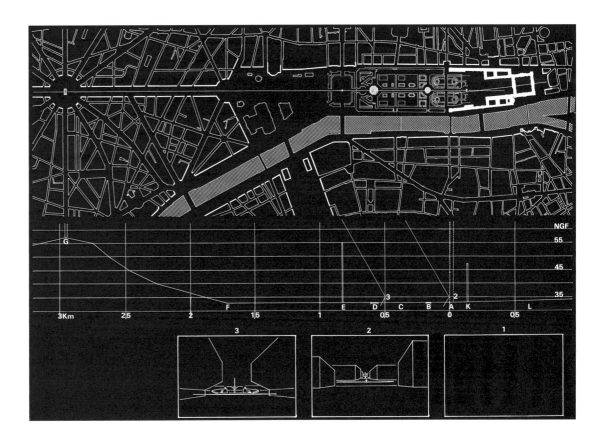

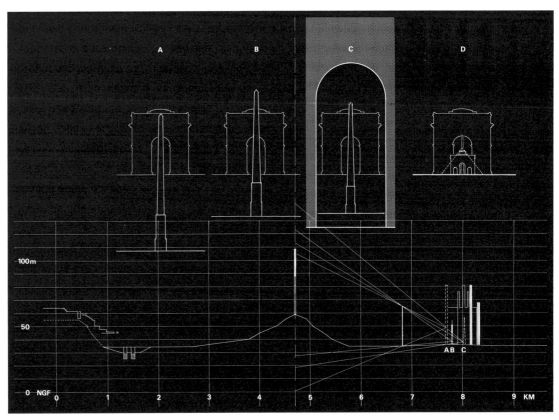

The obelisk on the Place de la Concorde (E) in the
view along the spatial axis from the Jardin des
Tuileries (1, 2, 3) to the Arc de Triomphe on the Butte
de Chaillot (G)

Perspectives along the spatial axis with the arches

A   from the Palais des Tuileries

B   from the portico in the Arc du Carrousel

C   from the Louvre

D   normal projection of the two arches at their actual size

perspective reaching to the horizon was interrupted by the erection of a monument at the point where the Grand Cours intersected with the axis to the Madeleine. The view across the square was blocked by further monuments at the intersections of the Madeleine axis with the two diagonals of the *patte d'oie*. In fact, the most important points for experiencing the vistas were occupied by monuments. As a result, the vista conceived by Le Nôtre was nailed down to the square by these monuments.

Framing the view

Initially the Grand Cours lay outside the city, running through fields and vegetable gardens as an avenue lined with elm trees. Later, after 1709, the area along it, which had then come to be called the Champs Élysées, a name that still later would be bestowed on the axis itself, was planted with trees. At the same time that the Place de la Concorde was laid out, between 1758 and 1767, the 150-meter wide axis through the Champs Élysées was once again planted with elms and lime trees. Particularly the north side, lying on dryer ground, was heavily used for ball games, parties and strolling. In 1770 the axis was extended past the Butte de Chaillot by Jean Perronet, director of the École des Ponts-et-Chaussées, so that it now ran on to the Seine. The Pont de Neuilly was built at this point. In order to obtain an even grade over the whole route the Butte de Chaillot was reduced by about five metres between 1768 and 1774. The octagonal square on this hill, which still dated from the time of Louis XIV, was changed into the Place de l'Étoile, a circular junction where five streets came together.

In the course of the 18th century numerous ideas were put forward for erecting a monument on the Place de l'Étoile. Finally, after his return from Austerlitz in 1806, Napoleon ordered the erection of two triumphal arches, one for peace and one for war. Both had to located on the axis of the Palais des Tuileries. On the west side of the palace the Arc de Triomphe on the Place de l'Étoile was erected as an entrance to the city, placed at the toll boundary of 1784. On the east side of the palace the Arc du Carrousel served as an entrance to the Tuileries. The size of the arches was coordinated with their distance from the palace. In the original situation this relation could only be seen from the interior of the palace.

The Arc du Carrousel was quickly built from plans drawn up in 1808 by the architects Charles Percier and Pierre F.L. Fontaine. The realisation of the Arc de Triomphe on the Place de l'Étoile took from 1806 to 1836. The design by Jean F.T. Chalgrin (1806-1809) displays three interesting differences from the Arc du Carrousel. The design for

the Arc du Carrousel was inspired by the classical Roman triumphal arch of Constantine, from 312, with three openings. The monument is modest in size (14.62 meters high, 17.87 meters wide, 6.54 meters deep), richly detailed, and given a row of four columns on high plinths or socles. In contrast, the Arc de Triomphe comprises one arch, 25 meters high, open on all four sides, in a colossal block 50 meters high, 45 meters wide and and 22 meters deep. The ornamentation is sober and it is without any columns, as mandated by the court architect Fontaine: "pilasters are unnecessary for an arch which will be seen from so far away, the size and mass of which constitutes its special beauty". In the absence of columns, which enable one to read the proportions, it is impossible to determine the scale of the arch. In this respect the arch is similar to the figure of Hercules which often marks the horizon in the classical villa.

On the spatial axis of the Tuileries the top of the Butte de Chaillot initially was the point where heaven and earth met. The slope of the Grand Cours brought this point forward visually. The reduction of the hill impaired this optical effect, but the hill continued to be the limit of the field of vision. The central perspective now dissolved into the atmosphere. Even though it is impossible to determine the scale of that arch, by placing an arch on the natural horizon the accent in the space shifts to the material object; the form of the arch as it were blocks out the true contact between heaven and earth. But at the same time the opening in the arch suggests a horizontal continuation of the main axis. The extension of the axis accomplished by Perronet however remained out of sight from the section between the Louvre and the arch. In a deeper sense, the framing of the view restricted the horizon, so that it became a virtual vanishing point.

Dismantling the mirror image

Napoleon's Arc de Triomphe on the horizon of the Champs Élysées was also to serve as a gateway for his 'Via Triumphalis', running from the old city to a new city – the new imperial city he planned for the hills west of Paris, reaching as far as the Seine. Napoleon's departure from the stage interrupted the realisation of these plans.

During the Second Empire (1852-1870) Napoleon III, together with his prefect Georges-Eugène Haussmann, began a gigantic operation to modernise the city, which then already counted more than a million residents. Until then east-west traffic had followed the original route along the Seine which lay higher, to the north of the Louvre and Tuileries palaces. In order to solve the traffic problem in the heart of Paris, between 1854 and 1855 Napoleon III extended the new Rue de Rivoli,

The Arc du Carrousel, between the Louvre and the Jardin des Tuileries, with the Arc de
Triomphe in the background

which had been started by Percier and Fontaine along the north wing of the Louvre, to the east, to the Place de la Bastille, the Place de la Nation and the Bois de Vincennes. In addition, the section of the city between the Tuileries and the Louvre was demolished, which at the same time allowed the realisation of the northern wing connecting the two palaces. With the completion of the Rue de Rivoli, the Jardin des Tuileries, which on the north had initially abutted the back of the buildings there, received a new architectonic side wall and access from the city.

The Champs Élysées, which had become municipal property in 1828 and been furnished with pavements and gas lights, became the favourite promenade for Parisians. Strolling, horseback riding, carriages and ball games all contributed to the lively bustle. *Café-concerts*, restaurants, winter gardens, panoramas, circuses, puppet theatres and finally even international exhibitions appeared on the site. The Place de l'Étoile became the hub of a new western district. Like the Place de la Concorde, l'Étoile lay where a boulevard, in this case the former toll boundary of 1784, intersected with Le Nôtre's spatial axis. In 1857 the round Place, 240 metres in diameter, was enlarged with seven new avenues which would form a framework for a new district running out toward the fields of Passy, so that it now became a star with twelve avenues radiating from it. The German-French architect Hittorff was responsible for designing the twelve uniform façades around the Place de l'Étoile. Compared to the Arc de Triomphe, they are small in scale; it is speculated that Haussmann had the triple rows of trees planted around l'Étoile to restore the scale.

The urban development which arose along the new avenues linked the most important axis of Paris with the Bois de Boulogne, which had been redesigned in 1852, and the Place du Trocadéro, opposite the Champ de Mars, in the south, and to the villas around the new Parc de Monceau, built in 1860, in the north. This was accompanied by the migration of the wealthy bourgeoisie and aristocracy to this western district.

Haussmann's reorganisation of the city resembled an urban version of the 17th century reorganisation of the medieval landscape around Paris. In this earlier intervention, a new network of avenues was laid out over the fragmented landscape, resulting in regional coherence. These avenues were connected to one another by *rond-points*. In the 17th century woods with their radiating paths, the *rond-point* made it possible to range quickly over the hunting grounds, and monitor what was happening in all directions from strategic points. Haussmann's Place de l'Étoile is a *rond-point* in the city. Like the straight new avenues, more than 30 meters wide and lined with uniform façades, its

primary function became facilitating the flow of traffic. Though originally a visual axis, the Champs Élysées, which now ended at the Place de l'Étoile, had had a route for traffic laid out along the middle of the axis. From being a *tapis vert* fringed by trees, it was now transformed into a metropolitan artery which, framed by walls of uniform buildings, formed the backbone of a whole urban district. The whole length of the axis – 3800 meters, including the horizon – came to lie within the city. With the transformation of the tree-lined avenue, the landscape that was the décor for the vista disappeared, as did the original visual series from culture to nature which was the foundation for Le Nôtre's spatial axis. The mirror image he created between the city and the landscape and nature, had now been dismantled.

The disappearance of the horizon

Beyond the Arc de Triomphe, on the other side of the Butte de Chaillot the axis continued as a straight line over the Pont de Neuilly to the Rond-Point de la Défense, on the other side of the Seine. But these points played no role in the view that one had from the Louvre through the open *portico* of the triumphal arch. For a century the monumental arch stood alone on the horizon, and framed nothing other than sky.

In 1931 the Département de la Seine organised a competition for proposals for the design of the axis from the Place de l'Étoile to the Rond-Point de la Défense. Among those who submitted ideas was Le Corbusier, but the Second World War prevented any of the ideas being elaborated further. In 1956 it was decided to extend the axis through the flats at Nanterre, across the island of Chatou in the Seine and through the flats of Montesson, as far as St. Germain. This extension meant – for the time being, only on paper – that it would be more than doubled in length, to a total of 17 kilometres. As a first phase of the project the EPAD, a public authority that was established in 1958, was to restructure the area around La Défense, and construct a new commercial district there. Once again the area involved in the plan was the intersection of an axis with a boulevard, now the Boulevard Périphérique. The old *rond-point* there was transformed into a civil engineering megastructure with separate levels for through auto traffic, local streets, parking places (underground) and pedestrians (above ground). Competing to be the tallest structure, office towers arose, spread across the zone along the axis. An elevated platform of about 100 × 1200 meters, descending to the Seine in steps, connected the stores, restaurants and public amenities that were accommodated on the raised pedestrian level among the tower blocks.

La Défense became the antithesis of le Nôtre's Jardin des Tuileries.

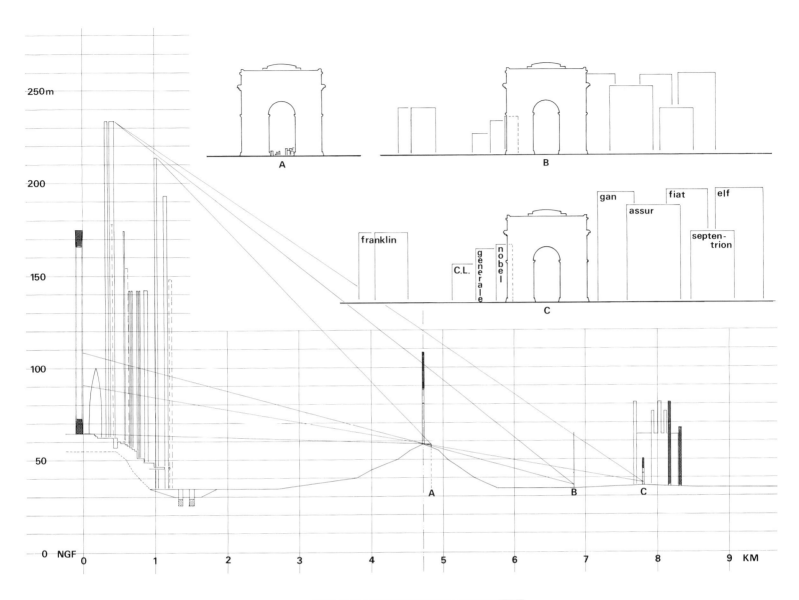

250m

200

150

100

50

0   NGF

0   1   2   3   4   5   6   7   8   9   KM

A — from a point in front of the Arc de Triomphe
B — from the Champs Élysées
C — from the portico of the Arc du Carrousel

Perspectives along the spatial axis, looking toward the towers of
La Défense

There the landscape and the city formed an architectonic unit, oriented solely to *otium*. In La Défense this unity was replaced by the spatial cacophony of today's *negotium*. On a clear day, it could even be seen from the Louvre. Despite being eight kilometres away, in this prospect the towers, as much as 200 meters tall, were visible as objects on either side of the Arc de Triomphe, just about equalling it in height. The presence of these objects made the displacement of the background, far beyond Le Nôtre's horizon, visible in the old city. This shift threw the spatial effect out of balance, and the 'infinity' of the 17th century formal spatial axis became a paradox. The axis was longer than ever before, but was negated visually by the disappearance of the horizon from the landscape.

The materialisation of the vanishing point

Although the Arc de Triomphe no longer stood alone on the horizon, the portico remained empty. The central zone of La Défense had carefully been kept free of anything that would rise above the horizon, and therefore be visible in the portico. Again in 1979 and 1980, when various architects were invited to produce a new design for an element on the axis, one of the basic conditions was that their structure could not be taller than 35 meters, so that it would not be visible in the open portico of the Arc de Triomphe, seen from the Tuileries. The height limit was only dropped when it appeared that with that condition no structure could be realised that would hold its own against the other towers.

In an international competition, held in 1982-1983, it was precisely the void, which until then had been carefully safeguarded as a historical monument, that became the subject of the design. An international communication centre (of about 45,000 m²) and two new ministries (about 75,000 m²) were formulated as points in the programme. In the jury's report detailing their evaluation of the 424 projects submitted, it was noted that the new project must 'break with the unitary morphology of the towers'. The Dane J.O. Spreckelsen was awarded first prize for his design, 'La Grande Arche'. His idea was to place a cube with an open front and back at the head of the axis, like 'a new Arc de Triomphe'. The dimensions of the plan (100 × 100 × 100 meters) and the angle of the cube on the axis referred to the corresponding measurements and angle of the great Louvre court at the other end of the axis.

La Grande Arche comprises a box of massive square concrete 'plates'. Offices are housed in the two verticals; the horizontals form a covered square and roof garden. The outside walls of the cube have a smoothly polished surface. The most important architectonic aim of the whole was the creation of a 'keystone'. With regard to this, the architect spoke of 'a window to the world', 'a meeting among peoples' and 'a view

of the future'. Because it rises over 100 meters above the pedestrian plaza, from the Jardin des Tuileries the structure is visible in the portico of the Arc de Triomphe, over the Butte de Chaillot. As one moves along the Champs Élysées, first descending and then rising again, the cap moves like a horizontal bar in the perspective framed by the portico of the Arc de Triomphe.

The form in which the new structure appears in the vista – a horizontal line – is even more abstract and devoid of scale than the Arc de Triomphe. It therefore remains impossible to gauge the depth of the spatial axis. Nevertheless, Spreckelsen's arch moves the end of the perspectival construction from the Butte de Chaillot to La Défense. This has caused a crucial displacement in the disposition of the foreground, middle distance and background along the original spatial axis. The background is now, more strongly than before, formed by La Défense. Like a coulisse, the Arc de Triomphe lies in the middle distance. Le Nôtre's whole original plan is reduced to foreground. As far as the arch, the buildings of the city are pushed forward. The visual reach of the axis has been increased from three to eight kilometres, but this has not been accompanied by an increase in the spatial depth effect. The vanishing point has been materialised, the landscape telescope has changed into an urban view. As a result of all this, the spatial depth is no longer illusionary but real and the tension between appearances and reality is broken.

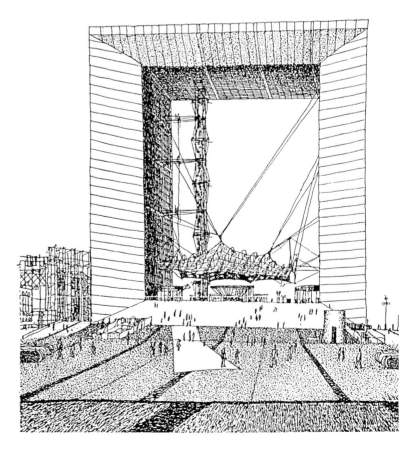

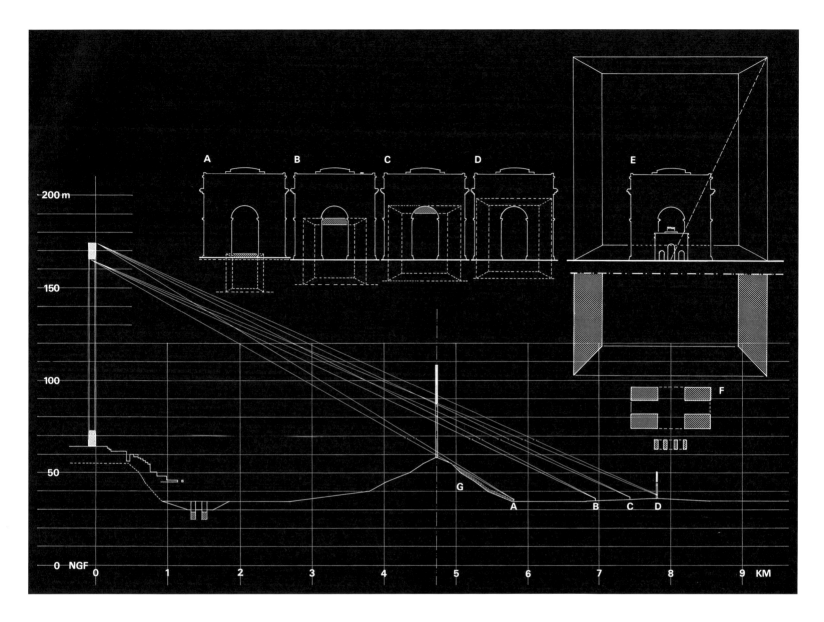

A, B, C — from the Champs Élysées
D — from the Arc du Carrousel
E — normal projection of the three arches in their actual size
F — the three ground plans

The visibility of the Grande Arche in the Arc de Triomphe

← Concept for the Grande Arche, drawing by J.O. von Spreckelsen

Looking back from the Grande Arche, in the direction of the Arc de Triomphe

The representation of the horizon

The 'spatial telescope' from the old heart of Paris to the top of the Butte de Chaillot that André le Nôtre devised in the second half of the 17th century was a new and spectacular construction. Unlike at Versailles, the axis of view was projected in the direction that the city was growing. The axis was an attempt to preserve a relationship with the open landscape which had been contested for centuries already by the centre of the growing city, and would be challenged ever anew, and give it potential for growth. As the city grew out over the axis, the formal space was included in the urban morphology, step by step. Finally, the 'spatial telescope' became an urban space. La Défense and Spreckelsen's arch definitively blew up the axis and put an end to the illusionistic spatial picture.

When the city grows over the horizon, the possibilities of the formal landscape growing with it appear to be limited. Increasing the scale of the formal spatial axis to beyond the horizon is accompanied by substituting an object-linked monumentality for spatiality. In formal landscape architectonic spatial design, it is apparently not without reason that the modelling of space stops beyond the horizon. There the spatial axis dissolves into atmospheric perspective and the regional system of avenues. The formal spatial axis cannot be expanded further in landscape architectonic terms, but as an element in the composition it is a repeatable entity, related to the scale of perception.

Seen from the perspective of urban planning, the axis, quite apart from its original spatial effects, can also be considered as a strategic line of force lying in the Seine valley, embodying the city's dynamic and the direction of its growth, and constantly providing new stimulus for it. In that sense, the landscape architectonic axis worked as a catalyst for urban development, and was flexible enough to transform itself into an urban form, step by step. That is why what was in its genesis a formal system in the landscape continued to be tied up with the successive stages of the city's growth, although the relation between the two was never clear.

There were also other places where the spatial axis was overtaken by urban development. Through the construction of a new network of urban avenues, promenades and boulevards under Napoleon III, coupled with a system of parks and woods, the 17th century formal system came to lie entirely within the domain of the new urban agglomerate. It too had to prove its strength anew.

Parc des Buttes Chaumont, ligne de Petite Ceinture

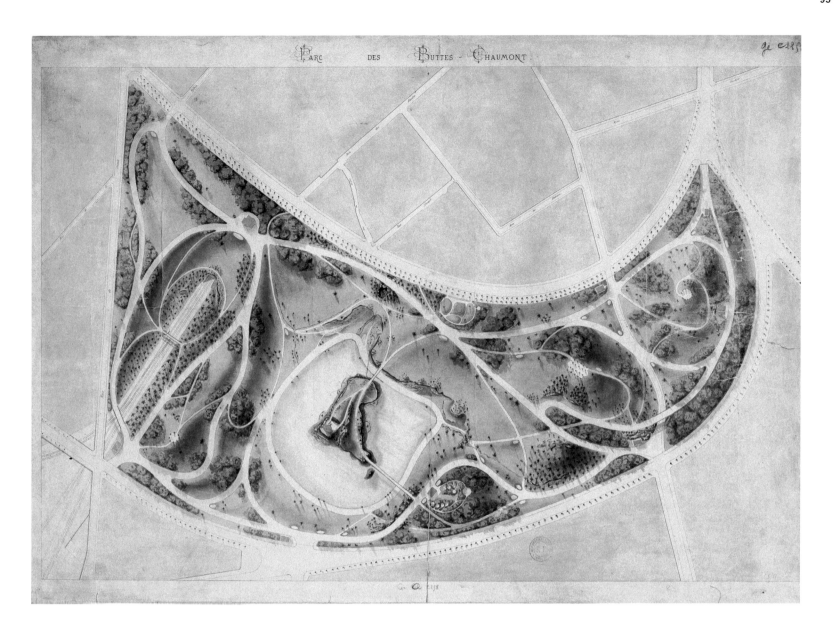

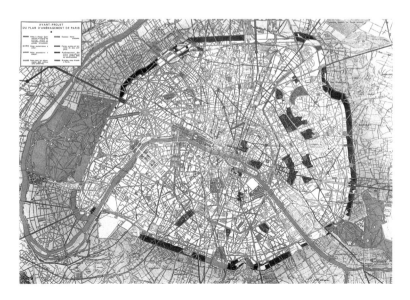

Parc des Buttes Chaumont, Jean-Charles Alphand 1867-73 (Bibliothèque nationale de France, Cartes et Plans, Parc des Buttes Chaumont, GE C- 2258, [nd])

Avant-projet du plan d'aménagement de Paris, 1938 (from Pinon e.a., *Les plans de Paris - histoire d'un capitale*. Paris 2004)

The horizon in the technical universe

As was already indicated in the discussion of the transformation of the Place de l'Étoile, great changes took place in the time of Napoleon III, under the direction of Georges-Eugène Haussmann (1809-1891) as a city planner, Jean-Charles-Adolphe Alphand (1817-1891) as landscape architect and civil engineer and Jean-Pierre Barillet-Deschamps (1824-1873) as landscape architect and gardener. The city was expanded with eleven new districts and provided with new defences, the last in a long series. These were finished in 1845.

A new design for the existing city, involving demolition and driving new streets through the old neighbourhoods, created a system of new *allées*, avenues and promenades with star-shaped intersections. For instance, the Avenue de l'Impératrice (now Avenue Foch) was built in 1854 to connect the Bois de Boulogne and the Place de l'Étoile. This avenue was 140 meters wide and comprised of three vehicular and pedestrian lanes with lawns, sycamores, chestnut trees and all sorts of shrubs. A new boulevard planted with trees was constructed along what was called the Fermiers Généraux, the route of the obsolete toll boundary. A visit to London gave the Emperor the idea for a system of parks and squares distributed across the city.

Alphand and Barillet-Deschamps designed and realised three new public parks. These were, successively, the Parc des Buttes Chaumont, the Parc Montsouris and the Parc de Monceau, all of them in new districts of the city. The urban infrastructure of avenues, promenades and rail lines ran right through the parks. The Parc des Buttes Chaumont, 25 hectares in size and intersected by a recessed railway line, was built between 1864 and 1867 on the site of a former stone quarry, with major differences in elevation, grottos, cascades, panoramas, etc. The Parc Montsouris, 15.5 hectares in size, was built on a hill, and is also intersected by a railway line. The Parc de Monceau, at 8.5 hectares, was the last to be built, and replaced the originally much larger garden of the Duke of Chartres, a curiosity cabinet designed by the painter De Carmontelle, with an Egyptian pyramid, a Dutch windmill, a minaret, a temple of Mars, Chinese bridges, and other follies. Part of it is preserved in the present park on the Boulevard de Courcelles.

Between 1853 and 1869 a total of 24 green squares were built in various quarters of the city, often at intersections. In general they were of limited size, usually less than two hectares, and surrounded by a fence. They were designed in a 'gardenesque' style, with plenty of flowers, ponds, fountains and rocks.

As former hunting parks, both the Bois de Boulogne (873 hectares)

Avenue Hoche, which runs through from the Arc de Triomphe into the Parc Monceau

The spatial axis of Meudon in 1764

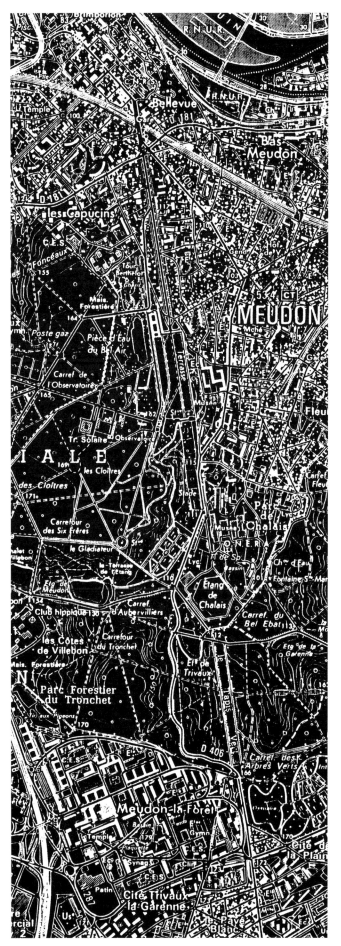

The spatial axis of Meudon in 1981

and the Bois de Vincennes (875 hectares) were redesigned for the public. Napoleon III personally set out the guidelines for the Bois de Boulogne. The Emperor wanted to have something like The Serpentine in London's Hyde Park. Alphand and Barillet-Deschamps laid out two large lakes there, at different heights, so as to create cascades, grottos, etc. They also provided the park with new, winding footpaths and roads for vehicles, and numerous pavilions and kiosks. Parts of the woods were leased to specialised institutions, for instance for a zoo and a horticultural garden. In fitting out the exhibition grounds for the 'Universal Exhibition' of 1867, on the then Champs de Mars, in addition to the building Alphand designed an intricate labyrinth of curving roads, water features and plant beds, bewildering in its complexity, and like the exhibition building intended to astonish visitors through the wonders of technology.

In 1903 Eugène Hénard launched a proposal to transform the outermost defensive belt into a 'Boulevard à redans', a ring with twelve new parks. In 1919 the city acquired the defences, and by 1932 the demolition of the fortifications had been completed. Despite all the fine plans, by then the ring had already been divided up into innumerable parcels for public buildings, hospitals, schools and apartment houses. Later sports fields, cemeteries and the Boulevard Périphérique were also built in this zone. All these Grands Travaux can be regarded as an effort to get the growing city under control and improve hygiene.

The distinction between nature and culture, between horizon and foreground, as represented by the formal system, evaporated into a 'technical universe'. That was also reflected in the growing network of paved roads, locomotives and smoking chimneys in the urban landscape. The city and landscape were once again united, now however not only by geometry, architectonic objects or the morphology of the landscape, but also through the products of technology. Within the technical universe the horizon continued to exist as the measure of the city in the landscape. The spatial staging of the horizon even took on new importance as a possibility to escape the dominant technical character of the city.

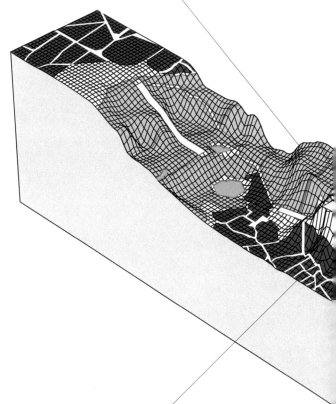

The formal and the urban network

With the growth of the *banlieue* in the 20th century the formal system became hemmed in entirely. On all sides it was confronted with a growing urban area of increasing density, an urban network that was expanding, and a programme for the creation and retention of natural areas in the urban sphere that was oriented to recreational needs. One example of this confrontation in the region around Paris is Meudon.

The fragmented spatial axis of Meudon, with the urban panorama and the landscape horizon (photo's: Hans Stotijn)

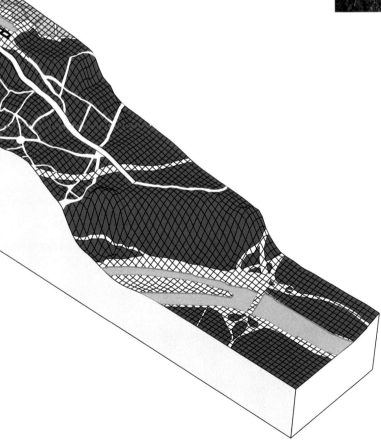

The eastern retaining wall of the great terrace

For more than three centuries the original scheme of the spatial axis, the garden, the woods with their radiating paths and the estate, had been exposed to neglect and pressures from urbanisation. The estate was entirely hemmed in by suburban development. Infrastructural amenities of urban life penetrated to the heart of the park and cut through the spatial axis at various spots. The Étang de Chalais, formerly an open water feature that was the deeply recessed hinge point on the original spatial axis, became wholly surrounded by woods and undergrowth.

The system of axes has largely been fragmented and obscured. Only a skeleton of the main axis remains, consisting of the entrance drive rising from the Seine valley, the high, tree planted terrace, and a lower grassy parterre with a reflecting pool in the foreground and a simple *tapis vert* surrounded by trees in the background. The lake which lies between them, and the adjoining sports facilities and green space in the woods are no longer visible from the terrace. Although incomplete because of the absence of the middle ground, the essence of the spatial axis – the tension between the foreground and the horizon – has remained intact, so that the form is reduced to the essence. This more or less spontaneous, unplanned reduction is the antithesis of the planned transformation of the axis of the Jardin des Tuileries in the heart of the city. The results of the two transformations are also antithetical. Despite its fragmentation and reduction, the main axis of Meudon does retain its elementary spatial power. Unlike in the Jardin des Tuileries, there, in the middle of a metropolis, one can experience the horizon within the landscape as originally intended. At Meudon confrontation with the dynamism of the city exposed the elementary force of Le Nôtre's spatial construction, anchored in the geomorphology. The *genius loci* unexpectedly appears in the generic landscape of the expanding city.

The map of Paris reveals scores of other overlaps, collisions and confrontations between the 17th century formal network and the present urban network. With a landscape architectonic treatment of them, the horizon can be given a new place in the metropolis as a timeless element in the landscape.

The formal network and the urban infrastructure

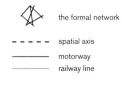

the formal network

- - - - -   spatial axis
————   motorway
————   railway line

A   Clagny
B   Grand Trianon
C   Luxembourg
D   Marly
E   Meudon
F   Saint Cloud
G   Saint-Germain-en-Laye
H   Sceaux
I   Tuileries
J   Versailles

1   Aéroport de Paris-Le-Bourget
2   Aérodrome Velizy
3   Aérodrome de Toussus le Noble

0   2   5km

The aqueduct at Marly

The formal network and urban green spaces

 the formal network

urban green spaces

1   Belleville
2   Bois de Boulogne
3   Bois de Monteclin
4   Bois de Vincennes
5   Bois des Gonards
6   Bois du Pont Colbert
7   Butte Montmartre
8   Champ de Mars
9   Cité Internationale Universitaire
10 Esplanade des Invalides
11 Forêt Domaniale de Fausses Reposes
12 Forêt Domaniale de la Malmaison
13 Forêt Domaniale de la Marly-Le Roi
14 Forêt Domaniale de Louveciennes
15 Forêt Domaniale de Meudon
16 Forêt Domaniale de Saint-Germain-en-Laye
17 Forêt Domaniale de Verrières
18 Forêt Domaniale de Versailles
19 Forêt Régionale de la Butte Pinson
20 Fort de Charenton
21 Fort du Mont Valérien
22 Forum des Halles
23 Jardin d'Acclimatation
24 Jardin du Trocadero
25 Jardin des Plantes
26 Jardin du Ranelagh
27 Les Batignolles
28 Palais Royal
29 Parc André Citroën
30 Parc de Bagatelle
31 Parc de Bercy
32 Parc de la Villette
33 Parc de Loisirs
34 Parc de Loisirs
35 Parc de Maisons-Laffitte
36 Parc de Monceau
37 Parc de Saint-Cloud
38 Parc Départemental
39 Parc Départemental de La Courneuve
40 Parc des Buttes Chaumont
41 Parc des Guilands
42 Parc Edmond de Rothschild
43 Parc Henri Sellier
44 Parc Jean Moulin
45 Parc Montsouris
46 Square de Choisy
47 Square George Brassens

0   2   5km

REGENT'S PARK
LONDON 1811

The landscape scenography of the city
John Nash
The pictural ensemble

The landscape of the Thames
The morphology of the Thames valley

The urban transformation of country life
Rus in urbe
Circus, crescent, urban route and belvedère

The integration of the landscape into the urban pattern
The division of London
The parks along the Thames
Commons
Pleasure gardens
Squares

The Grand Design
London estate development
The development of Marylebone Park
The landscape architectonic transformation of the topography

Regent's Park
The development of Nash's design
The topographic framework
The 'Theatrical Panorama'
The image of a park landscape
A residential programme for aristocrats

New Street
A complex transformation
The scenography of the urban route

The capstone on the Thames
The scenic staging for Buckingham Palace
The formal relation with the old city

The continuity of city and landscape
A prototype of the public park
Inscribing the landscape in the city

Upper Regent Street, Regent's Park and Primrose Hill (aerial photo: P. van Bolhuis/Pandion)

The landscape scenography of the city

Regent's Park lies in London's West End, about three miles to the north-west of St. Paul's Cathedral. With an area of 166 hectares, it is today one of the largest parks in London. It was created around 1810 as the most significant component in an extensive and ambitious project which also included Regent Street and St. James's Park, and led to the emergence of one of the most important urban landscapes of the first half of the 19th century.

The strategy behind what was called the Grand Design was to develop a former royal game preserve, Marylebone Park, thereby raising money for the Crown. In addition to providing a site for a royal summer palace, the project was to create a space for an attractive residential environment for the upper classes – in particular, the friends of the Prince Regent. A second objective was to connect the royal palace with this new residential area, and restore the contact between the centre and the agricultural landscape to the north of Westminster. It was to be a regal manner of establishing the boundary of the city and thus bringing the scale of the growing city under the control of the court. Finally, it was to take up the question of the relationship between the new royal palace, the centre of government and the urbanised districts of Mayfair and Westminster in the western section of London. This came down to nothing less than a landscape architectonic reordering of Westminster, and in a deeper sense, of the whole of London.

The Grand Design was in essence based on a landscape architectonic transformation of the spatial structure of both an existing agricultural landscape and the existing urban fabric. A task of this extent and complexity demanded a command of the design instruments of landscape architecture that was stunning for that day. The park is named for the Prince Regent, the title that the later King George IV (1820-1830) bore from 1811 to 1820. He was a fanatic developer of building projects and acted as patron of the architect John Nash, the creative genius behind this project. Nash understood the strategy and tactics of this intricate chess game like a grandmaster. Analysis reveals how it was played and which brilliant moves were made successively to bring the form of the growing city under control.

John Nash

John Nash (1752-1835) was probably born in London to a craftsman's family that had come from Wales. When he was fourteen an uncle found him a place in the offices of the renowned architect Sir Robert Taylor, where according to the custom of the time Nash remained for

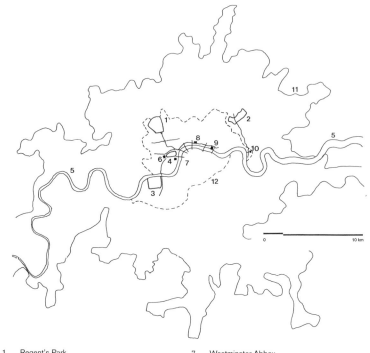

1	Regent's Park	7	Westminster Abbey
2	Victoria Park	8	St. Paul's Cathedral
3	Battersea Park	9	Tower
4	St. James's Park	10	Limehouse
5	Thames	11	Greater London 1927
6	Buckingham Palace	12	Boundary of London in 1843

Regent's Park in London 1927

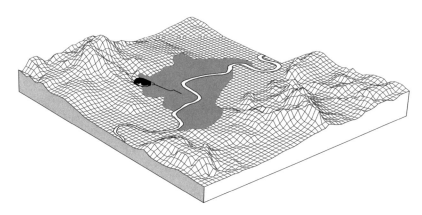

The Grand Design in the morphology of the Thames Valley

→ Topography

subway station
subway line
railway line

urban pattern

motorway
important road

Royal Park
other parks and urban green space
water

1	Bushy Park	5	Richmond Park
2	Greenwich Park	6	St. James's Park
3	Hyde Park	7	The Green Park
4	Kensington Gardens	8	The Regent's Park

 0   2   5km

about a decade, until he went into practice for himself in 1775. In 1794 he met Humphry Repton (1752-1818), who in terms of both practice and theory was the most important landscape architect of England in that day. When in 1796 Repton was asked to oversee the rebuilding of Corsham Court in Wiltshire, he recommended Nash as the architect. Their collaboration lasted until 1805 and was of decisive importance for Nash, although Nash never gave Repton the acknowledgement he deserved, and several times even appropriated Repton's work for himself.

As well as being an architect, Nash was a draughtsman and structural engineer; for instance, he also designed and built the massive brick sewer system under Regent Street and designed the Highgate Archway Bridge. In addition, he was a skilful financier, who after an initial bankruptcy had learned how he could take risks without going too far. Nash was already 58 years old when he began with his Grand Design, and he worked on it with unbounded energy for a period of more than 15 years, from 1810 to 1826. He possessed a well-developed sense for ensemble architecture and a talent for uniting various expertise and opinions in new combinations. New Street was almost entirely his own work, and in the transformation of Marylebone Park Nash was always the one who produced the spatial concept.

The pictural ensemble

Regent's Park marked the birth of a new spatial type, combining urban and rural elements. In terms of typology it was a transformation of the 18th century landscape garden. Through relativising the position of the house and a differentiation of the architectonic typology of the structure, elements of which were then arranged in spatial ensembles, the individual landscape garden was transmuted into a collective urban residential form containing scenic elements. Initially conceived as a profit-making venture exploiting Crown land, as a result of the unique confrontation between urban living and the scenic backdrop, and through the effective deployment of landscape architectonic techniques, it became a direct forerunner of the 19th century city park. Using the techniques of pictural composition, the dissimilar urban and scenic elements in this design were united into a new pictural ensemble and coherent spatial scenography.

Back of the 'stage scenery' of The Quadrant

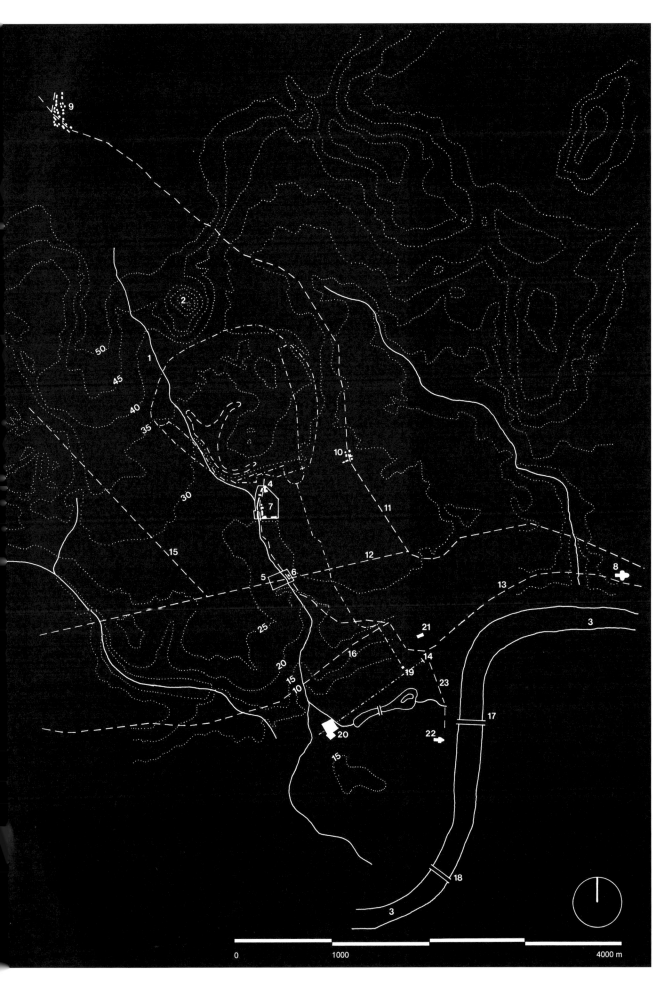

1 Tyburn
2 Primrose Hill
3 Thames
4 Tyburn Manor House
5 Village of Tyburn
6 St. John's Church
7 Marylebone
8 St. Paul's Cathedral
9 Hampstead
10 Tottenham Court
11 Tottenham Court Road
12 Oxford Street
13 The Strand
14 Charing Cross
15 Edgware Road
16 Piccadilly
17 Westminster Bridge
18 Vauxhall Bridge
19 St. James's Palace/Carlton House
20 Buckingham Palace
21 St. Martin-in-the-Fields
22 Westminster Abbey
23 Whitehall

Topography of London's West End

The landscape of the Thames

The most important geographic feature defining London is the Thames, the greatest navigable river of England. It rises in the Cotswold Hills, about 175 kilometres west of its estuary, runs through a gap between the White Horse Hills and the Chiltern Hills, and then meanders through London between lower hills. Further to the east, at Southend-on-Sea, the river empties into the North Sea through a broad estuary.

The morphology of the Thames valley

The Thames is a tidal river with a rather wide flood plain surrounded by the undulating swells of Parliament Hill, the Addington Hills and Primrose Hill. The river was previously much wider and shallower, with extensive marshes; particularly at high tide the river was as much as five times as wide as it is now. The tidal action of the far distant North Sea is noticeable as far inland as Teddington, south-west of the city.

At Hampton Court the river is narrow and winds in great curves through what were once extremely rural villages like Twickenham, Richmond, Kew, Chiswick and Barnes. Today these towns have all been swallowed up by Greater London. On the other hand, in the centre of London the valley is very broad, fringed by undulating hills. The landscape here slowly rises out of the wide river valley, rolling northwards in the direction of the boulder clay plateau of Hampstead, Highgate and Harrow. A small tributary of the Thames, the Tyburn, rose on Primrose Hill. Its lower course split into two branches, both flowing into the Thames, one to the north and one to the south of today's Westminster.

Since Victorian times the river has been confined by embankments; many of its small feeders now run underground. A large part of London remains vulnerable to flooding. In the course of time this threat has only become more serious, with the slow but steady rise in the sea level. To avert this danger, between 1974 and 1984 the Thames Barrier, a moveable flood barrier which can be closed at extremely high tides, was constructed east of the city, at Woolwich.

Regent's Park, Chester Terrace

Geomorphology and the urban domain

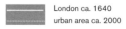
London ca. 1640
urban area ca. 2000

N   0   20   40km

Bath, Royal Crescent

Geomorphology, urban pattern and parks

	urban pattern
	park
	water

Elevation (metres)

	120 - 140
	100 - 120
	90 - 100
	80 - 90
	70 - 80
	60 - 70
	50 - 60
	40 - 50
	30 - 40
	20 - 30
	10 - 20
	0 - 10

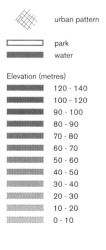

0   2   5km

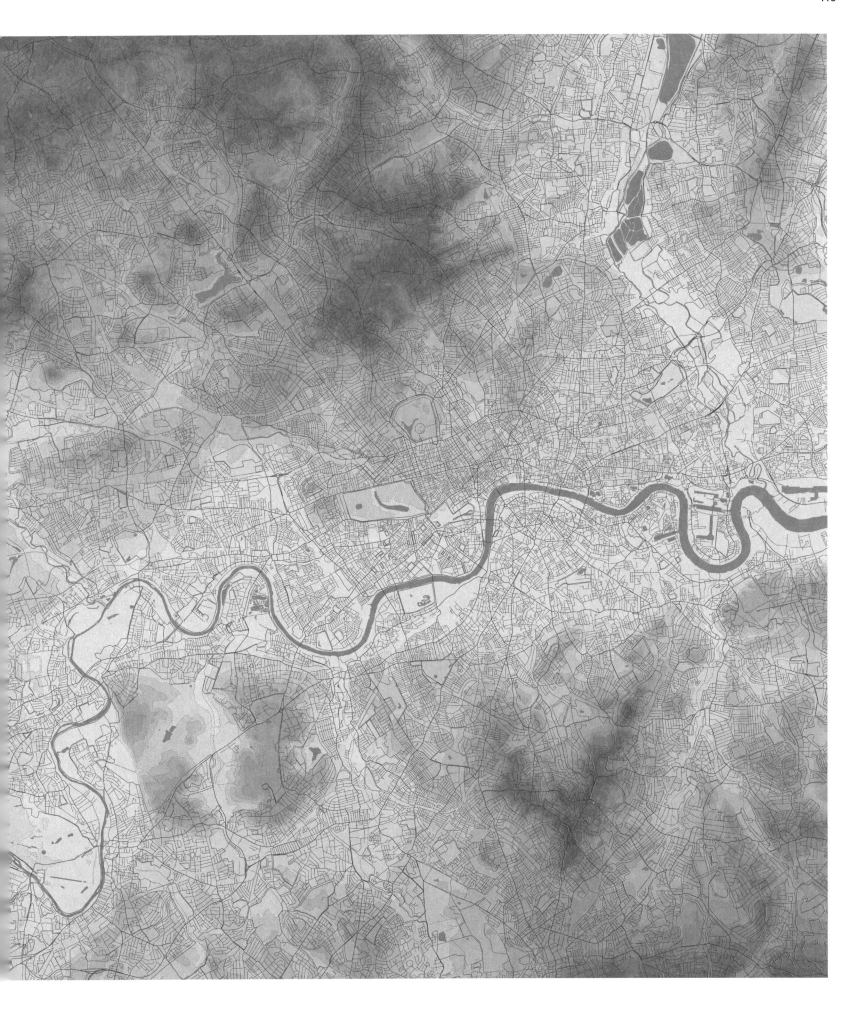

The urban transformation of country life

Rus in urbe

The classical ideal of *rus in urbe* was an important motif in the development of the 18th century city. There was a quest for a new lifestyle in which the the qualities of the city and countryside were united. If in the 17th century the urban residence was still the model for the rising culture of country life, now the influence ran in precisely the other direction: new urban residential forms were derived directly from the neo-Palladian country home.

The spas and seaside resorts, which were strongly in the ascendency under Queen Anne at the beginning of the 18th century, were laboratories for new urban experiments. For instance, within a few short years there were initiatives toward new residential forms in Bath, Clifton, Tunbridge Wells and Brighton. Not much later these would be adopted on a large scale in major cities, namely Edinburgh, Dublin and London.

As a result of renewed attention for its hot springs, Bath, which had already been noted in Roman times for its *thermae*, became a fashionable resort for the aristocracy, the gentry and wealthy commoners. This created a wave of speculative building under the direction of the Master of Ceremonies of Bath, Richard 'Beau' Nash, who gave the businessman and building tycoon Ralph Allen a free hand to make Bath a profitable enterprise. Allen provided the construction material, particularly the sandy-coloured Combe Down stone, out of which the new resort was erected. John Wood the Elder (1704-1754) drew up the plans. In doing so he made use of the experience he had gained in the building and expansion of the country house at Bramham. He had a vision for the transformation of the country seat into a collective urban residential form, in which the advantages of the urban residence were combined with the views only a landowner had. He had to take into account differing budgets and lifestyles of his customers, though, because the dwellings were sold on the free market.

Circus, crescent, urban route and belvedère

With the earliest London squares, such as Covent Garden and Grosvenor Square, as his point of departure, between 1728 and 1736 John Wood the Elder designed Bath's Queen Square, a square of 93 × 96 meters, with three walls in the 'palatial style'. The corners are open, so that the streets bounding the square run through.

The second transformation of the country house took place in his plans for King's Circus, erected between 1754 and 1758, a round court 97 meters in diameter at the end of Gay Street. The Circus is made up of three equally long segments of a circle, each standing opposite a free view along a street. One of these streets ran toward the centre of Bath, the other two pointed in the direction of the still undeveloped hill landscape. This design has a more egalitarian character. The hierarchic scheme of the façades of Queen Square has been abandoned; the façades here form an homogeneous urban wall. Behind them were dwellings that varied in width and depth. The circular shape of the space of the Circus is neutral, a turning point in the urban circulation pattern.

John Wood the Elder died in 1754 and was succeeded by his son, John Wood the Younger. He crowned the trend of his father's thinking with the design of the Royal Crescent between 1767 and 1774. With this design the process of opening the city to the landscape reached a new high point in which the urban building block was directly connected to the scenic panorama of the landscape. Its half-ellipse is the geometric translation of the principle of equal views over the landscape from every dwelling in the block. The strictly neutral scheme of the façades of King's Circus is partially abandoned again in favour of the architectonic articulation of the collective residential building. One of the streets running out of King's Circus provides access to the Crescent, and leads along in front of it so that the visitor suddenly stands face to face with both the colossal structure and the overwhelming panorama, just as he would in approaching a country house. The relation to the panorama did demand that the Crescent be freed up from the urban fabric, and positioned in the landscape morphology. The Royal Crescent was therefore situated above the old city, parallel to the contours of the hills that bound the valley of the Avon. A section of the landscape was kept free as a foreland, which like that of a country estate was zoned by means of a lawn, bounded by a ha-ha, a meadow and a wilderness in the form of a plantation of trees. This all lay downhill, with accelerated perspective.

With this development the landscape garden, until now an element of country life on a rural estate, was fundamentally transformed and tied in with the organisation of urban residential forms. Moreover, these forms were links in a purposefully designed series. Queen Square, King's Circus and Royal Crescent do not stand alone, but are connected by an 'urban route' which carries one from the constriction of the city centre to the scenic panorama. At its end, the Royal Crescent thus also becomes the belvedère of the city.

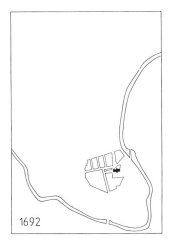

1692

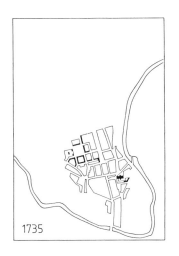

1735

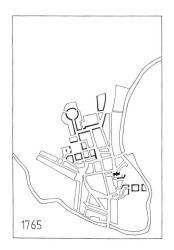

1765

1810

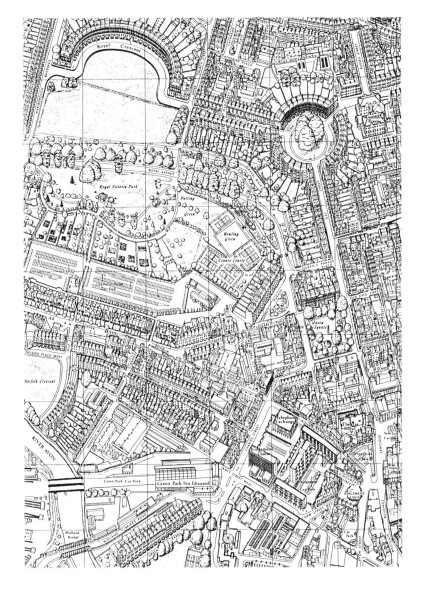

The development of Georgian Bath (from J. Galjaard, *Bath bijvoorbeeld.*
Unpublished study, Department of Architecture [Delft 1983])

Bath: Square, Circus, Crescent (Map of Bath 1971)

Bath, King's Circus and Royal Crescent

The integration of the landscape into the urban pattern

Roman Londinium was founded in 43 CE on the route from Dover to Chester, at a point near the tidal limit in the Thames. The river could be forded here, and the gravel bed provided a good footing for a bridge. In his writings Tacitus called London a trading city. During the rebellion led by the Celtic queen Boudica in 60 CE, Londinium was burnt to the ground. After this misfortune, in 61 CE the first city wall was built as a defence against new attacks. These walls were expanded by the Romans in the 3rd century. In the 9th century King Alfred (the Great) rebuilt the walls around London to protect the city against the Vikings. After the Norman Conquest in 1066, London, Westminster and Southwark (the latter name meaning 'south fort') together came to form the capital of England, with the Thames as shared space. Many of the mediaeval streets ran at right angles to the Thames, ending there as water gates, with mooring places for boats.

The division of London

Paradoxically, precisely as a consequence of the small size of the defended city – the Roman *urbs* – in the Middle Ages London became what Rasmussen called a "scattered city", a city outside the walls. This was comprised of various 'townships', grouped around the two poles of the cities of London and Westminster. Westminster, which according to one hypothesis grew out of a place where in earlier times the kings administered justice in an open-air court, became the seat of government. Gradually the most important governmental institutions, such as the Royal Treasury, the Supreme Court, and finally the Parliament, were moved to Westminster. The royal game parks, including Marylebone Park, which would later be transformed into Regent's Park, therefore all lay on the west side of London. From the earliest times the landed nobility also lived to the west of London along the Thames, or in the West End; later, high-ranking civil servants and wealthy bourgeoisie also gravitated there. In contrast, the City of London developed as a centre for commerce and maritime trade. Docks and workshops developed in the East End, downstream along the Thames. The area between London and Westminster gradually filled in, but this polarity continued to exist, and was even intensified by later industrialisation.

The parks along the Thames

For the most part, the castles and country houses along the Thames were located in visually strategic spots, on the foot hills that bounded the Thames valley. They not only looked out on the Thames, but eventually, with the aid of a belvedère higher in the hills, also had views of one another and of the dome of St. Paul's, which marked the centre of London. The visual network of this country estate landscape, reminiscent of that in the Tiber valley in Rome, dominated the long stretch of the Thames valley westwards.

Among these parks and hunting reserves were Hyde Park, Kensington Gardens, St. James's Park, Green Park, Greenwich Park, Richmond Park, Regent's Park and Primrose Hill, the Kew Botanical Gardens, Hampton Court and Bushy Park. Many of these gardens and parks lay on the Thames, so that this river began to form a chain of parks, as it were, which linked the city to the landscape. In response to the growing need for open space in the expanding city, in the 17th century many royal parks were opened to the public.

The region around London was originally part of the extensive Middlesex Forest, of which Highgate Wood and Holland Park are remnants. After the dissolution of the monasteries by Henry VIII in 1536, the whole area became the property of the Crown. Henry VIII had 223 hectares of it enclosed with a wall and fence with fifteen gates (the roughly circular shape of the area can probably be credited to this), and used the Marylebone Park thus formed as a hunting reserve. This situation continued until 1649, the beginning of the Commonwealth. All Crown lands were sold off under Cromwellian rule. The forest was very soon felled for use in constructing a fleet of warships. After the restoration of the monarchy and Charles II ascension to the throne in 1660, Marylebone Park reverted to the Crown and was leased out for agricultural purposes. When it had been a hunting reserve, Marylebone Park had not been a part of the country estate landscape, and moreover lay higher in the hills, without visual contact with the Thames. Because of its strategic location with regard to the seat of the court in Carlton House, the centre of government in Whitehall and the centre of London, it was nevertheless an obvious spot for anchoring places representative of the landscape in the urban structure of London.

As such, the Grand Design was the crown of a process that had already been going on for centuries, in which sections of the landscape were more or less methodically included in the city. In addition to the parks along the Thames, other typical elements for London were the commons, pleasure gardens and squares.

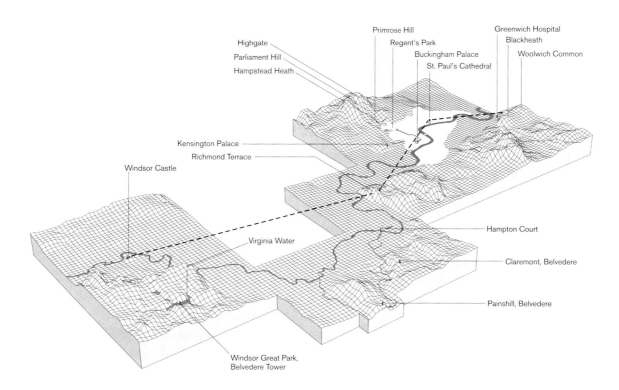

Highgate
Parliament Hill
Hampstead Heath

Primrose Hill
Regent's Park
Buckingham Palace
St. Paul's Cathedral

Greenwich Hospital
Blackheath
Woolwich Common

Kensington Palace
Richmond Terrace

Windsor Castle

Hampton Court

Virginia Water

Claremont, Belvedere

Painshill, Belvedere

Windsor Great Park,
Belvedere Tower

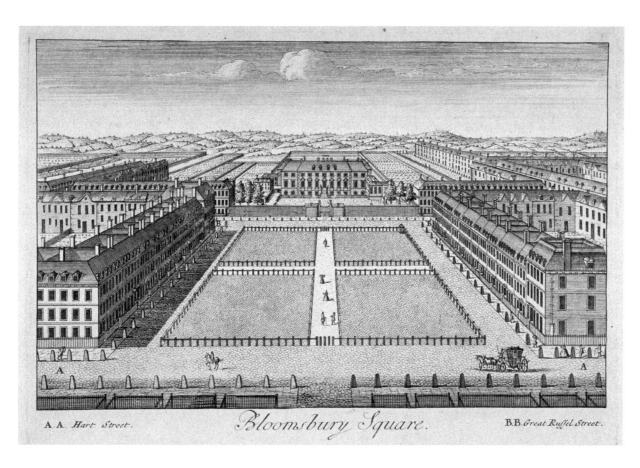

A.A. *Hart Street.*   *Bloomsbury Square.*   B.B. *Great Ruſſel Street.*

The chain of gardens and parks along the Thames

Bloomsbury Square, London, around 1727 (London Metropolitan Archives, Main Print Collection Pr.H4/BLO)

Commons

More than in other cities, in London utilitarian elements from the agricultural landscape were woven into the urban pattern. One example of this were the traditional commons. These were originally tracts of untilled land that were used 'in common' as grazing land. As a result of the Wimbledon and Putney Commons Act of 1871 a large number of commons continue to be preserved as open places in the city.

Pleasure gardens

Around the Roman *urbs* lay various open sites that since the Middle Ages were used as places for public entertainment, recreation and exercise. These continued to be kept as open spaces in later urban expansions. In the course of the 17th century the area became increasingly built-up. To the north of the city lay Moorfields, originally a bog, later filled in with refuse, drained and planted. As early as the 15th century this had become a public pasture, likewise protected under the Green Belt law as public space.

Theatre and drama were developing in the reign of Elizabeth I, first by travelling companies and later in purpose-built theatres, which for various reasons were not permitted north of the Thames and ended up in Bankside, south of the river. At the end of the 16th century and in the early 17th century Southwark was the most important centre for entertainment in London, drawing large numbers of spectators. Another attraction in Southwark were the pleasure gardens and park theatres like Vauxhall Gardens. This was an entertainment venue with a garden where the public could relax, drink tea, converse and stroll. There was music and other diversions in a pleasant environment. Vauxhall Gardens continued to exist until 1859.

In the 18th century the residents of neighbourhoods like Mayfair and Soho also sought entertainment on the north-west edge of the then city, in the southern part of Marylebone Park, among other places at an inn called The Jew's Harp. In 1649 the Marylebone Pleasure Gardens were opened behind Tyburn Manor House, with a garden, bowling green and refreshment room. The garden quickly became a much frequented place of entertainment, particularly for the wealthier residents of Mayfair. By the end of the 18th century the Marylebone Pleasure Gardens had been surrounded by the growing city.

Squares

Around 1630 Inigo Jones designed Covent Garden Piazza, presumably reaching back directly to Italian models. His design for several houses at Lincoln's Inn Fields in 1635 launched the concept of a square with dwellings behind a palace façade. This project was lost during the great fire of 1666. After the fire various plans were made for the reconstruction of the city, of which Sir Christopher Wren's was the most important. None of these plans were realised in their entirety because of problems with acquiring the land for them.

In the course of the 17th century, as the city expanded a number of the country estates in the immediate vicinity of Westminster and London were surrounded by new development. The forecourts of these mansions were subdivided into lots, and the land around them distributed as separate plots. Many of these built-up estates came to stand as autonomous 'villages' in the urban fabric. This form of urban development produced the 'square', a new urban spatial type characteristic of Westminster, comprising a generally rectangular square with the former noble house in a dominant position, and with the other walls formed by residential buildings uniformly designed as an architectonic entity. This model of the square was normative for the development of Mayfair. The earliest of these squares were Covent Garden, Soho Square, Bloomsbury Square, St. James's Square and Grosvenor Square.

A certain pattern emerged in the development of the squares. The simplest form was comprised of an extension of the forecourt of the noble house. St. James's Square and Bloomsbury Square originated from a palace or country house surrounded by the growing city. The house itself continued to stand free and with the forecourt had its own private grounds. In front of that lay a square with residential dwellings, the façades of which formed an architectonically consistent urban wall. In later developments the square was bounded on all four sides by houses with a equipollent architectonic form, on the model of the earlier Italian *piazza* and the French *place*. This provided the aristocracy with a comfortable residential space with a high degree of privacy. The central square was sometimes paved, but also sometimes planted as a communal garden, surrounded by a fence, and accessible only to residents on the square. The layout of the squares was initially formal, but followed fashion. For instance, Humphry Repton produced new designs for Bloomsbury Square, Sloane Square, Cadogan Square and Russell Square. Toward the end of the 19th century many squares acquired a more public character. The squares of Mayfair and the ensemble architecture of the urban landscape of Bath were the most important ingredients for Nash's Grand Design. In it, the integration of the landscape into the city would reach a new architectonic climax.

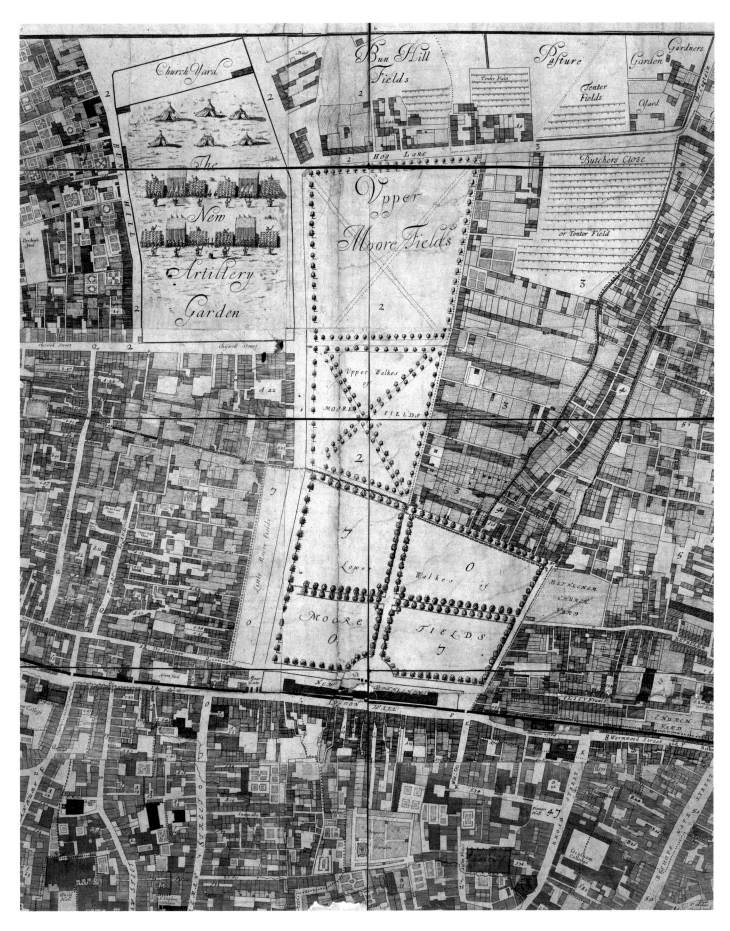

Moorfields, to the north of the old city (John Ogilby, 1677. Large and accurate map
of the city of London. Ichnographically describing all the Streets, Lanes, Alleys, Courts,
Yards, Churches, Halls and Houses, &c. British Library Maps C.7.b.4.)

The Grand Design

The development of Marylebone Park was not a matter of sheer chance, but had its impetus in part in the growing imbalance in the urban pattern of Mayfair. As a result its rapid growth, any contact between the centre of Westminster and the surrounding landscape, where the aristocrats in the House of Lords had previously had their London estates, had been severed. The continuity of the system of roads leading to the city was disrupted by the development projects undertaken by the nobility, which lay at sixes and sevens with respect to one another. Moreover, within Mayfair itself there was demand for new dwellings for the aristocracy and wealthy merchants; this translated into lucrative building projects, from which everyone except the Crown profited. It was high time that the Prince Regent capitalised on this development too.

Nash's plan had to provide answers to all these problems at the same time. It provided a new residential area for the aristocracy on what was then the edge of the city, with views of the pastoral landscape and designed like an urban landscape garden, with a ceremonial route which ran through from the park to the centre of government, connecting them with one another and to the rest of Mayfair. The theatrical New Street was the backdrop for this route and for urban life, just as the landscape garden was the background for country life. Later the Grand Design was expanded with a scenic treatment of Buckingham Palace and the government ministries in Whitehall. Finally, with the rebuilding of Haymarket and Charing Cross a new cultural centre for the city was even included in the Grand Design, although this plan was only partially realised.

The restoration of visual contact with the surrounding landscape and the theatrical staging of public space played a central role. In accomplishing these aims, Nash made use of the concept of landscape theatre, as it had been first conceived by Bridgeman in the early 18th century landscape garden, developed further by Kent and Capability Brown, and transformed for urban settings by two generations of the Wood family in Bath.

London estate development

Already since the early years of the 17th century most of the land available for building in London was being developed by large land-owners and the owners of country houses and estates. Until the second half of the 19th century municipal authorities had almost no role in urban development. With this system, residential construction was left in the hands of landowners and speculators. Rather than selling the estates to the municipality or coming up with a plan themselves, large landowners leased parcels of land to a project developer, which was often a combination formed for that specific purpose, made up of a financial speculator, a building contractor and an architect. The project developer divided the land into lots, built the houses and rented them out, with the objective of making as much profit as possible in a short time. After the expiration of the lease, the land, with the houses on it, reverted to the landowner. It was in Mayfair, at the end of the 18th century, that the consequences of this system first clearly revealed themselves. The larger and smaller projects were scattered about higgledy-piggledy, without good access and with no logic in the road system. As a result, the differentiation and coherence of the urban pattern – and the functional and representative pattern of the court and governmental centre in Westminster – slowly began to feel the pressure.

An entirely new approach to the question of design for the city was necessary in order to create space for the development of urban public life. Nash's Grand Design effected an increase in scale in the urban pattern in a spatial sense, breaking through the cramped conditions of the 18th century city, and created space to accommodate the modernisation of public life there. For that reason it was aptly also termed 'Metropolitan Improvement'.

The development of Marylebone Park

In 1786 legislation was passed, creating a commission to administer the widely scattered and often poorly defined Crown lands and draw up a plan for their management. In 1793 this commission presented its report, which included the recommendation to turn the management of the lands over to a standing committee of three, under the supervision of the Treasury. The idea for developing Marylebone Park came from John Fordyce, one of the members of the committee and Surveyor General to His Majesty's Revenue, in the service of the Prince Regent. This presented an opportunity to bolster the finances of the Crown; if built upon, the land would provide much more revenue than it did as agricultural land. Fordyce also sought to secure the interests of the Crown against those of the Duke of Portland, who owned land both to the north and south of Marylebone Park.

Fordyce however was not purely interested in the financial aspects; he had an integral vision of the significance this project would have for the development of London as a royal residence. For instance, among the things he considered necessary was a direct link between the royal palace and the parliament building in Whitehall. He commissioned studies to demonstrate the feasibility of this comprehensive plan.

London, 1843, with the completed Grand Design (London. 1843. Drawn & engraved from authentic documents & personal observation by B.R. Davies, 16 George Street, Euston Square. London, published Nov. 1, 1843 under the superintendence of the Society for the Diffusion of Useful Knowledge, by Chapman & Hall, 186 Strand (1844). David Rumsey Historical Map Collection, www.davidrumsey.com)

The 1809 study by John White is the best-known of these; it is interesting because it is a literal translation of the effort to impose a definitive limit on the city. It foresees various forms of urban development to the far end of Portland Place, which then changes into a landscape park such as Capability Brown might have designed. In the design the outer edge of the park, facing the landscape, was surrounded by rural villas.

Shortly before his death in 1810 Fordyce wrote a memorandum to the Treasury in which all of the basic conditions for the project were set forth. In 1811, just before the Duke of Portland's lease on Marylebone Park would expire, the standing committee of three, recommended as far back as 1793, was finally constituted, uniting the departments of Woods and Forests and Land Revenues under the chairmanship of Lord Glenberrie, who received parliamentary authorisation. Leverton and Chawner, architects employed by the Department of Land Revenues, and Nash and his assistant Morgan, a partnership formed specifically for this purpose from the Department of Woods and Forests, were immediately commissioned to work out plans for the project. Both pairs produced a design in March, 1811. In 1812 the standing committee produced its first report, which included the proposals by both Leverton and Chawner and by Nash and Morgan. The development of Marylebone Park is recorded in five reports by the standing committee, the last of which appeared in 1826. What Nash had in mind was never ultimately realised; the committee slowly arrived at the conclusion that Nash's development plan could not be carried out in its totality.

The landscape architectonic transformation of the topography

Over the duration of this project Nash became a master in the transformation of existing urban and rural topography. One of the most important keys to his success probably lay in this capability. In the process, Nash used techniques from Repton and his predecessors. He raised the transformation and integration of the topography, one of the characteristics that distinguishes the 18th century landscape garden from the formal garden, to a metropolitan level.

The transformation took place in four phases. Regent's Park was begun in the first phase. In Regent's Park the new residential buildings and the park together formed a theatrical landscape. Nash called this ensemble the 'Theatrical Panorama'. For it he drew on the palatial architecture (or 'palatial style') that the Woodses had developed some seventy years before in Bath. The second phase was formed by New Street, the link between the royal palace and the new residential area. The third phase was initiated by the construction of Buckingham Palace,

a new palace after the coronation of the Prince Regent as George IV in 1820. It included the stage-dressing of the most important ceremonial government buildings, on the other side of St. James's Park (the Horse Guards, designed around 1750 by William Kent in collaboration with John Vardy, the Royal Mews, the Admiralty, and the Houses of Parliament). The fourth and final phase, included in the last report that the standing committee issued in 1826, comprised of a reorganisation of Haymarket and Charing Cross and a new connection with the area around St. Paul's Cathedral.

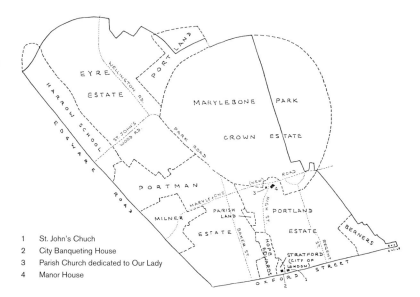

1   St. John's Chuch
2   City Banqueting House
3   Parish Church dedicated to Our Lady
4   Manor House

The various estates around Marylebone Park around 1800 (from A. Saunders, *Regent's Park. A study of the Development of the area from 1086 to the Present Day*, London 1969)

A   Regent's Park
B   The New Street
C   Buckingham Palace
D   St. James's Park
E   Haymarket
F   Charing Cross

1   Edgware Road
2   New Road
3   Tottenham Court Road
4   Oxford Street
5   Piccadilly
6   Hyde Park
7   Westminster Bridge
8   The Strand
9   Thames

0   250   1000 m

The transformation scheme (assembled from Map of London 1746, James Crew's Survey
1753, plan for Regent's Street, Nash 1814; Benevolo 1816; plan Charing Cross Nash
1826; plan St. James Park, Nash 1828; Regent's Park, Nash 1828; and OS 1:25.000)

Regent's Park

Marylebone Park lay on a southern foothills of the plateau comprising Hampstead, Highgate and Harrow. Immediately to the north lay Primrose Hill, the summit of which rises about 35 meters above the average height of the terrain, and the source of the Tyburn River. The morphology of Marylebone Park itself was dominated by a ridge of hills from 5 to 10 meters high which ran next to a lower, poorly drained section of the valley of the Tyburn. In the centuries after the departure of the Romans the village of Tyburn lay where the Tyburn was crossed by a Roman road (today Oxford Street) running east and west. Around 1250 a manor house was built nearby. Around 1400, in connection with the development of new farm land, this village shifted northward in the direction of the manor house and a newly founded church consecrated to St. Mary. This led to a change in its name: the settlement took on the name of Marybone or Marybourne, later Marylebone, probably a corruption of St. Mary-on-the-bourne.

In the 18th century the vast majority of the southern section of the park was used as pasture and hay fields by Willian's Farm, Kendall's Farm and Rhodes' Farm, previously Allaley's Farm, on the transition from the Thames terrace to the hard to till boulder clay of the plateau. The residents of Mayfair and Soho also sought amusement in the southern part of Marylebone Park, at The Jew's Harp inn and other places of entertainment.

The development of Nash's design

The plan produced by Leverton and Chawner in 1811 was still rather traditional in conception. It was an elaboration on the grid of Mayfair, with its streets and squares. They had already submitted a plan in 1806 for a link with the centre, and in the light of this new commission saw no reason to change it. They did not believe that any plan for a canal running on through to the Eastern Docks (the Grand Junction Canal) was feasible. The first rough plan by Nash from 1811 on the other hand already reveals the germ of a new approach to the task. This plan was not a continuation of the pattern around Cavendish Square, but was described by Nash as an "exclusive, self-contained residential area". It is urban in character, apparently based in part on the studies and plans by George Dance, who as early as 1767 had designed a miniature triad of a square, circus and crescent for London modelled on that in Bath.

An arrangement of urban blocks enclosed park-like inner courts with villas. A double circus on a hill was designed for the centre of the composition; this was retained in later versions of the plan. According

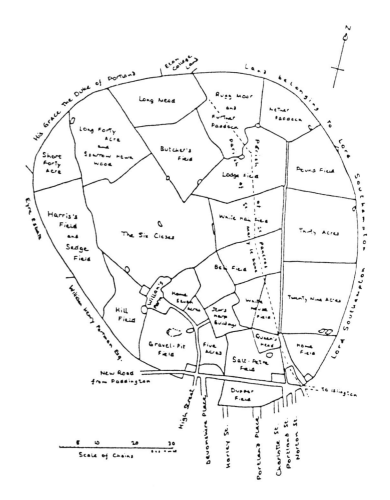

The parcellation of Marylebone Park, around 1789 (from A. Saunders, *Regent's Park. A study of the Development of the area from 1086 to the Present Day*, London 1969)

Hampstead, Highgate and the New Road seen from Devonshire Street; right, The Jew's Harp (Samuel Hieronymus Grimm, 1793. British Library Additional MS 15542 f.136)

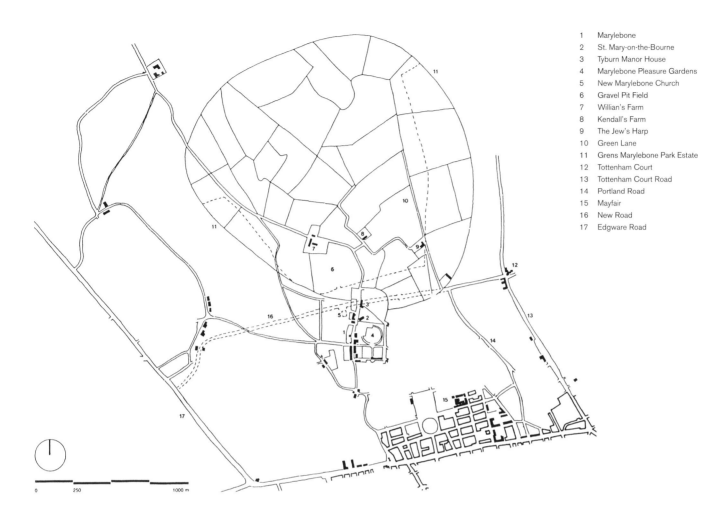

1 Marylebone
2 St. Mary-on-the-Bourne
3 Tyburn Manor House
4 Marylebone Pleasure Gardens
5 New Marylebone Church
6 Gravel Pit Field
7 Willian's Farm
8 Kendall's Farm
9 The Jew's Harp
10 Green Lane
11 Grens Marylebone Park Estate
12 Tottenham Court
13 Tottenham Court Road
14 Portland Road
15 Mayfair
16 New Road
17 Edgware Road

The topography of Marylebone Park (assembled from data from the Map of London 1746 and James Crew's Survey 1753)

The Boating Lake

to Nash this was to be the apex of the planned area, with a national monument devoted to British heroes in the middle, analogous to the British Worthies at Stowe. The park was crammed with a large number of villas, each with its own pleasure grounds surrounded by a screen of trees. Other striking features in the first rough plan are the Boating Lake, adopted from John White's 1809 plan, and the ingenious integration of the Grand Junction Canal. In this rough plan the landscape was still subordinate to the arrangement of the blocks of buildings; the open space had not yet taken on an autonomous form.

A comparison of this first version with a second, still from 1811 (several intermediate versions also exist) reveals a decisive change. The image shifts in the direction of a landscape garden. The number of villas was reduced from 56 to 26 (of which ultimately only six were built). The building density as a whole was also reduced. The Boating Lake became autonomous as the visual centre of the scenic composition; the Grand Junction Canal is run along the edge of the area.

The differentiation in the building forms, which was worked out still further in later versions, transformed the urban block arrangement of the first design into a 'park city'. In it the landscape stands in opposition to the architecture of the residential buildings. This produced a synthesis of the English landscape garden and neo-classical Regency architecture, in which the 18th century typology of Bath was turned into a 19th century urban villa park.

The topographic framework

By damming the Tyburn the boggy area near Willian's Farm was magically transformed into a Boating Lake, analogous to Capability Brown's lakes. The double circus (today the Botanical Garden) was situated on the top of the central hill as the visual centre of the park. South Villa was a transformation of the striking siting of Willian's Farm.

The country road between Marylebone High Street and Willian's Farm was transformed into York Gate; the new Marylebone Church was given a classical portico by Nash and used as a backdrop. Green Lane returned in the design as a promenade, called The Broad Walk. At the point where The Broad Walk cuts through the hill crest Nash designed The Guinguette, a summer pavilion for the Prince Regent, opposite Cumberland Terrace. A pool between them served the new section of the city as a reservoir for drinking water.

In this transformation Nash used all the morphological and topographic elements of the former agricultural landscape, except for the belvedère on Primrose Hill which, because of the ownership relations at the time, could be involved in the development of Marylebone Park

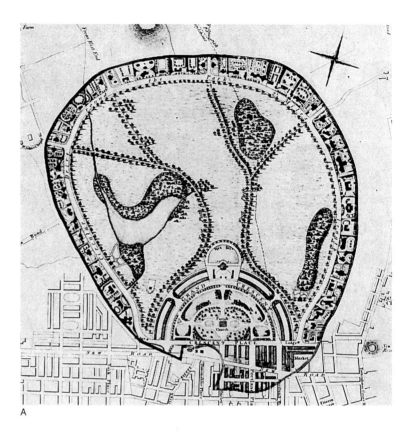

A

B

A White's plan, 1809

C Leverton and Chawner's plan, 1811

B Nash's first plan, 1811

D Nash's second plan, 1811

(from A. Saunders, *Regent's Park. A study of the Development of the area from 1086 to the Present Day*, London 1969)

C

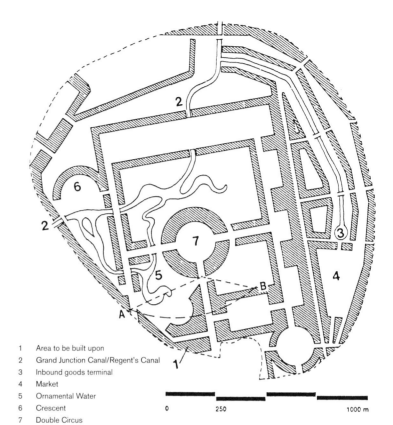

1   Area to be built upon
2   Grand Junction Canal/Regent's Canal
3   Inbound goods terminal
4   Market
5   Ornamental Water
6   Crescent
7   Double Circus

0   250   1000 m

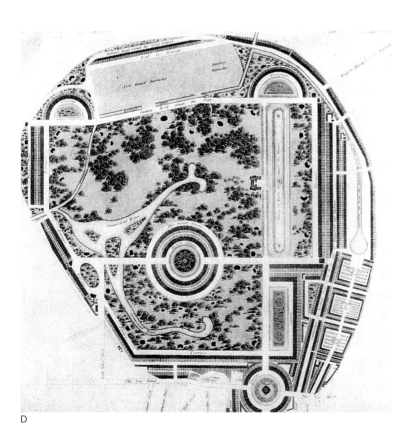

D

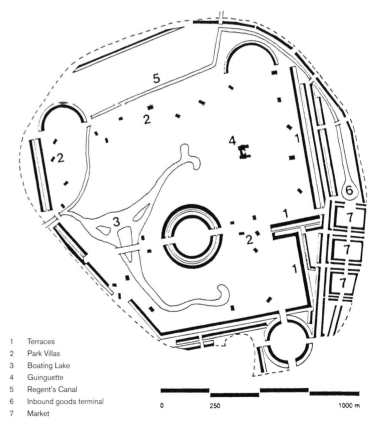

1   Terraces
2   Park Villas
3   Boating Lake
4   Guinguette
5   Regent's Canal
6   Inbound goods terminal
7   Market

0   250   1000 m

Plan, from the first design (March, 1811)

Plan, from the second design (November, 1811)

only as an external observation point. This relation between Regent's Park and Primrose Hill still exists today. The elementary composition of landscape architectonic elements was a reference to the original topography of the spot, and moreover permitted the area to fit in well with the uncertain morphological development of the city. In accomplishing this, the design fulfilled one of the important conditions for a successful transformation.

The 'Theatrical Panorama'

Every design tool to be found in the 18th century landscape garden was employed in staging the 'Theatrical Panorama' of Regent's Park. Summerson calls it a 'Bathonian concept', by which he refers to a direct visual confrontation between collective residential buildings and the landscape. The terraces and the villas each had their own unobstructed view of the park. This was not however a one-way visual relation, but rather one of reciprocity. The various residences were simultaneously both stage and décor. In his 'Theatrical Panorama' Nash consciously emphasises and plays with this ambiguity between 'seeing' and 'being seen'.

The terraces enclose the park landscape with the villas. Seen from the villas, the monumental façades of the terraces, divided up into middle class dwellings, formed an architectonically elaborated 'urban horizon'. Conversely, seen from the terraces, the Park Villas formed a part of the rustic décor. The Park Villages fringing the Regent's Canal were in turn an idyllic rural backdrop along the edge of the residential area, and formed the transition to the agricultural landscape outside the park. Seen from Park Road, Primrose Hill was part of the pastoral panorama, and emphasised the open visual relation with the landscape of Hampstead, Highgate and Harrow. Conversely, from Primrose Hill one could survey both Westminster and central London (Soho).

Two visual foci can be distinguished in the staging of the 'Theatrical Panorama'. The one focal point was the proposed double Inner Circus, while the other was formed by The Guinguette, Cumberland Terrace and the Reservoir. Park Road, with its ever-changing perspective on the 'Theatrical Panorama' and landscape, was a transformation of the composition scheme of the 'circuit walk' of the 18th century landscape garden. With this, Nash went even a step further than the scenic staging of the Royal Crescent by John Wood the Younger in Bath; Park Road became an urban pictural composition, a chain of scenic views of the city and landscape which would form the basis for the later Victorian city park.

In the 'Theatrical Panorama' the visual contrast between the city and the landscape is played out architectonically to its end, but at the same time the functional opposition is abandoned. With this, its design of urban space takes on the character of a continuum running from the landscape to the urban.

The image of a park landscape

The planting in Regent's Park was intended as an embellishment for the residential landscape. Nash took responsibility for the planting of the building sites before they were sold. Following Repton's precepts, he used a limited assortment of trees and shrubs, with a specific shape and texture, in order to obtain a certain unity. In general the planting consisted of two sorts of trees, supplemented by bushes. He adapted his choice of trees to the immediate soil conditions. Two planting schemes were applied. Where construction was expected later, he planted trees in a grid so that it was possible to thin the stand, as in a woods; around the villas, the Boating Lake and the canal he used looser clumps of trees for decorative purposes, and to frame the views of the principle space.

Nash himself characterised the image he created as a "general unity of park-like character". He also saw the Park Villas and Park Villages, the borders of rustic cottages on the north-east side of Regent's Park along the Regent's Canal, as urban housing, consistent with the continuing series of urban images. This assembling of such wholly different residential forms was related to the 'Gardenesque' style developed by Repton, who brought together a sampler of various thematic gardens in one total design at Ashridge and Woburn Abbey. As the antithesis of this there was the Inner Circus, according to Bacon the architectonic recapitulation of the outward form of the park. As the ideal collective form it replaced the individual stately home, thus becoming the nucleus in the transformation of the landscape garden into an urban park.

→ **York Gate, view of Marylebone Church** (from Tho. H. Shepherd and J. Elmes, *Metropolitan Improvements; or London in the nineteenth century: being a series of views, of the new and most interesting objects, in the British metropolis & its vicinity: from original drawings by Mr. Thos. H. Shepherd: with historical, topographical & critical illustrations by James Elmes M.R.I.A.* London 1827. Library, Rijksmuseum, 116 D 20)

The transformation of Marylebone Park

1 > 1' Tyburn/Gravel Pit Field > Boating Lake
2 > 2' Hill crest > Double Crescent
3 > 3' Highest point > Guinguette
4 > 4' Willian's Farm > South Villa
5 > 5' Green Lane > The Broad Walk
6 > 6' Marylebone High Street > York Gate
7   The Jew's Harp
8   Kendall's Farm
9   Edgware Road (?)
10   New Road
11   Tottenham Court
12   Hampstead/Tottenham Court Road
13   Boundary Marylebone Park Estate
14   Clarendon Square

A residential programme for aristocrats

In principle, Regent's Park was intended for a dual function. In addition to being a new residential area, it was conceived as the final element in a ceremonial series which connected Carlton House, then the royal residence, and the Guinguette, earmarked as the summer resort for the Prince Regent. The latter idea was dropped when the Prince Regent indicated his preference for demolishing Carlton House and rebuilding Buckingham House as the royal palace.

The zoning of the programme was primarily oriented toward rural living in the city. The terraces and the villas each had their own pleasure grounds as well as the right to use the park, and were linked directly with Whitehall.

The 'open market' section on the east side of the park provided for the everyday necessities of life, as a shopping mall would today. It had dwellings for the suppliers and service personnel for the residents of Regent's Park. It continued the pattern of Mayfair; for it Nash used variations on the repertoire of spatial forms that one finds there, such as streets, places and squares.

Nash laid out the Regent's Canal along the edge of the park. This had originally been intended by Charles Rennie as the Grand Junction Canal, which would carry goods from the eastern docklands area to the west of London, and vice versa. In Nash's plan, worked out by one of his assistants, James Morgan, the chief engineer of the Canal Company, the Regent's Canal was however joined up with the Grand Union Canal, which connected Birmingham with the harbours of London. Moreover, the canal provided for the delivery of foodstuffs and consumer goods directly to the market area, which was designed with an inbound goods terminal. Regent's Canal was also to surround a barracks and parade ground for the Life Guard and Artillery which was then located in the northern part of the park, and connected with the anticipated summer palace by the Broad Walk and Park Road. These plans were also dropped, along with the plans for the summer palace.

The terraces were accessible from both the city side (i.e., the outside) and Park Road. The double circus in the middle could be reached from Park Road by a crossroad, which included an inner ring around the double crescent.

Originally unwritten law provided that only The Broad Walk in the southern part of the park was open to the public. Furthermore, in Nash's design the pattern of paths was not intended for public use. After the park was opened to the public around 1845, with the exception of a zone surrounding the villas built in the park, a crisscross network of 'wild paths' developed. Park Road became the public access for coaches.

The park formed the scenic framework for a collective urban residential programme. This new urban residential landscape united the qualities of the landscape and the city.

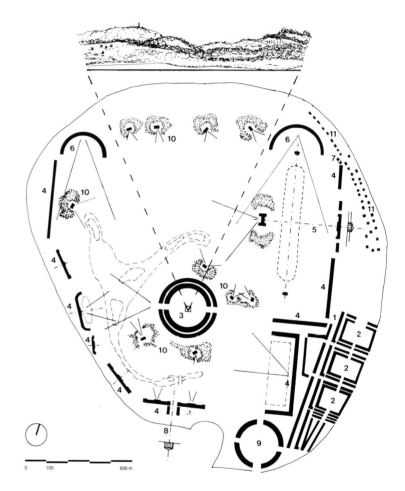

0   100   500 m

1   Streets
2   Markets
3   Double Circus
4   Terraces
5   Guinguette/Cumberland Terrace
6   Crescent
7   Gloucester Gate
8   York Gate/Marylebone Church
9   Park Circus
10   Park Villa's
11   Cottages (Park Villages)

Staging the Theatrical Panorama

A

B

C

D

E

F

The Park Villas: A The Holme   B Grove House (from Tho. H. Shepherd and J. Elmes, *Metropolitan Improvements; or London in the nineteenth century: being a series of views, of the new and most interesting objects, in the British metropolis & its vicinity: from original drawings by Mr. Thos. H. Shepherd: with historical, topographical & critical illustrations by James Elmes M.R.I.A.* London 1827. Library, Rijksmuseum 116 D 20 (B) and University Library, Vrije Universiteit Amsterdam, Special Collections, HQ.05032.- (A)).

**C Entrance to Chester Terrace   D The Regent's Canal
E The Broad Walk   F Park Village East**

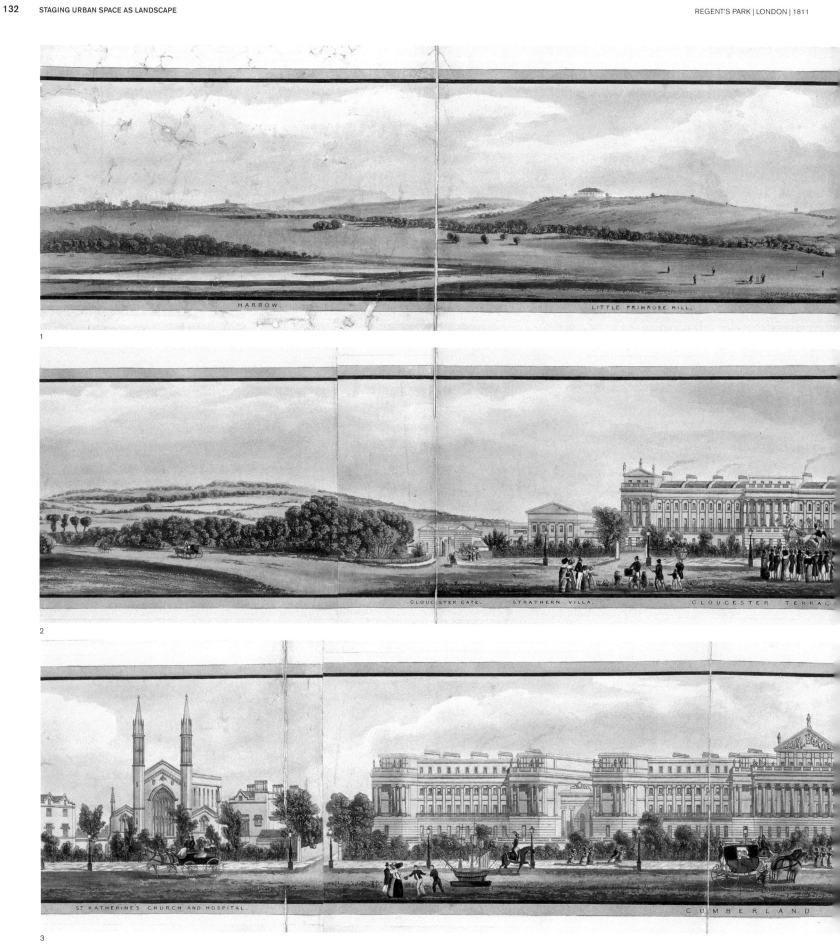

1

HARROW.

LITTLE PRIMROSE HILL.

2

GLOUCESTER GATE.   STRATHERN VILLA.   GLOUCESTER TERRAC

3

ST. KATHERINE'S CHURCH AND HOSPITAL.   CUMBERLAND

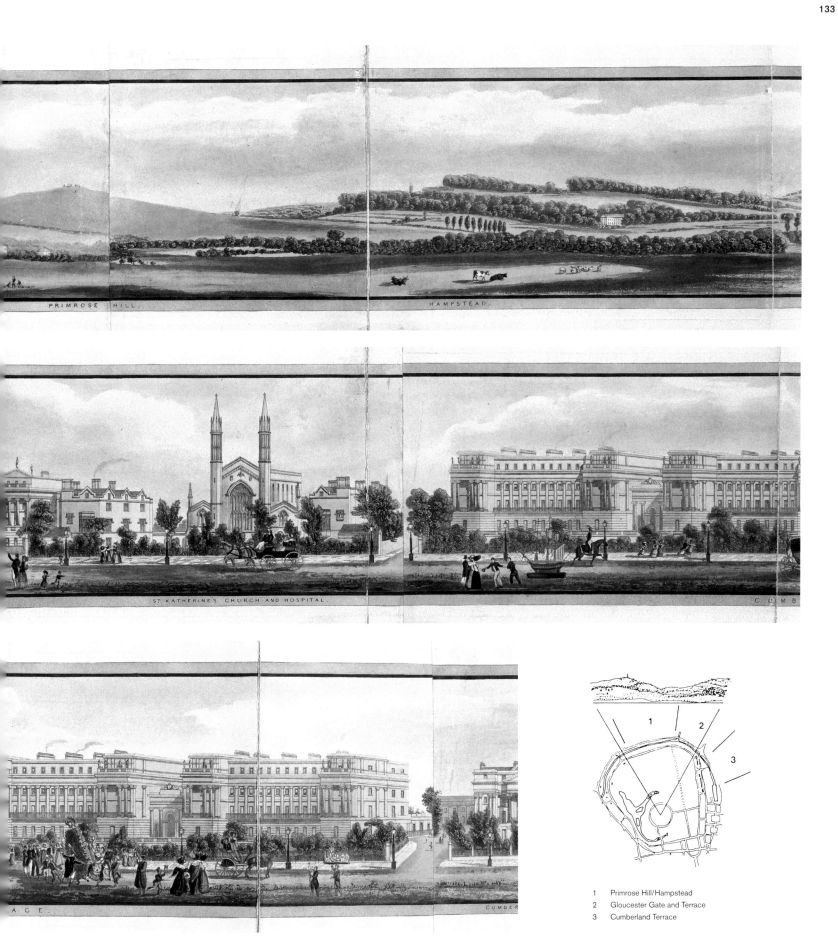

PRIMROSE HILL.   HAMPSTEAD.

ST KATHERINE'S CHURCH AND HOSPITAL.   CUMB

ACE.   CUMBER

1   Primrose Hill/Hampstead
2   Gloucester Gate and Terrace
3   Cumberland Terrace

The theatrical and pastoral panorama (British Library Maps 14.a.29)

New Street

New Street was intended as a 'Triumphal Avenue', a regal link between Carlton House, which was then the palace of the Prince Regent, and his summer palace in the newly developed Regent's Park. What initially seemed to be a relatively simple matter of breaking through a few blocks of buildings grew into one of the most complex components of the Grand Design.

The first rough drafts by Nash from 1812 included the section between Carlton House, near St. James's Park in the south, and Portland Place, a street already existing bordering on Regent's Park, in one monumental composition. In it New Street was conceived as a classic 'straight' street with continuous colonnades, intersecting with important cross streets by means of rectangular or round plazas (Oxford Circus, Piccadilly Circus), sometimes with a statue in the middle.

The second design, from 1814, was a more pictural composition, modelled on Oxford High Street. This design was more complex spatially, and also involved more urban development and technical aspects for its realisation. At the north end the plan was expanded to include the entrance to Regent's Park; at the south end Waterloo Place, the formal square in front of Carlton House, appeared, as did the links with Whitehall and the old city.

A complex transformation

New Street thus brought about a three-part transformation of the existing pattern in Mayfair. In cutting through the pattern of streets in Mayfair for this new space, some streets were replaced (for instance Swallow Street by The Quadrant), while others were included in the design (for instance Portland Place). Moreover, New Street formed a new metropolitan axis on the boundary between Soho, the old, dense and poorer district, and the wealthier Mayfair which lay to the west. Nash reorganised the relation between these two districts by designing a theatrical space at the point of transition, and selectively involving the streets and squares which lay behind his New Street. The spaces of the streets and squares were a stage, so to speak, on which the people of London could appear; the façades, gates and monumental buildings were the sets that hid the poorer streets and opened up access to the richer squares. A third important aspect of New Street was the connection it provided with the landscape outside London. Formerly the population of Soho had gone out of the city via Portland Road (rechristened Portland Place as part of the restructuring, and still later Portland Street), to reach The Jew's Harp inn via Green Lane.

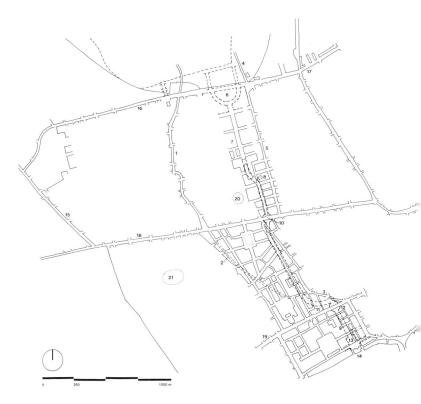

1   Marylebone Highstreet
2   Marylebone Road
3   Swallow Street
4   Green Lane
5   Portland Street
6   Park Crescent
7   Portland Place
8   Langham Place/All Souls Church
9   Regent Street
10   Oxford Circus
11   The Quadrant
12   Piccadilly Circus
13   Waterloo Place
14   Carlton House
15   Edgware Road
16   New Road
17   Tottenham Court
18   Oxford Street
19   Piccadilly
20   Cavendish Square
21   Grosvenor Square

The transformation of Mayfair

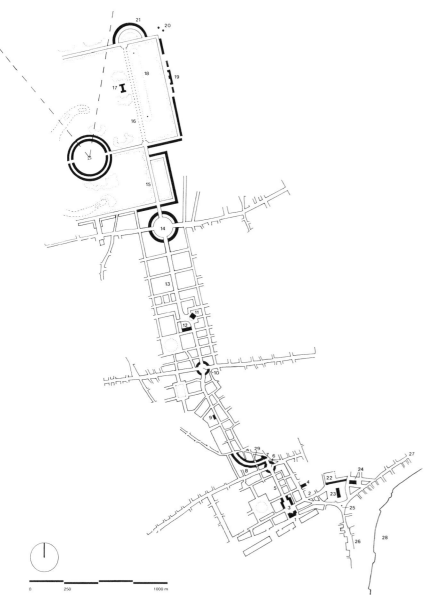

1	Carlton House	21	Crescent
2	Pall Mall	22	National Gallery
3	Waterloo Place	23	Royal Academy
4	Haymarket Theatre	24	St. Martin-in-the-Fields
5	Regent Street	25	Charing Cross
6	Piccadilly Circus	26	Whitehall
7	County Fire Office	27	The Strand
8	The Quadrant	28	Thames
9	Hannover Chapel	29	Air Street
10	Oxford Circus/Oxford Street		
11	All Souls Church		
12	Foley House		
13	Portland Place (existing)		
14	The Regent's Circus/New Road		
15	Park Drive		
16	The Broad Walk		
17	The Guinguette		
18	Reservoir		
19	Cumberland Terrace		
20	Gloucester Gate		

The scenography of the Triumphal Avenue in the second design

Waterloo Place, looking toward the former Carlton House (Thomas Hosmer Shepherd. View of Regent Street from Piccadilly, with pedestrians and horse-drawn transport. 1822. London Metropolitan Archives, Main Print Collection, Pr.W2/REG)

Waterloo Place, looking in the direction of the County Fire Office (Thomas Hosmer Shepherd. View of Waterloo Place and part of Lower Regent Street. 1828. London Metropolitan Archives, Main Print Collection, Pr.W2/WAT/pla)

The Quadrant, with the County Fire Office (Anon. View of The Quadrant on Regent Street, Westminster. Circa 1830. London Metropolitan Archives, Main Print Collection, Pr.W2/REG)

The 'Triumphal Avenue' added a ceremonial aspect to this, a 'royal' transformation of the historic link between the city and the landscape, which as public space would be of importance for all of Westminster.

The scenography of the urban route

The scenography of New Street (today Regent Street) gave the illusion of a spatial (visual) continuity; one walked from the centre on the Thames slowly upward, as it were, out of the city to an Arcadian landscape in the hills. In a certain respect this was an enlargement of the urban route from the centre of Bath to the Royal Crescent. The starting point was Carlton House, for which Nash provided a larger square, Waterloo Place, analogous to the forecourt of an 18th century country manor. In a deeper sense the end point was not the summer palace in the park, but Primrose Hill, from which one could return to the city in the valley of the Thames.

Nash used no trees in his design for New Street, as Alphand would do in his design for the boulevards of Paris forty years later. The continuity was sustained by the architectonic treatment of the façades bordering the street at visually strategic spots, which made it an architectonic route at those points. Nash articulated the offsets in the route with the aid of a number of transitional sections which were derived from the visual arsenal of the landscape garden. At Piccadilly Circus, for instance, the County Fire Office functioned like a grotto as the visual terminus to the view from Carlton House, over Waterloo Place and Lower Regent Street. The building was given five (today three) gates, one of which afforded a picturesque glimpse into the old city, as if a *nymphaeum* lay behind it. The connection between Piccadilly and Regent Street was The Quadrant, a theatrical street in the form of a quarter circle, in which the intersections with streets regarded as important enough for the treatment, such as Air Street, were marked by means of arch-shaped gates in the frontage along the street.

The north end of Upper Regent Street is visually defined by the semi-circular colonnade of All Souls' Church, comparable with the rotunda at the end of the Great Lime Cross Walk at Stowe. The street is connected with the then already existing Portland Place by means of an offset; in turn, the south end of Portland Place is closed visually by Foley House. The link between Portland Place and Regent's Park was designed as 'The Regent's Circus', which later was realised as the open, semi-circular Park Crescent.

The 'Triumphal Avenue' was continued in Regent's Park as a public promenade. This carried on past The Guinguette, where the Theatrical Panorama unfolded on either side. In Nash's second design The Broad

A

B

Walk was closed at its far end by an *exedra* in the form of a crescent, which apparently was in part intended to frame the pastoral panorama to the north side with the view of Primrose Hill.

A Stair to St. James's Park, on the site of Carlton House
B Lower Regent's Street, from Waterloo Place
C The built-over arcade of the County Fire Office, with a view of the old city
D Upper Regent Street with All Souls Church
E The Quadrant

C

D

E

The capstone on the Thames

With the death of the old king, George III, in 1820 and the coronation of the Regent, the Prince of Wales, as George IV, the construction of a new palace became urgent. Regent's Park and New Street had brought about such a far-reaching reordering of Mayfair that a re-evaluation of the location of the royal palace was also considered necessary. The decision was made to rebuild the existing Buckingham House, where the new king had been born. Nash prepared a design for this; Carlton House was demolished. This in turn required a rearrangement of the relation between the new palace and the centre of government around Whitehall. In 1814 the Treasury had already extended a commission for the redesign of St. James's Park.

The scenic staging for Buckingham Palace

St. James's Park originally belonged to a leper asylum, St. James's Hospital. It consisted of marshy meadowland with ponds and clumps of trees, and was probably regularly flooded by the Thames. In 1532 Henry VIII had the area drained and walled in. Around 1660, under Charles II, the area was enlarged. A park was laid out, probably by Mollet, with a formal Grand Canal (in which the king is reputed to have swum publicly), as well as tree-lined avenues and an early croquet court. In 1663 St. James's Park became one of the first royal parks to be opened to the public.

Buckingham House stood at the end of the already existing Mall, a lawn bowls green in St. James's Park which already is to be found on Bridgeman's drawing from 1725. Moreover, it lay at the 'hinge' in the series of parks comprising St. James's Park, the Palace Gardens/Green Park, Hyde Park, and the gardens of Kensington Palace. A new palace in this spot meant it was farther from Whitehall and the headquarters of the royal bodyguards, the Horse Guards, while at the same time being better embedded in the series of parks.

The new palace was set opposite the government buildings, with St. James's Park as a public landscape between them. A logical consequence of this was that Whitehall too was included in the scenic landscape. Following an earlier proposal by Capability Brown, Nash transformed the formal canal into a Serpentine Lake, asymmetrical in shape, the eastern end of which is somewhat widened, with receding planting, in order to frame Whitehall as seen from Buckingham Palace and frame the park. The choice of the Mall as the main axis required that the relation of Buckingham Palace with Whitehall had to be finished off on a diagonal. The crescent and terraces designed by

Nash for Birdcage Walk, along the southern end of St. James's Park (never realised) were intended to strengthen this diagonal as a second important axis in the composition.

The formal relation with the old city

The formal relation between Buckingham Palace and Charing Cross (today Trafalgar Square) and The Strand is defined by the Mall, the main axis of the composition, which in fact runs at a slight angle to the façade of the palace. A stair, with the Duke of York's Column added later, on the site where Carlton House had stood, formed an insert for connecting the Mall and New Street (now Regent Street).

The final piece in the Grand Design was an improvement in the relation between Buckingham Palace, Whitehall and The Strand and St. Paul's Cathedral through the reconstruction of the area around Haymarket and Charing Cross, at the far end of the Mall. This proposal, included in the final report from the standing committee of three in 1826, was only realised in part. (The area to the east of Haymarket was Crown land.)

Nash's idea was to tie the various parts of the city together compositionally by means of a new formal square near Charing Cross, a three-way junction which then still retained its mediaeval pattern. This would have provided the Mall and The Strand with a formal terminus at the square, to which Regent Street could also have been connected. The square at Charing Cross was conceived as a new cultural centre for the city, surrounded by important public buildings and institutions. In the middle, on the axis from Whitehall, Nash designed a Pantheon, intended for the Royal Academy. He placed the National Gallery on the north side of the square, with a colonnade as a screen in front of an existing garrison barracks. With the demolition of a couple of blocks of houses, St. Martin's Church (St. Martin-in-the-Fields) would come to stand alone, flanked by an Atheneum. Later Charing Cross was renamed Trafalgar Square, to commemorate the historic victory by admiral Horatio Nelson over the Spanish and French in 1805, dominated by the statue of the Admiral himself.

The transformation of St. James's Park

1 Pall Mall
2 St. James Square
3 Vroegere St. James's Palace
4 Carlton House
5 Carlton House Terrace
6 Buckingham Palace
7 The Mall
8 Palace Gardens
9 Green Park
10 Birdcage Crescent
11 St. James's Park
12 Admiralty
13 Horse Guards
14 Whitehall
15 Haymarket
16 Charing Cross
17 National Gallery
18 Hyde Park
19 Piccadilly
20 Westminster Abbey
21 Westminster Bridge
22 The Strand
23 Thames
24 Houses of Parliament
25 Big Ben

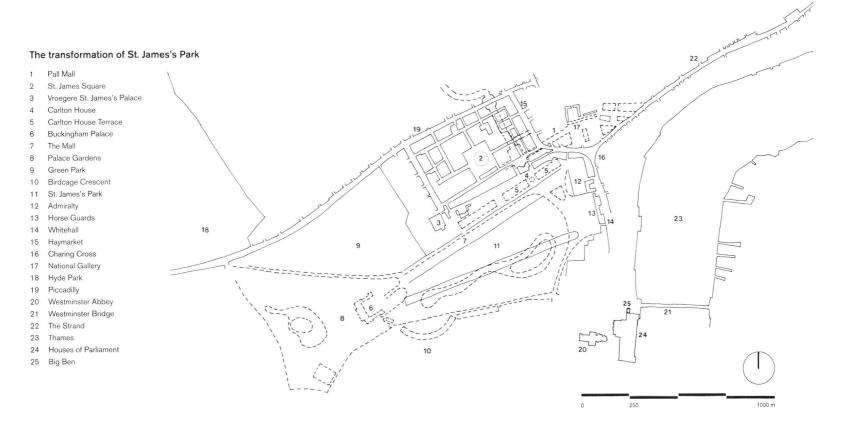

St. James's Park, view of the Horse Guards (The British Museum, Prints & Drawings, 1880,1113.2317)

View of the Horse Guards today

The continuity of city and landscape

John Nash's Grand Design is a 19th century continuation of the landscape architectonic tradition which works out the spatial relation between the city and the landscape. From this perspective, the Grand Design can be compared with the plan that linked the Piazza della Signoria and the Uffizi with the Arno and the landscape beyond it in 16th century Florence, and with Le Nôtre's 17th century Jardin des Tuileries that connected the Louvre with the Seine landscape to the west of Paris. In a deeper sense there is even a comparison to be made with the relation between the Horti Farnesiani and the Via Triumphalis in imperial Rome.

On the other hand, the significance of the Grand Design for urban design also permits a comparison with Versailles, because what Versailles was for formal French urban design in the 17th and 18th centuries, Regent's Park was for the pictural urban design of the 19th century; both plans established the visual relation between a royal palace, the city and the landscape in a normative form.

Nash provided a stage for public life according to the standards of the aristocracy. He created an 'Picturesque Manifesto' in the tradition of the 18th century landscape garden, in which public space was transformed into an 'urban theatre'. It proved to be possible to apply the techniques of the 18th century landscape garden successfully in urban design. In this sense the Grand Design was the next step beyond the 'Bathonian concept'. It testified to visionary power and royal ambition. In Regency London the possibilities of pictural landscape design were tested on a metropolitan scale for the first time.

A prototype of the public park

Nash's Grand Design had immense influence on the development of urban planning in the second half of the 19th century, especially because Nash succeeded in transforming the ideal of country life into an urban lifestyle. The importance of landscape architecture for providing a setting for public life in the city was demonstrated all the more by this design.

Without Regent's Park as a prototype, the public park, one of the most effective strategies for transforming the public domain amidst the architectonically almost unmanageable growth of the 19th century city, would have been unthinkable. With it, the coupling of the civil engineering and landscape architectonic aspects of park design, already found with Nash, gradually became an important issue.

However, notwithstanding its present use, Regent's Park in itself is still not a 19th century city park, in a landscape architectonic sense of the word. The stage-managing of the public function of the park was not yet crystallised. For instance, there is no urban programme, and the system of foot paths designed to promote circulation, which is an invariable characteristic of the public parks to come, is lacking. Neither is there a close relation between the planting, the open space and the pattern of paths. In Regent's Park the planting and the open space were still directly connected with the design of the terraces and the villas. The zoning of the various types of buildings, so characteristic of the 19th century city park, is present in a rudimentary form, but the polarisation of the 'city' over against the 'wilderness' was not yet fully worked out within the boundaries of the park. That would only happen for the first time in England in Joseph Paxton's 1843 design for Birkenhead Park at Liverpool.

Although the prospect out over the pastoral landscape in Regent's Park was kept open, with the 'Theatrical Panorama' the 'urban wall' as the horizon appeared in a landscape park for the first time. With this, the most important step had been taken; it is perhaps particularly for this aspect of his design that Nash is one of the devisors of the 19th century urban landscape. Scarcely twenty years later the public park, as a landscape architectonic type, was complete.

The Grand Design was very quickly confronted with a new reality. London grew at an ever increasing rate; with the arrival of the railway and industrialisation the configuration of the city was already changing drastically. In a deeper sense, with its theatrical urban space, the Grand Design sounded the final chord of the 18th century, a look back to the century of the Enlightenment, in which landscape architecture had played an important role.

Inscribing the landscape in the city

Much has changed since the time of John Nash. Regent's Park has become a public park. That was accompanied by the introduction of all sorts of recreational, but also educational and representative functions. As a result of this, the crisscross pattern of paths has developed further. The northern part of the park, which once housed the Life Guards, is now the home of the London Zoo and the headquarters of the Zoological Society of London. Various public flower and botanical gardens have been laid out in the park, the most important of which is Queen Mary's Gardens in the Inner Circle, where Nash's double crescent was to have stood. This garden also accommodates an open-air theatre and a café. Room has been found in the park for a range of sports, such as tennis, hockey, football, rugby and cricket. Regent's

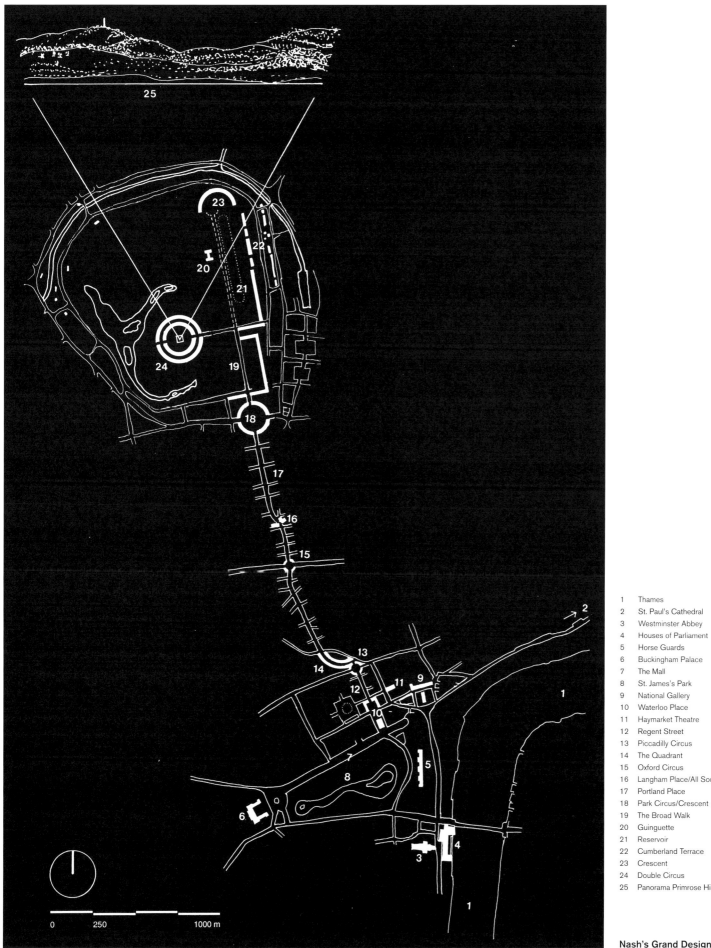

1   Thames
2   St. Paul's Cathedral
3   Westminster Abbey
4   Houses of Parliament
5   Horse Guards
6   Buckingham Palace
7   The Mall
8   St. James's Park
9   National Gallery
10 Waterloo Place
11 Haymarket Theatre
12 Regent Street
13 Piccadilly Circus
14 The Quadrant
15 Oxford Circus
16 Langham Place/All Souls Church
17 Portland Place
18 Park Circus/Crescent
19 The Broad Walk
20 Guinguette
21 Reservoir
22 Cumberland Terrace
23 Crescent
24 Double Circus
25 Panorama Primrose Hill/Hampstead

Nash's Grand Design

College, a large complex of buildings housing several important schools for university level economic studies, lies south of this, near the Boating Lake. The houses behind Park Crescent, by the southern entrance to the park, have largely been re-purposed as offices. Winfield House, one of the few original villas (and presently the residence of the American ambassador to the Court of St. James), stands on private land in the western part of the park. Between 1988 and 2004 six new villas were built along the western edge of the park, between the Regent's Canal and Park Road (now called Outer Circle). They were designed in various classic styles, including Corinthian, Ionic, Gothic, Tuscan – and Regency. Close by stands the London Central Mosque, better known as Regent's Park Mosque, with its dome and minaret.

Despite all the architectonic simplifications, the wear and tear, and the pressure of motorised traffic, the parts of the Grand Design which Nash's genius has left to us are still among the most important public spaces of London. With this project he left his stamp on the scenic identity of the city. The Grand Design is also important as a landscape architectonic model for a possible continuity in the transition from urban to more rural forms of space, something which remains highly relevant today. The key to this is the painstaking and detailed application of the technique of landscape architectonic transformation of the existing topography. Unlike with the urban balcony of the Horti Farnesiani in Rome or the geography of the system of avenues in Paris, in London a complete merger of the urban and rural landscape pattern took place, in a purposefully designed series, which links urban space with the landscape. With this topographic scenography Nash has inscribed the landscape in the city in a lasting manner.

Park Crescent, at the entrance to the park

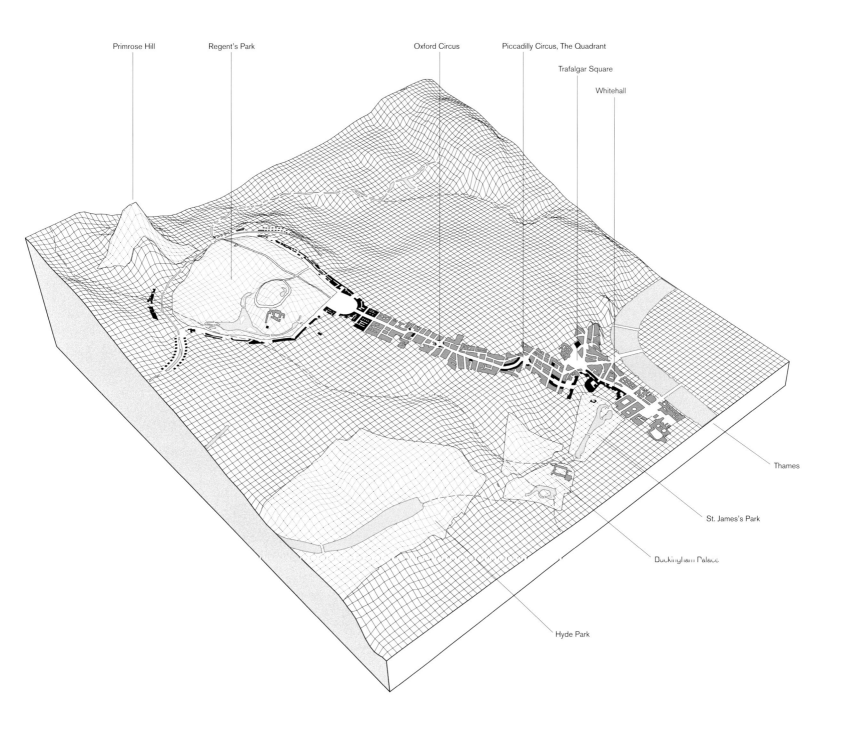

Primrose Hill

Regent's Park

Oxford Circus

Piccadilly Circus, The Quadrant

Trafalgar Square

Whitehall

Thames

St. James's Park

Buckingham Palace

Hyde Park

The Grand Design in the morphology of the Thames Valley

THE GARTENREICH OF POTSDAM BERLIN 1826

The landscape theatre
Peter Joseph Lenné
Karl Friedrich Schinkel
An urban Arcadia

The post-glacial landscape
Palaeovalleys
Glacial plateaus

The system of axes and avenues
The Tiergarten
The Grunewald
Potsdam
Sanssouci

Charlottenhof as a transformation model
The fragmentation of the axis
The liberation of the open space
The differentiation of the programme
The subjectivication of the image
A landscape architectonic étude

The great water theatre
The Neue Garten
The Pfaueninsel
Glienicke
Babelsberg
Sacrow
Nikolskoe

The Gartenreich of Potsdam
Hills, woods and heath
Farms, fields and villages
The Gartenreich as landscape theatre
The integration of Berlin into the Gartenreich

The limits of the garden realm
The scope of the visual instrumentarium

The Pfaueninsel, with the Schloss in the foreground (aerial photo: FTB - Werbefotografie)

The landscape theatre

Charlottenhof Park (1826-1836) was a 19th century expansion of
Sanssouci Park, the royal estate in Potsdam, near Berlin, which during
the 18th century had grown into a garden complex where experiments
were conducted with new ways of organising the landscape. The
landscape architect Peter Joseph Lenné played a central role in
this, often in collaboration with the architect Karl Friedrich Schinkel.
Among Lenné's projects as the royal *Gartendirektor* was the Havel
landscape between Berlin and Potsdam, as *Landschaftsverschönerung*,
conceived as a complete fusion of nature, the agricultural landscape,
architectonic and urban elements. In 1840 he drew up a plan for the
Stadtverschönerung of Berlin that encompassed the whole urban
region, and was intended to complement the *Landschaftsverschöne-*
rungen around Potsdam. The most important projects that formed
the basis for this series of new plans at an ever larger scale were the
transformation of the park at Sanssouci in Potsdam, and that of the
Tiergarten into a landscape park.

Peter Joseph Lenné

Peter Joseph Lenné (1789-1866) was one of the most important garden
and landscape architects of the 19th century. He was in Paris as a
student in 1811 and 1812, acquiring a knowledge of botany from André
Thouin, the director of the Jardin des Plantes. There he met Gabriel
Thouin, who was working on plans to include the baroque garden of
Versailles in a still much larger ideal landscape which was to take in the
whole of human society, with dwellings, work, agrarian pursuits, forestry
and gardens. He also took a course in architecture with Durand at the
École Polytechnique. In 1822 Lenné visited England to see works by
William Kent, including Stowe, and Caton Hall, designed by Humphry
Repton. In London he examined St. James's Park, Hyde Park, Green
Park, Kensington Park and the work being done on Regent's Park.
Later, in Italy he visited Isola Bella in Lago Maggiore, the castle park in
Caserta, and the Borghese, Medici, Doria Pamphili, Ludovisi and Mattei
villas in Rome.

Lenné's work comprises all scales of landscape architectonic design,
from gardens, streets and squares to large parks and whole man-made
landscapes. He worked not only in Berlin, but also in other German
cities. In recognising and dealing with the new tasks presented by the
city, he was a pioneer with a passionate social vision. For instance, he
designed the 'Kloster Berge' *Volksgarten* in Magdeburg (1821), one of
the earliest German city parks, which was an expression of his effort to
open up the landscape park for the urban working population.

Topography

parks by Lenné
A Babelsberg
B Klein-Glienicke
C Neue Garten
D Pfaueninsel
E Sacrow
F Sanssouci
G Tiergarten

historic and *Volks*parks
1   Botanische Garten
2   Britzer Garten
3   Der Insulaner
4   Fischtalpark
5   Freizeitpark Marienfelde
6   Görlitzer Park
7   Gutspark Britz
8   Gutspark Marienfelde
9   Heinrich-Lähr-Park
10 Kleine Tiergarten
11 Lessinghöhe
12 Lietzenseepark
13 Lustgarten
14 Marienhöhe
15 Naturpark Südgelände
16 Nuthe-Park
17 Olympiapark
18 Preussenpark
19 Rehwiese
20 Rudolph-Wilde-Park
21 Schillerpark
22 Schloss Niederschönhausen
23 Schlossgarten Charlottenburg
24 Schlosspark Lichterfelde
25 Schlosspark Marquard
26 Schlosspark Tegel
27 Schweizerhofpark
28 Spektepark
29 Stadtpark (Werder)
30 Stadtpark (Spandau)
31 Südpark
32 Thielpark
33 Viktoriapark
34 Villa Borsig
35 Volkspark Anton Säfkow
36 Volkspark Friedrichshain
37 Volkspark Hasenheide
38 Volkspark Humboldthain
39 Volkspark Jungfernheide
40 Volkspark Lichtengrade
41 Volkspark Mariendorf
42 Volkspark Rehberge
43 Volkspark Schönhölzer
44 Volkspark Wilmersdorf
45 Volkspark Wittenau
46 Zitadelle

airport

subway station
subway line
railway line
• railway station
— motorway
- - - - tunnel
— important road

urban pattern

park by Lenné
historic and *Volks*parks
other urban green space
water

0   2   5km

Karl Friedrich Schinkel

Karl Friedrich Schinkel (1781-1841) also travelled south, visiting Italy between 1803 and 1805 for studies there, and moreover was interested in Durand's new architectonic system and his ideas about Greek, Roman and Renaissance architectural forms.

Berlin was the sphere of activity where the two designers met. Here the 17th century axial garden landscape, with Potsdam as its heart, awaited a new integration into the growing 19th century city. For them, Charlottenhof Park was a training ground in miniature, as it were, for this new, integral urban landscape. There Schinkel and Lenné could imagine the ideal of the new post-revolutionary society in an experimental landscape composition. Together they created an ideal landscape based on philosophical ideas about the *Verschönerung* of nature and society, derived from thinkers like Fürst Hardenberg and Wilhelm von Humboldt, the older brother of the geographer Alexander von Humboldt.

An urban Arcadia

In addition to Sanssouci and Charlottenhof, the Neue Garten and many *Schmuckanlagen*, old and new, in the much wider vicinity of Potsdam were also rejuvenated, added to and connected with one another. The guiding thought behind this was to surround the Havel lake system with a continuous park landscape from the Karlsberg to the Pfaueninsel, and thus recreate Berlin as a *Gartenreich*, or Garden Realm, one great, coherent landscape theatre, so as to achieve a new balance among nature, the agricultural landscape, the royal parks and the city.

There can be no doubt that the *Gartenreich* of Wörlitz and Dessau, the life's work of Duke Leopold Friedrich Franz von Anhalt-Dessau, developed between 1760 and 1830, served as a model. It lay in the basin of the Elbe and Mulde, 60 kilometres from Magdeburg and less than 130 kilometres away from Berlin and Magdeburg, where Lenné concentrated his work. Leopold Friedrich Franz von Anhalt-Dessau and Frederick II, king of Prussia, were neighbours, so to speak. Through literature and art criticism the Dessau *Gartenreich* had a major influence on social and urban life in Germany. In it, elements of the Enlightenment were connected with the ideas of Johann Wolfgang von Goethe (1749-1832) and German Romanticism. In addition to the natural sciences and the social elevation of the working population in cities and rural areas, the idea of a reconciliation of city and countryside played a large role in this mix.

The ideal of the *Gartenreich*, an urban Arcadia in which the morphology of the natural landscape, the agricultural landscape and the city were transformed into one coherent formal system at the regional level found its widest spatial development and most impressive realisation in Lenné's work around Berlin and Potsdam. Charlottenhof was an idyllic element in this system, the germ of a fragile thought and growth process in which the intimacy and intellectual inspiration of this Arcadia took shape in a new landscape architectonic composition.

Panorama of the park at Wörlitz

The post-glacial landscape

The North German Plain, the vast landscape region between the coasts of the Baltic and North Seas and the German Central Uplands, was chiefly formed during the last glacial period in Europe, the Weichselian ice age, about 10,000 years ago. In this glacial landscape, glacial moraines formed along the sides and at the front of the ice cap. This resulted in the deposit of sedimentary layers of sand and gravel more than 20 metres thick. The landscape is further strewn with boulders, large and small. It slopes downward from the south to the north. At the end of the Weichselian ice age the Scandinavian ice cap ran up against the upward slopes of the Central Uplands, so that the meltwater could only drain briefly toward the south, and then had to find its way along the edge of the ice cap to the North Sea basin, which was then dry, as a result of the low sea level.

Palaeovalleys

Palaeovalleys run through this post-glacial landscape: extensive low lands which were created at the front of the Scandinavian ice cap during the ice age by the meltwater draining away along the ice. The Berlin palaeovalley was formed at the end of the last glacial period, the Weichselian ice age, as part of the Warsaw-Berlin palaeovalley. The valley is bounded in the north by moraines, and in the south by gravel sediments and glacial detritus. The primary direction of the flow in the Berlin palaeovalley is from east to west. There are side valleys, such as the Baruther and the Nuthe (or Potsdamer) palaeovalley, which apparently had drained meltwater away briefly before the Berlin palaeovalley had been formed. These side valleys are bounded at the front by terminal moraines.

Palaeovalleys should not be confused with glacial troughs or meltwater valleys, which are created under the ice. A glacial trough is formed by the erosive force of the meltwater, particularly when the ice runs up against rising terrain and normal drainage is obstructed. This meltwater, a product of the ice age summers, sought the quickest route to the edges of the glacier through gaps and fissures under the ice. The water was under massive pressure, and exerted enough force on the ground beneath the glacier to erode it, particularly if it was comprised of loose sediments. In ice age winters the channels closed, because the ice was pressed into the trough. These ice blocks continued to exist after the glacier melted, forming what are called pingos, which kept the channel from caving in. After the pingos finally melted too, their paths became lakes or longer – sometimes kilometres long – or shorter channels, with or without water.

Schematic overview of the water system in the vicinity of Berlin

		rivers
1	Dahme	
2	Dosse	
3	Elbe	
4	Havel	
5	Neisse	
6	Oder	
7	Nuthe	
8	Plane	
9	Rhin	
10	Spree	

		canals
A	Elbe-Havelkanal	
B	Grosser Havelländischer Hauptkanal	
C	Havelkanal	
D	Landwehrkanal	
E	Oder-Havelkanal	
F	Oder-Spreekanal	
G	Rhinkanal	
I	Teltowkanal	

Geomorphology and the urban domain

Berlin ca. 1650
urban area ca. 2000

0   20   40km

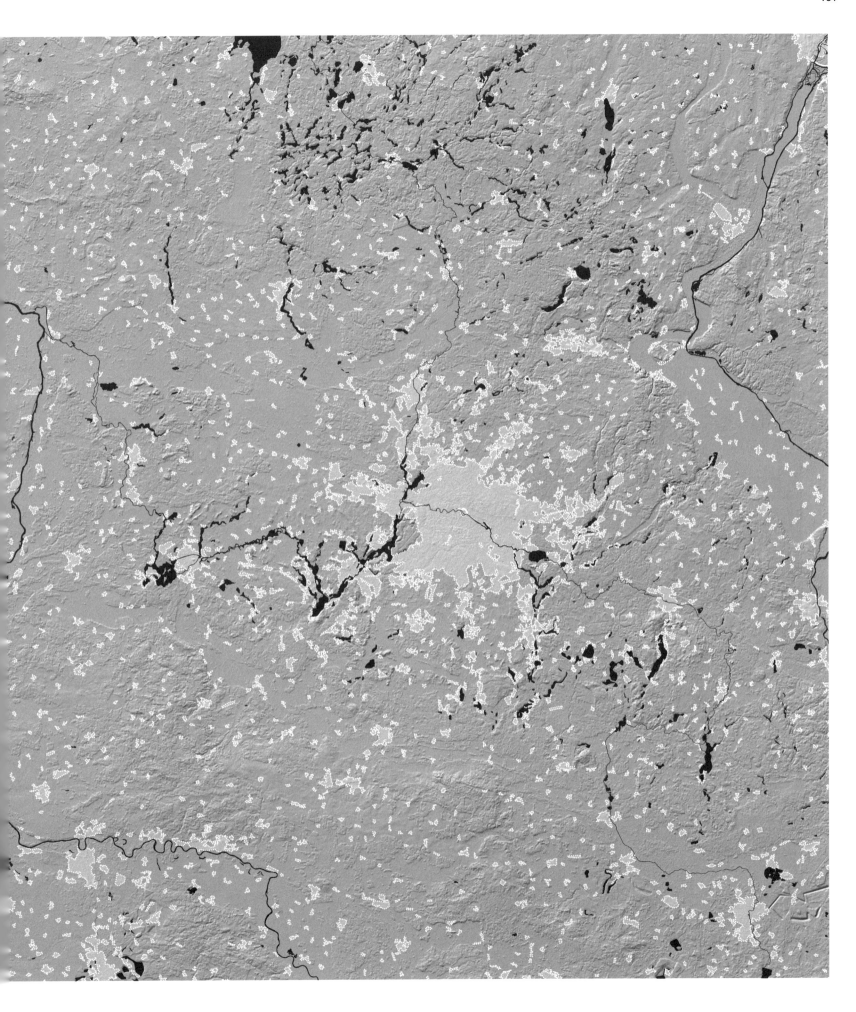

Glacial plateaus

The natural boundaries of the Teltow plateau are the Dahme River to the east, the River Spree to the north, the Nuthe-Havel to the west, and the Baruther palaeovalley to the south. The plateau came into existence during the last ice age, when the water from the melting glacier left behind a thick, shallowly rolling layer of boulder clay, sand and boulders between the Fläming terminal moraine and the Baruther palaeovalley, which had already been formed.

The Barnim plateau is a range of hills formed in the ice age, with a ground moraine, a terminal moraine and a small *sandr* or outwash sand apron between the Berlin palaeovalley in the south and the Eberswalder palaeovalley in the north. Several glacial trenches cut across the plateau. The highest point on the plateau is the Prenzlauer Berg, with a maximum elevation of 158 metres above sea level.

The vestiges which the ice age left behind in the soil include glacial dust, boulder clay and glacial erratics. A ground moraine is comprised of glacial detritus, gravel, clay and boulders, sediment that is carried along by the glacier as it moves and deposited in the base of the glacier.

The urban structure of Berlin in part follows the pattern of the plateaus. Comparatively small rivers, such as the Spree, Dahme, and more to the west, the Havel, now flow through the palaeovalley which once carried vast streams of meltwater. Important sections of present-day Berlin lie on the Teltow and Barnim plateaus, which border the palaeovalley to the north and south. The historic centre of Berlin lies in the narrowest part of the palaeovalley, where the Spree river runs from east to west, then flows into the glacial trench of the Havel at Spandau. The Havel cuts through the urban region in a north-south direction like a great, elongated lake, forming the western boundary of Berlin. Near Potsdam, where the Havel is somewhat broader, there was space for parks along the shores.

Geomorphology, urban pattern and parks

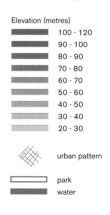

Elevation (metres)
100 - 120
90 - 100
80 - 90
70 - 80
60 - 70
50 - 60
40 - 50
30 - 40
20 - 30

urban pattern

park

water

N   0   2   5km

The system of axes and avenues

The name Berlin is perhaps derived from the Slavic word *birl*, which means swamp. During the Middle Ages castles stood at strategic points, such as where the River Spree joins the Havel, at Spandau. Growing out from these castles, upstream along the River Spree, a city began to develop. It initially was comprised of two settlements, Cölln on the left bank and Berlin on the right. In 1359 Berlin-Cölln became one of the Hanseatic cities, participating in this league of European commercial centres. With its favourable location on waterways and roads, the city flourished.

Elector Frederick II of Brandenburg (ruled 1440-1470) established his court there, at which time the city became a royal seat. In the reign of Elector Frederick William I (ruled 1640-1688) and his successor Elector Frederick III (ruled 1688-1713, from 1701 to 1713 as King Frederick I of Prussia), the city was laid out formally in the landscape. As a result, during the course of the 17th century the natural landscape of Berlin took on its first architectonic definition. A system of views, avenues and axes created a new, artificial cohesion. This formal system generally followed the structure imposed by the watercourses, but added a new order and coherence, which enlarged its scope. Two parks played a central role in this: the Tiergarten, just outside the old city, and the park Sanssouci, at Potsdam. Between them lay Grunewald, an extensive forest, and the Havel landscape.

The Tiergarten

The Tiergarten was originally a walled hunting park or game preserve to the west of the old city. Hunting was then a royal prerogative, reserved for the Elector. In 1647 the Elector had an avenue built, Unter den Linden, to provide some shade in the open field. Initially the avenue did not lead anywhere, but in 1698 Elector Frederick III had it extended, on the model of Le Nôtre's Champs-Elyseés, from the Cöllner Schloss to the citadel at Spandau. A section of this is still extant as a street in Alt-Moabit. With this extension Unter den Linden became the most important axis, a promenade 150 metres wide, fringed with six rows of trees, connecting the fortified city of Berlin with the Tiergarten, the royal hunting park outside the city. To the south of this, in 1688 Frederick III founded the independent suburb of Friedrichstadt, with the Friedrichstrasse as its most important north-south axis. Further to the west the main axis of the Tiergarten was connected with the axis of the new palace of Charlottenburg, built in 1695. At the same time the great star with eight radials was laid out in the Tiergarten.

Axes and lines of sight 1640-1750

1	1542 Jagdschloss Grunewald
2	1555 Schlosspark Tegel
3	1591 Hopfengarten
4	1594 Zitadelle
5	1594 Schloss Caputh
6	around 1600 Pirschheide
7	1646 Lustgarten/ Berlin
8	1647 Unter den Linden
9	around 1650 Bornim
10	1655 Kleiner Tiergarten
11	1662 Schloss Niederschönhausen
12	after 1664 Kronqut Bornstedt
13	after 1678 Hasenheide
14	1682-93 Schloss Glienicke
15	1689 Gendarmenmarkt
16	1697 Schlossgarten Charlottenburg
17	late 17th century Gutspark Britz
18	around 1700 Lustgarten/ Potsdam
19	1703 Montbijou-Park
20	17th - 20th century Tiergarten
21	1720-22 Plantage
22	1722 Nauenschen Plantage
23	1730-32 Jagdschloss Stern
24	1730 Gärten der Charité
25	1732-38 Leipziger Platz
26	1734 Pariser Platz
27	1734 Belle-Alliance-Platz
28	1734-45 Bassinplatz
29	1744 Luisenplatz
30	after 1745 Park Sanssouci
31	1748 Gärten am Invalidenhaus
32	1748 Ruinenberg
33	1751 Königin Plantage
34	1755 Nauener Tor
35	1764 Küster Palm
36	1770 Brandenburger Tor/Potsdam
37	1770-72 Belvedere Klausberg
38	1773 Schloss Sacrow
39	1775-80 Bebelplatz
40	1786-90 Park Bellevue
41	1786 Neue Garten
42	1789-91 Brandenburger Tor
43	1792 Unter den Eichen
44	after 1793 Pfaueninsel
45	1795 Marquardt
46	before 1799 Benediktinerinnenkloster
47	after 1800 kurfürstliches und königliches Jagdrevier
48	cemetery
49	Grunewald
50	Weinberg
51	Grosser Tiergarten

▬▬▬	woods
———	visual axis around 1640-1750

urban pattern around 1640-1750

urban pattern, late 20th century

▬▬▬	water

Landscape elements 1524-1800
▬▬▬	park / wooded park
▬▬▬	squares

N   0   2   5km

The road to Schloss Charlottenburg connected with the Charlotten-burger Chaussee at right angles. Because this crossed the Grunewald-graben, a subsidiary glacial trench, a second approach to the castle was built there, today's Otto-Suhr-Allee, which was continued as a visual axis through the woods and across the fields to a hill near Tegel. In 1697 the French garden architect Siméon Godeau designed two visual axes from Charlottenburg to the citadel at Spandau and to Schloss Niederschönhausen, supplemented by visual axes to Jungfernheide, then a hunting park. Still further west the axis ran through to Grunewald, along the Havel. With this the main axis of Berlin formed an artificial line which, quite separate from the valley of the Spree river, now connected the old city with the Havel landscape. After 1740 Georg Wenzeslaus von Knobelsdorff designed avenues and open spaces for the Tiergarten, and it was opened for the public.

The Grunewald

In the 16th century Grunewald was a hunting park for Elector Joachim II, who had a hunting lodge built there in 1542. Originally the woods which made up the reserve continued to the north of the Spree river in the forest of Tegel, which later vanished as a result of the Siedlung Siemensstadt and the airport. The woods was bounded on the west by the extensive lakes of the Wannsee and the Havel. On the east lie a series of long, narrow woodland ponds. Running from the north-east to the south-west, the woods is transected by Die Allee, a main axis that runs from Schloss Charlottenburg to the Wannsee, near Potsdam. This system of avenues was repeatedly altered over the course of the centuries.

In 1849 Grunewald was walled in as a hunting ground for the King of Prussia. The characteristic orthogonal division was already present before 1874. To the south-west the system of avenues reached beyond Grunewald to Potsdam, where in 1744 Frederick the Great began the construction of a garden which would be the genesis of Sanssouci. Toward the end of his reign the park extended over two kilometres from east to west.

Potsdam

The most important hub in Berlin's system of axes, outside the city itself, lay at Potsdam. This town, then still called Potztupimi, was granted status as a city in 1345. It lay at a junction in the lake landscape formed by the Havel to the south-west of Berlin. Under Elector Frederick William I, in the middle of the 17th century it became the second residence of the Hohenzollerns, and moreover a garrison city. The development of its

garden and park system began with this decision. In the time of the Electors there were already numerous avenues in the region of Potsdam that provided possibilities for hunting. One of them ran to the Stadtschloss of Potsdam.

In a letter dating from 1664 Johann Moritz van Nassau-Siegen, counsellor to the Elector of Brandenburg in the area of art, recommended that the *'gantze Eyland'* (whole island) of Potsdam be transformed into a *'Paradies'*. A series of pleasure gardens were to be built around Potsdam, including one in Caputh, on the banks of the Havel opposite the extreme south end of the island.

Sanssouci

In 1715 Frederick William I had a vegetable garden laid out to the north-west of Potsdam, with a small summer residence that he also called Marly. In 1745 his son Frederick II (Frederick the Great) had a vineyard planted on the slope opposite his father's garden, with curving terraces oriented toward the sun, and crowned with the summer palace Sanssouci (1745-1747). It afforded a wide vista over the Havel landscape. The garden was extended in an east-west direction, parallel to the chain of hills that lay about 40 metres above the Havel. To the south of this, at their foot, a main axis about two kilometres long was laid out, with an obelisk at its starting point at Potsdam and the Neue Palais (1763-1769) at its other end. This subordinated all the other elements to the palace. Until 1763 the park was still intersected by straight avenues. Its transformation in the landscape style began after that date, and the Sanssouci park was expanded with the Charlottenhof Park, among other projects, in which the new design principles took further shape.

Strasse des 17. Juni, from the Brandenburger Tor, continuing Unter den Linden

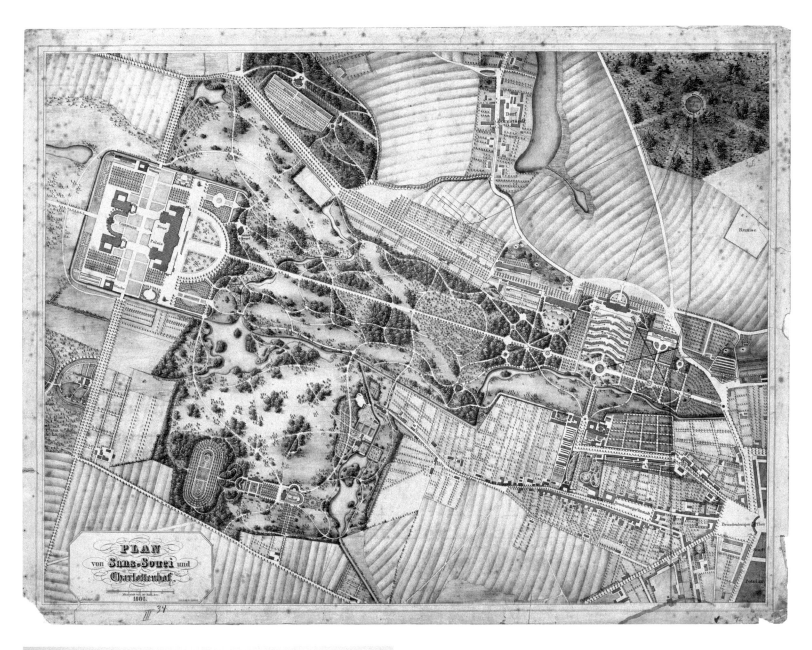

The Park at Sanssouci, with the Charlottenhof to the south as an expansion of the agricultural area ("Plan von Sans-Souci und Charlottenhof". Sign.:"1836. Entworfen von Lenné. Gez. u. lith. v. G. Koeber". Stiftung Preußische Schlösser und Gärten Berlin-Brandenburg, Plansammlung Inv.-Nr. 3683. Foto: SPSG)

The transverse axis, toward the summer palace of Sanssouci

The transverse axis, in the opposite direction

Charlottenhof as a transformation model

Charlottenhof Park lies to the south of the older park at Sanssouci, and was conceived as an expansion of that park. It was the first park design over which King Frederick William IV (1840-1861) had a decisive influence and was a training ground, as it were, for the larger landscape around Potsdam and Berlin. In 1825 Frederick William III (1797-1840) purchased a parcel of damp, sandy agricultural land of about 100 hectares for the crown prince to the south of the Neues Palais and the great park at Sanssouci. The crown prince had steeped himself in the letters Pliny the Younger and Roman villa architecture, and wanted to realise a private residence that would be a studied counterpoint to both the majestic Neue Palais and the existing gardens at Sanssouci.

As the primary designers, Schinkel and Lenné were assisted in the drawing and design work by the architect Friedrich Ludwig Persius (1803-1845), a pupil of Schinkel, and the landscape architect Hermann Sello. Between 1826 and 1829 Schinkel began with the conversion of the old mansion, and together with Lenné decided on the further expansion of the gardens and terraces, as well as the visual relations between the house and the park. At the same time the construction of a larger park began, stretching eastward to a new lake designed by Lenné. Schinkel designed the Gärtnerhaus on the north side of this park, a gardener's dwelling with a tea pavilion, terraces and a small garden of its own. This complex was completed by Schinkel and Persius with the addition of the Römische Bäder (Roman Baths, 1829-1836).

The land to the west of Charlottenhof was only acquired later. The Hippodrome was built here in 1836. In 1841-1842 this was followed by the Pheasantry, with a home for the manager designed in the Italian style. Charlottenhof Park has largely been preserved as it was built. Several components, such as the Italienisches Kulturstück (Italian agricultural garden) in front of the Römische Bäder, have disappeared.

The fragmentation of the axis

On the north and east the site where the Schloss Charlottenhof was to be realised was bounded by the Schafgraben, a canal to the Havel, which also ran past the royal gardens of Sanssouci. The southern boundary was the road to Potsdam, which at the Brandenburger Vorstadt branched off from a major avenue running from Potsdam along the Havel to the Pirschheide. To the west the site adjoined several country estates along the great entrance avenue to the Neue Palais. The western edge was separated from the park by relatively thick planting.

In the design for the park, the southern and eastern sides of the site were worked out with the aid of two modest architectonic axes which crossed one another at an angle of slightly more than 90 degrees. The direction and position of the first, southern axis was conditioned by the existing, small 18th century mansion. Schinkel rebuilt this structure as the Schloss Charlottenhof, a small, stylised, temple-shaped villa. The house was also included in an east-west axis linking a series of extremely diverse elements: successively a hippodrome surrounded by woods, a carp pond with *exedra*, the Dichterhain (a grove dedicated to the memory of great poets), the house with its terraces and *exedra*, a rose garden and a steam driven pumping station.

The *Maschinenteich*, an artificial lake which was linked with the Havel by the Schafgraben, was the most important element connecting with the second, eastern axis. Its position and direction was dictated by the course of the canal to the Havel. The heart of this axial series was formed by Schinkel's design for an Italianate gardener's dwelling, the Gärtnerhaus, a small-scale complex with a tea pavilion, terraces and small gardens. This was extended on the north with the Römische Bäder, with their accompanying courts and a geometric utility garden with three fish ponds.

Still further to the north, on the edge of the park, was the *Meierei* (an old farmstead) and the court nursery. On the south, via a court bordered by an arcade and a tea pavilion with a portico, the Gärtnerhaus was linked with the view out over the artificial lake. In the vicinity of the Gärtnerhaus and Römische Bäder the original canal was transformed into a system of geometric ornamental canals, ponds and a 'water arcade'. Where the two axes joined, in the south-east corner of the park, the canal was broadened and fashioned into a scenic lake with two islands, one larger and one smaller. On the north side of the site, closest to the Neue Palais, the original canal was redirected and transformed into a scenic water feature which functioned as a transition between the new park and that of Sanssouci. A major, carefully composed route passing the architectonic elements in this border zone marked the richly elaborated edge of the new park. Within it the old pattern of the fields was erased, and transmuted into a continuous park landscape.

In comparison with Sanssouci, in Charlottenhof the axial arrangement was reduced in relative importance, and fragmented. The axis was divided up into pieces that have a subordinate role and position in the composition as a whole, and functions here as a support for an 'architectonic series'.

↗ **The 1839 plan of Charlottenhof, with the Schloss, the Gärtnerhaus, and an artificial lake between them** (Gerh. Kober, Plan von Charlottenhof oder Siam, 1839. Stiftung Preußische Schlösser und Gärten Berlin-Brandenburg, Planslg. 3705. Foto: SPSG)

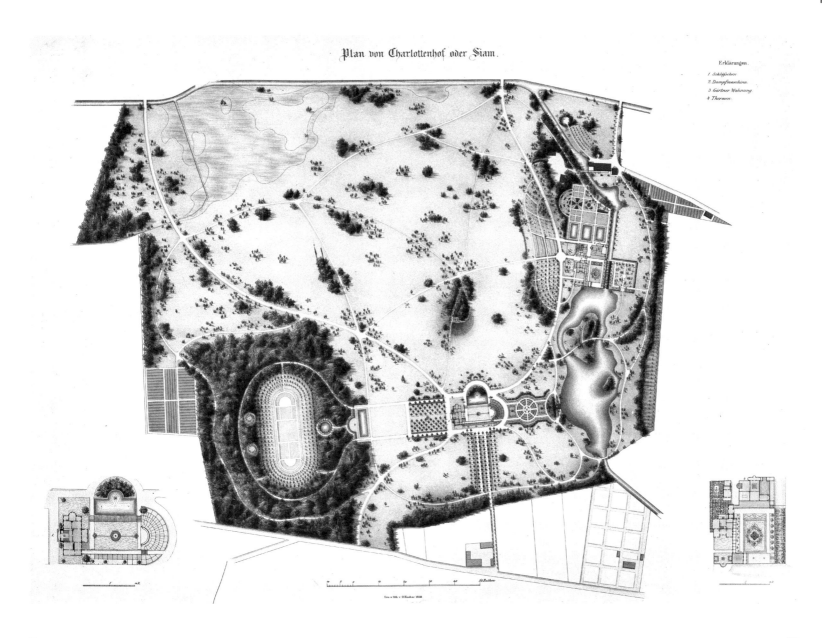

Plan von Charlottenhof oder Siam.

Erklärungen.
1. Schlößchen.
2. Dampfmaschine.
3. Gärtner Wohnung.
4. Thermen.

View of the house from the park

View from Schloss Charlottenhof toward the Neue Palais

The liberation of open space

Schloss Charlottenhof stands within the field of view from the Neue Palais. This was taken into account in the reconstruction of the old country home. To the east of the house the ground level was raised by one storey with a terrace. This was closed with a large *exedra* with a bench, from which the seated viewer could see the façade of the villa, with the Neue Palais in the distance. The old mansard roof of the house was removed and the outside walls somewhat increased in height, to obtain purer geometric proportions. A new, two storey high portico with Doric columns was constructed on the west side of the house. The central *impluvium* with a fountain between the stairs to the first floor is reminiscent of the classic Roman house.

The house does not assume a dominant position in the axial chain of spatial forms. Because of the transitional spaces of the terraces and *exedras* and the slight differences in height, the house is accepted smoothly in the architectonic series. The spatial series from the hippo-drome to the artificial lake ends with the smokestack of the steam mill, which Schinkel designed as a classical column standing alone in space.

In the composition of the park as a whole the southern spatial series, with the classical Schloss Charlottenhof, is also opposed to the eastern series, with the Gärtnerhaus, designed as a rustic Italian house with a four-storey high tower and sunken court and kitchen garden. The open forecourt has a raised *exedra* oriented toward the entrance, and a bench next to a stair leads to the arcades behind the house. The spaces in the Gärtnerhaus are not organised hierarchically along an axis, but are rather equipollent, juxtaposed with one another. The spatial core of the complex is formed by the sunken conservatory between the arcades and pergolas along the house and the canal.

Between 1834 and 1840 Persius added the Römische Bäder to the north side of the complex, with an *atrium*, *impluvium*, *caldarium* and billiard room with a fireplace. All the spaces are decorated with frescos and antique Roman and Pompeiian fragments, are lit from above, and have unexpected views and landscape scenes, including the Bay of Naples. The roof terrace of the Römische Bäder is the climax of the spatial series, with a prospect out over the gardener's house and tea house, toward Schloss Charlottenhof. One can also observe the arrival of boats by the water arcade in the sunken conservatory.

The technique of reciprocal views, as it is developed in the spatial series, particularly through the placement of *exedras*, also plays an important role in the spatial organisation of the park as a whole. The structures in the edges of the park not only provide views of the central space in the park, but are also, at the same time, backdrops, visible from the central area. The open space of the central area runs through to the buildings and terraces. The area itself is spatially articulated by clumps of trees, which function as coulisses to frame the views, blocking out some elements while creating new, reciprocal connections among others. The park route links the park landscape together and puts the various parts into a scenographic context.

The differentiation of the programme

Christian Cay Lorenz Hirschfeld's five volume *Theorie der Gartenkunst* appeared between 1779 and 1785. Like Durand's work on architectural theory, the book was encyclopaedic in nature. Analogous to Durand's classical, functionally differentiated architectural theory, Hirschfeld categorised gardens not only according to character, form and season, but also according to function (park, cemetery, spa, monastic garden) and user (common citizen, noble, royalty). In the course of this, he became the first to systematically distinguish the new design tasks involving landscape in relation to the city. Experiencing the landscape garden could no longer remain the privilege of royalty and enlightened landed aristocrats, but must also be designed for a new urban public that embraced all classes.

The form of the programme for the Charlottenhof park reflects this growing range in design. It extends from a royal palace to a gardener's dwelling and farm yard. It includes urban, industrial-technical functions such as a steam pumping station, alongside activities such as agriculture, market gardening, arboriculture, aquaculture and small animal husbandry. Recreational activities such as riding, strolling, sports and bathing are also included in the programme and integrated into the design. These activities are accommodated in the spatial series along the edges of the park and constantly alternate with, or are accompanied by moments of rest and contemplation on the terraces and in the *exedras*, arcades and courtyards. The all-embracing park route accesses the whole park programme which lies along it, and separates the edge of the park, with its richly varied programmes, from the central, free, open space. There the unprogrammed world of nature rules, binding all the separate activities and movements together, and absorbing them in a larger whole.

In Charlottenhof the traditional programme of utility and representative functions inclined more toward multiple, differentiated forms of use that encompassed the whole social scale. This programmatic pluralism, coupled with various forms of zoning, brought the park, as a spatial type, within the functional organisational pattern and heterogeneous experience of the city. Conversely, as an integrative model the park had the potential to restore spatial coherence in the increasingly further fragmented 19th century city.

The green arcade in the Römische Bäder (Wilhelm Grüzmacher nach Karl Friedrich Schinkel. Die grosse Laube der Römischen Bäder im Park Sanssouci, Potsdam. Karl Friedrich Schinkel, Sammlung architektonischer Entwürfe. Heft 24. Berlin 1835. Uit Harri Günther, Sibylle Harksen (Bearbeiter); Heinz Schönemann (Hrsg.) Peter Joseph Lenné. Katalog der Zeichnungen. Wasmuth, Tübingen / Berlin 1993)

The forecourt, with bench, from the Gärtnerhaus and the Römische Bäder, covered with rustic latticework (Nach Karl Friedrich Schinkel. Das Schloss Charlottenhof im Park Sanssouci, Potsdam. Karl Friedrich Schinkel. Sammlung architektonischer Entwürfe. Heft 18. Berlin 1831. Uit Harri Günther, Sibylle Harksen (Bearbeiter); Heinz Schönemann (Hrsg.) Peter Joseph Lenné. Katalog der Zeichnungen. Wasmuth, Tübingen / Berlin 1993)

The Gärtnerhaus and the arcade on the artificial lake

The subjectivication of the image

In Charlottenhof the crown prince wanted to revive contact with the classic world and with nature. On the second storey of the Gärtnerhaus a guest room was reserved for the naturalist and founder of physical geography, Alexander von Humboldt (1769-1859). Between 1845 and 1862 he published his *Kosmos – Entwurf einer physischen Weltbeschreibung*. Von Humboldt regarded nature not as an immutable system, but as a continuing process of creation. He argued that the understanding of nature is based on both a careful study of plants, animals and minerals in all their vast diversity, but also on an understanding of human perceptions of nature as these have been developed in philosophy, poetry and art. Thus he wrote to Goethe: "Nature must be felt; someone who merely sees and abstracts… could be sure of having described nature, but nature itself would forever remain alien to him." In accordance with this concept, Italian and German poets, represented as classic *hermae,* were given a place of honour in the Dichterhain next to Schloss Charlottenhof.

For the principle form of the Schloss its designers reached back to the French Maison de Plaisance, an elegant house with one storey, which made direct contact with nature possible. As visual elements, the portico with the *impluvium*, the terrace, the arcade, the *exedra* and the hippodrome were all derived from the Laurentian and Tuscan villas from the descriptions in Pliny the Younger.

The Gärtnerhaus is a curio cabinet full of rare objects, strange plant species, ancient fragments and architectonic motifs, a lesson by Schinkel regarding the manner in which the classic and the rustic, the analytic and the intuitive, architecture and nature can be united in design and brought into balance. This is expressed most wonderfully in the forecourt, which, unlike the formal portico at the Schloss, is not covered with a classic temple pediment, but with a rustic latticework along which grape vines grow. As a re-interpretation of the classic Roman *thermae* on a domestic scale, the Römische Bäder add a new dimension to this. Moreover, an *Italienisch Kulturstück* was originally planned for the transition from the Gärtnerhaus to the open central area of the park, an artificially constructed piece of rolling Italian agricultural landscape with crops such as maize, grapes, figs and olives.

The park comprises a vast wealth and diversity of styles and cultures, which are mixed with one another to form one great landscape. The tension between the formal palace (the Schloss) and the simple farm dwelling (the Gärtnerhaus) is resolved in a harmonic and equal relationship. In a deeper sense, the park is a model of the new world after the French revolution. Here human and social diversity is brought together in a new, relaxed order. Behind this lies the concept of the orderly, calming and reconciling power of nature. The crown prince aptly called Charlottenhof 'Siam', the land that he had gotten to know in his youth as a model of Eastern political liberty. The image of an objective, rational order was transmuted into a subjective, idyllic world, onto which every individual could project his dreams.

A landscape architectonic étude

The most important ingredients of the landscape architectonic transformation of Berlin's 17th and 18th century formal landscape are already present in embryonic form in the design of Charlottenhof. Reducing the relative importance of the formal system of axes, the self-sufficiency of the landscape space, the differentiation and zoning of the programme, and the subjectivication of the experience of nature were also going to play a large role there, on a larger scale.

A lake was created in Charlottenhof Park, because it seemed essential as a natural tableau with the potential to orchestrate and bind the various important elements of the composition together with one another. As a water feature, this artificial lake refers to the most important characteristic of the wider Havel landscape, the series of natural lakes with its larger and smaller islands. In that sense too Charlottenhof Park can be regarded as a practice round for the shaping of the great water theatre around Potsdam.

Seating in the park, Charlottenhof

→ **The artificial lake, near the Gärtnerhaus**

→ The forecourt with raised seating, at the Römische Bäder
→ The interior of the Römische Bäder
→ Ornamental waterspout in the forecourt of the Römische Bäder

The great water theatre

During the first half of the 19th century, many of the older parks around Potsdam were transformed, and new ones laid out. They were concentrated in the water landscape of the Havel. In a period of about 50 years, the water landscape was recreated as one great water theatre, with parks at outstanding scenic spots along the banks. The tension of the older Berlin-Potsdam axial system was assimilated into this new landscape architectonic treatment, refined, and connected with the natural morphology of the water landscape. The latent natural form of the lake landscape was brought to life, as it were, in a water theatre of unprecedented proportions.

Under the patronage of the monarch, one grand, coherent water park was created, with six parks as its most important vehicles: the Neue Garten, the Pfaueninsel, Glienicke, Babelsberg, Sacrow and Nikolskoe. With the water as the stage, numerous architectonic set pieces were built along the banks in the parks, marking, and thereby making it possible to experience the continuity of the space in the landscape, and its expanse. The dark, monotonous pines along the banks were replaced by broad-leaved trees, including willows, weeping willows, Lombardy poplars and birch trees. Here too the most important designers were Schinkel and Lenné.

The Neue Garten

The first large landscape park that was built on the banks of the Havel was the Neue Garten, north-east of Potsdam, on a flat stretch of land along the Heilig See, which functioned as a lake within the park, with views to the north of the larger Jungfernsee. It was built by Frederick William II, who was an admirer of the Dessau-Wörlitzer *Gartenlandschaft* and took on the designer of the gardens at Wörlitz, Johann August Eyserbeck (1762-1801), as his designer.

Between 1787 and 1793 Eyserbeck created a landscape garden richly furnished with buildings. The accent lay on the design for the banks and the route past them. The core of the design was the Marmorpalais, which stood mid-way along the banks of the Heilig See, with terraces projecting out into the water. This prominent position was stressed even more by its high dome topped by a gilded sculptural group visible from a great distance. To the north-east the panorama stretched out along a canal dug through a hollow in the landscape between the Heilig See and the Jungfernsee, reaching as far as the Pfaueninsel.

After 1816 Lenné designed great diagonal vistas through the park,

The great water theatre, ca. 1850

Neue Garten
1   Marmorpalais
2   Church designed as a temple
3   Dutch village
4   Gothic library
5   Pyramidal ice cellar
6   Red house
7   Green house
8   Grotto
9   Meierei
10 Hermitage
11 Moorish Temple

Pfaueninsel
12 Schloss
13 Ferry house
14 Steam pumping station
15 Water reservoir
16 *Volière*
17 Danziger house
18 Fasanerie
19 Meierei
20 Buffalo pasture

Park Glienicke
21 Schloss
22 Casino
23 Grosse Neugierde
24 Steam engine/water tower/Gärtnerhaus
25 Jägerhof
26 Glienicke bridge

Park Babelsberg
27 Schloss
28 Kleine Schloss
29 Steam engine and waterworks
30 Gerichtslaube
31 Matrosenhaus
32 Flatowtoren

Sacrow
33 Schloss
34 Heilandskirche
35 Exedra
36 Ferry house

Nikolskoe
37 Church of SS. Peter and Paul
38 Russian blockhouse

Potsdam
39 Schloss/Kirche

	Potsdam
	building
	park
- - - - -	potential sight line
————	road
....	avenue
----------	contour line, figures in metres
	water

A   Heilige See
B   Tiefe See
C   Jungfernsee

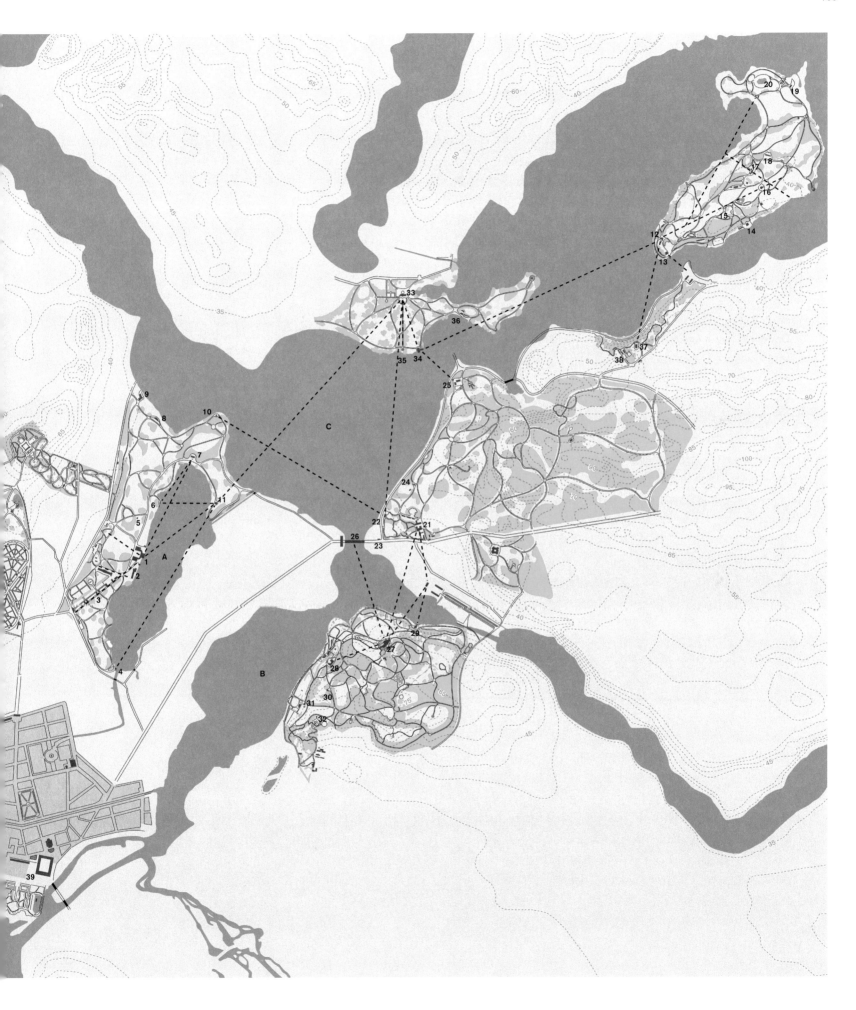

connecting the relatively narrow garden (which also included agricultural land) with the breadth of the surrounding landscape. The numerous structures that ornamented the park were also united by sight lines to form an ever-changing scenic composition. This also brought various historical and geographic elements along the Heilig See (such as a Dutch village, a kitchen built in the guise of a half-sunken temple, an ice cellar in the form of a pyramid, a red house and a green house) into play, essentially as set dressing.

On the south bank of the Heilig See the Gothic Library was erected opposite a Moorish Temple on the north bank, transforming the entire shore of the lake, with the Marmorpalais in the central position, into a space which could be experienced visually. The link with the Jungfernsee in the north was made through the Meierei (traditional farm), a *grotto*, and the Hermitage, in a thick woods on a point of land thrusting out into the water.

The Pfaueninsel

The Pfaueninsel, lying four kilometres further to the north-east, provided a scenic background for the Neue Garten. The name Pfaueninsel was derived from the peacocks which were then kept on the island. The island lies in the Havel, which broadens out at that point, and visually closes the view in the north-easterly direction with its naturally curved shoreline. Its isolation, the natural plant cover, and the centuries-old stand of oaks made a suitable background for the small manor that Frederick William II had built there between 1794 and 1796. A ruinous, pseudo-medieval façade, which when seen from the Neue Garten

→ **Composition scheme of the Pfaueninsel**

1	Schloss Pfaueninsel
2	Schweizerhaus
3	Kastellamtshaus
4	Rosengarten
5	Gärtnerei
6	Fregattenhafen
7	Rutschbahn
8	Maschinenhaus
9	Fontäne
10	Kavalierhaus
11	*Volière*
12	Winterhaus
13	Jagdschirm
14	Luisentempel
15	Meierei
16	Pferdestall

building
planting
– – – sight line
.... avenue
water

The Meierei in the Neue Garten (Wilhelm Barth, *Die Meierei im Neuen Garten*. 1844. Stiftung Preußische Schlösser und Gärten Berlin-Brandenburg GK I 6708. Photo: Gunter Lepkowski, 1985)

View from the Marmorpalais in the Neue Garten

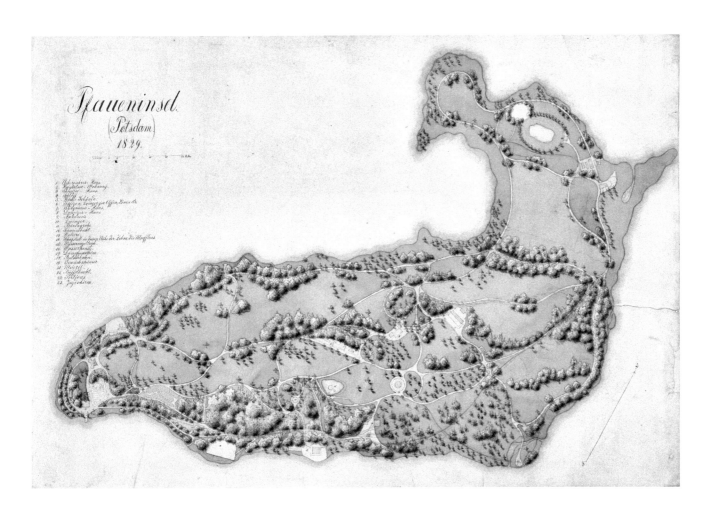

Drawing of the Pfaueninsel by Lenné (Stiftung Preußische Schlösser und Gärten Berlin-Brandenburg, Planslg. 3782. Photo: SPSG)

The Pfaueninsel, seen across the water from the south (photo: Stephanie Holtappels)

functioned as further stage-dressing, was placed in front of the house.

Under the aegis of Frederick Wilhelm III, after 1829 the island was transformed by Lenné into a landscape park with shore roads, coulisses of woods and views. Exotic structures such as the Palmenhaus (1829-1831), decorated as a Burmese pavilion, and the Kavalierhaus, the façade of which came from a Late Gothic patrician's home in Danzig, arose in the middle of the island, embedded in a diagonal view formed by coulisses of trees. The character of the park was defined by the rich variety of plants and animals; among the fauna were apes, a *volière*, a bear pit, water birds and a pheasantry. At the extreme southern tip stood a ferry house, and on the south-eastern shore there was a steam engine which pumped water into a reservoir farther north on the island. On the north shore of the island lay a Meierei, with an elliptical pasture for buffalo.

Glienicke

The central water element in the series of lakes upon which the parks are hung is the Jungfernsee. Along its long eastern bank, on the western tip of a large island surrounded by different branches of the Havel, lies Glienicke Park, a large landscape garden that extends far inland.

The original estate was acquired in 1814 by the Prussian Prime Minister Fürst Hardenberg. At his request Lenné did an initial re-design for the garden near the house. After Hardenberg's death in 1822 the area came into the possession of Prince Carl, the brother of Frederick William IV. Prince Carl had travelled to Italy and been impressed by the harmony of the landscape, architecture and ancient history he found there.

Schinkel and Lenné worked together on redesigning the buildings and park. Schinkel rebuilt the earlier country home as the Schloss Glienicke, on the road that ran from Berlin to Potsdam via the Glienicker Brücke. The park at the Schloss took the form of a classic landscape garden, with a sequence of flower garden, pleasure gardens, a wooded park and a *Wildgarten*. Schinkel's plan for the transformation of the old Billardhaus into an Italian Casino created the most important architectonic accent on the east bank of the Jungfernsee. Rising just above the surface of the lake, the building stands like a white Italian villa, with pergolas and terraces affording a magnificent view of the lake. Further to the north, along this same shoreline, stands the Dampfmaschinenhaus, with a water tower, and the Gärtnerhaus. The extreme northern point is marked by the Jägerhof.

The most intensively elaborated section of the park is found in the south-west corner and the edge along the Havel, where the path along

the steep banks affords superb views of the Neue Garten, Pfaueninsel, Sacrow, and the hills which lie further away. The crown of the whole was the Grosse Neugierde, a rotunda opposite the Glienicker bridge, at an important junction in the water series.

Babelsberg

The landscape park Babelsberg lies opposite Glienicke Park, to the south where the Havel splits into three branches. The banks of the Tiefe See form the north-west boundary for the hilly site. Still further to the east the original course of the Havel, now a blind arm of the river, is connected by a canal. In 1833 Frederick William III purchased the site for his son William (later Emperor William I), who was married to princess Augusta von Sachsen-Weimar, a great admirer of the Gothic style.

The location for the new Schloss Babelsberg, on the northern slope of the site, with views over the Havel and the Glienicker Brücke, was chosen in consultation with Lenné. Between 1834 and 1835 Schinkel designed the castle in the English Gothic style. Lenné laid out a system of paths for the park so as to create an intensive spatial relation between the morphology of the site and the many beautiful views along the banks and over the lake from the heights. A park drive ran around the whole edge of the park. Prince Hermann von Pückler-Muskau, who was involved with the park after 1840, added a network of narrow footpaths with numerous views. Further up in the park one finds small stands of trees and spacious meadows. The most eye-catching

View of the Pfaueninsel from Sacrow (photo: Stephanie Holtappels)

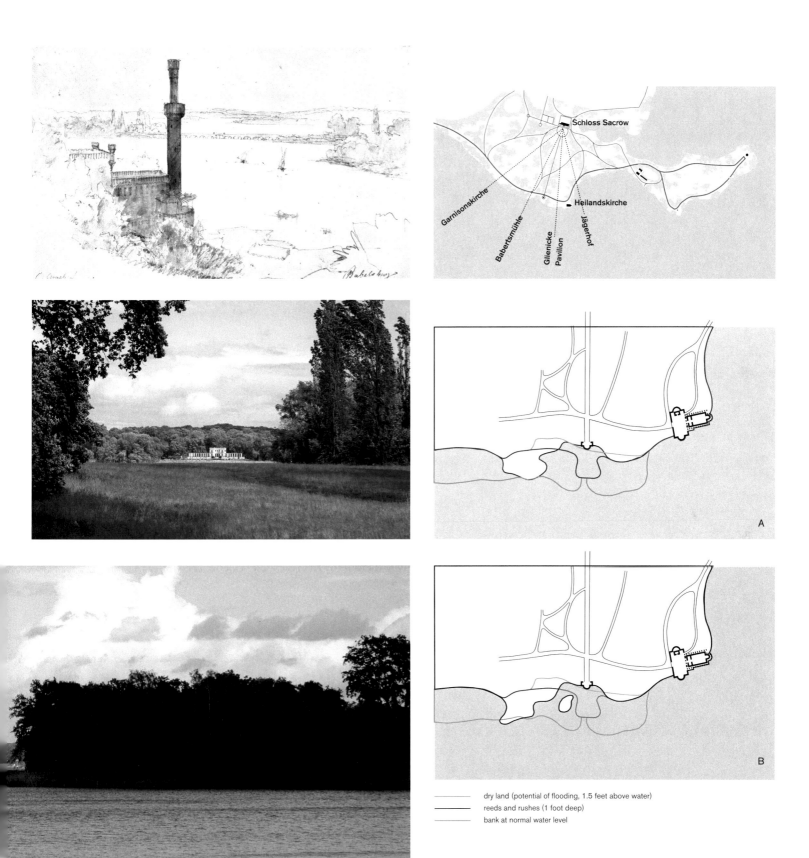

The engine house and waterworks in Babelsberg around 1844 (Carl Graeb, Maschinenhaus im Babelsberger Park. Stiftung Preußische Schlösser und Gärten Berlin-Brandenburg,
PK 4093. Photo: Daniel Lindner, 2008)

The Casino in Glienicke, on the bank of the Jungfernsee, seen from the Neue Garten
(photo: Stephanie Holtappels)

Sacrow, with the sight lines across the Jungfernsee

Scheme for the modelling of the bank by Lenné, near the exedra at the end of
the main axis of Sacrow. A: existing; B: new

element on the northern edge of the park, at a cove on the Havel, is the Maschinenhaus, with its water tower in the form of a medieval tower.

On the steep west bank, along the Tiefe See, lie the Kleines Schloss, reconstructed parts of Berlin's Gerichtslaube (courthouse), and the Matrosenhaus, with its Gothic façade, a copy of that on the town hall in Stendal, in that order. The closing piece in the series, in the south-west corner, is the tall Flatow tower, the shape of which was borrowed from the tower of the 15th century Eschenheimer city gate in Frankfurt am Main.

Sacrow

The landscape park at Sacrow lies on the north bank of the Jungfernsee, and as a projecting peninsula forms a scenic link between the Neue Garten, Glienicke and Pfaueninsel. In 1840 Frederick William IV bought the country home then on the site. Lenné sought to link the already extant house from 1773, standing higher on the hill, with the Jägerhof and Casino in Glienicke, Babelsberg and the Marmorpalais in the Neue Garten by means of four vistas with coulisses of trees. The middle vista was a narrow, funnel-shaped space, oriented toward an *exedra* in the form of a large Roman bench on the bank of the Jungfernsee. From here one could look back to the house, and across the water. The Heilandskirche, a church built on the shore by Persius between 1841 and 1844 in the form of an early Christian basilica with a free-standing *campanile* on an Italian model, was included to one side of the wide vista toward Glienicke. The church lies at the head of an inlet, like the prow of a ship projecting out into the water. Opposite it lies a ferry house, from which one could cross by boat to the other parks.

Nikolskoe

To complete the series of landscape parks along the banks of the Havel, on the bank between Glienicke and the Pfaueninsel there was finally the smaller Nikolskoe park. The name Nikolskoe is an homage to the daughter of Frederick William III, Charlotte, who was married to Czar Nicholas I of Russia. In 1819 a Russian blockhouse was built there, on a bend in the Havel. After 1833 Lenné was involved in the plan for the design of the area. On a higher plateau somewhat to the north of the blockhouse the church of Sts. Peter and Paul was then built, with a view out to the Pfaueninsel. Seen from a distance, the tower of this church, with its onion dome, is a striking visual element in the landscape. A route meandering through the narrow park connected the church with a dock for boats at the northernmost point on the bank, from which one could cross to the Pfaueninsel. Together the parks along the Havel

formed one great water theatre, which in turn formed the core of a man-made landscape fashioned through landscape architectonic means. Architecture and landscape were interchangeable quantities in this process, which could be manipulated as desired to shape an urban idyll.

The Heilandskirche in Sacrow in 1850 (Siegfried Massmann, Heilandskirche in Sacrow, 1850. Stiftung Preußische Schlösser und Gärten Berlin-Brandenburg, Aquarellslg. 2145. Photo: Daniel Lindner)

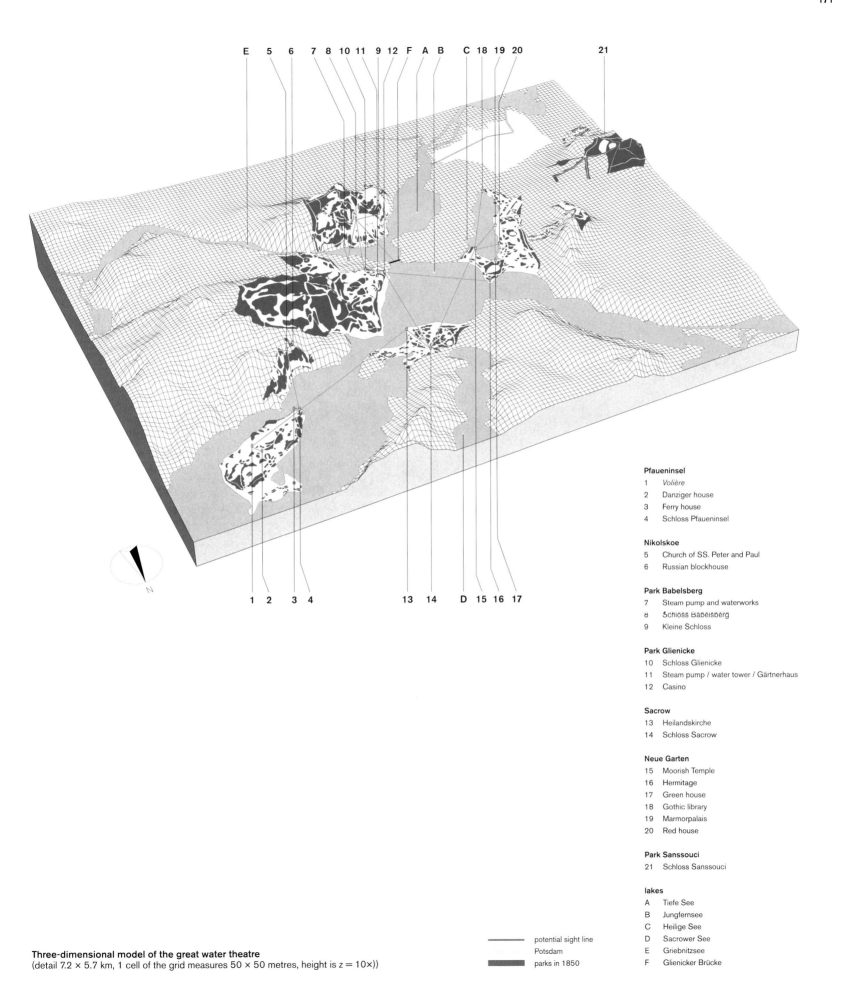

E 5 6 7 8 10 11 9 12 F A B C 18 19 20 21

1 2 3 4 13 14 D 15 16 17

N

Pfaueninsel

1 *Volière*
2 Danziger house
3 Ferry house
4 Schloss Pfaueninsel

Nikolskoe

5 Church of SS. Peter and Paul
6 Russian blockhouse

Park Babelsberg

7 Steam pump and waterworks
8 Schloss Babelsberg
9 Kleine Schloss

Park Glienicke

10 Schloss Glienicke
11 Steam pump / water tower / Gärtnerhaus
12 Casino

Sacrow

13 Heilandskirche
14 Schloss Sacrow

Neue Garten

15 Moorish Temple
16 Hermitage
17 Green house
18 Gothic library
19 Marmorpalais
20 Red house

Park Sanssouci

21 Schloss Sanssouci

lakes

A Tiefe See
B Jungfernsee
C Heilige See
D Sacrower See
E Griebnitzsee
F Glienicker Brücke

potential sight line
Potsdam
parks in 1850

Three-dimensional model of the great water theatre
(detail 7.2 × 5.7 km, 1 cell of the grid measures 50 × 50 metres, height is z = 10×))

The Gartenreich of Potsdam

The water theatre on the Havel did not involve just the river basin,
but also the landscape in the wider vicinity. At the request of Crown
Prince Frederick William, in 1833 Lenné drew up a plan for beautifying
Potsdam and its surroundings. After Frederick William IV ascended
to the throne in 1840 this plan became the basis for a regional park
landscape.

Lenné's 1833 draft plan covered an area of at least 15 × 20 kilometres. Its scope was determined by the natural morphology of the
Havel landscape, which locally consists of series of streams and lakes
which are sometimes connected by canals, and that surround various
larger and smaller islands and peninsulas. The largest are the island
of Potsdam in the west and the Glienicke island in the east, which
extends to the southern tip of Grunewald. The city of Potsdam lies at
the hinge point between these two islands. In addition to the gardens of
Sanssouci and the Pirschheide, the island of Potsdam had an extensive
hunting preserve in the south, and also agricultural land. Sand hills were
scattered among them. The Glienicke island was, to a great extent,
comprised of woods. As well as parks at strategic scenic spots, Lenné's
Verschönerungsplan also included a landscape architectonic treatment
of the hills, woods, heathland, farms fields and villages.

The Verschönerungsplan for the vicinity of Potsdam Lenné prepared in 1833
(Peter Josef Lenné (Entwurf), Gerh. Kober, (Zeichner): Verschönerungsplan von der
Umgebung von Potsdam, 1833. Stiftung Preußische Schlösser und Gärten Berlin-
Brandenburg, Planslg. 3639. Photo: Daniel Lindner, 2000)

The Gartenreich of Potsdam around 1850

Potsdam
1   Bassinplatz
2   Wilhelmplatz
3   Lustgarten
4   Plantage
5   Luisenplatz
6   Schloss/Kirche

landscape parks
7   Marlygarten
8   Schloss Sanssouci
9   Sanssouci
10   Neue Palais
11   Charlottenhof
12   Pfaueninsel
13   Nikolskoe
14   Sacrow
15   Glienicke
16   Neue Garten
17   Babelsberg

country estates
18   Caputh
19   Lindstedt
20   Villa A

hills
21   Pfingstberg
22   Ruinenberg
23   Heyne Berg
24   Zachlens Berge
25   Herzberg
26   Kahlenberg
27   Ehrenpfortenberg
28   Reiherberg
29   Heine Berg
30   Fuchsberge
31   Entenfangerberg

agricultural elements
32   Landesbaumschule

villages
33   Bornstedt
34   Bornim
35   Petzow
36   Der Tornow
37   Russian colony, Alexandrowka
38   Russian church
39   Werder

woods and heath
40   Nedlitzer Holz
41   Katharinen Holz
42   Raubfang
43   Königliche Wildpark
44   Great decoy
45   Pirschheide
46   Gross Wentorf
47   Sacrower Heide

████ woods/park, redesigned by Lenné
░░░░ woods/park by others
------ potential sight line
───── contour line, intervals of 5 metres
───── road 1850
  urban pattern ca. 2000

  water
 Potsdam

N   0   1   2km

Havel

Potsdam

Werder

Hills, woods and heath

Many of the small hills that were scattered over the area were subject to planting, to intensify the spatial effect of the landscape. Some, which were strategically placed in the landscape composition, received another architectonic treatment. Frederick the Great had an ensemble of artificial ruins reminiscent of ancient Rome erected on the Ruinenberg, to the north of Schloss Sanssouci: a wall like the Colosseum, a ruined temple and a pyramid, with three colossal columns in the foreground. Frederick William IV later added a Norman watchtower, with a panoramic view.

Lenné designed a network of winding routes to lookout points which offered views of the nearby village of Bornstedt on the Bornstedt lake, among other prospects. A steam-driven pumping station was constructed at the Borsig factory in Berlin, which could raise water to a reservoir at the top of the mountain, to provide water for the fountains in Sanssouci. At the instruction of the king, the engine house in the bend of the Havel in the Neustadt of Potsdam took the form of a mosque.

Further to the north-east lies the Pfingstberg, where Frederick William IV built his Belvédère palace from 1849 to 1852 and again from 1860 to 1862. Lenné drew up the first plans in 1849, which also included Schinkel's Pomona temple to the south. The Pfingstberg, together with the Ruinenberg, are links in a visual chain between Sanssouci, Bornstedt and the Neue Garten.

The landscape was framed by forests of various sizes, wooded plots and heaths, which together covered an area that was almost as large as that of the agricultural landscape. The largest of these were the forest to the east of Glienicke, the Sacrower Heide to the north of Sacrow, and the Königliche *Wildpark*, with the Pirschheide, south-west of Sanssouci. Smaller woodlands, which further subdivided the agricultural areas spatially, included the Katharinenholz and the Nedlitzer Holz.

Farms, fields and villages

A number of smaller, scattered farmsteads and country houses were rebuilt and embellished. After 1828 Lenné prepared a *Verschönerungs-plan* for Caputh, with vegetable gardens on the banks of the Templiner See. In Lindstedt, to the north-west of the Neue Palais, the old farm was converted into a country house in the form of an Italian villa, lying at the edge of the woods in an agricultural area (1859-1860). The arable land was itself involved in the *Verschönerung*; Lenné's plans here concerned not just beautification, but also restructuring of the farms and improved agricultural methods. Many roads and avenues were furnished with new planting, during which especially the shoreline of the islands, along the

banks of the Havel, were provided with beautiful, encircling routes with frequent views.

The fields themselves were fringed with hedges. The trees along the roads and the hedges served in part as windbreaks and to prevent topsoil from being blown away. Even the villages, such as Bornstedt, were beautified with planting and new architectonic structures and squares. In Bornim, on the northern edge of the island of Potsdam, Frederick William had a handsome official residence built for the mayor, with accompanying gardens, designed by Persius between 1844 and 1846.

In the years 1826-1827 the Russian colony of Alexandrowka arose north of Potsdam, a new village that was to confirm Prussia's friendship with Russia. Lenné designed the ground plan as a self-contained entity, in the form of a St. Andrew's cross of roads, one arm of which was an already extant, diagonally offset road. Wooden houses in the Russian style stood along these cross-roads. In 1829 a Russian church was built on a small rise to the north. This was connected with the Pfingstberg by a route which also ran past the Jewish cemetery.

The Gartenreich as landscape theatre

The parks, which as a landscape architectonic composition elaborate on the water series, formed the heart of the *Gartenreich*. Viewed across the water, they transmute the natural form of the water into a water theatre, an ideal scenic interior of the regional landscape. Inland, further from the water, this image is continued by landscape elements such as tree-covered hills and left-over corners, avenues, roads and canals, embellished steam pumping stations, farmsteads and country homes, beautified villages, and even new colonies, designed architectonically and stage-managed in the landscape.

The support for this spatial composition was the natural landscape and the topography derived from it, which permeates everything and takes up a multitude of historic, geographical, cultural and technical elements, combining them harmoniously. In the *Gartenreich* of Potsdam the natural landscape, the agricultural landscape and the city were united into one vast landscape theatre.

The integration of Berlin into the Gartenreich

Although the centre of gravity of the *Gartenreich* lay in the vicinity of Potsdam, the city of Berlin was also involved in the landscape project. The actual city was then still limited in size. Lenné devoted his talents to realise an urban organism ordered along the principles of a scenic landscape. In his *Projectirte Schmuck und Grenzzüge von Berlin mit*

The temple on the Kahlenberg (Carl Graeb, Der ehemalige Tempel auf dem Kahlenberge in Potsdam Stiftung Preußische Schlösser und Gärten Berlin-Brandenburg, Aquarellslg. 963. Photo: SPSG)

View of the Ruinenberg from the summer palace at Sanssouci

View across the Heilige See to Potsdam from the Neue Garten (Photo: Stephanie Holtappels)

Nächster Umgegend from 1840, he used a number of elements to integrate the city into the landscape harmoniously. In the plan technical elements such as canals and roads received a landscape architectonic treatment as promenades, avenues and boulevards. The plan included a semi-circular boulevard which would circumscribe the expansion of Berlin to the east and north. The Landwehrgraben, which could be widened to become a navigable canal, was proposed as the southern boundary for the city. He planned access to the Köpenicker Feld which lay between them by means of the Luisenstädtische Kanal, a link between the Landwehrgraben and the River Spree.

Just as with his plans for Sanssouci in Potsdam, Lenné began with proposals for the modernisation of the Tiergarten, the most important park. The heart of the development of a new relation with the landscape lay there, because for centuries the Tiergarten had been anchored in the landscape and the urban pattern by a system of axes. Working out

from this 'heart' in the landscape, reaching across the River Spree to the north (Pulvermühlengelände) and across the Landwehrkanal to the south (Köpenicker Feld), the city was tied into the landscape on the basis of the existing topography. Avenues, squares, gardens and parks played a role in binding the city with the landscape. The new layout was organically connected with the pattern of the old landscape, and at the same time, via the Tiergarten, formed a link between the River Spree and the Landwehrkanal. A new element appeared on the ring boulevard along the northern edge of the city, the later *Volkspark* Friedrichshain, where the system of footpaths was integrated into the city street plan. Particularly with the redesign of the Tiergarten and the inclusion of this centrally situated park in strips which ran through beyond it to link it with the landscape, but also through the construction of new parks, Berlin and the River Spree were integrated with the water theatre and the ideal landscape of Potsdam.

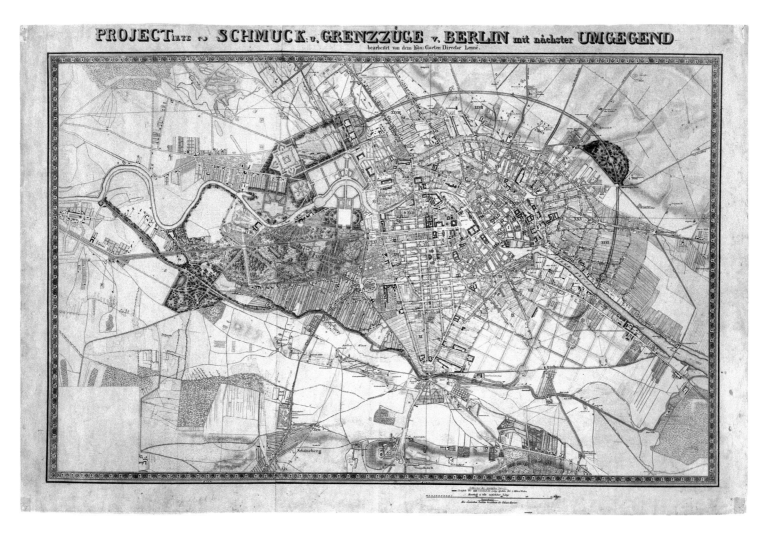

Lenné's 1840 plan for landscape interventions to beautify Berlin (Peter Josef Lenné, Projectirte Schmuck- und Grenzzüge von Berlin mit nächster Umgegend. Stiftung Preußische Schlösser und Gärten Berlin-Brandenburg, Planslg. 3817. Photo: Jörg P. Anders)

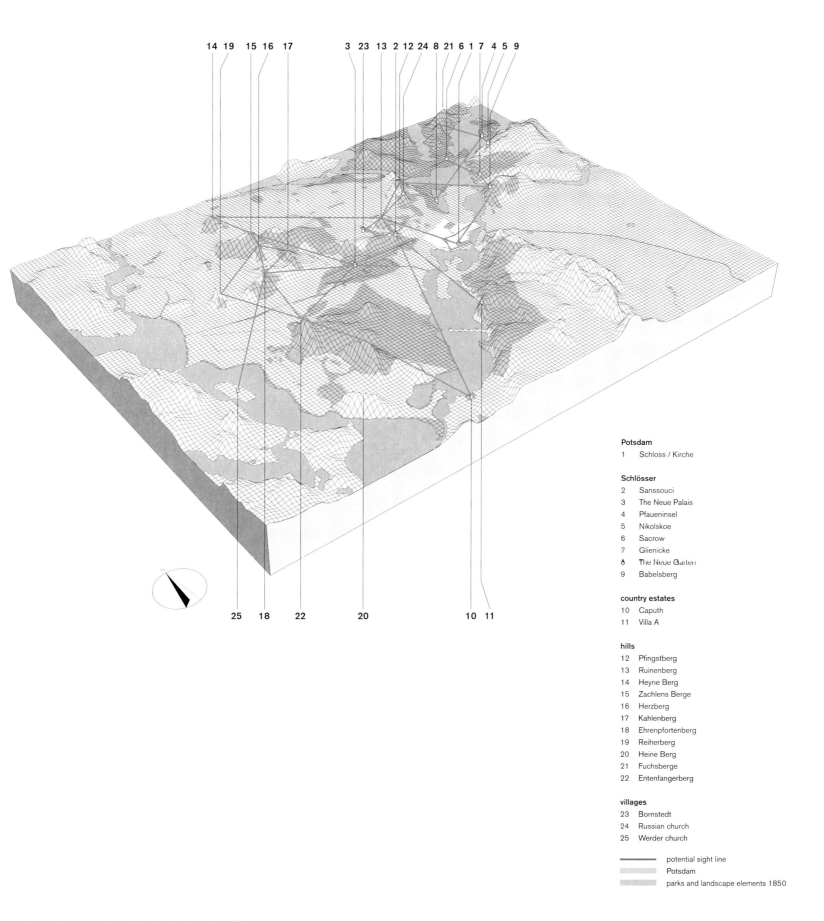

14 19 15 16 17   3 23 13 2 12 24 8 21 6 1 7 4 5 9

25 18 22 20 10 11

Potsdam

1   Schloss / Kirche

Schlösser

2   Sanssouci
3   The Neue Palais
4   Pfaueninsel
5   Nikolskoe
6   Sacrow
7   Glienicke
8   The Neue Garten
9   Babelsberg

country estates

10   Caputh
11   Villa A

hills

12   Pfingstberg
13   Ruinenberg
14   Heyne Berg
15   Zachlens Berge
16   Herzberg
17   Kahlenberg
18   Ehrenpfortenberg
19   Reiherberg
20   Heine Berg
21   Fuchsberge
22   Entenfangerberg

villages

23   Bornstedt
24   Russian church
25   Werder church

—————   potential sight line
     Potsdam
     parks and landscape elements 1850

Three-dimensional model of the Gartenreich of Potsdam
(detail 9 × 12 km, 1 cell of the grid measures 75 × 75 metres, z = 10×)

The limits of the garden realm

Berlin's 19th century urban landscape attained a critical balance among the city, the agricultural landscape and nature. The topography of the glacial landscape of rivers, lakes and hills played a central role in this. The landscape architectonic design included all scales of the topography, from the orchestration of the architectonic ensemble and the design of squares and streets to the planning of the entire city and structuring of the agrarian landscape.

In its context, Lenné's work illustrates most impressively the comprehensiveness of this landscape architectonic system. His plans built upon the natural and topographic potential that was present, and the formal qualities already realised in Berlin' landscape in the 17th and 18th centuries. For his work he employed the whole range of traditional landscape architectonic design instruments. The most important catalysts in this transformation were the Tiergarten in Berlin and the park at Sanssouci, near Potsdam, which were both integrated into the spatial continuity of the *Gartenreich*. They were public, and represented the new spatial concept of an uninterrupted urban landscape, in which the city, the agricultural landscape and nature are integrated.

This new urban landscape took on an experimental landscape architectonic form in the Charlottenhof park. The spatial design integrated the palace and the farmhouse in a single scenic idyll, and represented the ideal of an open world with harmonious relationships among all elements and cultures in the urban society. Landscape, which could absorb and unify different and even contradictory images, was an ideal medium for this task. The experimental ideal vision of Charlottenhof was then elaborated at a regional scale in the series of parks along the Havel, near Potsdam. Here, with considerable imagination and professional skill, a landscape theatre was created, with the sheets of water as the empty stage for the greenery which surrounded it and a multitude of architectonic set pieces. As a public prototype of an ideal world, the water theatre was the heart of the *Gartenreich*. Conversely, the whole world, including the city, was transformed into a garden in the Potsdam-Berlin *Gartenreich*. In that sense it was an enlarged and modernised version of the Wörlitz *Gartenreich* at Dessau, of the previous century.

The traditional formal instruments of landscape architecture were freely applied and transformed in an eclectic style, oriented toward incorporating new insights about the relations between architecture, landscape and the city. A new visual-spatial system arose from this, a regional landscape theatre with an autonomous form and character of its own, geared to urban living in an Arcadian setting. The German concept

of the *Gartenreich* is not to be found anywhere else in the world, in this form. It is remarkable that the concept of such a garden realm, which embraced both the city and agrarian landscape, should have developed precisely in a country that had not produced any design tradition of its own in landscape architecture that essentially distinguished it from Italy, England and France.

The scope of the visual instrumentarium

At the end of the 19th century this ideal, in essence still a function of the 18th century, was overtaken by industrial development. Industrial sites became larger, and were established chiefly along the water, inevitably leaving their stamp on the city. The Teltow Canal was dug as a part of a new industrial infrastructure, and new harbours were built. A number of towns to the west of the city, such as Wilmersdorf, Schmargendorf, Steglitz, Dahlem and Zehlendorf, grew into satellite cities. After the beginning of the 20th century these towns were increasingly tied into the urban fabric. The Kurfürstendamm was built as a artery for new, planned urban districts.

Between 1895 and 1910 the exclusive residential district of Grunewald arose along the Halensee, Königssee, Dianasee and Hundekehlesee. Motorways and a railway line were cut through the woodland itself, which came under the control of the city. Following the new building laws of 1925, which sought to guarantee air, light, and sun, new garden communities were built. Examples of these include the Hufeisensiedlung in Reinickendorf and Onkel Toms Hütte in Zehlendorf, built by Bruno Taut between 1926 and 1932, and the Siedlung Siemensstadt by Hans Scharoun in Spandau, built between 1929 and 1931. In Friedrichshain, Lenné had given the first impetus for this development. In addition, a series of new *Volksparken* were planned and introduced into the fabric of the city. Gustav Meyer and Erwin Barth were the most important of the designers for these parks. With the construction of these parks Berlin acquired a new landscape structure, for which the existing form of the landscape and the visual instrumentarium of landscape architecture was not longer the point of departure.

The explosive growth of the city and the urban infrastructure, combined with the democratisation of urban facilities, demanded a new programmatic concept. As compared with this, the Potsdam-Berlin *Gartenreich* bordered on an urban Arcadia, without any programme. But with this concept, Lenné and Schinkel had forever established the significance of the visual instrumentarium of landscape architecture in the design of the urban landscape.

View of the Schaeferberg from the Belvedère on the Pfingstberg

View of the Pfaueninsel from the Belvedère on the Pfingstberg (photos: Ulrich Orling)

Projects by Peter Joseph Lenné

0	1810 Lustgarten in Potsdam
1	1816 Park Sanssouci
2	1816 Neue Garten
3	1818 Bülowscher Garten
4	1819 Schloss Charlottenburg
5	1820 Kadettenanstalt
6	beginning 1820 Schlosspark/von Humboldt
7	1823 Parkanlage General von Witzleben
8	1823 Marquard
9	1824 Graefscher Garten
10	1825 Bassinplatz
11	1826 Russian Colony
12	1826 Kaserne des Lehrinfanteriebataillons
13	1828 Lindstedt
14	1828 Leipziger Platz
15	1828 Schloss Niederschönhausen
16	1828 Schlossgarten Caputh
17	1828 Garten des Palais des Prinzen Carl
18	1829 Ruinenberg
19	1829 Gärten Begas und Stier
20	1830 Prinz-Albrecht Garten
21	1830 Wilhelmsplatz
22	1830 Lustgarten in Berlin
23	1830 Pfaueninsel
24	1830 Pfingstberg
25	1831 Garten Kerll
26	1831 Wilhelmsplatz in Potsdam
27	1833 Park Bellevue
28	1833 Nikolskoe
29	1833 Kleine Tiergarten
30	1833-39 Tiergarten
31	1833 Park Babelsberg
32	1834 Charitégarten
33	1834 Park Klein-Glienicke
34	1835 Garten am Palais Redern
35	1835 Garten Jacobs
36	1835 Berliner Strasse
37	1836 Garten des Hofmarschalls von Maltzahn
38	1838 In den Zelten
39	1838 Hasenheide
40	1838 Lennéstrasse
41	1839 Pulvermühlengelände
42	1839 Garten de Freiherrn von Stein zum Altenstein
43	1840 Schmuck- und Grenzzüge von Berlin
44	1840 Garten Meyer
45	1840 Leipziger Dreieck
46	1840 Wildpark Potsdam
47	1840 Köpenicker Feld
48	1840/41 Der Tornow

49	1840 street design at Obeliskportal
50	1840 and 1842 Entenfang
51	1840/43 Garten Karl Heinrich Ludwig von Borstel
52	1841 Luisenplatz
53	beginning 1842 Moabit Zellengefängnis
54	beginning 1842 Bornstedter and Bornimer Feldflur
55	1842 Zoologische Garten
56	around 1842 Charlottenburger Chaussee
57	1842 Bell-Alliance-Platz
58	1843 lock between the Landwehrkanal and the Spree
59	1843 Kiezstrasse
60	1843 Bethanien
61	1843 Friedrichshain
62	1843-55 Spandauer Schiffahrtskanal
63	1843 Area around the Frankfurter Bahnhof
64	1844 Schöneberger Feldmark
65	1844 Bornim
66	1844 Brandenburgerstrasse
67	1845 Opernplatz
68	1845 Park Sacrow
69	1845-50 Landwehrkanal
70	1846 Grabenstrasse and Moritzhof [Badeanstalt]
71	1846 Garten Schumann
72	1846 Urbanufer
73	1847 Golmer Weinberge [Reiherberg; Ehrenpfortenberg]
74	1847 Schloss
75	1848 Bahnhof Wildpark
76	1848 Luisenstädtischer Kanal
77	1850 Plantage
78	1850 Villa Borsig
79	1850 Bornstedt
80	1850 Nauender Tor
81	1853 Marianneplatz
82	1853 Invalidenhaus
83	1854 Luisenplatz
84	1855 Area to the right of the Potsdamer Chaussee
85	1855 Urban Schlächterwiesen
86	1856 Villa Tiedke
87	1856 Schlosspark Steglitz
88	1856 Kemperplatz
89	1857 Hausvogteiplatz
90	1860 Kahler Berg
91	1863 Dönhoffplatz
92	1864 Evang. Johannisstift
93	1865 Area to the west of the Neue Palais
94	Kreuzbergpark
95	Forsthaus Templin

woods

water

urban pattern

urban pattern ca. 2000

projects by Peter Joseph Lenné 1816-1866

street

park

square

0   2   5km

Detail from: Plat of the seven ranges of townships being part of the territory of the United States, N.W. of the River Ohio [1796] (Library of Congress, Geography & Map Reading Room, G4080 1796. H8 Vault)

2 THE LANDSCAPE IN THE URBAN NETWORK

In the 19th century landscape architecture was confronted with the burgeoning growth of the city and the formation of an urban network. Urban expansion took on an autonomous form in the urban grid, which nevertheless was connected with nature and the topography of the landscape in various ways.

The most explicit landscape architectonic expression of this is the 19th century city park. Incorporated into the technical infrastructure, it played a major role in the interaction between the city and nature and the agrarian landscape. The parks were situated in diverse landscapes, and moreover could be self-standing or, on the contrary, be embedded in a series. Beginning from these conditions, they developed different forms.

Central Park, in New York, shows the democratisation and liberation of the 19th century city park as a new autonomous spatial type. The *genius loci* of the American wilderness was preserved in this park in the middle of the neutral grid of Manhattan. The contrast between the city and nature was raised to a maximum degree.

Cerdà's expansion plan for Barcelona consisted of an urban building kit, with plenty of open green space. Nevertheless, the spatial relation of the new city, laid out with its grid, and the landscape was chiefly determined by the careful modelling of the urban grid in the topography of the landscape and the architectonic elaboration of particular places in it.

Amsterdam shows us the 19th century urban expansion and the city park within it as a straightforward transformation of the matrix of the North Holland peat landscape. The type of the polder park arose out of the confrontation between English landscape architecture, which had been developed for a hilly landscape, and the sober, flat conditions of the peat landscape and the Dutch urban pattern of streets.

In the Emerald Necklace in Boston the concept of the city park was expanded into a coherent landscape series, linked together by parkways. This park system represented the different landscape types in the environs of the city and supported its further growth and the creation of new patterns and networks.

CENTRAL PARK NEW YORK 1857

Nature in the urban grid
Frederick Law Olmsted
The grandeur of the wilderness

A rocky peninsula
The bedrock
The peninsula

Birkenhead Park as model
Anchorage in the urban grid
Reshaping the image of the pastoral landscape

The growth of the urban grid
From New Amsterdam to New York
Wall Street and Broadway
The Commissioners' Plan of 1811
Opening up the hinterland
Densification and open space

The public planning process
The City Common Lands
The Greensward Plan, 1857
Realisation

The pastoral landscape as guide
A recomposition of landscape fragments
Staging the pastoral composition
Nature in the centre
The system of separated routes

The perfection of the park as urban spatial type
The democratisation of the programme
Swinging back the horizon
A print of the American landscape

Aerial photo of Central Park (aerial photo: Lee Ross, Sky View Pictures)

Nature in the urban grid

New York was founded in the 17th century (originally as New Amsterdam) on the spot now called Downtown Manhattan. In the second half of the 19th century America changed rapidly from an agrarian to an urban society. The plan for the growth of New York was set out in the expansion plan of 1811, comprising an urban grid based on city blocks of 50 × 200 meters, laid from the south to north over the whole island of Manhattan. When, around the middle of the 19th century, foresighted individuals perceived the threat of this urban grid filling entirely with buildings, the idea arose of safeguarding the original landscape in the urban layout in the form of a great park.

Central Park, about 320 hectares (843 acres) in size, was designed by the American landscape architect Frederick Law Olmsted in collaboration with the architect and landscape designer Calvert Bowyer Vaux (1824-1895), after they had won a competition in 1857 with their Greensward Plan. Central Park was the first urban park in America, and was built between 1857 and 1877.

Frederick Law Olmsted

Frederick Law Olmsted (1822-1903) was born in Hartford, Connecticut, from a colonial family which had been established there since 1636. Olmsted was a multi-faceted man, having led an adventurous life since his childhood. At the age of seven his father placed him in the home of a clergyman in another town, where he could receive a good upbringing. In the years that followed he was briefly enrolled at several different schools, and was successively an apprentice mechanic, clerk and seaman. In 1840 his father sent him to New York to begin work at a commercial firm, so that he could learn business practice. That was short-lived; already by 1843 he had signed on as a cabin boy on the barque *Ronaldson*, sailing to the Chinese port of Canton. This too proved to be a failure. Ill and emaciated, he returned to New York. Shortly thereafter he began academic studies in agricultural science at Yale University. After picking up the more practical side of things on a farm, in 1847 his father bought a farm for him in New Haven, on the coast of Connecticut. In 1848 he moved to a farm on the shores of Staten Island. It was on these farms that he gained his knowledge of agriculture, soil improvement, drainage and agrarian economics. He even devoted attention to the scenic presentation of his farm. In financial terms however the farm was no success.

In 1852 Olmsted made a six month tour around Europe, which he wrote up in his book *Walks and Talks of an American Farmer in*

Topography

Parks Frederick Law Olmsted
1   Central Park
2   Eastern Parkway
3   Forest Park
4   Fort Greene Park
5   Fort Tyron Park
6   Grand Army Plaza
7   Morningside Park
8   Ocean Parkway
9   Prospect Park
10 Riverside Drive
11 Riverside Park

airport

subway station
subway line
railway line

motorway
tunnel
important road

urban pattern

park
other green space
water

N   0   2   5km

England. In England he visited parks and landscape gardens designed by Humphry Repton and Capability Brown, the greatest landscape architects of their day. In Liverpool he visited the brand new Birkenhead Park, designed in 1843 by Joseph Paxton. In meticulous study there, he investigated the design principles and the tricks of the trade, such as the mechanics of moving soil, water management, and how to lay out a system of footpaths.

Back in America, as a correspondent for the *New York Daily Times* Olmsted made two trips to the American south, which was then still slave territory. He stayed there until 1854, writing news letters, as well as a longer critical analysis in book form. In 1857 however his publisher went bankrupt. Seeking a new job, he successfully competed for the position of Superintendent for Central Park in New York City, the land for which had been acquired in 1856. In this function Olmsted had to collect detailed topographic information about the designated site, see to the eviction of squatters (poor settlers who had built illegal homes and cabins there), and oversee the construction of a boundary wall. In the course of his duties he rode over the site on horseback, often by moonlight, until he was familiar with every detail, every rock, rill, morass and hill. In that same year Vaux invited Olmsted to join him in taking part in the competition for a design for the Central Park. Their Greensward Plan won the first prize, after which Olmsted was appointed as Architect-in-Chief for Central Park.

The grandeur of the wilderness

In Olmsted's eyes, urban growth was accompanied by negative effects such as lack of open space, overcrowding and an increase in traffic and noise. He argued for a large park in every city, in which the populace could completely separate themselves from urban life. This park had to be in a central spot, to be able to function optimally. The character of the park should be defined by a large, centrally located, lightly rolling open space, fringed by shady trees, which would screen out the sight of the city, with all its bad qualities.

Olmsted's views were especially influenced by Birkenhead Park as the first public city park in Europe, which had been designed as an integral part of the city's expansion, in both a spatial and social-economic sense. The sale of sites for homes around the park provided the money for the development of the park itself. In this way the wealthy assisted in paying for the furnishing of the park, and in exchange acquired the right to live directly on, or even in the park. Although the planning process for Central Park had a more public character, the composition scheme for it was still based on this first public city park.

The circumstances in America were however different from those in England. Birkenhead Park was in essence a suburban model, in which various residential forms could be advantageously combined spatially with a park landscape. In this respect it stood in the same tradition as Bath and Regent's Park. In the tumultuous growth of American cities however, it was a question of reserving a space and keeping it open as a neutral, free form for the whole city. A second difference was that in the English model nature had an idyllic character. For Olmsted, it was rather the authentic American nature, in all its wild grandeur, though tamed by man. Set in the ring of the park, nature was to sparkle like a raw diamond in the urban pattern.

Southern entrance to the park at 5th Avenue

A rocky peninsula

Hudson Bay is the edge of the Laurentian (or Canadian) Shield, a lake-studded plateau that is formed from gneisses, banded metamorphic rocks with a clear crystalline structure, which gradually slopes upward to the north, to attain a hight of about 600 meters above sea level. The plateau dates from the Paleozoic era, and is the oldest geological block underlying North America.

The bedrock

The Appalachian Mountains, to the west of New York, were folded upwards at the end of the Carboniferous period. Here the earth's crust is dozens of kilometres thick, and consists of rocks from various formations. Together they make up the bedrock, the hard substratum that is present everywhere, often covered with only a thin layer of soil. Most of these rock formations were originally deposited in horizontal layers, which were later deformed under pressure and crumbled away. For example, the rock formations in western New York State are composed of layers of sedimentary rock of various thicknesses which are tipped slightly to the south. The broad bands in that region are the result of the erosion of these tilted layers, which flattened them.

In the Adirondack Mountains of northern New York State the sedimentary layers became broad folds. The Taconic Mountains to the east of the Hudson River Valley are comprised of enormous pieces of the earth's crust that were pushed upwards from the east. Their serrated profile exposes the side of the fractures in these plates, created as they were pushed up. The formation extends from New England to past the edge of the Hudson Valley.

In more recent geological periods the ice cap played a large role in the formation of the landscape of New York. It retreated to the north between 20,000 and 10,000 years ago. Over the vast majority of New York State, the bedrock has been ground out and covered with deposits of boulder clay somewhat more than a meter thick, left behind by the ice cap that was perhaps two kilometres thick. This boulder clay consists of an indiscriminate mixture of clay, sand, pebbles and stones, deposited more thickly in the valleys than on higher areas. The Ronkonkoma and Harbor Hill moraines on Long Island dominate the landscape there, as the southernmost expansion of the ice cap. The Valley Heads Moraines close off the southern ends of the Finger Lakes.

The peninsula

The growing mass of the ice cap caused the sea level to fall. It was in this period that the continental plate was formed, with the moraines in the coastal landscape, such as those on Long Island, Fishers Island and Cape Cod. Rivers cut deep valleys in the landscape, which were later filled with sediment. A remnant of the Hudson Shelf Valley remained. When the ice melted, the sea level rose again and changed parts of this moraine landscape gouged out by river valleys into islands, which were then further transformed by wave action and currents.

Manhattan remained behind as a peninsula after these geological processes, connected with the mainland only be a thin strip of land. On the west flows the Hudson River, at this point a tidal estuary that forms the lower reaches of the Mohawk and Hudson Rivers; on the east is the East River, now actually an arm of the ocean, and originally a brackish inland sea. The shape of the peninsula was initially considerably narrower and more irregular. This has changed as a result of extensive landfills, comprised of material produced by levelling the surface of the island in the course of the city's expansion, among other things. Almost all of the zone containing the earlier docks is artificially created land. The peninsula was highest in the centre and drains to both sides, with the majority of the water running toward the East River. Originally there were also several marshy inlets and creeks on that side. The watershed lay about where Broadway now runs. From south to north the peninsula runs up to about 80 meters above sea level.

Geomorphology and the urban domain

New York 1811
urban area ca. 2000

N

0   20   40km

Geomorphology, urban pattern and parks

Elevation (metres)

	100 - 120
	90 - 100
	80 - 90
	70 - 80
	60 - 70
	50 - 60
	40 - 50
	30 - 40
	20 - 30
	10 - 20
	0 - 10

urban pattern

park

water

The confrontation with nature

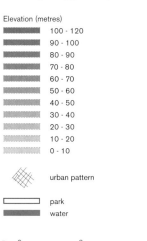

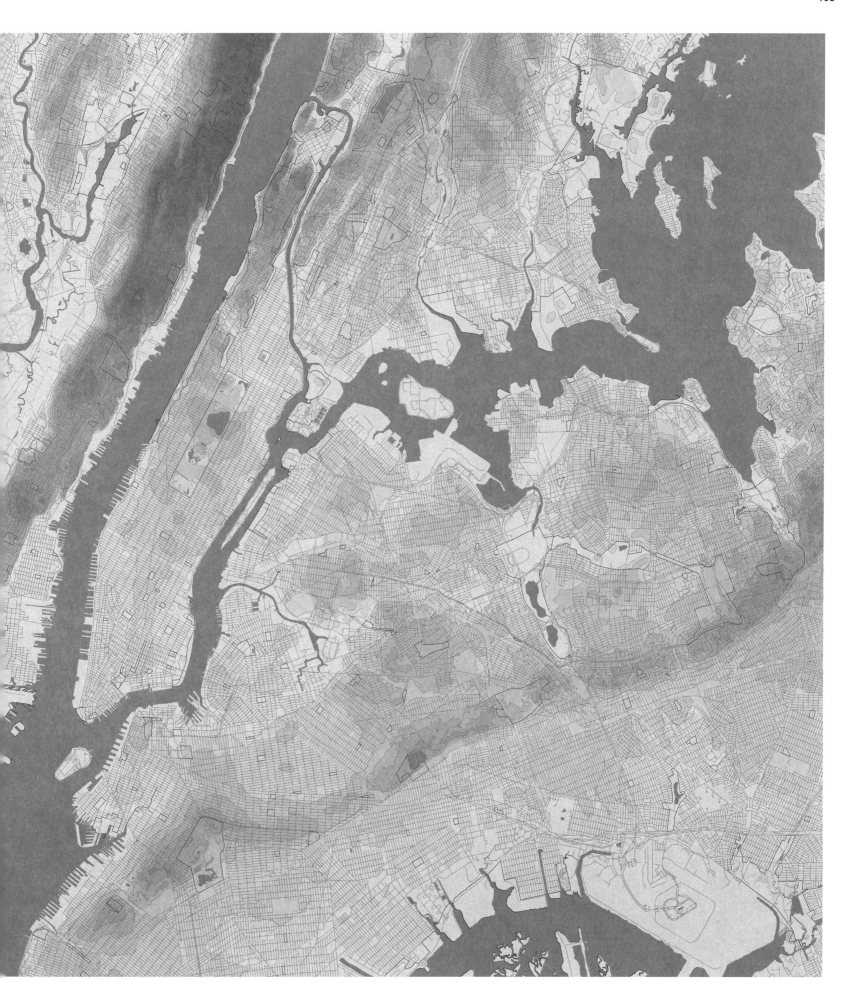

Birkenhead Park as model

After his visit to England, in his book *Walks and Talks of an American Farmer in England* Olmsted provided this description of Birkenhead Park: "Walking a short distance up an avenue, we passed through another light iron gate… Five minutes of admiration, and a few more spent in studying the manner in which art had been employed to obtain from nature so much beauty, and I was ready to admit that in democratic America there was nothing to be thought of as comparable with this People's Garden."

Birkenhead Park was designed in 1843 by the architect and general all-rounder Joseph Paxton (1803-1865), who, among other things, served as the gardener and landscape architect at Chatsworth House for over 26 years. It was a part of the development of Birkenhead, a new city opposite the rapidly expanding city of Liverpool, across the Mersey, an estuary with sea ports on either bank. The new port city was laid out on a rather flat area along the coast to the west of the town of Birkenhead. Hamilton Square was the heart of the city, and the point of departure for the urban grid. To the south, between Birkenhead and a higher sandy plateau with the villages of Claughton-cum-Grange and Oxton, lay a swampy hollow on loamy subsoil, in terrain that sloped upward to the south by about 18 meters. This was where a committee for urban improvement, composed of businessmen who had themselves purchased land there, in 1840 proposed the creation of a public park.

In a theoretical sense Birkenhead Park marks the end of the urban transformation of the landscape garden, which had seen the development of the city park as an autonomous form for the first time. As such, it benefited fully from the work of John Nash in Regent's Park in London, scarcely ten years earlier. The park had an immense influence on the expansion of the concept of the 19th century city park, both on the European continent and in the United States.

Anchorage in the urban grid

Paxton derived the design matrix of the park from the urban grid of Birkenhead. He drew diagonals between the points where the periphery of the park intersected the lines of the urban grid and the corners of the perimeter. The entrances to the park, with their lodges, were placed at these points. In this way he involved the various entrances with one another, and anchored the park into the grid of the new city. The ponds and crescents on the south were similarly included in the design scheme.

He also designated a pattern of zones for various kinds of dwellings in and along the edge of the park. Row houses for the working class bounded the low side of the park, as close as possible to the harbours. A border of terraces and crescents was projected for the higher side, which according to the 'Bathonian concept' of Regent's Park had views out over the park and, because of the difference in elevation, like the Royal Crescent in Bath, also had views of the Mersey and Liverpool on the opposite bank. The zone between the streets surrounding the park and the interior of the park was filled with detached houses.

The park's system of footpaths was related to the urban network of roads. The park was intersected by Ashville Road, a public urban thoroughfare. Park Drive, about ten meters wide and comprised of two loops, separated the private and semi-public section on the outside of the park and the public section on the inside. Paxton provided access to the crescents, terraces, villas and their accompanying gardens with branches off Ashville Road. An independent network of footpaths crossing to the central section of the park ran on through the wilderness in the middle of the lobes of the park. The pattern of paths which, in the landscape garden, had been focused on the house, was here transformed into an circulation pattern running around the whole park, stringing together various viewing points in a non-hierarchical manner.

Reshaping the image of the pastoral landscape

The park was intended first and foremost as a site for strolling, a diorama, as it were, in which one could walk around. In this, Paxton went a step further than Nash had done in Regent's Park. The common zoning of the landscape garden, comprised of the 'garden', the 'meadow' and the 'wilderness', was essentially turned inside out. With their gardens and parterres, the area in front of the crescents and terraces, on the outside of the Park Road, was now the 'garden'. The pleasure grounds were comparable to the 'meadow' of the landscape garden, suitable for cricket and archery, then popular sports for the more affluent. The planting along the inside of Park Drive screened the open, slightly concave, sun-lit 'meadow' from the denser edge zone. The wild and thickly planted ponds in the centre of the park formed an inwardly focused transformation of the wild nature, the 'wilderness', which had lain on the periphery of the landscape garden.

The soil which was excavated in digging the ponds was used to erect embankments five to ten meters high, which visually isolated the nature from the pleasure grounds. The embankments were furnished with planting, and the entrances were through masses of rock fashioned to obtain a sense of intimacy and illusion of naturalness that contrasted sharply with the open, refined character of the pleasure grounds. Islands in the whimsically shaped ponds prevented one from surveying them in their entirety, while permitting unexpected views. In this way nature was brought to the heart of the park, literally and metaphorically, compensating for the physical distance from real nature by a visual suggestion of nature that was all the more emphatic.

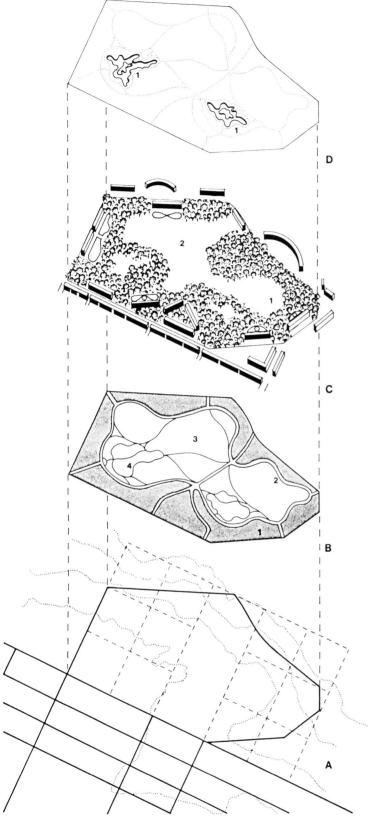

1	Liverpool		6	Oxton
2	Mersey		7	Conway Street
3	Ferry		8	Birkenhead Park
4	Birkenhead		9	Ashville Road
5	Claughton			

A The basis

B 'The garden'
1 The urban rim
2 Park Drive
3 Playing fields (Pleasure Grounds)
4 Footpaths

C 'The Meadow'
1 Planting
2 Open space

D 'The Wilderness'
1 Water and rocks

The zoning of the landscape in Birkenhead Park

The situation of Birkenhead Park in the topography

Engraving of Birkenhead Park (from: A. Alphand, *Les Promenades de Paris*, 1867. TUDL TRG 9411 E 01)

The growth of the urban grid

In 1609 the United East India Company (VOC) of the Dutch Republic of the Seven Provinces commissioned the English sea captain Henry Hudson to search for a north-east passage to India and China. He himself believed more strongly in the possibility of a north-western route, which, acting on his own authority, he decided to seek after going no farther than the North Cape. By way of the Faeroe Islands, Newfoundland and Nova Scotia, on 11 September, 1609 his ship *De Halve Maen* reached a bay along the coast of North America, presently Upper New York Bay. From it he sailed up a stream that would later bear his name, the Hudson River. It proved not to be the passage that he was seeking, but did provide access to a rich hinterland. On a manuscript map from 1610 the Indian tribes living along the river were called the Manna-hata. Around 1626 the island bearing their name, Manhattan, was purchased from the Indians by Peter Minuit, director of the West India Company (WIC), established in 1623, with the intention of founding a fur trading post there. The region became part of the province of New Netherland, and under the guidance of the surveyor Crijn Fredericksz van Lobbrecht work began on the construction of New Amsterdam on the southern tip of Manhattan, comprised of a fort and trading station. This was the first step in a process by which the settlement grew into the all-encompassing urban grid.

From New Amsterdam to New York

Against the wishes of the residents of New Amsterdam, in 1638 the fourth governor, Willem Kieft, started a war against the Indians. In the course of the hostilities much of what had been built up around the settlement was destroyed. This damaged the commercial interests of the colonists, who turned against the authority of the governor. The WIC found a new leader in Peter Stuyvesant, who was the governor of New Netherland from 1647 to 1664. Stuyvesant's colonial policies however could not prevent increasing numbers of English settlers from New England from establishing themselves in New Netherland, attracted by its more liberal religious climate. New Netherland thereby became a plaything in the rivalry between the Dutch and English for control of the seas, which led to three wars.

In 1651 England promulgated the Act of Navigation, in combination with attacks on Dutch trading vessels. This led to the First Anglo-Dutch War in 1652. With the ascension of Charles II to the throne in 1660 a second Act of Navigation was quickly adopted, with the aim of knocking the Dutch out of the Atlantic trade. On 8 September, 1664, the flag

of the WIC was lowered, and New Amsterdam was renamed New York, for the Duke of York, who later became King James II of England. Its capture proved to be the overture for the Second Anglo-Dutch War (1665-1667). After nearly three years of hard fighting the Dutch Republic surrendered its claim to New Netherland to the English. In exchange for this the islands of St. Eustatius and Saba were returned to the Dutch, and England also conveyed Surinam to the Dutch Republic. In 1672 war broke out again with the English. During this Third Anglo-Dutch War the Dutch would briefly recapture New York in 1673-1674, but very shortly after they had renamed it New Orange, in November, 1674, it was definitively ceded to the English.

Wall Street and Broadway

Around 1650 there were already more than 300 brick houses on the southern tip of Manhattan, surrounded by gardens and orchards. In 1653 a wall was built on the north side of the settlement, as protection against the Indians who still lived on the island. The adjoining street was called Walstraat, later to become Wall Street. In this phase of the development the topography still defined the settlement's structure. The streets were laid out according to the 'cow path method'. This meant that houses were built along the roads running to the fields outside the city, and to other settlements farther north. These roads were relatively flat, running through the valleys or along the crests of hills. In this way, the settlement grew outward locally.

In 1686 the Dongan Charter established the city of New York as the governmental authority for the whole island of Manhattan. This charter also decreed that land which had not previously been sold or granted to private individuals – that is to say, especially land to the north of the present 23rd Street – became the property of the city. In the century which followed, to raise funds the city now and then sold off portions

**Building and density of the urban grid,
prior to the construction of Central Park**

A   Jones Wood Estate

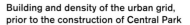 vacant blocks
blocks not yet laid out
blocks under 20% built up
blocks under 40% built up
blocks under 60% built up
blocks under 80% built up
blocks under 90% built up
blocks almost 100% built up

river banks largely occupied by industry
river banks still accessible to the public
- - - Hudson River Railroad

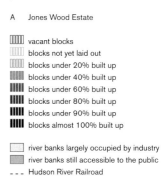

0   1   2.5km

1811

1836

1852

of this land. Around a century later, by this process the colony had grown into a succession of various settlements, each with its own street pattern, extending from the Hudson River to the East River for about a mile inland. Many of the sites had been levelled; the material which this produced was used for fill along the shores of the island.

One of the most important country roads from time immemorial was Bloomendale Road, later to become Broadway, which ran along the spine in the middle of the island to the hamlet of Bloomendale, with Harlem beyond it, a popular place for summer homes. Many country homes arose along Bloomendale Road. To the east, between Broadway and the East River, lay the dwellings of the lower classes, who worked in the harbour. Many squatters lived outside the built-up area, constantly being pushed north by the city's expansion. As the most important through road, Broadway was the link between the built-up and undeveloped areas.

The Commissioners' Plan of 1811

In 1804 New York had a population of 80,000. The city was growing rapidly; in the previous decade its population had doubled. To accommodate its new population, the city was spreading steadily northward. The scattered farms and country estates were subdivided into ever smaller plots and sold off to builders or speculators. As the city grew, streets were being marked out entirely without planning. The Common Council of New York had no binding authority over the layout of streets. Therefore they called on the state government for assistance. In 1807 New York State enacted a statute which granted the Commission of Streets and Roads the power "to lay out streets, roads, and public squares, of such width, extent and direction, as to them shall seem most conducive the public good, and to shut up, or direct to shut up, any streets of parts thereof which have been heretofore laid out.. [but] not accepted by the Common Council."

This led to the Commissioners' Plan, which was presented and adopted in 1811. It comprised a uniform urban grid which was laid over the whole island from south to north. This put an end to the growth of the mosaic of smaller urban expansions just above the existing city on its southern end, which had been oriented more to the local topography. The rigid new grid regulated the spread of the city, but nonetheless reflected a liberal vision. Within the neutral framework there was complete freedom and space given for commerce and entrepreneurship.

The plan called for twelve long, wide avenues running parallel to one another from south to north. At right angles to them there were to be more than 150 parallel east-west streets, intended to facilitate traffic

between the Hudson River and the East River. This division resulted in rectangular, roughly east-west oriented building blocks, which formed the module for the grid. The avenues were all 100 feet (about 30 meters) wide. Most of the streets were 60 feet (about 18 meters) wide; 15 streets were 100 feet wide. The distance between the avenues was not in all cases equal. The location of the avenues and streets was in part determined by the roads which had already been built, and by parcels of land which had previously been sold. There were also minor adjustments in the grid, which overall appeared entirely regular, to take account of different situations and the natural conditions.

The differences in the dimensions within the grid can in part be explained by the economic importance of the frontage in the vicinity of the shoreline and piers. The avenues also had to connect with the tip of Manhattan, which had already been built up. 10th Avenue was extended to the extreme northern end of the island, at Kingsbridge. The extension of the grid all the way to the north was in part determined by a planning strategy which was oriented to discouraging speculation. The commission foresaw that land in Harlem, where there was already a village, would be built on sooner than the hills which lay south of it, which afforded a more difficult site for construction. They wrote, "To some it may be a matter of surprise that the whole island has not been laid out as a city. To others it may be a subject of merriment that the Commissioners have provided space for a greater population than is collected at any spot on this side of China. They have in this respect been governed by the shape of the ground. It is not improbable that considerable numbers may be collected at Harlem before the high hills to the southward of it shall be built upon as a city; and it is improbable that (for centuries to come) the grounds north of Harlem Flat will be covered with houses. To have come short of the extent laid out might therefore have defeated just expectations; and to have gone further might have furnished materials to the pernicious spirit of speculation."

Opening up the hinterland

The Commissioners' Plan received an extra stimulus through the development of better connections with the American hinterland. Between New York City and the agrarian wealth of the Middle West lay the Appalachian and Allegheny Mountains. Transport of goods was very difficult; by horse and wagon it could take several weeks. To improve this, the Erie Canal was built, running more than 350 miles (560 km) between the Hudson River and Lake Erie, opening in 1825. It was now possible to convey goods within a week, and for only a fraction of the previous cost. With the Erie Canal products from the Middle West

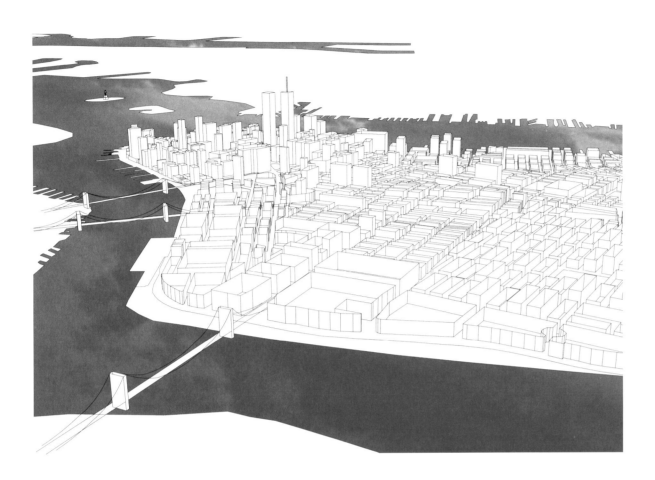

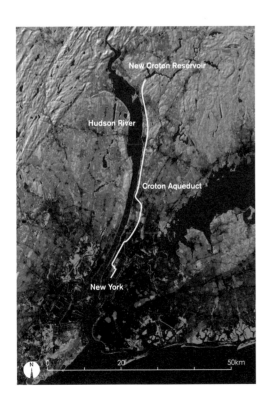

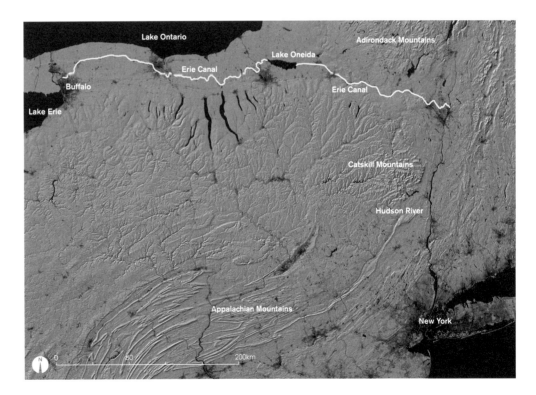

The urban development on the southern tip of Manhattan

Croton Aqueduct

The Erie Canal

could be carried to New York, and then transshipped for European destinations.

This led to New York quickly becoming the economic centre of America. Within a decade of the opening of the canal one third of American exports, and two-thirds of all imports, were moving through New York. The Erie Canal became the backbone of the rising industrial north, with New York as its heart. In 1862 the canal was deepened and widened. The establishment of the first regularly scheduled service between New York and Liverpool by the Black Ball Line in 1817 also promoted the importance of New York as a transit port. The service rapidly proved successful, and other operators followed suit. It soon became less expensive to ship goods from Boston, Philadelphia, Baltimore and Norfolk to England via New York than to do so directly. In 1851 the New York and Erie Rail Road opened a railway connection from the Hudson River to Buffalo, on Lake Erie, which further speeded up the transport of goods. Telegraph lines from the whole of America came together in Lower Manhattan.

Densification and open space

There were only a handful of open spaces included in the Commissioners' Plan. It was not believed that more parks and squares were necessary, because the estuary in which Manhattan lay was so large that there was enough room for both recreation and health, and for trade. There were spaces kept open for a water reservoir, an observatory, a military parade ground, a market and several small squares and park. The reservoir had to be on high ground; the site of a salt marsh, which would not produce enough revenue as building sites, was chosen for the market. A canal in the middle would serve both for draining and reclaiming the site, and as access for market boats.

By 1825 the population of New York had reached about 170,000. As the economic and industrial centre of America, the city was growing enormously. It was not only expanding, but rebuilding itself. Dwellings and small offices and workshops around Wall Street and Broadway were demolished and replaced by banks and insurance companies. This created the first business district in the world. There was however still no sewer system, no regular police, fire department, drinking water supply, rubbish collection or public transit.

On the evening of 16 December, 1835, a fire broke out in a warehouse on Pearl Street, in the business district. The volunteer fire services could not pump enough water to combat the flames and, to make the disaster total, the water actually froze in the hoses and pumps. One quarter of the area went up in flames, including the last Dutch houses, which had survived earlier fires during the Revolutionary War. A year later the whole area was rebuilt. The fire and several cholera epidemics prompted the municipal authorities to replace the outdated water system with the Croton Water Works. Water was brought in to New York from the Croton River, north of the city, via tunnels and aqueducts. Once it arrived it was first stored in a Receiving Reservoir, lying in what was later to become Central Park. From there it was piped to a Distributing Reservoir at 42nd Street.

Because of the enormous demand for workers, New York continued to attract people. Immigrants arrived daily, ending up in the poorest neighbourhoods of the city, where they lived packed together, with minimal services. The streets were packed with factories, workshops, warehouses and tenements. Landlords divided the dwellings into ever smaller units. Wooden huts – and later whole tenements – sprang up in what had been back gardens. In the poor districts the population density reached more than 750 inhabitants per hectare, five times higher than had been foreseen in the Commissioners' Plan in 1811. In 1851 there were already more than 500,000 residents south of 23rd Street, in buildings no more than five storeys high. The banks of the Hudson and East Rivers were inaccessible because of the wharves and docks. This ever-increasing population density created a dire shortage of open space.

View across The Lake to the western wall of the park

The public planning process

The first public criticism of the lack of open space in the city came in 1844. In that year William Cullen Bryant (1794-1878), a poet and editor, and as the son of a doctor an advocate of fresh air and movement, visited London and its parks. As a consequence of this visit, in his newspaper, the *Evening Post*, he began arguing for the construction of a large park in New York. His arguments were well received; various justifications for such a park were presented from all sides, varying from health to morals, and from speculation to culture.

A heated discussion over the location and financing of the park ensued. For instance, Jones' Wood, a summer retreat bounded by 66th and 75th Streets and 3rd Avenue and the East River, was proposed. It would have been easy to create a park by buying up various parcels of land there. Although a law authorising this was passed, the discussion about another, more central location went on for months. Councilman Henry Shaw and the Chairman of the Croton Aqueduct Board, Nicholas Dean, proposed that building a park and construction of a new water reservoir should be combined, which, they argued, would keep the costs down. In August, 1851, there was a proposal to enlarge the Battery, for 25 years a favourite promenade on the southern tip of Manhattan. This stirred up the discussion still further.

Andrew Jackson Downing (1815-1852), one of the leading landscape architects in the United States, also joined in the debate. Downing, who lived in the Hudson Valley north of New York, had published his first book in 1841, *A Treatise on the Theory and Practice of Landscape Gardening adapted to North America*. In 1845 he became the editor of *The Horticulturist and Journal of Rural Art and Rural Taste*. In 1850 he made a study tour to London. Downing thought Jones' Wood much too small. Moreover, it would be very expensive to acquire that length of shoreline, and a park there would be difficult to combine with a new water reservoir.

The City Common Lands

In January, 1852, a Special Committee on Parks advised that a large central park be built between 5th and 8th Avenues and 59th and 106th Streets. Acquiring this land would not be more expensive than that in Jones' Wood, because the rock outcrops and swamps in the landscape made it almost useless as lots for building. Moreover, the City already owned a section of the land for the construction of the new reservoir. The whole area had originally been owned by the city, a part of the City Common Lands. Thus fewer parcels of land had been sold there, and

they had not been subdivided as thoroughly as was the case in other sections of the city. Acquisition began in November, 1853; the process was completed by July, 1856. By this date the edge of the built-up section of Manhattan had reached 38th Street.

The Greensward Plan, 1857

The first plan for Central Park was drawn up in 1857 by Egbert Ludovicus Viele, a civil engineer, who had been appointed by the city as Chief Engineer for Central Park. The plan in fact consisted of a topographic survey, and attracted considerable criticism for its lack of imagination. One of the leading critics was the landscape architect Calvert Vaux, just at the beginning of his career, who had recently succeeded Downing, who had been drowned in a shipwreck in 1852.

Exposed bedrock in the park

→ **Map of the original landscape of Manhattan on the site of the park** (Egbert L. Viele, Sanitary & Topographical Map of the City and Island of New York. New York, 1865. David Rumsey Historical Map Collection, www.davidrumsey.com)

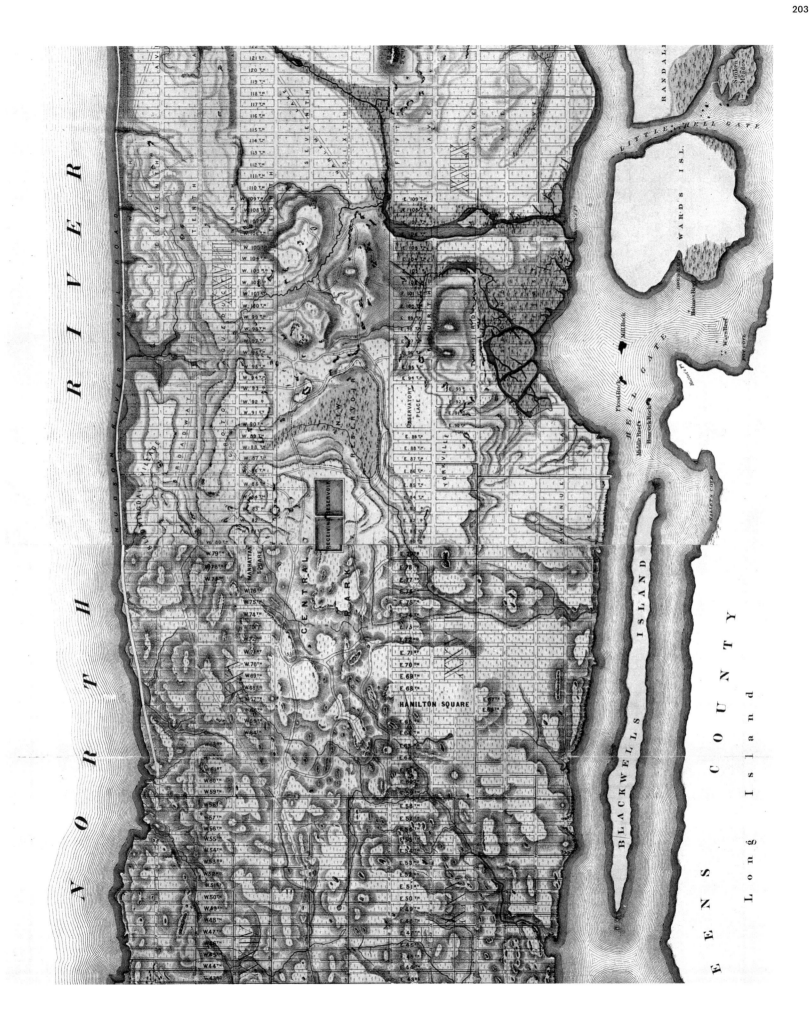

Following this critical reception, later that same year the city authorities organised a public competition for a design for Central Park. Out of the 33 submissions, the Greensward Plan by Olmsted and Vaux was chosen as the winner. Vaux had invited Olmsted, who in September, 1857, had been named as Superintendent of Central Park, and in that capacity had explored the terrain thoroughly, to join him in participating in the competition. Response to the plan was largely positive, because of the ingenious manner in which the city traffic was conducted through the park by means of sunken transverse roads.

The name Greensward, which Olmsted and Vaux chose for their plan, refers to a characteristic component in the English landscape garden, the meadow as a pastoral landscape element of wide grassy fields and lakes, in sharp contrast to the unruly image of the wilderness, the picturesque forms of rough, steep rocks, wild vegetation and nature. The park was to be a place where the city-dweller could find rest and escape from the pressures and commotion of urban life. The beauty and drama of the scenic and natural tableaux had to relieve the artificiality and oppressive effects of the city. Users from all social classes should be able to enjoy the same atmosphere and the same scenic images, increasing social freedom and equality.

Realisation

A team of specialists was formed to support the designers in the realisation of the winning plan. The team included the horticulturalist Ignatz Pilat (1820-1870) who worked on the park until his death, the hydraulic engineer George Waring (1833-1898) and the British born structural engineer and architect Jacob Wrey Mould (1825-1886), who was responsible for the various buildings and bridges. From 1857 to 1871 the Central Park Commission, with Andrew Haswell Green (1820-1903) as its president after 1860, had administrative responsibility for the construction of the park. Green saw to it that the Greensward Plan was realised in a form as close as possible to the original design. He was also responsible for the expansion of the park's size in 1863, when the northern boundary was moved from 106th Street to 110th Street. In 1859 there were 3666 labourers working on the preparation of the site. Some rock ledges were blown up, and there was a large amount of soil moved to level parts of the site for the creation of rolling, grassy fields.

The park was opened to the public in the winter of 1859. Thousands of New Yorkers came to skate on the newly constructed lakes. The full realisation of the Greensward Plan took another twenty years. Because the park was a public facility, there were scores of political imbroglios during its construction, several of which led the designers to submit

their resignations. Moreover, in 1861, with the secession of the southern states from the Union to form the Confederacy, the American Civil War broke out. With his critical stance toward slavery, Olmsted withdrew as architect-in-chief and spent two years with the United States Sanitary Commission, set up to oversee the health of the Union troops. Vaux left in 1863. After the Civil War, in 1865, the new partnership of Olmsted, Vaux and Company was appointed as the advisory bureau for the Central Park Commission. Olmsted's involvement with Central Park ended definitively in 1877. Vaux continued to be involved with the park until his death in 1895. The annual reports from the Commission included maps which showed which sections of the park had already been finished. The 1870 map was the first to show a completely realised park. Olmsted had designed the park for the future, when it would lie in the heart of a city of two million people. Olmsted's expectations were amply exceeded; by 1879 the park was already largely surrounded by urban development.

→ **The Greensward Plan, 1858**
(NYC Department of Parks and Recreation, Photo Archive. Image 61692.)

→ → **Central Park around 1870, extended by four blocks**

⌣	bridge
⁄⁄	tunnel
⌐	wall surrounding the park
○	ponds and lakes
⅋ ∘ ℅	solitary trees and small group of trees
	woods
ᴑ	rocks
●	buildings
	paths
⌒	drives
	bridle paths
	walks
❂	terraces
	transverse roads
⊔⊔	surrounding buildings
⌐⌐	fort
⋅—⋅	sight lines

0		500		1000m

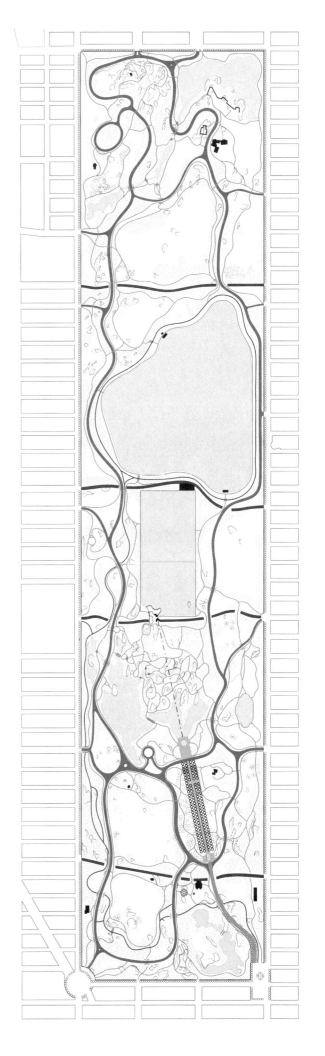

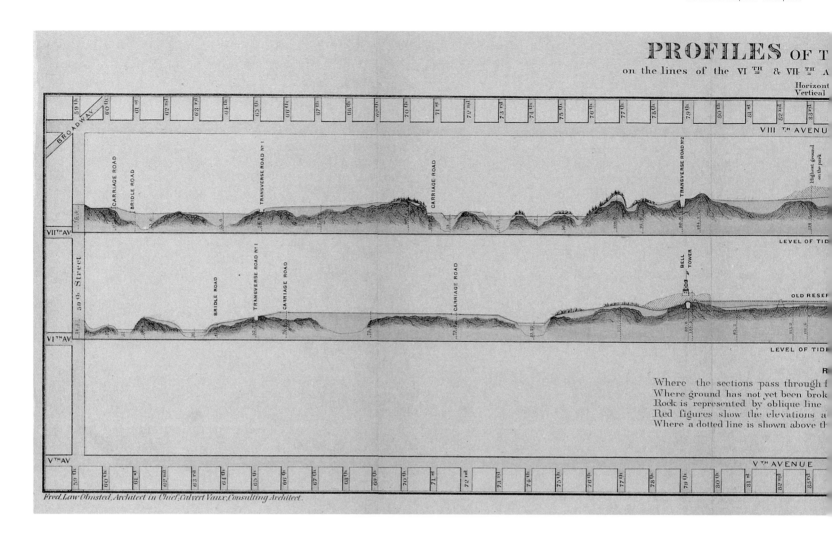

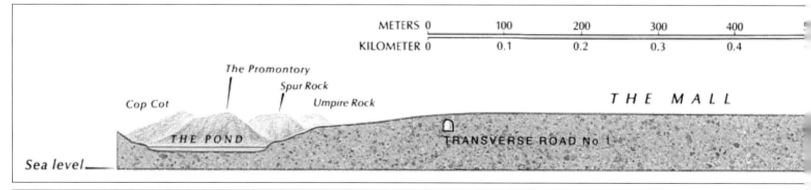

Longitudinal profiles along the lines of 6th and 7th Avenues, from 59th to 110th Streets ('Profiles of the Central Park on the lines of the VIth & VIIth Avenues prolonged from 59th to 110th Street', from *THIRD ANNUAL REPORT OF THE BOARD OF COMMISSIONERS OF THE CENTRAL PARK*, 1860 (New York: C. Bryant & Co.). 1859. New York, Metropolitan Museum of Art. Lithograph.© 2011. Image copyright The Metropolitan Museum of Art/Art Resource/Scala, Florence)

Cross-section of Central Park, from south to north (cross-section on the map of George Colbert & Guenter Vollath (Greensward Foundation 1994))

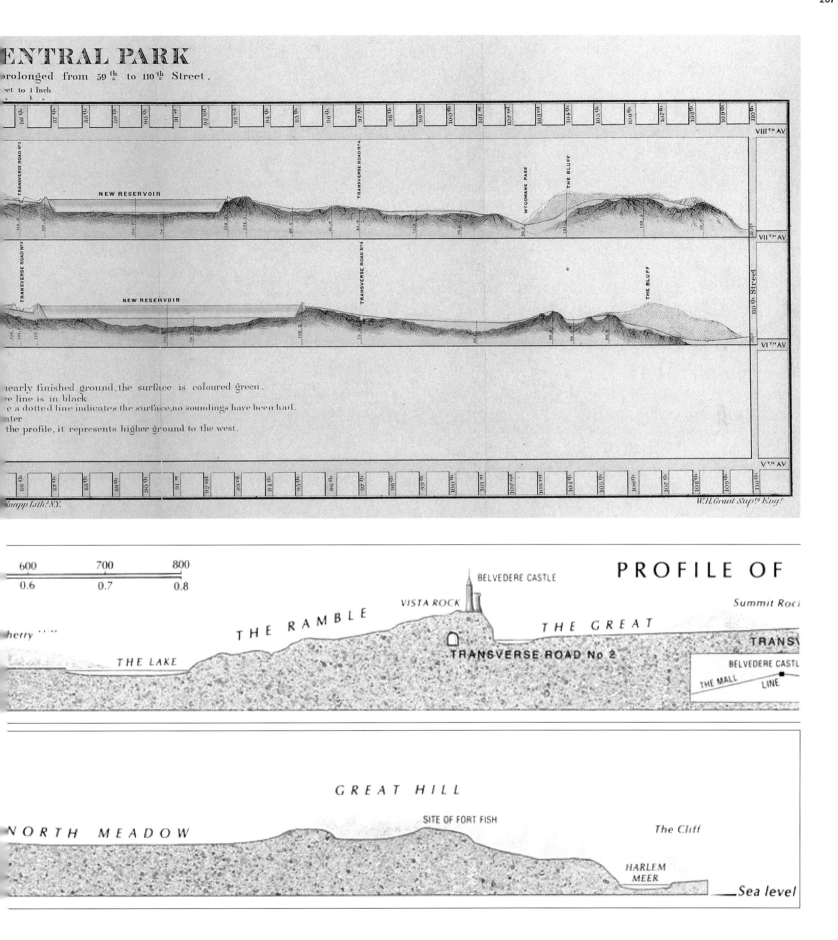

ENTRAL PARK

prolonged from 59ᵗʰ to 110ᵗʰ Street.

et to 1 Inch

TRANSVERSE ROAD Nº3

NEW RESERVOIR

TRANSVERSE ROAD Nº4

Mᶜ COWANS PASS

THE BLUFF

VIII ᵀᴴ AV.

VII ᵀᴴ AV.

TRANSVERSE ROAD Nº3

NEW RESERVOIR

TRANSVERSE ROAD Nº4

THE BLUFF

110 ᵗʰ Street

VI ᵀᴴ AV.

nearly finished ground, the surface is coloured green.

e line is in black

e a dotted line indicates the surface, no soundings have been had.

ater

the profile, it represents higher ground to the west.

V ᵀᴴ AV.

Knapp Lith. N.Y.

W.H.Grant Supᵗ Engᵣ

600   700   800
0.6   0.7   0.8

PROFILE OF

BELVEDERE CASTLE

VISTA ROCK

THE RAMBLE

Summit Rock

herry

THE GREAT

THE LAKE

TRANSVERSE ROAD No 2

TRANS

BELVEDERE CASTLE

THE MALL

LINE

GREAT HILL

SITE OF FORT FISH

NORTH MEADOW

The Cliff

HARLEM MEER

Sea level

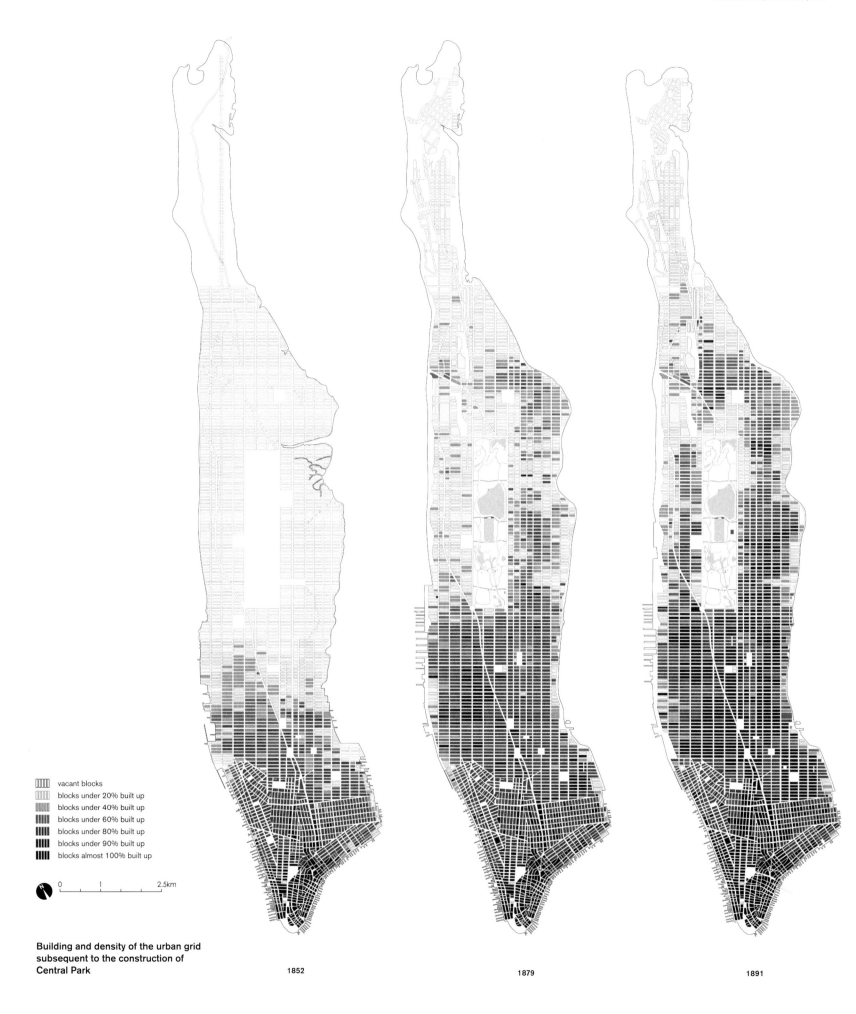

vacant blocks
blocks under 20% built up
blocks under 40% built up
blocks under 60% built up
blocks under 80% built up
blocks under 90% built up
blocks almost 100% built up

0   1   2.5km

**Building and density of the urban grid
subsequent to the construction of
Central Park**

1852

1879

1891

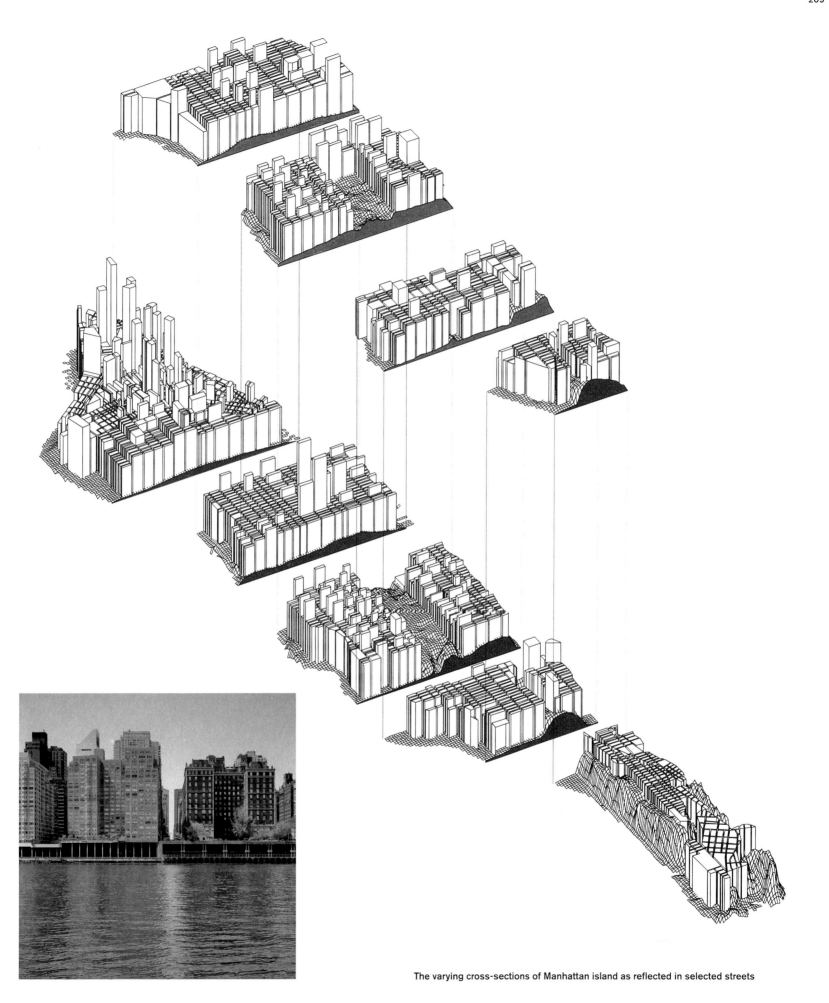

The varying cross-sections of Manhattan island as reflected in selected streets

The pastoral landscape as guide

Central Park lies in the heart of the geometry of the urban grid, slightly off centre in the direction of the Hudson River, like an abstraction of the shape of Manhattan island itself. The urban grid reduced the local diversity of the landscape to its elementary geographic characteristics, which still play a role at the scale of the city as a whole. It confronts the length of the island with the shorter breadth, restricted by the water; cross sections of the island are visible in the streets. The frequency of the streets is greater than that of the avenues running the length of the island. As a result, the urban blocks run transversely, across the island. In contrast, the block of the park lies longitudinally. With its 320 hectares the rectangle of the park is the largest single area that is derived from the dimensions of the urban plan, and at the same time is a representative slice of the island's original nature.

The park is bounded on the east by Fifth Avenue, the central axis of Manhattan, once called Middle Road, which begins at Washington Square in Lower Manhattan and is aligned with Mount Morris to the north of the park. This avenue, with its luxury shops and clubs, where the most prosperous New Yorkers have traditionally lived, has an entrance at the south-east corner of the park. Broadway, which followed the natural morphology along the spine of the island, cuts across the urban grid as a diagonal line more than 25 kilometres long, from the southern tip of the island to its north-west end. Half way along its route it touches the south-west corner of the park, where Columbus Circle, at the intersection of Broadway and 8th Avenue, also has an entrance. Thus the entrances to the park at its southern corners lie at two important points in the grid.

The northern edge of the park originally lay at 106th Street. This was one of the wider streets in the grid. With this as the boundary the rectangular Croton Reservoir, likewise defined by the lines of the grid, lay precisely in the middle of the park. The larger New Reservoir, completed in 1862, was sited north of the old one, while the boundary of the park moved north to 110th Street. This preserved the balance between the areas allotted for the Lower and Upper Park. The boundaries were spacious enough on all sides to allow the creation of a pastoral landscape as a medium between the city and wild nature.

A recomposition of landscape fragments

The terrain that Olmsted found was comprised in part of a still wild hill landscape with precipices and rock outcrops. The area was intersected from the west to east by four streamlets which originated near

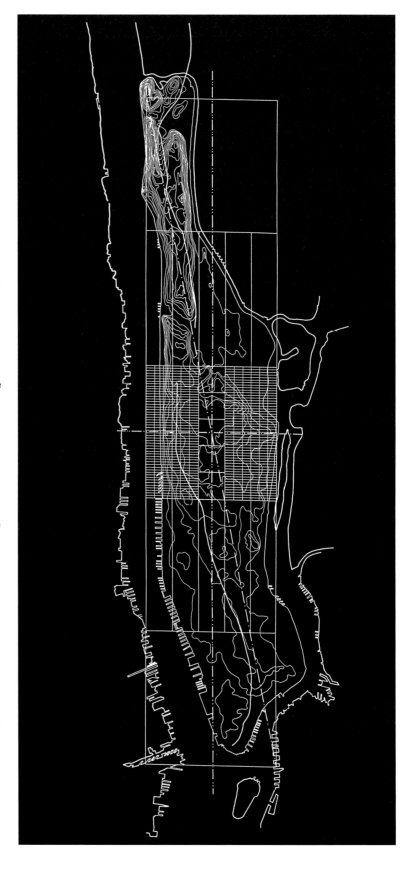

The park rectangle in the geometry of the urban grid and the island as a whole

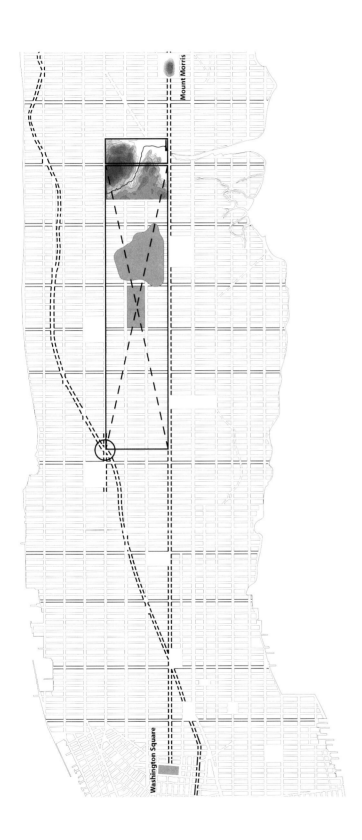

Mount Morris

Washington Square

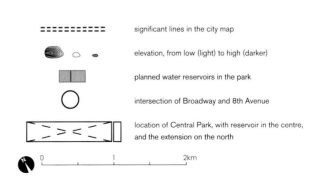

significant lines in the city map

elevation, from low (light) to high (darker)

planned water reservoirs in the park

intersection of Broadway and 8th Avenue

location of Central Park, with reservoir in the centre, and the extension on the north

0   1   2km

The position of the Park in the urban structure of Manhattan

Broadway and discharged into the the East River via creeks. The north-east corner of the park was originally part of an inlet, which was later drained. When the park was laid out, this area became the Harlem Meer, at the foot of Mount St. Vincent, fed by the water that came down the slope of Bogardus Hill in Montayne's Rivulet.

Several thousand squatters had settled in the area, homeless individuals living in primitive huts in the midst of stone quarries, foetid swamps, rubbish heaps, pigs and a slaughterhouse-cum-glue factory. Seneca Village, a village founded by free Negroes, with three churches, a school and two cemeteries, lay near the intersection of 8th Avenue and 82nd Street. In 1857 the last of its residents were evicted. In the northern part of the park, the Upper Park, there were several rocky crags from which one could survey the East River, the Hudson and Long Island Sound. During the Civil War, between 1861 and 1865, an arms depot was built on these heights, and garrisoned by soldiers. During the American Revolution, between 1775 and 1783, and again during the War of 1812, between 1812 and 1815, there had also been military fortifications built there, parts of which are still extant in the park today.

The existing streamlets were dammed and widened, creating a series of lakes and water features in the park, following its north-south orientation. The New Reservoir, occupying the site of a large, enclosed swampy hollow, supplied the primary accent. The series of lakes was embedded in parts of the original natural landscape by means of a variety of artificially levelled rolling fields, adapted to the terrain. This system formed the basis for a continuous pastoral landscape.

The whole was held together by the park's access system, defined by the east-west oriented transverse roads and the lines of the north-south oriented Park Drive. Together these form a flexible grid that follows the morphology of the terrain, frames the scenic series, and anchors the park into the geometry of the city's grid. The spatial dimensions of the Lower Park, with a total length of about 2000 meters to the New Reservoir, are such that in principle it could function as an independent park. Despite its smaller size, the Upper Park nevertheless provides its own unique contribution to the spectrum of landscapes in the park.

Staging the pastoral composition

The design by Olmsted and Vaux shut the city out. Where in Regent's Park and Birkenhead Park there was still a deliberate, planned spatial relationship between the city and the park, Central Park turned inward on itself. The need to give the landscape its own character and to isolate it as a separate urban space in the growing metropolis was felicitously expressed by Olmsted himself. In the commentary accompanying the Greensward Plan he wrote, "Considering that large classes of rural objects and many types of natural scenery are not practicable to be introduced on the site of the Park, – mountain, ocean, desert and prairie scenery for example, – it will be found that the most valuable form that could have been prescribed is that which may be distinguished from all others as pastoral. But the site of the Park having had a very heterogeneous surface, which was largely formed of solid rock, it was not desirable that the attempt should be made to reduce it all to the simplicity of pastoral scenery. What would be the central motive of design require of the rest? Clearly that it should be given such a character as, while affording contrast and variety of scene, would as much as possible be confluent to the same end, namely, the constant suggestion to the imagination of an unlimited range of rural conditions.

"The question of localizing or adjusting these two classes of landscape elements to the various elements of the natural topography of the Park next occurs, the study of which must begin with the consideration that the Park is to be surrounded by an artificial wall, twice as high as the Great Wall of China, composed of urban buildings. Wherever this should appear across the meadow-view, the imagination would be checked abruptly, at short range. Natural objects were thus required to be interposed, which while excluding the buildings as much as possible from view, would leave an uncertainty as to the occupation of the space beyond, and establish a horizon line, composed, as much as possible, of verdure."

The internal spatial structure of Central Park was based on the pastoral composition as Paxton had applied it in Birkenhead Park, with zoning into three spatial categories, the 'garden', the 'meadow', and the 'wilderness' respectively. This scheme, which is carried on through the whole park, provides a spatial coherence for the different parts of the park, making it one unified landscape. Spatially, the New Reservoir plays a subordinate role in this, because the surface of the water lies too high to work together visually with other parts of the park. It is a sort of intermediate space, withdrawn into itself, lifted out of the park, as it were.

Columbus Circle, the entrance in the south-western corner, where the park touches Broadway, and Grand Army Plaza, on the south-east corner, at the intersection of Fifth Avenue and 59th Street, were designed as special urban spaces. At Grand Army Plaza you are led into the park diagonally, via the Drive. The Drive brings you to the Mall. This is the 'garden', the architectonically most elaborated transitional space between the city and the landscape, comprised of a wide promenade 400 meters long, fringed with elms. At its end stairs lead under the 72nd Street Transverse to the Terrace, a richly ornamented plaza with a mooring place for boats, lying down at the side of the Pond.

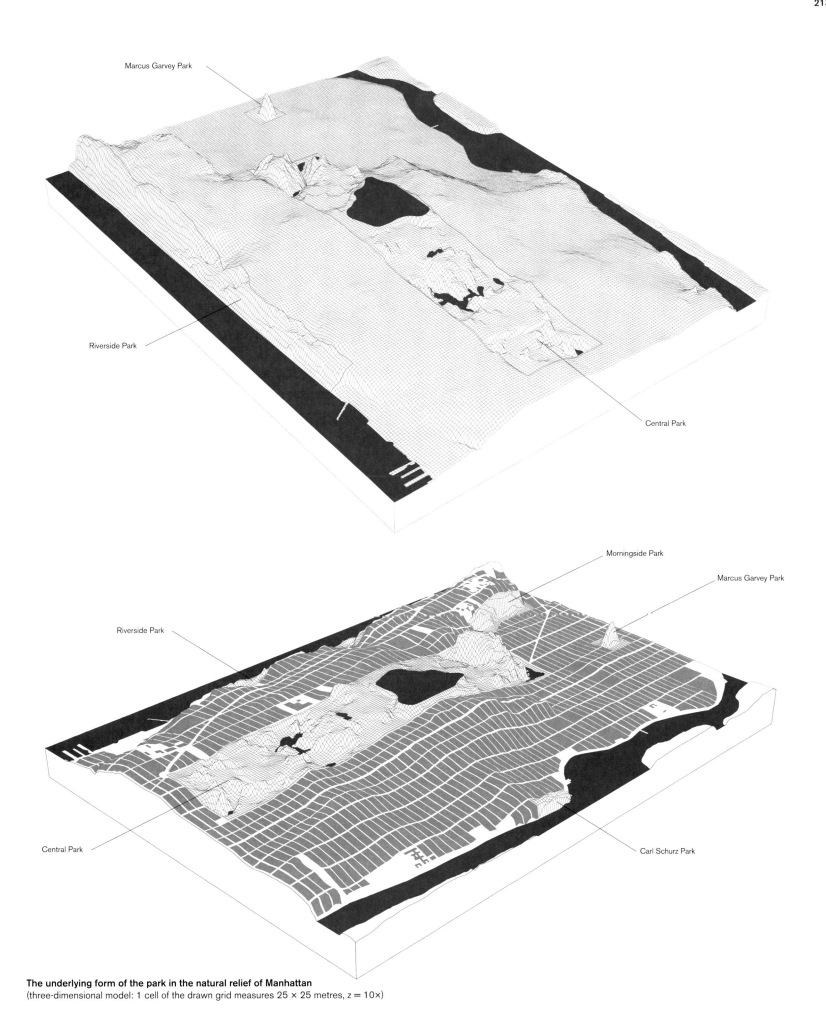

Marcus Garvey Park

Riverside Park

Central Park

Morningside Park

Marcus Garvey Park

Riverside Park

Central Park

Carl Schurz Park

The underlying form of the park in the natural relief of Manhattan
(three-dimensional model: 1 cell of the drawn grid measures 25 × 25 metres, z = 10×)

The sight lines from the Terrace over the Lake and the Ramble, a wild and hilly natural fragment, are focused on the high Vista Rock behind them. Within only a few years Vista Rock was no longer visible as a result of the growth of the trees in the Ramble, so Olmsted and Vaux decided to build Belvedere Castle on the top of the hill. In a single movement the Mall brought visitors to the park from one of the most important avenues in the city to the 'wilderness' in the heart of the park, enabling them to survey the park landscape from a belvedère. Looking back from this central position, the 'wilderness' of the Pond, at the beginning of the Mall, formed the background for the pastoral landscape of the Lower Park.

At the northern end of the park, the Great Hill was the highest point, and the Ravine, with a 'runnel', Montayne's Rivulet, the most picturesque, elaborated accent in the pastoral scenography of the Upper Park. The 'wilderness' around the Pool, the Ravine and the Harlem Lake was carefully separated from its surroundings, so that from the Great Hill you saw it as an intriguing piece of 'scenery', with the sight of the 'meadow' in the background. In the north-west corner of the 'wilderness' was the Cliff. This steep, rocky landscape was such a major natural obstacle that it became one of the reasons for shifting the northern boundary of the park from 106th to 110th Street. It was in this northern section that Olmsted's park ideal was perhaps to be found in its purest form: great open playing fields fringed by the suggestion of deep forest, transitions such as Montayne's Rivulet with its picturesque décor, and no architectonic structures that would distract attention from the pastoral character.

Nature in the centre

The cultural and ethical appreciation of nature in the design fit into a discussion regarding the antithesis between nature and culture, or between the landscape and the city. During the Enlightenment the paradigm of the Fall and original sin and the tainted nature that resulted from it was transformed into the idea that civilisation must be held responsible for this taint, and the source of unaffected purity must be sought in nature. Implied in this was a critical attitude toward the city as the stage for pollution, sickness and poverty. The idea of the invigorating landscape was given concrete form in the way the city was screened out. The green wall was the first step in a visual series that was designed to lead one from the city to nature. The pastoral landscape within it, based on the picture of human use of the landscape in an harmonious balance with nature, was the second step. The 'wilderness' was the third step. Here lay the core of the visual series in the design:

the original, unspoilt American nature of the island was placed at the centre.

The design and planting of the Ramble, between the Lake and Vista Rock, appears to have been determined by the original wooded landscape. The soil is damp; it is sheltered, and the image is defined by large masses of rocks. The earlier vegetation was rich and complex, and the terrain was strewn with stones. When the area was being cleared, and in the construction of the paths, care had to be taken that valuable plants were left in place. Nevertheless, much of the original vegetation was lost during the construction of the park. Various species of plants proved not to be usable. Olmsted himself still lacked experience in dealing with natural planting. For instance, after a short visit to Panama in 1863, in a letter to Pilat he gave instructions as to how he should transform the North American woodland landscape of the Ramble into a "Panamanian Jungle". In 1875 Olmsted designated the Ramble as the best place for a wild garden, an gave orders for the planting of snowberries, Bermuda grass and crocuses, without making any distinction between native and exotic plants. On the side toward the Lake openings were made which permit the wanderer to catch a glimpse of the water. The path that leads from Vista Rock, through the Ramble, over Bow Bridge and along the banks of the Lake to Bethesda Terrace is designed to accentuate the natural scenes and differences that come together in this section of the park.

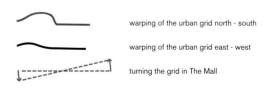

→ **The interaction of the park design with the natural differences in elevation, watercourses and creeks** (projection of the park design on Viele's 1865 map of the watercourses)

→ → **The warping of the urban grid in the park design**

warping of the urban grid north - south

warping of the urban grid east - west

turning the grid in The Mall

zoning of Central Park, based on the avenues

0   400   1000m

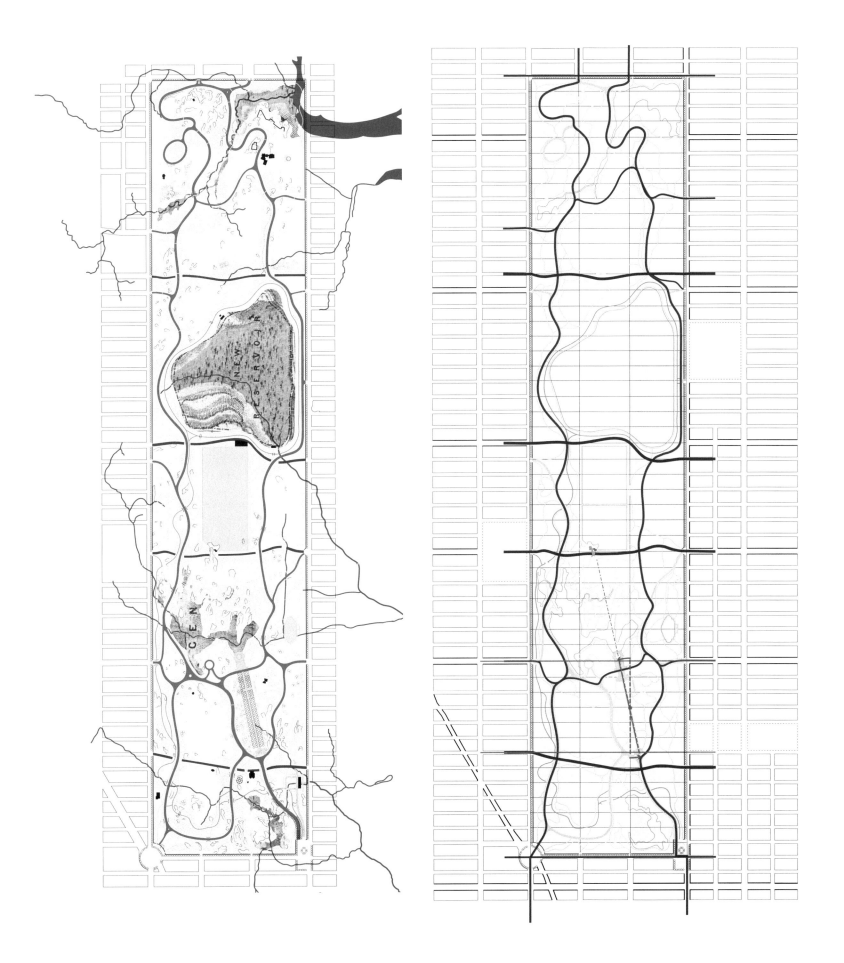

The programme that the Park Commission had drawn up was minimal. It did include three playing fields of from one to four hectares, a site that could be flooded in winter as a skating pond, a parade ground of from 8 to 16 hectares, an exhibition and concert hall, an observatory, a flower garden and a large fountain. Various public buildings appeared along the outside, and just inside the edges of the park, such as the American Museum of Natural History, across from the Park at 8th Avenue and 81st Street, and the Metropolitan Museum of Art, which was opened in 1872 after an initiative by the publisher George Palmer Putnam.

The system of separated routes

In the Greensward Plan Olmsted and Vaux had designed a system of routes for carriages, all of which had footpaths running along them. To make it possible for city traffic to cross the park in the east-west direction, transverse roads were planned at regular intervals. These transverse roads were to be sunken about two meters below the park level, so that bridges and traffic would not obstruct the views or annoy strollers in the park. Two weeks after the announcement of the winning plan, Robert J. Dillon, a member of the Commission, supported by August Belmont, proposed seventeen changes, which they had picked up from other submissions. Dillon and Belmont found the contrast between a rural park and the city grotesque. The park could become more urban if the system of paths would make more intensive use possible. Among other things, they wanted a long, straight boulevard running across the park diagonally, from the entrance at Fifth Avenue and 59th Street to the Great Hill, so that the reservoirs were not hidden away, but would be included as a visual element in the park's design. They also believed the sunken transverse roads were unnecessary. There should be a bridle path for horseback riders that ran around the whole park instead of only around the New Reservoir, and the system of Drives, Walks and Rides must be separated. On footpaths along the carriage drives, pedestrians would be exposed to the commotion, dust and danger of the carriages. An intense public debate ensued, after which the authorities ordered that the system of routes should be separated, and the bridle path should be lengthened. As a result, more emphasis was placed on circulation. Olmsted here designed the first separated traffic system, in which the different routes for pedestrians (The Promenades and Walks), horseback riders (The Saddle), carriages (The Drive) and through traffic (The Street, initially also for carriages) were segregated from one another. The East Drive and the West Drive together formed a circuit about ten kilometres long. There were five transverse roads through the park, at 66th, 72nd, 79th, 84th and 97th

Streets, which connected to important streets on the west and east sides of the park. Thirty bridges and eleven overpasses were necessary to achieve this. Each of the bridges was designed differently, with different constructions and architectonic motifs, in a variety of materials including cast iron, brick, granite, brownstone and wood. Alongside the reservoirs Olmsted had the least space for running the routes. There was only a narrow strip available to the east of the New Reservoir. The idea was put forward to lead the Drive through an arcade here, with shops under it and a view out over the reservoir and Fifth Avenue from the top. This idea to visually open up the park route to the city was never realised. The route system was to tie the park into the city's traffic system, without disrupting the scenic illusion.

→ **The composition scheme of the park, with garden, meadow, and wilderness**

Garden

pond

garden

wall

dike – footpath around The Reservoir, with entrances

entrance, mall, terrace and belvedère

Meadow

open grassy field

Wilderness

rocks and woods

water

0   500   1000m

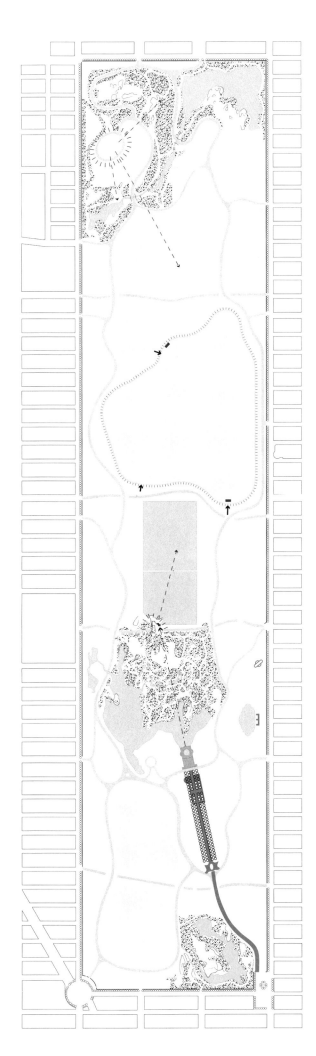

Wilderness

Meadow

Garden

Vista Rock with Belvedere Castle, viewed from the north

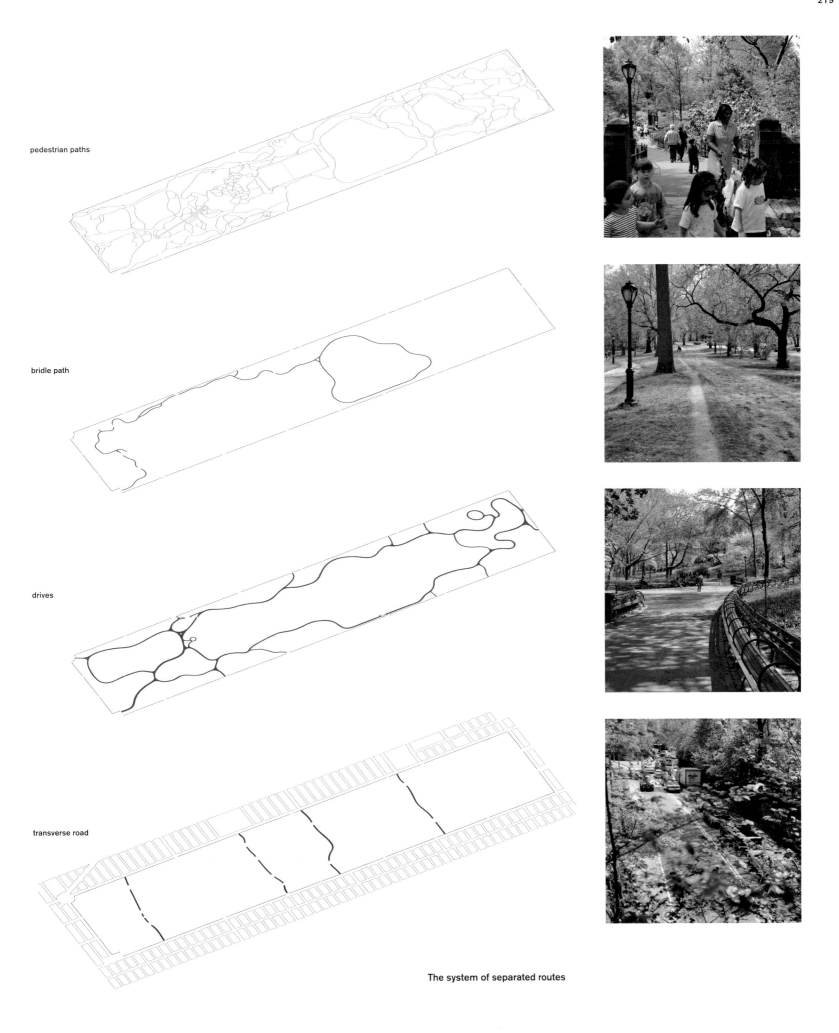

pedestrian paths

bridle path

drives

transverse road

The system of separated routes

Bridges at the intersections of park routes

The original park programme and subsequent alterations

→ Original programme

 promenade

carridge paths

bridle paths

 foot paths

 ice skating

 rowing

 model boat pond

'children's mountain' (playground)

music pavillion

zoo

 sports fields

→ → Alternations and additions

 jogging, bicycling, rollerskating

 jogging

bridle paths

 foot paths

 ice skating

 rowing

 model boat pond

 swimming

 playgrounds

M T museum, theatre

zoo

 sports facilities, incl. tennis and baseball

 garden

0   500   1000m

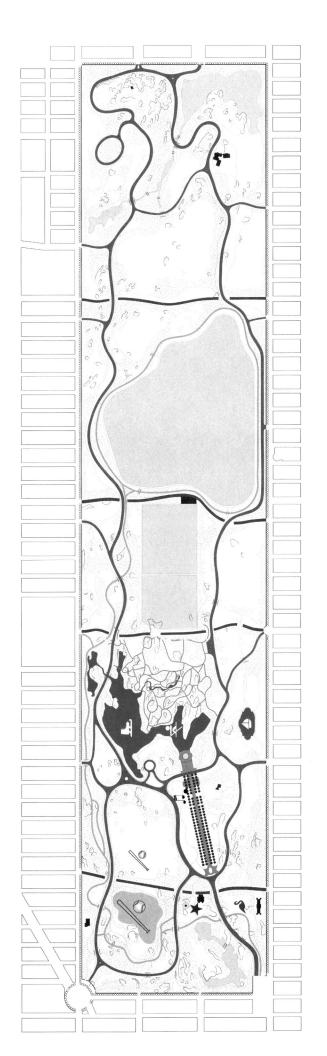

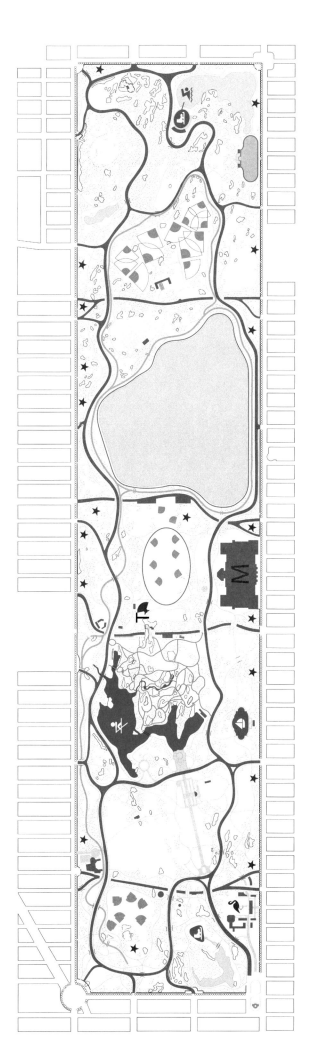

The perfection of the park as urban spatial type

In the Central Park envisioned by Olmsted and Vaux, being 'out of the city in the city' took on a new, democratic form. In Central Park, the evolution of the city park, which had begun with Regent's Park and ran on through Birkenhead Park, was carried forward and completed. The essence of the liberation of the city park as a separate landscape architectonic spatial type lay in the staging of the *topos* over against the dynamism of the city. The park placed the *longue durée* and the morphogenesis of nature over against the dynamism and changeability of the urban structure, and in so doing achieved its own content, form and meaning.

The democratisation of the programme

The architectonic backdrop of aristocratic urban living that constituted the urban street wall was dismantled. The urban grid, like Thomas Jefferson's plan for Washington, D.C., offers minimal preconditions that are the same for everyone. The egalitarian topography of the grid relativised the preference for sites and neutralised the architectonic form. This broke with the concept of the 'Theatrical Panorama' of Regent's Park and the English public park, in which the landscape and forms of urban building had been placed in tension to produce an architectonic entity. The only thing that still counted in Central Park was the landscape scenography of the park, which addressed the visitor directly.

In this process the city and the park came to stand diametrically opposed to each other. The form of the buildings in the city was more and more defined by the laws of functionality, efficiency, technology and building economics. This led to the development of the skyscraper as the building type that most fully exploited the potential of the urban grid. Over and against that stood the park. Olmsted spoke of an 'inner' and an 'outer' park. The outer park in fact was comprised of a green wall, that might be opened only if doing so did not disrupt the scenic illusion of the inner park. The mystery of the American landscape was preserved in the presence of the original geomorphology – rocks, vegetation, and water – in the inner park. The origins of the city in the landscape lay in the opulence of unspoilt nature. In the park, the city was reduced to its *topos*, its original natural form.

The Greensward Plan included almost no programme for active recreation. The design for Central Park had stretched the 'programmeless' strolling park, oriented to cultural interchange and the internalisation

The development of the park in the city

→ **The present density of the urban grid**

vacant blocks
blocks under 20% built up
blocks under 40% built up
blocks under 60% built up
blocks under 80% built up
blocks under 90% built up
blocks almost 100% built up

0   1   2.5km

→ → **Changes in the park after 1870**

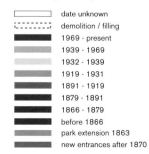

date unknown
demolition / filling
1969 - present
1939 - 1969
1932 - 1939
1919 - 1931
1891 - 1919
1879 - 1891
1866 - 1879
before 1866
park extension 1863
new entrances after 1870

0   500   1000m

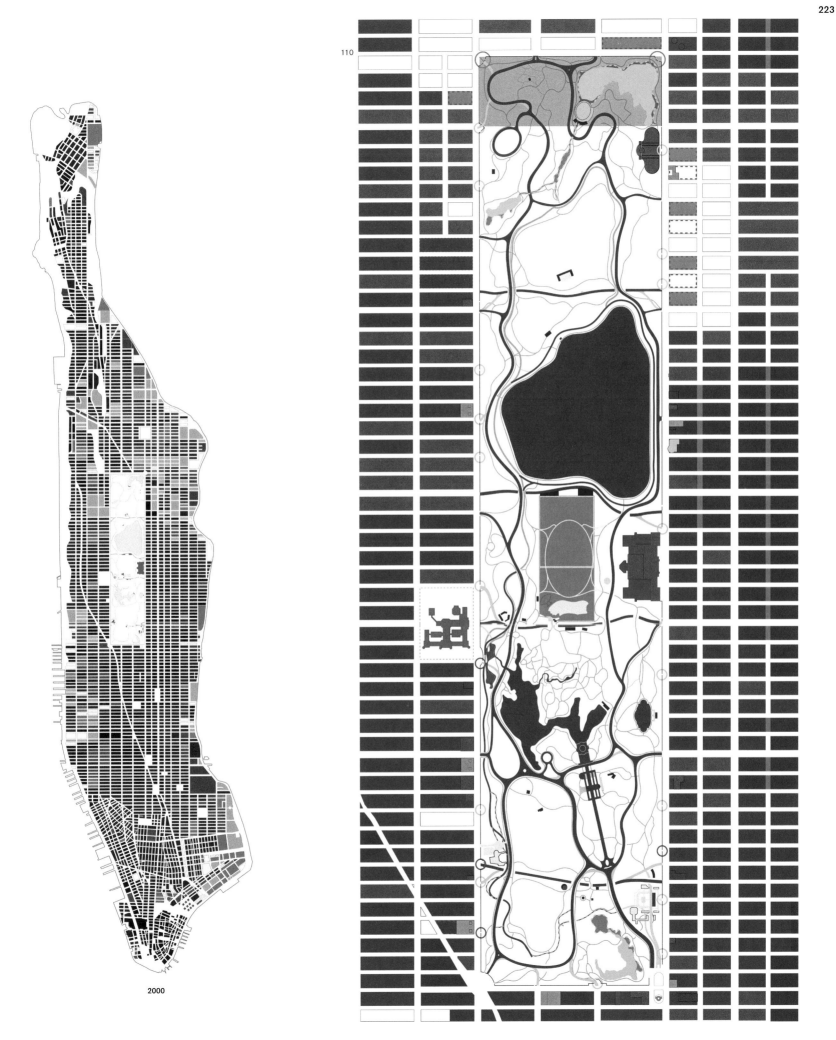

110

2000

of nature, to its maximum extent. Toward the end of the 19th century however demand arose for more recreational space in the park, and the drives were paved in connection with the arrival of the motor car. In 1926 a children's playground was opened, and the first playground equipment appeared, but for the rest the park began to take on a bedraggled aspect as a result of the neglect of the planting and general maintenance.

The appointment of Robert Moses as the Commissioner of a unified Department of Parks for all of New York in 1939 marked a turning point in this. Moses, who had designed the first parkways to Long Island and Jones Beach, implemented a vigorous policy of modernisation. In his view, the park should not be English or French, classic or romantic, but uncompromisingly American – and above all else that meant efficient and functional. He gave priority to recreational facilities over natural tableaux. Under his reign nineteen playgrounds appeared in the park, with sandboxes, baseball diamonds, handball courts and roller-skating rinks. He was also able to raise money for equipping special places, placing sculptures, and renovating buildings in the park and zoo. The old Croton Reservoir was cleared away and replaced by the Great Lawn. As a result of this expansion of its programme, the park became a part of everyday life in the city, more than it ever had before.

After 1960, following Moses' departure from the park commission, the park became increasingly overrun. Scores of urban facilities and public buildings appeared both inside and just outside the edges of the park, threatening to exceed the carrying capacity of Olmsted's composition. In 1980 Mayor Edward Koch announced the formation of the Central Park Conservancy, which in 1998 signed a management contract with the city, raised massive sums of money, and organised donors and volunteers from different parts of the city to restore the park to its former glory and continue to maintain it.

Swinging back the horizon

The unimaginable growth of the city, the anonymity of the urban wall and the dismantling of the classic architectonic form of the city have taken on considerably more dramatic aspects than Olmsted could have foreseen. Downtown Manhattan grew into a forest of skyscrapers. The development of high-rise buildings around the park altered the spatial and visual relation between the park and the city. Gradually views of striking buildings and ensembles from within the park itself became commonplace.

The visual relation between the park and Manhattan as a whole also changed. The highest buildings appeared at the south end of the island.

Buildings

1   Tavern on the Green
2   Site of Ballplayers' House
3   Carousel
4   Chess & Checkers House (former Kinderberg)
5   Dairy (Visitor centre and gift shop)
6   The Arsenal
7   Naumburg Bandshell
8   Kerbs Boathouse
9   Loeb Boathouse
10 Ladies' Pavillion
11 79th Street Yard
12 Swedish Cottage
13 Delacorte Theater
14 Belvedere Castle
15 Fire Alarm Station
16 Metropolitan Museum of Art
17 South Gate House
18 86th Street Shops
19 Tennis House
20 North Gate House
21 North Meadow Recreation Center
22 Lasker Rink and Pool
23 Blockhouse
24 Charles A. Dana Discovery Center

Bridges and arches

25 Greyshot Arch
26 Dalehead Arch
27 Pine Bank Arch
28 Dipway Arch
29 Site of Spur Rock Arch
30 Driprock Arch
31 Playmates Arch
32 Gapstow Bridge
33 Inscope Arch
34 Green Gap Arch
35 Denesmouth Arch
36 Willowdell Arch
37 Site of Marble Arch
38 Riftstone Arch
39 Bow Bridge
40 Trefoil Arch
41 Glade Arch
42 Ramble Arch
43 Bank Rock Bridge
44 Balcony Bridge
45 Eaglevale Arch
46 Winterdale Arch
47 Greywacke Arch
48 Southeast Reservoir Bridge
49 Southwest Reservoir Bridge
50 Claremont Arch
51 Gothic Bridge
52 Springbanks Arch
53 Glen Span
54 Huddlestone Arch
55 Mountcliff Arch

Park components

56 The Ball Ground
57 Heckscher Playground
58 Kinderberg
59 The Promontory
60 The Pond
61 East Green
62 The Mall
63 Sheep Meadow
64 Strawberry Fields
65 The Lake
66 Cherry Hill
67 The Terrace
68 Pilgrim Hill
69 Conservatory Water
70 The Glade
71 Cedar Hill
72 The Ramble
73 Vista Rock
74 Belvedere Lake
75 Summit Rock
76 The Great Lawn
77 The Reservoir
78 South Meadow
79 North Meadow
80 East Meadow
81 Conservatory Garden
82 The Mount
83 The Ravine
84 The Pool
85 Great Hill
86 The Cliff
87 Harlem Meer

The park in the city today: buildings, visual elements and park components

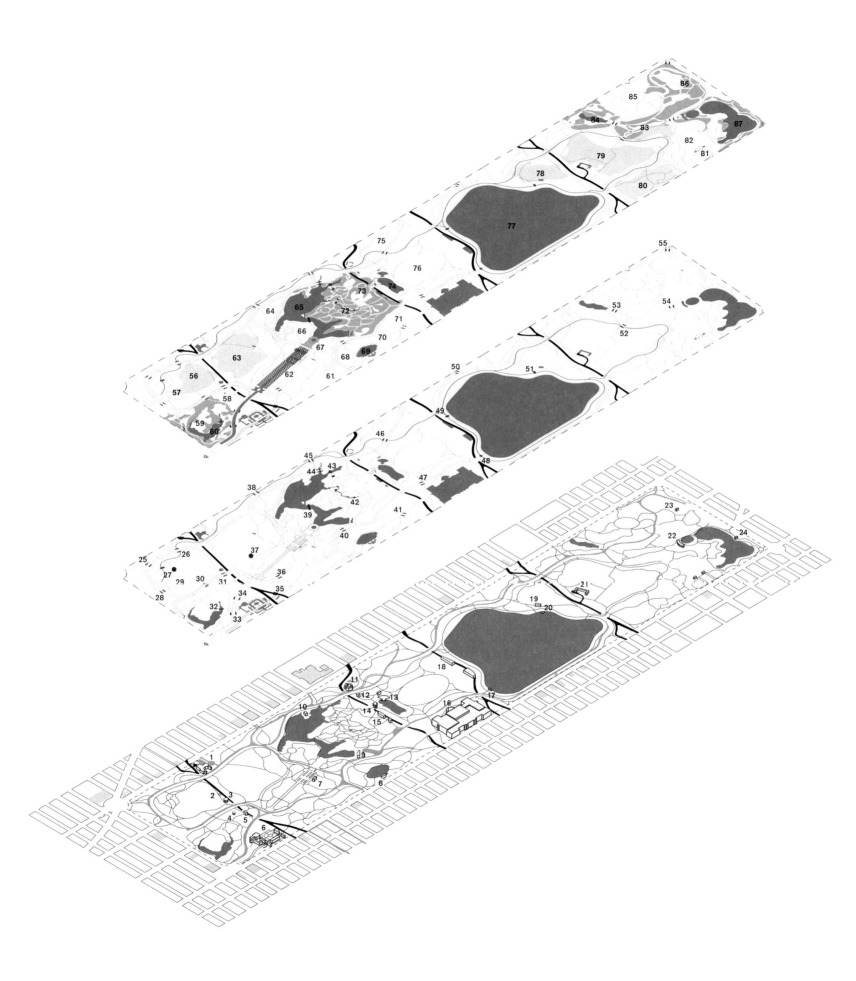

The natural relief in the park rises in the opposite direction, to the north. As a result of the growth of the skyscrapers to the south, the urban skyline increasingly became the opposite of the natural relief, and, quite differently than Olmsted could have suspected, the city appeared ever more prominently on the stage of the park.

The park became an urban *vide*, an open space around which the internal skyline of the city unrolled itself. This could be seen even from the heart of the 'wilderness', where the confrontation between the city and the landscape is most intense. Conversely, seen from the skyscrapers, Central Park is today nothing more than a foreground for the great urban water landscape of New York. But Central Park has survived this altered status, and accepted it into its form.

A print of the American landscape

After the completion of Central Park, Olmsted was involved in the design of various other parks in New York. Riverside Park, a long, narrow strip along the banks of the Hudson in the north-west of Manhattan, was intended as the beginning of a continuous landscaped treatment of the shores of the island. Because of its great elevation, Riverside Park afforded views out over the low-lying docks and rail lines to the vast panorama of the landscape of New Jersey lying behind them. Following Olmsted's train of thought, Riverside Park could be connected with Morningside Park, Central Park and the Manhattan Bridge over the East River by a park drive, and then onward to Prospect Park, and via Ocean Parkway even to the beach at Coney Island.

With the advent of the automobile, under Robert Moses this system took on a whole new dimension. It was elaborated into a network of parks and parkways, with playgrounds and open-air baths, that also embraced the shoreline and water's edge. The New Deal, the economic stimulus programme set up by president Roosevelt after 1932 to pull the country out of the Great Depression, expanded this urban system to encompass a nation-wide programme of national parks and parkways. In time, via the Hudson River Valley National Heritage Area, this system even penetrated Manhattan. In this modern, green network, the expressive power of Central Park, as a print of the American landscape in the heart of the metropolis, has remained as convincing as the design of the ideal city of Sforzinda was in the architectonically virgin landscape of Europe in its time.

5th Avenue, with the promenade along the edge of the park

→ **Significant buildings presently along the edges of the Central Park**

1	Time Warner Center	18	Cooper-Hewitt Museum
2	Former Gulf & Western Building	19	Church of the Heavenly Rest
3	The Century	20	National Academy of Design
4	Lutheran Church of the Holy Trinity	21	Guggenheim Museum
5	Congregation Shearith Israel	22	Metropolitan Museum of Art
6	The Majestic	23	The Frick Collection
7	The Dakota	24	Temple Emanu-El
8	The San Remo	25	Knickerbocker Club
9	Unitarian Universalist Church	26	Hotel Pierre
10	American Museum of Natural History	27	Metropolitan Club
11	The Beresford	28	Sherry Netherland Hotel
12	The Eldorado	29	General Motors Building
13	First Church of Christ Scientist	30	Plaza Hotel
14	Schomburg Apartments	31	Park Lane Hotel
15	Museum of the City of New York	32	Essex House
16	The Jewish Museum	33	NY Athletic Club
17	Convent of the Sacred Heart		

0   400   1000m

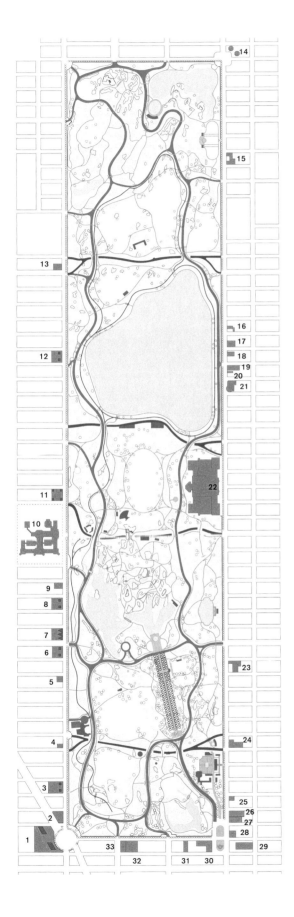

The illusion of wilderness in the metropolis

The park as metropolitan void (three-dimensional model, z = 10×)

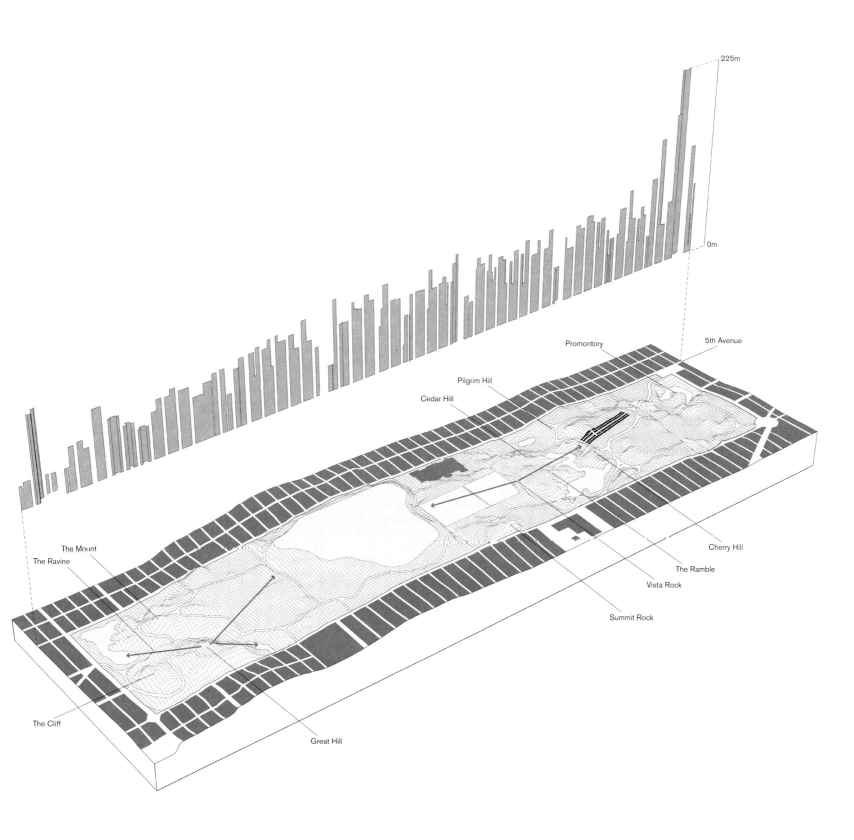

225m

0m

Promontory

5th Avenue

Pilgrim Hill

Cedar Hill

Cherry Hill

The Mount

The Ramble

The Ravine

Vista Rock

Summit Rock

The Cliff

Great Hill

The park relief and the metropolitan park wall (three-dimensional model, 1 cell of the grid measures 15 × 15 m, height of buildings and relief z = 5×)

EIXAMPLE
BARCELONA 1859

The topographic grid
Ildefons Cerdà i Sunyer
The grid design as hybrid form

Coastal plain and river delta

The topographic map as plan drawing
The Viles Noves
The 1855 topographic map
The first rough plan
The 1859 plan
Adaptations of 1863

The urban building kit
The orderly structure of the framework
The diagonals

The interplay between grid and topography
The geometric reduction of the topography
El Clot as a topographic enclave

The landscape architecture of the urban grid
Nature and the grid
The architectonic expression of grid and topography

View from the north-west over the Eixample, with the old city in the upper right
(aerial photo: LTCE / Getty Images 110437358)

The topographic grid

Cerdà's 1859 plan for the expansion of Barcelona, known as the 'Ensanche' or 'Eixample' (Spanish and Catalan, respectively, for 'expansion'), changed Barcelona from a compact city in the centre of a swarm of villages on the plain at the mouth of the Llobregat and Besòs rivers into a city based on a grid which embraced the entire plain and integrated the separate elements into one rational whole.

The industrialisation of the 19th century brought many immigrants to Barcelona, who could not be absorbed within the city's walls. The residential density in the old city rose alarmingly to 890 residents per hectare, as compared to, for instance, 350 in Paris and 380 in Madrid. People lived in six storey houses, while the widest street, the Carrer Ample, was not more than eight meters wide. The demolition of the walls of the old city presented Barcelona with the opportunity to formulate an expansion plan which would regulate its growth.

In 1854 the commission studying the expansion of Barcelona assigned Cerdà to make a map of the estuarial plain, where building had previously been prohibited for strategic reasons. He prepared an exceptionally detailed map of the city and its environs, the *Plano de los alrededores de la ciudad de Barcelona levantado por orden del gobierno para la formacion del Proyecto de Ensanche*. This map would be the point of departure for the expansion plan.

Ildefons Cerdà i Sunyer

Cerdà (1815-1876) was born in Centelles, a town in the north of Catalonia, about fifty kilometres north of Barcelona, not far from the Spanish-French border. He was the third son in a family of entrepreneurs who traded with the American colonies. In 1841 he completed his training as a civil engineer at the Escuela de Ingenieros de Caminos, Canales y Puertos in Madrid, a liberal school with many modern ideas.

In 1848 he settled in Barcelona, where he married. A sizeable inheritance after the death of his brother enabled him to develop his multiple interests and talents. He resigned from the civil service, entered politics, and began an intensive study of urban planning. He devoted the remainder of his life entirely to the design of a new urban plan for Barcelona. He died penniless in 1876, in Caldas de Besaya, near Santander, on the Bay of Biscay.

In 1854 Cerdà was appointed as civil engineer for the Treasury, and became a member of a commission tasked with the preparation of an expansion plan. At the same time we was writing a study entitled *Monografía de la clase obrera* (A Monograph on the Working Class), on the conditions under which the working class in the old city lived and worked. His conclusion was that the existing city was completely unfit for the new era of steam power, industrialisation, communication, transport and mobility. To his mind, these developments demanded a new type of city. Cerdà began to collect data and to organise his ideas, inspired by the American and French Revolutions. In 1867 this systematisation finally resulted in his *Teoría General de la Urbanización* (General Theory of Urbanisation).

The grid design as hybrid form

Cerdà sought the Enlightenment ideals of liberty, equality and fraternity in the 'egalitarian' city, for which a new balance between the city and the landscape also had to be found. "Make the urban rural, make the rural urban" was his motto. The ideal image which lay behind this was the free-standing house in the landscape. A grid plan was the basis for a city with homogeneous public space which could support a wide variety of different kinds of development. What was unusual in this was that his plan incorporated the existing towns and neighbouring communities, so that it was not only the city council of Barcelona that had to approve the proposals. The central government also had to act on them. After considerable wrangling, in 1860 the Spanish government gave the definitive go-ahead, though with several new instructions and conditions.

Realisation of the plan did not go smoothly. Land owners found the public amenities too lavish and were unwilling to bear the financial burden for creating them. There was also fierce criticism of the plan from the business world; there they believed it was monotonous. Cerdà defended himself by insisting that form and diversity would come with the architecture. Moreover, the plan created a divergent hybrid form, between the new structure of the city and the topography of the landscape. The existing topography was not only represented incidentally in the form of parks, but was also expressed in the design and elaboration of the grid itself. The forms of the city and landscape were united in a 'topographic matrix'.

Topography

	airport
	subway line
	railway line
	motorway
	tunnel
	important road

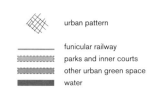

	urban pattern
	funicular railway
	parks and inner courts
	other urban green space
	water

Parks

1 Jardines de la Cuidadela
2 Parque de Montjuich
3 Parque del Clot
4 Parque Güell
5 Parque Joan Miró

Streets and squares

8   Avinguda Diagonal
9   Avinguda del Parallel
10 Avinguda Meridiana
11 Gran Via de les Corts Catalanes
12 Plaça d'Espanya
13 Plaça de les Glòries Catalanes

Rivers

6 Besòs
7 Llobregat

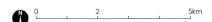

Coastal plain and river delta

Barcelona lies on the north-east coast of the Iberian peninsula, on the Mediterranean Sea. The city stands on a plateau about five kilometres wide and 20 kilometres long, sloping gradually toward the sea, and between the Llobregat River in the south and the Besòs River in the north. The lowest point, the beach at Pla de Palau, is five meters above sea level. The hills of the Serra de Collserola form the background, the highest point being the Tibaldo, with an elevation of 512 meters. This ridge of hills separates Barcelona from the plain of Vallès, and is part of the Catalan coastal zone, formed by two parallel mountain chains that were created by tectonic upheaval during the Palaeozoic era. The coastal plain on which the city is built includes innumerable lower hills which have given their names to the districts around them, including Carmel (267 meters), Monterols (121 meters), Putxet (181 meters), Rovira (261 meters) and Peira (133 meters). Montjuich (173 meters), on the southern edge of the old city, was once a fortress.

Barcelona was planted about in the middle of the plain between the two river deltas. Originally this plain was intersected by a large number of smaller streams which ran into a belt of swamps and lagoons along the coast, separated from the sea by a narrow row of sand dunes immediately along the shore. Rich in waterfowl, as early as the beginning of the 15th century these were a favourite hunting ground for Martín I, the last King of Aragon and Count of Barcelona. They were also, however, a hotbed for malaria. Midway through the 19th century the battle against malaria, which would remain endemic in Barcelona far into the 20th century, led to the the last swamps, such as El Clot, La Llacuna and El Cagalell, being filled in.

In the historic centre of the city, the relation between the streets and the former streams can still clearly be seen, for instance between the Rambla and the Torrent de Bargalló (formerly the Cagalell), the Via Laietana and the Torrent de Creu d'en Malla, and the Rambla de Raval with the Riera de Magòria. Somewhat less clear, but still readable, is the deformation of the grid pattern of the Eixample by the course of the river in the section between El Camp de l'Arpa del Clot and the old Icaria. The Carrer de Rogent, for example, follows the course of the Torrent de Bogatell.

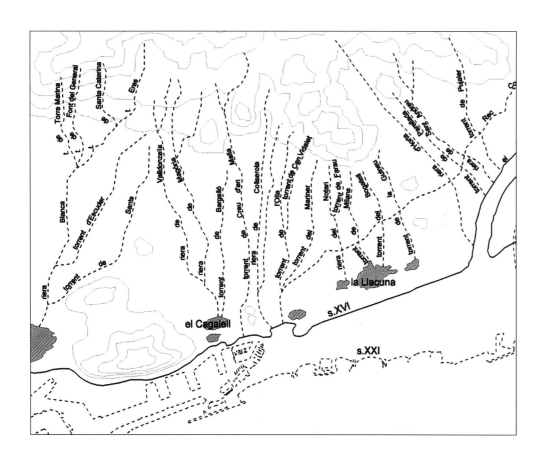

The streams formerly in the coastal plain (from J. Busquets, *Barcelona: the urban evolution of a compact city*. Rovereto 2005)

Geomorphology and urban domain

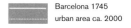

Barcelona 1745
urban area ca. 2000

N
0   20   40km

Geomorphology, urban pattern and parks

Elevation (metres)

480 - 560
400 - 480
360 - 400
320 - 360
280 - 320
240 - 280
200 - 240
180 - 200
160 - 180
140 - 160
120 - 140
100 - 120
80 - 100
60 - 80
40 - 60
20 - 40
0 - 20

urban pattern

park

water

Parque Güell, a balcony with views of the coastal plain

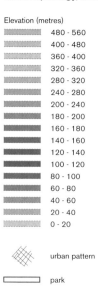

0   2   5km

The topographic map as plan drawing

There is evidence of human habitation on the hill of Montjuich for almost 10,000 years. In the fifth century BCE the first trading settlements developed. In the first century CE it became a Roman colony called Barcino. The hill was easily defended, but without drinking water or streams. (The district at the foot of the hill is known as Poble Sec, or 'dry town'.) For that reason the Romans chose a small, projecting hill crest on the north-east side of Montjuich, the Mons Taber, as the site for their fortifications. Later a modest provincial city appeared here, one of the many along the Via Augusta, the consular trading route that connected Rome, via the south coast of France, with Gerunda (Girona), Barcino (Barcelona), Tarraco (Tarragona), Saguntum (Sagunto), Valentia (Valencia), Carthago Nova (Cartagena) and Gadez (Cádiz).

Initially the Romans had only a slight interest in the place, because of its shallow harbour and distance from the consular route. Still, in consequence of its advantageous location on the coast, the settlement grew. In the third century CE its residents acquired the rights of Roman citizens, and it was renamed the *Civitas Julia Augusta Paterna Faventia Barcino*. To mark this momentous occasion, the fortifications were reinforced with towers and a moat, to protect the city against attacks by the Goths.

In the 9th century the city began to develop outside the walls. New parishes were founded, including Sant Andreu in Palomar, Sant Genis in Agudells and Sant Vincent in Sarrià. Barcelona's flowering was interrupted in 985, when Al-Mansur plundered the city and razed it to the ground during the caliphate of Córdoba (929-1031).

The Viles Noves

In the Middle Ages the old city wall was restored and a castle was built at each entrance gate in order to better defend the city. With this revival came the Viles Noves, new extensions outside the walls, such as Vila Nova de Mercandal, Vila Nova de Sant Cugat and Vila Nova del Mar (later Santa Maria del Mar). The most dynamic growth took place to the east of the old Roman city, by the harbour. In 1260, under James I (The Conqueror) a new city wall was built around the Viles Noves, about on the lines where the Citadel, the Carrer Santa Anna and the Rambla now run. The structure of this city was made up of an irregular pattern of long, continuous streets. Aside from the streets there was no public space; any squares were initially simply broader sections of the street. Here and there squares eventually appeared on the site of demolished buildings.

In the course of the 14th and 15th centuries, during the Catalan dynasty, a new urban structure arose. Until into the 15th century the Jewish neighbourhood was the cultural centre of Barcelona, an independent city with schools, hospitals, bathhouses, two synagogues and its own city gates. After the expulsion of the Jews in 1492 a new wall was begun to surround the western suburb of Raval, which was only completed with the construction of the Sea Wall under Charles V (1553-1563).

What later became the Rambla arose in the strip between the walls built by James I and the walled Raval. In the Middle Ages it was still a drain, which carried away the excess water from the Collserola during storms, and was known as the Cagalell (literally, sewer). The name Rambla – like Raval – comes from the Arabic, in which it means 'dry channel', while Raval means a 'market place and orchard'. The channel originally ran into a lagoon, one of the many along the coast of the Besòs delta. Some of the names of sections of Barcelona recall them, such as El Clot, an old Catalan word for an swamp, and La Llacuna. During the 16th century new monasteries were established here, which were involved in draining the swamps in the river plain.

The 1855 topographic map

During the first half of the 19th century discussions arose anew about the expansion of the city. In 1854 the walls around the Ciudad Vella were demolished, along with their 66 towers and ten entrance gates. At the same time Cerdà was assigned to prepare a topographic map of the vicinity of Barcelona, which could serve as a basis for an expansion plan that would include the whole coastal plain. This map was ready in 1855, and provides a picture of the underlying landscape, as it existed at the time. Two of Cerdà's previous designs, for a road that connected Sarrià with the centre and for a railway line to Granolles via El Clot, were also drawn in on it. The mapping was carried out on separate sheets, enabling the differences in elevation to be shown down to one meter. Each survey was repeated separately and checked by at least three technical experts. As a consequence, the map was exceptionally precise. The municipal authorities rewarded Cerdà for his work with a gold medal, in thanks for the services rendered. The 1859 plan which will be discussed below is the plan as it was approved; the project proposal from 1863 is a revised version of the same, based on the comments and suggestions of the advisory committee at the time of its approval. All three of the maps are cartographic masterpieces, drawn in colour on a scale of 1:5000.

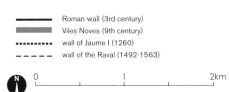

	Roman wall (3rd century)
	Viles Noves (9th century)
	wall of Jaume I (1260)
	wall of the Raval (1492-1563)

N 0   1   2km

The old city

Plaza Real, on the boundary between the old city and the Viles Noves

The first rough plan

Cerdà's topographic map of 1855 was accompanied by a rough plan on transparent paper that could be laid over the map so that one could see the effect of the plan on the topography. This transparent plan has been lost; the information that we have about it comes from a memorandum with accompanying drawings in which it is reported. The rough plan included an encompassing drainage canal at the foot of the mountains, which was also drawn onto the topographic map and retained in the 1859 plan. The canal was intended to protect the plain against flooding, and at the same time irrigate agricultural land on the edges of the newly built-up areas. From a budget proposal from the City Council, it appears that several important streets retained in the definitive plan were already included in the rough plan, such as the Meridiana, the Parallel, the Rambla de Catalunya and the Gran Via, which was to connect the harbour and the old city with the through road across the two river deltas, previously the consular Via Augusta, today the A7 motorway. It probably also included proposals for the basic urban block of the later plan.

The 1859 plan

The most important aspect of the new 1859 plan was the standardisation of the blocks of buildings and streets of the grid. The old city and the harbour were no longer the centre of the plan, to which all roads led, but were only a section of the new city. The historic axis between the sea and Gràcia, which had appeared in the rough plan of 1855, was replaced by the present Passeig de Sant Joan, a new central axis along the lines of the grid, now a tangent to the old city. The most obvious new detail was the Avinguda Diagonal, which was not oriented to the harbour, but to the Plaça de les Glòries Catalanes, the intersection of the Gran Via and the Meridiana.

Adaptations of 1863

The basic concept and the traffic structure remain unchanged in the revised plan of 1863. The urban blocks were however changed in response to the commentary and directions of the royal advisory council. The residential blocks might not be taller than 16 meters and had to be built at a greater density. That led to a differentiation in the buildings erected on the proposed blocks. One interesting aspect of the revised plan was that the railway lines cut through the larger parks. Cerdà wanted to 'domesticate the locomotive', as he put it, by integrating the rail connections into the urban grid, and thereby into urban life, rather than keeping them outside the city. Because Cerdà

used the topographic map as a sketch plan, in his plan the urban grid was directly confronted with the existing topography. This led to all sorts of topographic transformations and adaptations to the urban building kit, which were connected with the grid.

Beth Gali; El Fossar de la Pedrera. A quarry on Montjuich transformed into a cemetery

↗ **Cerdà's topographic map, 1855** (Cerdà, Ildefons. Plano de los alrededores de la ciudad de Barcelona. Copy from ca. 1861. Institut Cartogràfic de Catalunya, Mapes de Catalunya (s. XVII-XX), RM.267959)

→ **Cerdà's plan, 1859** (Plano de los alrededores de la cuidad de Barcelona y Proyecto de su Reforma y Ensanche : escala 1:5000 / El Ingeniero Ildefonso Cerdà-1859. Real Academia de Bellas Artes de San Fernando, Archivo-Biblioteca, Pl-6153)

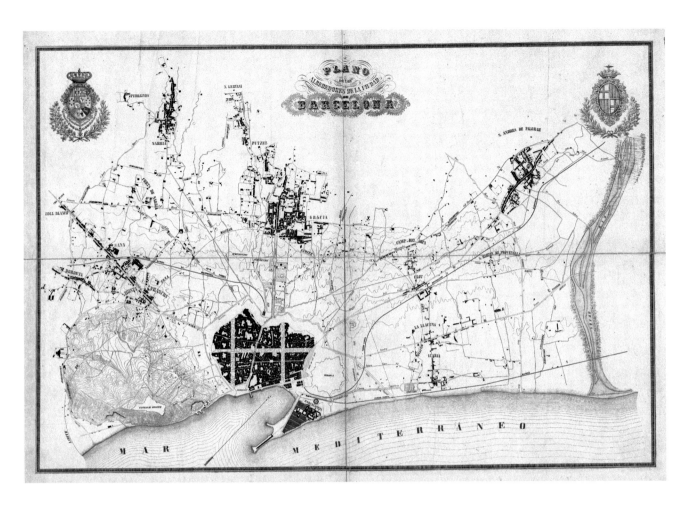

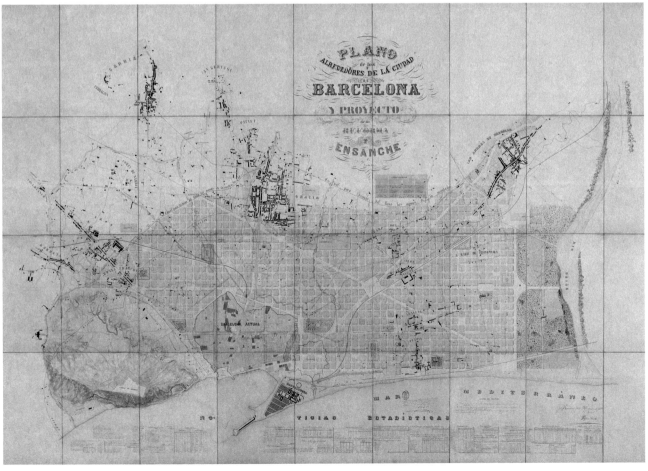

The urban building kit

In Cerdà's vision, the house, as the 'smallest city', was the starting point for the composition of the city as a whole. At the next level, he regarded the grid pattern as the most advantageous condition for an egalitarian and efficient city. In his 1859 project he was already focusing his attention on the development of an ideal model for the urban block and the street. The most most appropriate size for the individual module in the grid was derived from that, being 113 × 113 meters.

Traffic was likewise an important concern for Cerdà. Normal streets between the urban blocks were 20 meters wide. In addition to these, he designed streets 30 meters, and even 50 meters wide for heavy and intensive traffic. Cerdà divided the profile of the standard street up into a pedestrian section of 14 meters, with separate footways for porters, with a six meter carriageway in the middle for vehicular traffic. By cutting the corners of the blocks at an angle he created octagonal plazas at the intersections, which provided space for shops and public amenities. Clocks and fountains were to be placed at these social meeting points.

The orderly structure of the framework

If we simplify the grid as a design scheme and include the parks along the Besòs to the north in it, it comprises a huge rectangle of 70 × 20 modules. The central longitudinal axis, the Gran Via, touches Montjuich and the historic centre, while a number of the transverse axes subdivide it into 14 large squares of 10 × 10 modules. The Passeig de Sant Joan, which also touches the old city, is one of these transverse axes. They are emphasised by the particular morphology of the buildings on either side.

Two large squares, with 2 × 10 × 10 modules or urban blocks, were reserved for the parks along the Besòs, 12 × 10 × 10 modules were given over for building purposes. In this way the parks received their unique status within the orderly measurements of the urban grid. The modules which were intended for residential construction can be further subdivided into three districts of 4 × 10 × 10 modules, each with two district parks, a hospital and several governmental or commercial buildings. Each district was again subdivided into four sections of 10 × 10 modules, which each contained a market. Each of these sections was in turn subdivided into four neighbourhoods or *manzanas* of 5 × 5 urban blocks, with a church, school, pre-school and poorhouse. An ever varying arrangement of squares and public facilities gave each neighbourhood its own identity.

In Cerdà's design for the urban blocks, he did carefully fix the dimensions, but within the blocks the arrangement of the buildings was

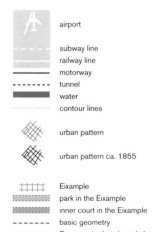

The geometry of Cerdà's plan in the topography

airport

subway line
railway line
motorway
tunnel
water
contour lines

urban pattern

urban pattern ca. 1855

Eixample
park in the Eixample
inner court in the Eixample
basic geometry
Roman axis (*cardo* and *decumanus*)
Dunkirk-Paris-Barcelona meridian

Towns, ca. 1855
1   historic city
2   harbour
3   Icaria
4   El Clot
5   San Andreu
6   Gràcia
7   Sarrià
8   Sans

N   0   2   5km

left unspecified. Apartment blocks could be a maximum of 16 meters tall and 20 meters deep. Only two sides of the block could be built on, in connection with admitting light and fresh air. The residential blocks could be built parallel with one another, or in an L-shape or U-shape. In the centre always lay a large, open interior space. In the 1859 plan the dwellings were all arranged parallel, so that the public space in the blocks ran through freely from one to the next. Cerdà saw the urban blocks as wholly open, as a condition for a 'green' city.

The diagonals

This openness was further enhanced by a number of important diagonal axes in the grid. The most significant, the Meridiana and the Parallel, which cut through the grid at a 45° angle, already appeared in Cerdà's first rough plan of 1855. The third axis, the Diagonal, which appeared in the 1859 plan, cuts through the grid at an angle of about 30° and with its intersection with the Meridiana fixes the site of the Plaça de les Glòries Catalanes as the central junction in the new city. The Meridiana, the Parallel and the Diagonal became the through arteries and were intended to provide structure for the whole plan and guarantee the coherence with the region around it. In this sense the geometric model of the Eixample was a synthesis of two different urban patterns, the grid and the radial pattern.

The square is the perfect form of equality, and has no particular architectonic effects. Therefore the grid, in combination with the diagonals, allows the different subdivisions, right down to the level of the residential block, to be in harmony with the through arteries, without the internal coherence of the plan being lost. Like an infinite flowchart that can adapt to changing circumstances and which permits a compromise to be found between the scale of the city and that of any particular spot, it gave the urban building kit the characteristic of an autonomous framework.

Parque del Clot, the diagonal pedestrian route transecting the park hill and connecting the edges

→ View of the old city and harbour from Plaça Catalunya

The interplay between grid and topography

The grid also has a dimension that relates to the landscape, and generally reflects the topography. Longitudinally the streets and avenues run parallel to the sea and the mountains, following the contour lines. In principle, the transverse streets run parallel to the many streams and creeks that cut across the contour lines on their way to the sea. They therefore have an optimal orientation for the sun and the sea breezes. The diagonals connect the deltas of the two rivers with each other crosswise. Moreover, Cerdà projected his grid in such a way that it connected all the settlements on the plain with one another: Barcelona and Icaria along the coast, La Bordeta and Sans in the south, Sarrià, Gràcia and San Andreu in the west, and Badalona in the north. With the two large park squares the Besòs landscape was also given a place in the grid.

The geometric reduction of the topography

A free-hand sketch that Cerdà included in his 1859 *Teoría de la construcción de las ciudades aplicada al projecto de reforma y enscanche de Barcelona* reveals his first ideas about the links among the towns around Barcelona. From it, it would appear that it was initially his intention to construct a network of triangles that could connect all the towns with each other and at the same time with the expansion of Barcelona. Its centre lay near the harbour and the historic heart of the city. In this pattern the Meridiana and the Parallel were already present in rudimentary form. They were intended to connect the plain with the El Vallès corridor along the river valleys of the Llobregat and the Besòs, where at one time the Roman Via Augusta had run. This scheme of connections was taken over almost unchanged in the plan, albeit that the two longitudinal axes – the central axis that links Bordeta with Badalona across El Clot, and the axis along the rim that links Sans, Gràcia and San Andreu – do not run entirely parallel with each other. In the grid plan of 1859 the central longitudinal axis no longer coincides with the *intervia* that connects Bordeta with Badalona. The axis along the western edge of the grid does not touch San Andreu, and Sarrià falls outside it. Nevertheless, the first sketch contributed to the definitive geometric system, in particular with regard to the importance of the diagonals.

The Avinguda del Parallel was possibly the first radial line that Cerdà drew, by extending the existing Carrer de Sants. The second important axis that he involved in his considerations was perhaps the Roman *decumanus*, presently the Carrer Ciutat and Carrer del Bisbe. Cerdà plotted the Meridiana at right angles to the Parallel from the notional point where this axis intersected the latter. It is interesting that Cerdà derived this name from the Meridian of Paris, which runs through Barcelona. The meridian was measured by Méchain and Delambre in 1789 for the French Assembly as a reference for a universal metric system, which had been adopted in Spain only in 1855. The bisector of the right angle between the Meridiana and the Parallel basically corresponds to the *decumanus* of the Roman settlement. In this sense one could say that Cerdà's grid followed the Roman colonisation grid, as if the Romans then already knew the direction of the 'healthy breeze' that Cerdà describes in the commentary accompanying his 1855 plan. Using the Meridiana as a pure diagonal, one could then plot the ideal line for the central longitudinal axis, the Gran Via, the centre line of the plain, which touches Montjuich and the old city too. Apparently Cerdà drew in the transverse axes to distinguish the districts from one another from the point where the Meridiana and the Gran Via intersect. It is unclear whether the Passeig de Sant Joan touches the historic centre by chance, or whether it was on the other hand definitive for the ideal block measurement of 113 × 113 meters.

In a certain sense the Diagonal was also already present in Cerdà's original scheme of connections, in the form of the link between Sarrià and Gràcia. With the Plaça de les Glòries Catalanes as the central junction, the Diagonal, running obliquely through the geometry of the grid, denoted the extent of the landscape of the new city between the deltas of the Llobregat and the Besòs. What viewed superficially appears to be an abstract geometric model, was in reality a design that took the geomorphology and topography of the region into account.

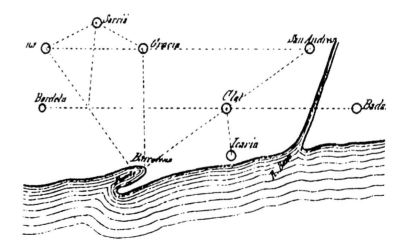

Schematic drawing of the lines connecting the towns around Barcelona (Teoría de la construcción de las ciudades aplicada al proyecto de reforma y ensanche de Barcelona. Barcelona, 1859. Archivo General de la Administración (AGA). Uit: Busquets, J., *Barcelona: the urban evolution of a compact city*. Rovereto 2005)

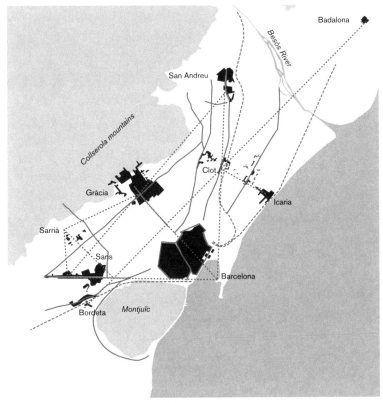

1. Potential connections in the existing topography

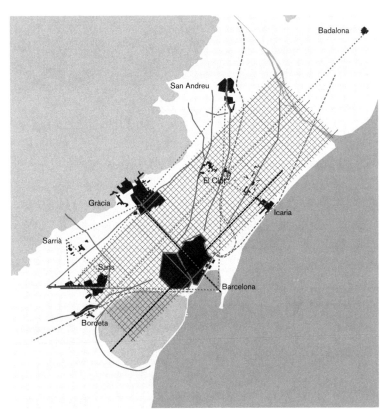

2. Connections and the grid

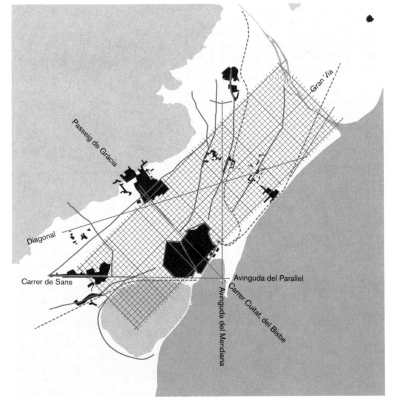

3. Resulting radials and the grid

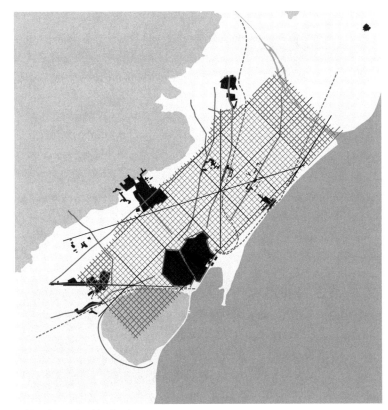

4. Adaptations to the grid at the edges

The situation of the urban grid in the topography

The grid itself adapted to these conditions by expanding and contracting along the edges, so that it breaks loose from the rigid geometry of the districts, without losing its logical coherence.

The way the grid adapts to include the existing towns is also interesting. Some existing towns along the edges of the grid were merged into it, but some of the towns in the middle of the expansion plan, such as La Llacuna and San Martin de Provencals, were more or less erased. Only at El Clot and Icaria were several existing roads worked into the plan, such as the Carrer del Clot, as well as the Carrer Pere IV and the Carrer Marià Aguiló. Half of San Andreu de Palomar was absorbed into the grid. A space between six urban blocks was left empty around Camp de l'Arpa. The Barcelona-Granolles and Barcelona-Martorell railway lines, which were a derivative of the old topography, were included in the grid by an anomalous design for the urban blocks. The same was the case for the road between Barcelona and Gràcia in the mountains, which required an adjustment to a whole series of blocks.

El Clot as a topographic enclave

The development of the town of El Clot and its environs is an example of the way in which the grid collided with topographic reality. The natural landscape slopes gently toward the sea. The rail line and the station at El Clot lie at the bottom of the slope, and follow the orientation of the contour lines and the old town structure. The old arterial roads from Barcelona to the north, still recognisable in the Carrer del Clot and Carrer de Ribes, in fact have the same orientation as the railway line. Cerdà's grid, on the other hand, is oriented to the coast line and at an angle with the roads and rail line. The historic heart of El Clot is wedged between the Avinguda Meridiana and the Gran Via de les Corts Catalanes; the present Parque del Clot is the connection between them. The narrow streets in the old town centre differ strikingly from the roads in Cerdà's grid, and cut through the urban pattern. With its own topographic logic, the town has expanded around its historic core, and is only partially integrated into the grid.

If one crosses the Avinguda Meridiana heading west, one enters El Camp de l'Arpa del Clot, another district that clearly diverges from the pattern through its own morphology. On three sides the area is defined by old roads, which prior to 1855 linked the northern part of the old centre of Barcelona and the core of the town of El Clot with the town of San Andreu de Palomar. Not only do the boundaries betray the old pattern, but the urban morphology here has also developed entirely according to the old topography, for instance, to the north of the Carrer

de la Muntanya, where the street pattern runs parallel to or at right angles to the slope. All the roads, and the buildings along them, more or less follow the course of one of several small rivers that drained the area toward the sea.

In his 1859 plan Cerdà did not seek to achieve a detailed adaptation to the existing topography. The only existing urban elements that he drew into his plan were the Carrer del Clot and the station along the railway line that connected the centre of Barcelona with Granolles. In contrast to that, the buildings along the Carrer de Freser were ignored. Cerdà was very well aware that such thickly built-up areas would create a complex design problem, but offered no solutions to it. Rather than doing so, he left the space around it free, as he did at the train station, or he made such an area part of an undefined 'macro-block', as in the case of El Camp de l'Arpa del Clot. As a consequence, these places could maintain themselves within the grid, and develop, as striking topographic enclaves.

Adaptations to the topography in Cerdà's original plan (above) and in the current urban grid (below)

Towns ca. 1855

1	Bordeta
2	Sans
3	Coll Blanch
4	Corts de Sarrià
5	Sarrià
6	San Gervasi
7	Putxet
8	Gràcia
9	Camp de l'Arpa del Clot
10	El Clot
11	La Llacuna
12	Icaria
13	San Martin de Provencals
14	San Andreu de Palomar
15	Barceloneta

---------- contour line

water

road

------------ railway line

Cerdà's grid, 1859

topography ca. 1855 (above), current topography (below)

existing urban pattern ca. 1855

Roman city

Adaptations to the topography

adaptations to the existing pattern
other adjustments
expansion of the grid

0　　　　　1　　　　2km

El Clot, the Cerdà plan (1859)

	urban morphology in the Cerdà plan	a	Carrer del Clot
	existing built-up areas ca. 1855	b	railway station
		c	Carrer de Freser
		d	El Camp de l'Arpa del Clot

El Clot

| | present urban morphology |

El Clot: the Cerdà plan projected on the present urban morphology

	present urban morphology
	urban morphology in the Cerdà plan
	existing built-up areas ca. 1855

El Clot as a topographic exception in Cerdà's grid

El Clot, the present urban morphology and the earlier topography

| | present urban morphology |
| | existing built-up areas ca. 1855 |

0   500   1000m

Detail of El Clot as a topographic exception in the Cerdà grid

Existing topography ca. 1855

- - - - contour line
water
buildings
street
railway line

Present urban pattern

present Cerdà grid
adaptations to the topography
other adjustments

Passeig de Maragall

Carrer de Freser

Carrer de las Navas de Tolosa

Carrer de la Muntanya

Avinguda Meridiana

Carrer de Bofarull

Carrer dels Enamprats

Carrer de Rogent

Carrer del Clot

Carrer dels Escultors Claperós

Carrer de la Verneda

Carrer de Ribes

Carrer de Sant Joan de Malta

The landscape architecture of the urban grid

If we compare the 1859 plan with the situation today, we find that in practice many more deformations of the grid have occurred as a result of local circumstances. The structure of the grid is robust, but the towns are still recognisable as exceptions to its regularity. The old pattern of roads, pre-dating 1855, has been preserved in it, and locally has even become a bearer for the urban morphology. From the perspective of urban planning, the expansion plan has unified Barcelona and the towns scattered around it, by taking up the larger structure of the landscape as the point of departure for the grid. The lines in the grid follow the main lines of the topography of the plain between the river deltas, the mountains and the sea, so that it has assumed the elementary logic of the landscape itself. The old landscape has not lost out to the abstraction of the grid and the unpacking of the urban building kit, but as *genius loci* has achieved a place in the urban order in various ways.

Nature and the grid

It is a remarkable paradox that the green inner courts and parks that Cerdà provided for in his plan played no significant role in this relation between the grid and the landscape. The present garden courtyards were created by slum clearance and the redevelopment of courtyards which had been filled with buildings. Today they form 'hidden landscapes', often not visible from the street. Around 1995 the municipal authorities of Barcelona launched a plan to 'revitalise' the Eixample, in which the redevelopment of the degraded inner courtyards was a part. Like a belated echo of Cerdà's original ideal of a continuous green space, in the future every resident will be able to wander in natural surroundings within 200 meters of his house.

Nor did much come of the parks Cerdà proposed within the grid. Without a topographic basis in the landscape they apparently could not hold their own. The Ciutadella park lies on the site of the earlier military citadel, which now contains the parliament building, zoo and various museums. With its 203 hectares, Montjuich, likewise an enclave anchored in the landscape, is presently Barcelona's largest park, comprised of various thematic, historical and urban components, directly adjoining with the city centre.

In the early years of the 20th century Parque Güell (Güell Park), designed by Antonio Gaudí and Josep Maria Jujol i Gibert, was created on the northern edge of the grid, on Carmel hill in the district of Gràcia, in the Collserola. It has views out over the whole of Barcelona and the bay. When Count Eusebi Güell conceived the plan of building a house in this area, it was because of the healthy air and magnificent views that Montaña Pelada afforded. The park itself was originally intended as a garden city. Count Güell extended the commission to Gaudí for its design in 1900. Gaudí responded with a 'magic garden' built up of terraces, a wonderful interweaving of nature and architecture achieved as the distinctions between them dissolved amid its pergolas growing out of rocks, dramatically landscaped stairs and undulating terraces. Equally striking are the market under the square, the entrance with the gatekeeper's house, the colonnade with slanting columns, the double stairs with the Salamander (also known as the Dragon), and the enormous, undulating balcony and sitting area with mosaics by Jujol. The garden city was never realised; as a public park, Parque Güell has been on the UNESCO World Heritage List since 1984.

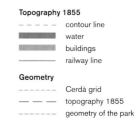

Parque del Clot, topography and geometry

Topography 1855
- – – – – contour line
- ▬▬▬▬ water
- ▬▬▬▬ buildings
- ──── railway line

Geometry
- ─ ─ ─ ─ Cerdà grid
- ── ── topography 1855
- - - - - - geometry of the park

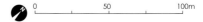

0　　　　　50　　　　　100m

Parque del Clot, design by Daniel Freixes and Vicente Miranda, 1985
(from: Hans van Dijk, 'Stedelijke theaters: De continuïteit van het Barcelonese experiment',
in: ARCHIS, November 1989)

Beginning in the 1980s many areas with disused buildings that had lost their function have been refitted as urban parks, like the Parque Joan Miró, built in 1983 on the site of Barcelona's old municipal slaughterhouse, and the Parque del Clot, constructed in 1986. For the Parque Joan Miró the abstract urban grid and the natural differences in elevation were taken as points of departure and adapted and refined in the landscape architectonic design. On the other hand, in the Parque del Clot it was precisely the topographic exception in the grid that was the starting point for the design.

The architectonic expression of grid and topography

The Parque del Clot was designed by Daniel Freixes and Vicente Miranda on the site of the station that was built at El Clot in 1858. The park follows the contours of the old town's buildings and the railway line, which are both oriented to the old topography. Where it links up with the outer edges of the surrounding urban structure, this orientation is confronted with the orientation of the grid. The spatial transition between the lines of the grid and the original town was once again raised for consideration by the design. The park separates itself from its surroundings, and in defining its limits adds a new dimension to the spatial confrontation between the topography and the grid. Two diagonals, oriented to an old factory chimney, cut through the park and restore the broken connection between the earlier running lines and the surrounding urban morphology. Internally, the park combines urban and rural elements. The most important urban element is the centrally located, sunken plaza, suitable for various activities. The most important element from the landscape is an otherwise bald grassy hill, with a *bosco* on it. The plaza functions as an urban theatre, which in terms of both form and materialisation is set off against the vegetation and the hill. Remnants of the factory along the edge, including a wall with arches, enhanced by various water features, are incorporated into the composition.

The architectonically active components of the city and landscape are 'anatomised', as it were, and employed anew as visual elements in a composition on a scale that is within the visitor's faculty for perception. Because of this, the confrontation between the grid of the city and the landscape becomes timeless. This is worked out emblematically on a smaller scale in the labyrinth which was designed. In this way the park provides an architectonic expression at several levels for the already long-slumbering confrontation between the grid and the original topography of the landscape, between then and now. Via an antithesis, the two spatial categories, city and landscape, enter into a synthesis that bears within itself the characteristics of both. To be sure, the urban grid of the Eixample as a whole has taken over characteristics of the landscape, but as the mediator between the city and the landscape it has ultimately attained a landscape architectonic form only in the design of this park.

Factory buildings transformed into a patio in the northern corner of the Parque del Clot

Parque del Clot, diagonals in the park as mirror images of the diagonals in the urban grid

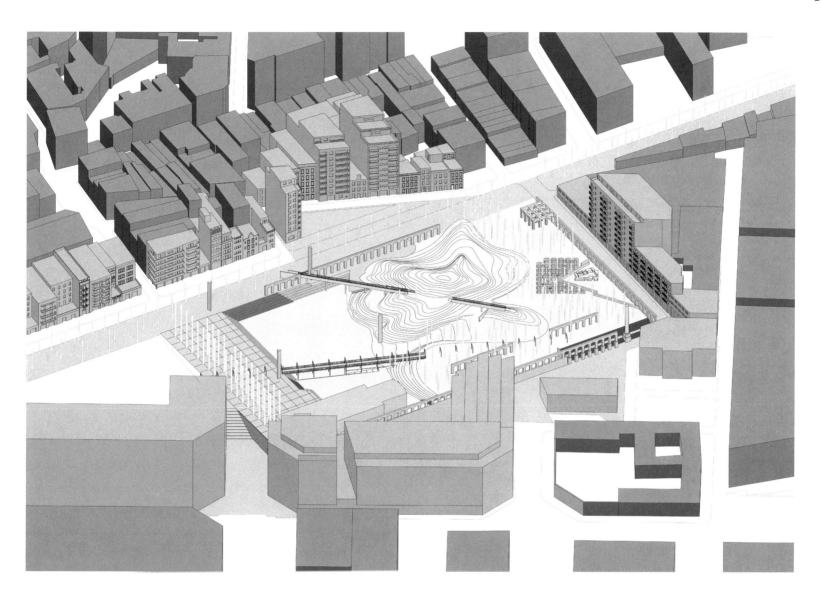

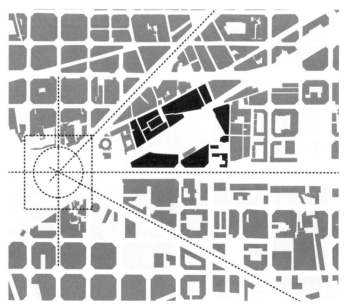

Parque del Clot, the spatial transition between the park, the old topography and the urban grid. The zone along the edge of the park adds a new dimension to this

Parque del Clot, the labyrinth in the park as emblem and reproduction of the urban pattern

VONDELPARK AMSTERDAM 1865

The agricultural landscape as an urban pattern
The Zochers
From agricultural polder to urban spatial form

The polder landscape
The peat polder landscape

The urban transformation of the peat polder
A city at the dam
The ring canals
A city of streets in the peat polders

Three phases of the 'free extension' into the peat polder
A modest beginning, 1865
The expansion of the park between 1867 and 1872
The expansion of 1877

The omphalos of the peat polder city
The height of the streets
The park is beheaded

The modulation of the peat parcel
Polder technology
Winding lowland forms
A sober spatial form
A Dutch carriage and pedestrian park

The polder park
Stage-managing the agricultural landscape
A model for the polder metropolis

The Vondelpark (aerial photo: Marco van Middelkoop, Aerophoto-Schiphol)

The agricultural landscape as an urban pattern

Around 1830 Amsterdam began to feel the need for a park where the upper middle-class citizens could escape from the bustle of the city, to stroll and refresh themselves in mind and spirit. This was further fed by the success of the strolling paths which Haarlem and Utrecht for instance had laid out on the site of their demolished city walls, which had not only given these cities a new look but also added a new dimension to recreation for the city's residents. The first plans for a new park were made by the lawyer F.A. van Hall, later a government minister, but were never realised.

In 1863 Christiaan Pieter van Eeghen (1816-1889), the director of the Nederlandsche Bank and philanthropist, announced a plan for the construction of a park in the Binnendijkse Buitenveldertse polder. A year later the Vereeniging tot Aanleg van een Rij- en Wandelpark te Amsterdam (Association for the Construction of a Carriage and Pedestrian Park in Amsterdam) was founded in the city hall on the Oudezijds Voorburgwal, with eight active members. A number of parcels of land in the peat polders to the south-west of Amsterdam, just outside what were then the city limits, were to be purchased for the construction of the park. The park was to counterbalance the unrestrained growth of the 19th century city. It was conceived not only with an eye to general public health, but also as a backdrop for a planned suburban residential development for wealthy Amsterdammers and new cultural amenities.

The low-lying park of about 45 hectares represented the low, flat and watery peat polder landscape around Amsterdam, a typically Dutch landscape which had been reclaimed over the centuries and developed into a polder landscape with a finely calculated system of agricultural parcellation and water management. These characteristic peat polders were transformed into a strolling park and refashioned into an urban nature idyll by landscape architectonic means. The design tools were borrowed from the English landscape parks and the way these had been transformed into public parks. The combination of the Dutch polder form and English landscape art created a new Low Lands variant of the 19th century city park.

The Zochers

The park was designed by the landscape architects Jan David Zocher and his son Louis Paul, who had developed a peculiarly Dutch landscape style. The Zocher family, originally from Saxony, produced three generations of architects and garden architects, respectively the father Johann David Zocher, Sr. (1763-1817), his son Johan David

Topography

parks
1   Amstelpark
2   Amsterdamse Bos
3   Artis
4   Baanakkerspark
5   Beatrixpark
6   Bijlmerpark
7   Bijlmerweide
8   Bilderdijkpark
9   Buiksloterbreekpark
10   Christoffel Plantijngrachtpark
11   Darwinplantsoen
12   Diemerbos
13   Diemerpark
14   Eendrachtspark
15   Erasmuspark
16   Flevopark
17   Frankendaal
18   Frederik Hendrikplantsoen
19   Frederiksplein
20   Gaasperpark
21   Gerbrandypark
22   Geuzenbos
23   Gijsbrecht van Aemstelpark
24   Hortus
25   Jachthavenweg
26   Jan de Louterpad
27   Kasterleepark
28   Martin Luther Kingpark
29   Museumplein
30   Noorderpark
31   Oosterpark
32   Park De Kuil
33   Prins Bernhardpark
34   Rembrandtpark
35   Sarphatipark
36   Schellingwouderbreek
37   Siegerpark
38   Sloterpark
39   Stadspark Osdorp
40   Vondelpark
41   W.H. Vliegenbos
42   Wertheimpark
43   Westerpark

water
44   Amstel
45   IJ
46   IJ-meer

airport

railway line

motorway

tunnel

important road

    urban pattern

    park

other urban green space

water

Zocher, Jr. (1791-1870), and grandson Louis Paul Zocher (1820-1915). Johann David Zocher, Sr. had come to The Netherlands from Strasbourg with his parents around 1780, where he had been apprenticed to Johann Georg Michaël (1738-1800), and married his daughter. Like Michaël, he was an architect and nurseryman.

The Zochers regarded themselves first and foremost as architects. In 1807 Johann David Zocher, Sr. was appointed as court architect by Louis Napoleon, and worked on the gardens of Huis ten Bosch, Soestdijk Palace and Amelisweerd. In 1809 his son, Johan David Zocher, Jr., won the Prix de Paris, which had been created by King Louis Napoleon. This allowed him to study in Paris at the École des Beaux Arts, and later also in Rome. In conjunction with this he also visited England, where he established contacts with professional colleagues. In 1838 he became a member of the Royal Institute of British Architects, an exceptional honour for a foreigner.

The family lived in Haarlem; in 1817 Johan David Zocher, Jr. settled on the site of his father's abandoned nursery Rozenhagen, outside the Kennemerpoort. The majority of the works by Zochers are also to be found in the vicinity of Haarlem. As the designer of Vondelpark and the Commodity Exchange in Amsterdam, Johan David Zocher, Jr. is the best known of the three. He worked together with his son Louis Paul from about 1850 until his death in 1870 at the Vondelpark. His architectonic training comes through clearly in his garden and park plans. They are characterised by their lucid spatial division and logical, well thought-out structure. The planting is compact, using a limited variety of species. The influence of Lancelot 'Capability' Brown (1716-1783), the most celebrated landscape architect of his time, is perhaps recognisable in this. Flowers and blooming shrubs are used sparingly, placed against a background of closed groups of trees. According to Leonard Springer, Zocher also often consulted *De la composition des paysages*, written by the Marquis de Girardin, who designed Ermenonville, in 1777.

From agricultural polder to urban spatial form

The park was realised in phases, in each of which the back boundary was extended further to the south-west, until the park ultimately ran from the Singel to the Kostverloren Vaart, the old inland limit of the peat bog reclamation begun from the Amstel River. In this way the park reaffirmed the centuries-old relationship between Amsterdam's urban landscape and the surrounding landscape of polders reclaimed from the peat bog, which were gradually included in the urban pattern of Amsterdam in various processes. The Vondelpark marks the moment when the peat polder parcel, as an elementary building block for the agricultural landscape, began to define the basic form of urban space. It is a point of reference in the development of the spatial forms which link the city of Amsterdam with its peat matrix and the *genius loci* of the Low Lands, making it a polder city.

The large pond as a prolongation of the P.C. Hooftstraat

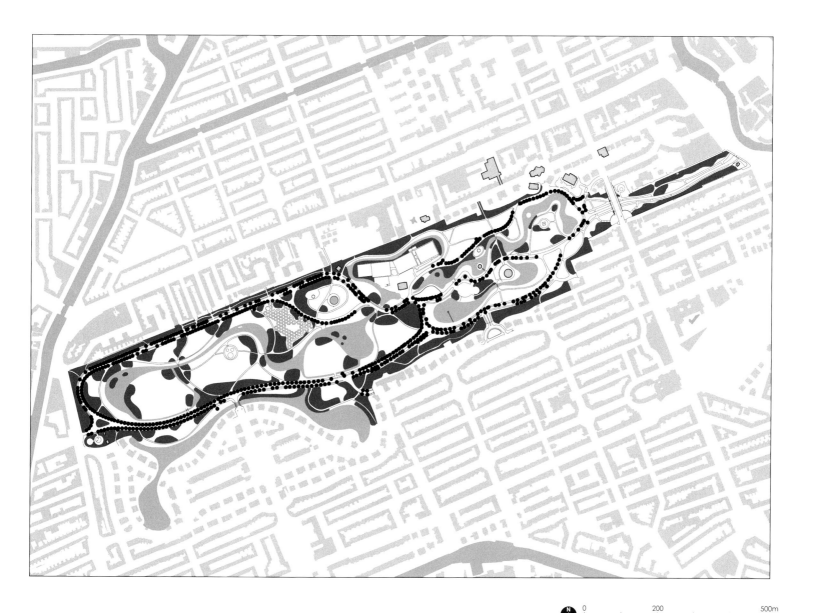

The present plan of the Vondelpark

The polder landscape

The landscape of the Dutch Low Lands was created by the dynamics of water, the most important creative energy behind the pattern of sand, clay and peat bogs which comprises the natural landscape. The dynamic of the water however also formed a threat for its inhabitants, so that they had to protect themselves against it. The paradox of the polder is that precisely these necessary protective measures hindered the natural drainage of the water and created a water management problem, which ultimately led to the characteristic mosaic of the polder landscape.

The first important formative force for the Dutch Low Lands was the sea, which with its masses of water also proved the most dynamic. With the rising sea level of the Holocene epoch, the sea, with its wave energy, tidal effects and currents, transported and regrouped material from the sea floor and sediments delivered by the rivers, creating the coastal landscape of the Low Lands, zoned by beach ridges. A second formative force, operating more regularly, was the supply of rain and meltwater from the hinterland by the river system of the delta, the most important of the streams being the Rhine and the Maas. In its lower reaches this river system flows through a sedimental plain, with little drop. Here, on the average, sedimentation is greater than erosion, so that the rivers branch into various – and often varying – channel belts. A third, still more subtle formative force was the standing water of the swamps. Here it was not the dynamics, but precisely the stagnation and the seeping, gradual drainage of the rain water which created the conditions for the emergence of the peat bogs.

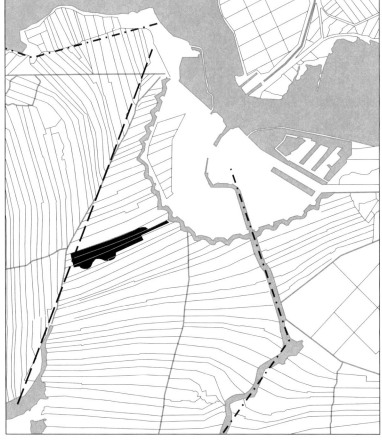

base for the reclamation (Amstel, IJdijk)

back dike (Kostverlorenkade)

peat parcel drainage ditches

drained polder or sand fill (Amsterdam centre)

The Vondelpark in the peat polder parcellation

Geomorphology and urban domain

Amsterdam ca. 1850
urban area ca. 2000

polders higher than 1 m above NAP
polders -0.5 - 1 m NAP
polders -2.5 - -0.5 m NAP
polders deeper than -2.5 m below NAP

N   0   20   40km

The peat polder landscape

The peat polder landscape emerged after about 800 CE from the reclamation of the wild peat bogs which had developed behind the beach ridges throughout what are today the provinces of North and South Holland and even further. It had branches in the river landscape and, with the exception of the estuaries and rivers, encompassed almost the entire delta. The drainage caused the peat to sink. The peat reclamations became polders, with artificial drainage systems, comprised of a very complex system of watercourses, dams, dikes, windmills to pump the water, and sluices.

The IJ separated the two parts of Holland, each of which came to form independent hydraulic entities. To the north of the IJ lay Zaanland and Waterland. Zaanland was comprised of peat islands, surrounded by dike rings, within which smaller peat polders lay. Waterland, to the north-east of Amsterdam, was an extensive peat region, intersected by bog streamlets and surrounded by the Waterland Dike Ring. Many of the lakes in the Waterland, such as the Buikslotermeer, Broekermeer and Belmermeer were drained. The Buikslotermeer lies today entirely within the city limits of Amsterdam. To the south of the IJ the reclamation landscape is comprised of various polder complexes, larger landscape entities containing different polders, often from various historical periods, but with a common geomorphological background and reclamation history. The Haarlemmermeer complex includes the Haarlemmermeerpolder, a large 19th century drained lake, surrounded by smaller lake bed polders and peat polders. More to the south-east lies Amstelland, on either side of the Amstel River. Here drained lake bed polders such as the Watergraafsmeer and the Bijlmermeer are to be found, and larger peat polders like the Rondehoep and the peat lakes and polders of the Ronde Venen.

The Vondelpark lies in the Binnendijkse Buitenveldertse polder, a peat polder that belongs to the Haarlemmermeer complex. The parcellation of this peat reclamation stretched from the Amstel in the east to the Kostverloren Vaart and the Schinkel in the west. A cluster of parcels of more than 1000 meters in length along the Overtoomse Vaart formed the base for the future park in the matrix of the peat polder.

The staging of the agricultural landscape in Vondelpark

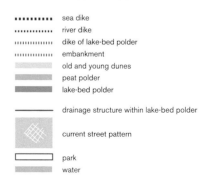

Geomorphology, urban pattern and parks

- sea dike
- river dike
- dike of lake-bed polder
- embankment
- old and young dunes
- peat polder
- lake-bed polder
- drainage structure within lake-bed polder
- current street pattern
- park
- water

The urban transformation of the peat polder

In the development of Amsterdam the urban transformation of the peat polder landscape always went hand in hand with the formation of a new urban morphology. The physical properties and spatial characteristics of the peat polder landscape played an important role in this process. On the basis of the differences in these transformations one could theoretically distinguish the different phases, each with its peculiar relation to the original peat polder landscape. The dam across the Amstel was the first step in the regulation of the water management in the peat lands. Like the lake bed drainage projects, the ideal scheme of the 17th century canal city broke the pattern of the peat polders which had the peat parcel as their basic module. The streets and urban blocks of the 19th century city followed the peat parcellation in a more pragmatic way.

A city at the dam

Amsterdam appeared around 1200 at the spot where the Amstel, then a peat bog rivulet, discharged into the IJ. The city was still limited in size, but had a strategic location in relation to a potentially rich hinterland. The first buildings arose along the banks of the Amstel. The sea dike along the IJ curved inland at the Amstel, where the bog river was cut off from the open IJ with a dam. This dam shifted the mouth of the river inland, as it were, thus forming a natural harbour where goods could be transshipped from seagoing vessels to boats plying the river. The city around the river's mouth, which had previously had an open connection with the tidal channels of the IJ, thus gained a controlled water regime, initially still based on natural drainage.

During the Middle Ages the peat region in the vicinity of the city was reclaimed. As a result of its drainage the peat soil subsided, and the inhabitants of the area encountered increasing problems from the surrounding water. In the 13th century they began to build dike rings around the sinking peat landscape and to dam the estuaries of other nearby rivers. The pattern of the reclamations was defined by the comb structure of the drainage ditches, running at right angles to the main direction of the river, at their far end connected by a watercourse running across the back of the peat parcel. Immediately along the Amstel the parcellation curved along with the bends in the river. The city expanded in phases onto the strips of land between the Amstel and the drainage ditch at the back of the parcels, parallel to the river. The peat polder parcellation was thereby transformed into a system of ditches,

alleys and streets at right angles to the watercourses. Trade, storage and transport developed along the watercourses, while dwellings, stores and workshops sprang up along the secondary network of streets. This pattern was based on the direct interpretation and subdivision of the pattern of the original peat polders. The drainage function of the Amstel was taken over by two new watercourses parallel with the river, which connected the Binnen-Amstel with the IJ by means of outlet sluices in the dike. In a technical sense the urban area became a polder system, like the surrounding peat polders. The dam, dikes and artificial drainage defined the form of the city, which fit into the peat polder. The existing landscape pattern of ditches, avenues and paths was absorbed into the built-up area, with gardens, orchards, yards with planting and inner courtyards.

The ring canals

After the end of the 16th century Amsterdam developed into an international trading metropolis. This necessitated a major, planned expansion of the city, with easy access by water as a central condition. In 1609 the city fathers approved plans to expand the city and provide it with new fortifications. The city surveyor Lucas Sinck laid out the plan on the ground. In phases an orderly pattern of new canals was dug around the old city and the ground level raised above the maximum water level in the *boezem* with sand from the dunes and the Gooi. Here the rich merchants established themselves, with their warehouses. The water level in the canals was the same as that in the Amstel; the Buitensingel, like the ring canal around a lake bed polder, was the transition between the city, with its canals, and the surrounding peat landscape. The water level within the city was controlled with the aid of windmills and sluices. The city fathers required that the regional water board, the Hoogheemraadschap Amstelland, not raise the *boezem* level, which was the same as that of the surrounding agricultural polders, above a certain maximum, to prevent flooding in the city. The tidal fluctuations on the IJ, which was connected with the North Sea via the Zuiderzee, were exploited for flushing out the canals.

The rational plan of the 17th century ring canals broke through the existing peat parcellation. An ideal plan was projected onto the landscape, which, in its rationality, shows similarities with the plans of 17th century North Holland lake bed polders. Within the city, all of the original peat polders except those in the Jordaan were entirely re-parcellated. A culture of urban gardens developed, particularly on the ring canals. Planting appeared in public spaces, and an intensive country life developed, in which wealthy urbanites built country homes

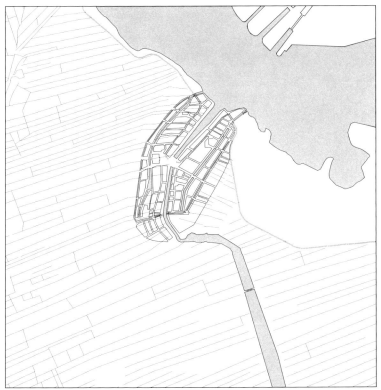

The city at the dam

The canal city

The peat polder city

The lake-bed polder city

Stages in the urban transformation of the peat polder landscape

in the wider environs of the city, along the peat rivers and the edges of the inner dunes, often conjoined with new reclamation projects such as lake bed polders. In parts of the ring canals that were still undeveloped special kinds of public gardens appeared, such as the estates and pleasure gardens in the Plantage. Country homes, pleasure gardens and a squash court appeared in the new lake bed polders closer to the city, such as the Diemermeer (Watergraafsmeer). The Buitensingel, along the Schans, was planted with a double row of trees. Here one could stroll for an hour or so, enjoying a world of contrasts and interesting scenes. On the one side one saw the city with its towers, surrounded by imposing gates and bulwarks topped with windmills, and with its planting, regular but still each section with its own character. On the other side was the peat meadow landscape with its small canals, paths and many industrial windmills, farms, summer homes and market gardens.

A city of streets in the peat polders

In the last quarter of the 19th century, when industrialisation got off the ground, Amsterdam began to burst its 17th century seams. The first dwellings already started appearing outside the Buitensingel around 1860, without any sort of urban expansion plan. Windmills, existing cottages and gardens were cleared away and the drainage ditches filled in. In their place came new streets. At first this still involved the building of separate houses; later whole blocks of tenements followed. In a couple of decades the relatively open environs, outside the city as delineated by the Buitensingel, changed into a building site without a clear boundary, overrunning the landscape.

In 1866 the city council instructed the city engineer J.G. van Niftrik to prepare an Expansion Plan. This plan, submitted in 1867, included an imposing belt of squares, public gardens, residential neighbourhoods and public parks outside the Singel. The Vondelpark was an important link in this, flanked by an extensive residential development. It was also exceptional for its length, extending far outside the width of the belt, a sort of forward post thrust into the peat landscape. But the city council rejected the plan because they thought it too ambitious, and because they did not have the legal means at their disposal to expropriate the land and impose their will on private builders. In 1877 a considerably more pragmatic expansion plan by the Director of Public Works, J. Kalff, was accepted. This plan followed the existing peat polder parcellation as closely as possible, because this considerably simplified the acquisition of land for building by project developers. At its outer edges the pattern of city blocks and streets ended randomly, without a clear

limit. It did create a uniform pattern of closed urban blocks, streets and cross streets, bounded by lines of infrastructure. Within it there was space left open for small parks, such as Sarphatipark (1886) and the Oosterpark (1891). Westerpark (1890) was created in the space left over between the sharp edges of the 17th century infrastructure and the new railway lines.

The Vondelpark assumes a special place in the 19th century urban expansion primarily because it arose out of a private initiative and the land was acquired even before there was a plan drawn up for the area. Given the relationship between its width and length, Vondelpark spans the whole depth of the urban expansion into the peat polders and therefore belongs to the basic pattern of the 19th century city. Within it the park received a landscape architectonic expression which sought the greatest possible contrast with the morphology of the streets, squares and urban blocks around it. This collective project of wealthy individuals, for whom the experience of nature was reserved, was as it were a new phase in the reclamation of the peat landscape.

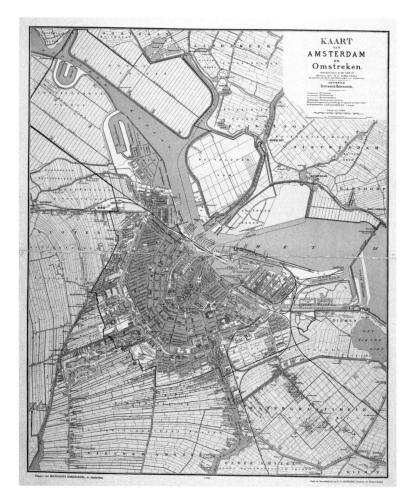

The Vondelpark as an outpost in the peat polder landscape (Kaart van Amsterdam en Omstreken (Seyffardt's Boekhandel, Amsterdam 1881). Stadsarchief Amsterdam, bestandsnr. 01003520006353)

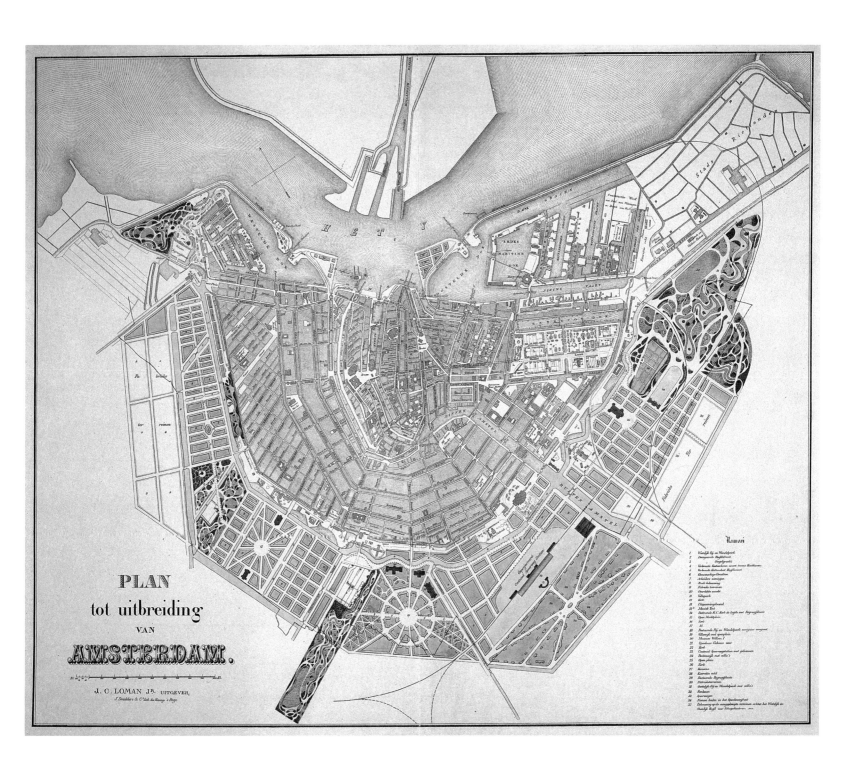

J.G. van Niftrik, Plan for the expansion of Amsterdam, 1867 (Stadsarchief Amsterdam, toegangsnr. 10035)

Three phases of the 'free extension' into the peat polder

The plans to build Vondelpark were in part prompted by the sale of the city-owned gardens in the Plantage. Until the construction of Vondelpark the Plantage, with the Hortus Botanicus (1632) and Artis (1838), was the prime section of the city for sauntering and sitting, seeing and being seen. As early as the 17th century the Plantage had been divided into fifteen privately held gardens with avenues between them, which could not be built upon, so that this pattern was long maintained. In the 19th century many pubs and theatres opened there, so that the neighbourhood also became a site for night life. In 1858 the city sold off the gardens and rescinded the ban on building in the Plantage. With that the only place left for strolling and entertainment within the 17th century walls disappeared.

In 1863 Van Eeghen entered the scene with his plan for a new park. The choice of its location seems to have been determined by the availability of several parcels of land in the Binnendijkse Buitenveldertse polder, just outside the Singelgracht, between the Zandpad and the Schapenburgerpad. Perhaps the foliage of the Leidsebosje and the gardens of the De Hereeniging clubhouse, Eyerhoven, Tivoli and Malta, already present nearby, suggested the possibility of further similar use and even expansion, particularly as a location for building. There were also country homes on the Amstelveenseweg. And there were still further advantages connected with the location. Those living along the ring canals could reach the park without having to cross a lower-class neighbourhood like the Jordaan. In 1864 Samuel Sarphati tried to have his Paleis van Volksvlijt linked to the proposed Carriage and Pedestrian Park by a boulevard. The city fathers however turned down the idea.

A modest beginning, 1865

The Park Commission entered into a contract with the garden architects J.D. Zocher, Jr. and his son L.P. Zocher. From the very beginning it was the intention that the park would extend to the Amstelveenseweg, but the construction would take place in a number of phases. In 1865 the first ten hectares of the park were laid out after gifts were received from 938 donors. The members of the Vereeniging themselves contributed a third of the money needed. About eight of the ten hectares were bought from the industrialists Stumpff and Von Baumhauer, who had let their concession for the construction of a gasworks run out. Between 1862 and 1922 the Parks Commission published a biannual report on the progress of the project.

In the first phase the park reached to the Kruitwetering, a drainage canal at the Kattenlaan, on which a steam pumping station was placed. The pump had a capacity of two horsepower, and pumped water in the ponds to a depth of 8 to 9 palms (with the introduction of the metric system in 1820, the equivalent of ten centimetres, thus a total of 80 to 90 centimetres) under ground level. The capacity of the pump proved to be insufficient, so that it had to be replaced. The bushes and trees were supplied by the Zochers' Rozenhagen nursery, at Haarlem. The firm of J.D. Zocher and Voorhelm Schneevoogt, at Sassenheim, supplied the flowers and bulbs. On 15 June, 1865, the New Park, as it was called, then still only a half parcel deep and only five parcels wide at some points, opened to the public.

A map of the first part of the construction drawn by P.H. Witkamp is included in the Park Commission's reports. The parcels which were to be acquired for the expansion of the park are also indicated on it. Because the park lay largely in the adjoining town of Nieuwer Amstel, on 19th century maps of the city it was generally drawn in only as far as the Amsterdam city line. Sometimes, as a place of interest, it was shown in its entirety as an insert, albeit rather inaccurately. The map which accompanied the Kalff plan of 1881 offered an early rendering of the section in Amsterdam.

The expansion of the park between 1867 and 1872

In 1867 the park was expanded by another six hectares after the collection of 120,000 guilders, which provided for the construction of a flower garden beyond the extension of Vondelstraat and a meadow with a dairy. The parcels acquired once again reached to the Kruitwetering. In the same year a statue of the poet Joost van den Vondel (1587-1679) by the sculptor Louis Royer was erected, arranged by the Vondel Committee, of which P.J.H. Cuypers was a member. The Park Commission gave the land to the city, which in exchange paid for the foundation. Cuypers designed the pedestal. J.D. Zocher, Jr., died in 1870.

In 1872 a new collection was held for a further expansion of 16 hectares. Because the proceeds, at 130,000 guilders, fell short of expectations, the Park Commission began to speculate with land. They purchased pasture land outside the park and resold it for building purposes, for instance on the P.C. Hooftstraat. This was opened in 1872-1873, at which time the plans were tested against the urban plans of Van Niftrik and Kalff. As a result of this transaction the park gained a good entrance from the P.C. Hooftstraat. Initially the Commission wanted to build ten villas in the park along an extension of the P.C. Hooftstraat, on land in the town of Nieuwer Amstel.

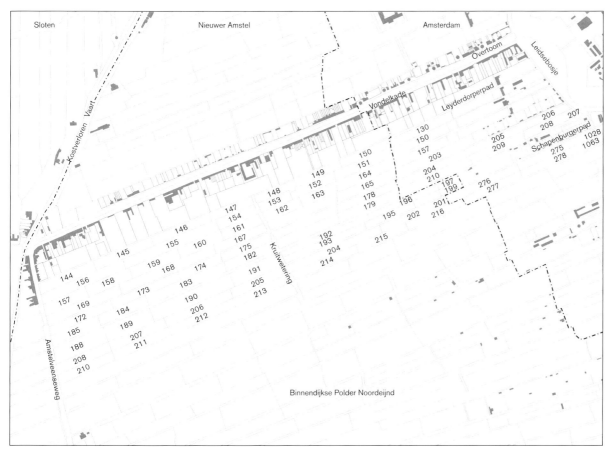

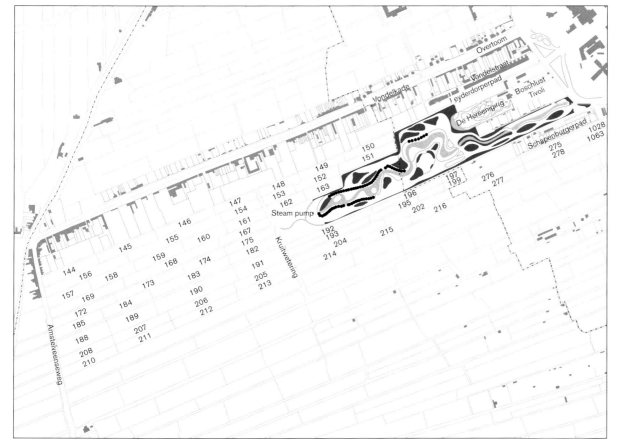

The Binnendijkse polder Noordeijnd, 1820. The Vondelpark and the P.C. Hooftstraat
were laid out on the numbered parcels

The genesis of the park in 1866, after Witkamp and Kalff

The expansion of 1877

In 1877 Vondelpark was extended from the Kruitwetering to the Amstelveenseweg. Work on filling in the Kruitwetering had begun already in 1876. A rough sketch of this extension made by L.P. Zocher has been preserved. This part of the park had a somewhat coarser structure, with meadows and lanes. It also necessitated the construction of a third pumping station of six horsepower, in an annex to the park superintendent's house on the Kattenlaan. In 1880 the Carriage and Pedestrian Park was renamed the Vondelpark.

The final phase in the development of the Vondelpark was ushered in by the realisation of L.P. Zocher's 1876 *Plan van bebouwing der landerijen naast het Vondelpark* (Plan for constlruction on the estates adjoining the Vondelpark, i.e., the Willemspark neighbourhood). It was ready for construction to begin in 1883, but sales of the lots proved difficult. It would be decades before the site would be built up entirely. The present course of the streets, with the flowing curves of the Koninginneweg, corresponds roughly with Zocher's design. In the same way that agricultural settlers had pushed steadily further into the wild peat bogs, the park was unrolled ever deeper into the peat polder. After the expansion of 1877 the park comprised a cluster of twelve parcels, two of which extended the whole length between the Singelgracht and the Amstelveenseweg.

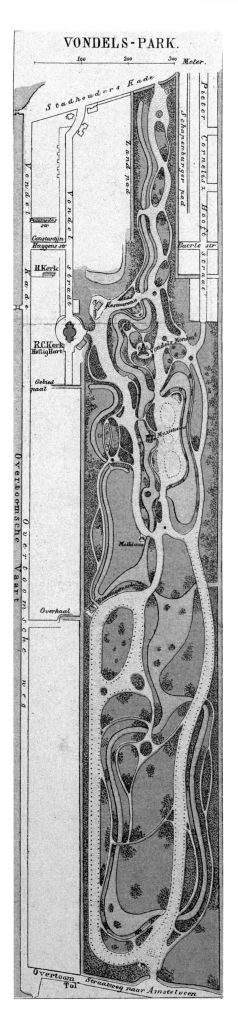

The Vondelpark as an insert in a general map of Amsterdam, 1877. A drainage ditch still runs along the side of the Van Eeghenstraat. The Vondelstraat ends at another drainage ditch, and there is a facililty for winching boats over the dike near the Kattenlaan
(A. Braakensiek, Amsterdam 1877. Stadsarchief Amsterdam,Kok collection, nr. 535)

The 1872 expansion, with the large pond following the line of the P.C. Hooftstraat
(source: Kalff Plan, 1881)

The 1877 expansion to the Amstelveensche Weg (after Scheltema)

The omphalos of the peat polder city

The Vondelpark and many of the streets around it were realised together. Civic leaders in Amsterdam lived in fear of their wealthy citizens fleeing the city – a concern made all the more real by the development of the railways. Luxury homes along the park could tie the more affluent to the city. The Park Commission gained partial control over the building on the streets around the park by acquiring the land around it, more than was necessary for the construction of the park itself. The eventual sale of this land was accompanied by covenants, for instance requiring sewers or banning pubs or the construction of workers' dwellings or factories. The profits from this land speculation were invested in the park.

The height of the streets

The Park Commission was very keen on keeping the level of the surrounding streets low, to obtain the best connections for the park, such as from the Zandpad. But with an eye to hygiene and preventing wet cellars, the Amsterdam building code prevented a low level for the Vossiustraat. The Vossiusstraat therefore makes a small jog; numbers 1-15 together form a lower lying ensemble, previously designed by the architect Isaac Gosschalk.

The streets on the south side of the park in Nieuwer Amstel, among them the Van Eeghenstraat and in the Willemspark neighbourhood, were laid out at lower levels, because the rules in Nieuwer Amstel were less strict. The Park Commission had no influence over the buildings and small streets between the park and the Overtoom, to the west of the Vondelstraat. There were many small factories there, and they swarmed with vagabonds. For many years the Commission was able to prevent the opening of any entrances to the Vondelpark from these streets. Until the opening of the fence at the Gerard Brandstraat in 1905, the Kattenlaan was the westernmost entrance on that side. The result was that the section of the park toward the Overtoom took on the character of a 'back end' while, with its monumental entrances, the side toward the Willemspark, where the buildings descended into the hollow of the polder, became the 'front entrance' from that exclusive urban domain.

The Vondelstraat thanks its existence to the architect P.J.H. Cuypers and his associates. In 1865 Cuypers moved from Roermond to Amsterdam on the advice of Alberdingk Thijm and Viollet-le-Duc. After its renovation, he moved into a former inn, the Nabij Buiten, near the Leidse Poort, at Tesselschadestraat number 31, on the corner of the Vondelstraat (replaced in 1884 by a new house designed by his son).

A park with a tea garden that Cuypers called the Leyerhoven belonged to it.

In 1866 Cuypers and N. Redeker Bisdom asked permission from the city to lay out a 15 meter wide street from the Singelgracht along the Leyderdorperpad. They were supported by others, who had previously submitted a building plan for the Vondelstraat. The city assented In 1867. The north side received row houses, while on the south side, on the Leiderdorperpad, free-standing homes with views of the park arose. In the same year Cuypers and Van der Biesen obtained permission to extend the Vondelstraat to the city boundary with Nieuwer Amstel, at the Anna Vondelstraat. The Vondelkerk was dedicated in 1873 and completed in 1876. Cuypers designed the Nieuw Leyerhoven for himself, at Vondelstraat 73-75, opposite the Vondelkerk, where he moved in 1878. Here the park received a second entrance, which lined up with a bridge over the Overtoom.

The park is beheaded

Van Niftrik's plan, like the later Kalff plan, provided for a circumferential road around the city centre, which was to be called the Ceintuurbaan over its whole length. When Cuypers and his associates received permission to lay out the Vondelstraat in 1866, there was one condition imposed: at the point where the future Ceintuurbaan was to cross their street, a gap of 30 ells (a Dutch el was equal to 68 centimetres) must be left, in which no brick building could be erected. As early as 1872 the Constantijn Huygensstraat (now the Eerste Constantijn Huygensstraat) was laid out along this route between the Overtoom and the Vondelstraat.

Very much against the will of Van Niftrik, beginning in 1878 the Vossiusstraat was built in phases. He had hoped to be able to expropriate, raise and reorganise all the land between Vondelstraat and P.C. Hooftstraat, including this as part of Vondelpark. It would have been a outstanding opportunity to add the gardens of the De Hereeniging club, among others, to the Vondelpark, as Samuel Sarphati had probably already planned to do when he purchased the Tivoli and De Hereeniging gardens in 1865. After Sarphati's death in 1866 Cuypers and Redeker Bisdom went through with the plan for the Vossiusstraat. With the construction of Tesselschadestraat and Roemer Visscherstraat the widening of the narrow part of Vondelpark was definitely out of the question. Cuypers and Redeker Bisdom wanted to fill the Leyerhoven, De Hereeniging and Tivoli gardens with free-standing homes. The Roemer Visscherstraat also had to have a gap of 30 ells at the point where it would intersect with the Ceintuurbaan.

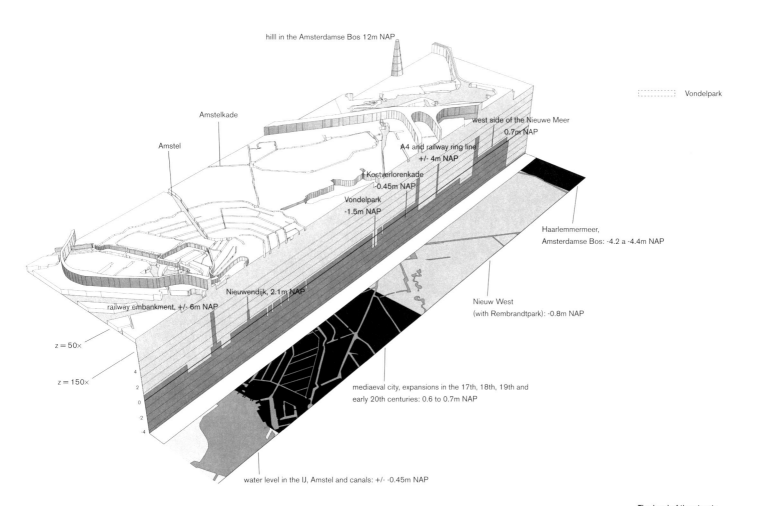

hilll in the Amsterdamse Bos 12m NAP

Amstelkade

Amstel

Kostverlorenkade
-0.45m NAP

Vondelpark
-1.5m NAP

A4 and railway ring line
+/- 4m NAP

west side of the Nieuwe Meer
0.7m NAP

⋯⋯⋯⋯ Vondelpark

Haarlemmermeer,
Amsterdamse Bos: -4.2 a -4.4m NAP

Nieuwendijk, 2.1m NAP

railway embankment, +/- 6m NAP

Nieuw West
(with Rembrandtpark): -0.8m NAP

z = 50×

z = 150×

mediaeval city, expansions in the 17th, 18th, 19th and
early 20th centuries: 0.6 to 0.7m NAP

water level in the IJ, Amstel and canals: +/- -0.45m NAP

The level of the streets

Streets constructed at a lower level at the
request of the Park Commission, to obtain better
connections with the park:
• Willemspark, Koninginneweg and Van Eeghenstraat: in
the town of Nieuwer Amstel streets could be constructed
at lower levels in relation to the NAP than in Amsterdam.
• Vossiusstraat, the first part (nrs. 1-15, architect Isaac
Gosschalk) are lower lying. Ultimately the city engineer,
Van Niftrik, wanted to expropriate all the land between
Vossiusstraat and the Zandpad, including this part of the
Vondelpark, to raise it.
• As far back as records exist, the Zandpad has been at
polder level.

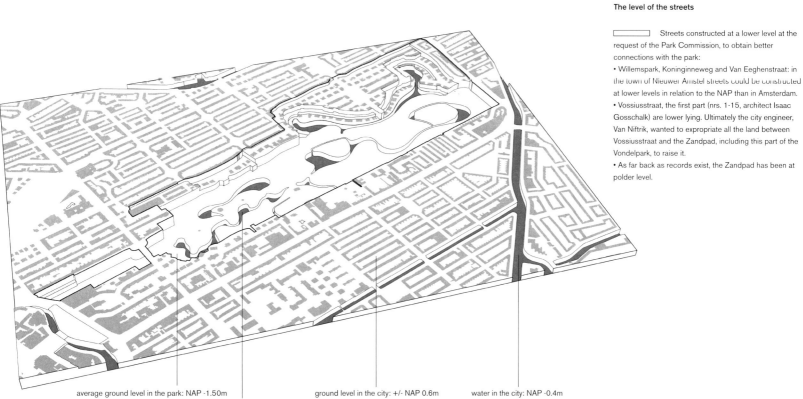

average ground level in the park: NAP -1.50m

park ponds / polder level: NAP -2.45m

ground level in the city: +/- NAP 0.6m

water in the city: NAP -0.4m

Water levels in the park and surrounding polders

The P.C. Hooftstraat was an initiative of the Park Commission. In 1871 the city approved its construction as far as the city line. Again, the street was subject to the same conditions as the Vondelstraat: a strip 30 ells wide had to remain open, for the Ceintuurbaan. In exchange for the ownership of the right of way, the city raised the terrain and provided the street furnishings. The sale of building plots made the expansion of the park possible.

Only with the completion of the bridge over the Vondelpark in 1947, one of the last bridges to be designed by Piet Kramer, were the Van Baerlestraat and the Constantijn Huygensstraat linked up with one another. With that, the noose around the neck of the park was finally tightened, and the park more or less decapitated. The connection with the old city, the entrance from Leidseplein via the Leidsebosje and the main entrance to the park, has remained problematic to this day. On the positive side of the balance, there is the fact that the Vondelpark, the landscaped omphalos of the peat polder city, is now connected to the whole of the 19th century Amsterdam by the Ceintuurbaan.

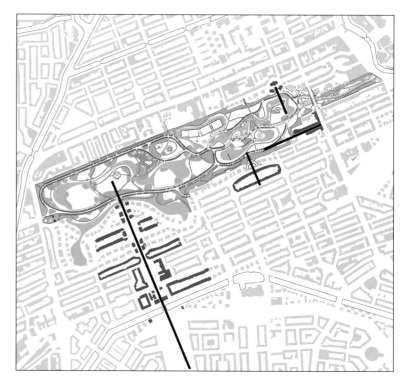

Entrance to Vondelpark from the P.C. Hoofstraat

Formal relations between the park and the city

View of the Vondelkerk above the monument

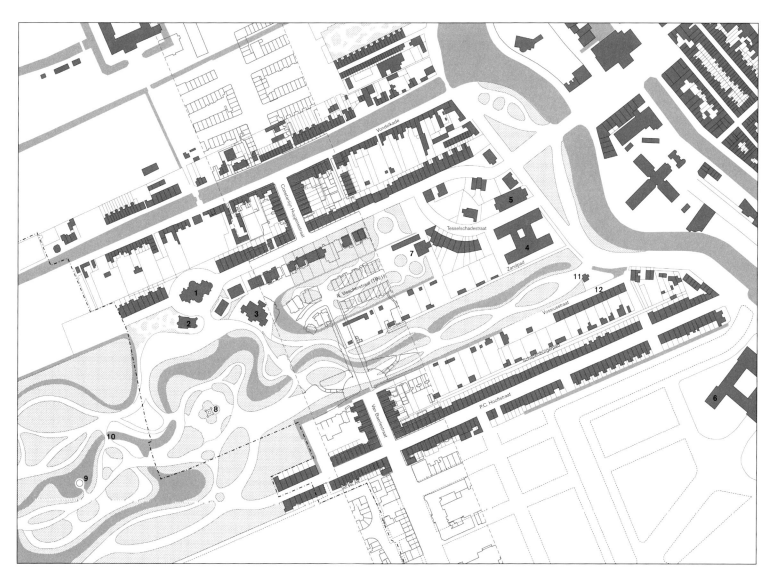

1   Vondelkerk, architect P.H.J. Cuypers (1876)

2   Nieuw Leyerhoven, architect P.H.J. Cuypers (1878)

3   Vondelpark Pavilion (Filmmuseum), architect Hamer (1881)

4   Orphanage, architect A.N. Godefroy (1882, later demolished)

5   Koepelkerk, architect A.J. van Beek (1884, demolished 1972)

6   Rijksmuseum, architect P.H.J. Cuypers (1885)

7   site of De Hereeniging clubhouse (in use from 1864 to 1889)

8   Vondel, sculptor L. Royer (1876)

9   bandstand, architect L.P. Zocher (1874)

10 bridge, architect Posthumus Meyjes (1889)

11 superintendent's residence, architect L.P. Zocher (1867)

12 Vossiusstraat 1-15, architect I Gosschalk (1879)

The Ceintuurbaan, through the park

The modulation of the peat parcel

Vondelpark is low lying, practically at the floor level of the original peat polder. Raising the ground level was so expensive that the park was built directly in the polder, two meters lower than, for instance, the Overtoom. If the park did not have its own pumping system, rain water and seepage from the Kostverlorenkade and Stadhouderskade would turn it into a lake. As a result of settling and oxidation of the peat soil, the ground level in the park has sunk further during the century-and-a-half of its existence. That can be seen, for example, on the banks in the Willemspark neighbourhood. These were once at the the level of the ponds; now they rise half a meter above the water. The decline in the ground level has decreased by now; in the course of the years the ground level has been raised, so that a certain balance has been achieved.

Polder technology

In terms of water management, the Vondelpark functions somewhat like a lake bed polder with a ring canal. The ring canal lies at a level half way between that of the park and that of the surrounding street. During the construction of the streets this canal assumed the function of a sewer, and was vaulted over. Because it lies under private property for most of its length, its precise route is not known.

Managing the water level in the park presented a dilemma. If the water table was too high, it would be detrimental to the planting, but it was too low the foundations of the adjoining houses would be subject to pile rot. This was resolved by constructing a wall running three meters deep into the soil around the edges of the park to hold back the water on the higher side, so that the foundations could be kept wet while the water level in the park could be better adjusted to the demands of the plants there.

Water for flushing out the ponds could be let in from the Stadhouderskade. Originally a long pipe carried the water to the pond near the Film Museum. On the west side of the park, the water can again be pumped out to the Kostverlorenkade. Today the water from the Singelgracht is let in under the Stadhouderskade and stored in an underground reservoir near the entrance to the park, where the silt and coarse material settles out. Then it is further purified by means of an underground filter, after which the clean water flows into the park via a 'waterfall' on the southwest side of the Vondelbrug on the Van Baerlestraat.

The final expansion of the park led to the construction of a new pumping station (the fourth) on the Amstelveenseweg. In 1912 the city assumed responsibility for the pumping of the park. The water level in the park was then lowered to 2.1 (and sometimes 2.4) meters below Normal Amsterdam Level. This was a half meter below that of the first plan. The present pumping station stands on the Sophialaan, at the Amstelveenseweg. From there the water is discharged into the Schinkel.

Winding lowland forms

Because the park was projected onto the parcellation of a peat polder, it takes on the outline of a cluster of peat parcels: deep and narrow, with straight edges. A collection of original cadastral maps from the years 1818-1822 shows the open polder landscape in which the Vondelpark was built. In terms of surveying, laying out the paths and water features in the Vondelpark was quite an achievement. A style developed for a hilly landscape was projected onto a polder landscape, creating a unique new style, in which the line technique was essential to the *écriture* of the park design. The handling of the lines of the paths and pond banks is on the one hand reminiscent of the serpentine line or 'line of beauty' in the theories of William Hogarth, set out in his 1753 book *The Analysis of Beauty*, or on the other an early prefiguration of Art Nouveau.

The Zochers tried to imitate a natural river landscape, but on a flat plane. With its curving water features, coulisses of trees and meandering paths, the park suggests a river valley, a continuing space, which in fact is limited in both its height and depth. The lawns are designed to be concave, so that they appear larger and visitors walking on them can look up into the higher-lying clumps of trees. In the parts of the park closest to and farthest from the entrance, the more natural winding forms of a stream were stylised into an artificial meander. The elongation and minimal amplitude of the winding forms of the paths and water features refers to the original dimensions of the narrow peat parcels, which stretched between the outer edges of the peat polder. The water features modulate the standard width of the peat parcels like contrapuntal musical notation, as it were, projected onto the matrix of the peat polder. Comparison of the design with the realised water features reveals that they have been simplified at a number of points, such as in the Willemspark and in the section where the second expansion connects up with the first. At other points, such as at the far end of the park by the Amstelveenseweg, the shape of the water features has become more elaborate.

A sober spatial form

The North Holland peat polder was an obstinate substratum on which to imitate an Arcadian landscape. To be sure, drainage ditches could be dug out to make a meandering river, the spoils heaped up into a mini-Parnassus, and trees placed freely in the field, but the vast, flat polder land was always dimly visible in the distance.

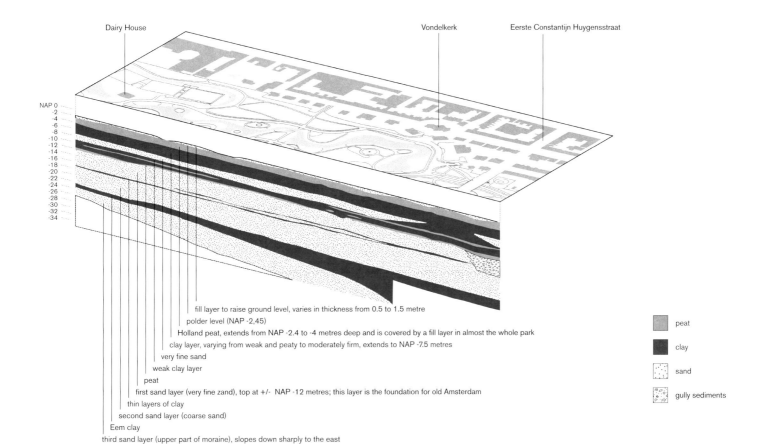

Dairy House   Vondelkerk   Eerste Constantijn Huygensstraat

NAP 0
-2
-4
-6
-8
-10
-12
-14
-16
-18
-20
-22
-24
-26
-28
-30
-32
-34

fill layer to raise ground level, varies in thickness from 0.5 to 1.5 metre
polder level (NAP -2,45)
Holland peat, extends from NAP -2.4 to -4 metres deep and is covered by a fill layer in almost the whole park
clay layer, varying from weak and peaty to moderately firm, extends to NAP -7.5 metres
very fine sand
weak clay layer
peat
first sand layer (very fine zand), top at +/- NAP -12 metres; this layer is the foundation for old Amsterdam
thin layers of clay
second sand layer (coarse sand)
Eem clay
third sand layer (upper part of moraine), slopes down sharply to the east

peat

clay

sand

gully sediments

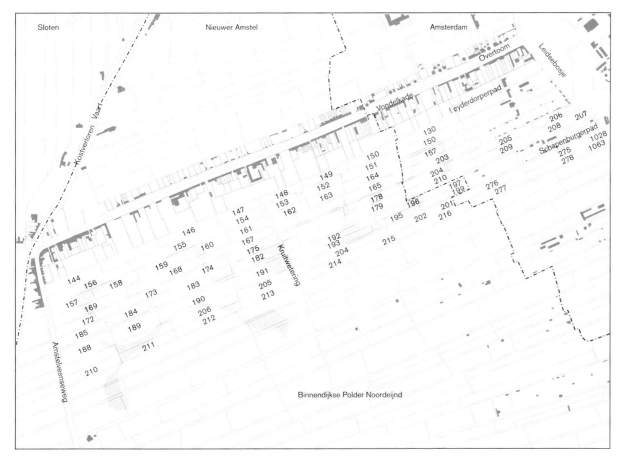

Soil profile between the Dairy House and the Eerste Constantijn Huygensstraat
(source: Omegam Geotechniek, commissioned by the district council Oud-Zuid, 1996)

The water features of the park projected onto the peat parcellation

As in the landscape garden, in Vondelpark too there is a belt, but here along the park boundary. The angularity of the contour betrays the Dutch situation with its straight lines separating the parcels. By planting along the edges and at the entrances, it was pretty much possible to turn the gaze back into the park; it opened outward only toward the Willemspark. In the oldest part of the park, which had been planned first, the space is intimate and smaller in scale. The farther one goes toward the Amstelveenseweg, the greater the spaces become, and the park takes on the character of a coulisse landscape. There were visual benefits to be gained from the expressive elements on the edges where it abutted the city. These were included in the views within the park to suggest continuity and greater dimensions. The continuous, flowing character of the water features was enhanced by the use of coulisses and grouped planting.

Not long after the construction of the park, the density with which the trees had been planted required that they be thinned out. In the spring of 1887 Zocher walked through the park with the park's directors to decide on which trees had to be cut. Since then this has been repeated annually. To a great extent, the planting chosen by the Zochers came out of nursery catalogues and was part of the standard repertoire for gardens and parks with entirely different soil conditions. Zocher acknowledged that the sodden soil had not always been taken into account in the selection of the plants. This problem was partially overcome through the trimming and replacement of plants. Thus there are few trees left in the park from its earliest years; the majority of the trees there today are no older than fifty years or so. In 1905 E. Heimans and Jac. P. Thijsse wrote of the choice of trees, "The Vondelpark will never become a Haagsche Bosch or Haarlemmerhout; the pulpy soil of Amsterdam will not allow that, nor is it necessary. Although we will have no majestic beeches or oaks, there are enough other species of trees that will reach upward to the sun, even on our wet soil; our poplars, maples and elms do that just as well, their shade is no less cool, their branches interlock just as well and provide comely avenues and dark green accents."

The most important route through the park was a avenue for carriages, planted with trees on either side, which ran for most of its length through the green belt along the edges of the park. The expansion of the park between 1867 and 1872 received two smaller, adjoining loops; in this section the park route crossed the water features. The second expansion, of 1877, was given a single loop which ran around the water in the open centre. The walking paths lay inside this, and meandered along – and occasionally, with bridges, over – the water. In the area of the first expansion the paths crossed one another frequently. Because pedestrians often stayed onto the carriage road, in 1888 walking paths

were also constructed alongside it. The paths were chiefly planned out with a view to the experience of the park landscape, and did not always connect with one another.

The slight differences in elevation and the native planting resulted in a sober spatial form. The construction in phases had a detrimental effect on the spatial continuity of the park. Nor was the spatial form of the park supported by a system of paths that was designed as a whole. As a consequence of all these factors, the spatial form became somewhat fragmented in character.

A Dutch carriage and pedestrian park

Quite early there were cultural amenities designed for the park, such as a band shell and a milk bar, designed as a farmyard with a cowshed and haystack for a rustic feeling, both by L.P. Zocher in 1874, a pavilion by the architect W. Hamer in 1881 (later the Film Museum), and a beer hall at the Vondelstraat, by Cuypers, in 1873. Horse lovers could go to the Hollandse Manege, designed in 1882 by Van Gendt, between the Vondelstraat and the Overtoom, with its own entrance to the park. The bridle paths are no longer in use. Further, there were technical facilities for the maintenance of the park, such as a barn for storing manure from the sheep and cow pastures and a workshop at the far end of the park, near the Amstelveenseweg. Zocher also designed the superintendent's house on the Stadhouderskade (1867). There is another superintendent's dwelling near the tennis court. Most of the cultural amenities accompanied the expansion of the park between 1867 and 1872, connected with the Vondelstraat. In contrast, the section approaching the Amstelveenseweg is more rural. The Willemspark, that adjoins this, has no public facilities, but does have the most impressive entrance gates.

The park has seven bridges, which play an important role in its visual structure. They are ornamental, as well as facilitating traffic circulation. That is also true for the cast-iron gates at the entrances, particularly on the Willemspark side, and obviously for the main entrance from the Stadhouderskade. Like the buildings in the park, they emphasise the monumental and exclusive character of the Vondelpark. The 1867 statue of Joost van den Vondel stands at a prominent spot close to the main entrance from the Stadhouderskade and symbolises the dedication of the park to the culture and illustrious history of Amsterdam.

After the beginning of the 20th century there were other facilities built in the park, such as tennis courts, playgrounds and an open-air theatre; while they have made the park more usable, they are not characteristic of it. It is still primarily the 19th century elements that underscore the original character of the park, a carriage and pedestrian park in nature, with a cultural purpose.

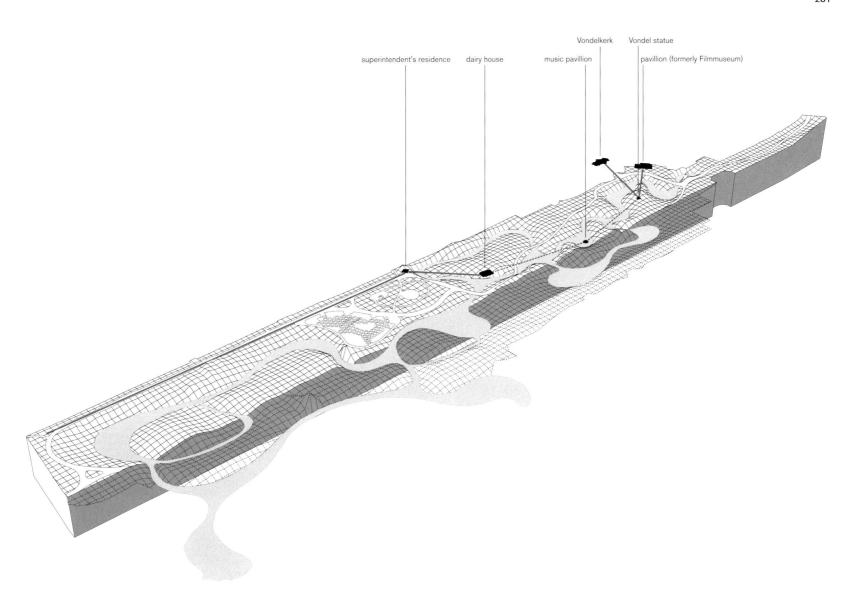

superintendent's residence   dairy house   music pavillion   Vondelkerk   Vondel statue   pavillion (formerly Filmmuseum)

A

B

C

↑ Three-dimensional model of the water features in the park relief (1 cell of the grid measures 20 × 20 metres, z = 200×)

A Meander of a Low Land stream in the park
B The staging of the pavillion
C Roadway in the park

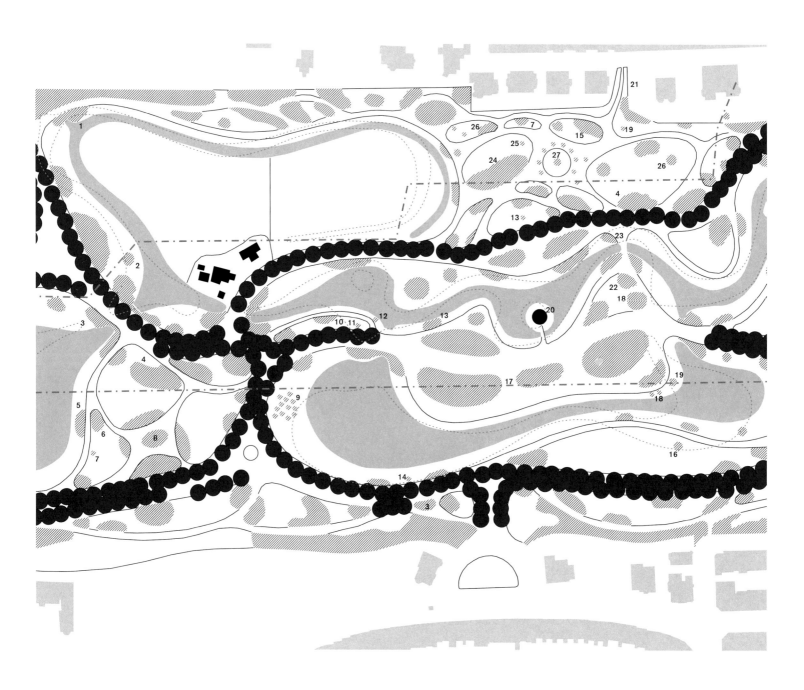

In this detail:

1	weeping willow	15	ginkgo
2	holly	16	Caucasian wingnut
3	male yew	17	the large playground
4	elm woods	18	golden ash
5	mountain ash	19	swamp cypress
6	ailanthus	20	bandstand
7	cork oak	21	the Comuslaantje
8	square with *Aesculus*	22	sweet chestnut
9	*Pavia* (red horse chestnut)	23	the Elm Bridge
10	Coppice	24	large thicket of evergreen shrubs
11	pyramid poplar	25	flowerbed with *Azalea mollis*
12	female yew	26	magnolias
13	birch	27	flowerbed with stone vase, with a ring of
14	hornbeam		sharp-leafed maples around it

In other parts of Vondelpark:

acacia
maple
almond tree
beech
yellow willow
catalpa
oak
alder
silver spruce
great beech
Gunnera scabra (Chilean rhubarb)
hazel
hornbeam 'with double leaves'

autumn lilac
holly-leafed barberry
hydrangea
flowering quince
crocus
lily of the valley
larch
hawthorn
horse chestnut
Pavia (red horse chestnut)
Pavia macrostachya (bottlebrush buckeye)
rhododendron
flowering currant

rose
field maple
spruce
tamarisk
box elder
pyracantha
willow leaf pear
black poplar

Planting in the Vondelpark in 1903 (detail)
Inventory by J.P. Thijsse and E. Heimans (1901), map after Scheltema (1903)

0   50   100m

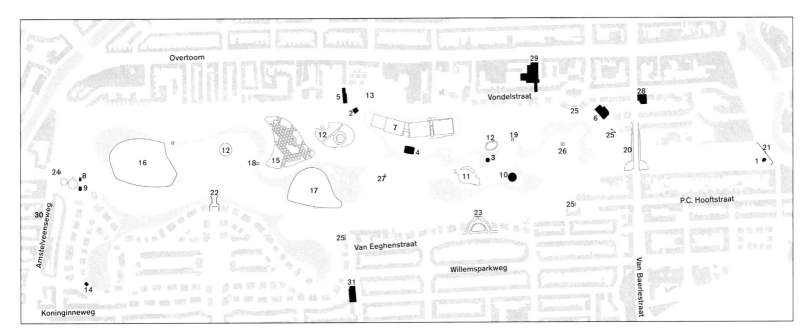

1   superintendent's residence (architect L.P. Zocher), 1867

2   superintendent's residence

3   bandstand (architect L.P. Zocher), 1874

4   Dairy House (architect L.P. Zocher), with cowshed, hayrick and pasture for 25 Lakenvelders, 1874.
    Renovated in 1937 (architects H.A.J. and J. Baanders). Cows were milked in the park until 1962.

5   double shed for manure storage on the Kattenlaan (architect Van Niftrik), 1884.

6   Vondelpark Pavillion (architect W. Hamer), 1881

7   Festina tennis club (founded 1904); the eastern part of the site was a dairy pasture

8   candy kiosk in Indonesian style (architects H. A.J. and J. Baanders), 1927

9   workshop (architects H.A.J. and J. Baanders), 1929

10 Blue Teahouse (architects H.A.J. and J. Baanders), 1936

11 open-air theatre, 1955; roof, 1984

12 playgrounds

13 tennis park

14 electric pump

15 rosarium (design E. Mos), late 1950s

16 cow pasture

17 sheep and lamb pasture

18 bridge (architect W. Hamer)

19 bridge (architect C.B. Posthumus Meyjes), 1889

20 Vondelbrug (architect P.L. Kramer, sculptures H. Krop), 1947

21 fence along the Stadhouderskade (architect A. Linnemann, sculpture of the patroness of the city by
    F. Schierholz), 1883

22 Koningslaan entrance, gate and bridge (architect J.L. Springer and/or A.L. van Gendt), ca. 1880

23 Van Eeghenstraat entrance, gate (architects W. and J.L. Springer), 1893

24 Amstelveensweg entrance (architect M. de Klerk), design 1915, executd later in a mor sobre style

25 entrance gates on the P.C. Hooftstraat, Vondelstraat, Roemer Visscherstraat and Koninginneweg
    (these look similar to the first gate that the Zochers designed for the Stadhouderskade)

26 statue of Vondel (sculptor Louis Royer), unveiled in 1867

27 Figure decoupée (Pablo Picasso)

28 Vondel Beerhall, at Vondelstraat 39-41 (architect P.J.H. Cuypers, commissioned by Heineken), 1873.
    Used by the Freemasons since 1904, and renovated by the architect W. Kromhout (number 39) and once
    again by the architect P. Heyn (1910-1911).

29 Hollandsche Manege (architect A.L. van Gendt), 1882

30 car barn for horse-drawn streetcars, Amstelveenseweg 134 (architect A. Salm), 1885 (in Russian style;
    G.B. Salm had restored the Czar Peter House)

31 car barn and stalls for horse-drawn streetcars, Koninginneweg (architects A.L. and J.G. van Gendt), 1893.
    Now a police station.

Design elements and amenities

0   200   500m

The polder park

The Vondelpark can be regarded as a model for the landscape architectonic transformation of the peat polder landscape. From the perspective of technology, it incorporates the pedological and hydraulic qualities of the peat polder, and the Low Lands' repertoire of the polder park was developed in its design. The plan for the park therefore contains the basic solutions for the landscape architectonic incorporation of the peat landscape into the city. The properties of the parcel, the basic module, the fundamental shape of a cluster of parcels and the asymmetry of the extended reclamation here take on a significance in the ground plan of the park.

The park's low-lying position, intensified by the planting along its edges, formed the point of departure for the spatial form. Slight differences in elevation were obtained by excavation and locally raising the ground level, and then utilised in the spatial composition. The spatial form of the park is also based on a modulation of the peat parcel across the width of the cluster; the water features and the system of paths made optimal use of this. Botanically, the initial planting was not based on the local circumstances, but the relation between soil and species selection was improved in the course of the park's long-term development.

The visual structure of the park refers to the Dutch agricultural landscape and nature with attractions such as the fenced pasture and the dairy. The technology of the polder system played no role of importance in the references; the pumping station was hidden behind a screen of trees. The transformation of the peat polder landscape nevertheless received a normative landscape architectonic form in the Vondelpark. Within the limitations of the soil conditions of the peat landscape and the narrow margins of the cluster of parcels, the ensemble of the water features, the pattern of paths and planting created an entirely unique form: the polder park as a nature idyll for the Low Lands.

Stage-managing the agricultural landscape

In 1953 the Park Association could no longer bear the costs of maintaining the park, and conveyed it to the city. A plan had to be made for the restoration and redesign of the park; in it, the choice was made for practical solutions, which in the light of the wear and tear on the park and increasingly intensive use appeared necessary.

The radical possibility of raising the floor of the park to street level proved unfeasible. None of the trees would have survived that, and all the structures in the park would have had to be raised with the ground level. Egbert Mos, who as the designer directed a reconstruction in 1959, had the ground level raised locally by sometimes more than a half meter. Almost a fifth of all the trees were cut down. About 9000 shrubs and 1900 young trees, primarily fast-growing species such as willows and poplars, were planted in their place. In the course of the redesign the structure of the walks was sharply simplified in a process "whereby the shortest paths between all the entrances to the park were sought." Functional considerations that emphasised access and the hierarchy of the paths in the pattern weighed most heavily in this, with the result that the flowing course of the paths was locally affected.

In 1996 Vondelpark became the first public park in The Netherlands to be designated as a "national monument of great natural, cultural/historical and urban planning value". In the light of this designation, during its most recent renovation, which lasted eleven years and was rounded off in 2010, under the supervision of the landscape architect Michael van Gessel the spatial character of the park was again restored and brought into accordance with the Zochers' original intentions. Erik de Jong was asked to assist in the interpretation of the design history of the Vondelpark. The water was restored to its role as the support for the continuing spatial form. The "grass was brought to the water", as Van Gessel put it, so that the surface of the water again worked more strongly as a reference point for the slight differences in elevation in the low-lying park, and it "appeared as if the park was floating". This illusion was further enhanced by making the banks concave in the outside curves and convex in the inside curves.

Alterations to the design of the park

Changes in the water features since 1903 (above)
Small diferences in position are sometimes the result of less careful measurements carried out around 1900

ponds in 1903

surface water today

places with important changes

Routes of paths and roadways in 1903 (middle) and today (bottom)

paths and roadways

boundaries of the successive phases in the park's construction

0   200   500m

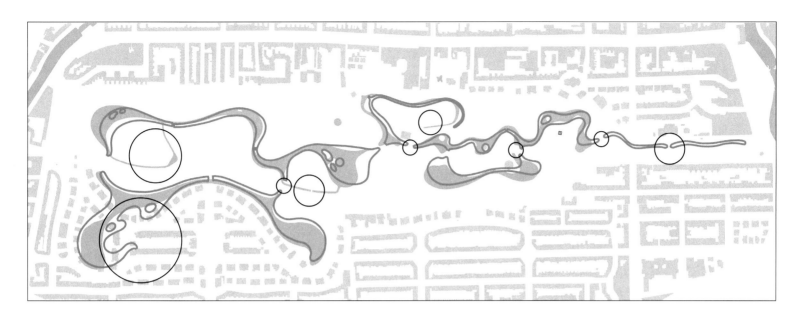

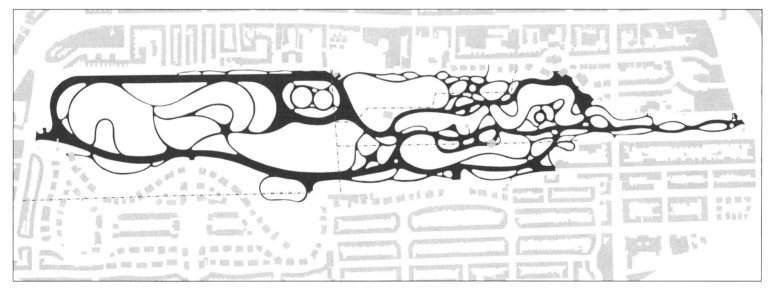

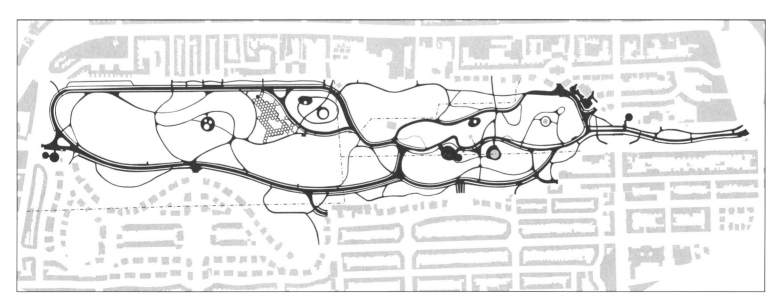

On the basis of the results of the previous adaptations, the alternation between thick planting and open spaces was more strongly accentuated, overgrown paths were cleared, sharp curves rounded off, and views across the water opened up. The Film Museum is once again reflected in the somewhat broadened pond around the statue of Vondel. In order to lengthen the life expectancy of some of the new trees, they were underpinned by platforms supported on piles. The original differentiation in the path system was restored by relaying the original semi-paved paths. With this one of the park's most important functions was restored: that of an urban illusion of nature based on a refinement of the agricultural landscape of the Low Lands.

A model for the polder metropolis

If we hypothetically think through the further development of Amsterdam and expand that to the development of the Randstad, then the question presents itself as to whether a new, metropolitan polder park can be conceived that does not erase the basic form of the peat landscape of the delta, but rather gives it a new face. The urban development of Amsterdam since 1900, in combination with the model of Vondelpark, offers various clues.

In the Expansion Plan South (between 1905 and 1911) and the Expansion Plan West (1922) by the architect and urban planner H.P. Berlage the lines of the infrastructure that constituted a part of the composition of the city map were monumentally related to the peat polder as a vast landscape plane. Moreover, the avenues and canals marked particular places in the peat plain, such as the old river mouth near Sloterdijk and the point where Watergraafsmeer touches the Amstel near the Berlagebrug. The 1934 Algemeen Uitbreidingsplan or A.U.P. (General Expansion Plan) for Amsterdam encompassed a plan for a whole city with radial green zones. The location of these green wedges was primarily based on the water pattern of the surrounding peat landscape with its rivers, peat streams and dike rings, such as the IJ, the Zaan, the east edge of the Haarlemmermeer, the Amstel, the Gaasp and the Vecht.

These developments once again raised the question of the relation between the form of the city and the polder landscape, but now on a larger scale and in the light of modern urban planning requirements. The dimensions of the Watergraafsmeer, for example, were almost as great as those of Amsterdam inside the Singelgracht. Another novelty was that at the level of the expansion plan as a whole there were connections with prominent features in the peat landscape, as in the case of the Sloterplas, which as a transformed lake bed polder in the heart of the planning area was developed into the central space in an urban park. The Amsterdamse Bos is also an outstanding example of this kind of transformation. In this way the landscape structure of the peat polder continued to be a presence in the modern city, and the modern park supported the urban pattern. In each of the periods of development, and in each of the sections of the urban plan, the basic form of the peat polder landscape was treated differently. This created a differentiated morphological pattern, the boundaries and form of which are still derived from the original polder landscape. It is for this reason that one can consider Amsterdam as a whole a polder city.

The Vondelpark is an experimental landscape architectonic model within this urban landscape system. The character of the North Holland peat polder is completely present in the park, not only in its low level, the vegetation and the water, but also in the staging of the agrarian landscape. The form is utile, transparent and inevitable. Just as in a real polder, through its plain architecture the landscape architectonic form is reduced to an abstract scheme. In this, the Vondelpark teaches us how the typology of the polder landscape can be the point of departure for a landscape architectonic concept for the city today, and in particular for the Randstad as a polder metropolis.

The basic constituants of the polder metropolis

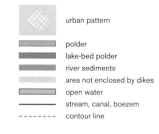

urban pattern

polder
lake-bed polder
river sediments
area not enclosed by dikes
open water
stream, canal, boezem
contour line

0   10   20km

EMERALD NECKLACE
BOSTON 1876

The landscape as urban framework
Frederick Law Olmsted
The park system

The estuary of the Charles River

Boston Common as the starting point
Boston Common
Outwharfing
Back Bay
The Public Garden

A municipal or a metropolitan park system?
Desirability and scope of a park system
The Park Commission plan of 1876
The effect of the landscape architectonic design

The water chain
The Back Bay Fens
The Muddy River Improvement
Jamaica Pond

The parks in the hills
The Arnold Arboretum
Franklin Park

The tail piece on the ocean, and the parkway
Marine Park
The parkway as the string of the Emerald Necklace

The first urban park system
The park system as the landscape backbone of the city
Charles Eliot's metropolitan park system
An unbreakable chain of landscapes

The Boston Park System, with the Public Garden in the foreground and Jamaica Pond to the left of the centre in the background (aerial photo: SuperStock 1566-275140)

The landscape as urban framework

The origins of the Boston Park System lay in a public debate initiated by the Boston Park Movement after the construction of Central Park in New York. The idea for the park system took form in the *Proposed Park and Parkways*, an 1876 plan by the Boston Park Commission. The Boston Park System was the first complete park system, built according to a comprehensive plan and anchored structurally in the city and in the landscape. Unlike any other city in the United States, Boston had a long tradition of land reclamation and horticulture, two important building blocks for the park system. It was tied in with the water management, land reclamation and levelling of the landscape that had been under way in Boston for more than a century. The parks were connected with one another by parkways, wide, landscaped roads with a differentiated profile for different sorts of traffic, from which it was possible to obtain scenic views out over the park landscapes. These qualities made it a catalyst for the growth and development of the city.

Frederick Law Olmsted had a decisive influence on the selection and cohesion of the places in the landscape topography, the landscape architectonic development and the anchoring of the park system in the urban pattern. He had already been involved in the planning of a park system in Buffalo, at the eastern end of Lake Erie, one of the first in the United States. This was comprised of one large, composite main park, from which various parkways radiated to smaller parks and green squares, with The Front, a green square on a steep hill with a prospect out over Lake Erie, as the climax. Olmsted had also been consulted with regard to plans for a park system in Chicago.

Frederick Law Olmsted

After Olmsted (1822-1903) had left Central Park in New York in 1877, he worked on scores of commissions in the United States. In the meantime, at the invitation of the Park Commissioners he had become involved with the Boston Park System in 1875. In 1878 he signed an agreement with the Park Department there for preparing a design for Back Bay Park, after which he was also called in for other parts of the park system. In 1883 Olmsted moved to an old farm in Brookline, near Boston, where he opened a new professional landscape architectural agency. Two of his sons, John Charles (1852-1920) and Frederick, Jr. (1870-1957) were trained in the discipline there. The agency carried out many commissions, spread across the whole United States, including the plan for the 1893 World's Columbian Exposition in Chicago. When Olmsted retired from the agency in 1895, the Boston Park System was largely completed.

Topography

parks in the Municipal Park System
1   Arnold Arboretum
2   Back Bay Fens
3   Boston Common
4   Commonwealth Avenue Mall
5   Fort Independence/Castle Island (Pleasure Bay)
6   Franklin Park
7   Jamaica Pond
8   Olmsted Park (Leverett Park)
9   Marine Park (Pleasure Bay)
10   Public Garden
11   The Riverway (Muddy River Improvement)

other parks and urban green space
12   Blue Hills State Park
13   Columbus Park
14   Cutler Park
15   Doublet Hill Conservation Area
16   Middlesex Fells Reservation
17   Mill Pond Reservation
18   Newton Lower Falls Park
19   Prospect Hill Park
20   Stony Brook Reservation
21   Wrights park

water
22   Charles River
23   Chestnut Hill Reservoir
24   Everett River
25   Fresh Pond
26   Muddy River
27   Mystic Lakes
28   Mystic River
29   Neponset River
30   Pleasure Bay

streets
31   Arborway
32   Beacon Street
33   Columbia Road
34   Commonwealth Avenue

airport

subway station
subway line
railway line
railway station
motorway
tunnel
important road

urban pattern

park in the Municipal Park System (Olmsted)

still existant park in the Metropolitan Park System (Eliot)

Eliot's park system: existing parks and green space in 1893

Eliot's park system: plan for new parks and green space, 1893

other parks and urban green space

water

0   2   5km

The park system

In addition to Boston Common and the Public Garden which already existed in the old city, the plan encompassed six new parks in a wide ring around Boston Neck, the narrow tongue of land that connected the old city with the mainland. Changes in the location and size of the proposed parks ensued during the implementation of the plans. Ultimately the Back Bay Fens, the Muddy River Improvement, Jamaica Pond, the Arnold Arboretum, Franklin Park and Marine Park were realised.

Olmsted worked during the 'urban explosion' in America. He was convinced that carefully composed natural scenes were a remedy against the pressures and stress of urban life: "Landscapes move us in a manner more nearly analogous to the action of music than to anything else… Gradually and silently the charm overcomes us; we know not exactly where or how."

Olmsted's ideal was to create 'natural scenery', the dramatisation of the original, natural scenes as a counterweight to the dynamics and turmoil of the city. Just as in the case of Central Park in New York, but now on the scale of the agglomerate, in the Boston Park System he sought a balance between the pastoral landscape (the meadow) and wild nature (the wilderness). He endeavoured to interpret both with an eye for the agricultural landscape that was already present, the geological qualities of the terrain, and the possibilities for planting native species. In addition, he had to take into account the pressures of increasing use by the growing urban population (the garden).

The Public Garden (photo: C.H.E. van Ees)

→ **Sketch map of Olmsted's plan for Buffalo, as one of the first park systems in America** (Buffalo & Erie County Public Library, Central Library 33M-18 1 NONFICTION Grosvenor Room-Rare Books)

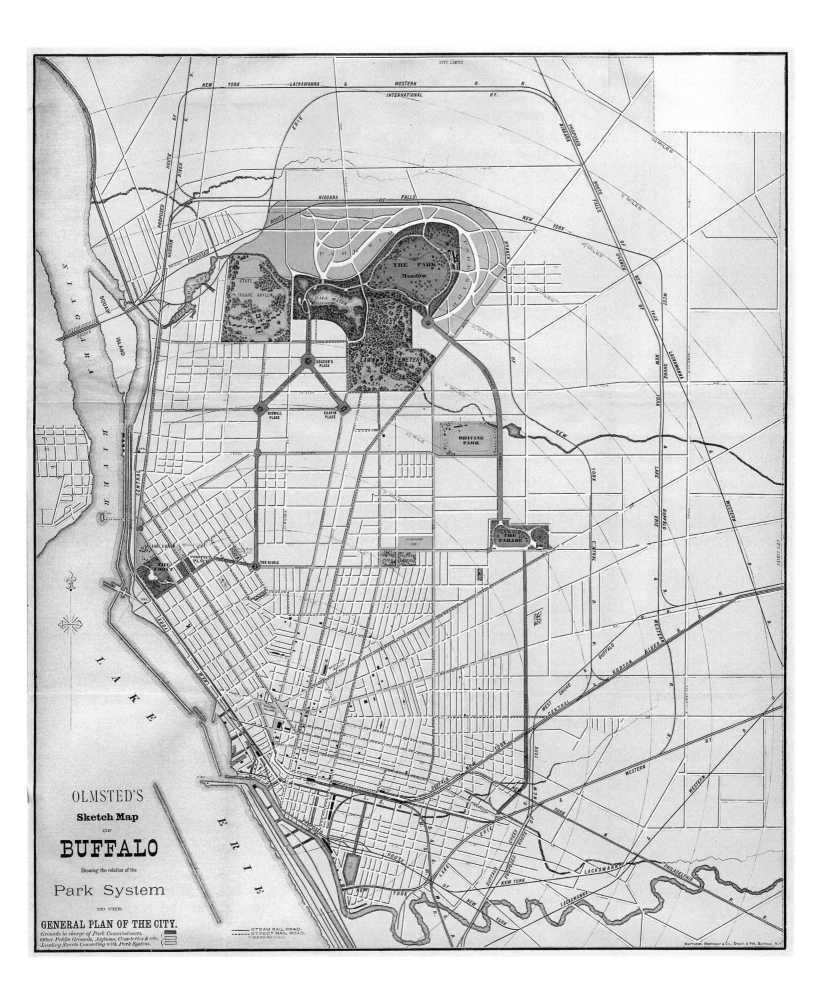

OLMSTED'S

Sketch Map

OF

BUFFALO

Showing the relation of the

Park System

TO THE

GENERAL PLAN OF THE CITY.

Grounds in charge of Park Commissioners.
Other Public Grounds, Asylums, Cemeteries & etc.
Leading Streets Connecting with Park System.

STEAM RAIL ROAD.
STREET RAIL ROAD.
SCALE 1000 feet =1 Inch.

Matthews, Northrup & Co., Engrs & Prs. Buffalo, N.Y.

The estuary of the Charles River

The state of Massachusetts in New England, in the north-east of the United States, extends from the Appalachian Mountains in the west to the sandy beaches and rocky coasts of the Atlantic Ocean. During the Wisconsin glaciation, during which the present landscape was formed, the whole region lay under the ice. It is largely covered with boulder clay and is in many places characterised by typical ice age formations such as glacial lakes, drumlins (elongated glacial drifts running in the direction of the ice flow), *eskers* (meltwater ridges) and stony moraines.

The land slopes from the west to the east and rises from the south to the north. The highest point in the state is Mount Greylock, at 1064 meters. In the south-west corner of Massachusetts the Taconic Mountains, which are part of the Appalachian chain and form the western border with New York State, are about 800 meters high. The Housatonic Valley separates this mountain range from the Hoosac and Berkshire mountains, a wide ridge of steep hills, southern foothills of the Green Mountains of Vermont extending on to the south into Connecticut. East of the Berkshires, separating it from the rest of Massachusetts, lies the Connecticut River Valley, also known as the Pioneer Valley. This old geological fault zone originated in the Mesozoic era, when the Americas separated from Europe and Africa. Basalt rocks and abrupt changes in elevation of up to 300 meters testify to the tectonic forces involved.

The coastline of Massachusetts is deeply indented with bays, coves and estuaries, separated by narrow capes, of which the Cape Cod peninsula is the largest. Some of these provided natural harbours, which sometimes grew into port cities such as Newburyport-Gloucester, Salem, New Bedford and Boston.

Boston lies in a basin which was formed by old deposits of volcanic ash, clay, slate and compressed rock fragments which were alternately ground up and left behind by different ice ages. The pattern of deep channels, the many islands, and the peninsula of Boston itself, the Shawmut Peninsula, were the result of the rise in the sea level after the last ice age, about 10,000 years ago. The land behind Boston is drained by three rivers, respectively the Mystic River, the Charles River and the Neponset River, which discharge into channels fringed by swampy tidal basins and salt meadows. Together they make up the great estuary of the Charles River, in which land reclamation has defined the layout of Boston, and the form of its park system.

The water landscape of the Back Bay Fens (photo: C.H.E. van Ees)

→ **Geomorphology and urban domain**

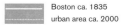 Boston ca. 1835
urban area ca. 2000

N   0   20   40k

Geomorphology, urban pattern and parks

Elevation (metres)

	180 - 200
	160 - 180
	140 - 160
	120 - 140
	100 - 120
	90 - 100
	80 - 90
	70 - 80
	60 - 70
	50 - 60
	40 - 50
	30 - 40
	20 - 30
	10 - 20
	0 - 10

urban pattern

park

water

Franklin Park (photo: C.H.E. van Ees)

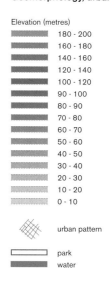

0   2   5km

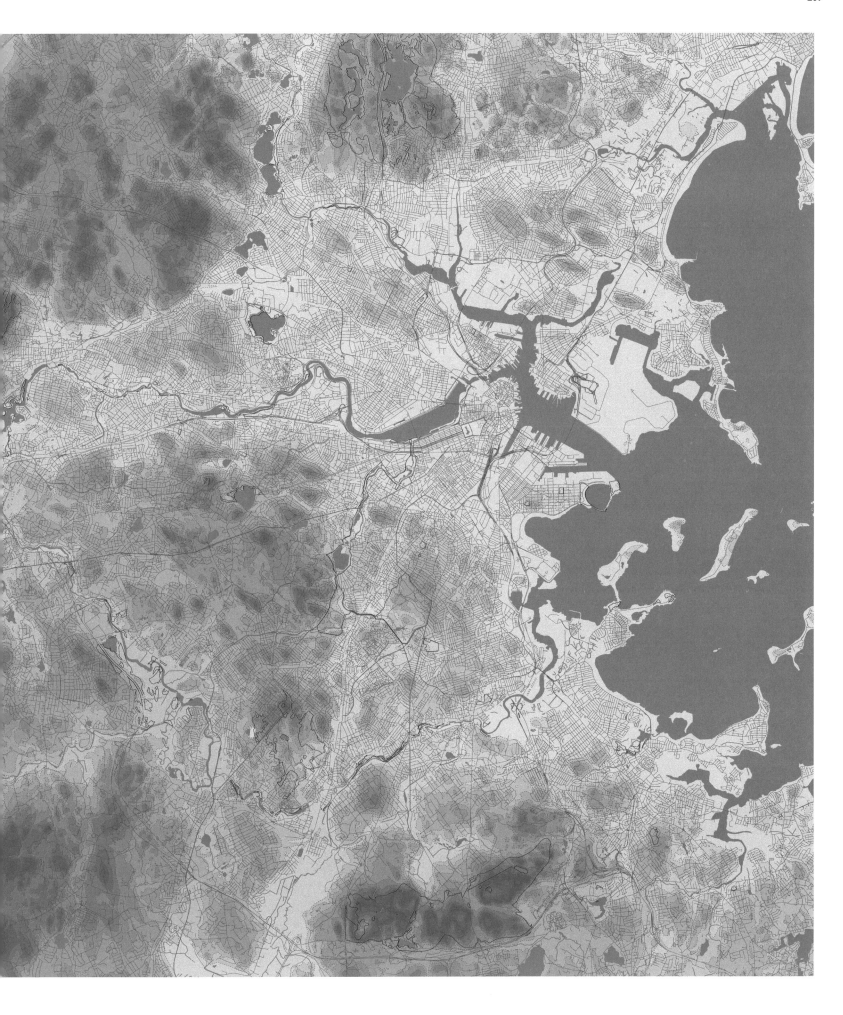

Boston Common as the starting point

In 1625 the Anglican clergyman William Blaxton settled as a hermit on Beacon Hill, one of the higher points on the Shawmut Peninsula in the bay. Five years later his reclusive existence was broken by new neighbours, the Puritans of the Massachusetts Bay Company, who as migrants from England settled in Charlestown, on a peninsula somewhat to the north, and from there also colonised the Shawmut Peninsula. The peninsula was connected with the mainland only by a narrow tongue of land called The Neck, and was thus easily defended; moreover, it offered outstanding natural conditions for a harbour. In the 18th century Boston became famous as the Cradle of Liberty, when what has gone down in history as the Boston Tea Party provided the spark to set off the resistance to English authority that would result in the American Revolution (1775-1783) and eventual independence.

Boston Common

The Puritans established themselves on the north side of the Shawmut Peninsula and renamed it Boston. The construction of the Long Wharf, an embankment extending far into the natural bay, created the city's first harbour. On the south side lay the farm of William Blaxton in Boston Common, a large, almost treeless area without clear boundaries that served as a common pasture for livestock.

On a map from 1722 one can see that the built-up area had already spread across the whole peninsula, leaving the Common by Beacon Hill as the only open area. To the south-west lay a large tidal plain, almost as big as the peninsula itself, and enclosed by Boston Neck. This plain was a part of the wider estuary at the mouths of the Charles River, Stony Brook and the Muddy River, with its mud flats and salt marshes. This section of the estuary would later be known as the Back Bay. The Mill Pond, a large bay on the north-west side of the peninsula, was closed off by the Mill Dam, in order to be able to harness the rise and fall of the tides for powering mills. By around 1790 the city had about 18,000 residents, for the most part living in wooden houses. Construction of a new State House on Beacon Hill, with a view out over Boston Common, began in 1795.

Outwharfing

Between 1790 and 1825 Boston's population tripled. Bridges were built to link the city proper with nearby settlements on the other bank of the Charles River, such as Charlestown and Cambridge. Because there were not yet any railways or automobiles, the built-up area on the opposite banks remained limited. Developers and speculators focused primarily on the exploitation of the new land created by filling in natural creeks and coves, and land created by the process called outwharfing, where embankments were first built out at right angles to the shore, and then the area between them filled in. Mill Pond, for instance, was filled in with material obtained by digging away the top of Beacon Hill. A part of Copp's Hill was also dug away to create new land along the shore of the North End.

The water landscape of Boston in 1777. The Muddy River and Stony Brook still flow into the Charles River without obstruction (Henry Pelham, 1777. A plan of Boston in New England and its environs, ... Harvard College Library, Harvard Map Collection, MAP-LC G3764.B6S3 1777 .P4.

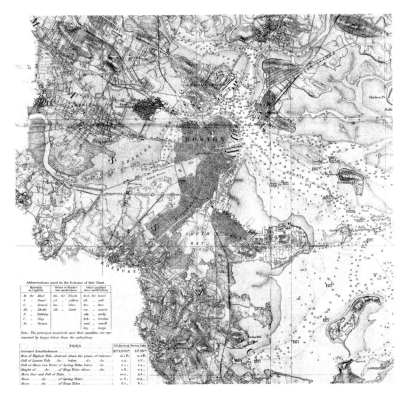

Back Bay with the Mill Dam (and other dams) along the Charles River, before the 'outwharfling' (from: A. Krieger, D.A. Cobb, A. Turner & D.C. Bosse, *Mapping Boston*, Cambridge, Mass. 1999)

View of Boston Common, with the Public Garden on new land in the foreground (John Bachmann, Bird's eye view of Boston, 1850. Library of Congress, PGA - Bachmann-Bird's-eye view of Boston)

The levelling of Beacon Hill in Boston Common to provide spoil for the outwharfing ('Beacon Hill, from Mr. Vernon St. near the head of Hancock St.' from 'Old Boston : [five chromo-lithographs from sketches of Beacon Hill, taken in 1811 or 1812] / J.H. Bufford's Lith. ...', Boston : Smith, Knight & Tappan, 1857, 1858. Boston Public Library Central - Fine Arts, Folio/Oversize, CAB. 23.18.10)

The coming of the railway brought with it vast changes. Between 1825 and 1850, with the many immigrants from Ireland the population grew from 58,000 to 137,000. This growth was the impetus for the great land reclamation projects of the second half of the 19th century, such as Back Bay and South End, on either side of Boston Neck.

Back Bay

With the filling of Mill Pond in the north-west, the water mills on the old Mill Dam became unusable. Therefore in 1821 a new, larger Mill Dam was built in the Back Bay, in combination with a barrage that divided the basin in two. The Full Basin, a balancing reservoir with creeks, into which the Muddy River and Stony Brook discharged, and into which water was also pushed at high tide, comprised the smaller section. The other section, the Receiving Basin, held the water that provided constant power for the mills. It did not function as such for long, however; beginning with the middle of the 19th century it too was filled in to create new land.

Land reclamation also took place on the south-east side of Boston Neck, so that the narrow tongue of land became embedded between two new residential neighbourhoods, Back Bay and South End. The most important streets of the South End ran parallel with Washington Street, originally the only access road to Boston over the Neck. The street pattern of Back Bay ran parallel with the Mill Dam, which formed the new coastline.

The Public Garden

Originally, on its south-west side Boston Common was bounded by the waters of the Back Bay. In 1794 the city granted permission to a rope manufacturer to use the shore along the Common as a ropewalk. With the construction of the dams and basins in Back Bay, and the later filling of the Receiving Basin, the old Common occupied a central position between the old and new land. In 1839 the Receiving Basin had been only partly filled in, and still lay a meter below street level. A group of horticulturists led by Horace Gray obtained permission from the city fathers to set up a public botanical garden on the new land adjoining Boston Common. The landscape architect Andrew Jackson Downing was approached for the preparation of a Public Garden which at the same time could function as a scientific arboretum. The soil conditions on the site however proved so problematic that it was only in 1859, after the survival of the garden had been secured under law, that a definitive plan was drawn up, commissioned by the city. This plan, by the architect George F. Meacham, was comprised of a central axis with a main building, oriented to Commonwealth Avenue, the new axis of Back Bay. Across the axis he designed a curved pond encircled by a walk, and several other garden components. The plan was adapted by the city engineer James Slade. A greenhouse was built along Charles Street, and the main building was replaced by an equestrian statue of George Washington. By 1860 the Public Garden was ready. It lay entirely on new land and formed a link between Boston Common and Commonwealth Avenue, running through the reclaimed land of Back Bay and ending at the mouth of the Muddy River. The area around the mouth of this stream now became the next focus for a further expansion of the park system.

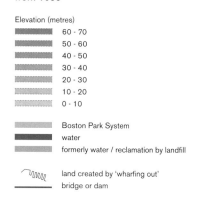

Overview of the land reclamation process, from 1630

Elevation (metres)

	60 - 70
	50 - 60
	40 - 50
	30 - 40
	20 - 30
	10 - 20
	0 - 10

	Boston Park System
	water
	formerly water / reclamation by landfill
	land created by 'wharfing out'
	bridge or dam

0   1   2km

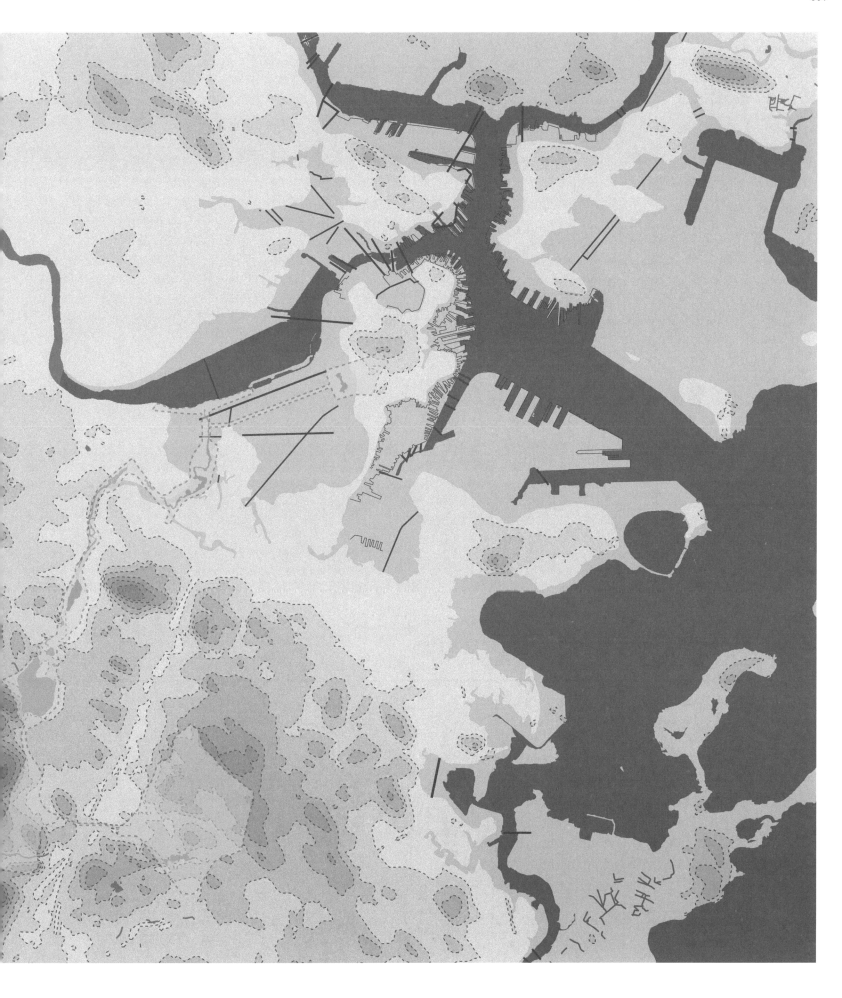

A municipal or a metropolitan park system?

Already at the beginning of the 19th century Boston was one of the most important horticultural centres in America. There were many estates with exceptional planting, famous nurseries and many amateur horticulturists. Many of the latter were members of the Massachusetts Horticultural Society. Their interest in horticulture was accompanied by a special interest in parks. For them, the realisation of Central Park in New York was a signal that something of that nature had to be done in Boston too.

Not only did the city's population increase rapidly with the construction of railways and highways, but so did the area it covered. A number of the surrounding cities and towns were annexed, such as Roxbury (1868), Dorchester (1870), Charlestown and Brighton (1873). This extension of the city's boundaries threatened ever more agricultural landscapes and natural areas. In 1869 a group of citizens, including a number of prominent amateur nurserymen, presented a petition to the city fathers requesting the construction of a public park. Upon receiving it, the City Council appointed a committee to report on the matter. After several hearings the committee advised the City Council to investigate the legal possibilities for acquiring land for the construction of a large park, and several smaller ones.

Desirability and scope of a park system

In the meantime the landscape architect Horace W.S. Cleveland (1814-1900) had published an article in the *Boston Advertiser*, in which he argued that Boston was not so much in need of a central park, as of a system of scenic improvements in the surrounding landscape, based on the natural elements present and the existing agricultural landscape and the accompanying farms. The lawyer Uriel H. Crocker argued for a linear park extending along the Charles River, the design of which could incorporate natural elements present locally, such as hills, the river banks and lakes. The landscape architect Robert Morris Copeland (1830-1874) envisioned a park system comprised of various large and small parks, connected with one another by parkways. Copeland also suggested that the varied topography of Boston was best served not with one large park, as with many smaller ones. Various other park plans also appeared in the years after 1869.

In 1870 the Park Act, the proposed law which permitted the acquisition of land for the parks, was rejected by the Boston City Council. With this, a private organisational and administrative aspect came to the fore. Disagreements arose about the question of on whose territory the

parks lay and who should help pay for them. The distinction emerged between a municipal and a metropolitan park system. A municipal park system would only include parks in the communities that fell under one and the same civic administration, that of Boston. A metropolitan park system, on the other hand, could also include parks in communities that indeed had their own municipal administration, but fell within Boston's sphere of influence. Moreover, the difference between a municipal and a metropolitan park system changed over time. Some communities that were a part of metropolitan Boston in 1869 became a part of the city of Boston proper after their annexation. On the other hand, Brookline, for example, lay in the middle of Boston, as it were, but remained an independent city, and therefore was part of metropolitan Boston.

In 1874 the city of Boston appointed a new committee to study the question of parks. Once again hearings were held. Ernest W. Bowditch,

Charles Davenport's proposal (1875) for the banks of the Charles River, on the model of the Alster in Hamburg (The Boston Athenaeum, Prints and Photographs Dept., C B64B6 M.b.(no.1))

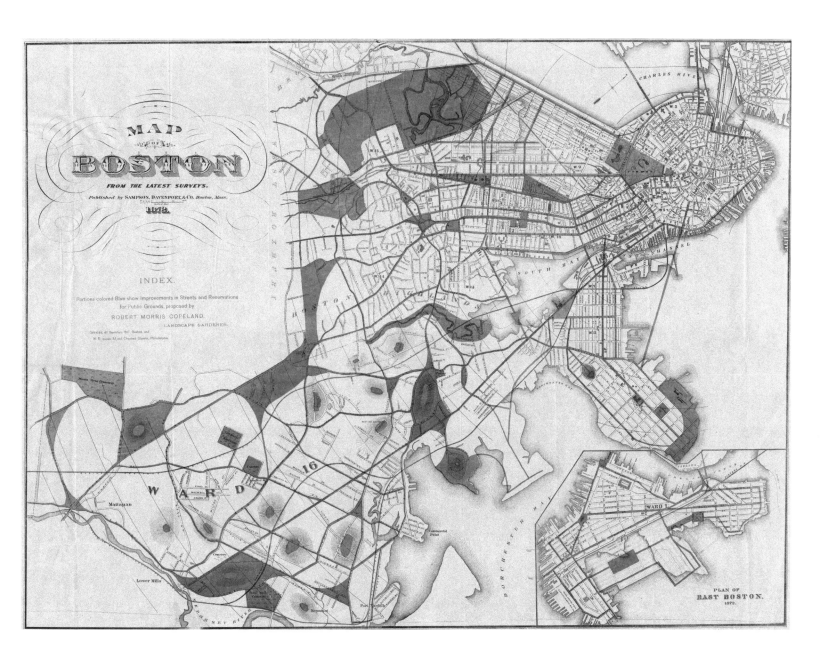

Robert Morris Copeland's proposal (1872) for a park system
(Harvard College Library, Harvard Map Collection, MAP-LC G3764.B6 1872 .S31)

a young engineer who had worked with Robert M. Copeland, published a plan called *Rural Parks for Boston*, with a wide circle of parks around Boston, from Chelsea Beach in the north to Squantum in the south. Measures for the protection of the metropolitan water system were included in this plan.

The Park Commission plan of 1876

In May, 1875, the Park Act was approved, after which a new Park Commission was named for the acquisition of land within the city's administrative boundaries. This body once again organised hearings, during which many potential sites and possible plans once more passed in review. At this point Olmsted also appeared on the stage. In October, 1875, he was invited by the Commissioners to join them in visits to the proposed sites. They did this again in April, 1876, shortly before the Commission published its final report. This contained a long-term blueprint for the park system, based on considerations involving population density, the economy and public health. The sites for the parks were in part selected on the basis of their accessibility for people of all classes, whether they were coming on foot, by carriage or on horseback, or by steam carriage, horse car or railway.

The plan included several separate inner city parks and suburban parks in the recently annexed areas. There were also several 'outer parks', including the Chestnut Hill Reservoir, places that stood out for their natural beauty and rural character. The Park Commission's plan fell within the city's administrative boundaries. In addition the commission advised that areas should already be secured for a metropolitan park system, comprised of a wider ring of suburban parks, six to eight miles from the centre of the city. This really fell outside its remit, because to do so would require the cooperation of adjoining cities and communities.

The backbone of the plan was made up of the suburban parks, an encircling chain of parks, from the north side of the Neck at Boston Common, along the Charles River, to the ocean on the south side at Boston South End. This ring of parks opened up a much larger urban domain in a wide belt. The form and relationship of the parks was still indicated rather schematically in this plan. Over about the next twenty years, with some interruptions, work was done on the park system at different places. Over the course of this work the original cohesion envisioned by the plan, anchored in the landscape, was expanded into an urban fabric, further reinforced by the construction of a linking parkway. From Boston Common to the Back Bay area this cohesion was founded on the shape of the reclaimed land along the Charles River. This is where the connections were made with the historic city. From Back Bay to Jamaica Pond the cohesion was based on an artificially created 'river', a continuous chain of water features that was part of the urban drainage system. Still further inland the accent lay on the topographic relationships in the existing agricultural landscape. Here Franklin Park, lying in the highest part of the hills, formed the climax of the whole system. The final piece of the chain through the landscape was Marine Park, an public seaside resort on the ocean.

The effect of the landscape architectonic design

The plan was approved by the City Council, but after that went onto the back burner. The Commission had asked for an appropriation of five million dollars to purchase the land. The city had to borrow the funds for this by issuing bonds, but the financial situation after the economic crash of 1873 was bad. Moreover, at the same time massive investment in a new sewer system was necessary. At last, in 1877 the city made $450,000 available for the purchase of land for a park in the Back Bay. Because of the limited sum available, the Commissioners were forced to buy the worst land, with the deepest creeks, and then resell as much land along the edges for building purposes as possible.

In March, 1878, the Commission had title to the land needed, after which a public competition was held for the design. This Back Bay Park Competition produced 23 submissions. The first prize of 500 dollars went to the florist Herman Grundel. However, the Commissioners did not want to use this plan, which the *American Architect and Building News* had described as 'childish'. Olmsted was then commissioned to prepare a plan for the Back Bay. This first design laid the foundation for the realisation – and the success – of the governmental park plan.

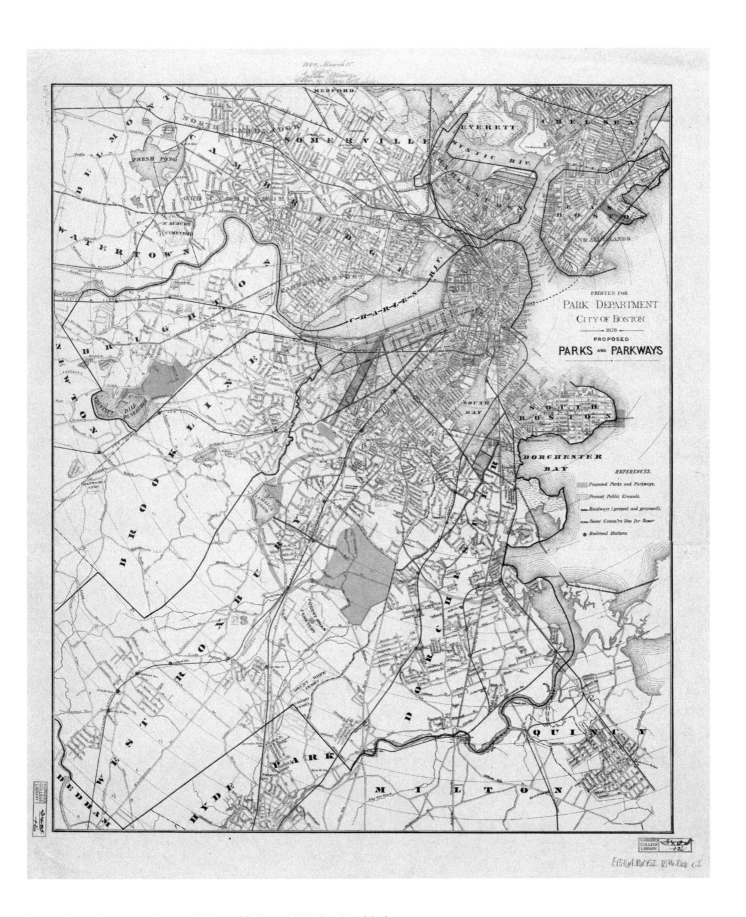

The Park Commission plan, 'Proposed Parks and Parkways', 1876, for a 'municipal park system' (Harvard College Library, Harvard Map Collection, MAP-LC G3764.B6G52 1876 .B66)

The water chain

Commonwealth Avenue ends at the Back Bay Fens, the lowest lying part of the park system along the drainage system. This system included the low-lying, brackish tidal area of the Fens, the somewhat higher basin of the Muddy River, and above that several lakes, of which Jamaica Pond was the most important. Olmsted used the 'natural' structure of this water chain as a means of reinforcing the visual-spatial coherence of the park series, but was careful in doing so that at the same time the natural drainage would become part of the urban drainage system. In this way he created both a functional-technical and a scenic-compositional coherence in this part of the park system, which then continued in the urban layout.

The Back Bay Fens

When Olmsted began with his plans for the Back Bay Fens in 1878, the Receiving Basin, as it had been formed in 1821 with the construction of the great Mill Dam and the barrage, had already been filled in. The area involved in his plan lay next to it, covering the eastern half of the Full Basin, with the two small streams, the Muddy River and Stony Brook, which together drained a large area of Roxbury, Dorchester and Brookline. Both were subject to tidal influence far inland. This was a problem particularly along the Stony Brook in Roxbury, because the stream's valley was narrow and the surrounding land relatively low. Moreover, both streams served as open sewers for the adjoining residential areas. The residue ended up directly in the Full Basin, to be carried out to sea with the ebbing tide. The construction of the Mill Dam, however, had interfered with the circulation of water from the ocean. This was complicated all the more by the construction of several railway embankments between 1830 and 1850. The water stagnated and at low tide the sewer sludge spread across the mud flats and into the winding creeks in the basin. As a result, the area was slowly becoming a threat to public health.

In the Park Commission plan of 1876 the park was shown schematically as a narrow strip between the Charles River and Parker Hill, crossing the salt marshes and mud flats of the Full Basin. After consultation with the city's engineer for sewer works, J.P. Davis, in his *Proposed Improvement of Back Bay* Olmsted revised the plan for this strip at a number of points. The core of his proposal was an ingeniously designed drainage system which made optimal use of the natural morphology.

The Boston Fens, with the new parks under construction (View of Boston, Massachusetts 1880. Drawn & published by H.H. Rowley & Co. Lith. by Beck & Pauli. Library of Congress G3764.B6A3 1880 .R6)

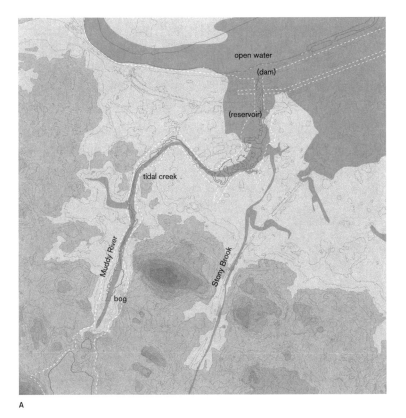

A

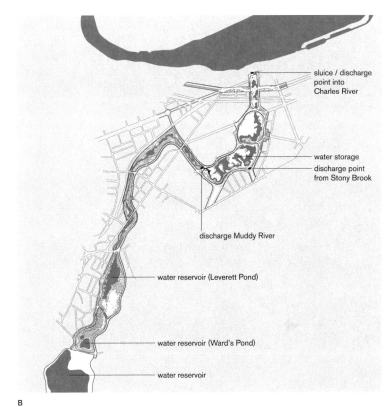

B

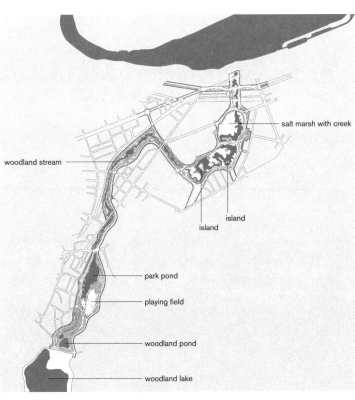

C

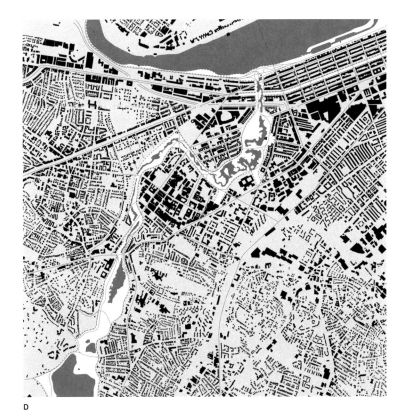

D

The transformation of natural water features into an urban park system

A   Tidal creek/streamlet (reconstruction)

B   Regulated water system

C   'Natural' park with through route

D   Present urban context

The discharge from the Muddy River and Stony Brook was separated from the creek system in the park and conducted directly to the Charles River and the sea by separate pipes.

The intake of water from the Muddy River and Stony Brook into the park's creek system was regulated by two small sluices on the south side. If the water level in the rivers rose above the water level in the park, for instance as the result of heavy rain, the valves to the Fens automatically opened. In this way the park's creek system functioned as an overflow and holding reservoir for the two rivers. On the side of the park toward the sea, a sluice was also built on the Charles River. The intake and discharge of salt water to and from the creeks in the park was regulated via this sluice. By means of openings and gates, the tidal fluctuations inland were reduced to about 30 centimetres. This was enough to prevent stagnation and keep the creek system in the park flushed with salt water. On the other hand, it was little enough to prevent wave action and erosion from the gently sloping mud banks that Olmsted carefully designed. In cases of high water (as a result of flooding or overflow from the two rivers) a larger part of the marshes in the park could be flooded, without the water level rising more than a couple of feet (about 60 centimetres). When the tide fell, the extra water could be released into the Charles River through a gate under Beacon Street. If necessary, the creek system in the park could also be drained entirely. The whole hydraulic system for regulating the water was adjusted in such a way that it worked automatically.

The movement, quality and level of the water was regulated, without destroying the image of a natural salt marsh landscape. It is true the creek system in the park was derived from the existing natural pattern, but it in fact had been redesigned. Within the boundaries of the park, stretches of the old creeks were linked up to create a continuous stream with the right dimensions, at the right level. The new creek was dredged to the ebb tide level and embedded in a large salt marsh that was raised with the spoils from the creek. Together they covered almost the whole surface of the park. The outline of the park was also adjusted with regard to the new creek, with several bulges in edges of the ground plan at the points where it was connected with the two small rivers.

The planting of the marsh was another question entirely, and demanded the specialist knowledge of outsiders. Barren mud banks could be prevented by not allowing the water level fluctuate too much. More species were planted than would be found in a natural salt marsh landscape: in the marsh itself, grasses, mixed with goldenrod and asters, and on the banks various varieties of salt-tolerant wild flowers and low shrubs. Along the edges of the park, beyond the reach of the salt, bushes and shade trees were planted as a transition to the adjoining residential areas. An access system was designed for the outside, comprised of a footpath, a park drive, a bridle path and city streets planted with trees that crossed through the park at several points via bridges and dams.

The realisation of the park was completed in 1895. In fact, it did not resemble a normal park; Olmsted therefore urged that it not be called Back Bay Park but Back Bay Fens. The space here was too limited for the composition of a complete landscape park with a 'garden', 'meadow' and 'wilderness'. Here Olmsted placed the 'wilderness' directly in the urban space, almost without any envelope.

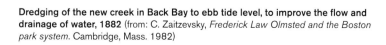

Dredging of the new creek in Back Bay to ebb tide level, to improve the flow and drainage of water, 1882 (from: C. Zaitzevsky, *Frederick Law Olmsted and the Boston park system*. Cambridge, Mass. 1982)

The present appearance of the creek in Back Bay (photo: C.H.E. van Ees)

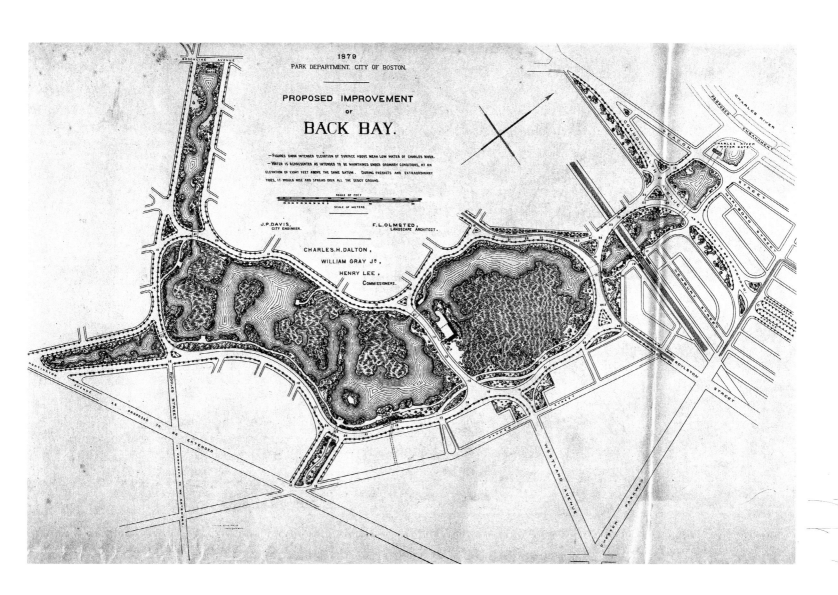

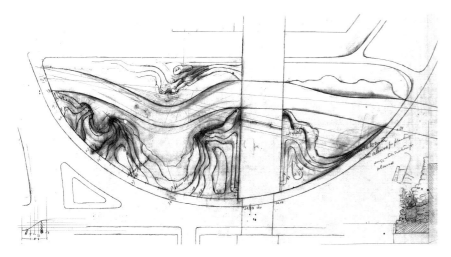

Olmsted's plan for the Back Bay Fens, 1879 (Olmsted National Historic Site, Olmsted Plans and Drawings Collection)

Design study for a bank in Back Bay by Beacon Entrance, by John C. Olmsted, 1882 (Olmsted National Historic Site, Olmsted Plans and Drawings Collection)

The Muddy River Improvement

The Muddy River was not a part of the Park Commission's 1876 plan, in which Back Bay Park along the east side of Parker Hill was linked with Jamaica Pond. But the reorganisation of Back Bay and the changes in the water management programme necessarily involved the Muddy River, which ran along the west side of Parker Hill, so that its rearrangement was obvious too. The Muddy River was the natural boundary between Boston (Roxbury) and Brookline. On the Brookline side, Longwood was an attractive residential area, and the Brookline Land Company wanted to develop new land for dwellings. On the Boston side there was a wooded bank with suburban development and a view out over the valley. Collaboration between the park commissions of the two communities was a prerequisite for the development of any plan.

Initially Olmsted came up with a suggestion to redesign the banks. In 1880 he made a first schematic plan entitled *Suggestion for the Improvement of Muddy River*. In this plan the twists of the old tidal stream were replaced by the lightly meandering pattern of a brook. The large bog between the upper and lower reaches of the stream was replaced by a lake (Leverett Pond) which was connected with Ward's Pond by a small rivulet. After this plan was approved, the site was carefully surveyed, and in 1881 Olmsted's agency prepared a *General Plan for the Sanitary Improvement of Muddy River*. Later Olmsted altered this plan several times to enlarge its tight boundaries and fit it into the topography as sympathetically as possible. To obtain the optimal scenic route for the Muddy River Olmsted even proposed redrawing the boundary between Boston and Brookline.

Muddy River was comprised of two sections, the lower reaches, where tidal effects and salt water still played a role, and the upper reaches, which took the form of a freshwater brook. The lower reaches extended from Leverett Pond to the Back Bay Fens, the freshwater section from Ward's Pond to Leverett Pond. Leverett Pond, originally a brackish swamp still reached by salt water only at spring tide, lay on the boundary. Above Leverett Pond the land rose with a series of small, wooded hills to Ward's Pond, a 'kettle hole' or small glacial lake. Before the regulation of the water system in the Back Bay Fens, the tidal effects in the lower reaches of the Muddy River had already been decreased as a result of the construction of the Mill Dam. That had led to the water becoming stagnant, brackish and a breeding place for mosquitoes. Moreover, the stream, like the Back Bay, had become overloaded with sewer water, causing flooding with high tide and heavy rain storms.

Olmsted's plan placed the source of the Muddy River at Ward's Pond, the level of which was maintained by an overflow from Jamaica Pond.

Through a chain of ponds and small dams, water from Ward's Pond was conducted in a narrow stream to Leverett Pond, which had been deepened by dredging. To assure it of sufficient water, the Brookline Town Brook was also directed there through a conduit. A dam with a spillway was built on the north side of Leverett Pond, at the transition point between the upper and lower reaches, to regulate its water level. A whole new stream bed with sloping banks was dug for the lower course of the Muddy River, broadening out here and there. Through a sluice with an overflow (the Muddy River Gate House) the water was ultimately discharged into the Back Bay Fens. Laying out the plan in the terrain was an exacting task, and the earthworks and slopes had to be executed with precision.

The park's boundaries were extremely narrow. To still guarantee some degree of separation from the adjoining neighbourhoods, a thickly planted earthen embankment was raised on the west side, between the railway line and the pedestrian path, and planted islands were introduced into the widened stream at some points. Further, the whole length of the banks were planted, and there were only a few smaller open fields. Only at Leverett Pond was there a larger meadow. Scores of bridges were built where the roads that linked the area with the city crossed the park. In fact, the park was comprised only of a park route, for which the watercourse provided the continuity in the landscape. In the legend to his 1881 plan Olmsted himself termed it "a continuous promenade between Boston Common and Jamaica Pond".

Construction of the new bed for the Muddy River (1891) (from: C. Zaitzevsky, *Frederick Law Olmsted and the Boston park system.* Cambridge, Mass. 1982)

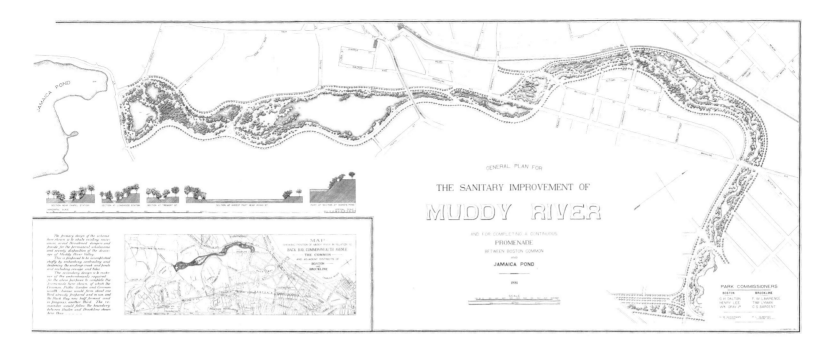

Olmsted's plan for the Muddy River Improvement, 1881 (Olmsted National Historic Site, Olmsted Plans and Drawings Collection)

The present appearence of the Muddy River (photo: C.H.E. van Ees)

Jamaica Pond

Jamaica Pond, a large glacial lake, was such a powerful natural feature that it was given a place in most of the park plans that were developed after 1850. In the Park Commission's plan Jamaica Pond was even the most important link between Back Bay in the north and Franklin Park in the south. Until 1848 the lake was an important fresh water reservoir for the city. One could go boating there, and skate in the winter. Jamaica Plain, the landscape around the Pond, was a favourite place for country homes and summer houses for the wealthier residents of Boston. Several large country homes and private estates bounded on the lake, such as Holm Lea, the estate of Ignatius Sargent, whose son later became director of the botanical garden at Harvard, and of the Arnold Arboretum. Around 1870 there were also two ice factories along the shores of the lake, which more seriously threatened to disrupt the rustic scene, and were also a source for water pollution. This was reason for the Park Commission to include Jamaica Pond in its plans, thus securing the future of a unique piece of nature. Because the majority of the land around the lake was in private hands and commanded huge prices, the Park Commission however could only acquire a relatively narrow strip around the lake.

Retaining the unique natural character of the site was the first concern in the design that Olmsted and his agency prepared for the lake in 1892. It had to be made accessible for the public, with as few interventions as possible. To this end, here and there small areas along the banks were filled in to create space for a path encircling the lake. The glacial landscape of 'knobs' and 'kettles' on the north and south sides was left as it was, thereby retaining much more of a small-scale character than the landscaped slopes and meadows that Olmsted normally worked with in his parks. For the planting, to a great extent he made use of the existing groves of pines, birches and other species along the shores.

Although in this park too the wilderness – now in the form of a natural glacial lake – was the heart of the plan, there were also several garden elements included. Directly opposite the entrance at Pond Street lay a boat house; a bathhouse that was planned for the south-west corner was, however, never built. Olmsted retained two of the houses which were already present on the site, for recreational purposes, one on the north and one on the south side. The unobtrusiveness of these elements only reinforced the overwhelmingly natural appearance of the lake. Jamaica Pond was an impressive final chord in the water chain that Olmsted had designed. At the same time, this park around the lake formed the transition to the grander landscape of Franklin Park, the main park in the Boston Park System.

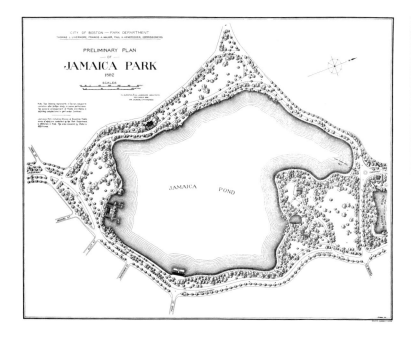

Olmsted's tentative plan for Jamaica Pond, 1892 (Olmsted National Historic Site, Olmsted Plans and Drawings Collection)

View of Jamaica Pond near Pond Street around 1892 (from: C. Zaitzevsky, *Frederick Law Olmsted and the Boston park system*. Cambridge, Mass. 1982)

The present water landscape of Jamaica Pond (photo: C.H.E. van Ees)

The parks in the hills

In the 1876 Park Commission plan, the climax of the series of parks was to be Franklin Park. This was the large and complete park that Olmsted believed every great city must have. Only in a vast landscape park like it could the city dweller really come in contact with nature. The scale had to be spectacular, but the image simple and rural. The space had to be large enough to screen off the surrounding buildings and evoke the illusion of boundlessness. In addition to giving it these elementary characteristics, in Franklin Park Olmsted designed a place for the active forms of recreation that were becoming increasingly popular.

The Arnold Arboretum, between Jamaica Pond and Franklin Park, the component of the Boston Park System which lay farthest inland, likewise covered a relatively large area, but its function as a park remained secondary. In fact it was an extra attraction, a place where the real plant-lover could enjoy a rich collection of trees and bushes. Both parks represented the agricultural landscape – the Arnold Arboretum horticulture, which in that day had many avid followers, and Franklin Park the pastoral landscape and the wild nature that was a part of it.

The Arnold Arboretum

The Arnold Arboretum in West Roxbury was not a part of the original plan of the Park Commission in 1876. Its contours were defined by the topography of the agrarian landscape and more or less random property boundaries, which reflected the history of their evolution. The history of the arboretum went back to the Benjamin Bussey Farm, a farm which in the beginning of the 19th century grew into an estate with a number of farms, with several woods and a fine collection of trees. Additionally, the area was intersected by streams, and there were several hills, including Hemlock Hill, Peters' Hill and Bussey Hill. Bussey Farm was open to the public and functioned as an informal park.

In 1842 Bussey left the estate to Harvard University, to be used as an agricultural college. There was however no funding for this, until in 1868 the amateur horticulturist James Arnold left a legacy of $100,000 for horticultural purposes. George B. Emerson, one of the administrators of the legacy and author of *Trees and Shrubs Growing Naturally in the Forests of Massachusetts* (1846), proposed that the money be used to establish an arboretum, a scientifically organised collection of trees and shrubs. In consultation with the Harvard Botanic Garden, it was decided that the money would be devoted to setting up such a collection at Bussey Farm. The botanist Charles Sprague Sargent (1841-1927), who around 1872 became director of the botanical garden at Harvard, was placed in charge.

Sargent understood that the financing of the necessary construction work and eventual management required a broader base of support. He therefore began negotiations with the city of Boston with regard to the conditions under which the park could be transferred to the city. To add force to his argument, Sargent needed a good plan that not only recommended itself for its extraordinary collection of plants but also for its fine landscape design. While Sargent negotiated with Harvard and Boston, Olmsted began to draw up a plan. In 1882 the parties reached an agreement in which the city acquired the land and committed itself to making several adjoining sites available, and also to the maintenance of the infrastructure. The city then leased the facility to Harvard for a thousand years, and made it available for scientific purposes.

Olmsted's design was very restrained, consisting only of the route system and an arrangement of the collection of trees and bushes. Within the fragmented contours of the site, Olmsted sought to accentuate the natural morphology of the land and thus restore continuity. The Public Drive, which linked the park with the city, made optimal use of the relief. This was laid out so that it ran in a winding fashion along the two small streams on the sides of the arboretum before making a large loop around Bussey Hill. At the foot of the hill a side branch ran to the top, from which one could survey all of Boston over the trees.

Franklin Park

Franklin Park was originally a piece of untouched agricultural landscape containing a dozen small farmsteads. The landscape was typical for Massachusetts, its principle element being a rolling, open valley about 1600 meters long and averaging about 400 meters in width, enclosed by wooded hills. It lay between two railway lines; the New York and New England Railway on the east and the Boston and Providence Line on the west provided excellent access. Because the city fathers hoped that the costs of building the park would be covered by a bequest from Benjamin Franklin, they had changed the name of the area from West Roxbury Park to Franklin Park. Acquisition of the land began in 1881, but ran into a number of problems because of high damage claims. Moreover, it proved difficult to raise enough funds to compensate for the appreciation in land values.

After the surveying of the site was completed in 1883, Olmsted began to develop his plan. The area was surrounded by wide roads, but the buildings of West Roxbury did not yet extend to the boundaries of the park. In 1886 the Park Commission approved Olmsted's plan. In his design the outer edges of the park were surrounded by avenues. Internally it was comprised of two sections, the Ante-Park and the Country Park.

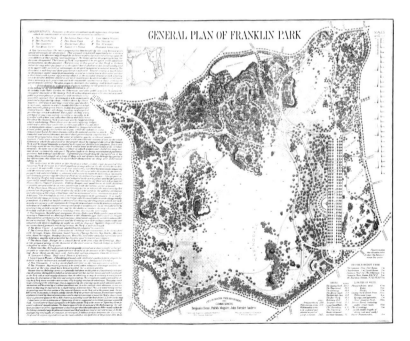

Olmsted's plan for the Arnold Arboretum, 1879 (Olmsted National Historic Site, Olmsted Plans and Drawings Collection)

Olmsted's plan for Franklin Park, 1885 (Olmsted National Historic Site, Olmsted Plans and Drawings Collection)

The wooded landscape of the Arnold Arboretum (photo: C.H.E. van Ees)

Present appearence of the Country Park in Franklin Park (photo: C.H.E. van Ees)

The Ante-Park functioned as a forecourt for the Country Park, and contained facilities for sports and other activities that, in Olmsted's opinion, did not belong in the actual park. The most important space in the Ante-Park was the Playstead, a twelve hectare playing field for school sports in the northern point of the park, in a somewhat levelled natural meadow, with a 150-meter long raised terrace for spectators on the west side. A second important component of the Ante-Park was the Great Mall, also called the Greeting, an 800-meter long promenade with paths for pedestrians, carriages and horses. Places were planned on the outer edge of the Ante-Park for an amphitheatre, a zoo, a deer park, a playground and an open sports field (Sargent's Field).

The Country Park occupied about two-thirds of Olmsted's design for Franklin Park. In his vision, this was the real park, where one was not distracted by decorative arrangements, or bothered by other activities or noise. Here one could experience nature and the landscape directly. The most important space in the Country Park was a great north-south oriented valley, with a smaller, east-west oriented side valley, Ellicottdale, at an angle to it. To enhance the pastoral image, sheep were to graze in these valleys. On the rocky soil of the upper rim of the valleys lay wooded slopes with thick undergrowth, to shut out the city.

The Ante-Park and the Country Park were separated from one another by Glen Lane, an urban route (later an auto road) that cut through the park from north to south. Two park circuits lay on either side, on the west the Park Drive in the Country Park, and on the east the park route in the Ante-Park. The two circuits touched each other at two points, with crossings over Glen Lane. The entrances to the Country Park at those points were gated, so that it could be closed at night.

The zoning of the classic English landscape park is clearly recognisable in the division of Franklin Park. The Ante-Park, with all its facilities and structures for active recreation, corresponds to the 'garden'. The 'wilderness' is represented in the thickly planted and rocky edges of the valleys in the Country Park. The pastoral landscape of the open valleys in the central section of the Country Park makes up the 'meadow', the support for the spatial form. By his distinction between an Ante-Park and a Country Park within one compositonal entity, Olmsted made a final attempt to secure the pure image of the real landscape and intact nature in the park, against the growing demands for recreational space made by the encroaching city.

The sightlines over the valleys unite the two sections of the park, and also run on through outside the park, in the north-south direction to Forest Hill and the Blue Hills of Milton, and in the east-west direction to Refectory Hill and the Arnold Arboretum. With these views, which were to always remain open and undeveloped, Olmsted created the illusion of an uninterrupted landscape. But this could not conceal the fact that internally the balance had in fact already tipped to a division in functions, which is the hallmark of the utilitarian park. The unadulterated image of Arcadia had lost ground to everyday practice and the multiformity of urban life.

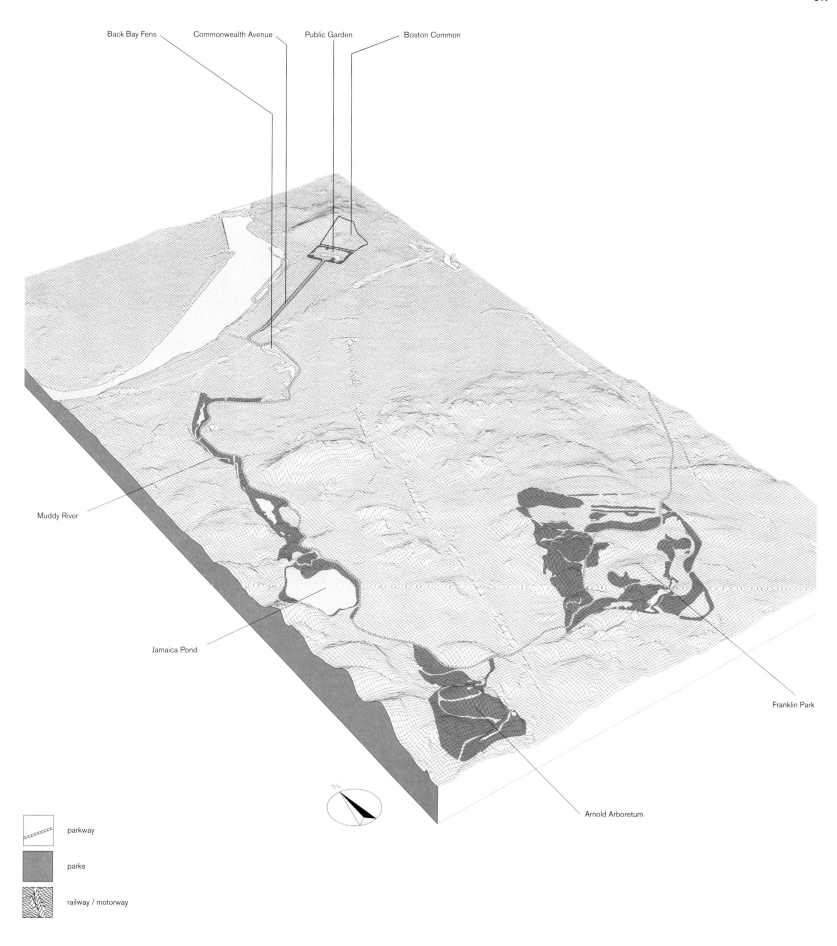

Back Bay Fens

Commonwealth Avenue

Public Garden

Boston Common

Muddy River

Jamaica Pond

Franklin Park

Arnold Arboretum

N

parkway

parks

railway / motorway

Three-dimensional model of the Emerald Necklace
(detail 4.9 × 8.9 km, one cell of the grid measures 25 × 25 m, z = 5×)

The tail piece on the ocean, and the parkway

Although the series of parks found its natural climax in Franklin Park, with its vistas that dissolved into the surrounding landscape, the park system conceived by the Park Commission in 1876 still had a final piece in a park outside the coastline, at the head of Boston's South End, connected with the other parks by a parkway.

Marine Park

Marine Park was planned for a wider spot in a strip along the ocean near Dorchester Point, obtained through filling out from the shore, in combination with the construction of a broad embankment running out to Castle Island, which lay off the coast. Olmsted's first sketches from 1883 already established the main lines of the design. On the south side Olmsted foresaw a curved pier as a promenade and play area for children. The soil needed would come from dredging operations in the shallow mud flats, which were regularly exposed at low tide. In this way a protected bay was to be created, nearly encircled by a long beach in the form of an open-air theatre.

Because of the importance that the federal government attached to Castle Island and Fort Independence, which stood on it, it was however not until 1920 that the island was connected with South Boston. Nevertheless, even in Olmsted's day Marine Park was already the most popular park in Boston. It offered a wonderful opportunity to spend a day by the ocean, to play, swim and sail. One could also enjoy the views out over the ocean from the tree-lined drive along the whole shore, with the beach and bay in the middle distance. Olmsted did not regard Marine Park as a park in the real sense of the word. In the terminology of Franklin Park we could call it an Ante-Park, or a garden. Olmsted himself called it Pleasure Bay, to indicate that here the accent lay on recreational uses.

The parkway as the string of the Emerald Necklace

The Boston Park Commissioners' plan of 1876 also included a number of smaller parks and playgrounds with a more local function within the already densely built-up sections of the city. These parks all lay on the water; most of them on fill along the shore. Among them were Charlesbank Park along Back Bay, Wood Island Park on the coast by East Boston Harbor, Charlestown Heights on the slope of Bunker Hill on the Mystic River, and North End Park in North End, the northern harbour section of old Boston. The parks of the Necklace, which were

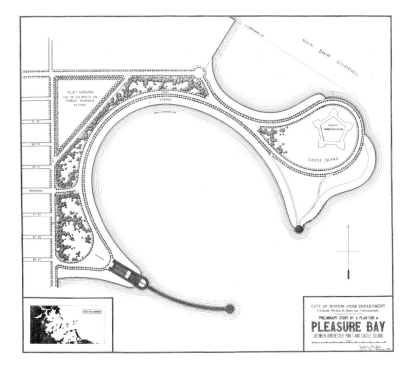

Olmsted's tentative plan for Pleasure Bay, 1883 (Olmsted National Historic Site, Olmsted Plans and Drawings Collection)

The pier at Pleasure Bay in 1892 (Olmsted National Historic Site, Olmsted Plans and Drawings Collection)

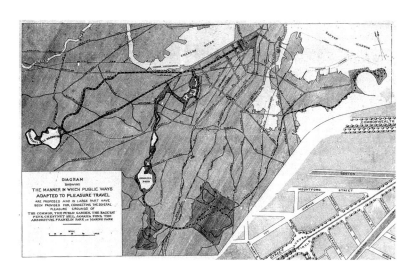

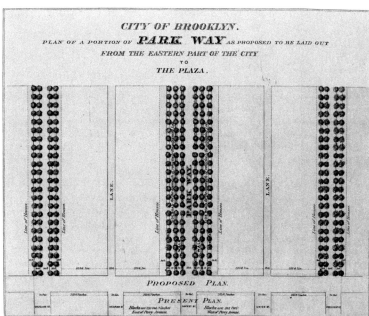

Diagram with the connecting parkways to Marine Pond and Chestnut Hill Reservoir (Olmsted National Historic Site, Olmsted Plans and Drawings Collection)

Olmsted's plan for a parkway in Brooklyn, NY (from: C.E. Beveridge, P. Rocheleau & D. Larkin, *Frederick Law Olmsted: designing the American landscape*. New York 1995)

Ocean Parkway, Brooklyn, NY, ca. 1894 (City of New York - Parks & Recreation, Photo Archive. Image AR1099.)

intended for all the city's residents, were distinguished from these by their location, size and facilities, but more particularly because they were connected with one another by parkways.

A parkway was then a spaciously conceived, broad avenue with a differentiated cross section supported by planting. The avenues constructed under Hausmann (1809-1891) in Paris, such as the 120-meter wide Avenue de l'Impératrice to the Bois de Boulogne, played an important role as models. Olmsted divided the traffic which would make use of the parkway into pedestrians, horseback riders and vehicles. The vehicles could move along the Drive; for the pedestrians he furnished Promenades on either side of the Drive. Horseback riders used the Saddle, which lay between the Drive and one of the Promenades. There was also often a street which ran parallel to the parkway behind the buildings which faced onto it. This street was intended for the 'dirty' urban through traffic.

Olmsted's *Diagram showing the manner in which public ways adapted to pleasure travel are proposed*, from 1887, shows a parkway running through from Boston Common and the Public Garden, via Back Bay, Jamaica Pond and Franklin Park, out to Marine Park. The Chestnut Hill Reservoir in Brighton was also linked with this system by parkways. The first part of the route was formed by Commonwealth Avenue, a wide, formal avenue over the newly reclaimed land in Back Bay, between Boston Common and the Back Bay Fens.

Olmsted conceived the route of the parkway as a single entity, comprised of segments with a varying landscape character derived from the local circumstances. He called the parkway along the edge of the Back Bay Fens, with an open character and views over the Fens, the Fenway. The parkway along the east side of the Muddy River, with a more intimate and woodsy character, he called the Riverway. The next section, the Jamaica Way, curved along the lake and was open to the water. Near the Arnold Arboretum the parkway became the Arborway, a woods way, to then enter Franklin Park as a monumental avenue. There it ran along the edges of the Country Park, to veer of in a north-easterly direction at the start of the Greeting. Via the Dorchesterway the parkway connected with the Strandway, a grand new land extension along the coast of South Boston with magnificent views over the ocean. This parkway was built in stages. In 1895, when Olmsted retired, the system was in principle complete. One could indeed then justly speak of an Emerald Necklace, a chain of emerald green around the neck of Boston.

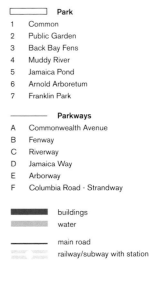

The park system and the parkways in the present urban morphology

	Park
1	Common
2	Public Garden
3	Back Bay Fens
4	Muddy River
5	Jamaica Pond
6	Arnold Arboretum
7	Franklin Park

	Parkways
A	Commonwealth Avenue
B	Fenway
C	Riverway
D	Jamaica Way
E	Arborway
F	Columbia Road - Strandway

buildings
water

main road
railway/subway with station

0   500   1000m

The first urban park system

Between 1878 and 1895 the Boston Park System, as it was conceived in the plan of the Park Commission, was realised step by step, being changed and adapted constantly in the process. Olmsted's insight into the spatial potential of the landscape at hand, his concept of the park as a mirror image of the city, and his disciplined and purposeful deployment of landscape architectonic design instruments played a decisive role in this. Through his perseverance not only was Back Bay Park changed from an ornamental park into an civil engineering project with a unique expression in the landscape, but the whole Necklace became a coherent park system which, through its technical and scenic quality, could serve as a framework for a new city.

The park system as the landscape backbone of the city

The starting point for the Municipal Park System was a collection of outstanding sites in the landscape. Olmsted succeeded in catching the character of these places in a landscape architectonic concept and anchoring them in the memory of the city as a design. The *genius loci* of the city was exposed at a number of critical spots, which were then linked into a landscape chain in the Emerald Necklace. As though it were a typological series, this chain contains the entire diversity of the landscapes around the city, and inscribes them in the city's morphology.

In Boston the individual city park, like Central Park, which was still defined in terms of a single place, grew into an series of urban landscapes, which represented the *genius loci* on the scale of the whole city. Rather than the continuity of the urban grid, the continuity of the landscape in the park system became the backbone for the city's morphology. Olmsted's idea for accomplishing this was based on a merger of the park series with the city's infrastructure, so that the parks at the same time formed the antithesis of the urban grid. By taking the existing landscape typology as his point of departure, he created a firmly anchored park system, which could accept both the changes in the pattern of the city and the changes in the pattern of park usage without being lost.

Olmsted could not have foreseen that his design for the salt marsh of the Back Bay Fens would only exist for 15 years. As part of the regulation of the whole Charles River estuary, in 1910 the Charles River Dam was completed, so that the estuary became fresh water and the tidal fluctuations disappeared. The park had to be redesigned, and became neglected. Although radical changes have also taken place in the Muddy River Improvement, such as a fly-over at the intersection with South Huntingdon Avenue, the creation of a large parking area where it connects with the Fens, and the levelling of the meadow at Leverett Pond for a sports field, the concept of the park has held up.

At Jamaica Pond, and in the Arnold Arboretum, Olmsted's original design has largely remained intact, albeit that with high-rise buildings the urban skyline has now intruded in the picture, and the Arnold Arboretum has expanded with the acquisition of additional land. The most thoroughgoing changes have taken place in Franklin Park. As early as 1891 Scarboro Pond was dug in the south-west of Country Park as an extra attraction. On the contrary, because of a lack of funds the Greeting, which Olmsted had intended as the most important bearer for urban activities in the park, was never realised.

Olmsted had endeavoured to keep the Country Park pure by segregating the active forms of use in a separate section of the park. But the enjoyment of nature alone proved to be too weak a foundation. The park was 'abused' for other purposes, such as sports, mass gatherings and attractions. Security also became an issue. The city's answer was to increase the number of attractions still more, with a golf course, a stadium, a rose garden and a zoo. On the other hand, despite changes made during its realisation, the concept for Marine Park, where Olmsted had allowed the active use programme to prevail, has held its own.

These two parks illustrate that, quite apart from the increase in the scale of the city and the acceleration in the pace of its growth which had caused the development from a simple city park to a park system, there was also an internal revolution that occurred in the spatial structure. In the shift from the enjoyment of nature to a park for active use, as this began in and with Franklin Park, a functional green structure was already revealing itself. Design with this in mind would henceforth no longer depart primarily from the qualities of the landscape at hand, but from the recreational programme and the habitation structure of the city.

Charles Eliot's metropolitan park system

The 1876 park plan was carefully fitted in to the administrative boundaries of the municipality of Boston. After the completion of this plan toward the end of the century, there was renewed interest in a much greater metropolitan park system that would also include other communities within Boston's sphere of influence. The Chestnut Hill Circuit, with the Chestnut Hill Reservoir and its accompanying parkways in the community of Brighton, which had already been drawn in in the municipal park plan, were in fact the impetus for this. The decisive step for the creation of a metropolitan park system was taken by the

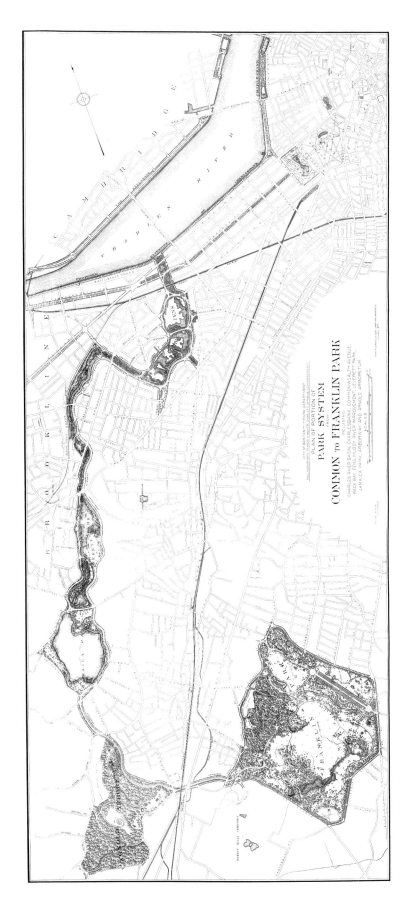

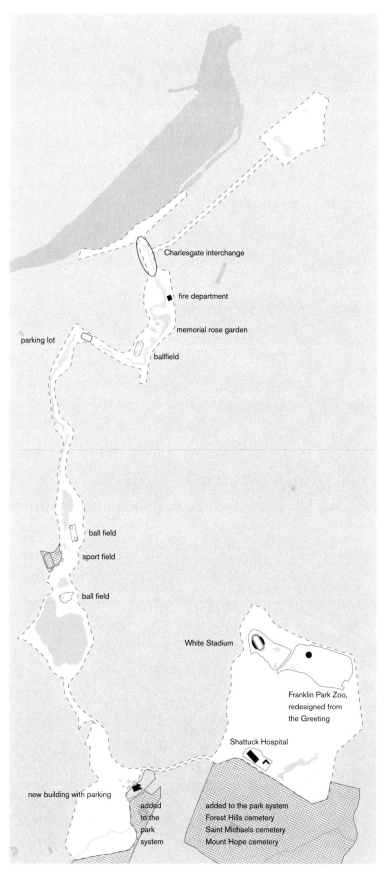

Charlesgate interchange

fire department

memorial rose garden

parking lot

ballfield

ball field

sport field

ball field

White Stadium

Franklin Park Zoo,
redesigned from
the Greeting

Shattuck Hospital

new building with parking

added
to the
park
system

added to the park system
Forest Hills cemetery
Saint Michaels cemetery
Mount Hope cemetery

The Emerald Necklace in 1894 (left) and later changes and additions (right) (Olmsted
National Historic Site, Olmsted Plans and Drawings Collection)

landscape architect Charles Eliot, when in 1890 he took the initiative in establishing the Trustees of Public Reservations. The aim of this group was to undertake a large-scale inventory of available spaces that were of public importance, and attempt to acquire them.

Charles Eliot (1859-1897) was born in Cambridge, Massachusetts, where his father, Charles Eilliam Eliot, was president of Harvard University. In 1883 Eliot entered the employ of Olmsted's agency as a trainee, where the projects he worked on included the designs for the Back Bay Fens (1883), Franklin Park (1884) and the Arnold Arboretum (1885) in Boston. In 1885, on Olmsted's advice he made a tour through Europe to look at the landscape there and study the work of famous landscape architects like Capabillity Brown, Humphry Repton, Joseph Paxton and prince Pückler-Muskau. Among the sites he visited in the course of his trip was the basin of the Alster in Hamburg, now closed off with a dam. Back in Boston, in 1886 he opened his own agency together with Henry Sargent Codman. After Sargent's death, in 1893 Eliot finally joined Olmsted's agency, and as Olmsted's health declined rapidly became its leading figure.

In 1892 Eliot's initiative led to the founding of a Metropolitan Park Commission, on which he sat as an advisor. The *Metropolitan Park Report* from this commission in 1893 was based on a proposal by Eliot, and contained a regional plan with various reserves to be acquired within a radius of about 15 kilometres around Boston. These included woodland reservations (Middlesex Fells, Stony Brook, Blue Hills), river reservations (Charles River, Neponset River, Mystic River) and sea coast reservations (Reserve Beach). With this, the plan contained the principle elements of the physical-geographical structure, connected with one another by parkways. Moreover, it provided for parkways connecting the municipal and metropolitan park systems, such as for instance the West Roxbury Parkway as a link between the Arnold Arboretum and the Stony Brook Reservation. This resulted in a regional structure of landscape reservations based on selection and protection, management and improvement, somewhat akin to today's concept of 'main ecological structure'. The increase in scale in the park system to the metropolitan level did not however mean that the landscape architecture also began to manifested itself at this scale.

An unbreakable chain of landscapes

Eliot used modern analytical methods and described the landscape as an accumulation of various systems: cultural, economic and ecological. He also added a new 'strategic' vocabulary to the discipline. Where Olmsted thought and wrote about 'landscapes', designed landscapes such as landscape parks, parkways and pastoral refuges where one could retreat and feed on nature, Eliot chiefly used the term 'scenery', existing, beautiful cultural landscapes that were useful for the urbanite, and matching structural concepts, to conserve them and secure them as public space. The emphasis here lay not on the design, but on the protection and management of the landscape in landscape reservations, as the starting point for a recreational experience of nature. Eliot's concept of the importance of landscape architectonic design consisted of planning local interventions, distributed across a large area and focused on the enhancement of experience. The question of how landscape architecture could get a grip on the regional structure of metropolitan landscapes was not asked, let alone answered.

The significance of Olmsted's work, on the other hand, lies precisely in the quality of his designing, in the manner in which he was able to transform the scheme of the Park Commission in 1876 into a landscape architectonic composition, and was able to link this with civil engineering and urban systems. He designed an unbreakable chain of landscapes, thereby bringing the concept of a park system, essentially a matter of urban planning, within the scope of landscape architecture.

Charles Eliot's proposal for a Metropolitan Park System (Boston Public Library, Norman
B. Leventhal Map Center, G3764.B6E63 1893.W3)

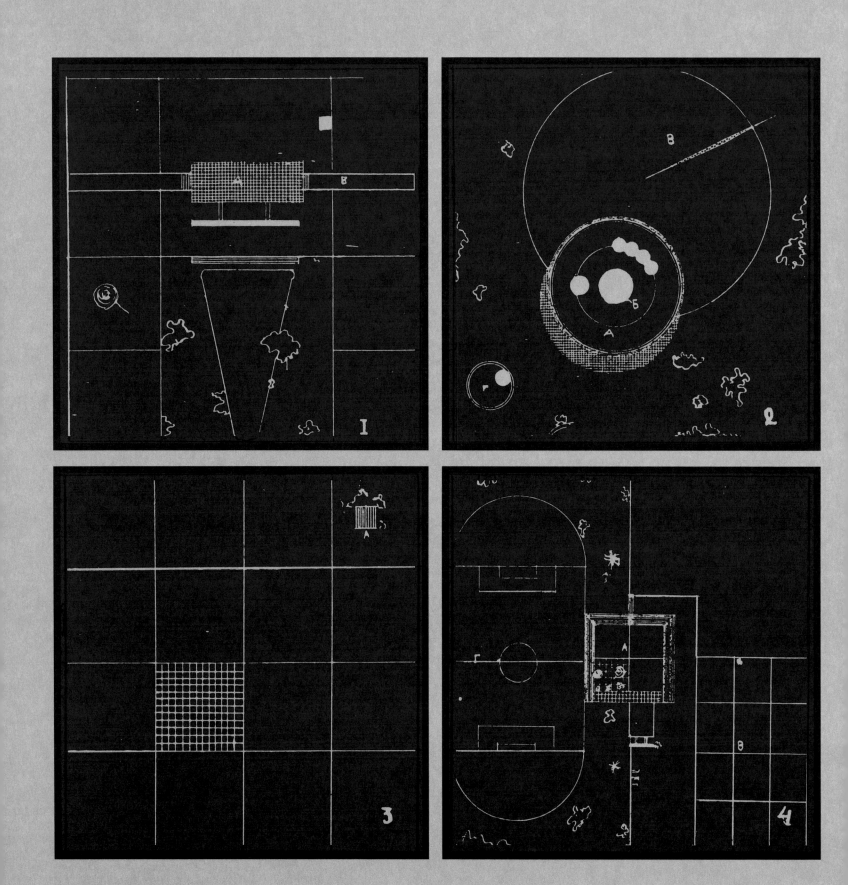

Collage of the plan for a Palace of Culture in the form of a Volkspark, to be laid out
the site of the Simonov monastery, Moscow. Ivan Leonidov, 1930 (from A. Kopp, *Ville
et révolution: architecture et urbanisme sovietiques des années vingt*. Paris 1967)

3 LANDSCAPE FORM AND URBAN PROGRAMME

In the modern city of the 20th century landscape architecture, rooted in the tradition of the 19th century city park, was confronted with mass residential development and with a new, hierarchical system of recreational facilities. In the design of green space an increasingly sharp break began to appear with both the topography of the landscape and the standard landscape typology of the 19th century city park. The quest for a functional form in combination with a gradually more thoroughgoing zoning and differentiation of the recreational programme led to solutions in which the form of the urban landscape began to gradually orient itself to the urban pattern and urban morphology.

The Stadtpark Hamburg played a decisive role in the transformation of the 19th century city park into a functional, recreational Volkspark for the urban masses, in which the landscape architectonic paradigms of the park form were called into question.

Frankfurt demonstrates how this process developed toward the creation of the settlement park, an urban landscape in which a new balance was sought between the house, the garden and the landscape, as original constituent elements of the man-made landscape. This led to rethinking the balance between functional-productive and contextual-topographic aspects. The urban landscape broke away from the stylised landscape typology of the 19th century city park through a return to the agricultural landscape as a reference point for the spatial organisation of the settlement park.

On the other hand, in the green belts and green radials of Cologne the city park as an autonomous spatial type dissolved into a multitude of green spatial forms. Urban green space detached itself from its landscape context and became a programmatically standardised, spatially zoned network of recreational landscapes. In the process its landscape architectonic form developed from the specific to the generic, leading to a series of repeatable spatial constructions.

STADTPARK HAMBURG 1902

Monumentalising the practical landscape
Fritz Schumacher
Leberecht Migge
The functional form as an artwork

The Elbe in the North German Plain

Toward a functional design for urban space
Villas and working-class neighbourhoods along the Alster
A cemetery as model

The debate over functional form
The Senate Commission's programme
A competition for ideas
Schumacher's compromise

An urban recreational landscape
An enclosed spatial series
The recreational machine
A celebration of a common space

The Volkspark
The differentiation of otium
Zweckgebilde (the visualisation of functional form)
The limits of landscape architectonic form

Stadtpark Hamburg in Winterhude (aerial photo: Matthias Friedel Luftbildphotographie)

Monumentalising the practical landscape

The 19th century walking park, termed a *Volksgarten* in German, provided the opportunity for strollers to meet one another and experience the beauty of nature, to be reinvigorated by the idyllic scenes and tableaux. In his *Theorie der Gartenkunst* Christian Cay Lorenz Hirschfeld wrote that it was the place for social encounters and conversation. The *Volksgarten* could, he thought, imperceptibly cleanse the urban dweller from the baleful influences of the city. During the 19th century the *Volksgarten* increasingly took on a social significance. This was visible in rudimentary form in the Volksgarten Klosterberge in Magdeburg, designed by Peter Joseph Lenné in 1824 as a commission from the city. In addition to dramatising the *Auenlandschaft* (the meadow landscape with oaks outside the dikes) of the River Elbe, public welfare, health aspects, accessibility for the urban population and technology as a symbol of social progress had also already begun to play a role in this park.

The beginning of the 20th century saw the rise of an urban reform movement that from its inception was permeated by emancipatory social ideals; they wanted a park 'of the people and for the people', characterised by a pursuit of simplicity and efficiency. The park was to be designed as a great open-air home for the people, with various spaces for the most diverse activities by groups, but also by individuals. The spaces had to be arranged with regard to one another in such a way that the whole was more than the sum of the parts, and resulted in a beautiful park landscape.

The Hamburger Stadtpark was a prototype for this new, functional city park. The plan development and design occupied a period of eight years, between 1902 and 1910. During these years design concepts were produced, experts consulted, and debates carried on in a wide circle with regard to the points of departure for the design. The architect Fritz Schumacher played a decisive role in the creation of the final design.

The design for a public garden in the northern suburb of Fuhlsbüttel by the garden architect Leberecht Migge in 1913, several years after the design of the Stadtpark, went still another step further in the development of a functional landscape form that fit into the morphology of the city.

Fritz Schumacher

Fritz Schumacher (1869-1947) was born in Bremen. His father was in the diplomatic corps, and he spent parts of his youth in Bogotá, Colombia, and in New York. After studies in Munich and Berlin he worked as an architect, and from 1896 to 1901 was attached to the *Stadtbauamt* (city planning department) in Leipzig. In 1903 he became a professor at the Technische Hochschule at Dresden. In 1907 he was one of the founders of the Deutsche Werkbund, an association of artists, craftsmen and industrialists who strove to promote better design of everyday appliances. In 1908, at the age of 39, he became the *Baudirektor* (city architect) of Hamburg, remaining in that post until 1933. In this position the new Stadtpark was one of the most important challenges he had to deal with.

Leberecht Migge

Leberecht Migge (1881-1935) was born in Danzig, the son of a wholesaler, and studied horticulture in Hamburg. From 1904 to 1913 he worked as a garden architect for Jacob Ochs's company Gartenbau in Hamburg, together with the architect Muthesius planning and realising private gardens at the villas of their wealthy clients. In 1910 he made a study tour of England, after which he established his own agency in Hamburg. In 1909 he gave a first airing of his social ideals in a pamphlet entitled *Der Hamburger Stadtpark und die Neuzeit: Die heutigen öffentlichen Garten − dienen sie in Wahrheit dem Volke?* (The Hamburg Stadtpark and modernity: today's public gardens − do they truly serve the people?).

The functional form as an artwork

The design of the Hamburger Stadtpark was preceded by the planning of the Ohlsdorf park-cemetery by the architect Johann Wilhelm Cordes. As a sort of intermediate form between the strolling park and the functional park, it was a foreshadowing of the new *Volkspark*. Like the Stadtpark, it lies on the east bank of the Alster, and brings the upper course of this river within reach of the city. Through these designs the significance of the Alster River as a support for Hamburg's urban landscape was considerably increased.

The Stadtpark was to be a transcendent *Gesamtkunstwerk*. Representivity and monumentality therefore played an important role in its design. To achieve these, the design reached back to a formal plan which, stripped of its historic content, could provide a spatial arrangement for a new programme. The structure reflected the ideal of modern, industrial production; the park must be organised like a factory in order to accommodate the large numbers of city-dwellers in an ordered pattern of activities, moving them through a well-oiled series of actions, not unlike the production lines being introduced at the time.

In his 1928 book *Ein Volkspark* Schumacher wrote, "The goal of the

The Grosse See, with the playing fields and water tower in the background

park's design was achieved not only by successfully constructing an area for pleasant strolls, but also by allowing this area to be enjoyably occupied. 'Occupied' here means claiming the area for various functions related to 'recreation'. The possibilities had to be tailored to the needs of large numbers of people, and the special relationship the urban dweller has to nature, which has gradually evolved from his circumstances, had to be taken into account. This relationship is not one of enjoying landscapes which nature in her true fashion almost endlessly offers us, but primarily that of some sort of outdoor activity that has replaced a casual stroll. Even the largest artificial arena cannot meet this need without eventually wearing out. Games, sports, camping, boating, water activities, horseback riding, dancing, or even the enjoyment of music, art, flowers, physical pleasures, these are the activities which should be enjoyed in a park."

It is true that the Stadtpark was conceived by Schumacher as a functional, urban construct, but the form still remained connected with the scenic image of the landscape and the idea of the garden. The burgeoning modernity within which he thought and worked reacted against the idyll of the 19th century city park. In part through its greater historical distance, the scheme of the formal French garden, which in fact conceptually preceded the landscape garden, lent the park design a suggested objectivity. In essence however it lacked the logic of the formal plan, and likewise that of modern design, and could therefore easily degenerate into empty monumentality. Nevertheless, this form was used as a framework for accommodating the ways urban-dwellers would use the park. As a result, the design of the Stadtpark became a confrontation between landscape architectonic instruments and urban forms of land use.

Topography

airport	
subway station	
subway line	
railway line	
• railway station	
motorway	

  - - - - tunnel
important road

 urban pattern

park

other green space

water

Parks

1	A.-Lütgens-Park	54	Mansteinpark
2	Alter Botanischer Garten	55	Meyers Park
3	Alter Elbpark	56	Ohlendorffs Park
4	Alsterpark	57	Öjendorfer Park
5	Alstervorland	58	Ossenmoorpark
6	Altonaer Balkon	59	Platz der Republik
7	Altonaer Volkspark	60	Pulverhofspark
8	Amsinckpark	61	Rathenaupark
9	B.v.Suttner Park	62	Reemtsmapark
10	Baurs Park	63	Römischer Garten
11	Berner Gutshof	64	Roosens Park
12	Blohms Park	65	Rosengarten
13	Bolivarpark	66	Saseler Park
14	Bonnepark	67	Schleepark
15	Bornpark	68	Schöns Park
16	Botanischer Garten	69	Schröders-Elbpark
17	Dr.-H.-Thieleke-Park	70	Seelemannpark
18	Donners Park	71	Sola-Bona-Park
19	Eichenpark	72	Stadtpark
20	Eichtalpark	73	Sternschanzenpark
21	Eilbeker Bürgerpark	74	Stolten-Park
22	Eimsbütteler Park	75	Sven-Simon-Park
23	Elbpark	76	Tarpenbekpark
24	Eppendorfer Park	77	Teetzpark
25	Gorch-Fock-Park	78	Thörls Park
26	Goßlers Park	79	Tierpark Hagenbeck
27	Große Wallanlagen	80	Trauns Park
28	Gut Wendlohe	81	Unnapark
29	H.-Ch.-Andersen-Park	82	Von-Eicken-Park
30	Hammer Park	83	W.-Möller-Park
31	Hauptfriedhof Ohlsdorf	84	Waldpark
32	Hayns Park	85	Waldpark Falkenstein
33	Hellwigpark	86	Waldpark Marienhöhe
34	Hennebergpark	87	Wehbers Park
35	Henry-Vahl-Park	88	Wassermannpark
36	Herbstscher Park	89	Wasserpark
37	Hessepark	90	Wesselhoeftpark
38	Hindenburgpark	91	Westerpark
39	Hirschpark	92	Wilh. Rathauspark
40	Hohenbuchenpark	93	Wohlerspark
41	Horner Park		
42	Innocentiapark		**Water**
43	Jacobipark	A	Alster
44	Jenfelder-Moorpark	B	Aussen Alster
45	Jenischpark	C	Elbe
46	Katthorstpark		
47	Kellinghusens Park		**Places**
48	Krupunder Park	D	Altona
49	Lattenk.-stieg	E	Barmbek
50	Liliencronpark	F	Eimsbüttel
51	Lise-Meitner-Park	G	St. Georg
52	Lunspark	H	St. Pauli
53	Lutherpark	I	Winterhude

0   2   5km

N

The Elbe in the North German Plain

The River Elbe flows through the North German Plain, a vast landscape lying between the coasts of the North Sea and the Baltic on the one side and the Central Uplands of Germany on the other. It was formed chiefly in the course of the various glacial periods of the Pleistocene epoch, during which the Scandinavian glaciers covered the region. With the retreat of the glaciers drifting dunes formed, later anchored by vegetation. The relief is flat to rolling. Human influence lead to the creation of heathland. As a result of deforestation and peat cutting, the soil became impoverished over large areas. The deepest point of the plain lies in the bogs and old mud flats between the younger mud

flats raised by more recent sedimentary accretions and the edge of the Pleistocene sand ridges. Here, just a in the north of the Netherlands, extensive peat bogs formed, which then settled after they were drained.

The Elbe was formed by the valleys of primaeval rivers which carried off the meltwater from the different periods of glaciation. The land to the north and south of the river consists of higher-lying sandy soil, created by sand and grit sediments from the meltwater rivers during the glacial period. In the estuary of the Elbe lie salt marshes, subject to tidal influences. Some of these flats were diked in (with names such as Koog or Polder). Hamlets in the undiked flats stand on low hillocks or *Halligen*. The diked in flats are kept dry by a drainage system comprised of ditches, canals, pumping installations and sluices.

Geomorphology and urban domain

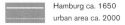 Hamburg ca. 1650
urban area ca. 2000

The harbour at Hamburg

N   0   20   40km

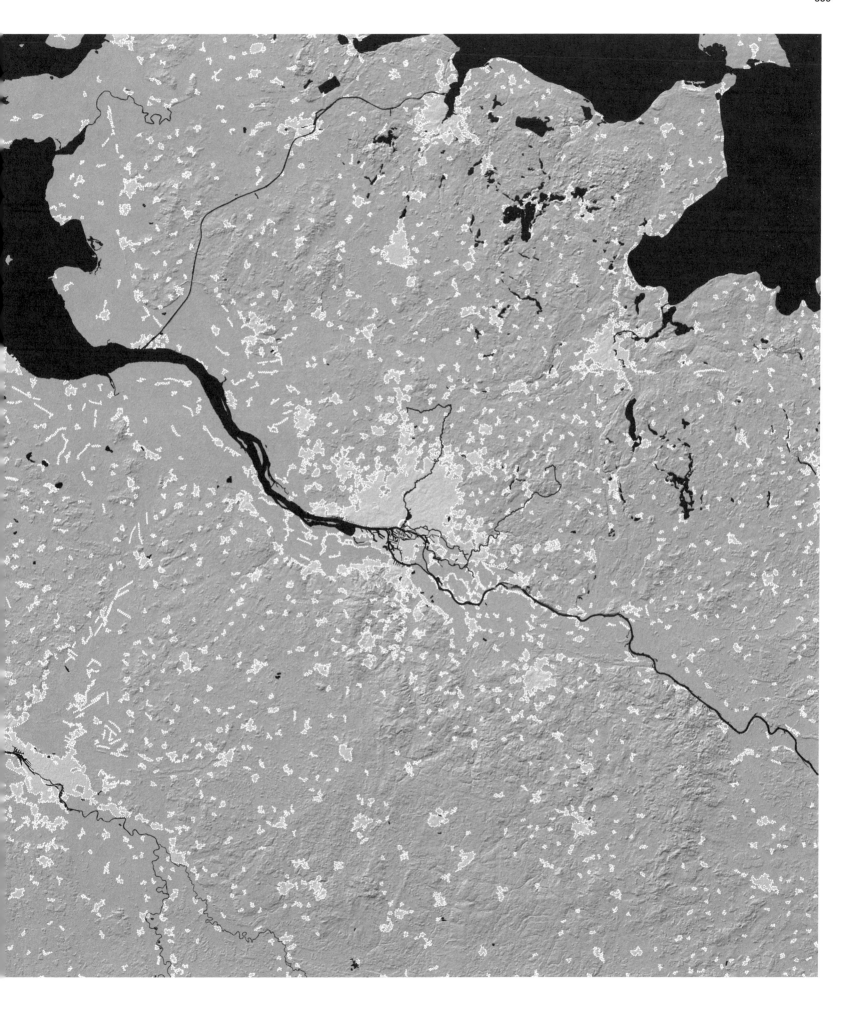

Geomorphology, urban pattern and parks

Elevation (metres)

140 - 160
120 - 140
100 - 120
90 - 100
80 - 90
70 - 80
60 - 70
50 - 60
40 - 50
30 - 40
20 - 30
10 - 20
0 - 10

urban pattern

park

water

Perspective sketch for the island in the Grosse See (from: F. Schumacher, *Ein Volks-park: dargestellt am Hamburger Stadtpark*. Munich 1928)

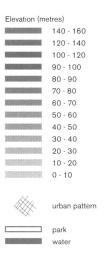

0   2   5km

Toward a functional design for urban space

Hamburg lies on the lower reaches of the River Elbe, which empties into the North Sea about 100 kilometres further down, but is still subject to tidal action at this point. Two tributaries of the Elbe, the Alster and the Bille, from northern Schleswig-Holstein, enter the main stream at Hamburg.

The original harbour of Hamburg lay between the mouths of the Alster and the Bille. Around 810 Charlemagne (747-814) had a baptistery built there for the Christian mission effort in the north, near which the castle Hammaburg was built on the Alster. In the 12th century Adolf III, Count of Schauenburg and Holstein, founded a trading settlement there. Since 1190 the Alster has been artificially dammed up, in order to power a flour mill.

The Emperor Frederick Barbarossa (1122-1190) granted the city harbour rights and trading privileges, after which it developed into a flourishing centre for trade during the Middle Ages. In the 14th century Hamburg became a Hanseatic city and the most important point for warehousing and transshipment between the North Sea and the Baltic. In the 17th century fortifications were constructed by the Dutch architect Jan van Valckenburgh. These circular walls cut across the impounded waters of the Alster, dividing it into the Binnenalster and Aussenalster. The settlements of St. Georg and St. Pauli developed outside the gates.

Villas and working-class neighbourhoods along the Alster

The demolition of the walls and the construction of the first parks began in 1804. After a major fire in 1842 the region of the city around the Binnenalster was rebuilt, which also presented an opportunity to lay a new water system. After 1872 new parks were also laid out to the west of the Alster. Great villas with gardens rose on the roads along the banks of the Aussenalster. Further up, suburbs were spreading quickly.

The transition from sail to steam changed maritime trade and traffic. Hamburg became an international port with lots of industry. At the end of the 19th century the harbours along both sides of the Elbe were expanded. Many residents of the old harbour neighbourhoods were housed in tenements around the old villages outside the city. Between them ran the old farm roads that radiated outward from the old city. This was the origin of densely built-up working-class neighbourhoods like Barmbek, Eimsbüttel and Hammerbrook with their terraced houses packed close together to fill the whole block on narrow, dead-end alleys which branched off the actual streets like wishbones, just as

elsewhere in the old city. Further to the north, in Hohenfelde, Uhlenhorst, Winterhude, Harvestehude and Rotherbaum, lay working-class neighbourhoods with row houses and flats.

The city then counted 700,000 residents, and after Berlin was the largest city in the German Empire. Beginning around 1890 a discussion arose in the city about the lack of open space and parks in the suburbs. In a letter written back while travelling in Stockholm in 1897, Alfred Lichtwark, director of the Hamburger Kunsthalle, the city's art museum, pondered whether the city could remain fit for habitation if there was no large new city park in prospect. As the municipal architect, Schumacher criticised the lack of regulations requiring open space between buildings. Moreover, there were few parks in the area east of the Alster. In his book *Ein Volkspark* he wrote, "Even though the tree-lined Alster flows though the centre of Hamburg like a mighty park, you cannot delude yourself into forgetting that on both sides huge neighbourhoods of stone rental houses have arisen behind this mass of trees. Working-class areas have begun to spread out like cities in themselves, primarily to the north-east. The creation of a large green central area in the middle of this mass of houses had become an unavoidable necessity."

Hamburger Stadtpark. View across the Grosse See from the boating island

Hamburg in 1895 (Hamburg und Umgebung: Sect. Barmbeck, Eppendorf, Hamburg, Hamm. Vermessungsbureau der Baudeputation, 1895)

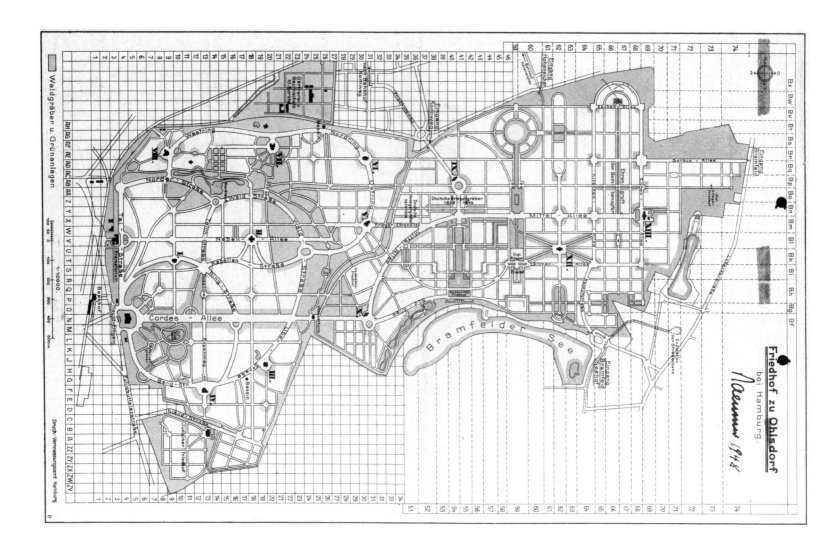

A cemetery as model

As a result of the intense growth in its population in the second half of the 19th century, the cemeteries around the churches in the city were rapidly running out of burial space. In 1875 the city acquired a site of 130 hectares, about ten kilometres outside the city centre in the vicinity of Ohlsdorf on the east bank of the Alster. It was comprised of fields, pastures and heathland, with centuries-old walls of mighty oaks and birch trees between them. In the years after 1879 Johann Wilhelm Cordes (1840-1917), an architect with the city's *Ingenieurwesen*, designed the new Ohlsdorf cemetery there, which attained fame throughout Germany and the world. The plan was organised around two purposes projected onto one another, a strolling park and a cemetery. The principal element in the plan was a 900-meter-long axis, the Cordes

Allee, to stretch between the main entrance on the Fuhlsbütteler Strasse, with the cemetery's service building, and the planned water tower further up. The strolling park consisted of a system of curving park routes, such as would be found in a landscape park. In contrast, the fields of graves were based on a rectangular grid of 50 × 50 meters. The existing walls of trees and geological peculiarities were integrated into the plan. This created a functionally designed park, adapted to the character of the site, which at the same time was a pleasant place to walk. Cordes himself called it a *Zweckmässigkeitsentwurf* (functional design). His design, in which efficiency was given equal standing with the enjoyment of nature, was a foreshadowing of the new form of park, which would be developed further in the Stadtpark.

Parkfriedhof Ohlsdorf. Left, the plan by Cordes, right the later extension by Otto Linne
(Friedhof zu Ohlsdorf bei Hamburg met uitbreidingen van Cordes en Linne. Staatsarchiv Hamburg 720-1 141-20= 16/1948.1a)

The Binnen- and Aussenalster, seen from the Nikolai Church in the old city.
The Hamburger Stadtpark is in upper centre

The debate over functional form

After investigating various possible locations, in 1901 the city began the purchase of land for the construction of a large new park in the suburbs at Winterhude, about five kilometres north of the old city. The area lay on the east bank of the Alster, to the east of the built-up part of Winterhude-Nord, surrounded by the routes of various railway lines. The site was connected with the rest of the city by the municipal railway. Measuring 128 hectares in area, the site was comprised of a higher wooded area in the west and an area that was more open, sloping away to the east. It was the intention to entirely surround the park with building projects in order to maximise the profits from the views over the park. In 1902 *Oberingenieur* (Senior Municipal Engineer) Eduard Vermehren, as the head of the municipal *Ingenieurwesen*, produced the first sketches for the park. These showed a main axis running east-west, with a large, symmetrical body of water in the west and two restaurants, one at each head of the axis. The designs by the *Ingenieurwesen* however provoked more questions than they answered, and were never carried out.

The Senate Commission's programme

In the years that followed an extensive discussion took place regarding the content, form and costs of the park. In 1904 the city assembled a Senate Commission which included the experts Vermehren, Lichtwark, Brinckmann and Cordes, to advise on the most appropriate form for the park. This commission developed a programme and produced a number of new sketches. Lichtwark cited the St. Cloud park in Paris as a possible model and, with the support of Cordes, argued for a reassessment of the baroque French garden. A baroque garden, stripped of its aristocratic aspects, would be suitable for providing space for large masses of people, and at the same time could be an all-inclusive *Gesamtkunstwerk*. This idea was in keeping with a general tendency to monumentalisation and representative forms, in which a park as 'monument to the German people' fit well.

A large lawn to which the visitors would have access, something like a contemporary form of the medieval tournament field or a 17th century formal *parterre de gazon* emerged as the most important functional element. A *Volkswiese* like this would afford the city-dweller the possibility for balanced development of the body and psyche, making the city park a social centre for the whole community. In contrast, Lichtwark and Brinckmann favoured rustic farm garden motifs, surrounded by *boskets*. This fit with the *Heimatbewegung* (homeland movement) which arose after 1900, with its revaluing of folk traditions and a romantic conception of pre-industrial, rural life.

A competition for ideas

Because the Senate Commission could reach no agreement about a plan as a body, the Senate was advised to hold a competition for ideas, with several basic conditions. For instance, existing natural features, such as soil, water, heath and woods, as well as historic elements of the man-made landscape such as tree walls, had to be respected. Further, a water tower had to be included, standing on the highest point, facing the park. The competition, announced in February, 1908, drew 66 submissions. The jury, which included members of the Senate Commission and others, decided not to award a first prize. Three designs (*Elbau*, *Aap* and *Suum Cuique*) shared the second prize, and three shared the third prize. They further recommended the purchase of several designs, including the design *Ein Pfau*, by the architect Max Läuger, from Karlsruhe. Läuger's design had a monumental, architectonic character, founded on geometric forms. It was based on an axial succession, and was characterised by a rigid symmetry that was not really adapted to the morphology of the site. Functionally, however, the design was a breakthrough, because numerous activities were specified in it.

The majority of the jury though could not imagine an architectonic design like this as a *Volkspark* for all classes in the population. Extensive discussions once again flared up, extending over the city and the whole professional community. In these proponents of the new, functional trend, among them Lichtwark, Muthesius, Encke and Migge, and its opponents, such as Sperber and Jürgens, who wanted to see a further development of the landscape park concept, sharply disagreed with one another.

Schumacher's compromise

Among the first tasks confronting Schumacher after his appointment as municipal architect in Hamburg in 1908 was to break the stalemate and seek a compromise. The Senate Commission directed him to work out a joint proposal with Sperber. The plan was ready in January, 1910, and was approved by the Senate shortly thereafter; with this, construction began, to extend over two phases. The first ran from 1910 to 1914, with the realisation of the earthwork and all the larger elements of the park. Studies were done for the modelling of the base using maquettes at scale, on which the effects of planting and the placement and form of structures could also be studied. The 38-meter-tall water tower,

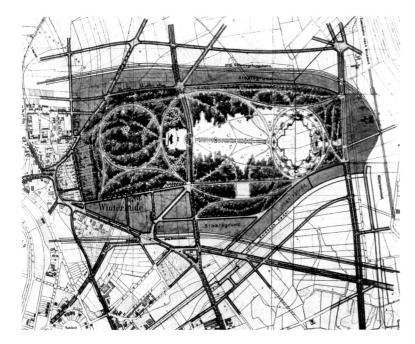

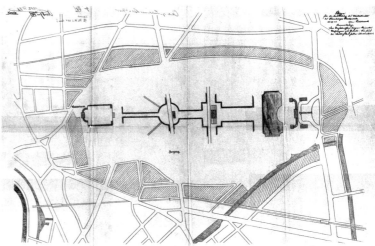

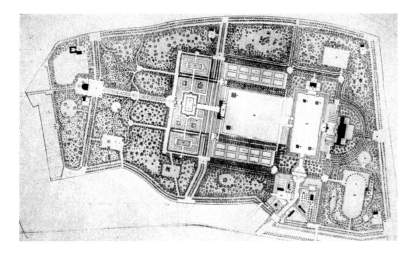

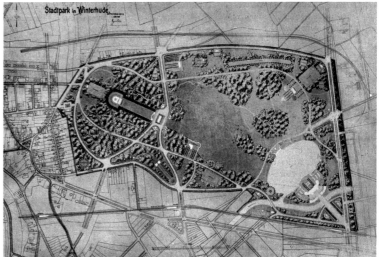

Plan by Vermehren for the Stadtpark in Winterhude, 1902 (from: M. Goecke, *Stadtparkanlagen im Industriezeitalter, das Beispiel Hamburg.* Hannover 1981)

Plan of the axis of the park, by A. Lichtwark, 1905 (Staatsarchiv Hamburg Senat Cl. VII Lit. Fh Nr. 2 Vol. 1 Conv. I)

The competition submission by M. Läuger, 1908 (from: M. Goecke, *Stadtparkanlagen im Industriezeitalter, das Beispiel Hamburg.* Hannover 1981)

The design by F. Sperber, 1909 (from: F. Schumacher, *Ein Volkspark: dargestellt am Hamburger Stadtpark.* München 1928)

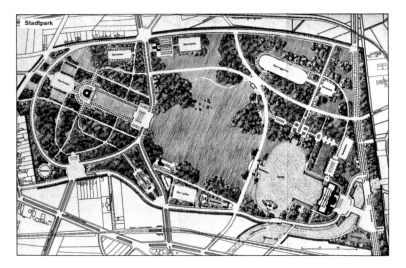

designed by the architect Otto Menzel, was built in 1913-1914.

In 1912 Schumacher made a study trip to England, during which he devoted particular attention to the smaller flower gardens and the spatial execution of the central playing meadow or *Volkswiese*. He decided that the latter required a border of some sort, a clear boundary such as one found around the great meadows in the English landscape gardens. The second phase began after the First World War, with the construction of the smaller architectonic gardens, the racecourse, the water playground and the open-air theatre with its seating. A planetarium was installed in the water tower in 1929. During the Second World War the Hamburger Stadtpark was used as a military base. The main restaurant, the dairy, café and cascade were destroyed by Allied bombardment.

The design adopted, drawn by the Ingenieur- und Hochbauwesen, 1910
(from: Architekten- und Ingenieur-Verein zu Hamburg, *Hamburg und seine Bauten unter Berücksichtigung der Nachbarstädte Altona und Wandsbek*. Bd. 2. Hamburg 1914)

Perspective sketch for the central axis (from: Schumacher, F., *Ein Volkspark: dargestellt am Hamburger Stadtpark*. München 1928)

The connection with the Alster and the city

I	Winterhude
A	Alster
B	Goldbeckkanal
1	Flurstrasse
2	Marie Luisenstrasse
3	Borgweg

	city expansion
	urban green space
	woods
	parkways
	urban pattern
	water
••••••••••	trees / avenues

0   250   500m

An urban recreational landscape

The elongated, roughly rectangular park lies in a bend of the Alster, about one kilometre to the east, at angles to the flow of the river. It measures about 1800 × 850 meters, is about 150 hectares in area, and is surrounded by residential neighbourhoods and streets on all sides. Several through streets cut across the park in a north-south direction. A railway line runs along the south edge. The site slopes considerably. Schumacher reported that the north-west section was the highest, at 26 meters above sea level, gradually falls by 16 meters, to its lowest point in the south-east section, at 10 meters above sea level. The Goldbeck Canal, which carries water from the Alster, and the large rowing lake have the same water level as the Alster.

An enclosed spatial series

The basic form of the plan is determined by the direction and position of the central axis of symmetry, which is projected onto the base diagonally, stretching from the highest point on the site, with the water tower, to the lowest point, with the lake and Stadthalle (civic hall). This main axis indicates the greatest dimensions in length and width that are possible in the given terrain. Transversely, the geometry of the axis is continued as far as possible toward the edges. There a transitional zone assures that this geometry is adapted to the irregularities in the shape of the site.

The organisation of the axial zone is defined by a sequence of spaces along the main axis. The series begins on the south-east corner, outside the park, at the point where the axis cuts across the Flurstrasse at a sharp angle. Here the Goldbeck Canal has been broadened out into an urban water basin with a mooring for boats, while a bridge connects the forecourt on the city side with the bastion of the plaza of the Stadthalle. This building had the form of a palace, with a higher central section and wings to the sides, blocking views into the park behind it. On the park side lay a tree-planted terrace, arcades and stairs on the Grosse See, a large oval lake sharing a water level with the Alster. Together with the terraces the Stadthalle provided space for 10,000 visitors.

The surface of the lake is the lowest-lying space in the park. At the terrace the difference in height, here something more than three-and-a-half meters, is overcome by stairs and retaining walls; farther up in the park this is accomplished by sloping banks with planting. A cascade on the main axis, connected with a higher body of water by unseen pipes, formed the transition to the great playing meadow of 30 hectares, in the shape of a vast rectangle surrounded by a double row of trees. Moving

toward the west end, the meadow narrows in two stages, becoming an extended *tapis vert*, surrounded by coulisses of woods. This is closed off by the 38-meter-tall water tower, with behind it, out of sight, a stadium and an open-air theatre.

The structure and the form of the axis, and the spatial articulation along it, is somewhat reminiscent of the spatial axis of the formal French garden, particularly at Vaux-le-Vicomte. In both cases there is an elevated standpoint (the terrace behind the Stadthalle) and an upward sloping background (the *tapis vert* in front of the water tower). The length of 1000 to 1500 meters is rather similar, and in both Vaux and the Stadtpark the difference in height in the terrain are between 20 and 30 meters. But there are also considerable differences. Here, unlike at Vaux, the main axis is not a spatial axis that links the system of the garden with the structure of the greater landscape. Here the horizon is dominated by the massive presence of the water tower, from which no avenues radiate further into the space. The spatial axis, and the other axes, are locked in between structures at their starting and end points. The successive spaces and areas are also simpler in terms of their organisation and texture; the foreground passes over abruptly into the background. The most important difference however is that the axial space is not empty, like an abstract stage, but is filled with people. In this park the spaces along the axis do not function as tableaux, in which nature opens up and is reflected, but as an outdoor urban plaza, intended for a teeming crowd. This accent on the programme is only reinforced by by the fact that the main axis is surrounded by a wreath of various smaller spaces, each with their own content, form and orientation. These are connected with the central space by a number of larger and smaller transverse axes.

The recreation machine

According to Schumacher, the urbanite really had to be able to take possession of the park; it must be able to be used for the most diverse recreational activities, both by individuals and by groups. The programme has a zoned structure; similar programme elements are repeated in different variations and forms and arranged in zones around the central area. Clearly articulated entrance spaces are to be found along the outer edges at regular intervals, and at important junctions with the urban road network. The most important of these is the main entrance, with stops for public transit and docking facilities for boats and excursion steamers.

The central element of the programme is the 30 hectare playing field, surrounded by trees. Sports facilities such as the great rowing

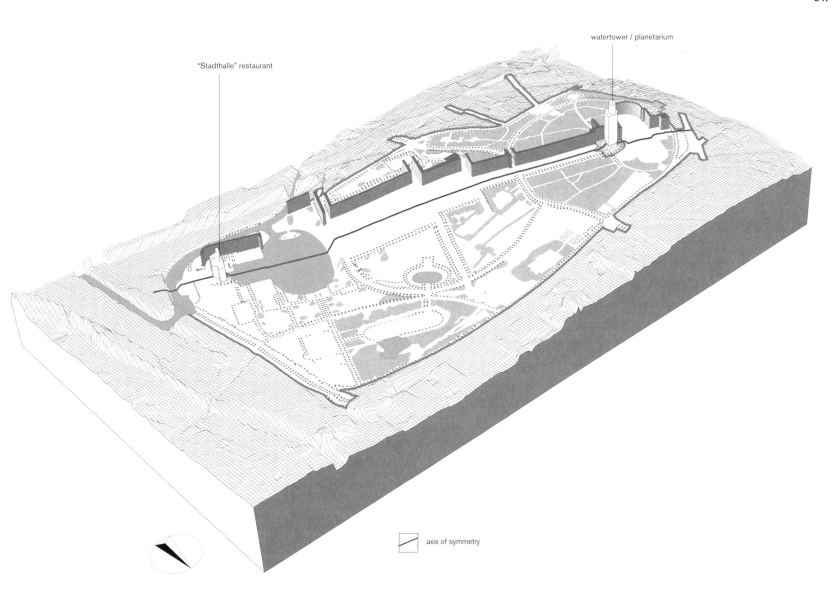

"Stadthalle" restaurant

watertower / planetarium

axis of symmetry

Three-dimensional model, with cross-section along the park axis (1 cell measures 10 × 10 metres, z = 8×)

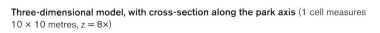
The island, with the boat rental

The quay along the Grosse See

and swimming lake, boat rental, sports fields, a racecourse with a grandstand, a show jumping course and bridle paths are tucked into the woods in the intervening zone. These were interspersed with playgrounds and sitting areas, a water playground, architectonic gardens and flower gardens. Cafés were distributed around at convenient points between the recreational facilities, each with its own character: the Stadthalle as an urban restaurant, the café on the north bank of the lake as a small country estate, a rural inn in the farm on the south side, a dairy on the north edge of the park, and on the south edge a *Trinkhalle* with a health spa where mineral water could be consumed. The main routes, in the form of wide, curving avenues, link the north and south edges of the park with one another and with the city. In addition to these – and intersecting with them – smaller park routes connect the programmatic facilities with each other. The water tower is an exceptional element. It falls outside the actual park programme, but is the pivot that links the park with the technical system of the city.

As an open-air *Volkshaus* and recreation machine, the park became a component in the programme of urban activities. Its architectonic form was directly linked to an industrially organised recreational 'productivity'. The recreational programme had assumed the role that nature and scenic topography had formerly played as the unifying factor in parks.

A celebration of a common space

The visual structure of the park does not reflect a direct, individual identification with nature, but permits the people collectively to reach back to their historical roots, to the *Heim*, the landscape as a communal space, a late echo of the thought of the philosopher Johann Gottfried Herder (1744-1803), regarded as the founding father of 'Germanic culture'. To accomplish this, the designers used stylistic means which referred to a regal residence, but for the people rather than a monarch. The Stadthalle, at the point where the main axis begins, had the shape of a palace – but for the people – with an open entrance and a raised *piano nobile* from which urbanites could survey the park as their collective domain. Another characteristic is the changed attitude toward nature. In terms of the composition, the people's palace was placed opposite nature, represented by a 'forest' at the other end of the axis. However, that was visually dominated by a water tower, which functioned as a piece of urban technology. At a deeper level, then, this hinted that the culture-nature antithesis was abandoned and the park landscape as a whole belonged to the urban realm. The pastoral antithesis between nature and culture was still worked out visually on a smaller scale within the primary urban form in various garden elements.

On the transverse axis of the largest body of water, the Stadtcafé, in the form of a villa, is placed opposite an island planted with Italian poplars, like the Rousseau-Insel in the landscape garden of Wörlitz. In order not to disrupt this idyll, the dock for boat rental is pushed to the back of the island, out of sight from the café.

Programmatically, the *Volkspark* was in part influenced by a burgeoning nationalism which sought its inspiration in history. Spread along the edges of the park are visual elements that refer to the German cultural landscape around Hamburg. Among them are a rustic inn in the form of a north German brick country home, with its enclosed garden and orchard, and a dairy in the form of a half-timbered farmhouse from Lower Saxony, with espaliered lindens, a walk under an arch of foliage, an orchard and gardens. The German spa, and the health cult which accompanied it, is also represented in the park with the dome-shaped *Trinkhalle*. To the north of the Stadthalle lay a series of small architectonic gardens and flower gardens as separate artworks. The scene here is however dominated by the *Volkswiese*, a communal space fringed by native species of trees, reminiscent of the traditional Germanic landscape with sacred oaks. The formal framework of the French baroque garden not only provided the recreational landscape with an urban form, but was also the vehicle for celebrating the historic landscape of the nation.

The park programme

	Entrance
1	main entrance
2	mooring place for boats
3	other entrances
	Sports
4	sports field
5	racecourse
6	tribune
7	Grosse See/swimming, rowing
8	boat rental
9	show jumping course
	Play
10	playing fields
11	water playground
	Relaxation
12	flower gardens
13	woods
14	*Trinkhalle*/spa
	Eating/drinking
15	Stadthalle
16	Stadtcafé
17	Landhaus
18	Milchwirtschaft

0   150   300m

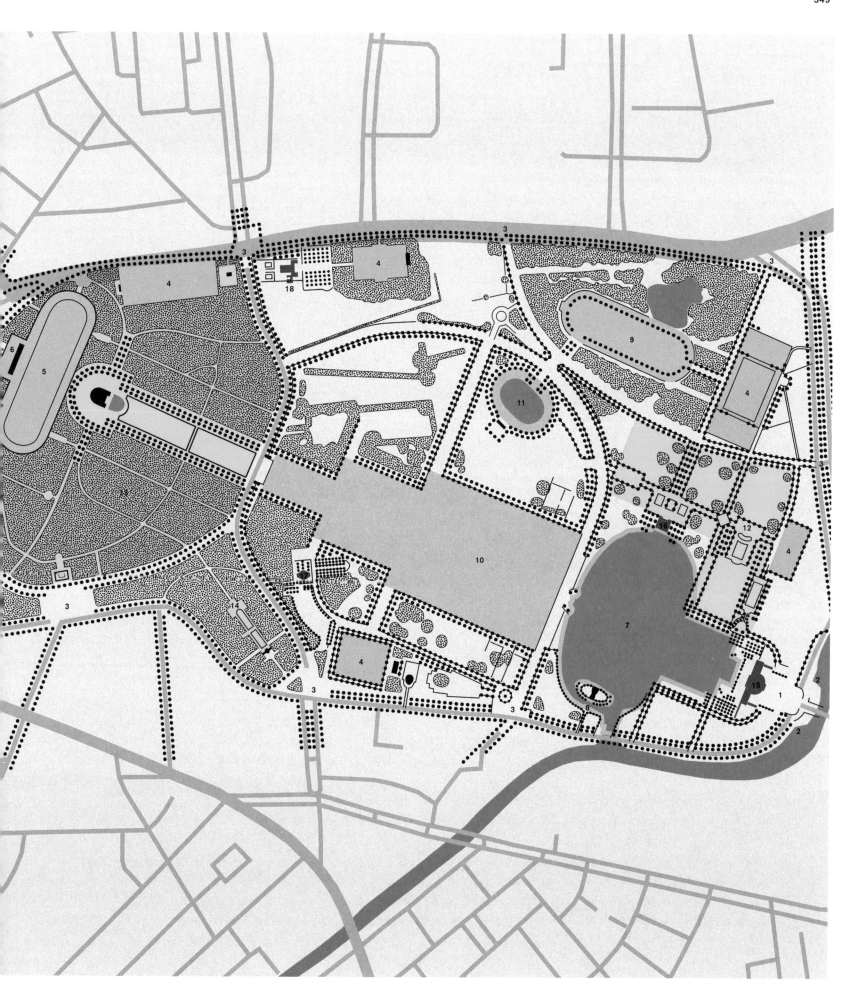

The Volkspark

The development of the functional plan in the *Volkspark* was the most important change that occurred in respect to the 19th century *Volksgarten*. In terms of its design, however, the *Volkspark* was influenced by the French formal garden, although influences of the landscape park could also be traced, particularly in the design of the system of paths. In this sense the *Volkspark* was still a complete city park with a 'garden', a 'meadow' and a 'wilderness', albeit that these constituents had undergone a radical transformation in their relation to one another. The 'garden' had become the support for the specific recreational programme and the 'meadow' the central, multifunctional playing field, while the 'wilderness' was included in the wooded rim as a botanical garden.

The differentiation of otium

The basis for such a functional plan lay in a differentiation of *otium*, the separation and spatial zoning of elements in the urban recreational and cultural programme. In the Stadtpark the cultural and contemplative functions were allotted places in the protected edge, while a multi-functional space appeared in the centre, flanked by avenues suitable for sauntering. In 1913, several years after the construction of the Stadtpark had begun, the garden architect Leberecht Migge, who was also working in Hamburg, wrote, "Our masses do not want a museum of trees and shrubs in the park which belongs to them; they quite rightly want to actively use it and not merely to look at it. The contemporary community garden will be a creation with a purpose and will invite a majority of people to enjoy it in very specific ways. The people will actively put this into practise both on workdays and during their free time – we do not need Sunday gardens! The people must really be able to romp around in the people's park."

Zweckgebilde (the visualisation of functional form)

Migge's 1913 design for an *Öffentlicher Garten* (public garden) in Fuhlsbüttel, a suburb of Hamburg, is an example of the way in which he tried to connect the classic art of the garden and modern urban planning at the beginning of the 20th century. The public garden has a trapezoidal footprint and is bounded by public thoroughfares on two consecutive sides. On the other two sides it abuts back gardens. The garden consists of a composition of a raised area reached by a formal stair and a playing field or *Tummelwiese*, which is not furnished but left as free space that can be appropriated by the users. The raised area

includes a number of classic elements such as a fountain, *boscos*, flowerbeds, a balustrade and a stair. The *Tummelwiese* is bounded on two sides by a similarly somewhat elevated *berceau*. The third side is accessible from the street and planted with trees. The field can also be entered from the raised platform and the corners of the tree-covered walks. The formal entrance, with an arcade and two loggias, is at the corner of the two public streets.

The playing field is soberly furnished: a minuscule formal element in the axis of the platform, a large tree with a bench under it, that is all. Diagonal paths, which appear to be worn into the lawn by the users themselves, cut across the field, coming together at the tree. It is a picture that reminds one of the landscape of an African savannah. This archetypal image of a free, informal space must make the active appropriation (*körperliche Inbesitznahme*) obvious, and was deliberately opposed to the formally treated parts of the park.

Here Migge not only designed a free and functional plan, but he also visualised the concepts of freedom and efficiency. In this plan the informal character of the *Tummelwiese* was effectively set off against the monumentality and formal representativity of the raised platform. The form of Migge's common space self-evidently evokes freedom and mobility. As a result, form and function became extensions of one another.

The limits of landscape architectonic form

Migge's design took the development of a purely practical form a step further. The landscape space melted into the coherent, functional spatial system of the city. This calls up several questions which touch upon the core of the city park as a landscape architectonic concept. To what extent does the park form have a formal essence of its own, which distinguishes it from urban space?

In Schumacher's design for the Hamburger Stadtpark, in a deeper sense the park was still a space with a distinguished from, and separated from, the city, in which the 'garden', the 'meadow' and the 'wilderness' were articulated and in which the formal organisation underscored the monumental character of the programmatic form. The park was still anchored in the topography of the landscape, hung on the Alster River, and it was a component of a radial system of green spaces conceived by Schumacher, in which the topography of Hamburg as a river delta was readable. Within the Stadtpark this topography can also be read from the position of the main axis of the park, which connects the highest point in the local landscape with the water level of the Alster. The visual vocabulary of the park also still referred to the landscape.

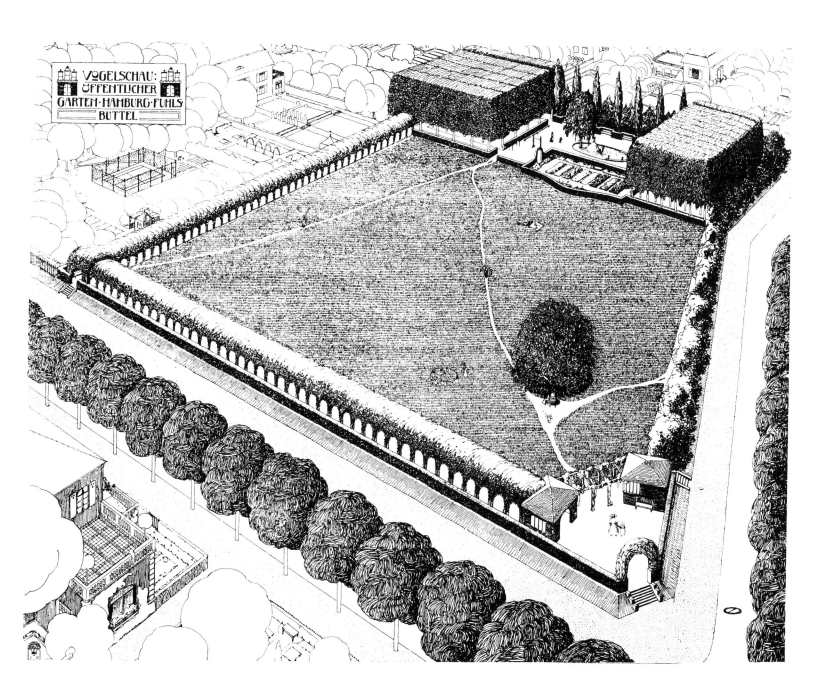

VOGELSCHAU:
ÖFFENTLICHER
GARTEN·HAMBURG·FUHLS
BÜTTEL

Migge's design for a public garden in Fuhlsbüttel, 1913 (from: Gesamthochschule
Kassel Fachbereich Stadt- und Landschaftsplanung, *Leberecht Migge 1881-1935;
Gartenkultur des 20. Jahrhunderts*. Lilienthal 1981)

It was chiefly at the level of the functional programme that the contrasts with urban space disappeared.

In Migge's design the contrast with urban space was reduced to the use of materials, greenery and planting in place of stone and steel. Of the constituent elements of the city park only one, the meadow, still remains here, albeit in a metaphorical sense. The landscape architectonic treatment of the landscape topography was replaced by an adaptation of 'the landscape' in time and space, as a plastic category in the topology of the city. With the archetypal landscape of the *Tummelwiese*, urban space assumed the character of a landscape. The monumentality of the park design was reduced to a garden architectonic frame. The informal and undefined character of the *Tummelwiese* indeed did still refer to the garden as an experimental landscape playground but, more than was the case with the Hamburger Stadtpark, shifts in the direction of an urban spatial form. With this Migge reached the limits of the landscape architectonic form of the city park.

In a certain sense, Schumacher's design for the Hamburger Stadtpark had created the conditions for this. The balance between the landscape and urban forms made it a classic functional design, in which everyday use was given a monumental expression. Migge's design was a critical gloss on this, from a deeply founded perception of the organic dynamics of landscape space, placed over and against the collectivity and uncompromising planning of the modern city.

The central playing field

View across the park from the former site of the Stadthalle (now a pond)

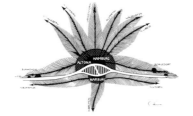

urban green space, woods, open landscape
urban expansions 1919-1931
historic centre
water

urban pattern

Fritz Schumacher's proposal for green space in Hamburg, plan and present topography (from: K. Müller-Ibold & Baubehörde Hamburg, *Stadt im Fluss; städtebauliche Entwicklung am Beispiel Hamburg*. Hamburg 1978)

0   2   5km

THE NIDDA VALLEY FRANKFURT 1925

A productive urban paradise
Ernst May
Leberecht Migge
The concept of urban farming

Rhine, Main and Nidda
The Nidda

Folding the edge of the city inward
The 1927 expansion plan
Migge's 1928 Grünflächenplan
The 1930 expansion plan
The articulation of the Nidda Valley
Landschaftssteigerung

The *Siedlung* as an architectonic settlement form
The actualisation of the topography
The landscape as urban interior
An unpretentious homogeneity
The functional unity of house and garden

The settlement park
The functional transformation of the classic landscape theatre
Urban living as a settlement process
The revival of urban farming

The valley of the Nidda, viewed from the south (aerial photo: Stadtvermessungsamt Frankfurt)

A productive urban paradise

In the expansion of Frankfurt am Main in the first half of the 20th century, its urban landscape took on a form based on the ways it was originally used: the house, garden and landscape. The process was permeated by the concept of rational means of production: the industrial production of the homes, and production of food through intensive forms of urban farming. After the First World War Germany was confronted with massive problems in both providing adequate housing for its people, and with its food supply. Because of antiquated production methods, its agriculture was barely able to feed the growing population. The construction of housing, which had come to a halt during the war, also was unable to meet demand, while the shortage of housing in urban areas became even more critical as a result of the stream of workers drawn to the cities by the industry there. After the financial reorganisation following the Dawes Plan of 1924, which was a response to the economic crisis and hyperinflation of 1922-1923, the economic situation in the Weimar Republic improved. Under Gustav Stresemann, who was briefly the Chancellor of the Republic, new initiatives were made to rationalise and industrialise agriculture and housing production.

As the intermediary between architects and industry, the Deutsche Werkbund stimulated new architectonic and urban development experiments. This, for instance, resulted in the *Schematischer Stadtplan* (schematic city plan) by Bruno Taut, in which he explored a more efficient structure and zoning for the mass housing projects and industrial zones in the constantly growing metropolis. The residential projects in Frankfurt am Main from the years 1925-1930 mark an important point in this search for a new form and relationship between urban mass housing and food production. The architect Ernst May and the landscape architect Leberecht Migge were involved in this as the most important designers.

Ernst May

Ernst May (1886-1970) studied architecture in Munich, meeting modern architects of the Deutsche Werkbund such as Peter Behrens there. Around 1910 May worked with Raymond Unwin, the designer of the English garden city of Letchworth, and attended conferences of the International Garden Cities and Town Planning Federation. From 1919 to 1921, as the technical director of the Schlesischer Landesgesellschaft (Silesian Land Scoeity), May built residential neighbourhoods in rural communities and began to publish the journal *Schlesisches Heim*. Among the subjects studied and discussed in it were economical construction methods, the standardisation of dwelling types and parcellation, urban aesthetics and urban expansion.

May proceeded from the idea that as things stood the metropolis inflicts "indescribable damage" on people, and yet saw increasing growth of the cities. Therefore the shortcomings and flaws of the big city must be eliminated, by developing the city in such a way that the natural conditions of life for man could be realised as perfectly as possible. To achieve that required both the building of healthy dwellings

Topography

airport

subway station
subway line
railway line
• railway station
motorway

- - - - tunnel
——— important road

urban pattern

park
other green space
water

Parks

1	Adolf von Holzhausen Park		48	Opelzoo
2	Bethmannpark		49	Ostpark
3	Biegwald		50	Palmengarten
4	Boehlepark		51	Park Louisa
5	Bonifatiuspark		52	Pflanzenpark Arboretum
6	Botanischer Garten		53	Quellenpark (Bad Soden)
7	Brentanopark		54	Quellenpark (Kronberg im Taunus)
8	Brüning-Park		55	Rebstockpark
9	Bürgerpark		56	Riederwald
10	Büsingpark		57	Rothschildpark
11	Cäcilia-Lauth-Park		58	Scheerpark
12	Carl-von-Weinberg Park		59	Schloss Friedrichshof
13	Erholungspark		60	Schlossgarten
14	Freizeitgelände Schneckenberg		61	Schlosspark (Heusenstamm)
15	Freizeitpark		62	Schlosspark (Rumpenheim)
16	Freizeitpark Eichwiesen		63	Schwanheimer Wald
17	Freizeitpark Kalbach		64	Seehofpark
18	Freizeitpark Oberwiesen		65	Sinaipark
19	Freizeitpark Unterwiesen		66	Solmspark
20	Fritz-von-Unruh-Anlage		67	Sommerhoffpark
21	Gimmersberg		68	Spielpark Sindlingen
22	Goetheturm		69	Spielpark Tannenwald
23	Goldsteinpark		70	Stadtteilpark Niederrad
24	Graubnerpark		71	Südpark
25	Günthersburgpark		72	Tiergarten
26	Hanny-Franke-Anlage		73	Tiroler Park
27	Heinrich-Kraft-Park		74	Unterwald
28	Höchster Stadtpark		75	Volkspark
29	Huthpark		76	Volkspark Niddatal
30	Kurpark (Bad Homburg)		77	Von-Bernus-Park
31	Kurpark (Bad Soden)		78	Wasserpark
32	Kurpark (Bad Vilbel)		79	Weseler Werft
33	Leonhard-Eißnert-Park		80	Wörthspitze
34	Lohrpark		81	Zoologischer Garten
35	Martin-Henrich-Anlage			
36	Martin-Luther-Park		**Places**	
37	Martin-Luther-King Park		A	Bad Homburg
38	Meisterpark		B	Bad Soden
39	Miquelanlage		C	Bad Vilbel
40	Museumsufer Sachsenhausen		D	Königstein
41	Naussauer Hof			
42	Neuer Kurpark		**Water**	
43	Nieder-Erlenbacher Wald		E	Main
44	Nieder-Eschenbacher Wald		F	Nidda
45	Niedwald			
46	Nizza-Gärten		**Other**	
47	Nordpark		G	*limes*

N   0   2   5km

with gardens, but also opening up the city as a whole. For the latter May reached back to the 1910 Great Berlin competition and the models that the urban planners Rudolph Eberstadt, Bruno Möhring and Richard Petersen developed for it, with wedge-shaped strips of greenery reaching to the centre. According to May, however, such green strips were no alternative for the necessary open space. He argued for a model of urban expansion with decentralised cores, in the form of satellites, "like the planets around the sun: free bodies that nevertheless depend on the central star for many functions."

In 1925 May became the head of the newly established municipal development bureau in Frankfurt. In this function he designed a new structural plan in which the locations for new residential development were carefully defined in relationship with the landscape. The expansions were based on various new planning strategies, including measures to discourage land speculation, the prefabrication of building components, establishing housing cooperatives and public relations. A new periodical entitled *Das neue Frankfurt* was to spearhead the latter effort. In Frankfurt May worked together with the landscape architect Leberecht Migge.

Leberecht Migge

Leberecht Migge (1881-1953) was born in Danzig and studied horticulture in Hamburg. From 1904 to 1913 he worked as a garden architect for Jacob Ochs's company in Hamburg. After a study tour of England in 1910, in 1913 he started his own agency in Hamburg, and in 1920 established a school, the Siedlerschule Worpswede, for the study and development of small-scale, intensive market gardening. Its periodical *Siedlungswirtschaft* (Settlement Economy) served as its forum for exchanging ideas, delving into concepts and discussion. In the years between 1922 and 1926 Migge drew up plans for Kiel, among other cities, for urban green spaces which would use the land productively. In 1926 he opened an office in Berlin, where he came into contact with modern architects like Martin Wagner, Bruno Taut and Ernst May.

The background for these developments was a resistance to what was called 'scientific management', or Taylorism, named after its pioneer Frederick Winslow Taylor (1856-1915). Taylor argued for the rational organisation of the industrial production process, characterised by a thoroughgoing division of labour in which people were reduced to a factor in production. The production of automobiles in Henry Ford's factories, organised along the assembly line, was an example of this. The dehumanisation of this extreme division of labour led to a sense of powerlessness, futility and alienation. Leberecht Migge here suggested gardening as a way to reconnect with real life, and worked out this idea himself in his experimental home and garden Sonnenhof, in Worpswede, near Bremen. He wrote, "We need... firm ground

under our feet again; we are fighting for that. The main point is to re-establish the lost connection with real life." A second important aspect in his thinking was a theoretical orientation to communism, which resounded in his questions involving the issue of public housing (the *Siedlungsbewegung* – settlement movement). He wrote on these social questions in the periodical *Die Tat*, under a pseudonym he chose for himself, *Spartakus im Gr n*. He saw *Bodenreform* (land reform) as a third way, an alternative to capitalsim and communism. In his opinion, a revolution, such as had happened in Russia, would not be necessary if people were afforded the possibility of producing the food to meet their own needs, right in the immediate vicinity of their homes: *Jedermann Selbstversorger* (Every man a self-sustainer).

The concept of urban farming

In his text *Deutsche Binnenkolonisation – Sachgrundlagen des Sied-lungswesens* (German internal colonisation – functional fundamentals of settlement) Migge argues for 'urban farming', in which green spaces in the city could retain their function in agrarian production, so that the city was assured of the basic food supply it needed. Conversely, in this relationship urban farming would involve a guaranteed income, production of waste and water, which would be supplied by the city. The engine driving urban farming was a perpetual cycle of these products, including the preparation of compost from the waste generated by the city, so that it would be possible to actually increase productivity when switching over from agriculture to intensive market gardening. According to Migge, urban farming was a means to solve many urban problems, including unemployment, food shortages and waste disposal. In these plans domestic gardens and allotment gardens played a crucial role, as the smallest units in the urban cycle of food production. For Migge the 19th century strolling park was finished; he regarded this type of park as useless, unnecessary and without cultural value; if one wished to contemplate nature, this was better done outside the city, where it was found in its true form.

Migge's urban farming fit perfectly with May's ideas about the rationalisation of mass housing projects in the new urban entities and the landscape space which accompanied them. Through his collaboration with May in the expansion plans for Frankfurt, urban farming developed into a concrete form, the settlement park, which took on both productive content and architectonic form. Urban farming became the foundation for open space, which had to provide for an articulation of the new urban areas in orderly entities, or *Siedlungen*. In this concept the house, the garden, the city and the landscape were involved with one another in their original context, and transformed into a productive and architectonically controlled urban paradise.

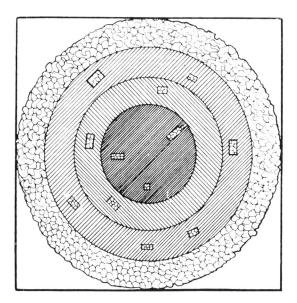

A. Concentric urban expansion

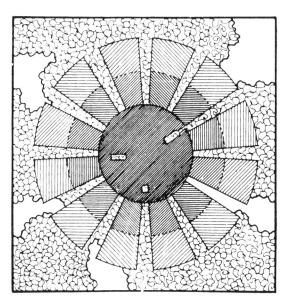

B. Radial urban expansion

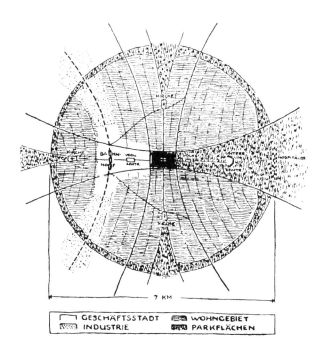

GESCHÄFTSSTADT   WOHNGEBIET
INDUSTRIE   PARKFLÄCHEN

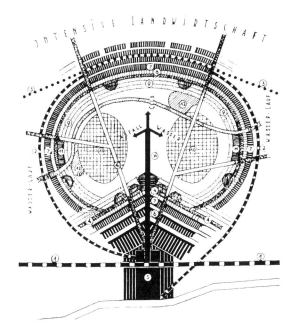

Transport

1   railway
2   tram
3   bus connections
4   foot routes

Buildings

5   city centre
6   areas with high-rise building
7   areas with low-rise building

Gardens

8   ring of domestic gardens
9   ring of allotment gardens
10 core with intensive market gardening

Sports and recreation

11 sports fields
12 swimming pools
13 school garden complexes
14 green areas

A and B: Eberstadt, Möhring and Peterssen: plans submitted for the competition for Greater Berlin, 1910 (from: H. Engel, E. van Velzen & TU Delft Faculteit der Bouwkunde, *Architectuur van de stadsrand, Frankfurt am Main*, 1925 - 1930. Delft 1987)

Bruno Taut: schematic city plan (from: K. Junghanns & Bauakademie der DDR Institut für Städtebau und Architektur, *Bruno Taut 1880-1938*. Berlin 1983)

L. Migge: municipal colonisation park, 1928 (from: H. Engel, E. van Velzen & TU Delft Faculteit der Bouwkunde, *Architectuur van de stadsrand, Frankfurt am Main*, 1925 - 1930. Delft 1987)

Rhine, Main and Nidda

Frankfurt lies on the lower reaches of the Main near the point where it runs into the Rhine, which here flows through the Upper Rhine Plain. This plain is 300 kilometres long, from Basel to Frankfurt, and at places 40 kilometres wide, and forms the central part of an enormous geological rift zone which extends from the Dogger Bank in the North Sea to the mouth of the Rhone on the Mediterranean Sea. This fault zone has many side branches, including the Roer rift, which runs through The Netherlands. On the north the Upper Rhine Plain is bordered by the Taunus Mountains, a low mountain range that is part of the Rhenish Slate Mountains.

A rift is caused by tension stress that tears the earth's crust apart. The strain and crustal thinning leads to the creation of a rift or graben, in which the central section sinks between two normal faults. As this decline occurs, the earth's crust also rises along the edges of the rift. Along the Upper Rhine Plain this tectonic uplift has created the rift shoulders, the Black Forest to the east and the Vosges to the west. The downfaulted floor of the rift formed a great basin which has largely been filled by sedimentation. The Rhine carried clay along with it, while erosion from the rift shoulders on either side provided a further source for this material. At the same time this erosion has caused a levelling of the relief caused by the tectonic uplift.

The Nidda

The present landscape around Frankfurt is strongly defined by the wide, deeply incised valley of the Main and by the valley of the Nidda, which flows into the Main at Frankfurt. Along the lower course of the Nidda, the height of the valley walls varies from 90 to 150 meters above sea level. To the north-east the valley narrows, with a broad bend to the

An old meander of the Nidda

→ Geomorphology and urban domain

Frankfurt ca. 1650
urban area ca. 2000

N   0   20   40km

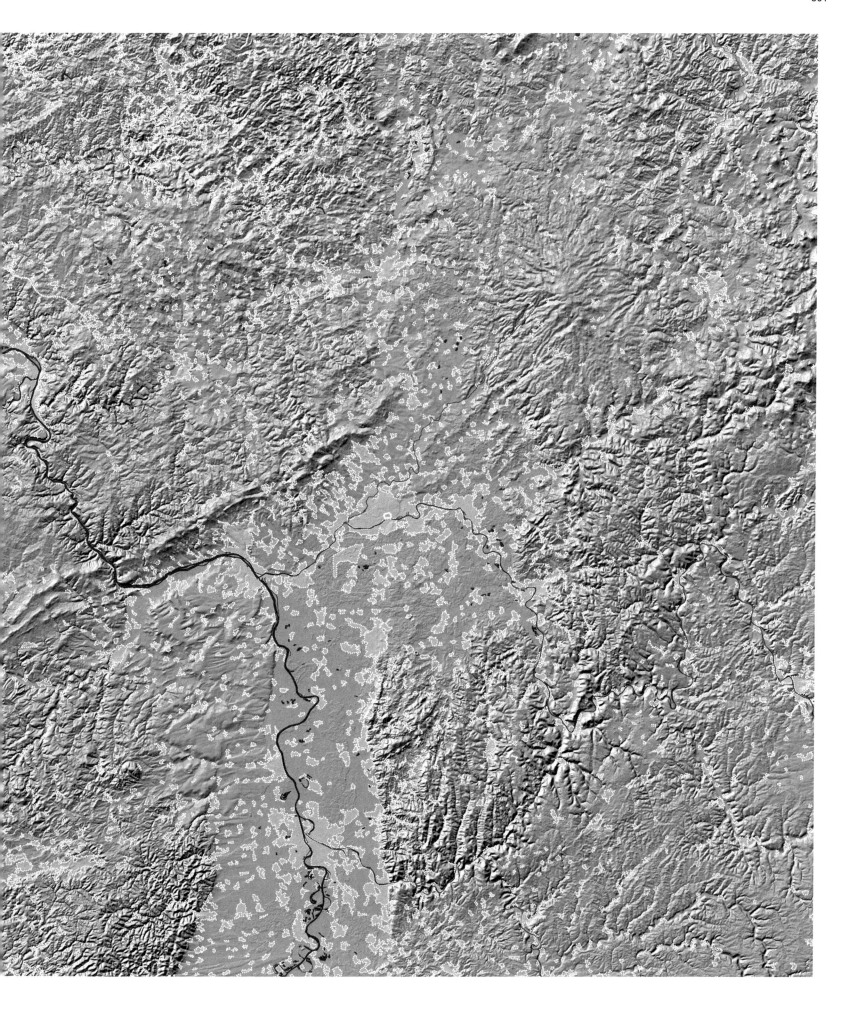

upper reaches in the hills. The steepness of the slope also varies, so
that streams from the Taunus Mountains to the north-west flow into the
Nidda. The wet valley floor is bordered by higher, fertile loess soils and
wind-borne sand deposits.

Regularly recurring floods necessitated the regularization of the
river. As part of this effort the river bed was deepened and the course
shortened by eliminating bends. Locks were included in the dams which
were necessary for the regularization, in order to make the whole course
navigable.

The valley along the lower course varies in width. Constrictions at
Eschersheim and Rödelheim create three basins over its length: an
upper basin around Bonames, a central basin and a wide lower basin
around where it discharges into the Main. This articulation into basins
and the old sections of the river cut off from its new course, with the
islands between them and the new course, were used in the plans for
the residential projects and the green belt.

Allotment gardens along the edge of the Nidda valley

Geomorphology, urban pattern and parks

Elevation (metres)

720 - 800
640 - 720
560 - 640
480 - 560
400 - 480
360 - 400
320 - 360
280 - 320
240 - 280
200 - 240
180 - 200
160 - 180
140 - 160
120 - 140
100 - 120
90 - 100
80 - 90

urban pattern

park

water

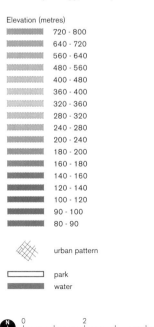

0   2   5km

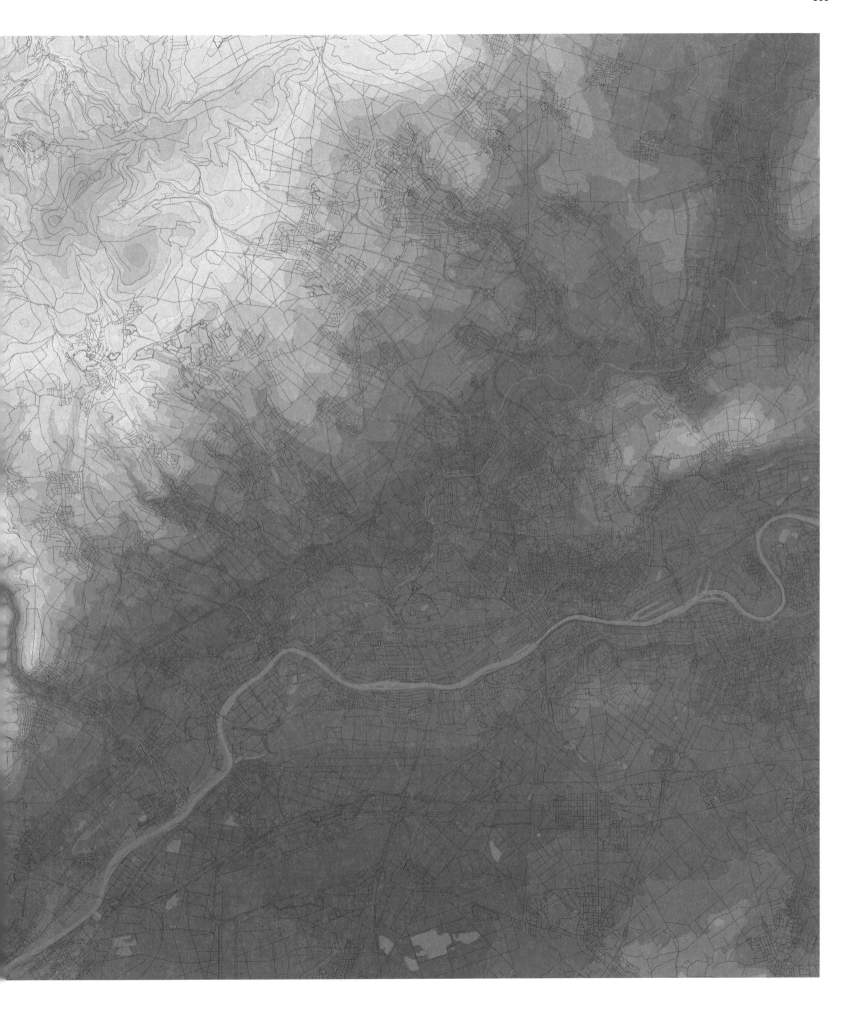

Folding the edge of the city inward

Frankfurt developed at a point where it was still relatively simple to cross the river. The suffix *furt* (English: ford) denotes a shallow area on a river that can be crossed on foot or horseback. In Roman times the area was a strategic zone in the valley of the Main, just to the south of the *limes*, the boundary of the Roman Empire, which ran along the crest of the Taunus Mountains. Many Roman villas lay in the vicinity, while the city of Wiesbaden was at that time already a spa known as Aquae Mattiacorum. In the Middle Ages Frankfurt was a Carolingian administrative centre; its first walls were built under the Emperor Barbarossa (1122-1190). With its favourable location, the city developed into an important hub for trade, with a stock exchange and many banks. In the 18th and 19th century a number of spas with springs, villas, parks and hotels developed outside the city in the Taunus Mountains. Industrialisation arrived rather late. At the end of the 19th century new neighbourhoods were rising on the edges of the city, with a lot of land speculation and uncontrolled expansion along the old country roads radiating out from the city.

During the tenure of Franz Adickes, burgomaster from 1890 to 1912, an autonomous Municipal Housing Department and Department of Urban Development were established. The uncontrolled expansion of the city was rationalised into a concentric development with monumental avenues and parks, including the Ostpark. In addition, areas around the city were annexed on a large scale and added to the municipality of Frankfurt, the area around the Nidda, with the towns of Berkersheim, Eckenheim, Eschersheim, Hausen, Herdernheim, Praunheim and Rödelheim being the largest.

Under burgomaster Voigt (1912-1924) the idea of a green belt around the city was proposed. To the south of the city it was to connect with the natural woodland, on the west to the valley of the Nidda, and on the east to the Ostpark. At the same time, work was begun on the regularization of the channel of the Nidda. In 1925, after Ludwig Landmann was elected burgomaster, a ten-year-plan for residential projects and a general building plan were drawn up. Following that, 8396 dwellings were realised in Frankfurt with public financing from1926 to 1928, and another 3396 in 1929. The director of this extensive residential building programme was Ernst May, who had been appointed head of the new Department of Urban Development in 1925. May brought in various specialists, including Herbert Boehm as an urban planner and Max Bromme for the parks and cemeteries. Leberecht Migge had great influence on shaping the landscape in the master plan and designed the gardens with the homes and the allotment gardens.

The 1927 expansion plan

In the 1927 expansion plan residential construction was still largely concentrated in existing, smaller units near the towns and in prime locations in the topography, such as along the Nidda Valley. At that point the city had already grown to far outside its old fortifications, and in the north-west had reached the valley of the Nidda near Heddernheim.

This early expansion plan is reminiscent of May's previous plan for Breslau. In this design submitted in a competition, the city is surrounded by twelve satellites, often expansions of existing towns, with an articulated edge to the city. In contradistinction to the formlessness of the 19th century urban expansion, May proposed that the city be organised in comprehensible units. Therefore the size of the satellite cities had to be fixed in advance, so that they would stand in the landscape as well-defined entities.

Migge's 1928 Grünflächenplan

Migge's regional *Grünflächenplan* (urban green space plan) from 1928 proceeded from the idea of the growing city as a coherent landscape, with the historic core as the centre. Around this were a succession of different zones. The first was the promenade zone, the part of the city just outside the fortifications. Next was a zone with parks, which were linked to one another by parkways. Outside of that lay a large, productive green and *Siedlung* zone. His *Siedlungen* here were not so much separate entities lying in the landscape, but formed a frame of landscape units. The various parts were connected with each other by green routes.

Migge worked out his idea for a "fundamentally new suburb of 5000 to 10,000 dwellings" further in an idealised scheme for a municipal settlement park. In it a zone with low-rise housing surrounds an open area of 500 to 1000 hectares. Railway lines go around it, bus lines run into the residential areas, pedestrian routes go through them. The gardens of the low-rise homes are oriented to the open centre, which is surrounded by a wide ring of allotment gardens for the residents of high-rises. The garden ring was interrupted at rhythmic intervals by sports fields, outdoor swimming pools and school gardens. The largest part of the inner area was intended for intensive market gardening. Migge regarded this plan as a model for a new, productive and inexpensive form of agriculture, for which the city ought to make funds, waste products and water available. At the same time it formed a new, productive type of park, a real and inexpensive *Volkspark*. A fruitful satellite of this sort could also include farms which lay further out, converting them for more intensive agriculture and thus growing into a productive green city.

Topographic map of Frankfurt assembled from two map pages, 1906-1908
(Topographic map 1:25,000 (shown at 1:40,000) Hessische Verwaltung für Boden-management und Geoinformation)

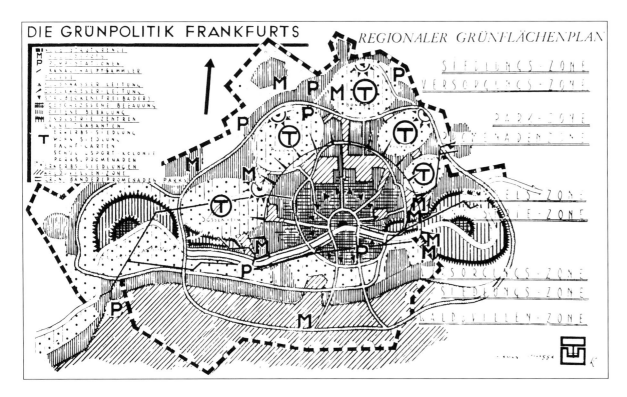

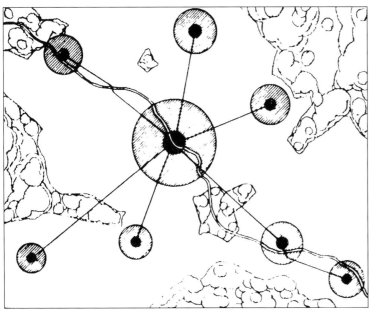

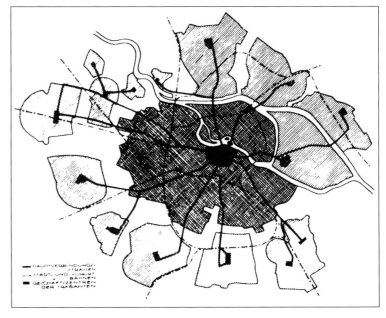

L. Migge: Grünflächenplan Frankfurt (1928) (from: H. Engel, E. van Velzen & TU Delft Faculteit der Bouwkunde, *Architectuur van de stadsrand, Frankfurt am Main, 1925-1930.* Delft 1987)

May and Boehm: schematic plan for satellite cities (1922) (from: H. Engel, E. van Velzen & TU Delft Faculteit der Bouwkunde, *Architectuur van de stadsrand, Frankfurt am Main, 1925-1930.* Delft 1987)

Schematic proposal accompanying the expansion plan for Breslau by May and Boehm (1920) (from: H. Engel, E. van Velzen & TU Delft Faculteit der Bouwkunde, *Architectuur van de stadsrand, Frankfurt am Main, 1925-1930.* Delft 1987)

The expansion plan of 1930 in the wider landscape

- urban pattern
- planning area 1930
- green basins of the Nidda valley
- other green space
- allotment gardens
- industry 1930
- built-up areas in 1930, with the new *Siedlungen* and the towns incorporated in them
- later expansions
- water
- contour lines

N   0   2   5km

The 1930 expansion plan

Migge's influence on the 1930 expansion plan is easy to discern. The expansions were to take place primarily to the north of the Main. In the south they were more modest in size, because the extensive woodlands there formed an impediment. These woods were the basis for a landscape belt around the new city. In the west they could be fit into the open valley of the Nidda, while a large number of the projected expansions lay in the upper reaches farther to the north-east of there. Still farther to the north-east the belt was comprised of several wedge-shaped zones pointed toward the centre, in which an open landscape could be maintained to far into the city. Because this landscape belt was fitted into the natural morphology and topography of the agricultural landscape, it was the obvious bearer for the expansions. Many towns along the arterial roads, and also along the Nidda, were included in it. They in part determined the form and the siting of the expansions, articulated in the landscape as neatly arranged entities.

The articulation of the Nidda Valley

The towns in Nidda Valley lay in favourable positions between the hills and the river valley. Between the city and the towns, the valley itself was a large open area in which there had thus far been little built. The sites and the dimensions of the zones for building were based on this strategic location of the towns and the natural articulation of the Nidda Valley into different basins. This articulation was further enhanced in the plans by the Department of Parks and Cemeteries. New planting was limited to several supplements in order to preserve the character of the river valley. In contrast to this, the new, canalised course was accentuated by planting walls of trees with openings for views. Old arms of the river and islands that had been created when the river was regularized were refurnished and included in the plan. Existing swimming areas in the Nidda were expanded and the islands were transformed into new swimming facilities, playgrounds and sports fields and special nature reserves, connected with one another by paths along the banks. The Brentano Park, on the banks of the Nidda at Rödelheim, designed in 1929 by Max Bromme, is an example of a swimming area of this sort in an old, cut off meander. The park had originally been laid out in 1770 as a garden for the Prussian Hofrat F. W. Basse. The Brentano family, wealthy Frankfurt merchants, bought the property in 1808 and considerably expanded the garden. The *Petrihäuschen*, on the Nidda, dates from this period. The city acquired the park in 1926, after which the Brentanobad was constructed in conjunction with the regularization of the Nidda.

The uppermost basin of the Nidda at Bonames was partially designed as a recreation area with sports fields and playgrounds for the northern city expansions. Depending on the location and the soil conditions the largest part of the area was reserved for market gardening and intensive agriculture. The lowest basin, at the mouth of the Nidda between Rödelheim and Höchst, was not sharply framed by built-up areas. There the Rebstockerwald, the Biegwald and the municipal woods at Nied were combined and linked with the city park of Höchst, as the terminus of the green belt on the north-western bank. The middle basin, to the south of Heddernheim, lay favourably with regard to the old city and was the most developed spatially. Here the open landscape of the valley was retained to provide a place for mass gatherings in the open air. The more intensive forms of use were situated along the edges, so that the large open space was not be cut up. In terms of their sites and form any buildings were carefully coordinated with the morphology of the landscape. Particularly the slopes were built on, in new, well-organised units that marked off the landscape space and provided new edges for the towns.

Scheme of the 1930 expansion plan 1930

urban pattern

built-up areas in 1930, with the new *Siedlungen* and the towns incorporated in them
pattern of older towns and structures along the Nidda valley
industry 1930
later expansions
green basins of the Nidda valley
other green space
allotment gardens
water
contour lines

0   1   2km

Here the river valley has the form of a broad, asymmetrical eroded meander, with a steeper slope on the west side and a gentler declivity on the east. The buildings are clustered in various groups, the contours of which follow the form of the valley. In the northern part of the basin, between Heddernheim on the west bank and Eschersheim on the east, the natural narrowing of the valley is accentuated by the buildings, which here almost touch one another. In the southern part the new margins of the town of Hausen accentuate the bend in the river and introduces the narrowing of the valley there. On the eastern bank the dispersed urban expansion around the towns of Bockenheim and Ginnheim is forged together by new tracts of buildings into units with a clearly defined contour along the valley, with branches from the space of the valley inwards. The town of Praunheim marks the westernmost bend of the river's meander. If existing country roads could not be used, new roads were adapted to the contour lines.

Landschaftssteigerung

The buildings and streets of the new *Siedlungen* run parallel to the contour lines of the valley. Moreover, the valley walls and the differences in elevation present are accentuated even more by the decreasing height of the buildings in the direction of the valley. This accentuating of the relief was appropriately termed *Landschaftssteigerung* (landscape movement). The edge of the landscape was marked by the long, white walls of the façades of the new *Siedlungen* at the top of the slopes. The valley itself, lying below, was kept open. Contrariwise, from the *Siedlungen* one has a grand view out over the valley and the urban panorama of Frankfurt which lies behind it. The contrast between the open valley and the residential area is further intensified by designing the residential areas as one connected architectonic wall with the repetition of similar elements in the façades and the floor plans. Just as in old Frankfurt, where the rows of houses along the banks of the Main involve the river with the city, the series of dwellings along the Nidda Valley transform the landscape into a new, shared architectonic space. With the precisely calculated size and positioning of the urban units with regard to each other, the landscape is changed into an emphatically urban space and the edge of the city is folded inward. The most pronounced expression of this spatial reversal between the city and the landscape is in the Siedlung Römerstadt, where, just as in a classic villa in Rome, bastion-shaped balconies in the edge intensified the view of the enclosed landscape.

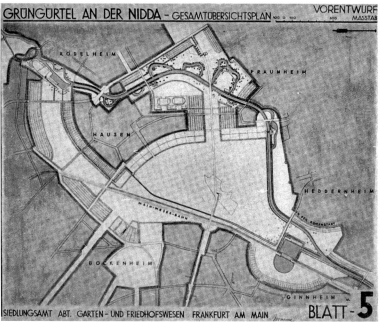

Existing structures included in the new expansions

Detail of the central basin, with the Brentanopark to the upper left (from: H. Engel, E. van Velzen & TU Delft Faculteit der Bouwkunde, *Architectuur van de stadsrand, Frankfurt am Main, 1925-1930*. Delft 1987)

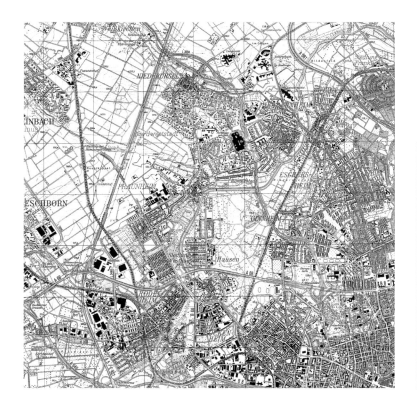

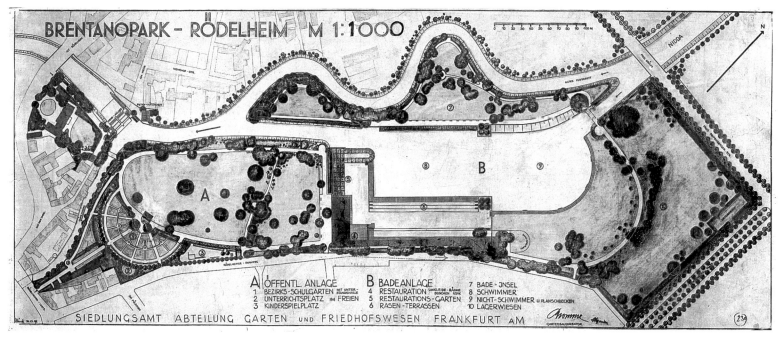

Hausen, Praunheim and Römerstadt on the Nidda (topographic map 1:25.000 1995, Hessische Verwaltung für Bodenmanagement und Geoinformation)

Allotment gardens at the foot of the retaining wall at Römerstadt

M. Bromme, design for the Brentanopark (Institut für Stadtgeschichte Frankfurt am Main)

The Siedlung as an architectonic settlement form

The Siedlung Römerstadt stands on a spot where in Roman times a part of the fortified settlement of Nida lay. It was built in 1928 and is comprised of a total of 1220 dwellings. Ernst May played a key role in both the urban development plan and its architectonic elaboration. Leberecht Migge designed the gardens. In Römerstadt the relation between the *Siedlung* and the landscape was worked out as a single entity, both programmatically and landscape architectonically.

The actualisation of the topography

Römerstadt is the northernmost of the three settlements which gave the western edge of the central Nidda basin a new, architectonic boundary: from south-west to north-east, Westhausen, Praunheim and Römerstadt. All three of the ground plans were designed to be approximately parallel with the contour lines of the valley. Westhausen has the most rational plan, a rectangle with roughly north-south oriented strip parcellation. The more or less rectangular ground plan of Praunheim lies at right angles to it and curves farther eastward with the valley. Together they form a right angle, an architectonic treatment and enclosure of the bend in the canalised Nidda and the old, cut off arms of the river which lie in front of it.

Römerstadt has a ground plan that curves along with the forward thrust of the main shape of the valley at that point. The ground plan is about one-and-a-half kilometres long and comprised of two narrow sections along the valley. A slightly curved road runs between the two, curling obliquely up out of the valley over the contour lines as a sort of arabesque. Each section is composed of several residential streets running parallel with the valley, with rows of single family houses and gardens. With several jogs, the straight streets in the western section follow the contour lines running the length of the valley, while in the eastern section the streets curve with the bend in the river. In this way the original topography is actualised in the urban layout.

The landscape as urban interior

The rows of houses lie on a rising series of terraces between the river valley and the centre of the neighbourhood to the east of the old cemetery of Heddernheim. The height of the buildings is greatest at the top of the valley wall; here there are strips with middle-rise flats. The *Siedlung* bounds the river valley with a long, curved retaining wall. This is studded at regular intervals with platforms reminiscent of bastions,

offering a grand panorama of the valley and the city lying behind it. The bastions are connected with the residential area lying behind it by footpaths crossing the residential streets, and with the valley by stairs running down obliquely. Looking out across the valley, this effect creates a spatial series from small-scale and closed to large-scale and open. As a result, each dwelling is individually connected with the landscape of the Nidda. At the foot of the retaining wall, between the residential neighbourhood and the valley, lies a promenade planted with lime trees, which marks the curving longitudinal contours of the valley. The promenade, the bastions, the retaining wall, the terraces and the rising

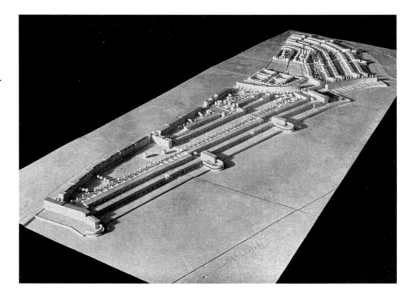

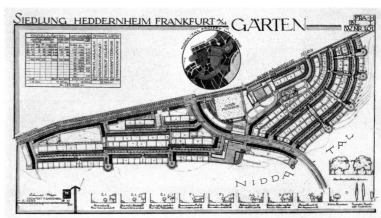

Three-dimensional model of the Siedlung Römerstadt (from: J. Buekschmitt, *Ernst May.* Stuttgart 1963)

Design by Leberecht Migge for the gardens and open space in Römerstadt (*Gartenschönheit* 9/2[1928] 48-51, Farbbeilage, o.P. p.49. Universitätsbibliothek TU Berlin.)

Scheme of the central basin
of the Nidda valley in the 1930
expansion plan

▰	expansions up to 1930
▰	later expansions
▰	green basin of the Nidda valley
▱	other green space
⊞	allotment gardens
▬	water
░	infrastructure
——	railway line

0   500   1000m

rows of houses accentuate the natural form of the valley wall and give it a new architectonic form. Conversely, from the valley, the edge of the city manifests itself as an architectonic ensemble, draping itself around the space of the landscape and bringing it into the domain of the city. With this, the edge of the city formed the borders of an urban interior.

An unpretentious homogeneity

To a great extent the visual structure of the *Siedlung* was defined by a repetition of architectural elements which resulted from the standardisation in its construction. According to May, this, like other technical and economic changes, was unavoidable. New construction techniques tended toward an ever more rationalised form of production for homes and building elements. May thought that one should encourage this development in order to make housing construction less expensive and to create forms of living that would also be within the reach of less well-off families. In his view, it was the task of the architect to catch the essence of the building assignment and develop standard types that did justice to the demands of life and the technology of the times, rejecting every form of ornamentation altogether. A standard type offered enough possibilities for further development and refinement, without having to degenerate into visual cacophony. According to May, through the potential for variation in interior furnishings, the dwelling type also still offered the residents sufficient possibilities for individuality.

With regard to the visual/spatial relation between the city and landscape he wrote, "The image of the city will unquestionably change fundamentally as a result of the rationalisation of the building process… In place of the endless varieties that lead to agitated urban effects, there will be a thoroughgoing restfulness, an unpretentious homogeneity, to be seen in the uninterrupted image of white stuccoed façades and the sober contours of the flat roofs which mark the edge of the city as an elementary form in the landscape."

The functional unity of house and garden

Not only residential living, but also the unity of house, garden and production landscape as this had been developed by Leberecht Migge, contributed to defining the programmatic form of the *Siedlung*. Migge started from the idea that gardens are "cure for the misery and vices of life in the metropolis". The garden is the simplest way back to nature, by which Migge did not mean primal nature, that one can contemplate outside the city, but the original human existence, in which men worked the land with their own hands and gathered in its bounty – in short, before they became urbanites. Migge regarded the garden

as an essential extension of domestic space, and moreover as an indispensable supplement to one's livelihood. In that, he distinguished himself from many others in the garden city movement. For them the garden city remained bogged down in a romantic rejection of the city by building villages, and offered no solutions for the questions of mass residential projects. In that sense, for him the garden was not so much an aesthetic or architectonic form, but a *Zeichen des Machens*, an expression of industry.

Just as Ernst May was in search of the essence of the domestic floor plan in a typological composition of mass housing, Leberecht Migge sought to find the elementary typology of the garden as the basis for various necessities of life and production purposes. In his view, as vital components in a residential neighbourhood gardens should be designed as responsibly as the houses, and realised with the same technical perfection. Migge even took the technical execution of this idea so far that according to him a suburban area, with enough gardens for recycling waste products, could do without sewers. A good garden with a low-rise building should not be too small, not smaller than 200 to 300 m². A wide band of allotment gardens for the use of the residents in the flat buildings were projected for the bottom of the retaining wall along the valley. In this way the functional zoning and structure of the residential neighbourhood was to a large degree defined by the garden as the smallest production unit of agricultural work. Through this the city, in the form of the *Siedlung*, also took on a new, productive significance as an architectonic settlement form for the original agricultural landscape.

The spatial transitions and connections between the dwellings above and the Nidda valley below

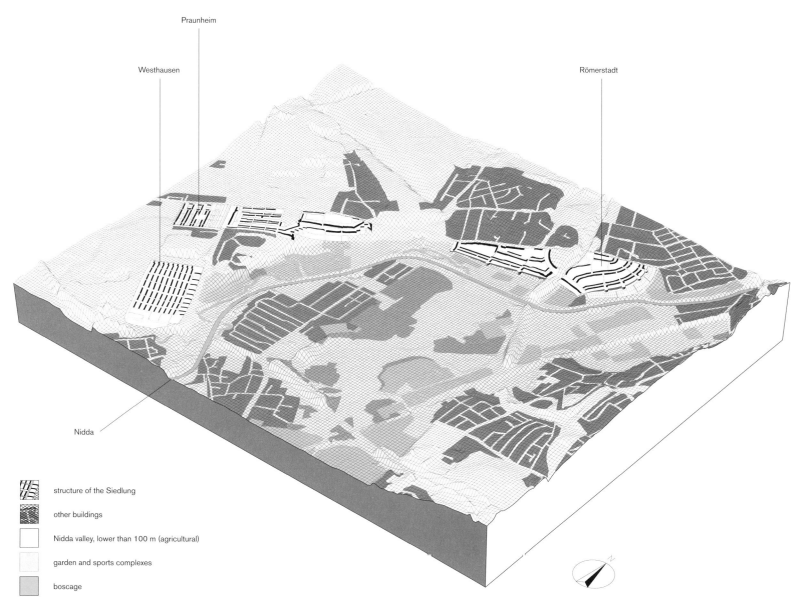

Praunheim

Westhausen

Römerstadt

Nidda

▨	structure of the Siedlung
▨	other buildings
☐	Nidda valley, lower than 100 m (agricultural)
☐	garden and sports complexes
▨	boscage

Three-dimensional model of the Siedlungen in the landscape relief (1 cell measures 20 × 20 metres, z = 9×)

The settlement park

The mass housing projects in Frankfurt am Main in the years 1925-1930 were based on a rationalisation of the domestic floor plan and urban planning parcellation for industrial building production. To achieve this, it was necessary to reduce the dwelling to a reproducible standard type. Two aspects made this typological reduction and repetition a unique landscape architectonic experiment. First, there was the exceptional attention given in the planning and design process to the stage-managing of the new *Siedlungen* in the landscape. A second aspect was the logical development of the outdoor space through a functional transformation of the garden and the agricultural landscape of the Nidda.

The functional transformation of the classic landscape theatre

The articulation of urban expansion into *Siedlungen* as well-organised entities led to a new, direct relation between residential entities and the landscape. In their spatial interaction with the old towns, the *Siedlungen* were an ambitious architectonic transformation of the existing topography. The rationalisation of residential construction led to the deconstruction of traditional urban forms of building such as the residential block. What remained were the essential building blocks of urban housing, which in the increase in scale involved in urban development could be regrouped into pure architectonic forms that could enter into a new functional and visual relation with the landscape.

Essentially, classic design instruments were used in the staging of these elementary urban building blocks in the landscape. Like villas, the *Siedlungen* lie at prominent positions in the Nidda landscape, and together they form a modern functional landscape theatre in which the views over and the use of the landscape were democratised. Agriculture, defined by the natural form of the valley, played its role on the landscape stage as a wholesome and invigorating activity, incorporated spatially into a park-like scene – just as in the *villa rustica*.

Urban living as a settlement process

The collaboration between May and Migge led to the creation a new, urban production landscape, a renewed settlement of the landscape by an urban form of living, which, as well as having an architectonic dimension also had an elementary landscape dimension. What was most unusual about the experiment in Frankfurt is that it gave a production landscape a place in the urban pattern. Based on their location and the soil conditions, large parts of the Nidda Valley were reserved for market gardening and agriculture. On the slopes along the edge of the open Nidda Valley, adjoining the built-up areas, long strips were designed as allotment gardens for food production. The majority of the pasture land in the valley was preserved and retained an agrarian purpose. Rather than transforming the agricultural landscape into a park landscape, it was once again made productive, intensified spatially and incorporated into the city. Occasionally this productive, agricultural function was supplemented by recreational facilities such as swimming areas and sports fields, in which an effort was made to achieve a good interaction between the natural and technical characteristics of the production landscape. In connection with the rationalisation of the ground plans for housing, the layout of gardens was also rationalised. Both ecological/productive considerations, and considerations with regard to domestic functions, played a role in this. The garden returned to the urban landscape as a basic, practical domestic resource and as a catalyst for the social process of living. In addition, the allotment garden also was given a functional, standard form. Folded in strips around the *Siedlungen*, they formed a practical, collective, productive space as a transition to the larger agricultural landscape.

In the Stadtpark Hamburg the design task was primarily focused on the spatial accommodation of new social and recreational functions. This design tacked between the new programme and an historical landscape architectonic concept, yet without that leading to a new, coherent landscape architectonic form. That did succeed in Frankfurt. Here a new relationship arose between the landscape architectonic form and the content of urban living, in which bringing land under cultivation and the practical ecology of the urban landscape were also involved. The result was the creation of an ecologically rooted, productive and enjoyable urban landscape that not only served as a backdrop for recreational functions, but in which the original relation

The regional park landscape

green belt, open fields
woods
urban pattern
Siedlungen 1926-31
water
limes

N   0   2   5km

between *otium* and *negotium*, between the enjoyment and exploitation of nature, was restored.

In the course of this the elementary relationship between house, garden and landscape was reassessed and the relation between the city and the landscape was released from its one-sidedly idyllic character, as that had been established in the 19th century city park. Here the design question of the urban landscape was uncoupled from the city park and emphatically placed in the tradition of the agricultural landscape, as a settlement process in which urban living was understood as the next phase in the reclamation of the natural landscape. Migge himself spoke of a settlement park, in order to indicate that this was a whole new park form in which the settlement of the landscape was embedded in the the building process of urban expansion.

The revival of urban farming

In the late 1980s proposals were made in Frankfurt for a new park in the central basin of the Nidda Valley. The old agricultural land in the heart of the valley became a nature reserve, while the edges were more thickly planted, and various facilities and objects were located there. The site in the northern part, adjoining a motorway that cut across through Römerstadt, became home to the *Bundesgartenschau* (national horticultural exhibition, a temporary exhibition). This all meant the abandonment of the original concept of the settlement park as an integral urban landscape. Perhaps Migge had overestimated the binding, community-forming character and the economic capacity of urban farming. The modern concept of urban farming was traded in for 'virgin' nature, supplemented with park-like facilities. In a deeper sense, this meant a return to the 19th century park type.

What apparently can no longer be done on the scale of the city expansion, is however being tried anew on the regional scale with other means. In the Regionalpark Rhein-Main (2004), which includes the whole region, Frankfurt is embedded in a public urban landscape in which nature, agricultural landscapes and recreation are woven together. The development of this *Zwischenstadt* (in-between city and landscape) is oriented toward redesigning open spaces and linking them with one another, with the goal of creating a harmonious connection between their various functions. In this however it is no longer a matter of domestic coherence among house, garden, city and landscape, but of bridging the growing discrepancy between the dynamics of urban development and nature, in which the agricultural landscape is assigned a role as a mediator. In many other big cities too the concept of urban farming, in whatever form it may take, is

being advanced again. It was the accomplishment of Ernst May and Leberecht Migge that they were able to give the agricultural landscape a place in the functional structure of the modern city. Their settlement parks provide indispensable landscape architectonic design keys for a revival of urban farming in the framework of a productive urban pleasure landscape.

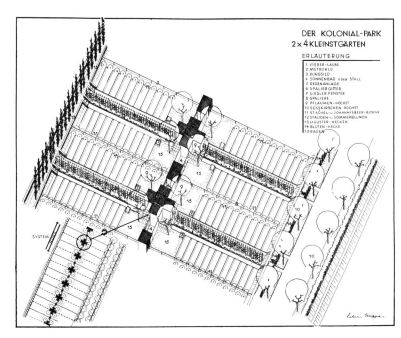

Layout of allotment gardens at Römerstadt
Composition of the gardens in the Kolonial-Park (both from: *Leberecht Migge 1881-1935. Gartenkultur des 20. Jahrhunderts.* Worpswede 1981)

→ **View into the Nidda valley near Römerstadt**

THE GRÜNGÜRTEL COLOGNE 1925

Green structure as an artificial landscape form
The concept of the green belt
Fritz Encke
The development of the park form within the green structure

The Lower Rhine

The first green belt as a boulevard
The first ring of fortifications (1650)
The second ring of fortifications (after 1815)
The boulevard or Prachtstrasse

The second green belt and the spatial articulation of the city
The third defensive ring (after 1873)
Schumacher's Freiflächenplan

The third green belt and the functional zoning of the green
The development of the scheme
The green radials

A green matrix
Schmuckplätze and Erholungsplätze

The park form dissolves
A catalogue of nature
Deconstructing the pastoral landscape
Standardising the programmatic form
The park as a green link

Urban green space as a generic landscape
The break with the agricultural landscape
Dismantling the park scheme
Between form and norm

The outermost green belt of Cologne, at the Decksteiner Weiher (aerial photo: Bilderbuch Köln)

Green structure as an artificial landscape form

The urban landscape of Cologne is based on an artificial green structure in which the form of the city's fortifications is repeated three times at different scale. This green structure has profoundly affected the relation between the city and the landscape. The growth of the city constantly broke through the attempts to fix its edges. In this growth process, however, the successive belts of fortifications created spatial margins for the city, which later afforded the possibility of developing a coherent pattern of green spaces which were consistent with the growth, scale and differentiation of the city, and which moreover provided an articulation for the city as a whole.

The concept of the green belt

With Martin Wagner's 1915 dissertation *Das Sanitäre Grün der Städte* (Urban green space for public health) and follow-up study *Städtliche Freiflächenpolitik* (The politics of urban open space), likewise from 1915, the question of the form of the park landscape shifted to the benefits, quantity and spatial organisation of the green in the city. Urban green became a separate category in the systematic expansion of the city. In the development of plans the word 'green', or green space (*Grünfläche*), began to supplant the word 'park'. While the cultural and representative functions were not entirely eclipsed, it was now chiefly the social and urban development significance of green space that occupied the foreground. In the designs by Fritz Encke the park developed from a spatially defined exercise into a functional component of a green structure that encompassed the various stages of the growth of the city and its increasing range of scale as an artificial landscape.

Fritz Encke

From 1890 to 1913 Fritz Encke (1861-1931) was an instructor at the Landschaftsgärtnerei at the Königliche Gärtnerlehranstalt in Wildpark, near Potsdam. This school had been established in 1823 as an initiative by Peter Joseph Lenné and played an important role in professional discussion. In 1900 Encke visited the Exposition Universelle in Paris and acquainted himself with the great formal gardens of Le Nôtre, such as Versailles and Chantilly. In 1903 he became *Gartendirektor* in Cologne, where until his retirement in 1926 he produced designs for parks and squares within the context of a greater, likewise planned green structure. Encke's work falls into a period in which the second and third belts of fortifications around Cologne were removed, creating considerable new

space in the city. The heart of his work therefore lies in the new suburbs and in the area along the edge of the city, in and around the outermost green belt.

The development of the park form within the green structure

The concept of the green belt took on new content in Fritz Encke's park designs. The belt developed from an urban promenade for the beautification and framing of the city into a green zone integrated into the whole plan for the city, playing a role in the pattern of the city's functional services. Landscape architecture had to provide a new content and form for this artificial green structure.

Topography

airport	tunnel
subway station	important road
subway line	urban pattern
railway line	park
railway station	other green space
motorway	water

Parks

1	Abteipark	41	Kölner Rugby Park
2	Aguilapark	42	Kulturpark
3	Äußerer Grüngürtel, Decksteiner Weiher	43	Kurt-Burnhoff-Sportpark
4	Bayer Erholungshauspark	44	Leo-Amann-Park
5	Beethovenpark	45	Lis-Böhle-Park
6	Blücherpark	46	Lörsfelder Schloßpark
7	Böcking-Park	47	Mediapark
8	Botanischer Garten/Flora	48	Merheimer Heide
9	Bürgerbusch	49	Naherholungsgebiet Fühlinger See
10	Bürgerpark	50	Nordpark
11	Bürgerpark Sudetenstraße	51	Oberländer Werft
12	Burgpark	52	Olof-Palme-Park
13	Burgpark	53	Park der Menschenrechte
14	Burgpark Gleuel	54	Parkanlage Rheindorf-Nord
15	Carl-Duisberg-Park	55	Pyramidenpark
16	Chorbusch	56	Quartierspark
17	Deutzer Stadtgarten	57	Rheinpark
18	Dünnwalder Wald	58	Rheinpark
19	Finkens Garten	59	Riehler Aue
20	Forstbotanischer Garten	60	Rochuspark
21	Freizeitgelände Entenfang	61	Römerpark
22	Freizeitpark	62	Schloßpark
23	Friedenspark (Hindenburgpark)	63	Schloßpark
24	Friedenswäldchen	64	Schloßpark
25	Fritz-Encke-Volkspark (Volkspark Raderthal)	65	Schloßpark Gymnich
26	Galopprennbahn Köln-Weidenpesch	66	Schloßpark Stammheim
27	Graf-Berghe-von-Trips-Stadion	67	Schloßpark Türnich
28	Grüner Hof	68	Stadtgarten
29	Grünzug Quettinger Feld	69	Stadtpark
30	Hindenburgpark (Leverkusen)	70	Stadtwald
31	Hiroshima-Nagasaki-Park	71	Südpark
32	Hitdorfer Laach	72	Tierpark an der Lutherstraße
33	Humboldtpark	73	Toni-Steingass-Park
34	Innerer Grüngürtel	74	Trude-Herr-Park
35	Jahnwiese	75	Volksgarten
36	Japanischer Garten	76	Vorgebirgspark
37	Johannes-Giesberts-Park	77	Weidenpescher Park
38	Jugendpark	78	Weißhaus
39	Kennedy-Ufer	79	Worringer Bruch
40	Klettenbergpark	80	Wuppermannpark

0   2   5km

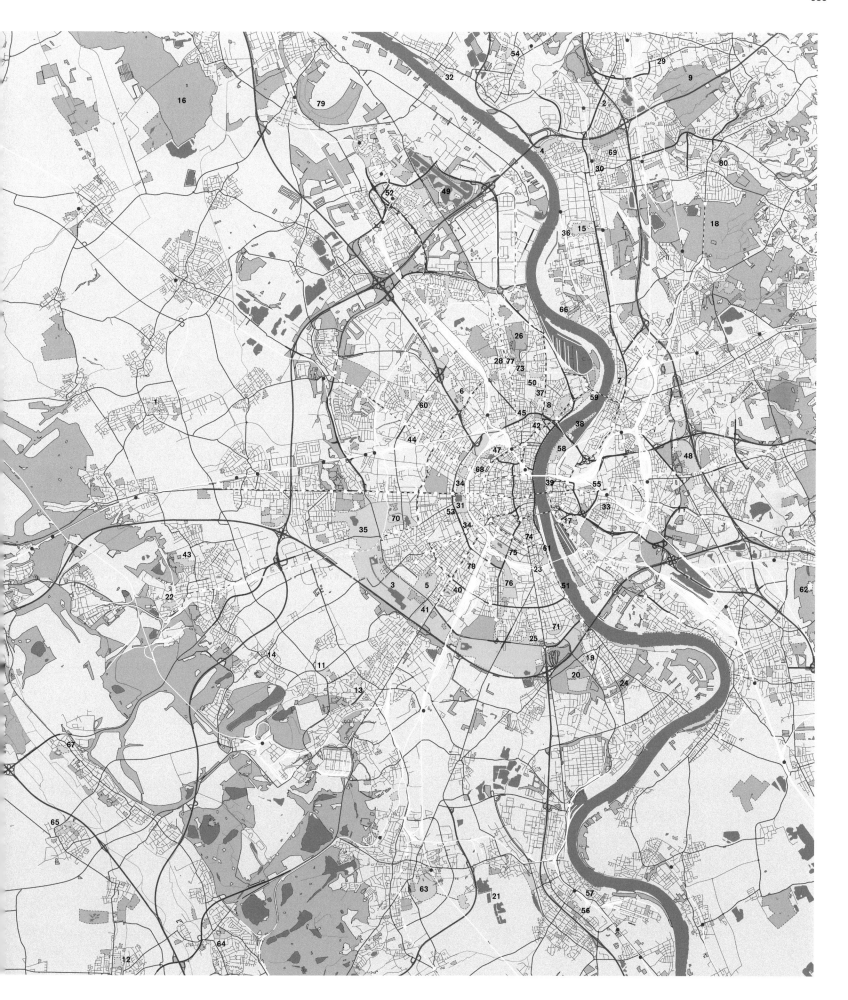

The Lower Rhine

The Lower Rhine forms the lowest, northern part of a geological fault zone, a rift that stretches from the Dogger Bank in the North Sea to the mouth of the Rhône on the Mediterranean Sea. On the south the plain of the Lower Rhine is bounded by the low Taunus Mountains and the Eifel Plateau. The rift of the Rhine Valley is largely filled with sediment, primarily clay which the Rhine has carried down with it.

Cologne lies on a slight bend in the Rhine, at the point where the Rhine Valley opens out from the higher, slate Eifel Plateau to the lower hill country and low lands to the north-west. The river changes here into a meandering stream, whose amplitude is determined by the hills that border the valley, about 25 kilometres across. The transition from the middle reaches to the lower course meant that goods on boats which could easily reach this point had to be transshipped at Cologne. The landscape slopes down toward the river at a rather steep angle, then changes over into a terrace of loam and loess sediments, with an island off the river bank. The flood plain is comprised of layers of lignite, covered with gravel and river sediments. During the last ice age a fertile layer of loess was deposited in the region. Here the stream bed was only 600-700 meters wide, making it relatively simple to link the banks by bridges. The soil pattern is characterised by old stream belts and winding forms which arose as a result of variations in water drainage, currents, erosion and sedimentation. The city's green belts, which connect to the Rhine, form artificial green meanders, as it were an extension of this old river pattern.

Lignite mine near Hambach, to the west of Cologne (photo: Johannes Fasolt)

Geomorphology and urban domain

Cologne ca. 1650
urban area ca. 2000

0   20   40k

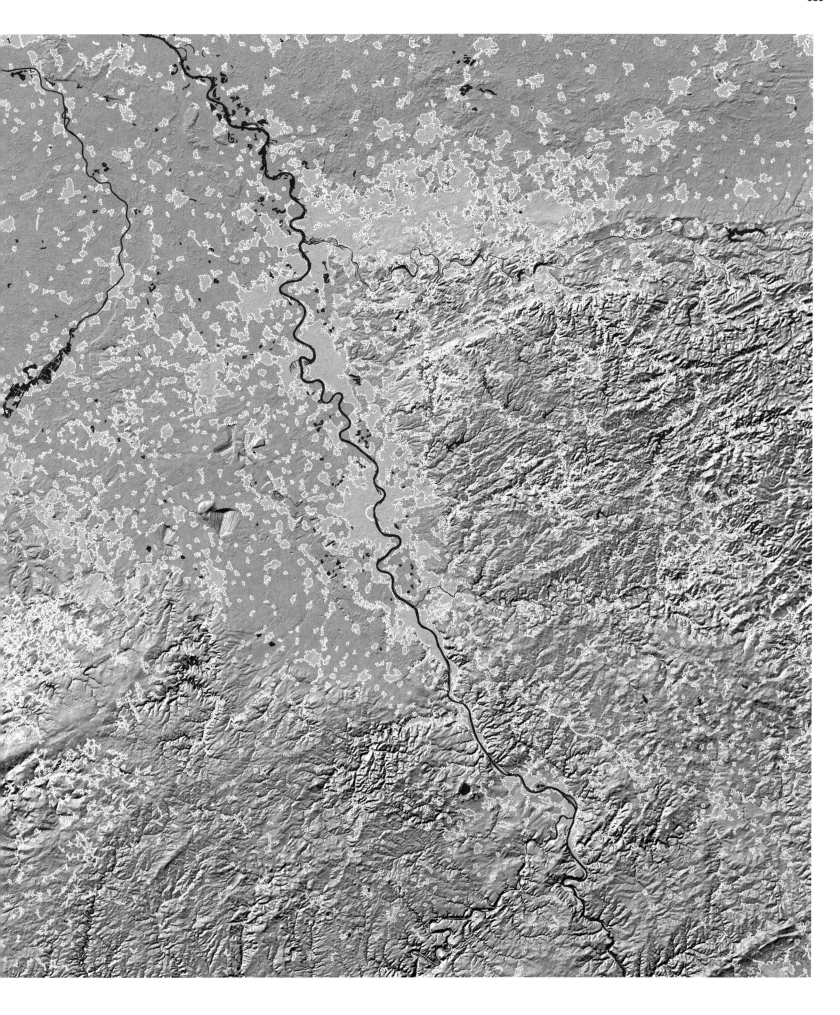

Geomorphology, urban pattern and parks

Elevation (metres)

	200 - 240
	180 - 200
	160 - 180
	140 - 160
	120 - 140
	100 - 120
	90 - 100
	80 - 90
	70 - 80
	60 - 70
	50 - 60
	40 - 50
	30 - 40
	20 - 30
	10 - 20
	0 - 10
	-10 - 0

urban pattern

park

water

Pond in the Stadtwald (photo: Bilderbuch Köln)

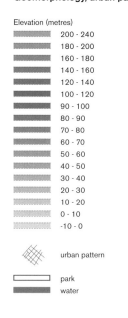

0   2   5km

The first green belt as a boulevard

From around 50 BCE the Rhine formed the boundary between Gallia, part of the Roman Empire, and Germany. Cologne (Colonia) was founded in 38 BCE by Agrippa, the son-in-law of Emperor Augustus, as a part of the *limes*, the northern border of the Empire. The city was populated by Ubii, who settled here after the destruction of the revolting Eburones. For that reason the city was also called Oppidum Ubiorum, the city of the Ubii. The city plan was formed by a rectangular grid with two main axes, the one roughly parallel with and the other at right angles to the Rhine, the *Cardo* and the *Decumanus Maximus,* on which the most important buildings and the Forum lay. The Romans regarded agriculture as the foundation for prosperity. Various villas – *villae rusticae* – were built around the settlement. There were also agricultural areas supplied with water from the hills and drainage canals to the Rhine. The successive fortifications, which formed the basis for the later green structure, reflected the original, semi-circular Roman colony on the Rhine.

The first ring of fortifications (1650)

Under Charlemagne (747-814) Cologne became the seat of an archbishop, who was also the administrator of the city. With its wealth of relics, including the staff of St. Peter and the remains of the Three Kings (the latter having been brought from Milan to Cologne under the Holy Roman Emperor Frederick I Barbarossa of Hohenstaufen [1122-1190]), it also became a goal of pilgrimage, which further increased its prosperity. Furthermore, the city was a starting point or way station on European pilgrimage routes which ran on to Jerusalem, Rome or Santiago de Compostela.

In terms of area, after the construction of its new city wall in 1180 Cologne was the largest German city in the Middle Ages, with flourishing arts and crafts and the most important markets. The city soon reached the heights of its importance, with its Dom (cathedral, begun 1248) and the Dom School with famed teachers such as Albertus Magnus (1200-1280). The semi-circular wall dating from 1180 was reinforced with bastions in 1650. A glacis was also constructed in front of the wall, a slope with on open zone on the inside, at the foot of the walls, creating a free fire zone. It was this system which formed the first fortification ring.

The second ring of fortifications (after 1815)

In 1815 Cologne became a fortress city in the kingdom of Prussia. A new ring of eleven forts and seven lunettes (detached earthwork bastions) were then built at a distance of about a kilometre out in the field of fire in front of the old city wall. Meanwhile – and particularly with the advent of the railways – the population grew explosively. In 1860 the city had already grown tight against the old wall. Moreover, at one kilometre the width of the circuit was no longer adequate for protection against artillery, which by then had a range of 6000 meters.

The need for a new defensive line became acute, both from military considerations and from the standpoint of urban expansion. Ultimately the city acquired the land under the old city walls, after which a new line of defence was realised by connecting the already existing forts from 1815. This created the second defensive ring. Complete with a moat and casements, this was built between 1882 and 1890, and ran from Fort I in the south to Fort XI in the extreme north. It had fourteen wide gates for vehicular traffic, and four passages for trains were included, while a railway was also built along the defence works. The Neustadt was built between the old city wall and the second belt of fortifications.

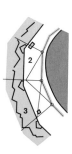
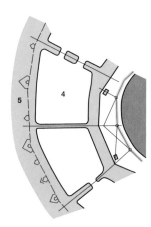

A	first ring of fortifications (1650)	B	second ring of fortifications (after 1815)	C	third ring of fortifications
1	old city core	2	Neustadt	4	suburbs
2	wall + bulwark + glacis	3	forts + wall + glacis	5	forts + Militärring

Scheme of the first, second and third ring of fortifications

Map of Cologne and vicinity in 1836 (Preußische Kartenaufnahme 1836-1850 5007 Köln, Bezirksregierung Köln)

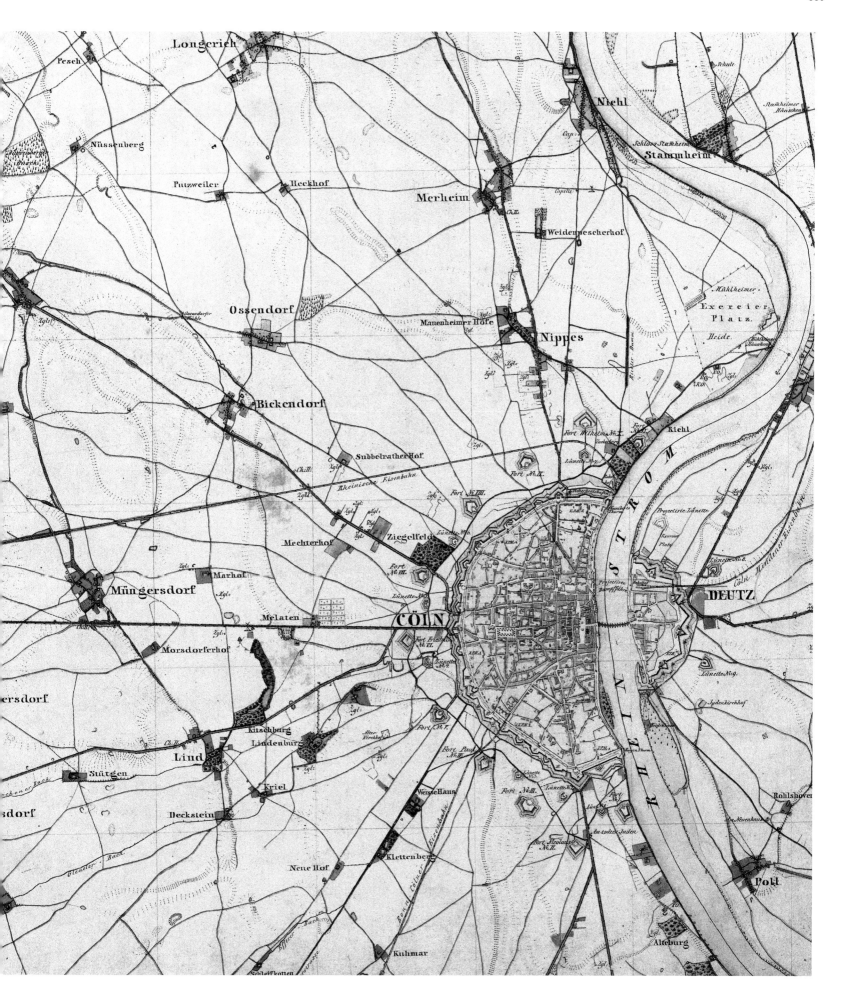

The boulevard or Prachtstrasse

Immediately after the first ring of defences were turned over to the city, the walls and gates were demolished, the embankments levelled and the moats filled in. In 1880 the city administration announced a competition for an urban development plan for the Neustadt. The design by Josef Stübben, which won the first prize, called for a ring boulevard six kilometres long on the site of the former medieval city wall, to be 35 meters wide and planted with four to five rows of trees. This *Ringstrasse* or *Prachtstrasse* displayed clear similarities – though with less allure – with the Wiener Ring, the broad boulevard with parks and squares that had been built in Vienna after 1858 on the site of its demolished defensive belt. The street profile, carefully worked out with the rows of trees, park elements and pedestrian paths, was strongly focused on the architecture of the façades along it. Children's playgrounds were laid out on several sections of the dry moat which had been left empty along the boulevard. Squares, with public buildings such as churches, museums and an opera house, were designed for prominent points. The *Ringstrasse*, with its promenade, flower gardens, fountains and monuments, formed a chain of festive spaces, the green backbone of the Neustadt.

Stübben also included radial arterial roads and diagonal streets in his plan, in part based on the system of paths present in the glacis outside the old walls. It was also his intention to give every important street a unique character with a view of some striking object. Among these objects were three parks and a number of green squares, distributed more or less regularly across the Neustadt. In the south came Römerpark (2.3 hectares). In 1888 the Stadtgarten (6.1 hectares), established in 1882 at the initiative of the city's beautification association, was redesigned as a walking park by the garden architect Adolf Kowallek (1852-1902), who also drew up a refurnishing plan for the Volksgarten (14.9 hectares) in 1887. In it Fort IV, in the second defensive belt along the outer edge of the Neustadt, was transformed into a café and included in the park. Outside the Neustadt and the second defensive belt, on an arterial road by the suburb of Lindenthal, a municipal woodland of 105 hectares was planted in 1895, likewise designed by Kowallek.

In Stübben's plan for the Neustadt the green belt, the green radials, the parks and green squares still had a traditional form, differing strongly from one another. Nevertheless, in principle they together already formed a complete, coherent green structure, which brought the elementary green spatial forms within the reach of the city.

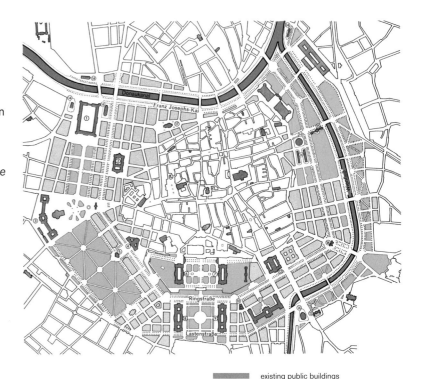

existing public buildings
planned construction
planned public buildings
public green space
water

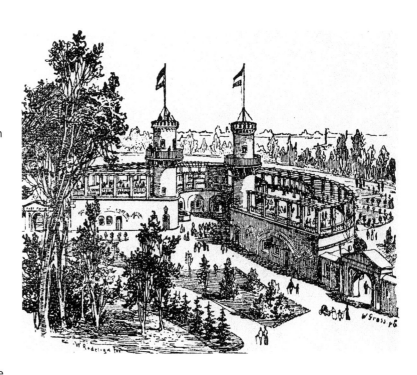

Scheme of the Wiener Ringstrassen zone, based on the plan approved in 1859 (from: K. Mollik, H. Reinig & R. Wurzer, *Planung und Verwirklichung der Wiener Ringstrassenzone; Kartenband.* Wiesbaden 1980)

The bulwark in the Volksgarten transformed into a café (from: H. Kier, *Die Kölner Neustadt; Planung, Entstehung, Nutzung.* Düsseldorf 1978)

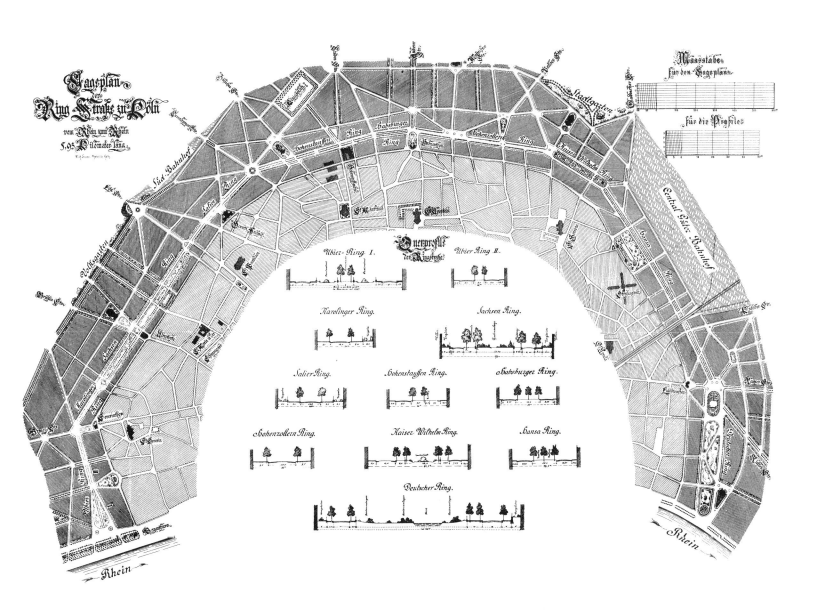

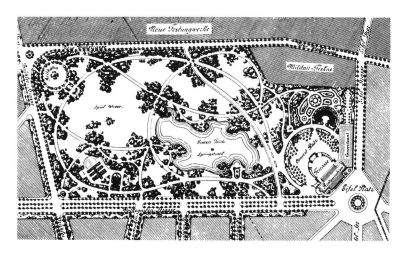

Joseph Stübben's plan for the Ringstrasse (from: Architekten- und Ingenieur-Verein für Niederrhein und Westfalen, *Köln und seine Bauten. Festschrift zur VIII. Wanderversammlung des Verbandes deutscher Architekten- und Ingenieur-Vereine in Köln vom 12. bis 16. August 1888.* Cologne 1984)

Adolf Kowallek's Volksgarten, with the restaurant on the Eifelplatz: a bulwark transformed into a café (from: H. Wiegand, *Entwicklung des Stadtgrüns in Deutschland zwischen 1890 und 1925 am Beispiel der Arbeiten Fritz Enckes.* Berlin 1975)

The second green belt and the spatial articulation of the city

Early on it was already foreseen that the second ring of fortifications was not sufficient for the defence of the city, so that even before it was realised construction began on a chain of new forts in a much more advanced position (1873-1881).

The third defensive ring (after 1873)

This ring, with a radius of more than five kilometres, formed the third ring of defences, a chain of forts along what was called the *Militärringstrasse*. This circular line of defensive works included about 185 independent fortifications. After the First World War it too was abandoned. In the meantime, as a result of lack of space in the city centre, the suburbs of Cologne, including Bayenthal, Lindenthal, Ehrenthal and Nippes, had grown very quickly. They developed primarily into industrial districts. A nearly solid ring of structures arose outside the Neustadt, so that the second defensive belt lost its function and changed into a neglected wasteland between the Neustadt and the suburbs.

In 1911 the state gave permission for the demolition of the second defensive belt. That left a vacant, ring-shaped zone eight kilometres long and an average of 70 meters wide, just outside the Neustadt. Carl

Rehorst (1866-1919) designed a first building plan for this area, with occasional parks, many green squares, open green inner courts and broad streets planted with rows of trees. In this plan two earlier forts were spared and reworked into parks by Fritz Encke. Fort I became the Hindenburgpark (1914), in which the great differences in the levels, the embankments, the trees and the walls are reminiscent of the fort. At Fort X (1919) too the existing geometric arrangement of the fort was taken as the point of departure and reworked into a small park with a spatial effect that still remains strong.

Because of his death, the outbreak of the First World War, and also the interference of burgomaster Konrad Adenauer, Rehorst's plan was never carried out. Adenauer took up the idea that "not the creation of showpiece streets and small, decorative squares, but the merging of public green space into large, usable green areas" should be one of the starting points for a new green belt in the urban development plan. Adenauer also found the political and financial means to realise this idea.

After the First World War Cologne was abandoned as a fortress city. A competition was now organised for the urban design of the area of the former second defensive belt. Fritz Schumacher (1869-1947), then the municipal architect in Hamburg, won the competition, was brought to Cologne by Adenauer, and given the assignment of drawing up a *Generalbebauungsplan* (master plan) for Cologne.

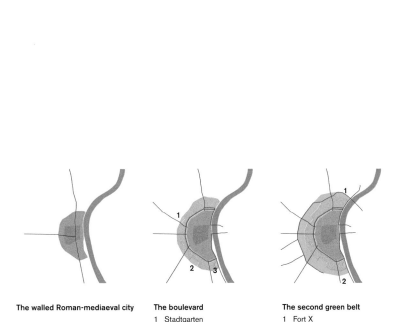

The walled Roman-mediaeval city

The boulevard
1 Stadtgarten
2 Volksgarten
3 Römerpark

The second green belt
1 Fort X
2 Fort I (Hindenburger Park)

Cologne's three green belts

The outermost green belt
1 Militärringstrasse
2 Chorweiler See
3 Decksteiner Weiher

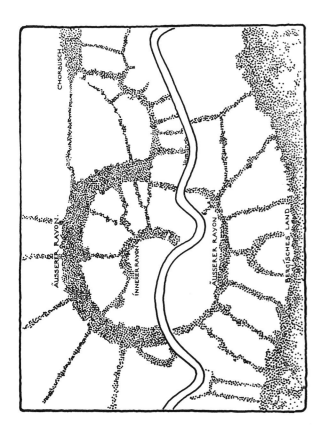

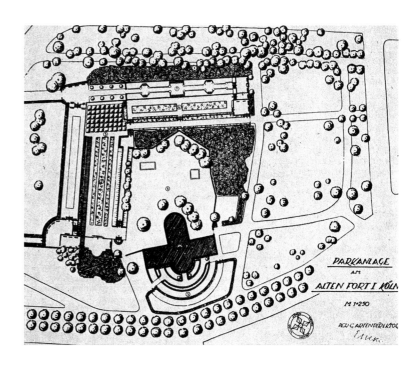

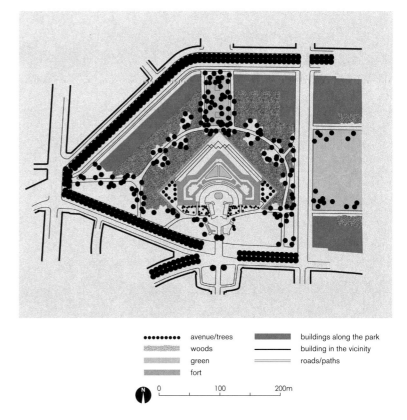

Fritz Schumacher's green scheme (from: F. Schumacher & W. Arntz, *Köln; Entwicklungsfragen einer Groszstadt*. Cologne 1923)

The Freiflächenplan or green structure proposed by Fritz Schumacher (from: F. Schumacher & W. Arntz, *Köln; Entwicklungsfragen einer Groszstadt*. Cologne 1923)

F. Encke, park design for the former Fort I, the Hindenburgpark (from: H. Wiegand, *Entwicklung des Stadtgrüns in Deutschland zwischen 1890 und 1925 am Beispiel der Arbeiten Fritz Enckes*. Berlin 1975)

Plan diagram of Encke's design for Fort X, ca. 1920

Schumacher's Freiflächenplan

With the *Freiflächenplan*, ready in 1923, one of the issues addressed by this *Generalbebauungsplan* was a green structure for the whole city. It was comprised of two concentric green rings, based on the former second and third defensive belts. Five green radials were planned between these green rings, of which three were realised (at the Aachener Tor, the Volksgarten and Fort X). The outermost green ring was in part justified as a screen against the lignite mining which was encroaching on the city from the west. Cemeteries, allotment gardens and sports complexes, but also private arable fields, pastures and woods complexes were included in the green system. While in 1914 there were still only 314 hectares of public green (4.8 m² per resident), the *Freiflächenplan* called for 3790 hectares (17.5 m² per resident), for an estimated total population of 2.16 million. Including the planned woods areas, this was even 31 m² per resident.

In the years 1923-1924 Schumacher prepared a detailed building plan for the demolished second defence belt, which served social as well as cultural and representative purposes. It was no longer a *Prachtstrasse* with decorative green squares, but was not yet an amalgamated functional green structure. The plan was comprised of an segmented axial succession of architectonic green spaces. The function and nature of the green was guided by the adjoining buildings, for instance decorative green by churches, playgrounds near community centres and sports fields, and allotment gardens.

There were provisions for public buildings on the axis of the most important green spaces. In this regard too there was a certain similarity between this plan and the Wiener Ring. The core of the green belt came to lie at the Aachener Tor, with a station, a business centre and a large body of water. At this point a promenade with trees and water, leading in the direction of the Stadtwald, joined the belt at right angles. Its purpose was to provide a representative entrance to the city. Schumacher's design was adapted, modified, and only partially realised. It cost the city considerable time and effort to acquire the land needed for the public buildings and green space. Nevertheless, with Schumacher's *Freiflächenplan* a decisive step had been taken in the development of a green structure as an integral component of an urban development plan; it was in fact the first green structure plan.

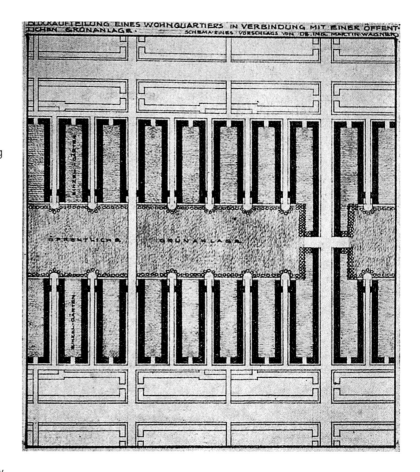

M. Wagner, green articulation; applied by F. Schumacher in his plan for the second fortification belt (from: H. Meynen, *Die Kölner Grünanlagen*, Düsseldorf 1979)

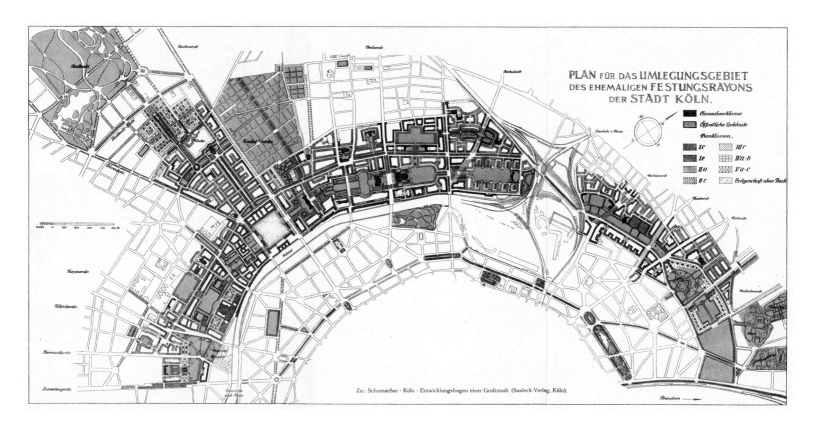

F. Schumacher: plan for the second fortification belt, with a spatial articulation of green (1923) (from: F. Schumacher & W. Arntz, *Köln; Entwicklungsfragen einer Groszstadt*. Cologne 1923)

The higher garden in the Hindenburgpark (Fort I) (from: H. Meynen, *Die Kölner Grünanlagen*, Düsseldorf 1979)

The entrance to Fort X

The third green belt and the functional zoning of the green

As early as 1910 there had been ideas floated to recreate the outermost defensive ring as a green belt of stature, for instance the proposal by A. Stooss, in his publication *Groszgrünflächennetz und Kleingrün-flächennetz* (Networks of large and small green spaces). In 1923 Fritz Schumacher had already included the former third defence ring in his *Freiflächenplan* as the outermost green belt. The total length of the belt was twenty-five kilometres, the average width one kilometre, and the area about 2300 hectares. Schumacher wanted to weave this new green ring in organically with the whole body of the city and with the landscape outside it. He designed green radials running into the city, in doing so making as much use as possible of existing parks, and also narrow green zones running to the hilly landscape in the west. According to him, the development of a green plan could "not stop arbitrarily at the boundaries of the city", because "the city is part of the landscape". Schumacher's outermost green belt was much less detailed than the second. Transversely, at right angles to the belt, he distinguished an articulation into three zones. Allotment gardens were accommodated on the city side, with sports fields, swimming pools and open-air schools in the middle zone. The outermost and broadest zone was comprised of woods, fields and meadows.

The development of the scheme

In 1925 Encke developed a plan for the further elaboration and arrangement of the outermost green belt (scale: 1:2500). This plan was later revised and only very partially implemented. The most important aim in his design was that it be usable for all classes in society, and for all age groups. Among the activities listed in his programme were walking, sports, play and nature education. Encke wanted a green belt with the continuous character as a park, while Schumacher wanted to retain its present character as fields and meadows, as much as possible. Encke designed what he called penetration zones between Schumacher's intensive and extensive zones, for instance by having park axes radiate far out into adjoining areas, as, for example at the Volkspark Raderthal. Over its length he divided the green belt into four main sections, with about the same basic facilities in each, so that no district of the city was too far from the most important facilities. Among the facilities in the intensive use zones were *Volksparks*, *Volksweiden*, beaches and swimming pools, open-air schools, allotment gardens and sports complexes. Encke worked out the former, largely demolished

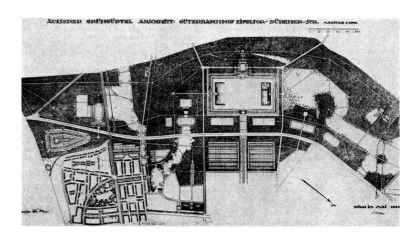

1	Klettenbergpark	5	Platz an der Bismarcksäule
2	Vorgebirgspark	6	De-Noel-Platz
3	Blücherpark	7	Botanischer Garten
4	Volkspark Raderthal	8	Zoologischer Garten

Fritz Encke's plan for the south-west sector of the outermost green belt, at the Klettenbergpark (lower left) (from: H. Wiegand, *Entwicklung des Stadtgrüns in Deutschland zwischen 1890 und 1925 am Beispiel der Arbeiten Fritz Enckes*. Berlin 1975)

The green radials in the suburbs

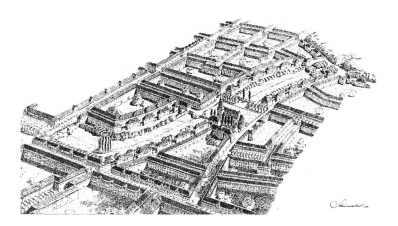

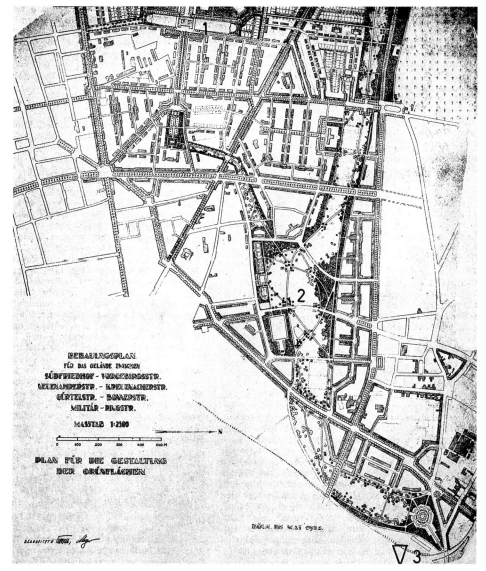

1 Volkspark Raderthal
2 Vorgebirgspark
3 Volksgarten

Sketch by Fritz Schumacher for a section of a green radial (from: F. Schumacher &
W. Arntz, *Köln; Entwicklungsfragen einer Groszstadt.* Köln 1923)

Plan by Fritz Encke for a green radial at the Vorgebirgspark (from: H. Wiegand,
*Entwicklung des Stadtgrüns in Deutschland zwischen 1890 und 1925 am Beispiel der
Arbeiten Fritz Enckes.* Berlin 1975)

forts, which lay about a kilometre from one another along the *Militärring*, as rest points. They were given a function, for instance as a sports complex, school or playground. The characteristic geometry of the forts was preserved in the design. The extensive areas were comprised of woodland and landscape zones with mixed woods, woodland parks, fields and cow pastures.

Theodor Nussbaum (1885-1956), who succeeded Encke in 1926, began with the elaboration of the outermost green belt at the Decksteiner Weiher (pond). Schumacher's transverse articulation was largely retained, but more than his predecessors Nussbaum emphasised physical exercise in the green, in the form of many sports fields and facilities for water sports. In his plans the contrast between the landscape and the geometric plan that Encke advocated 'melted' into a compromise. In the 1930s the work came to a halt because of a lack of funds.

The green radials

In his plans for the outermost green belt Fritz Encke devoted considerable attention to the green radials, the zones which connected the different green rings, the city and the landscape. In his view, a green belt could only function well if it were connected with the centre of the city by strip parks. Moreover, the green radials formed an articulation between the various suburbs, which along them could be connected with parks and green facilities at walking distance. The Blücherpark is an important element in the northern green radial. In the west the Stadtwald is an important point of contact for the central green radial. In the south the Vorgebirgspark and the Volkspark Raderthal play an important role. With the development of the outermost green belt and the green radials the *Groszgrünflächennetz* was completed. The green structure assumed the character of an urban development scheme that included all scales and green spatial forms. Furthermore this scheme could grow along with the development of the city.

The first, second and third green belts

1   Blücherpark
2   Volkspark Raderthal
3   Vorgebirgspark
4   Stadtwald
5   Decksteiner Weiher

urban pattern

park
other urban green
Grünflächenplan 1929
water

0   1   2km

A green matrix

The *Kleingrünflächennetz*, comprised of green squares, was also further elaborated by Fritz Encke. During the 19th century the urban square had lost a number of its earlier functions, such as being a market place and military drill field. The square, surrounded by urban walls, remained intact spatially, but received a different, often green décor. For instance, they might become a *Schmuckplatz*, a formally designed square or public garden in which their representative function and urban beautification were the central concerns, or an *Erholungsplatz*, for which the recreational programme was most important. By 1914 Encke had designed more than 30 squares in connection with construction activities in the suburbs. His first designs for squares were still in keeping with the 19th century tradition of the *Schmuckplatz*, but in most of his designs the social use function of the square occupied the foreground.

Schmuckplätze and Erholungsplätze

The Platz an der Bismarcksäule, a *Schmuckplatz* from 1903, in the suburb of Bayenthal and at the southern terminus on the Rhine of one of the ring streets, was one of the first designs Encke did. The square is comprised of a triangular lawn about 5000 m² in area, which is divided into two sections by an axis that ends in a 30-meter high column. The column stands on a raised platform enclosed by a yew hedge, with an *exedra* of oaks behind the column. The square serves as a 'salver', and as a green element has a purely decorative function.

The recreational squares, or *Erholungsplätze*, were designed as green islands in the midst of buildings. Within an architectonic framework, Encke here always distinguished the activities of various age groups: from children in the sandbox through youth horsing around to senior citizens, who had their own corner in the flower garden. One of the first recreational squares designed by Encke is the De-Noel-Platz, from 1904, of about 3500 m². The basic plan is comprised of a rectangle bounded by streets, with a central longitudinal axis. The square is divided into three parts, an arrangement which is found in most of Encke's squares. At the far north end lies a raised rectangular terrace for elderly people. In the centre lies a play field, consisting of a gravel bed surrounded by trees. At the southern end lies an elliptical, fenced-in play area for small children. The two far ends are screened off from the adjoining streets by thick planting, while the central section affords an open view through the sides to and from the surrounding buildings. The whole is framed by street trees. There is no playground equipment, just sandboxes and games tables. In this square the domestic function of the private garden, which was often lacking in the densely populated working-class suburbs, is moved to public space. Through the simplicity in form and the sobriety in the detailing, the *Erholungsplatz* fits in with the everyday life of the residents of the suburbs.

Encke wanted to have squares of this sort within a maximum of ten minutes walking distance – aptly termed *Kinderwagenentfernung*, i.e., the average distance mothers would push a pram – of all homes, so that all the residents of the suburbs could easily reach them. In that way a green matrix of play squares, woven into the matrix of the buildings, could replace the gardens with houses, and function as an intermediate step between the dwelling and the park. This system complemented the green structure of the belts and radials and anchored them in the pattern of the city.

Bird's-eye view of Platz an der Bismarcksäule (photo: Bilderbuch Köln 114065)

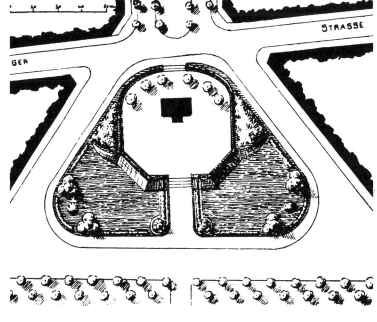

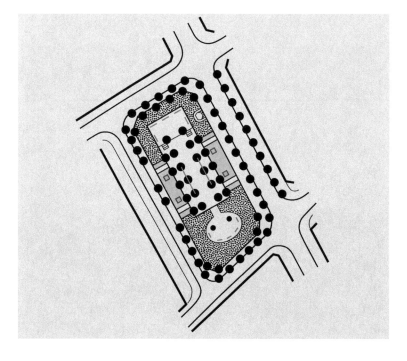

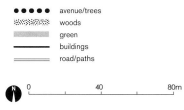

Schematic plan of the De-Noel-Platz from 1904, as an example of an *Erholungsplatz* by Fritz Encke

F. Encke, Platz an der Bismarcksäule, 1903 (from: H. Wiegand, *Entwicklung des Stadtgrüns in Deutschland zwischen 1890 und 1925 am Beispiel der Arbeiten Fritz Enckes.* Berlin 1975)

F. Encke, Manderscheider Platz (photo: Bilderbuch Köln 135383)

The park form dissolves

A development from the late 19th century 'mixed' style to an early 20th century functional form is clearly to be seen in Fritz Encke's designs. There is also a transition from a visual-spatial approach to the design problem, in which space provided opportunities for play and activities, to an approach in which analytic-programmatic and functional thinking began to define the spatial arrangement.

Changing economic relationships and social attitudes, and concern about public health and physical exercise, demanded open spaces in the city, where light and air invited residents to participate in an active and healthy life. The idyll of nature in the landscape city park was rejected as romantic; moreover, people who wanted to could go out into real nature for themselves. Moreover, in a practical sense, the flowing forms of the landscape park collided with the new programmatic division of sports fields, allotment gardens and playgrounds, which are rectangular and functional in shape – as were residential buildings. The attention became focused on mass recreation for the working class, the practice of sports as physical training, and on meeting the needs of various age groups in the population of the new neighbourhoods, as an extension of public health and public housing. Park design now became first and foremost a social democratic task; it was all about the uplift of the working class and determining the programme which could best accomplish that. In Cologne's urban green Encke tried to find an answer to these changes in the assignment. Through a number of intermediate steps Encke developed a form of his own, with an increasingly functional character.

A catalogue of nature

The Klettenbergpark was an early design that was done when ideas about a green structure for the city had not yet taken on a fixed form. The park was laid out in 1905 and 1906 in the southern suburb of Klettenberg. As with other Cologne parks, it is designed around an old gravel quarry, about ten meters deep. The plan has an area of about 3.5 hectares, is surrounded by residential façades, and is bounded on the short side by an important radial avenue to the centre. The form is comprised of a linkage of landscape and formally organised elements. The park is roughly triangular, has a central space, is surrounded by densely planted edges with clearly articulated entrances and views out to its surroundings. In the centre lies a lake (the former gravel quarry) with somewhat meandering banks, small islands on the edge, and a mooring place for boats. A more formally designed rose garden lies

in the acute angle at the head of the lake, with its longitudinal axis stretching on out across the water. There was also a café with a terrace and several children's playgrounds along the main route through the park. The park still has hardly any facilities for active recreation.

It was not however the suggestion of spatiality that was dominant in the landscape design, but the material presentation of nature. The park was actually a botanical garden of a sort; the lawns were originally indigenous plant communities. With this Encke, following the rising *Natur- und Heimatschutz* (nature and cultural heritage protection movement), wanted to imitate various indigenous natural landscapes, such as a heath landscape, a waterfall, a meadow with wild vegetation and a basalt quarry. These little landscapes were threaded together along the two main routes through the park, so that a stroll had an instructional purpose, as a lesson in natural history. The man-made landscape and nature coincided in a general 'cataloguing' of nature.

Deconstructing the pastoral landscape

The Vorgebirgspark was designed and built between 1909 and 1911. It lies in the south, between several suburbs, and would become part of a green radial to the outermost green belt. The park is comprised of only a few elements: a large central meadow, a pond in one corner and, along one street edge, a series of three different gardens, with a square surrounded by rows of trees. The whole is surrounded by a fringe of woods. The zoning is similar to that of Encke's *Erholungsplätze*, where the playing field in the middle was enlarged into a meadow with trees, and the shell of trees which connected the *Platz* with the planting along the street was expanded into a belt. The interior space was emphasised by a path along the edge of the woods. Several groves of trees were planted near the entrances to the main space and at the intersections of the paths, where they accentuated the functional play spaces. A faintly curving street runs across the park, its route separating the play meadow from the sunbathing lawn. The ground is raised slightly toward the west, intensifying the depth effect. The garden on the east side is a symbolic reproduction of the municipal garden. The design is not focused on the façades of the dwellings along the park, but is entirely turned inward. Only the system of paths connects the park with the urban fabric.

The Vorgebirgspark marked a turning point in the design of urban green. One could regard the park as Encke's first utilitarian statement. Although he continued to use native species of trees, the observation of nature slid into the background in the design while, conversely, sports and play became more important. Here the visitors are not led along

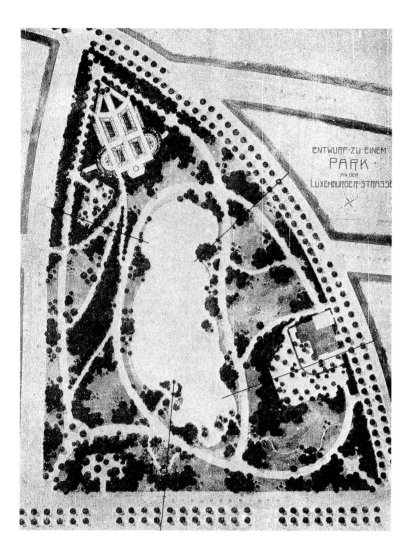

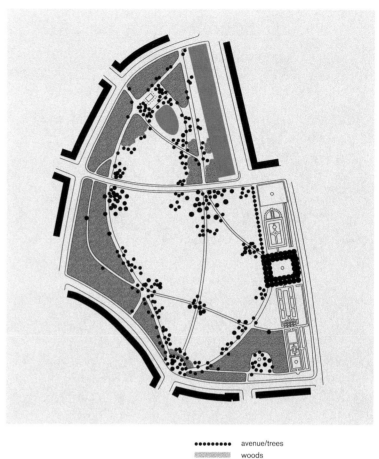

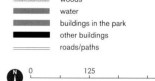 avenue/trees
 woods
water
buildings in the park
 other buildings
roads/paths

0　　　　125　　　　250m

The design for the Klettenbergpark (1905-1906) (from: H. Wiegand, *Entwicklung des Stadtgrüns in Deutschland zwischen 1890 und 1925 am Beispiel der Arbeiten Fritz Enckes*. Berlin 1975)

View into the garden along the edge of the Vorgebirgspark

Schematic plan of the Vorgebirgspark in 1910

The playing field the Vorgebirgspark

the paths, but are expected to actively use the space. The pattern of picturesque walking paths in the landscape park is here reduced to a system of functional connections. The contrast between the garden, the meadow and the wilderness disappears and dissolves into a hybrid green form in which the topography of the landscape plays a subordinate role. This resulted in a deconstruction of the pastoral landscape, a simplification to a recipe for a generic green space, not specific to the topography, which can be employed any and everywhere.

Standardising the programmatic form

The Blücherpark, constructed between 1910 and 1913, was the first *Volkspark* for the densely-populated industrial suburbs of Ehrenfeld and Nippes. The park forms a rectangle about 700 meters long and 200 meters wide, oriented on a south-east/north-west line, with a ten metre deep former clay pit on the east side which was transformed and included in the rim of the park. In the original plan this park also lay in the middle of an urban space, enclosed by residential buildings, and the main axis ran through into the street pattern. Like the Vorgebirgspark this park was also later included in a much more extensive green radial, where the main axis of the park supports the direction of the green radial. The Volkspalast, the core of the design, was never realised. With the construction of highways along two sides of the park, it has now come to lie in the axil of the urban traffic network.

Encke's original design was sober and rigidly formal in conception. It was constructed along an axis of symmetry, on which lay three connected compartments, successively increasing in size, creating a perspectivistic effect. These compartments were, respectively, a terrace with a water niche and flower garden, a large pond, and a large, somewhat elevated *Volkswiese*, closed off at the end of the axis by a viewing platform, accentuated by pillar-shaped Italian poplars. From this platform one could look back to the Volkspalast with its wings, which had been planned for the separation between the water niche and the pond. The *Volkswiese* and the pond were bordered by a double row of linden trees. The eastern part of the park, by the former clay pit, likewise had an axial structure, with tennis courts, a children's playground and a plant nursery. The whole park was surrounded by a woods, with pedestrian paths, play areas and resting places, and the transitional spaces to the street.

Like the socially inspired landscape architect Leberecht Migge and the architect Fritz Schumacher, in this design Encke regarded the formal geometric form as the most suitable for handling a large number of visitors and offering varied recreational opportunities in

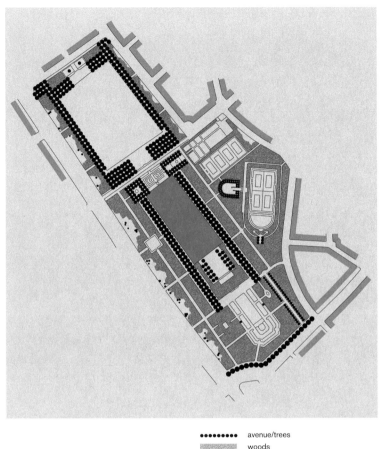

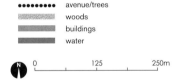

●●●●●●●●   avenue/trees
                   woods
                   buildings
                   water

N   0   125   250m

an edifying environment. This was the first time he applied these architectonic principles not to just a section, but to the whole of a park. The spatial concept appears similar to that of the Volkspark Hamburg, and is derived from the formal French garden. This too is a monumental *Volkspark*, with a perspectively arranged, 'regal' spatial series as the basis for a zoned, ever more particularised recreational programme. A comprehensive recreational programme was fitted into this compositional system, including canoeing, skating, a play meadow, children's playgrounds, a wading pool, tennis, ornamental gardens and gardens for relaxation, strolling paths and shaded promenades. Encke described this transformation as follows: "There places for the display of courtly brilliance, here places of relaxation for the masses of the big city." Obviously the concept of the *Volkspark*, as it was developed by Schumacher in Hamburg, could be repeated here, and the programmatic form could be standardised.

Schematic plan of the Blücherpark in 1910

The main axis of the Blücherpark

Avenue along the side of the *Volkswiese* in the Blücherpark

The park as a green link

The Volkspark Raderthal was built in 1923 and 1924. It lies on the southern edge of the city, on the inside of the outermost green belt. On two other sides it is bounded by allotment gardens, and on the final side by detached housing. In the southern direction the main axis connects with a sports centre with an athletics track and sports fields in the outermost green belt. The rationale for the design was the utilisation of four intact embankment rings from former powder magazines. These were retained and used as vertices in a rectangle with intersecting axes. The axes run on outside the park, contributing to the radiation of the park scheme into both the city and the outermost green belt. The main space itself was turned inward and surrounded by a wide promenade with trees.

The heart of the plan was a 300 × 200 meter *Volkswiese* at the intersection of the axes. On the north-south axis, which connects the city with the park, at the transition from the city, was a *Volkspalast*, obliquely bounded by two flower gardens with seating, included as a target and entrance from the city. Within the four thickly overgrown embankment rings there were sandboxes built for children, and a reading garden and dance floor for school classes and clubs. The *Volksweide* was surrounded by a fringe of woods with a separate children's playground, an open-air school, a flower garden with seating for families and a nature theatre in it. Encke made multi-faceted utility central to this design, with a great variety of recreational possibilities and activities for all age groups. He wanted to unite this versatility and practicality with compositional quality. The latter was understood as "Einfachheit und Einheitlichkeit" (simplicity and cohesion), resulting in a spatial composition with a rational-functional form, derived from the programme and the situation, a simple and well-rounded whole. The Volkspark Raderthal was however no longer a park in the 19th century sense of the word, with a 'garden', 'meadow' and 'wilderness' as representatives of the real agrarian landscape. Nor was it a complete *Volkspark*, in which all these elements were transformed and taken up in a formal-programmatic form. Only a few elements of this remained; the park was the envelope for a particular package of activities tailored to a specific place in the urban pattern. The park was first and foremost a link in a larger, programmatically conceived green structure. The design marks the moment at which the city park, as an autonomous, integral spatial type of landscape melts into a standardised system of green areas which were defined by the urban structure and the recreational programme. With this, the development of green space as a category in urban planning and urban development was in principle complete.

Volkspark Raderthal: former gun turret and ornamental garden

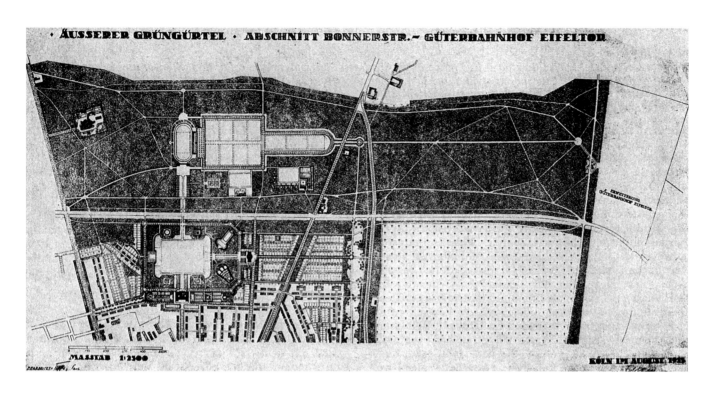

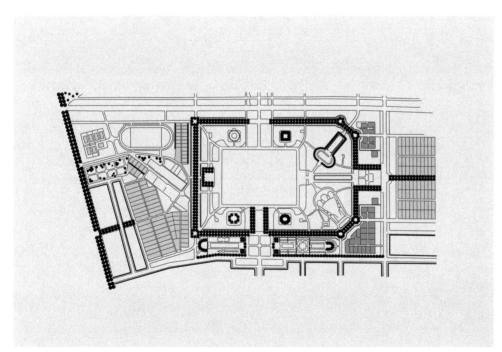

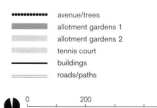

avenue/trees
allotment gardens 1
allotment gardens 2
tennis court
buildings
roads/paths

0   200   500m

The Volkspark Raderthal as a link to the outermost green belt (from: H. Wiegand, *Entwicklung des Stadtgrüns in Deutschland zwischen 1890 und 1925 am Beispiel der Arbeiten Fritz Enckes*. Berlin 1975)

Schematic plan of the Volkspark Radertal in 1924

Urban green space as a generic landscape

Cologne's *Prachtstrasse* suffered greatly during the Second World War. The 19th century architecture of its façades was damaged, and in the years that followed the height of the buildings along it increased. In the 1960s much of the layout yielded to traffic, and it lost its character as a promenade with continuous ranks of trees. The only testimony to the earlier sculptural quality of the second green belt is to be found in a few relics near the Aachener Tor. Fort X, with its decorative park, also continues to stand in the midst of an otherwise completely changed green belt. After the Second World War only the basic articulation of the green belt remained recognisable. Under the direction of Theodor Nussbaum, the successor to Fritz Encke, new plans for organising the city were drawn up. Built-up areas alongside the old city were abandoned. In their place came green hills created from the mountains of rubble from the ravaged city. As with the first belt, here too traffic has contributed to there being little of the concept originally designed by Schumacher still recognisable.

The break with the agricultural landscape

Through the transformation of the defensive rings, the green structure of Cologne, schematic on paper, was linked with the *genius loci* of the landscape, at least in a derivative sense. With its various rings as ever more distant echoes of the original shape of the city, the structure reflects the bend in the Rhine and the geomorphological boundaries of the Rhine Valley, while the radials confirm the location of the centre of the city on the spot where the Roman *urbs* stood.

In the reconstruction following the Second World War attention was primarily focused on the extension of the green radials, particularly to the north and the south. Work was still done on the outermost (third) belt, particularly in the north-west between the city and the Rhine Valley. The metro network, which follows the radial structure, guarantees easy access to the outermost green belt. The green structure of circular disks and radials, reflecting the concentric growth of the city, is firmly anchored in the urban pattern, the geometry of which leaves its stamp on the form and the organisation of the green space. Despite the green character, a new problem arose in the relation with the topography of the surrounding landscape. As a spatial category, the green belt came to stand between the pattern of the city and that of the agricultural landscape, and in a deeper sense it screened the city off from the landscape rather than connecting the city with it.

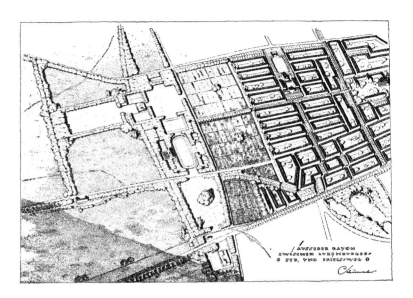

The idea of a concentric green structure was later expanded into a green belt of landscape on a regional scale. This regional structure is anchored in the topography and geomorphology of the landscape in which the city lies, much more than the three belts inside it were. It follows the edges of the Rhine valley, where large open pit lignite mines, transformed into recreational and nature areas, support a landscape zone around the city more than five kilometres wide. But there is no more of a guiding landscape architectonic concept for the development of this regional green belt as a spatially coherent urban landscape that could create a meaningful connection with the agricultural landscape and integrate it with the urban landscape than there was for its predecessors.

Dismantling the park scheme

In Cologne the question of the relation between the city and the landscape surfaced in the most emphatic way in the transition from the second to the third green belt. The enormous increase in scale, the rapid expansion of the city's population and the changing housing culture demanded a new design approach.

In his park designs Fritz Encke initially experimented with transitional forms between the composition of the landscape park and a composition based on a utilitarian programme, in which the landscape architectonic form increasingly became subordinate to the arrangement of the various recreational functions. The Klettenbergpark was designed as a sort of botanical garden, a popularisation of the concept and image of nature. In the Vorgebirgspark the pastoral landscape form of the

Fritz Schumacher's plan for the outermost green belt, Decksteiner Weiher sector, ca. 1920 (from: H. Meynen, *Die Kölner Grünanlagen*, Düsseldorf 1979)

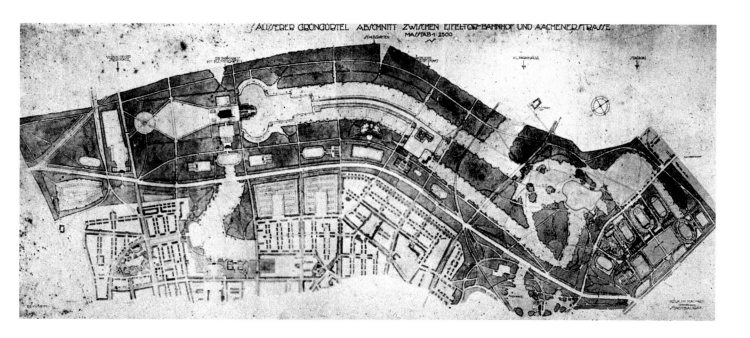

Plan by Theodor Nussbaum for the outermost green belt, Decksteiner Weiher sector, 1927 (from: H. Meynen, *Die Kölner Grünanlagen*, Düsseldorf 1979)

The outermost green belt, seen from the south, with the Decksteiner Weiher in the background to the left (aerial photo: Bilderbuch Köln)

19th century park was changed into a generic green space that could be employed anywhere in the city. In his Blücherpark design Encke reached back to the formal scheme of the formal garden as a basis for the development of a functional form. With this formal-functional form a step was taken toward a formal scheme for green space, which was not fundamentally different from other urban spatial forms of the time, such as streets and squares. Like the Hamburger Stadtpark, the design for the Blücherpark illustrated the repeatability and standardisation that were characteristic of this form of green space.

The Volkspark Raderthal saw the creation of a new, rational-functional form that was a neutral envelope for a particularised recreational sub-programme. The green was connected more with the structure of the urban pattern than with the landscape. In the design the *genius loci*, the character of the landscape of the place, only indirectly entered into the design in the reuse of several elements of the earlier fort. Encke's design for the Volkspark Raderthal therefore teetered on the edge of the city park as a spatial type. In a deeper sense, however, the city park here merged into the urban development amalgam of the green structure.

Fritz Encke's designs in Cologne reveal how the pastoral scheme of the 19th century city park was dismantled step by step and green space took on a generic, standardised form. The 'wilderness' was accommodated in the botanical garden. The 'meadow' became a rectangular, multifunctional play field, and the 'garden' took on the guise of a recreational facility. The elements constituting the park scheme would henceforth be used apart from one another, and worked out in a functional sense as needed. This arrangement was quantifiable and repeatable, so that urban green space could be divided up across a whole city in a quasi-rational pattern of rings and radials. It had therefore in principle become a standardised urban planning category. The break with the 19th century park scheme was complete.

Between form and norm

The urban planning structure of the green belts does not by itself lead to a spatially differentiated landscape with recognisable places. Landscape architecture is needed to create a compositional context that is effective at this scale, as it did in the Potsdam-Berlin Gartenreich or the Boston Emerald Necklace. The limit of the elasticity of a simple landscape architectonic form was reached in the third green belt. Nussbaum's design for the Decksteiner Weiher in 1927 demonstrates this in a striking way. The elongated meadow in the middle of the green belt, with its water feature reminiscent of a canal, bends along with the geographic curvature of the green belt. At more than two kilometres, the

water has reached the maximum length that can be surveyed between the walls of the woods, which curve along with it. The segment as a whole here reaches the limits of the landscape architectonic concept within which Encke projected the green belt as a series of parks.

The urban development plan of Schumacher's green structure was a challenge for landscape architecture. The design of Encke's parks still stood in the tradition of garden and landscape design. The relation between his park designs and the expansion of the green structure, with its ever more deterministic programme, was therefore problematic. In Cologne Encke was caught between standardisation and the distributive logistics of urban development planning and the historically defined landscape architectonic form of the city park. In this sense his work documents his struggle with the amorphousness of urban green space and its anonymity as a landscape.

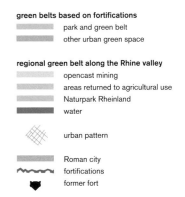

The regional fourth green belt

green belts based on fortifications
park and green belt
other urban green space

regional green belt along the Rhine valley
opencast mining
areas returned to agricultural use
Naturpark Rheinland
water

urban pattern

Roman city
fortifications
former fort

N   0   2   5km

METROPOLITAN LANDSCAPE ARCHITECTURE

The landscape architectonic conquest of the city
The basic spatial instruments
Typological differentiation
Toward a new experimental cycle

Keys to the design of metropolitan landscape
Landscape theatre
The flow landscape
The plantation
The montage landscape

Landscape architecture for the metropolis

A green periphery as strategy
Individual positions in the suburban field
Decomposition as landscape architectonic experiment
Reconstruction of the landscape as a catalyst
The fusion of infrastructure, landscape and architecture
Refolding the urban grid
Staging the high-rise landscape

The analyses of these studies lead to conclusions regarding the foundations of a metropolitan landscape architecture. On the other hand, experimental design practice has a dynamic which evades the analytic framework, and the outcome of which proves impossible to predict precisely.

In order to do justice to both these aspects, we have therefore followed two tracks in this, the closing chapter. Alongside the conclusions based on an analysis of the design history, drawing on a number of intuitively selected designs we have also sought to interpret the metropolitan process today, in the commentaries on each.

These two tracks complement each other, and are so closely connected, that in this concluding chapter they have literally been set alongside one another.

The landscape architectonic conquest of the city

Three phases can be distinguished in the development of urban landscape architecture, which together make up a complete experimental typological series or cycle. Successively, these phases are the formation of a set of basic spatial instruments and spatial prototypes, a differentiation of spatial forms and design instruments, and finally a standardisation and cataloguing of spatial design. With the completion of this cycle the city was in principle brought wholly within the landscape architectonic domain.

The basic spatial instruments

After the Renaissance the physically closed city was opened up visually and spatially, and the landscape pacified and domesticated. With its cultivation nature became a source of beauty and pleasure – and with that, the landscape became an important category in architecture. The city and landscape were united into one territory in the culture of country living. In several steps the landscape architectonic design instruments were reforged to make it possible to stage urban space in terms of landscape.

In the Horti Fanesiani the villa was transformed into a public garden at a prominent spot in the city, in which the layers of Rome's history were stage-managed and brought together in an architectonic route. The villa terrace was transformed into an urban balcony, from which the architectonic diorama was spread out to view, included in the great landscape space of the Seven Hills and the notional network of visual relations among strategically located and architectonically elaborated vantage points which defined the urban landscape of Rome.

In the Jardin des Tuileries the system of the formal garden received an urban form, in which the spatial axis that had been directed toward the horizon was taken up into the city and connected it with the landscape. The parterre garden in the foreground became an urban stage, and in the background the horizon in the landscape now came to lie within the boundaries of the city. The lines of the visual network that encompassed the city and countryside were materialised as physical axes, a formal framework that has been incorporated into the urban pattern of Paris, linking it with the lines of force in the geomorphology.

In Regent's Park the transformation of elements of the existing agricultural landscape into the model of the landscape garden became the driving force behind the design of an environment for aristocratic living in the city. With the typological differentiation and zoning of residential buildings and a differentiation of the route system this concept was developed further in Birkenhead, to become an urban

A green periphery as strategy

As a result of the continuous growth of the city, its edges became a sort of amorphous transitional zone, without a clear spatial structure. In London this transitional zone was given its own identity through the planned regulation of what came to be called the London Green Belt. In 1831 London was the largest city in the world. The development of the railway from 1836 on only increased its rate of growth. In 1914 London covered a circle with a radius of eight miles, centred on Charing Cross; by 1940 that was already twelve miles.

At the end of the 19th century the concept of a green belt around the city, modelled on the parkways and greenbelts in other European and American cities, became a topic of serious discussion. Since the 15th century writers and thinkers such as Sir Thomas More (1478-1535) and Robert Owen (1771-1858) had developed the idea that the ideal city must be functionally linked with the landscape, while being physically distinguished from it. Ebenezer Howard (1850-1928) conceived the Garden Cities, not just as cities *with* gardens, but also as cities *in* gardens. His Country Belt had various functions, including acting as a limit on urban growth and providing space for the practice of agriculture and gardening for the urban population, as well as recreation and urban beautification.

In 1901 William Bull published proposals for a green girdle around London, in which existing open spaces would be strung together in a park belt a half mile wide. In 1911 George Pepler connected the idea of a park belt with a parkway, a ring road system comprised of different sorts of roads, rail lines, paths and greenery. In 1919 the London Society put forward its Development Plan for Greater London, which also included a green belt. The Greater London Regional Planning Committee subsequently studied the possibility of regulating the growth of London by concentrating new development in what were called the New Towns, and in 1935 came up with a proposal for a Metropolitan Green Belt around London. The architect and urban planner Sir Raymond Unwin (1863-1940) concluded that there was an acute shortage of recreational areas in London and advised the construction of a chain of open spaces and playing fields around the city. Unlike Howard's Country Belt, Unwin's green belt was not a semi-rural, agrarian zone but a continuous ring of parks, which was to compensate for the shortage of open space and sports grounds in the centre of London. Despite major financial challenges, the realisation of the London County Council Green Belt Scheme began in 1935. The goal was to provide for a sufficiently large reserve of open space and recreational areas. In 1944 about 40 square miles, a large part of the projected Green Belt Scheme, with arable land, woods, hills, water and country estates, was was acquired.

strolling park as the basis for a suburban form of living in the city. The urban landscape of London took on a new form with the recomposition of the urban pattern of the West End in terms of a landscape, giving the urban route system a scenography, as previously found in landscape gardens.

In the Gartenreich at Potsdam-Berlin the 17th century formal framework was integrated into Lenné 19th century plans. This created an extensive landscape composition, with the system of lakes and rivers south-west of Berlin as the new vehicle. This composition became the stage for an idealised urban landscape, built up from architectonic set pieces and landscape backdrops. City and countryside were united into one great landscape theatre in which the contrasts between them were neutralised. In order to achieve the spatial coordination of this urban landscape the landscape architectonic design instruments from the preceding three models were combined, as it were, and integrated. A network of sightlines from outstanding topographic points accessible to the public, a system of axes and avenues incorporated into the city, and pattern of landscaped routes and places based on the morphology of the underlying landscape was elaborated spatially, its elements attuned to one another, and composed so as to form a unified entity.

In the confrontation with urban space the classic design instruments of garden art, detached from their original context, received a new urban content and significance. These transformations shaped the basic instruments and the first prototypes of urban landscape architecture, with a spatial range that went beyond the landscape boundaries of the city, and thereby already bore within itself the germ of the metropolitan landscape.

Typological differentiation

In the 19th century the landscape architectonic design instruments were confronted with a new wave of urbanisation. Migration to the cities led to their uncontrolled growth. The edges of the city became dynamic, a front line from which the settlement and urban exploitation of the landscape took place. The urban pattern changed into an open matrix which was rolled out over the landscape topography, street after street and block after block. The relation between the city and the landscape became a question for civil engineering. The construction of canals, railway lines and roads created an extensive, ramified infrastructural network that cut off and enclosed parts of the agricultural landscape. The agricultural landscape within these enclaves disintegrated and in turn became a part of the urban domain. The nature of the urban pattern was increasingly determined by these interventions. The physical conquest of the actual landscape was coupled with a romantic idealisation of its pastoral image. Nature was reconstructed in the urban

In that same year the Greater London Plan appeared, in which the architect Sir Patrick Abercrombie (1879-1957) once again advanced Howard's multifunctional Country Belt concept. According to Abercrombie a green belt must be put into place when the city reached its maximum or optimal size. The multifunctional country belt should not be comprised of sterile public green space, but of a productive landscapes in which the appropriate forms of ground usage were maintained. Moreover, recreational facilities for the residents of the city should be included in it. The Green Belt in Abercrombie's 1944 Greater London Plan covered a zone ten miles wide. In order to achieve the purposes of the Green Belt there was no longer an effort made to acquire the land, but merely to control its use. After 1950 the Green Belt was further developed as an instrument in the regional planning of London. It covered a considerable number of the communities outside the London agglomerate, growing into a zone of twelve to twenty miles, reckoned from the centre. In 1964 it was even as much at thirty miles wide in places.

The Green Belt has been under constant pressure from the need for land for residential construction and other urban functions. Any expansions of the zone in fact also imply an expansion of the urban region. With the aid of protective regulations and prohibitions, the agricultural landscape is used to reign in urban growth. This development is not guided by a landscape architectonic concept, which means that no new coherence can be created in the landscape. However, a transitional zone with a relatively large number of protective landscapes has been created, a green periphery, which contributes to the green character of Greater London, without it being clear what the end result will be, and how the urban landscape will take shape.

Individual positions in the suburban field

As a result of an untrammelled growth of infrastructure and suburban living, the landscape has changed into an urban field which extends across vast areas. In Los Angeles this led to an endless repetition of essentially identical urban development elements to form a metropolitan landscape that incorporated the physical-geographical lines of force from the original landscape – and even the ocean and desert – into city-centre spaces. This in turn led to a new metropolitan form of living, that chose an individual position in the anonymous suburban landscape.

In 1781 the new Spanish governor of California, Felipe de Neve, designated the place where the valley of the Los Angeles River opened up to the Pacific Ocean and Father Juan Crespi and his Mexican colonists had encountered the original Native Americans for the first time as the site for founding the Pueblo de Nuestra Senora Reina de Los Angeles de Porciuncula. This sandy coastal plain, with some hills

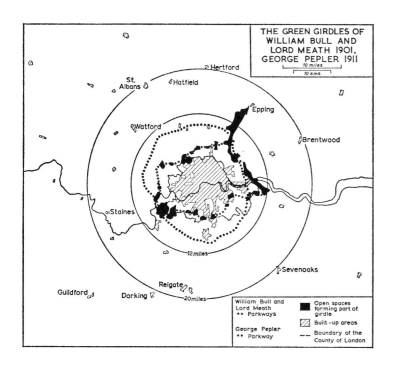

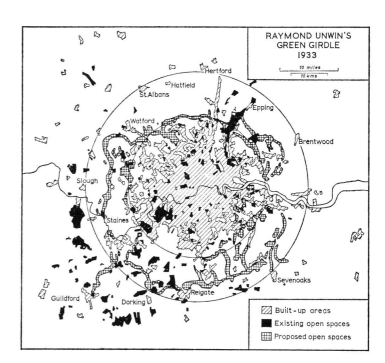

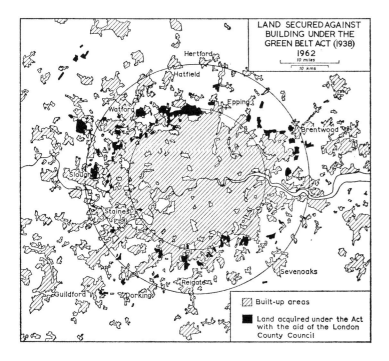

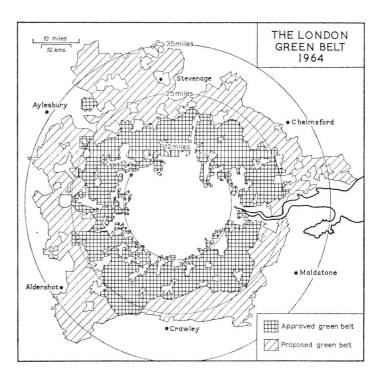

Atopy in various schemes for the London Green Belt (from: D. Thomas, *London's Green Belt*. London 1970)

park as 'wilderness', ostensibly beyond the reach of human intervention, but nevertheless incorporated within the matrix of the city. Landscape architectonic design for a park involved playing a consummate game with nature and the city.

In Central Park this led to a new spatial type, a city park that, unlike its European predecessors, was deliberately severed from the city around it, an autonomous composition involving nature in which the city's origins in the landscape were preserved as though in a shrine, as a sort of ennobled wilderness as a mirror for the technological development of the city. At the same time the park functioned as an advance post in the urban conquest of the landscape. This urban dynamic was carried by an urban grid that was projected onto the landscape; within it the park formed a landscape hallmark.

In the urban grid of Barcelona, Cerdà was seeking a system that could connect the old city and the towns around it with one another and include them in the scale of the coastal plain and natural delta landscape. The central element in this was the definition of the spatial relationship between the grid and the topography of the landscape. The urban grid was carefully oriented, bounded and calculated in size within the existing landscape space. Long diagonals anchored it to the key elements of the landscape. It could also be adapted to the topography of the landscape locally, on the scale of the building block. As a result, the grid indeed functioned as a mediator between the city and the landscape, but the space within it did not yet take on any landscape architectonic form.

In the case of the Vondelpark, the matrix and topography of the peat bog reclamation landscape were the starting points for both the urban layout and the park. Its content and design harked back to the scenic natural idyll that was customary all across Europe, but which here was artificially reconstructed and fitted into the peat polder landscape. A reference to the city's origins in the landscape was indirectly captured in the multiple layers of the park's landscape. In this sense the park was a snapshot of the ongoing urban transformation of the basic pattern of the landscape. The agricultural landscape was transformed, but remained recognisable in the urban pattern. This created an urban landscape the coherence of which was based on the grid and topography of the original agricultural landscape. The landscape architectonic composition of the park sealed this unique relation.

In the Boston Park System the urban landscape was unfolded in different parts, each with its own content, based on different local natural forms, reclamation forms and topographical patterns. The landscape architectonic treatments varied from civil engineering to highly architectonic, according to the role of the landscape element in

here and there, was divided up into Spanish-Mexican ranches for cattle raising, with several tracts of wild nature as common grazing land. The plan of the settlement was based on a grid of limited scope, oriented to the shape of the valley of the Los Angeles River.

About the same time the future American president Thomas Jefferson – then still a delegate to Congress from Virginia – expanded the authority of the nascent federal government significantly with the Land Ordinance Act of 1785, extending its control over the Mississippi River valley and the Great Lakes. As an answer to the confusing system of surveying that was then in use, Jefferson introduced a new orthogonal grid system, based on the square. The grid divided the existing land into sections of a square mile, each of 640 acres, and at the same time projected a system of measurements over still undeveloped land. Jefferson thereby laid the foundations for a continent-wide settlement grid, which also functioned as a large-scale framework for agricultural and urban development. This Act had an abiding effect on urban planning and land development. With the 'Jefferson grid' as its driving force land development could expand freely, and the tract house, the free-standing American home with a yard, a descendent of the 'homestead' which spread across the wilderness, could be repeated without obstruction in the suburban map.

In 1848 the front lines of settlement in the New World reached the American West Coast and Los Angeles, which then numbered 2500 residents. The settlement grid was rolled out over the old ranches as a network of roads, railroad lines and aqueducts. Within this grid a thousandfold repetition of the homestead grew into a suburb, which grew from its first million residents in 1915 to a 'superurb' of 17 million in 2003, with its 'downtown' where the old Pueblo had been.

This urban field, covering about 10,000 square kilometres, also enveloped the hills, which lay in and around the plain like a gigantic grandstand. Only at the ocean and the surrounding mountains did the super-grid collide with the Ur-nature, with Sunset Boulevard as the scenography for this confrontation. Here and there in the hills the settlement pattern of the free-standing house took on the character of an architectonic case study, an experimental investigation into a new relationship between architecture, the landscape and the boundless suburban field.

The Case Study Houses were part of a building programme which, already during the Second World War, was engaged in a search for new architectonic possibilities for the application of prefabricated steel constructions. One of the most striking examples is the Case Study House #22 from 1959, which stands against the slope of a hill that is

Location of the Case Study House #22 and Sunset Boulevard in the geographic texture of Los Angeles. Insert: Case Study House #22, P. Koenig.
(© J. Paul Getty Trust. Used with permission. Julius Shulman Photography Archive, Research Library at the Getty Research Institute 2004.R.10)

Pueblo

the city. The parts were connected by their origins in the landscape, and were linked with one another by parkways. Together they made up a park system comprised of a landscape-topographic series in which all the landscapes present in the urban domain were represented, and which could serve as a backbone for metropolitan growth.

The definition of the city park as an autonomous, public spatial type was an important step in the development of a specific formal typology within urban landscape architecture. The design instruments were transformed and sharpened to find the right balance between the drama of the scenic image and the generic, public character of the park. The local topographic and urban conditions led to a further differentiation of the set of design instruments within a typological series that was related to the metropolitan scope of the urban network.

Toward a new experimental cycle

The organisation of the modern city as a product of urban planning created a new urban continuity in the landscape through the creation of urban regions with satellite cities and self-contained units such as the garden city, with its autonomous form and surrounding buffer of 'air, light and space'. The intermediate agricultural landscape, initially still without a functional purpose, now had to serve as a green foil for the built-up urban pattern. The set of landscape architectonic design instruments were confronted with diverse aspects of urban growth, and particularly with a functional approach to urban living. After spatial aspects and the infrastructural network, the emphasis now came to lie on the urban programme as the basis for the structure of the city. City and landscape were united in a common functionality, in which the typology of the city park was stretched to its limits.

The Stadtpark in Hamburg was a watershed in this development. The content of the city park was freed from the original pastoral prototype; the experience of nature and cultural artefacts yielded to a zoned programme of recreational use, based on sociological research. The spatial scheme of the formal garden could serve as an empty shell for the accommodation of this programme for large groups of people. The scenography of the architectonic route changed into a series of functional connections between the different parts. Out of this arose the Volkspark as a new park type, which then developed into a pragmatic, functional form, derived directly from the content and organisation of the programme. With that the foundation was in place for a similarly functionally organised urban landscape, in which the urban park could be conceived as a component in a generic, planned system of public green space.

The 'Neue Frankfurt' was articulated as separate settlements, in which prefabricated, serially produced homes could be exploited to

part of the Hollywood Hills, the northern boundary of the coastal plain. The house is transparent and designed in such a way that 'Los Angeles is their great big front yard'. The space of the living room is directly confronted with the panoramic space of the suburban field. 'Modern Living' becomes dwelling in a world space.

Although the Case Study House #22 in fact lies within the city, it keeps its distance treats the city as an architectonic diorama. From its elevated position above the suburban plain, the city is reduced to a geographic texture; from this viewing platform the city appears in a new guise, as a landscape with its own geography.

Decomposition as landscape architectonic experiment

In the metropolis landscape architectonic design takes on a new significance as a laboratory for the design of urban space. The Parc de La Villette is an experimental landscape architectonic model of the dynamics and layeredness of metropolitan spatial forms.

In 1982 the Établissement du Parc de la Villette organised an international competition for an urban park on the site of a former abattoir on the Bassin de La Villette in Paris. The area is enclosed on the north and south sides by two arterial roads and is bounded on the east by the Boulevard Périphérique. A canal runs through the site, dividing it into two sections, but also connecting it with the city. Because according to those organising the competition the formula for the existing city park was outmoded, the new park should not be purely a recreational green facility, but a park of Discovery, Relaxation, Science and Culture. The programme actually embraced all the cultural activities associated with life in a city centre, except dwellings.

The winning park design by the architect Bernard Tschumi is organised in three layers 'thrown onto each other', comprised of points, lines and planes. He used a way of resolving the spatial form and the programme and reassembling them, to thus generate new activities and spaces by their unexpected combinations and encounters. Activities that require plenty of space, such as markets, sports and playing fields and mass entertainment, have their places on the planes. The bases of large structures, such as the Great Hall and museum, are also included in this layer. The second layer contains the linear elements such as canals, screens, axes and routes, including a promenade cinematique which winds through the park. The smaller programmatic components such as pavilions, kiosks, restaurants and service buildings are accommodated in the third layer, comprised of red folies, experimental and flexible architectonic compositions based on a $10 \times 10 \times 10$ meter cube, coupled to an activity or event. They mark the points of an urban grid of 120×120 meters that runs through into the park, and at some places also into the city. This layeredness is also carried over into the Jardin des

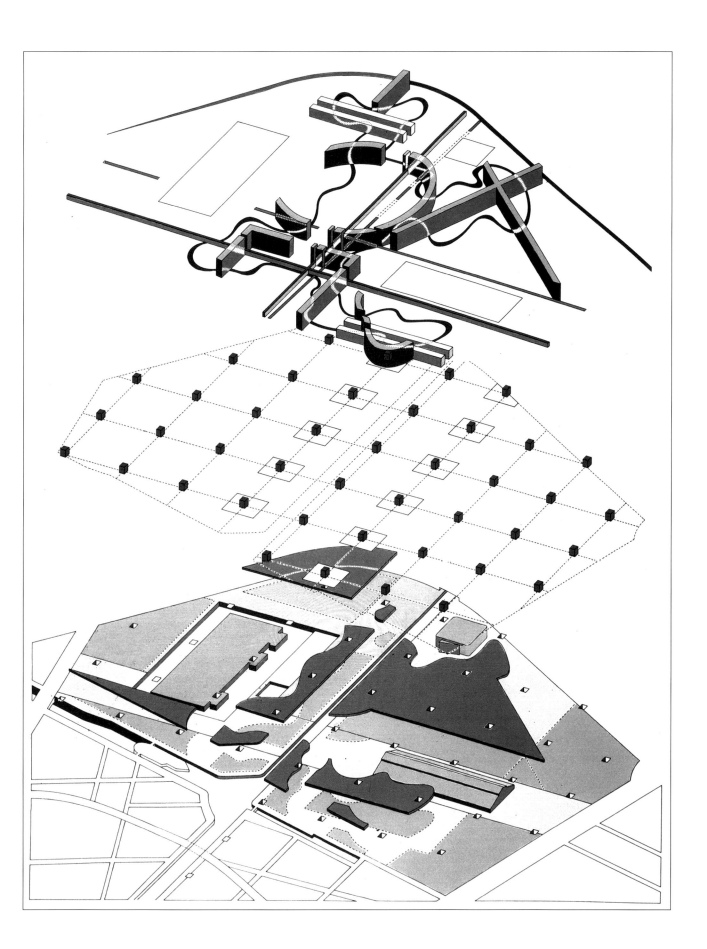

Composition of the dynamic in Parc de la Villette by Bernard Tschumi (Bernard
Tschumi Architects, International Competition for Parc La Villette, Paris 1983, 1st prize)

the fullest, and which could be fitted into the landscape topography as individual spatial entities. Characteristic elements in the city-countryside relation were given special landscape architectonic treatments, such as for instance the spatial transitions from the building sites at higher elevations down to the valley of the Nidda river. The urban landscape took the form of various architectonic ensembles, which were folded around the space of the landscape like stage scenery. Elements of the agricultural landscape had a unique place in this. Within the settlements they were worked out at the level of the individual home and the garden; around them, up to the level of the cultivated, productive landscape in which the city lay. Through the dynamic zoning of the productive and recreational programme, a new spatiality was developed within the existing topography. The instruments of landscape architectonic design were utilised toward a functional and spatial articulation of the urban landscape, where built-up urban areas, urban farming, vegetable gardens and recreational elements were grouped to form an intensified agricultural landscape.

In Cologne's Grüngürtel the 19th century city park dissolved into a zoned recreational programme and into tension between the planned character of the city's green structure and the landscape topography. The content and zoning of the green structure was derived directly from the centralistic articulation of the urban pattern and the urban programme. This led to an artificial form, the result of urban planning, in which the green structure was not based on the characteristics of the existing landscape, but on the zoning of the functional programme of the city, moving outward from the centre. Cologne's Green Belts were not a chain of landscape fragments received into the city, but a distributive system of green areas organised according to scale and accessibility. In the spatial and functional sense, this hierarchic ordering of urban green space implied the equivalence of the city and landscape.

In the integration of landscape architecture into urban topology the development of its unique set of instruments became increasingly marginalised. The design instruments could no longer be employed for the free, experimental expression and representation of the characteristics of the landscape, but were limited to the construction and cosmetic aspects of a green environment for recreational activities in the open air. With this standard catalogue of green spatial forms the landscape architectonic exploration of the city reached a dead end. With this the experimental cycle that began with the urban transformation of the basis set of instruments, and continued with the typological differentiation of the urban landscape also came to an end.

At the same time however this end meant the beginning of a new experimental cycle, which is focused on the exploration of today's metropolitan landscape. The specific formal instrumentarium of urban

Bambous, lying below grade level, created by the landscape architect Alexandre Chemetoff, which like a *giardino segreto* affords an escape from the urban elements of the park. Chemetoff reveals the bowels of the city in the form of the utility pipes that run across through the garden. Between them he projected the image of a jungle, represented by a *bosco* of 28 species of bamboo, supplemented with birdsongs and the sound of running and falling water.

In his design for the park Tschumi made free use of design means, as if he had plucked them from a catalogue. Elements of the formal and landscape repertoire are combined and linked with elements of the city. Park and city have become interchangeable; the park lies in the city, but at the same time the city is manifestly present in the park. In this design the decomposition of the metropolitan landscape takes on an experimental landscape architectonic form.

Reconstruction of the landscape as a catalyst

The reconstruction and redesign of the industrial landscapes of the Ruhr region, altered beyond all recognition by mining and heavy manufacturing, led to a new topography with its peculiar role in shaping a metropolis. In 1989 the Internationale Bauausstellung (IBA) selected the area along what had once been a small river, the Emscher, which now ran through the middle of the Ruhr region as a drainage canal, as the subject for a research and design project, with a time line of ten years. The regeneration of the landscape formed an important accent in the urban restructuring.

The Ruhr is part of a European coal belt which runs from Katowice in Poland, through Germany, The Netherlands and Belgium to the English Midlands. In the course of the 19th century the coal mining expanded

The industrial landscape as transformative topography

IBA Emscherpark
other urban green space
water
industry 1970
industry
spoil tips
mining

urban pattern

0   2   5km

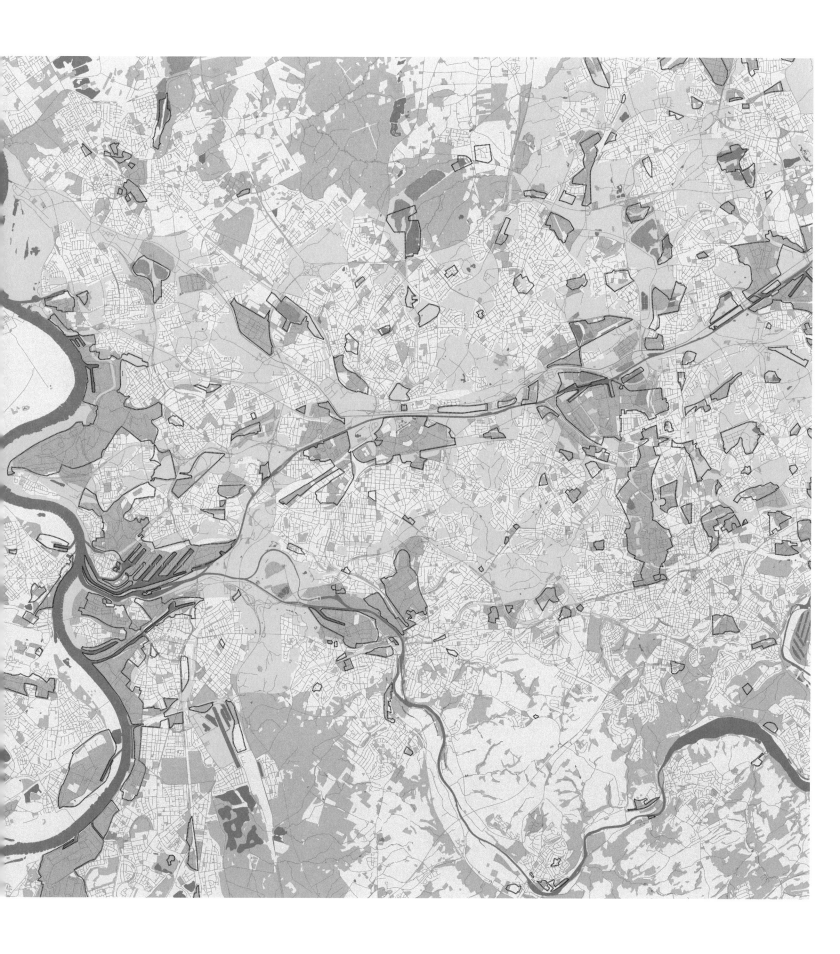

landscape architecture and the intermediate forms derived from it are available to it as material that can be recalibrated and applied experimentally, as the point of departure for the development of a metropolitan landscape architecture.

Keys to the design of metropolitan landscape

In the preceding cycle the point of application for landscape architectonic design shifted from urban space, to the urban programme, by way of the urban network. The landscape architectonic treatment of these generic urban structures created new intermediate forms, with their own content, form and scope. In the course of this process three basic intermediate forms or landscape modalities were created, which could anchor the spatial and systemic characteristics of the landscape in the metropolis: the landscape theatre, the flowing landscape and the plantation. They comprise the keys for landscape architectonic design for shaping the metropolitan landscape.

Landscape theatre

In the classic city the instruments of landscape architecture were employed to create a visual viewing apparatus that connected the city spatially with the landscape. The design was based on a theatrical staging of the landscape space, a landscape theatre, in which the panorama and the horizon were central. In a metaphorical sense, the landscape theatre is conceivable at every level within the panoramic range of scale. The 'theatre' refers to the principle of spatial staging, by which the scene, and also the relation between seeing and being seen, can change. Despite all sorts of shifts in accent, it continues to play a role in the spatial staging of nature, landscape and the horizon within the urban domain. The landscape theatre marks a spot in the urban landscape where place, time and the process by which the original landscape came into being can receive an architectonic expression. It includes the essential characteristics of the landscape and the crucial details that refer to the genius loci.

In today's metropolitan landscape, with its limitlessness, fragmentation and spatial dynamics, landscape theatre can take on a new significance. The inversion of the horizon to within the metropolitan field, in which it turns over to become an internal horizon or void, plays an important role in this. Visual elements such as 'metropolitan gardens' or "reference points and the marks which we establish in a contemporary landscape over which we have no control", as Michel Desvigne and Christine Dalnoky termed them, can be assembled in the encapsulated landscape

from the south to the north, to cover the whole region between the Ruhr and Lippe Rivers. The development of the mining followed the geology of the substrata. At first the mines lay close to the cities; later they came to be distributed across the whole countryside. Because iron ore was also mined in the region, blast furnaces were built near the coal mines, fed by coke distilled from the coal. These blast furnaces in turn attracted engineering works and factories. The first blast furnaces appeared along the old road system, such as Thyssen near Mühlheim and Krupp near Essen. Later, in connection with the supply of iron ore, they moved closer to the Rhine.

The process of industrialisation and the fragmentation of the landscape which accompanied it were accelerated by the construction of new roads, railways, canals and temporary harbours to serve the construction work, all aimed toward an expansion of the transport possibilities for industry and providing access to the hinterland. The series of cities along the Hellweg, the medieval trading route, with Duisburg, Essen and Dortmund, became overgrown with unplanned expansions and scores of new residential areas around the towns, close to the blast furnaces, factories and rail lines. Siedlungen for accommodating the industrial labourers arose everywhere, initially in the form of cottages, later in the 19th century more in terraced houses and tenements, and in the 20th century in the form of garden towns. Among them lay several Volksparken, more middle-class residential areas, and the villas of the factory directors and the industrial barons, such as the Villa Hügel, of the Krupp family, and Villa Thyssen.

After the Second World War region, heavily damaged during the war, underwent reconstruction. However, after 1957, as a result of a glut of coal on the world market, many mines were closed. This was followed by a surplus of steel in 1980, hastening the closure of more mines and leading to the demolition of surplus steel mills. Rail lines which had served them were abandoned, and previously coherent living and working districts disintegrated. The large coal and steel companies initially held onto their land to prevent it from falling into the hands of new firms. As a result considerable stretches of area became industrial wasteland. With this the disintegration of the topography of the landscape reached a dramatic climax. The agglomeration of conjoined cities, towns and industrial complexes was strewn with polluted, desolate manufacturing sites, mountains of mine tailings, decommissioned blast furnaces and abandoned mine shafts, water towers, generating plants and marshalling yards. It was in this situation in 1989 that the IBA-initiative launched a new planning concept alongside a a functional restructuring, directed toward the regeneration of the landscape. With this approach they sought a new landscape structure by interweaving east-west oriented industrial development lines

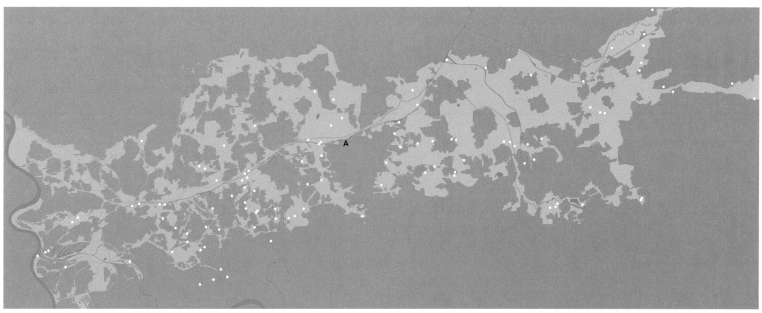

Industriekultur / landmarks

Emscher Landschaftspark

water

A   Hoheward spoil heap

View from Halde Hoheward (photo: Joachim Schumacher)

The IBA Emscherpark as a network of landscape projects

N   0   10   20km

space. In these fragments the information which is necessary to be able to understand the map that lies under the metropolis can be given a landscape architectonic form.

The flow landscape

In the 19th century city the point of application for landscape architectonic design lay in the collective pattern of the urban expansion and the creation of a technical, infrastructural network. The landscape architectonic treatment of an urban infrastructure can be designated as a 'flow landscape'. It is, in that sense, the ultimate enlargement and transformation of the route as the basis for a scenic composition, as this was invented in the landscape garden of the second half of the 18th century and came to flower in the urban park landscape and the parkway. With some shifts in emphasis, as a landscape scenography for movement within the topology and programmatic zoning of the city the flow landscape continued to play a role in the 20th century urban landscape.

In the metropolitan landscape today the infrastructure is becoming increasingly independent, occupying ever more space and becoming visually dominant, and as a result altering its significance for the residents' daily lives. The motorway is no longer merely a structure providing a service, but also a space with a landscape architectonic form, where one spends increasing time. Along with the adjoining spaces, it expresses countless individual time-space chains. Moreover, because of the speed with which one can move from one place to another, the flow landscape is connected with one's individual experience of a greater landscape space and the morphology of the natural landscape. The flow landscape is an intermediate form which connects, which ties the metropolitan landscape together visually at various scales into a topographic-landscape 'film' within a larger geographic order. In this sense it is the continuation of a development which began with Olmsted's American parkways.

with north-south oriented zones of suburbanisation. The most important support bearing this new urban landscape was the Emscher River.

The point of departure for the Emscher Landschaftspark was the regeneration of the river, which had become an open sewer, accompanied with the diking and draining of the area along it, much of which had subsided as a consequence of the mining. Further aims of the Landschaftspark were the integration of the open space, green zones and the redevelopment of the abandoned industrial sites. In this 'industrial nature' as vegetation and 'industrial forest' as a new form of the municipal woodland were to provide for a specific landscape texture. This landscape concept was elaborated in various sub-concepts and a large number of projects. Among these were the development of large-scale, supra-regional functions, such as shopping malls, sports arenas and cultural events integrated into the landscape, and new green dwelling forms in the former *Siedlungen*. A Route der Industriekultur 400 kilometres long was laid out past 25 'anchor points' such as the Landschaftspark Duisburg Nord, the Weltkulturerbe Zollverein, thirteen *Siedlungen* and fourteen mine heaps that offer wide panoramas. Within these anchor points the industrial structures were redesigned for recreational and cultural purposes and once again made accessible.

In this way mountains of mine tailings, conical hills, gigantic plateaus, shafts and towers, gasholders and blast furnaces, in combination with scores of artworks, formed a new landscape topography. As one of the most important determinants of the *genius loci* of the area, industrial history was brought to the fore and used as a catalyst in shaping a metropolitan landscape.

The fusion of infrastructure, landscape and architecture

In the parkway the line of flow in the infrastructure fused with the architectonic staging of landscape space. Through their extent and through the intensity of the experience of space that is connected with that, the flow charts of today's infrastructure inherently have a landscape character.

In 1999 the International Foundation for the Canadian Centre for Architecture (IFCCA) organised a competition for the redesign of a relatively isolated but intensively used part of Midtown Manhattan, an area of about 27 hectares between Pennsylvania Station and the Hudson River. The topography there is dominated by the proximity of the Hudson, the open cut where the railway line emerges from a tunnel under the river, followed by the platforms of Pennsylvania Station, and several other large-scale infrastructural elements which intersect with it. The aim of the competition was to develop a new architectonic

Urban infrastructure as architectonic landscape in Infrastructural Flow, by Jesse Reiser and Nanako Umemoto

The plantation

In the modern, 20th century city the point of application lay in the residential programme, the functional organisation and the green structure of the city. The design instruments of landscape architecture were utilised to zone this functional programme and give shape to an objective landscape form. The intermediate landscapes which were created as a result formed an urban 'man-made landscape', as it were, which ordered the urban activities into a rational settlement pattern. In analogy with 17th century land reclamation projects, one could term such an intensified man-made landscape an (urban) plantation. This urban densification and transformation of the settlement scheme of the 'reclaimed' landscape permitted the crush of the urban programme to be staged in terms of landscape. In this sense it is the opposite of the landscape theatre, where it is the emptiness that is central.

The zoning of built-up urban areas – in combination with components of the landscape such as avenues and canals, and textures such as woods and water – plays an important role in today's metropolitan landscape. Special functions, such as the natural landscape, infrastructure and residual landscapes, can be included and granted their own place in the basic plan of the plantation, so that the urban landscape which arises from it has a complete constellation of landscape elements. In the plantation the topographic logic of densities and variations is more important than the architectonic composition of spaces and volumes. The landscape architecture of the plantation therefore focuses on the recognition, classification and selection of usable topographic elements and on their adaptation and repetition to create a new landscape texture within the metropolitan field.

The montage landscape

The urban landscapes discussed in this book were all absorbed into an urban and landscape context of increasing metropolitan dimensions, so that they attained a new metropolitan position. This metropolitan space is not delimited or bounded and is characterised by a flexible and dynamic relationships among its components, densification, layeredness and the interpenetration of the city and landscape. The spatial form, the form of the network, and the programmatic form take on a new dynamism from this. Very different spatial conditions can coexist next to and mixed through one another, and receive their own landscape architectonic treatments. In this sense the metropolis can be understood as a landscape that is in the process of formation and that must be made into a new whole.

One could conceive the landscape architectonic form of this landscape as the result of a confrontation between landscape theatre, the flow landscape and the plantation as strategic interventions in the

vision with the existing, unique conditions of the place as the point of departure. To reinforce this starting point, the designers were free to develop their own programme for the area.

In their design *Infrastructural Flow* Jesse Reiser and Nanako Umemoto proposed a new relationship among architecture, landscape and infrastructure. In their eyes, with its extreme variations in scale, size and form the infrastructure creates a landscape with many new fields of action for architecture. More so here than elsewhere in Manhattan, the local scale of the urban morphology could be connected with the landscape scale of the Hudson and the island as a whole, through an architectonic reshaping of the form of the lines of flow of the railway and regional highway connections that penetrate the area.

The *Space Frame* that they designed transforms the lines of flow of the infrastructure into an undulating roof landscape that enters the space of the city in one continuous movement from the Hudson River to near 8th Avenue. Like an elevated, open park, the roof landscape of the Space Frame affords views over the river and along the shores of the island. Internally, in conjunction with Pennsylvania Station and the facilities in the vicinity, it provides for a gigantic 'event space'. This space too is designed as a landscape, so that it refers to the Meadow in Central Park. In their 'super meadow' Reiser and Umemoto are thus able to bring together a merger of the lines of flow of the river with those of the urban infrastructure, and the likeness of the open playing field of the park, all into one architectonic image.

Refolding the urban grid

However, the winning design in the 1999 IFCCA competition was the *Manhattan Fold* project by Peter Eisenman. In this project it is not so much the landscape architectonic potential of the infrastructure that Eisenman wants us to reconsider, as the relation between the landscape and the urban form. For him the geometric urban grid as the vehicle for that form is central. Step by step this grid is transformed into a landscape. Just as in the case of the design *Infrastructural Flow*, this leads to an elongated, wavy volume, which sometimes rises to the level of the roofs of the adjacent buildings. On the west it runs through to, and even out into the river with an open stadium; on the station end it terminates in a high-rise tower in which the wavy lines are continued vertically.

The difference from *Infrastructural Flow* is primarily in the way in which the volume is cut through with grid lines in a north-south direction, so that it is incorporated into the urban structure of Manhattan. In a way that is comparable with what happens in Central Park, here the undulating volume is intersected by the lines of the urban grid and the programme they accommodate. At these points the lines of the grid are

A fold in the city; Peter Eisenman, Manhattan Fold (Eisenman Architects, IFCCA Prize Competition for the Design of Cities, New York, 1999. Aerial plan view. Courtesy Eisenman Architects)

topography. In principle, the whole of the metropolitan field can be covered with the aid of these landscape architectonic interventions. They encompass the whole set of instruments and vital design strategies of urban landscape architecture, which can in this process be reassessed and deployed anew.

As a concept, montage offers the possibility of treating a heterogeneous field architectonically. It no longer strives for a harmonious linking of differing elements, but seeks out the hidden creative significance of the confrontation. It makes the frictions among the various forms visible, tangible and understandable as expressions of the metropolitan formation, so that they can be reconciled with one another on an architectonic level.

Landscape architecture for the metropolis

As the urban system became more extensive, it began to include ever more landscape architectonic points of application. With that, in many respects the metropolitan system appears to have become a landscape question. Recent studies have described the formation of metropolitan areas as a 'natural' process that is characterised by uncertainties, unforeseen reactions and capriciousness, rather than by stability and rationality. Models from landscape and systems theory which describe the complex systems and processes in nature would therefore seem to be more applicable to metropolis-formation than would rational planning and spatial design. Natural and urban processes can be integrated into one all-inclusive system, as it were, which could generate new, open networks and configurations. In this vision, the spatial form of the metropolitan landscape arises as a logical consequence of the integration of sustainable landscape techniques, systems and processes.

However, there is one crucial aspect missing from this approach. In this vision the landscape is, to be sure, a base for urban development, but it has no autonomous, formal status. From this point of view, form analysis, typological investigation and architectonic studies would not be necessary, and even undesirable. A systematic approach and a sustainable programme however do not turn into a spatial form on their own. The spatial design of the landscape demands a landscape architectonic thought process.

This is certainly also true for the relation between the metropolitan system and the original landscape. The generic character of systems theory, like that of the standardised urban development programme, ignores the *genius loci* and the architectonic culture within which the

warped; they provide for the continuity of the city underneath and at the same time link it with the landscape world above. There, from the roof landscape, the continuing flow of the open space from the river, over and through the stadium-cum-theatre, is palpable and visible.

In this design the composition scheme of Central Park is turned inside out, as it were. The limiting boundaries disappear; the landscape and nature are no longer a hidden treasure, but on the contrary, are placed on a stage. This undulating 'natural landscape' is the result of countless experiments and revisions; through displacing, rotating, overlapping and cutting through its elements, it has been designed step by step and assembled as an architectonic construction. Eisenman called this digital simulation of the landscape and nature a 'paradox of the present time'. In *Manhattan Fold* the urban grid and the form of the city that is derived from it is refolded to produce a landscape, and as a consequence a new layer of meaning is added to the relation between the city and the landscape.

Staging the high-rise landscape

High-rise structures are often seen as an undesirable side effect of urbanisation, with a negative impact on the landscape. A design study by Arnold Homan and Auke van der Weide, part of the research by design work at the Department of Landscape Architecture of the Delft University of Technology, demonstrates that the relation between high-rise building and landscape can also be developed in a positive sense by approaching the high-rise building itself as part of the landscape. The goal was to design a skyscraper as a villa landscape, with a vertically organised series of specific spaces and views. This experimental 'high-rise villa' was to be situated on Central Park, at Columbus Circle, where Broadway, as the representative of the original landscape topography, 59th Street, as the representative of the urban grid, and the subway, as the expression of the metropolitan system, all intersect and indicate the layeredness of the metropolitan landscape.

In order to realise the maximum interaction between the tower and the layered urban landscape, set pieces derived from the composition elements that manifest the relation between architecture and landscape in the classic villa are inserted in the various segments of the tower. As intermediary spaces, these transformed architectonic set pieces connect the interior with the high-rise landscape of Manhattan and confer a landscape character on the collective programme components in the tower.

The vertical division of the tower is composed of a wide urban programme, consisting of dwelling units, offices, stores and recreational facilities. In order to optimally utilise the visual qualities the open space is concentrated in the base and in the top of the tower, connected

The intersection of Broadway, 59th Street, 8th Avenue and Central Park, as location
for the High-rise Villa

specific spatial qualities of the landscape manifest themselves and develop. The role of metropolitan landscape architecture consists precisely in laying bare these hidden qualities and transforming them into a new landscape architectonic form.

Metropolitan landscape architecture is not a matter of aesthetics or a particular notion about form, nor is a matter of repeating old models, but rather of opening the technical form for consideration, as this arises out of the process by which the metropolis is formed. This generic technical form, with its own programmatic, functional and procedural logic, must be adapted to the conditions of the place and developed into a landscape architectonic form in which the *genius loci* receives a specific expression. In order to achieve that it must be placed within a landscape architectonic frame of reference, as that has been shaped by the normative models from the development of the discipline.

It becomes obvious from the series of examples in this book that the topographic memory of the city is not a static, given fact, but is characterised by constant reinterpretation and redevelopment. Like a palimpsest, new layers of meaning are continually being written over one another. Each stage in the development of the urban structure has its own points of departure in the topography of the landscape and requires a specific landscape architectonic treatment. The topographic memory of the city can only be maintained by continually renewing and expanding it. The design repertoire of urban landscape architecture plays a role in this unavoidable and necessary process as a collection of models in which countless landscape architectonic design experiences, discussions and experiments are stored.

The landscape contains a generative structure that can serve as a transformative framework for the metropolis. With the instruments of urban landscape architecture this can be utilised to transform the loss of the distinction between the city and the existing landscape into the shaping of a new, metropolitan landscape. That is its essence – and its most essential task.

with each other by lifts on the corners. In this way a balance is realised in the high-rise villa – just as in the classic villa – between *otium* and *negotium*; the practical, economic function of the place is combined with the enjoyment of the landscape. The scale of the architectonic design means is an interesting aspect of this scenography. The elements of the classic villa are enlarged horizontally and vertically. The size of the visual viewing apparatus is coordinated with the diverging sightlines from the position of the observer. The deeper the observer is in the interior, the more room is required for a spatial link between the interior and the world outside. The first segment contains a *grotto*, a *labyrinth*, a *piano nobile*, a *screen*, a *footbridge* and a *ramp* ascending from the ground floor level. The *piano nobile* is designed as an open area in the interior, just above the crowns of the trees, which can therefore be surveyed as a green plain. The second segment has no specific spatial orientation. A colonnade around the offices provides views in all directions. The third segment has two *loggias* fifteen storeys high on either side of the building. The vertical *loggia* frames the high-rise landscape as if in an artificial *ravine*. The fourth segment has a *vide* 50 meters high. The fifth contains a colossal *stair*, which works visually as a *cascade* descending to the park. It also contains a *reflecting pond* and a roof garden with a panoramic view over New York.

The set pieces enable one to experience the high-rise landscape of Manhattan in different ways. The play of distancing oneself and looking back is here organised as a 'vertical diorama' or kaleidoscope with the landscape. In the ascending route the panorama unfolds in a number of steps. High in the tower the leap in scale from the interior to the panorama can be made in one stroke. In the high-rise villa the metropolitan landscape attains the dynamic character of a geological pageant. One moves through a virtual landscape of infinite dimensions, which lays bare the visual characteristics of the metropolitan high-rise landscape and, moreover, through its position connects with the *genius loci* of the city.

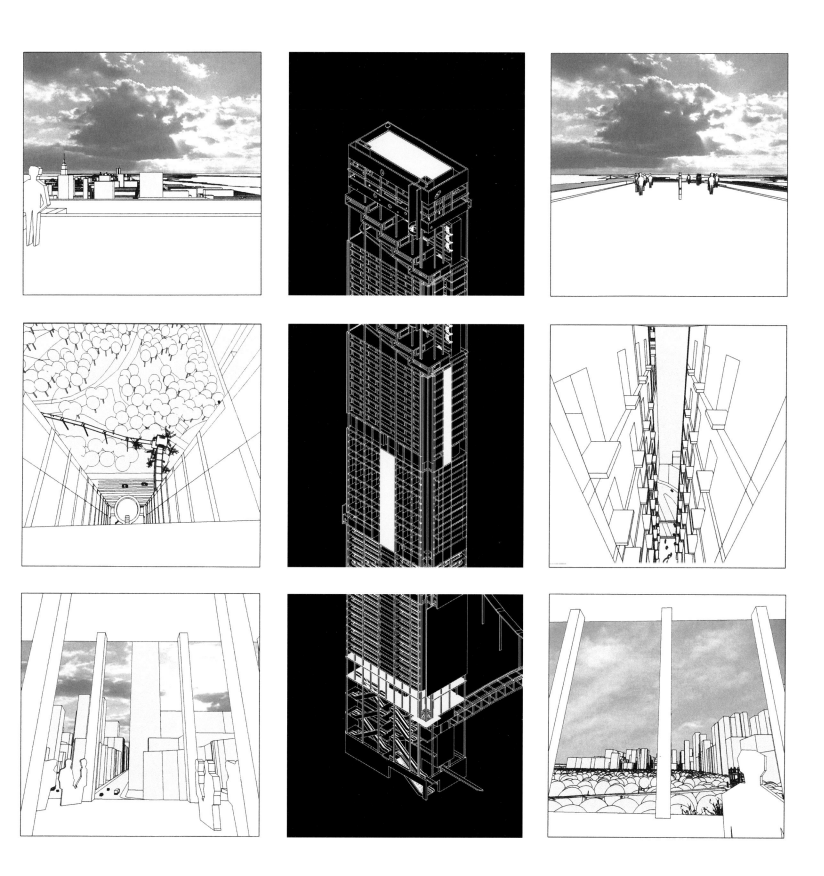

The High-rise Villa with (from bottom to top) the *piano nobile* with tree crowns as lawn, the loggia with the architectonic ravine, and the roof terrace with the horizon.

Indexes (numbers in **bold** refer to the illustrations)

Concepts

abstraction 19, 252, 210
accelerated perspective 82, 114
active recreation 312, 316, 402
agora 17
agricultural 378
agricultural garden 158
agricultural land 120, 158, 166, 172, 240, 378
agricultural landscape 15, 78, 106, 118, 128, 146, 148, 162, 174, 178, 183, 258, 260, 284, 286, 292, 302, 304, 312, 327, 376, 378, 406, 408, 413, 414, 420
allotment gardens 358, **362**, 364, **371**, 374, 376, **378**, 394, 396, 402, 406
amphitheatre 316
anamorphosis 82
aquae or spa 364
aqueduct 38, **38**, **40**, 42, 44, **62**, 78, **102**, **198**, 200
arabesque 372
arboretum 312, **313**
arboriculture 160
arcade 48, 82, **136**, 158, 160, **161**, 162, 216, 346, 350
Arcadia 148, 316
Arcadian landscape 15, 36, 136, 178, 278
arch 44, **46**, 54, 56, **87**, 88, 90, 92, 348
archaeological park 54
archaeological zones **62**
archetypal landscape 352
architectonic
    axe **55**, 158
    composition 56, 426
    diorama 413,418
    ensemble 178, 420
    entrance 28
    framework 400
    gardens 344, 348
    landscape **425**
    route 30, 50, 56, 60, 413
    screen 86
    series 158, 160
    set piece 164, 178, 414, 428
    settlement form 372, 374
    system 25, 148
    typology 108
architectonically active components 254
architecture and nature 15
architecture of the city 36
artificial green meanders 384
artificial lake 78, **158**, 160, **161**, 162, **162**
artificial landscape 76, 382
artificial meander 278
artificial wall 212
artificially created land 190
assortment of trees and shrubs 128
asymmetry 32, 70, 82, 284
atmospheric perspective 88, 94
atopy **415**
atrium 160
Auenlandschaft 330
authentic nature, American 188
autonomous form 178, 183, 194
avenue 36, 66, **77**, 78, 82, **84**, 90, 94, 156, 158, 174, 176, 198, 210, 214, 266, 270, 280, 286, 312, 320, 346, 348, 350, 364, **405**, 426
avenue, tree-lined 52, 78, 82, 88, 90, 138
axial
    arrangement 158
    organisation of space 66
    spatial series 54, 66, 158
    structure 404
    succession 342, 394
    system 164
    zone 84, 346

axiality 56, 60
axis 50, 52, 54, 56, 60, **65**, 66, **72**, 76, 74, **77**, 78, **81**, 86, 88, 92, 94, 138, **154**, 160, 240, 242, 340, **343**, 413
axis in the composition 138
axis of buildings **55**
axis of symmetry 52, 54, 78, 80, 82, 404
axis, fragmentation of the 158
axis, transverse 242, 246
backdrop 86, 120, 126, 160
background 86, 92, 192, 00, 214, 346
balcony 21, 38, 56, 78, **236**, 252, 370
baroque garden 146, 342
basic form 23, 260, 286
basic pattern 268, 416
basic spatial instruments 413
bastion 48, 54, 346, 388
beach ridge 262, 264
beautification 172, 174
beauty of nature 330
bedrock 190, **202**
belt 280, 304, 382, 388, 402
belvedere 114, 116, 126, **179**, 214, **218**
boating island **338**
Boating Lake **125**, 126, 142
boezem level 266
bog 126, 310, 334
bog river 266
bog streamlets 264
bosco 50, 254, 350, 420
bosquets 82, 84, **84**, 342
botanical garden 50, 140, 312, 350, 402, 408
boulevard 21, 78, 86, 90, 94, 96, 136, 176, 216, 270, 388, 390, **392**
bowling green 118
bridle path 216, 280, 308, 348
building blocks 376
bulwark **390**, **391**
caldarium 160
canal city, 17th century 266
Cardo 388
carriage and pedestrian park 280
carriage drives 216
cascade 78, 96, 98, 344, 346, 430
casino **169**
castle 80, 116, 154, 168, 238, 338
castle park 146
cemetery 98, 160, **240**, 340, 364, 372, 394
central allée 84
central axis 82, 210, 240, 246, 300, **343**, 346
central longitudinal axis 400
central perspective 88
central space 160, 286
centre of the composition 124
ceremonial backdrop, woods as 76
ceremonial entrance route 56
ceremonial parcours 78
ceremonial route 120
ceremonial series 130
chain
    of forts 392
    of gardens and parks **117**
    of open spaces 413
    of parks 116, 304
chalk cliffs or falaises 70
channel belts 262
château 76, 78
children's playground 224, 406
circuit walk 128
circulation of water 306
circulation pattern 140, 194, 216
circus 114, **115**
city boundary 264, 274, 302
city park 28, 140, 183, 194, 338, 406, 84

city park as a spatial type 410, 416, 418
city park with a 'garden', a 'meadow' and a 'wilderness' 350
city park, 19th century 108, 140, 183, 327, 378
city park, concept of 350
city park, Victorian 128
city wall 36, 38, 74, 76, 78, 80, 116, 232, 238, 390
city wall, demolished 82, 258
classic and the rustic, the 162
classical city 15, 17, 21, 32, 38, 52, 60, 422
classical column 160
classical portico 126
classical topography 52
classical villa 88, 370
clay pit 404
climax of the composition 56
clumps of trees 128, 138, 160, 260, 278
coast line 248, 294, 300, 318
coastal landscape 190, 262
coastal plain 32, 234, **234**, **236**, 238, 416, 418
coastal zone 234
collective residential building 114, 128
collective spatial form 25
colonisation grid, Roman 246
colonisation park **359**
colonnade 134, 136, 138, 252
common pasture 298
common space 348, 350
commons 116, 118, **299**
communal garden 118, 350
composition 15, 19, 25, 30, 50, 52, **52**, 56, 60, 134, 158, 160, 242, 408, 254, 348, 416, **417**
composition elements 428
composition scheme 128, **166**, 188, **216**, 428
compositional system 404
concept 17, 60, 128
    of a garden realm 178
    of a green belt **382**, 413
    of a metropolis 20
    of a park system 324
    of nature 66, 408
    of the 19th century city park 183, 194, 322
    of the settlement park 378
    of the urban landscape 25
    of urban farming 378
conservatory 160
construction of the park 214, 342
consular roads 36, 238, 240
continuing space 164, 278, 284, 428
continuity of the landscape 140, 142, 310, 322
continuous green space 252
continuous park landscape 148
contour lines 246, 248, 370, 372
cordonata or gentle stair 48, 54, 56, 60
coulisse 82, 92, 160, 280
coulisse landscape 280
coulisses of trees 170, 278
coulisses of woods 168, 346
Country Belt concept 414
country estate 78, 84, 114, 116, 118, 158, **172**, **177**, 198, 348
country estate landscape, regional 66, 76
country home 36, 160, 168, 170, 174, 198, 266, 270, 312
country house 80, 114, 118, 120, 116, 174
country life 114, 120, 266, 413
Country Park **313**
country road 126, 198, 370, 364

court 158, 160
court nursery 158
courtyards 40, 160
cove 170, 294, 298
cow pastures 280
cowshed and haystack 280
creek system in the park 308
creek 190, 212, **214**, 298, 300, 304, 306, 308, **308**
crescent 114, **115**, 136, 138, 194
croquet court 138
cross-section **57**, **206**, **209**, 210, **347**
cryptoporticus 42, 48, 50, **52**, 54, 56, 60
cultural landscapes 324, 348
dairy 270, 284, 344, 348, 348
decelerated perspective 82
decomposition 418, 420
deconstruction 376, 402, 404
decorative green 394
decorative squares 392
Decumanus Maximus 246, 388
deer park 316
defences, ring of 392, 396
defensive belt 388, 392, 394
defensive belt, demolished 390, 394
defensive works of the city 86
delta 238, 264, 286
delta landscape 416
design instruments 15, 17, 23, 376, 413, 418
design instruments of garden art 414
design instruments of landscape architecture 106, 426
design matrix 54, 194
design principles 156, 188
design process 15, 23
design scheme 194, 242
diagonal 78, 88, 138, 194, 244, 246, 254, **254**, 416
diagonal axis 82, 244
diagonal line 210
diagonal vistas 164
differences in elevation 254
differentiation of the programme 160, 327
dike 264, 266
dike rings 264, 266, 286
diorama 52, 194
district parks 242
domain of the city 19, 374
domestic gardens 358
double circus 124, 130
double crescent 130, 140
double Inner Circus 128
double stairs 252
drainage 186, 264, 266, **308**
drainage canal 240, 270, 388
drainage ditch 266, **272**, 268, 278
drainage, 262, 266, 306
drainage system 306, 334
drained lake 264
drive 224, 318, 320
drumlins 294
eclectic style 178
edge of the city 76, 120, 364, 370, 374, 382, 414
edge of the park 122, **226**, **255**
elementary
    building block 260
    composition 128
    form in the landscape 374
    geographic characteristics 210
    green spatial forms 390
    logic of the landscape 252
    typology of the garden 374
elements of the composition 94, 162
elevation, differences in **214**, 284
embankment 108, 194, 298, 310, 318, 390, 392, 406
enclosed garden 48, 348

court 158, 160
enclosed landscape, view of the 370
enjoyment of nature 322, 340
ensemble architecture 108, 118
entrance 44, **46**, 52, 54, **57**, 134, 160, 194, 216, 252, 274, 280, 312, 346, 348, **348**, **395**, 402, 406
    avenue 158
    drive 100
    gate 238, 280
    scheme 56
    stair **52**
    theatre 48, 54, 56, 58
    to the city 78, 88, 394
    to the park 142, **142**, **189**, 194, 210, 212, 274, 270, **276**, 284, 316
Erholungsplatz 400, **400**, 402
eskers or meltwater ridges 294
estate 76, 100, 118, 120, **122**, 168, 268, 402, 302, 312
estuarial plain 232
estuary 70, 108, 194, 200, 264, 266, 294, 298, 322, 334
event space 426
exedra or 'echo' 48, 54, 82, 136, 158, 160, 162, **169**, 170, 400
experimental landscape architectonic form 178, 420
experimental landscape architectonic model 286
experimental landscape composition 148
experimental typological series 413
eye-catching element 168
façade 15, 44, 90, 114, 118, 128, 134, 136, 138, 160, 166, 168, 170, 370, 374, 390, 408, 402
farm 166, 174, 186, 290, 298, 302, 312, 348, 364
farm land 124
farm yard 160
farmhouse 178
farmstead 174, 312
fer à cheval, or horseshoe shape 82
field of vision, limit of the 88
fish pond 42, 50, 158
flood barrier 108
flood plain 108, 384
flow landscape 422, 424, 426
flower garden 168, 216, 270, 344, 348, 390, 400, 404, 406
flowerbeds 48, 50, 350
follies 96, 418
foot hills 116, 124, 294
footpath 308
ford 116, 364
forecourt 118, 136, 160, **161**, 162, **163**, 316, 346
forecourt of the city 82
foreground 76, 82, 86, 92, 98, 100, 226, 346
foreshortening of the perspective 82
forest 116, 154, 156, 174, 214
forestry 76, 146
form as a framework 332
form of the programme 160
formal
    (French) garden 25, 122, 350, 382, 404, 413
    avenue 320
    balcony 56
    canal 138
    design instruments 94, 178
    entrance 350
    framework 413, 414, 348
    garden system 78
    geometric form 404
    landscape **74**, 94, 162
    layout 118
    model 82
    network 25, 100, **100**, **103**

reduction 84
scheme 23
space 94
spatial axis 92, 94
spatial design 66
square 134, 138
system 17, 66, 94, 96, 98, 148, 154, 162
typology 418
urban design 140
-functional form 410
-programmatic form 406
fortification 19, 80, 212, 266, 364, 392, **410**
fortification 54, 338, 382, 388, 392
fortification, demolition of the 98
fortification belt **394**, **395**
fortifications 238
fortified castles 76
fortress 80, 234, 388, **393**
forts, demolished 398
fountain 36, 42, 50, 54, 96, 160, 174, 216, 350, 390
fragmentation 90, 100, 422
Freiflächenplan **393**, 394
functional
form 327, 330, 342, 402, 410, 418
green structure 322, 394
landscape theatre 376
organisation 160, 426
park 330
pattern 17, 426
programme 352
game preserve 154
garden 40, 56, 60, 66, 82, 84 100, 138, 140, 146, 156, 158, 160, 164, 172, 176, 196, 212, 260, 266, 274, 300, 308, 316, 318, 350, **371**, 372, **395**, **403**
garden and park system 156
garden architectonic frame 352
garden as an experimental landscape 352
garden as an extension of domestic space 374
garden as the smallest agricultural production unit 374
garden city 21, 252, 356, 413, 418
garden city movement 374
garden communities 178
garden complex 28, 52, 146
garden composition 84
garden courtyards 252
garden elements 54, 312, 300, 348
garden realm 178
garden ring 364
garden towns 422
garden, meadow and wilderness **216**, **217**, 292, 406, 404, 410
Gardenesque style 96, 128
Gartenlandschaft 164
Gartenreich or Garden Realm 148, **172**, 174, **177**, 178, 178
gate 48, 54, 56, 116, **128**, 134, 136, 388
gates and bulwarks, planted 268
gateway 44, 88
generative systems 17
generative structure, landscape as a 21, 430
generic green space 404, 410, 418
generic landscape 100, 408
generic urban structures 422
generic, standardised form 410
genius loci 30, 42, 62, 84, 100, 183, 252, 260, 410, 422, 424, 428
genius loci of the city 322, 430
genius loci of the landscape 408
genius loci, expression of 430
geographic order 424
geographic texture **417**, 418
geological basin 70
geological fault zone 294, 360, 384
geometric
diagram 19
form 342

garden 50, 76, 80, 158
model 244, 246
reduction of the topography 246
scheme **55**, 82
system 246
geometry 76, 80, 98, **240**, **252**, 346, 398
geometry of the urban grid 212, **209**, 246
geomorphology **32**, **34**, 38, **70**, **72**, **74**, 78, 100, **110**, **112**, **150**, **152**, **190**, **234**, **236**, 246, **262**, **294**, **296**, **334**, **336**, **359**, **362**, **384**, **386**, 408
giardino segreto 50, 56, 60, 420
glacial lake, or 'kettle hole' 294, 310, 312
glacial landscape 150, 178, 312
glacial plateaus 152
glacial trenche 152, 156
glacial troughs or meltwater valleys 150
glacis 388, 390
golf course 322
Grand Design **106**, 120, 140, **141**, 142, **142**
gravel quarry 402
green
amphitheatre **84**
arcade **161**
areas 392
belt 280, 327, 362, 364, 368, **381**, 382, 388, 384, 390, 392, **392**, 394, 396, **396**, **397**, 398, 402, 406, **406**, 408, **408**, **409**, 410, **415**
girdle 413
matrix 400
network 226
periphery 413, 414
radial 327, 390, 394, 396, **396**, **397**, 398, 402, 404, 408
scheme **393**
space 100, 183, 327, 394, 406
space, organisation of the 408
space, standardisation of 410
squares 96, 290, 400
structure 382, 388, 390, **393**, 394, 398, 400, 402, 406, 408, 410, 426
system **394**
wall 214, 222
wedges 286
zone 382, 396, 424
grid 21, 80, 82, 183, 198, 212, 222, 232, 240, 246, **251**, 252
grid and topography 254, 246
grid pattern 242, 234
grid, deformations of the 252
grid, edges of the 248
grid, lines of the 210, 254
grid, module for the 198
grotto 36, 56, 96, 98, 136, 166, 430
ground plan 74, 80, 284, 308
Grünflächenplan **366**
ha-ha 114
Halligen or hillocks 334
harbour 238, 240, 246, 298, **334**
heath landscape 402
heathland 172, 174, 340, 342, 334
hermitage 166
hidden landscapes 252
high-rise building and landscape 322, 428
high-rise city 21
high-rise landscape 428, 430
High-rise Villa 428, **429**, **431**
hill crest 32, 78, 126, 302, 312, 238
hilly landscape 32, 114, 168, 183, 210, 278, 396
hippodrome 158, 160, 162
homestead 416
horizon 66, 78, 82, 84, **84**, 88, 90, 92, 94, 96, 98, 100, 140, 224, 346, 413, 422, **431**
horizon line 212
horizon within the city 90

horticultural garden 98
horticulture 290, 302, 312, 330, 378
hortus 21, 56
hunting ground 156, 234
hunting lodge 76
hunting park 96, 154, 156
hunting preserve **30**, 116, 172
hybrid form 232, 404
hydraulic system 308
ice cellar 166
iconography of the garden 82
idea of the garden 332
ideal city 17, 19, **20**, 21, 66, 226, 413
ideal landscape 146, 148, 176
ideal of country life 140
ideal polder city 21
ideal Renaissance city 19
idealised nature 19
idealised urban landscape 414
idyll of nature in the landscape city park 402
idyll of the 19th century city park 332
idyllic character 188
idyllic rural backdrop 128
idyllic scenes and tableaux 330
illusion of boundlessness 312
illusion of naturalness 194
illusion of wilderness **227**
image of a jungle 420
image of nature 408
image of the city 374
imperial city 88
imperial palace 42
imperial residences 44
imperial villas 36
impluvium 160, 162
in-between city 378
industrial forest 424
industrial landscape 420, **420**
industrial nature 424
industrial wasteland 422
inland sea 70, 190
inlet 170, 212
inner and an outer park 222
inner city parks 304
inner courtyards 252, 266
inner dunes, edges of the 268
intermediate landscapes 426
intermediate space 212, 428
intermediate spatial forms 15, 17, 422
inversion of the horizon 422
irrigation 240
kitchen garden 160
koog or polder 334
labyrinth **20**, 28, 84, 98, 254, **255**, 430
labyrinthine space of the city 60
lagoon 238
lake 21, 70, 78, 98, 126, 150, 156, 158, 162, 164, 168, **171**, 174, 204, 214, 264, 278, 290, 302, 306, 310, 312, 320, 346, 402
lake bed polder 19, 266, 278, 264, 268
lake landscape 156, 164
lake, artificial 158
land reclamation 19, 290, 294, 300, **300**
land reclamation projects, 17th century 426
landfills 190
landscape architectonic
building kit 23
composition 23, 25, 48, 174, 324, 416
concept 286, 322, 376, 410
design instruments 170, 178, 322, 258, 414, 418
design keys 378
domain 413
form 84, 254, 286, 327, 352, 376, 416, 408, 410, 430
model 142, 284
transformation 106, 142, 162, 284
treatment 164, 172, 422, 426
type 140

landscape architecture, English 183, 258
landscape architecture, instruments of 332, 420, 422
landscape as a communal space 348
landscape
backbone of the city 322
backdrops 414
belt, basis for a 368
boundaries of the city 414
composition 174, 414
concept 424
fragments 420
garden, (18th century English) 25, 120, 122, 126, 128, 140, 160, 164, 168, 188, 194, 204, 280, 332, 344, 348, 414, 424
garden, transformation of the 114
garden, visual arsenal of 136
horizon **98**
morphology 114
of gardens 40
park 122, 140, 146, 164, 168, 170, **172**, 258, 308, 312, 324, 340, 350, 402, 404
park concept 342
pattern 19, 266
relief **375**
repertoire 420
reservations 324
scenography 25, 106, 160, 222, 424
space 162, 352, 358, 368, 413, 416, 422
structure 178, 286
style 156, 258
telescope 92
texture 424, 426
theatre 25, 120, 146, 148, 174, 178, 376, 414, 422, 426
topography 290, 352, 404, 414, 420, 424, 428
types 183
typology 322
typology of the 19th century city park 327
landscaped routes 414
landscaped slopes 312
landscaped stairs 252
landscapes, spectrum of 212
landscape-topographic series 418
Landschaftssteigerung 370
Landschaftsverschönerung 146
lawn 96, 114, 138, 278, 342, 402, **431**
lignite mine **384**, 408
limes 364, 388
linear park 302
lines of flow 426
lines of force in the geomorphology 413
lines of sight **154**
lines of the topography 252
lines of the urban grid 428
locks 70, 362
locus 17, 62
loggia 48, 50, 350, 430, **431**
longitudinal axis 86, 246, 402
longitudinal profile 78, **83**, **206**
lookout points 174
low lands 19, 150, 384
low tide 306
lowland forms 278
main axis 19, 56, 60, 82, 88, 100, 138, 154, 156, **169**, 346, 348, 350, 388, 404, **405**, 406
main entrance 54, 276, 280, 340, 346
main gate 52, 54, 56, **60**
main park in the Park System 312
main route through the park 402
Mall 138, 212
management of perspective 52
man-made landscape 17, 146, 170, 327, 342, 402
mannerism 28, 50
manor house 124, 166

mansion 118, 158
market gardens 268, 358, 364, 368, 376
marshes 108, 308
mass housing projects 374, 376
mass recreation 402
mass residential projects 374
matrix 52
matrix of the city 416
matrix of the cultivated landscape 17
matrix of the peat polder landscape 183, 264, 278
meadow 114, 168, 194, 204, 212, 214, 270, 272, 292, 308, 310, 312, 316, 322, 344, 350, 352, 402
meadow landscape 330
meadowland, marshy 138
meander **279**, **359**, 368, 370
meandering river 384
meltwater rivers 334
meridian 246
metropolis 15, 21, 100, 212, 356
metropolis, in the heart of the 226
metropolis, life in the 374
metropolis, trading- 266
metropolitan
axis 134
dimensions 426
field 422, 426, 428
formation 428
gardens 422
landscape 20, 21, 23, 324, 414, 420, 422, 426, 430
landscape architecture 412, 414, 422, 428, 430
park system 302, 304, 322, **325**
polder park 286
space 426
water system 304
Metropolitan Green Belt 413
Metropolitan Improvement 120
metropolitan landscape, design keys for the 422, 424
mirror axis 76, 82
mixed style, late 19th century 402
moat 36
moat and casements 388
model 21, 42, 66, **67**, 194, 284, 320, 414
model city 19
model for a park 342
model of an ideal city **18**
model of an industrial city 21
model of the landscape garden 413
model of urban expansion 358
model, landscape architectonic 148
model, park as a 162
modulation of the peat parcel 278, 284
module in the grid 242
monastic garden 160
montage as a concept 428
montage landscape 426
moraine landscape 190, 150, 152, 294
morphological pattern 286
morphology 17, 92, **106**, 108, 124, **142**, 212, 242
morphology of the city 322, 330
morphology of the landscape 52, 66, 98, 148, 368, 414, 424
morphology of the site 168, 342
mountain lakes 32, 38
movement and perception, relation between 56
moving soil, mechanics of 188
mud flats 298, 318, 334
multifunctional space 350
municipal garden 402
municipal park plan 322
municipal park system **290**, 302, **305**, 324
municipal woodland 424
national parks, programme of 226
native planting 214, 280
native species 292

natural form 174, 376, 416
natural form, latent 164
natural
    fragment 214
    harbour 266, 294
    landscape 17, 154, 174, 212, 248, 262, 402, 426, 428
    morphology 164, 172, 210, 306, 312, 368
    plant cover 166
    planting 214
    scenery 212, 214, 292
    tableau 162, 224
nature 146, 148, 178, 204
nature education 396
nature idyll 284
nature reconstructed as 'wilderness' 416
nature reserve 368, 378
nature theatre 406
nature, 'cataloguing' of 402
nature, 'virgin' 378
nature, experience of 162
nature, morphogenesis of 222
nature, original 210, 214, 222
negotium 92
neo-Palladian country home 114
network
    of avenues 90
    of footpaths 168, 194
    of green spaces 396
    of landscape projects **423**
    of parks and parkways 226
    of sightlines 414
    of visual relations 62, 413
New Towns 66, 413
nodus 17
nymphaeum 42, 54, 56, 60, 136
obelisk 36, 156, **87**
objective landscape form 426
observation of nature 402
observation point 126
observatory 200, 216
ocean 212
open space 21, **85**, 116, 118, 126, 140, 156, 160, 188, 200, 202, 226, 286, 338, 358, 368, **371**, 378, 413
open-air baths 226
open-air home 330
open-air schools 396, 406
open-air theatre 38, 84, 140, 280, 318, 344, 346
optical effect 88
orchard 48, 196, 238, 266, 348
order of nature, illusionistic 82
organic landscape form 17
organisation of the programme 418
orientation of the grid 254
ornamental garden **406**
otium 92, 350
otium and negotium 378, 430
outdoor space 376
outdoor swimming pools 364
outer park 304
outlet sluices 266
outwharfing 298, **299**
oxidation of the peat soil 278
palace 28, 36, 42, 50, 52, 60, 80, 82, 86, 88, 90, 118, 134, 138, 154, 162, 178, 346
palaeovalley 152, 150
palatial architecture or 'palatial style' 122
palatial façade 118
palazzina 54
palazzo 28, 56
palimpsest 430
panorama 25, 56, 62, 76, 90, 96, 114, **149**, 164, 372, 422, 424
panorama of the city 30
panorama of the landscape 226
panoramic space 418
panoramic view 174
parade ground 130, 216
parcellation **124**, 264, 356, 258
parcellation of a peat polder 278

parcellation of the agricultural landscape 19
parcels of land 198, 202, 258, 270
parcels, cluster of 264, 284
park **30**, 56, **72**, 98, 106, **112**, 116, 120, 126, 130, 138, **146**, **149**, 152, **152**, 154, 158, **159**, **162**, 164, 168, 170, 172, 174, 176, 186, 188, **190**, 200, 212, **213**, **232**, **236**, 240, 242, 252, **255**, 258, **258**, 260, 264, 268, 292, **296**, 302, 310, 312, **332**, **336**, **355**, **362**, 368, 382, **386**, 402
park as a refuge 80
park as metropolitan void **228**
park axis **347**, 396
park belt 413
park city 126
Park Crescent 136, **142**
park drive 168, 194, 212, 226, 308
park form 327, 382, 402
park landscape 128, 160, 188, 214, 280, 382, 290, 330, 376
park landscape as urban realm 348
park landscape, continuous 158
park landscape, regional **376**
park programme 160, 216, **220**, 224, 342, 348, **348**
park programme 84
park route 160, 216, 310, 316, 340, 348
park scheme 306, 406, 408, 410
park series 306, 322
park squares 246
park system 183, **289**, 290, **292**, 294, 300, 302, **303**, 306, 318, **320**, 322, 418
park system, blueprint for the 304
park system, building blocks for the 290
park theatres 118
Park Villages 128
park villas 128, **131**, 270
parks and green squares 390, 392
parkway 304, 318, 424, 183, 224, 290, 302, **319**, 320, **320**, 322, 324, 364, 418
parterre 82, 100, 194
parterre de broderie 82, 342
parterre de gazon 82
parterre garden 413
pastoral
    character 214
    composition 212
    image 316, 414
    landscape 120, 140, 194, 204, 210, 212, 214, 292, 312, 316, 402, 408
    panorama 128, **133**, 136
    prototype 418
    scenery 212
    scenography 214
    scheme of the 19th century city park 410
pasture, pasture land 38, 60, 124, 168, 284, 270, 340, 376, 394, 398
path system 286, 368
patio **254**
patte d'oie 82, 88
pattern
    of activities 330
    of green spaces 382
    of park usage 322
    of paths 130, 140, 194, 284
    of the paths, hierarchy 284
pavilion 56, 98, 168
peat (meadow) landscape 268, 284, 286
peat bog 262, 264, 272, 334
peat bog reclamation 260
peat bog rivulet 266
peat cutting 334
peat islands 264
peat lakes 264
peat landscape 266, 286
peat matrix 260
peat parcel as basic module 266, 284

peat parcellation 266, **279**
peat parcels, dimensions of the 278
peat plain 286
peat polder 258, 264, 266, 268, 270, 278, 284, 286
peat polder city 274, 276
peat polder landscape 264, 266, **267**, **268**, 286
peat polder parcel 260
peat polder parcellation **262**, 266, 268
peat polders, transformation of 258
peat reclamation 264
peat rivers 266
peat streams 286
pedestrian lanes 96
pedestrian path 310, 390
pedestrian route **244**, 364
peninsula 170, 190, 294, 298, 172
people's palace 348
people's park 350
perfect order, illusion of 82
pergola 48, 160, 168, 252
periphery 36
perspectival construction 92
perspectival visual axis 28
perspective 19, 28, 50, 82, **83**, **87**
perspective and motion 28
perspective in the ground plan 82
perspective reaching to the horizon 88
perspective sketch **336**, **343**
perspective, framed 92
perspectivistic effect 404
perspectivistic image, notional 82
perspectivistic tableau 82
physical-geographical lines of force 414
physical-geographical structure 21, 324
piano nobile 348, **431**,430
piazza 42, 118
pictorial composition 108, 134
pictorial ensemble 108
pictorial landscape design 140
pictorial scheme 212
pictorial urban design 140
picturesque 204, 214, 404
pier 318
pingo 150
place 118
plain 232, 240, 246, 252
planning strategy 198, 358
plant beds 98
plant communities, indigenous 402
plant nursery 404
plantation 422, 428
plantation, basic plan of the 426
plantation, topographic logic of densities 426
planting 48, 140, 174, 194, 224, 260, 266, 278, **279**, 286, 312, 320, 280, 302, 308, 342, 346, 368, 400, 402
planting scheme 128
plateau 21, 78, 124, 170, 234, 384, 424
play area 318
playgrounds 226, 280, 316, 318, 348, 368, 390, 398, 402, 404
playing field 214, 216, 316, **331**, 346, 400, 402, **403**, 350, **352**
playing meadow 346, 404
plaza, octagonal 212, 242, 254
pleasure garden 56, 116, 118, 168, 268
pleasure grounds 126, 130, 194
point of view 86
polder 19, 258, 260, 264, 260, 266, **275**
polder city 260, 286
polder complex 264
polder form, Dutch 258
polder geometry 19
polder land 278
polder landscape 262, 278, 286
polder metropolis 286, **286**
polder metropolis, model for the
polder parcellation 19

polder parcels 19, **271**
polder park 183, 284
polder system 19, 266, 284
polis 17
pond 82, 96, 138, 158, 194, **260**, 278, 286, 300, 306, 310, **313**, **386**, 398, 402, 404
pool 54, 126, 214
portico 42, 90, 92, 158, 160, 162
position of the city 19
Prachtstrasse 390, 394, 408
prairie scenery 212
precipices 210
private arable fields 394
private estates 312
private garden 330, 400
private residence 158
productive green 364
productive green city 364
productive landscape 414, 420
productive urban pleasure landscape 378
profile of the standard street 242
programmatic concept 178
programmatic division 402
programmatic form 23, 350, 374, 404, 406
programme elements 346
programme for active recreation 222
programme, building blocks for the
promenade 48, 76, 84, 90, 94, 126, 154, 176, 202, 212, **226**, 310, 316, 318, 320, 390
promenade cinematique 418
promenade zone 364
promenade, shaded 404
promenade, tree-lined 80, 86, 372, 394, 406, 408
prototype of the functional city park 330
prototype of the public park 140
proto-urban domain 32
public (urban) park 25, 60, 84, 96, 188, 194, 252, 258, 268, 302
public botanical garden 300
public domain 17
public garden 28, 44, 268, **292**, **299**, 330, 350, **351**, 400, 413
public green 394
public green space, merging of 392
public landscape 138
public park 284
public pasture 118
public space 84, 118, 136, 140, 142, 232, 238, 244, 324, 400
public squares 198
public urban landscape 378
pumping station 158, 174, 272, 278, 334, 284
pumping system 278
pyramid 166, 174
quay 70, **347**
radial avenue to the centre 402
radial green zones 286
radiating avenues, star-shaped 78
radiating axes 86
radiating paths 100
railway embankments 306
rational settlement pattern 426
rational-functional form 406, 410
rationalisation of mass housing 358
ravine 214
ravine, architectonic **431**
ravine, artificial 430
reading garden 406
receding planting 138
reciprocal views 160
reclaimed land 300, 304, 320
reclamation forms 416
reclamation of the landscape 378
recomposition 44
recomposition of landscape fragments 210
recomposition of the urban pattern 414
recreation 118, 258
recreation and health 200

recreation area 368
recreation machine 348
recreational
    'productivity' 348
    activities 160, 346
    and nature areas 408, 413
    experience of nature 324
    facilities 224, 348, 376, 414
    functions 140, 376, 408
    landscape 348
    needs 98
    programme 322, 348, 350, 404, 406, 410
    space 224, 316
rectangular grid 340, 388
recursiveness 21
redevelopment of industrial sites 424
reflecting pond 100, 430
regeneration of the landscape 420, 422
regeneration of the river 424
regional green belt **410**
regional landscape theatre 178
regional park landscape 172
regional scale 178
regional structure of landscape reservations 324
regional system of avenues 66, 94
regularization 364
regularization of the river 362, 368
relation between city and landscape 78
relief **81**, 312, **213**, 226
Renaissance garden 82
Renaissance model of the 'ideal city' 19
repertoire of the polder park 284
representation of nature 19, 82
reservoir 70, 174, 216, 300, 308, 312
residential
    area 130, 370
    block 376
    building programme 364
    environment 106
    estates 76
    forms 128, 188
    landscape 128
    neighbourhood 268, 372
    space 118
residual landscapes 426
retaining wall 21, 48, 60, **98**, 346, **371**, 372, 374
ridge of hills 234, 294
rill 188
ring boulevard 176, 390
ring canal 19, 266, 270, 278
ring of defences, first 390
ring of fortifications **388**
Ringstrasse **390**, **391**
river 21, 32, 76, 84, 108, 116, 118, **150**, 152, 156, 168, 196, **232**, 248, 266, 286, 294, 308, 346
river (flood)-plain 32, 238, 384
river bank 370, 384, 302
river basin 172
river bed 80
river branches 108
river delta 234, 240, 246, 252, 262, 350
river landscape 78, 264, 278
river mouth 286
river pattern 384
river reservations 324
river valley 19, 21, 74, 108, 190, 246, 368, 370, 372, 278
river-mouth 266, 298
rivulet 214, 310
rock 96, 188, 204
rock formations 190
rock outcrops 202, 210
rocky landscape 214
rolling fields 204, 212
rolling hills 21
Roman road 124
Roman villas 364
rond-point 90

roof garden 92, 430
roof landscape 426, 428
roof terrace 160, **431**
rose garden 158, 322, 402
rotunda 136, 168
Rousseau-Insel 348
route 28, 42, **58**, 60, 164, 170, 174, 280
route system 216, 312, 413
rowing and swimming lake 348
rows of trees 390, 392
royal (game) park 106, 116, 138, 148
royal estate 146
royal gardens 66, 158
royal geography 78
royal palace 106, 120, 122, 130, 140, 160
royal residence 76, 120, 130
royal summer palace 106
ruined temple 174
ruins 28, 36, 38, 44, 48, 50, 52, 54, 60
ruins, artificial 174
rules of landscape architecture 23
rural
    character 304
    conditions, range of 212
    elements 254
    estate 114
    image 312
    landscape pattern 142
    life, enjoyment of the 76
    life, pre-industrial 342
    living in the city 130
    section of the park 280
    setting 15
    villages 108
    villas 122
rus in urbe 114
rustic
    cottages 128
    décor 128
    environs 15
    farm garden motifs 342
    inn 348
    Italian house 160
    latticework 162
    scene 312
sacred city **20**
sacred spot 42
Saddle 320
salt marsh 200, 298, 306, 308, 322, 334
salt marsh landscape 308
salt meadows 294
sand hills 172
sandbanks 70
sandr or outwash sand apron 152
sandy beaches 294
sandy plateau 194
satellite cities 178, 364, **366**
scale 15, 66, 88, 90, 92, 94, 146, 162, 254, 280, 292, 312, 382, 416, 430
scale of the city 106, 210, 244, 322
scale, increase in 94, 120, 324, 376, 382
scale, panoramic range of 422
scattered city 116
scenery 214, 324
scenic and tableaux 204
scenic
    backdrop 108
    background 166
    composition 126, 166, 424
    elements 108
    framework 130
    identity 84, 142
    idyll 178
    illusion 216, 222
    image of the landscape 204, 332, 418
    lake 158
    landscape 138, 174
    link 170
    panorama 114

quality 322
route 310
series, framing the 212
spots 164
staging 128, 138
topography 348
view 128, 290
water feature 158
scenic-compositional coherence 306
scenographic context 160
scenography 62, **135**, 416, 430
scenography of the architectonic route 418
scenography of the urban route system 414
schematic city plan 356, **359**, **366**
scheme for a municipal settlement park 364
scheme of the (French garden) 332, 410
Schmuckanlagen 148, 400
school gardens 364
scientific arboretum 300
screen 60, 86, 126, 284, 394, 430
sea coast reservations 324
sea dike 266
sea level 190
sea level, rising 108
seaside resort on the ocean 304
secret garden 50
sedimental plain 262
seepage 278
sequence of spaces 346
series
    of architectonic compositional elements 56
    of lakes 168, 212
    of parks 138, 178, 312, 318, 410
    of pleasure gardens 156
    of specific spaces and views 428
    of streams and lakes 172
    of terraces 372
    of urban landscapes 322
Serpentine Lake 138
serpentine line or 'line of beauty' 278
settlement 246, 298, 418
settlement grid, continent-wide 416
settlement park 327, 358, 376, 378
settlement process 378
shoreline 166, 168, 198, 202, 226
Siedlung 370, 372, **375**, 358, 422, 424
Siedlung zone 364
Siedlung, visual structure of the 374
sight lines 166, **169**, 214
skating pond 216
skyline of the city, internal 226
skyscrapers 224, 226, 428
sluice 310, 264, 266, 308, 334
soil conditions 284, 300
soil pattern 384
soil profile **279**
solid rock 212
source 124, 310
spa 160
Space Frame 426
space in time 62
space of the city 426
space of the landscape 374
spaces 414
spatial
    (visual) continuity 136
    arrangement 330, 402
    articulation along the axis 346
    articulation of green **395**
    articulation of the city 392
    autonomy of the garden 80
    axis 25, 66, **68**, 76, 78, 84, 86, **86**, **87**, 88, 90, **91**, **97**, **98**, 100, 346
    axis of the French garden 346
    axis toward the horizon 413
    axis, dissolving into atmospheric perspective 94
    axis, gauge the depth of the 92
    cacophony 92

category 212, 254
characteristics 21, 266
coherence 32, 160, 212
composition 30, 66, 76, 174, 284, 406
concept 108, 178, 404
construction 15, 100, 327
continuity 136, 178, 280
depth effect 92
depth of the axis 82
depth of the garden 82
dimension 62, 212
distribution 17
diversity 21
division 260
dynamics 422
effects 92, 94, 174
ensembles 108
form 15, 17, 23, 130, 160, 260, 278, 280, 284, 316, 413, 428
interaction 376
margins 382
organisation of the green 382
organisation of the park 160
patterns 15
prototypes 413
relation 15, 20, 21, 66, 140
scenography, coherent 108
scheme of the garden 418
series 160, 346, 372, 404
structure 78, 106, 212, 322, 413
system 17, 60
telescope 94
transition 254, **255**, **374**
type 108, 160, 183, 222, 327, 406
zoning 21, 350
spiral stair 48, 54, 56, 60
sports complex 394, 396, 398
sports facilities 100, 398
sports field 98, 316, 322, 348, 364, 368, 376, 396, 398, 402, 406
square 17, 42, 86, 88, 92, 114, **115**, 116, **117**, 118, 136, 138, 174, 176, 200, 238, 244, 268, 382, 402
square grid, Roman 74
square, circus and crescent 124
squares and streets 124, 130, 134, 146, 178, **232**, 410
stadium 322
Stadtverschönerung 146
stage 134, 346
stage and décor, both 128
stage scenery **108**
stage set 38
stage-dressing 166
stage-managing 140, 174, 376
staging 282, **130**, 426
stair 28, 30, 48, 50, 56, 138, 160, 212, 346, 350, 372
stairs 42
stairway 54
standard catalogue of green spatial forms 420
standard form, functional 376
standard type and individual variation 374
standard width of the peat parcels, modulating the 278
standardisation of dwelling types 356
star with eight radials 154
steam engine 168
steam mill 160
steam pumping station 160, 174, 270
stoa 82
stone quarry 96, 212
strategic interventions in the topography 426
stream 38, 212, 234, 238, 306, 310
stream bed 310, 384
stream belts 384
stream, reaches of the 310
street pattern 198, 248, 300, 404
street profile 390
strip parcellation 372
strips of greenery, wedge-shaped 358

strolling park, 19th century 258, 330, 340, 358
strolling park, programmeless 222
strolling paths 258, 404
structure of the urban pattern 410
stylistic means 348
subsidence of peat soil 266
suburb 21, 154, 238, 364
suburban
    concept 21
    development 100, 258, 310
    field 414, 416
    form of living 414
    landscape 21, 414
    model 188
    parks 304
    plain 418
suburbs 382, 392, **396**, 398, 402
suburbs, industrial 404
summer homes 198, 268
summer houses 312
summer palace 130, 134, 136, 156, **157**, **175**
summer pavilion 126
summer residence 156
summer resort 130
summer retreat 202
super meadow 426
super-grid 416
superurb 416
sustainable programme 428
swamp 154, 202, 212, 238, 262, 310
swamps and lagoons, belt of 234
swimming areas 368, 376
swimming pools 396
symmetry 54, 86, 138, 342
symmetry of the design 48
system
    of *allées*, avenues and promenades 96
    of avenues 142, 156
    of axes 78, 100, 154, 156, 176, 414
    of Drives, Walks and Ride, separated 216
    of foot paths 140, 176, 188, 194
    of avenues 84
    of functional connections 404
    of green areas, standardised 406
    of lakes and rivers 414
    of parks and squares 96
    of parks and woods 94
    of paths 168, 216, 284, 350, 390, 402
    of recreational facilities, hierarchical 327
    of routes 216
    of scenic improvements 302
    of separated routes **219**
    of views, avenues and axes 154
systems and processes in nature 428
tapis vert 78, 82, 90, 100, 346
tea garden 274
tea house 160
tea pavilion 158
technical landscape form 17
telescope 78, 82
templum 19
temporal dimension 62
tennis courts 280, 404
terrace 25, **46**, 50, 54, 56, 60, 78, 82, 84, **98**, 100, 124, 128, 130, 140, 156, 158, 160, 162, 164, 168, 194, 214, 252, 316, 346, 400, 402, 404
theatrical
    landscape 122
    Panorama 122, 128, **130**, **133**, 136, 140, 222
    space 134
    staging of public space 120
    staging of the landscape space 422
    street 136
    urban space 140
thematic gardens 128

thermae 114, 162
three-dimensional model **171**, **177**, **279**, **317**, **347**, **371**, **375**
tidal
    area 306
    basins, swampy 294
    channels 266
    effects 262, 310
    estuary 190
    fluctuations 266, 308, 322
    influence 306
    limit 116
    plain 298
    river 108, 310
tides, rise and fall of the 298, **308**
time and space 60, 352
time machine 62
timeless element in the landscape 100
time-space chains, individual 424
topographic
    basis 252
    conditions 418
    enclave 248
    exception **250**, **251**, 254
    framework 126
    grid 232
    information 188
    intersection 74
    logic 248
    map 238, 240, **240**, **364**
    map as plan drawing 238
    matrix 232
    memory of the city 430
    points, outstanding 414
    potential 178
    relationships 304
    scenography 142
    survey 202
    transformations 240
topographical patterns 416
topographic-landscape 'film' 424
topography 15, 19, 23, **30**, 32, 36, 42, 52, 62, **68**, **106**, **109**, **125**, **146**, 174, **186**, **195**, 196, **232**, **240**, **248**, **251**, **252**, **255**, **258**, **290**, 302, 327, **332**, **355**, **382**
topography of the landscape 183, 327, 232, 312, 350, 368, 408, 416, 422
topography, anchored in the 66
topography, convergence in the 76
topography, effect of the plan on the 240
topography, existing 142, 176, 240, 248
topography, fitting into the 310
topography, geometric reduction of the 246
topography, integration of the 122
topography, landscape reflecting 246
topography, local 198
topography, old 248, 254
topography, original 128, 254, 372
topography, prime locations in the 364
topography, scales of the 178
topography, transformation of the 122
topology of the city 17, 352, 424
topos 17, 222
traffic system, separated 216
transformation 23, 44, 48, 76, 78, **80**, 86, 90, 100, 108, 126, **129**, 134, **134**, 140, 146, 156, 168, 178, 183, 194, 266, 286, **307**, 324, 350, 376, 404, 413, 414
transformation model 158
transformation of
    the 19th century city park 327
    the agricultural landscape 126, 376, 416
    the basic instruments 420
    the country seat 114
    the defensive rings 98, 408
    the design instruments 418
    the lake bed polder 286
    the landscape 370
    the landscape garden 108, 128
    the landscape theatre 376

the peat polder landscape 284
the Renaissance villa 25
the route 424
the settlement scheme 426
the topography 376
the wild nature 194
transformation scheme **123**
transformation, royal 136
transformative framework for the
    metropolis 430
transformative topography **420**
transitional forms 408
transitional sections 160, 136, 212,
    404
transitional zone 346, 413, 414
transport axis 78
transverse axis 19, 346, **157**, 348
transverse roads 212, 204, 216
transverse streets 246
tree-covered walks 350
treillages 48
triclinium 48
Trinkhalle with health spa 348
triumphal arch 86, 88, 90
Triumphal Avenue 134, **135**, 136
Tummelwiese or playing field 350, 352
type 28
typological
    differentiation 413
    differentiation of the urban
        landscape 420
    investigation 428
    moment 23
    reduction and repetition 376
    relationship 23
    series 322, 418
    similarities 23
typology 17, 108, 126
typology of the city park 418
typology of the polder landscape 286
urban
    Arcadia 25, 148, 178
    axis 52, **55**
    balcony 25, 28, 30, 142, 413
    beautification 400
    block 124, 126, 240, 242, 248,
        266
    block, basic 240
    building block 114
    building kit 242, 244, 252
    context 23, **44**
    continuity in the landscape 418
    development **198**, 372, 392, 394,
        428
    development scheme 398
    domain **32**, **70**, **110**, **150**, **190**, **234**,
        262, **294**, 304, **334**, **359**, 414,
        418
    drainage system 304, 306
    fabric 106, 118, 178, 402
    farming 356, 358, 420
    field 416
    force field 20
    fragments 15
    framework 290
    gardens, culture of 60, 266
    geometry 19
    green 382, 402
    green space **103**, 327, 358, 364,
        408, 410, 420
    grid 19, 183, 186, 194, 196,
        196, 198, **208**, **214**, 222, **222**,
        428, **248**, 254, **254**, **255**, 322,
        416
    grid in the topography **247**

grid transformed into a landscape
    426
grid, geometry of the 210
grid, landscape architecture of the
    252
grid, measurements of the 242
grid, modelling of the 183
ground plan 19
horizon 128
illusion of nature 286
infrastructure **425**
interior 374
landscape 15, 17, 20, 21, 23, 25,
    40, 62, **62**, 66, 98, 106, 118,
    148, 178, 260, 327, 330, 356,
    376, 378, 382, 413, 414, 416,
    418, 420
landscape architecture 17, 23, 62,
    418, 413, 422
landscape architecture, design
    repertoire 430
landscape architecture, design
    strategies 428
landscape architecture, instruments
    of 430
landscape garden 120
landscape system 286
landscape, 19th century 140, 178
landscape, uninterrupted 316
layout 306, 372
mass housing and food production
    356
morphology 86, 94, 248, **250**, 252,
    254, 266, **320**, 327
morphology, local scale of the 426
nature idyll 170, 258
network, formation of an 183
open space, politics of 382
organism 174
panorama 56, **98**, 370
paradise 358
parcellation 19
park 128, 186, 254
park landscape 424
park system **307**, 322
pattern 19, 21, **34**, 52, 66, **72**, **112**,
    118, 120, **152**, 176, 188, **190**,
    236, 244, 248, **251**, **255**, 260,
    262, 286, **296**, 327, **336**, **362**,
    386, 413
pattern as an open matrix 414
pattern of streets 183
pattern, a specific place in the 406
pattern, anchoring of the park
    system in the 290
pattern, coherence of the 120
pattern, geometry of the 408
pattern, integration of the landscape
    into the 116
pictural composition 128
planning and land development
    410, 416
planning parcellation 376
planning structure 410
plantation 426
production landscape 376
promenade 382
recreational landscape 346
regions with satellite cities 418
residence 114
residential form, collective 114
residential landscape 130
route 114, 136
route, scenography of the 136
rural, rural 232

settlement landscape 21
skyline 66, 226, 322
space 86, 94, 128, 212, 308, 350,
    352, 404, 414
space, staging in terms of
    landscape 413
spatial form 260, 352, 410
spatial type 118, 222
stage 413
strolling park 414
structure 36, 152, **211**, 222, 238,
    254, 406
system 17, 20, 21, 324, 428
territory 20
theatre 140, 254
topography 74
topology 420
transformation 25, 86, **86**, 94, 266,
    267, 416
transformation of the landscape
    garden 194
typology 17
vide 226
villa park 126
wall 114, 118, 224
water basin 346
water landscape 226
urbs 17, 116, 118, 408
use zone, intensive 396
utilitarian park 316
vanishing point 88, 92
vantage point 50, 413
vegetable garden 48, 88, 156, 174,
    214, 420
vegetation 214, 254, 286
velabrum 48
Verschönerung 148, 174
Verschönerungsplan 172, **172**, 174
vertical diorama 430
via triumphalis 42, 88, 140
vide 430
view 50, **57**, **58**, 88, **128**, **159**, 160,
    166, 168, **168**, 174, **175**, **179**,
    236, 402
view of the park 128, **352**
viewing platform 404, 418
viewing points 194
views over fields 76
views over the river and the shores of
    the island 426
views, terminating visually 36
Viles Noves 238
villa **30**, 36, **38**, 40, **40**, 56, **62**, 90,
    126, 128, 130, 140, 142, 146,
    158, 162, 168, 174, 194, 330, 338,
    348, 376
villa architecture 25, 50
villa architecture, Roman 158
villa landscape 36, 38
villa rustica 376, 388
villa terrace 413
villa, transformed 413
village 118, 124, 172, **172**, 174, **177**,
    198
village, Dutch 166
village, founded by free Negroes 212
villages, beautified 174
villages, swarm of 232
villeggiatura 36, 38
vineyard 28, 38, 40, 48, 60, 76, 156
vista 56, 88, 90, 92, 156, 170, 318
visual
    axis 78, 90, 156
    cacophony 374
    centre 126

chain 174
confrontation 128
contrast 128
control, brought under 82
element **224**, 254
element in the landscape 170
form 23
instrumentarium 178
integration 54
network **60**, 76, 413
range of the urban domain 62
range, maximising the 82
reach of the axis 92
relation **38**, 52, 140, 128, 224
series 90, 214
spectacle 21
stimulus 56
structure 17, 280, 284, 348
suggestion of nature 194
system, 'carriers' of the 78
unity of the urban and scenic
    panorama 38
viewing apparatus 430
visually strategic points 76
visually strategic sites 38, 116
visual-spatial approach 402
visual-spatial coherence 306
visual-spatial system 178
void 92, 422
volière 30, **46**, 48, 54, 50, 56, **58**,
    80, 168
Volksgarten, 19th century 146, 330,
    350, **390**, **391**
Volkshaus 348
Volkspalast 404, 406
Volkspark **146**, 176, 178, **326**, 327,
    342, 364, 396, 404, 406, 422
Volkspark as a new park type 418
Volkspark, concept of the 406
Volkspark, functional plan in the 350
Volkswiese 396, 342, 344, 404,
    405, 406
Volkswiese as communal space 348
wading pool 404
walk 300
walking 396
walking park 390
walking paths 280
wall 54, 196
wall of the park **201**
wall with arches 254
walls and gates 390
walls of trees 340
wasteland 392
water arcade 158, 160
water axis 19
water basins 78, 82, **83**, 84
water chain 306, 312
water drainage, variations in 384
water features 82, 98, 212, 254, 278,
    279, 280, 284, **307**, 410
water features, shape of the 278
water gates 116
water landscape 82, 164, **294**, **298**,
    313
water level 266, **275**, 308, 310, 346,
    350
water level in the park 278, 308
water management 188, 258, 266,
    278, 290, 310
water management system 19
water niche 404
water park 164
water pattern 286
water playground 344, 348

water reservoir 200
water reservoir, construction of a 202
water series 168, 174
water system **150**, 200, 310, 338
water theatre 162, 164, **164**, 170,
    171, 172, 174, 176, 178
water tower 168, 170, **331**, 340,
    342, 348
water, stagnated 306
watercourses 154, **214**, 264, 266
waterfall 278, 402
watershed 70, 190
waterways 154
waterworks 38, **169**
wild garden 214
wild nature 210, 312, 416
wild paths, crisscross network of 130
wild thickets 52
wild vegetation 204
wilderness 114, 140, 183, 188, 194,
    194, 212, 214, 214, 226, 308, 312,
    316, 350, 292
wilderness, unruly image of the 204
Wildgarten 168
winding forms of a stream 278
winding forms, amplitude of the 278
winter gardens 90
wooded area 342
wooded bank 310
wooded hills 310, 312
wooded landscape 214, **313**
wooded park 168
wooded rim 350
wooded slopes with undergrowth 316
woodland landscape 214
woodland parks 398
woodland ponds 156
woodland reservations 324
woodlands 174, 178, 364, 398
woodlands, extensive 368
woods 90, 98, 100, 128, 156, 158,
    166, 172, 174, 312, 342, 348,
    398, 404
woods and heath **172**
woods and undergrowth 100
woods and water 426
woods complexes 394
woods way 320
woods with radiating paths 78
woods, fields and meadows 396
woods, fringe of 402, 406
woods, walls of the 410
yards with planting 266
zone with parks 364
zone, intervening 348
zoned network of recreational
    landscapes 327
zoned programme 346, 418
zones of suburbanisation 422
zones, pattern of 194
zoning 20, 160, 402
    of building types 140
    of residential buildings 413
    of the English landscape park 316
    of the functional programme of the
        city 374, 420, 426
    of the green structure 396, 420
    of the landscape **195**
    of the landscape garden 194
    of the productive and recreational
        programme 420
    of the programme 130, 162
    of the recreational programme 327
zoo 98, 140, 224, 252, 316, 322

Places

A7 Motorway 240
Aachener Tor 394, 408
Abruzzo, the 32
Accademia degli Arcadi 50
Addington Hills 110
Adirondack Mountains 190, **199**
Admiralty 122, **139**
Africa 294
Agudells 238
Air Street **135**, 136
Alban hills 154
Albano (mountain lake) **31**, 32
Alexandrowka **173**, 174
All Souls Church **134**, **135**, 136, **137**, **141**
Allaley's Farm 124
Allée de la Balustrade 76
Allee, Die 156
Allegheny 198
Al-Mansur 238
Alster (Hamburg) **302**, 324, **333**, 338, **345**, 346, 350
Alster Bank 340, 342
Alt-Moabit 154
Amelisweerd 260
America 294
Amstel **259**, 260, **262**, 264, 266, **275**, 286
Amstelkade **275**
Amstelland 264, 266
Amstelpark **259**
Amstelveenseweg 270, **271**, 272, **273**, 278, **279**, 280, **283**
Amsterdam **259**, **263**, **265**, **267**, **269**, **271**, **279**
Amsterdamse Bos **259**, **275**, 286
Aniene **31**, 32
Anna Vondelstraat 274
Ante-Park 314, 316, 318
Apollo, temple of 42
Appalachian Chain 294
Appalachian Mountains 190, 198, **199**, 294
Aqua Alexandrina 42, **63**
Aqua Claudia **39**, 41, 44
Aqua Felice 38
Aqua Paola 38, **39**, **41**
Aqua Vergine 38
Aquae Mattiacorum 364
Arborway **291**, 320, **321**
Arc de Triomphe **87**, 88, **89**, 90, **91**, 92, **93**, **96**
Arc du Carrousel **87**, 88, **89**, **91**, **93**
Arch of Septimius Severus **45**, **48**, **51**, 52, **55**
Arch of Titus 42, **45**, **51**, 52, **53**, 54, **55**, 56
Ardennes 70
Arno 80, 140
Arnold Arboretum **291**, 292, 312, 314, **315**, **317**, 320, **321**, 322, 324
Artis **259**, 270
Ashridge 128
Ashville Road 194, **195**
Athens 15, **16**
Atlantic Ocean 294
Auguratorium 42
Aula Isiaca 44
Aurelian wall 32, **33**, 36, **37**, 38, 39, **41**, **63**
Aussenalster **333**, 338, **341**
Aventine Hill 32, **33**
Avenue de l'Impératrice 96, 320
Avenue de l'Octogone 78
Avenue Foch 96
Avenue, 3rd 202
Avenue, 5th **189**, 202, 210, 212, 216, **226**, **229**
Avenue, 6th **206-207**
Avenue, 7th **206-207**

Avenue, 8th 202, 210, **211**, 212, 426, **429**
Avenue,10th 198
Avinguda del Parallel **233**, 240, 244, 246, **247**
Avinguda Diagonal **233**, 240, 244, **247**
Avinguda Meridiana **233**, 240, 244, 246, **247**, 248, **251**
Avon 114
Babelsberg **147**, 164, **165**, 168, **169**, 170, **171**, **173**, **177**, **181**
Back Bay 298, **299**, 300, 304, **308**, **309**, 310, 312, 318, 320
Back Bay Fens **291**, 292, **294**, 306, 308, **309**, 310, **317**, 320, **321**, 322, 324
Back Bay Park 290, 308, 310, 322
Badalona 246, **246**, **247**
Bagnaia 28
Baltic Sea 150, 334, 338
Baltimore 200
Bankside 118
Barcelona **233**, **235**, **237**, **241**, **243**, **247**, 416
Barcelona (old city) **239**
Barcelona-Granolles, railway 248
Barcelona-Martorell, railway 248
Barcino (Barcelona) 238
Barmbek 338
Barnes 110
Barnim plateau 152
Baruther palaeovalley 150, 152
Basel 360
Basilica of Maxentius 38, **43**, **45**, 50, **51**, 52, 54, **55**, 56, **57**
Basilica of St. Peter 36, **39**, **41**, 42
Bassin de la Villette 418
Bastione Farnesiano 48, **53**
Bath **112**, 114, **115**, 118, 120, 122, 124, 126, 128, 136
Bay of Biscay 232
Bayenthal 392, 400
Beacon Entrance **309**
Beacon Hill 298, **299**
Beacon Street **291**, 308
Belgium 420
Belle-Alliance-Platz **155**, **181**
Belmermeer 264
Belvedere Castle **206-207**, 214, **218**, **225**
Benjamin Bussey Farm 314
Berkersheim 364, **365**
Berkshires 294
Berlagebrug 286
Berlin **147**, **151**, **153**, **155**, 150, **151**, **176**, **181**, 338, **414**
Berlin palaeovalley 150, 152
Berlin-Cölln 154
Besòs 232, **233**, 234, 238, 242, 246, **247**
Bethesda Terrace 216
Biegwald 368
Bijlmermeer 264
Bille 338
Binnenalster 338, **341**
Binnen-Amstel 266
Binnendijkse Buitenveldertse polder 258, 264, 270
Birkenhead 413
Birkenhead Park (Liverpool) 140, 188, 194, **195**, 212, 222
Birmingham 130
Black Forest 360
Bloomendale 198
Bloomendale Road 198
Bloomsbury Square **117**, 118
Blücherpark **383**, **396**, 398, **399**, 404, **404**, **405**, 410
Blue Hills 316, 324
Blue Hills State Park **291**

Bockenheim 370
Bogardus Hill 212
Bois de Boulogne 96, **103**, **69**, 90, 96, 320
Bois de Vincennes **69**, 90, 98, **103**
Bonames 362, **365**, 368
Bordeta 246, **246**, **247**, **249**
Bornim **155**, **173**, 174, **181**
Bornstedt **173**, 174, **177**, **181**
Bornstedt lake 174
Borsig 174
Boschlust **271**, **273**
Bosco Parrasio 50
Boston 200, **291**, **297**
Boston (ca. 1835) **295**
Boston (water landscape, 1777) **298**
Boston Common **288-289**, **291**, 292, 298, **299**, 300, 304, 310, **317**, 320, **321**
Boston Fens **306**
Boston Neck 292, 298, 300
Boston Park System **288-289**, 290, 292, **297**, **301**, **321**, 312, 314, 322, 410, 416
Boston Parkway **321**
Boston Southend 304, 318
Botanical Garden 126
Botanischer Garten **383**, **396**
Boulevard de Courcelles 96
Boulevard Périphérique 90, 98, 418
Bow Bridge 216
Bramham 114
Brandenburger Tor **155**, **156**
Brandenburger Vorstadt 158
Brentano Park 368, **370**, **371**
Brentanobad 368
Breslau 364, **366**
Brighton 114, 302, 320, 322
Brittany 70
Broadway 190, 196, 198, 200, 210, **211**, 212, 428, **429**
Broekermeer 264
Brookline 290, 302, 306, 310
Brookline Town Brook 310
Buckingham House 130, 138
Buckingham Palace **106**, **109**, **117**, 120, 122, **123**, 138, **139**, **141**, **143**
Buffalo 290, **293**
Buikslotermeer 264
Buitensingel 266, 268
Bunker Hill 318
Bushy Park **107**, 116
Bussey Farm 314
Bussey Hill 314
Butte de Chaillot 82, **87**, 88, 90, 92, 94
Cabin of Romulus 36, **51**, 42, 60
Cacine 80
Cadogan Square 118
Caelian Hill 32, **32**
Caldas de Besaya 232
California 414
Cambridge, Massachusetts 298, 324
Camp de l'Arpa 248
Campagna Romana 32, 36
Campo Vaccino 28, **29**, 42, **47**, 48, 50, **51**, **51**, 52, 54, 56, **57**
Cancelleria 36
Cape Cod 190, **206**, 294
Capitol Hill 32, **32**, 38, 42, 52, 54, 56
Caputh 156, **173**, 174, **177**
Carlton House **109**, 116, 130, 134, **134**, **135**, 136, **136**, 138, **139**
Carmel 234, 252
Carrer Ample 232
Carrer Ciutat 246
Carrer de la Muntanya 248, **251**
Carrer de Ribes 248, **251**
Carrer de Rogent 234, **251**
Carrer de Sans 246, **247**
Carrer del Bisbe 246, 248, **250**, **251**

Carrer Marià Aguiló 248
Carrer Pere IV 248
Carrer Santa Anna 238
Carthago Nova (Cartagena) 238
Case Study House #22 416, **417**, 418
Caserta (castle park) 146
Casino del Belvedere 48, 50
Castle Island **291**, 318
Catalunya 240
Caton Hall 146
Cavendish Square 124, **134**
Ceintuurbaan 274, 276, **277**
Centelles (Catalonia) 232
Central Park (New York) 184-229, **184-185**, **187**, **189**, **197**, **203**, **205**, **206-207**, **208**, **209**, **210**, **211**, **213**, **215**, **217**, **219**, **221**, **223**, **225**, **227**, **228**, **229**, 290, 292, 302, 322, 416, 426, 428, **429**
Central Uplands of Germany 334
Cermalus 42
Champs de Mars **69**, 90, 98, **103**
Champs Élysées 88, 90, **91**, **93**, 154
Chantilly 382
Charing Cross **109**, 120, 122, **123**, **135**, 138, **139**, 413
Charles River **291**, 294, 298, **298**, **299**, 302, **302**, 304, 306, **307**, 308, 324
Charles River Dam 322
Charles Street 300
Charlesbank 318
Charlestown 298, 302
Charlestown Heights 318
Charlottenburg 154, 156
Charlottenburger Chaussee 156, **181**
Charlottenhof 146, 148, 156, **157**, **159**, 158, 162, **162**, **173**, 178
Château de Fontainebleau 66
Château de Richelieu 66
Château du Val 76
Château-Neuf 76
Chatou 90
Chelsea Beach 304
Chester 116
Chestnut Hill Circuit 322
Chestnut Hill Reservoir **291**, 304, **319**, 320, 322
Chicago 290
Chiltern Hills 110
Chiswick 110
Chorweiler See **392**
Circus Maximus 36, **37**, 42, **43**, 50, 52, **55**, **63**
Citadel 238
Ciudad Vella 238
Ciutadella 252
Clagny **69**, **75**, **77**, 78, **101**
Claughton-cum-Grange 194, **195**
Cliff, The **206-207**, 214, **229**
Clifton 114
Clivius Palatinum 42, 52, **53**, **55**
Clivius Victoriae 44, 48, 52, 54, **55**
Cöllner Schloss 154
Collserola mountains 238, **247**, 252
Cologne 382, **383**, 384, **385**, 388, **389**, 402, 408, 410
Colosseum 36, **37**, 38, **39**, **41**, **43**, **45**, **46**, **52**, **55**, 56, **63**, 174
Columbia Road **291**, **321**
Columbus Circle 210, 212, 428
Columbus Park **291**
Commodity Exchange 260
Commonwealth Avenue **291**, 300, 306, **317**, 320, **321**
Commonwealth Avenue Mall **291**
Condotta dell'Acqua Felice 42
Coney Island Beach 226
Connecticut 294
Connecticut River Valley 294

Constantijn Huygensstraat 274, 276, **277**, **279**
Constantinopel 36
Copp's Hill 298
Cordes Allee 340
Corsham Court (Wiltshire) 108
Cotswold Hills 110
County Fire Office **135**, 136, **137**
Cours de Vincennes 78
Cours-la-Reine **79**, 82, **83**
Covent Garden 114, 118
Covent Garden Piazza 118
Crescent **130**, **135**, **141**, **141**
Crescent (Bath) **115**
Croton Aqueduct **199**, 202
Croton Reservoir **199**, 210, 224
Croton River 200
Cryptoporticus of Nero 48, 50, **52**, **53**
Cumberland Terrace 128, **130**, **133**, **135**, **141**
Cutler Park **291**
Dahlem 178
Dahme **151**, 152
Dantzig 168
De Hereeniging 270, **271**, **273**, 274, **277**
Dechsteiner Weiher 398, **380-381**, **392**, **399**, **408**, **409**, 410
De-Noel-Platz **396**, 400, **401**
Dessau (Gartenreich) 148, **149**, 164, 178
Dianasee 178
Diemermeer 268
Dijon 70
Dogger Bank 360, 384
Domus Augustana 42, **51**
Domus Aurea 42, 44, **63**
Domus Flavia 36, 44, 50, **51**
Domus Livia 42, **51**
Domus Palatium 44
Domus Tiberiana 36, 42, **43**, 44, 48, 50, **51**, 52, 54, **55**
Domus Transitoria 42, 44
Dorchester 302, 306
Dorchester Point 318
Dorchesterway 320
Dortmund 422
Doublet Hill Conservation Area **291**
Dover 116
Downtown Manhattan 186, 224
Dublin 114
Duisburg 422
Dutch Low Lands 262
East Boston Harbor 318
East End 116
East River 190, 198, 200, 202, 212, 226
Eastern Docks 124
Eberswalder palaeovalley 152
Eckenheim 364, **365**
Edgware Road **109**, **123**, **125**, **134**
Edinburgh 114
Ehrenthal 392
Eifel 384
Eifelplatz **391**
Eimsbüttel **333**, 338
Eixample (Barcelona) 230-255, **230/231**, **241**, **243**
El Cagalell 234, 238
El Camp de l'Arpa del Clot 234, 248, **249**, **250**
El Clot 234, 238, **243**, 246, **246**, **247**, 248, **249**, **250**, **251**, 254
El Pueblo de Nuestra Señora la Reina de los Ángeles del Río de Porciúncula 414, 416
Elbe 148, **151**, 330, **333**, 334, 338
Ellicottdale 316
Emerald Necklace (Boston) 288-325, **317**, **323**
Emscher 420, 424

Emscher Landschaftspark **421**, **423**, 424
England 196, 200, 298, 344
English Midlands 420
Erie Canal 198, **199**, 200
Erie Lake 198, 290
Ermenonville 260
Eschenheimer city gate (Frankfurt) 170
Eschersheim 362, 364, **365**, 370
Esquiline Hill 32, **32**, 42
Essen 422
Étang de Chalais 100
Étang de Clagny 78
Europe 200, 226, 294, 416
Everett River **291**
Eyerhoven 270
Fenway 320, **321**
Fermiers Généraux **96**
Filmmuseum **277**, 278, 280, **281**
Finger Lakes 190
Fishers Island 190
Fläming 152
Flats at Nanterre 90
Flats of Montesson 90
Florence 140
Flurstrasse **345**, 346
Foley House **135**, 136
Forest Hill 316
Fort I (Cologne) 388, 392, **392**, **393**
Fort Independence 318, **291**
Fort IV (Cologne) 390
Fort X (Cologne) 392, **392**, **393**, 394, **395**, 408
Fort XI (Cologne) 388
Forum Romanum 28, **29**, **31**, 36, 38, 42, 50, 52, **58**, **63**
France 21, 238
Frankfurt **357**, **363**, **365**, **366**, **367**, **368**, 370, 418
Frankfurt (ca. 1650) **361**
Franklin Park **291**, 292, **296**, 304, 312, 314, **315**, 316, **317**, 318, 320, **321**, 322, 324
Frascati **31**, 32, 36, **34**, 38
Friedrichshain **147**, 176
Friedrichstadt 154
Friedrichstrasse 154
Fuhlsbüttel 330, 350, **351**
Fuhlsbütteler Strasse 340
Full Basin 300, 306
Gaasp 286
Gadez (Cádiz) 238
Gallia 50
Gartenreich 414
Gartenreich at Potsdam-Berlin 410
Gartenreich of Potsdam 144-101, **173**, **177**
Gärtnerhaus (Charlottenhof) 158, 160, **159**, **161**, 162, **163**, **165**, **171**
Gay Street 114
Gerard Brandstraat 274
German Central Uplands 150
Germany 388, 420
Gerunda (Girona) 238
Ginnheim **365**, 370
Glienicke 164, 168, **169**, 170, **173**, 174, **177**
Glienicker Brücke **165**, 168, **171**
Glienicker island 172
Gloucester Gate **130**, **133**, **135**
Goldbeck Canal **345**, 346
Gooi, het 266
Gràcia 240, **243**, 246, **246**, **247**, 248, **249**, 252
Gran Via 240, 242, 246, **247**
Gran Via de les Corts Catalanes **233**, 248
Grand Army Plaza **187**, **189**, 212
Grand Cours 78, 82, 84, 86, 88
Grand Junction Canal 124, 126, **127**, 130
Grand Union Canal 130
Grande Arche **67**, **92**, 92, **93**
Granolles 238

Great Hill **206-207**, 214, 216, **225**, **229**
Great Lakes 416
Great Mall 316
Great Wall of China 212
Greater Berlin 358, **359**
Greater Londen 110, 413, 414
Greater London (1927) **106**
Green Belt 413, 414
Green Lane **125**, 126, **134**
Green Mountains (Vermont) 294
Green Park **107**, 116, 138, **139**, 146
Greenwich Park 116
Grosse Neugierde **165**, 168
Grosse See **331**, **336**, **338**, 346, **347**, **349**
Grosvenor Square 114, 118, **134**
Grunewald 154, **155**, 156, 172, 178, **181**
Grüngürtel (Cologne) 380-410, **380-381**, **383**, **392**, **393**, **396**, **399**, **409**, **411**
Guinguette 126, **127**, **129**, 130, 130, **135**, 136, **141**
Haagsche Bosch 280
Haarlem 258, 260, 270
Haarlemmerhout 280
Haarlemmermeer **275**, 286
Haarlemmermeerpolder 264
Halensee 178
Hambach **384**
Hamburg 330, **333**, **335**, **337**, **339**, 338, 348, 350, **353**, 404
Hamburg (harbour) **334**, 338
Hamburger Stadtpark 410
Hamilton Square 194
Hammaburg (castle) 338
Hammerbrook 338
Hampstead **109**, 110, 124, **124**, 128, **129**, **133**, **141**
Hampton Court 110, 116, **117**
Harbor Hill 190
Harlem 198
Harlem Flat 198
Harlem Lake 212
Harlem Pond 214
Harrow 110, 124, 128
Hartford (Connecticut) 186
Harvestehude 338
Hausen 364, **365**, 370, **371**
Havel 148, **151**, 152, 154, 156, 158, 164, 166, 168, 170, 172, **173**, 174, 178
Havel landscape 146, 154, 156, 162, 172
Havelkanal **151**
Haymarket 120, 122, **123**, 130, **139**
Heddernheim 364, **365**, 368, 370, 372
Heilandskirche **165**, 170, **170**, **171**
Heilige See 164, **165**, 166, **171**, **175**
Hellweg 422
Hemlock Hill 314
Highgate 110, **117**, 124, **124**, 128
Highgate Archway Bridge 108
Highgate Wood 116
Hills of Viterbo 32
Hindenburgpark **383**, 392, **392**, **393**, **395**
Höchst 368
Hohenfelde 338
Hoheward (Halde) **423**
Holland 19, 264
Holland Park 116
Hollands(ch)e Manege 280, **283**
Hollywood Hills 418
Holm Lea 312
Honfleur 70
Hoosics 294
Horrea Margaritaria 54
Horse Guards 122, **139**, **141**
Horti Farnesiani 26-63, **26-27**, 28, **29**, **39**, **45**, **48**, **49**, **51**, **55**, **58**, **59**, **60**, **61**, **63**, 140, 142, 413
Hortus Botanicus **259**, 270
Housatonic valley 294

House of the Griffins 44, **51**
Houses of Parliament 122, **139**, **141**
Hudson 424, 426
Hudson Bay 190
Hudson River 190, 196, 198, **199**, 200, 210, 212, 226
Hudson River Valley 190, 226
Hudson Shelf Valley 190
Hudson Valley 190, 202
Hufeisensiedlung 178
Huis ten Bosch 260
Hundekehlesee 178
Hyde Park 98, **107**, 116, **123**, 138, **139**, **143**, 146
Icaria 234, **243**, 246, **246**, **247**, 248, **249**
IJ, the **259**, 264, 266, **275**, 286
Île de la Cité 74
Île St Louis 74
Inner Green Belt **383**
Isola Bella 146
Jamaica Plain 312
Jamaica Pond **288-289**, **291**, 292, 304, 306, 310, 312, **312**, **313**, 314, **317**, 320, **321**, 322
Jamaica Way 320, **321**
Jan Pieter Heijestraat 273
Janiculum 50
Jardin des Plantes 146
Jardin des Tuileries 64-103, **69**, **75**, **77**, **79**, **80**, **83**, **85**, **87**, **89**, **101**, 140, 413
Jerusalem 388
Jew's Harp, The 118, 124, **124**, **125**, **129**, 134
Jones Beach 224
Jones Wood Estate **197**, 202
Jordaan 266, 270
Jungfernheide 156
Jungfernsee 164, **165**, 168, **169**, 170, **171**
Kahlenberg **173**, **175**, **177**, **181**
Karlsberg 148
Katharinenholz **173**, 174
Katowice 420
Kattenlaan 270, 272, **272**, **273**, 274, **283**
Kendall's Farm 124, **125**, **129**
Kennemerpoort 260
Kensington Gardens **107**, 116
Kensington Palace **117**, 138
Kensington Park 146
Kew 110
Kew Botanical Gardens 116
King's Circus 114, **115**
Kingsbridge 198
Klettenberg **389**, 402
Klettenbergpark **383**, **396**, 402, **403**, 408
Kolonial-Park **378**
Königssee 178
Koninginneweg 272, **273**, **275**, **283**
Koningslaan **283**
Köpenicker Feld 176, **181**
Kostverloren Vaart 260, 264, **271**, **279**
Kostverlorenkade **262**, **273**, **275**, 278
Kruitwetering 270, **271**, 272, **273**, **279**
Kurfürstendamm 178
La Défense **67**, 90, **91**, 92, 94
La Llacuna 234, 238, 248, **249**
Lago di Bracciano 32
Lago di Vico 32
Lago Maggiore 146
Lake, The **201**, 214, 216, **225**
Landschaftspark Duisburg-Nord 424
Landwehrkanal **151**, 176, **181**
Langres Plateau 70
Latium 36
Laurentian Shield 190
Le Havre 70
Leidse Poort 274
Leidsebosje 270, **271**, 276, **279**
Leidseplein 276
Letchworth 356
Leverett Park **291**
Leverett Pond **307**, 310, 322

Leyderdorperpad **271**, **273**, 274, **279**
Leyerhoven 274
Limes (boundery of the Roman Empire) **357**, 364, **377**, 388
Lincoln's Inn Fields 118
Lindenthal 390, 392
Lippe 422
Liverpool 140, 194, 200
Llobregat 232, **233**, 234, 246, 246
Loire 76
Londinium 116
London **106**, **107**, **111**, **113**, **117**, **121**, 413, 414
London Central Mosque 142
London Green Belt 413, **415**
London-Brabant Massif 70
Long Island 190, 224
Long Wharf 298
Longwood 310
Los Angeles 414, 416, **417**, 418
Los Angeles River 414, 416
Louvre 74, **79**, 80, **81**, 82, **85**, **87**, 88, **89**, 90, 92, 140
Louvre axis **64-65**
Lower Manhattan 200, 210
Lower Park 210, 212, 214
Lower Regent Street 136, **136**
Lower Rhine 384
Lugdunum (today's Lyon) 74
Luisenstädtischen Kanal 176, **181**
Lupercal 36
Lutetia Parisiorum 74
Lyon 21
Maas 262
Mable 66
Madeleine (church) 86, 88
Madrid 232
Magdeburg 148
Magna Mater, temple of 42
Main **357**, 360, 364, **365**, 370
Mall 138, **139**, **141**, **206-207**, 214, **225**
Malta 270
Manderscheider Platz **401**
Manhattan 186, 190, 196, 198, **199**, 200, 202, **203**, 210, **211**, **213**, 224, 226, 426, 428, 430
Manhattan Bridge 226
Marine Park **291**, 292, 304, 318, 320, 322
Marine Pond **319**
Marly **69**, **72**, **75**, **77**, 78, **101**, **102**, 156
Marmorpalais **165**, **166**, **171**
Marne 70
Marylebone **109**, 125
Marylebone Church 126, **125**, **129**, 130
Marylebone High Street 126, **129**, **134**
Marylebone Park 106, 108, 116, 118, 120, 122, **122**, 124, **124**, 125, **125**, 126, **129**
Marylebone Pleasure Gardens 118, **125**
Marylebone Road **134**
Massachusetts 294
Massif Central 70
Mayfair 106, 118, **118**, 120, 124, **125**, 130, **134**, **134**, 138
Mediterranean Sea 234, 360, 384
Megara 15, **16**
Melun 70
Mersey 194, **195**
Meta Sudans 52, **55**
Metropolitan Boston 302, 304
Metropolitan Museum of Art 216, **225**, **226**
Metropolitan Park System **291**, 324, **325**
Meudon **69**, **75**, 76, **77**, 78, **97**, 98, **98**, 100, **101**
Middle Road 210
Middle West 198, 200
Middlesex Fells 324
Middlesex Fells Reservation **291**
Midtown Manhattan 424
Milan 388

Militärringstrasse 392, **392**
Mill Dam 298, **299**, 300, 306, 310
Mill Pond 298, 300
Mill Pond Reservation **291**
Milton 316
Mississippi 416
Mohawk 190
Mohawk River 190
Mons Caelius 44
Mons Taber 238
Montaña Pelada 252
Montayne's Rivulet 212, 214
Monte Janiculum 32
Monte Mario 32
Monte Palatino 32, **47**
Monte S. Egidio 32
Monterols 234
Montjuich 234, 238, **240**, 242, 246, **247**, 252
Montmartre 70
Moorfields 118, **119**
Morningside Park **187**, **213**, 226
Mount Greylock 294
Mount Morris 210
Mount St. Vincent 212
Muddy River **291**, 298, **298**, 300, 306, **307**, 308, 310, **310**, **311**, 317, 320, **321**
Muddy River Gate House 310
Muddy River Improvement **291**, 292, 310, **311**, 322
Mühlheim 422
Mulde 148
Mystic Lakes **291**
Mystic River **291**, 294, 318, 324
Nabij Buiten 274
Naples 50
National Gallery **135**, 138, **139**, **141**
Naturpark Rheinland **411**
Neck 298, 304
Nedlitzer Holz **173**, 174
Neponset River **291**, 294, 324
Netherlands, The 19, 196, 420
Neue Garten **147**, 148, **155**, 164, **165**, 166, **166**, 168, **169**, 170, **171**, **173**, 174, **175**, **177**, **181**
Neue Palais 156, 158, **159**, 160, **173**, 174, **177**, **181**
Neustadt **388**, 390, 392
New Amsterdam 186, 196
New Bedford 294
New England 190, 196, 294
New Haven 186
New Jersey 226
New Netherland 196
New Reservoir 210, 212, 216
New Road **123**, **124**, **125**, **129**, **134**, **135**
New Street 108, 120, 122, **123**, 134, 136, 138
New York 21, **193**, **199**, 430
New York (1811) **191**
New York (state) 294
New York and Erie Rail Road 200
New York and New England Railway 314
New York Upper Bay 196
Newburyport-Gloucester 294
Newton Lower Falls Park **291**
Nida 372
Nidda **357**, 360, **360**, 362, 364, 368, **371**, 372, **375**, 376, 420
Nidda Valley (Frankfurt) 354-379, **354-355**, **362**, **363**, **367**, **369**, **373**, **374**, **375**, **377**, **379**
Nied 368
Nieuw Leyerhoven 274, **277**
Nieuwe Park 270
Nieuwendijk 275
Nieuwer Amstel 270, **271**, 274, **275**, **279**
Nikolai Church **341**
Nikolskoe 164, **165**, 170, **171**, **173**, **177**, **181**
Nippes **389**, 392, 404
Norfolk 200

Normandy 70
North End 298, 318
North End Park 318
North German Plain 150, 334
North Sea 70, 110, 150, 266, 334, 338, 360, 384
North Sea basin 150
Nôtre-Dame 74
Nuthe **151**
Nuthe palaeovalley 150
Nuthe-Havel 152
Ocean Parkway **187**, 226
Ocean Parkway, Brooklyn, NY **319**
Ohlsdorf 330, **333**, 340, **340**
Oise 70
Olmsted Park **291**
Onkel Toms Hütte 178
Oosterpark 268
Opernplatz **181**
Oppidum Ubiorum 388
Ostia 32
Ostpark **291**
Otto-Suhr-Allee 156
Overtoom **271**, **273**, 274, 278, **279**, 280, **283**
Overtoomse Vaart 264
Oxford Circus 134, **134**, **135**, **141**, **143**
Oxford High Street 134
Oxford Street **109**, **123**, 124, **134**, **135**
Oxton 194, **195**
P.C. Hooftstraat **260**, 270, **271**, **273**, 276, **276**, **277**, **283**
Pacific Ocean 414
Palace Gardens 138, **139**
Palace of Nero 60
Palace of Tiberius 50, 60
Palais des Tuileries 80, 84, **87**, 88
Palais du Luxembourg 76
Palatine Hill 28, 32, **32**, 36, 38, 42, **43**, 44, **44**, 50, 54, 56, 60
Palazzo dei Conservatori 42
Palazzo Farnese 28, 36
Palazzo Nuovo 42
Palazzo Pitti 76
Palazzo Senatorio 56
Palazzo Venezia 36
Paleis van Volksvlijt 270
Pallante 36
Palomar 238
Parc de la Villette 418, **419**
Parc de Monceau **69**, 90, 96, **103**
Parc des Buttes Chaumont **69**, **94**, **95**, 96, **103**
Parc Montsouris **69**, 96, **103**
Paris 64-103, **64-65**, **71**, **73**, **75**, **95**, **101**, 140, 142, 232, 413, 418
Paris Basin 70
Park Crescent **134**, 142, **142**
Park Road 128, 130, 142
Parker Hill 306, 310
Parliament Hill 110, **117**
Parque de Montjuich **233**
Parque del Clot **233**, **244**, 248, **252**, **253**, 254, **254**, **255**
Parque Güell **233**, **236**, 252
Parque Joan Miró **233**, 254
Passeig de Sant Joan 240, 242, 246
Pearl Street 200
Peira 234
Pennsylvania Station 424, 426
Peters' Hill 314
Petrihäuschen 368
Pfaueninsel **144**, **147**, 148, **155**, 164, **165**, 166, **167**, 168, **168-169**, 170, **171**, **173**, **177**, **179**, **181**
Pfingstberg **173**, 174, **177**, **179**, **181**
Philadelphia 200
Piazza del Campidoglio 42, **55**
Piazza del Gesu 42
Piazza della Signoria 140
Piccadilly **109**, **123**, **134**, **139**
Piccadilly Circus 134, **134**, **135**, 136, **141**, **143**
Pioneer Valley 294
Pirschheide **155**, 158, 172, **173**, 174

Pla de Palau 234
Plaça de les Glòries Catalanes **233**, 240, 244, 246
Place de l'Étoile 88, 90, 96
Place de la Bastille 90
Place de la Concorde 86, **87**, 88, 90
Place de la Nation 90
Place du Trocadero 90
Plantage 268, 270
Platz an der Bismarcksäule **396**, 400, **400-401**, **401**
Plaza Real **239**
Pleasure Bay **291**, 318, **318**
Poble Sec 238
Poland 420
Pond Street 312, **312**
Pont de Neuilly 88, 90
Pont Neuf 70
Porticus Margaritaria 44
Portland Place 122, 134, **134**, **135**, 136, **141**
Portland Road **125**, 134
Portland Street 134, **134**
Potsdam **165**, **171**, **172**, **173**, **175**, **177**, **181**, 382
Potsdam (Neustadt) 174
Potsdam, island of 172, 174
Potsdamer palaeovalley 150
Potztupimi 156
Praunheim 364, **365**, 370, **371**, 372, **375**
Prenzlauer Berg 152
Primrose Hill **104-105**, **109**, 110, 116, **117**, 124, **126**, 128, **133**, 136, **141**, **143**
Prospect Hill Park **291**
Prospect Park 226, **187**
Providence Line 314
Prussia 388
Pulvermühlengelände 176, **181**
Putxet 234, **249**
Quadrant **108**, **134**, **135**, 136, **137**, **141**, **143**
Quartier de Marais 74
Queen Square 114
Quirinal Hill 32, **32**, 42, 56
Rambla 234, 238, 240
Rambla de Raval 234
Ramble **206-207**, 214, 216, **225**, **229**
Raval 238, **239**
Rebstockerwald 368
Receiving Basin 300, 306
Refectory Hill 316
Regent Street 106, 106, 108, **134**, **135**, 136, 138, **141**
Regent's Canal **127**, 128, 130, **131**, 142
Regent's Circus **135**, 136, 142
Regent's Park (Londen) 104-143, **104-107**, **110**, **117**, **123**, **143**, 146, 160, 188, 194, 212, 222, 413
Regionalpark Rhein-Main 378
Reserve Beach 324
Reservoir, The **135**, **141**, **206-207**, **211**, 225
Rhenish Slate Mountains 360
Rhine 262, 360, **383**, 384, **387**, 388, **389**, **399**, 400, **408**, **411**, 422
Rhine valley 384, 408, **411**
Rhodes Farm 124
Rhône 360, 384
Richelieu (ideal city) 66, **67**
Richmond 110
Richmond Park **107**, 116
Richmond Terrace **117**
Riera de Magòria 234
Ringstrasse 390, **391**
Riverside Park 226, **213**
Riverway **291**, 320, **321**
Rödelheim 362, 364, **365**, 368
Roemer Visscherstraat 274, 277, **283**
Roma Quadrata 36, 54
Rome 26-63, **63**, 66, **31**, **33**, **34**, **35**, **37**, **39**, 116, 140, 142, 238, 388, 413
Rome, ancient 174

Romeinse Campagna 38
Römerpark 390, **392**
Römerstadt 370, **371**, 372, **372**, **375**, 378, **378**, **379**
Römische Bäder 158, 160, **161**, 162, **163**
Ronde Venen 264
Rondehoep 264
Rond-Point de la Défense 90
Ronkonkoma 190
Rotherbaum 338
Rouen 70
Rousseau-Insel (Wörlitz) 348
Rovira 234
Roxbury 302, 306, 310
Royal Academy 138, **135**
Royal Crescent **112**, 114, **115**, 128, 136
Royal Crescent (Bath) 194
Royal Mews 122
Rozenhagen (nursery) 260, 270
Rue de Rivoli 88, 90
Ruhr 422
Ruhr region 420
Ruhr rift 360
Ruinenberg **155**, **173**, 174, **175**, **177**, **181**
Russel Square 118
Russia 358
Saba 196
Sabine hills 32
Sacrow **147**, 164, **165**, 168, **169**, 170, **170**, **171**, **173**, 174, **177**
Sacrow (park) **181**
Sacrower Heide **173**, 174
Saguntum (Sagunto) 238
Saint-Cloud **69**, 76, **77**
Saint-Germain-en-Laye **69**, **75**, 76, **77**, 78, 90, **101**
Salem 294
San Andreu **243**, 246, **246**, **247**, 248, **249**
San Martin de Provencals 248, **249**
Sans **243**, 246, **246**, **247**, **249**
Sanssouci 146, **147**, 148, 154, **155**, 156, **157**, 158, **171**, 172, **173**, 174, **175**, 176, **177**, 178, **181**
Santander 232
Santiago de Compostela 388
Sargent's Field 316
Sarphatipark **259**, 268
Sarrià 238, **243**, 246, **246**, **247**, **249**
Scalae Caci 42, **51**
Scarboro Pond 322
Sceaux **69**, **75**, **77**, 78, **101**
Schafgraben 158
Schapenburgerpad 270, **271**, **273**, **277**, **279**
Schinkel 264
Schleswich-Holstein 338
Schloss **165**, **173**, **177**, **181**
Schloss Babelsberg 168, **171**
Schloss Caputh **155**
Schloss Charlottenburg 156, **181**
Schloss Charlottenhof 158, **159**, 160, 162
Schloss Glienicke **155**, 168, **171**
Schloss Niederschönhausen **147**, **155**, 156, **181**
Schloss Pfaueninsel **167**, **171**
Schloss Sacrow **155**, **171**
Schloss Sanssouci **173**, 174
Schmargendorf 178
Sea Wall 238
Seine 70, 74, **75**, 76, 78, 80, **81**, 82, 84, 88, 90
Seine landscape 140
Seine terrace 82
Seine valley **72**, 76, 78, 84, 94, 100
Seneca Village 212
Septimius Severus, arch of 42
Septimontium 32, 36
Septizodium 44
Serra de Collserola 234
Sforzinda 17, **18**, 19, 226
Shawmut Peninsula 294, 298

Siam 162
Siemensstadt 156, 178
Simonov monastery **326**
Singel 260
Singelgracht 270, 272, 274, 278, 286
Sloane Square 118
Sloten **271**, **279**
Sloterdijk 286
Sloterpark **259**, 286
Soestdijk Palace 260
Soho 118, 124, 128, 134
Soho Square 118
Sonnenhof 358
Sophialaan 278
Sound 212
South Boston 320
South End 300
South Huntingdon Avenue 322
South Villa 126, **129**
Southend-on-Sea 110
Southwark 116, 118
Spandau 152, 154, 156, 178, **181**
Spree **151**, 152, 154, 156, 176, **181**
Squantum 304
SS. Venanzio e Ansovino 42
St Francesca Romana (monastery) 42
St Maria Nova (monastery) 42
St. Cloud (Paris) 342
St. Eustatius 196
St. Georg, suburb **333**, 338
St. James's Hospital. 138
St. James's Palace **109**, **139**
St. James's Park 106, **106**, **107**, 116, 122, **123**, 134, **136**, 138, **139**, **141**, **143**, 146
St. James's Square 118
St. Martin's Church of St. Martin in the Fields **109**, **135**, 138
St. Mary-on-the-Bourne **125**
St. Paul's Cathedral 106, **106**, **109**, 116, **117**, 122, 138, **141**
St. Pauli, suburb **333**, 338
Stadhouderskade 278, 280, **283**
Stadtcafé 348, **349**
Stadtgarten **383**, 390, **392**
Stadthalle 346, **347**, 348, **349**, **352**
Stadtpark Hamburg 328-353, **328-329**, **338**, **341**, **343**, 376, 418
Stadtschloss of Potsdam 156
Stadtwald **383**, **386**, 394, 398, **399**
Stammheim **389**
Staten Island 186
Steglitz 178
Stendal 170
Stony Brook 298, **298**, 300, 306, **307**, 308, 324
Stony Brook Reservation **291**, 324
Stowe 126, 136, 146
Strand **109**, **123**, **135**, 138, **139**
Strandway 320, **321**
Strasse den 17. Juni **156**
Street Transverse 72nd 212
Street, 106th 202, 204, 210, 214
Street, 110th 204, **206-207**, 210, **214**
Street, 23rd 196, 200
Street, 38th 202
Street, 42nd 200
Street, 59th 202, **206-207**, 216, 212, 428, **429**
Street, 66th 202, 216
Street, 72nd 216
Street, 75th 202
Street, 79th 216
Street, 82nd 212
Street, 84th 216
Street, 97th 216
Sunset Boulevard 416, **417**
Surinam 196
Swallow Street 134, **134**
Taconic Mountains 190, 294
Tarraco (Tarragona) 238
Taunus Mountains 360, 362, 364, 384
Teddington 110
Tegel 156
Teltow plateau 152
Teltowkanal **151**, 178

Templiner See 174
Terrace 214
Tesselschadestraat 274, **277**
Thames **106**, **109**, 110, 116, **117**, 118, **123**, **135**, 136, 138, **139**, **141**, **143**
Thames Barrier 110
Thames terrace 124
Thames valley **106**, 110, 116, **143**
The Serpentine 98
Tibaldo 234
Tiber **31**, 32, **32**, 36, 38, **61**
Tiber valley 32, 36, 38, 116
Tiefe See **165**, 168, 170, **171**
Tiergarten 146, **147**, 154, **155**, 156, 176, 178, **181**
Tivoli 32, 36, 50, 270, **271**, **273**, 274
Torrent de Bargalló 234
Torrent de Bogatell 234
Torrent de Creu d'en Malla 234
Torretta 48
Tottenham Court **109**, **125**, **129**, **134**
Tottenham Court Road **109**, **123**, **125**, **129**
Touraine 66
Trafalgar Square 138, **143**
Triumphal Arch of Constantine 88
Troyes 70
Tunbridge Wells 114
Tusculum 36
Twickenham 110
Tyburn (river) **109**, 110, 124, 126, **129**
Tyburn (village) **109**, 124
Tyburn Manor House **109**, 118, **125**
Tyrrhenian Sea 32
Uffizi 140
Uhlenhorst 338
Unter den Linden 154, **155**, **156**
Upper Park 210, 210, 214
Upper Regent Street **104-105**, 136, **137**
Upper Rhine Plain 360
Utrecht 258
Valentia (Valencia) 238
Vallès, El 246
Vallès, plain of 234
Valley Heads 190
Van Baerlestraat 276, **277**, 278, **283**
Van Eeghenstraat **272**, **273**, 274, **275**, **283**
Vatican enclave 32, 36
Vauxhall Gardens 118
Vaux-le-Vicomte 66, 346
Vecht 286
Versailles 66, **68**, **69**, **75**, 76, **77**, 78, 84, 94, **101**, 140, 146, 382
Via Appia 36, 44, **63**
Via Augusta 238, 240, 246
Via Aurelia 38, **63**
Via della Polveriera 56
Via di San Bonaventura 44, 52, 54, **60**
Via di San Gregorio 54
Via Flaminia 38, **63**
Via Laietana 234
Via Nova 48, **50**, **51**, 52, 54, **55**
Via Pia 36
Via Sacra 42, **51**, 52, **53**
Victoria, temple of 42
Vila Nova de Mercadal 238
Vila Nova de Sant Cugat 238
Vila Nova del Mar (later Santa Maria del Mar) 238
Viles Noves 238, **239**
Villa Aldobrandini **31**, **34**, 38, **39**, 41, **61**, **63**
Villa Aurelia 38, **41**, **61**
Villa Borghese **31**, 36, **39**, **41**, **63**, 146
Villa Colonna 38, **61**
Villa dei Cavalieri di Malta 38, **61**
Villa Doria Pamphili 36, **63**, 146
Villa Giulia 28, **39**, **41**, **61**, **63**
Villa Hadriana 36, 50
Villa Hügel 422
Villa Lante 28, 38, **61**
Villa Ludovisi 146
Villa Mattei 146

Villa Medici 38, **39**, **41**, **61**, **63**, 146
Villa Montalto 38, 42
Villa Quirinale 38, **61**
Villa Thyssen 422
Viminal Hill 32, **32**, 42
Vista Rock 214, 216, **218**, **225**, **229**
Volksgarten Klosterberge (Magdeburg) 146, 330
Volkspark Raderthal **383**, 396, **396**, **397**, 398, **399**, 406, **406**, **407**, 410
Vondel statue 270, **273**, **277**, 280, **281**, **283**, 286
Vondelbrug 278, **283**
Vondelkade **271**, **271**, **273**, **277**, **279**
Vondelkerk 274, **277**, **279**, **281**, 276
Vondelpark (Amsterdam) 256-287, **256-257**, **259**, **261**, **262**, **268**, **271**,

272, **275**, **276**, **281**, **282**, **285**, 416
Vondelstraat 270, **271**, **272**, **273**, 274, 276, 280, **283**
Vorgebirgspark **383**, **396**, **397**, 398, **399**, 402, **403**, 404, 408
Vosges 70, 360
Vossiusstraat 274, **275**, **277**
Wall Street 196, 200
Walstraat 196
Wannsee 156
Ward's Pond **307**, 310
Warschau-Berliner palaeovalley 150
Washington Square 210
Washington statue, George 300
Washington Street 300
Watergraafsmeer 264, 268, 286
Waterland 264

Waterland Dike Ring 264
Waterloo Place 134, **134**, **135**, 136, **136**, **141**
Weltkulturerbe Zollverein 424
West Drive 216
West End 106, **109**, 116, 414
West Roxbury 314
West Roxbury Park 314
West Roxbury Parkway 324
Westerpark 268
Westhausen 372, **375**
Westminster 110, 116, 118, 120, 128, 136
Westminster Abbey 106, **109**, **139**, **141**
Westminster Bridge **109**, **123**, **139**
White Horse Hills 110

Whitehall **109**, 116, 120, 130, 134, **135**, 138, **139**, **143**
Wiener Ring 390, 394
Wiener Ringstrasse **390**
Wiesbaden 364
Wildpark 382
Wilhelmplatz **173**, **181**
Willemspark 272, **273**, 274, **275**, 278, 280
Willemsparkbuurt 278
Willemsparkweg **273**, **283**
Willian's Farm **125**, 126, **129**,124
Wilmersdorf 178
Winterhude **328-329**, **333**, 338, 342, **343**, **345**
Winterhude-Noord 342
Wisconsin, 294

Woburn Abbey 128
Wood Island Park 318
Woolwich 110
Wörlitz **149**
Wörlitz Gartenlandschaft 148, **149**, 164, 178
Worpswede 358
Wrights park **291**
Yonne 70
York Gate 126, **129**, **130**
York's Column 138
Zaan 286
Zaanland 264
Zandpad 270, 274, **275**, **277**
Zehlendorf 178
Zoologischer Garten **396**
Zuiderzee 266

Persons

Abercrombie, Patrick 414
Adenauer, Konrad 392
Adickes, Franz 364
Adolf III, Count of Schauenburg and
    Holstein 338
Aeneas 36, 42
Agrippa, Marcus Vipsanius 388
Alberdingk Thijm, J.A. 274
Albertus Magnus 388
Alexander VI Borgia, Pope 36
Alfred (the Great), King 116
Allen, Ralph 114
Alphand, Jean-Charles **95**, 96, 98, 136
Amulius, King 36
Anhalt-Dessau, Duke Leopold Friedrich
    Franz von 148
Anne, Queen of Great Britain 114
Argan, Giulio Carlo **23**
Aristoteles 17
Arnold, James 314
Augustus, Emperor 36, 42, 50, 388
Averlino, Antonio di Pietro 17
Barbaro, Daniele 19
Barbarossa, Emperor (*see* Hohen-
    staufen)
Barillet-Deschamps, Jean-Pierre 96, 98
Barth, Erwin 178
Basse, Hofrat F.W. 368
Baumhauer, Albert Gillis von 270
Behrens, Peter 356
Belmont, August 216
Berlage, H.P. 286
Biesen, J.J.W. van den 274
Blaxton, William 298
Boehm, Herbert 364, **366**
Boni, Giacomo 50
Bordino, G.F. **37**
Boudicca, King 116
Bourbons, the 50
Bowditch, Ernest W. 302
Boyceau, Jacques 66
Brentano, family of merchants 368
Bridgeman, Charles 120, 138
Brinckmann, Justus 342
Bromme, Max 364, **368**, **371**
Brown, Capability 120, 122, 126, 138,
    188, 260, 324
Bryant, William Cullen 202
Bufalini, Leonardo 48
Bull, W. 413, **415**
Caligula, Emperor 36, 42
Capetian dynasty 74
Carl, Prince 168
Carmontelle, Louis de 96
Cathérine de Médicis 80
Cerceau, J. Androuet du 80
Cerdà i Sunyer, Ildefons 232, 238,
    241, 242, **243**, 244, 248, **249**, **250**,
    251, 252, **253**, 416
Chalgrin, Jean F.T. 88
Charlemagne 338, 388
Charles II 116, 138, 196
Charles V 80
Charles V, Emperor 42, 238
Charlotte of Prussia 170
Chartres, Duke of 96
Chawner, Thomas 122, 124, **127**
Chemetoff, Alexandre 420
Cleveland, Horace W.S. 302
Clovis, King 74
Colbert, Jean-Baptiste 78
Constantine, Emperor 36
Copeland, Robert Morris 302, **303**, 304
Cordes, Wilhelm 330, 340, **340**, 342
Crespi, Father Juan 414
Cromwell, Oliver 116
Cruyl, Lievin **29**
Cuypers, P.J.H. 270, 274, **277**, 280, **283**
Dance, George 124
Davenport, Charles 302, **302**
Davis, J.P. 306

Dean, Nicholas 202
Delorme, Philibert 80
Descartes, René 66
Dillon, Robert J. 216
Domitianus, Emperor 44
Downing, Andrew Jackson 202, 300
Duca, Giacomo del 28, 48, 54
Durand, Jean-Nicolas-Louis 146,
    148, 160
Eberstadt, Rudolph 358, **359**
Eeghen, Christiaan Pieter van 258, 270
Eisenman, Peter 426, **427**, 428
Eliot, Charles **291**, 322, 324, **325**
Elizabeth I 118
Emerson, George B. 314
Encke, Fritz 342, 382, 392, **393**, 396,
    396, **397**, 398, 400, **401**, 402, 404,
    406, 408, 410
Etruscans 36
Evander, King 36, 42
Eyserbeck, Johann August 164
Falda, G.B. 52
Farnese, Alessandro (°1467; Pope
    Paulus III) 28, 42
Farnese, Alessandro (°1520) 28, 42,
    48, 50
Farnese, Odoardo (°1573) 48
Farnese, Odoardo (°1635) 48
Farnese, Ranuccio (°1530) 28
Farnese, Ranuccio (°1612) 48
Filarete, Antonio 17, **18**, 19, 21
Filipini family, the 50
Fontaine, Pierre F.L. 88, 90
Fontana, Domenico 36
Ford, Henry 358
Fordyce, John 120, 122
Fouquet, Nicolas 66
François I 80
Franklin, Benjamin 314
Frederick II, Elector of Brandenburg 154
Frederick II, King of Prussia (=
    Frederick the Great) 148, 156, 174
Frederick III, Elector of Brandenburg
    (= King Frederick I of Prussia) 154
Frederick William I, Elector of
    Brandenburg 154, 156
Frederick William I, King of Prussia 156
Frederick William II, King of Prussia
    164, 166
Frederick William III, King of Prussia
    158, 168, 170
Frederick William IV, King of Prussia
    158, 170, 172, 174
Freixes, Daniel **252**, 254
French Kings 76
Gabriël, Jacques-Ange 86
Garnier, Tony **20**, 21
Gaudí, Antonio 252
Gendt, A.L. van 280, **283**
George III 138
George IV (= Prince Regent) 106,
    120, 122, 126, 130, 134, 138
Gérardin, René-Louis Marquis de 260
Gessel, Michael van 284
Glenberrie, Lord 122
Godeau, Siméon 156
Goethe, Johann Wolfgang von 148, 162
Gosschalk, Isaac 274, **275**, **277**
Gray, Horace 300
Green, Andrew Haswell 204
Gregory III, Pope 42
Grundel, Herman 304
Güell, Eusebi 252
Hadrianus, Emperor 44
Hall, F.A. van 258
Hamer, W. **277**, 280, **283**
Hardenberg, Fürst 148, 168
Haussmann, Georges-Eugène 88, 90,
    96, 320
Heimans, E. 280, **282**

Henard, Eugène 98
Henri II 80
Henri IV 80
Henry VIII 116, 138
Herder, Johann Gottfried 348
Hirschfeld, Christian Cay Lorenz 160,
    330
Hittorff, Jacques-Ignace 90
Hogarth, William 278
Hohenstaufen, Frederick I Barbarossa
    of 338, 364, 388
Hohenzollerns, the 156
Homan, Arnold 428
Hortensius, hortator 42
Howard, Ebenezer 21, 413, 414
Hudson, Henry 196
Humboldt, Alexander von 148, 162
Humboldt, Wilhelm von 148
James II, King 196
Jaume I, King 238, **239**
Jefferson, Thomas 222, 416
Joachim II, Elector 156
Jones, Inigo 118
Jong, Erik de 284
Jujol i Gibert, Josep Maria 252
Julius Caesar 74
Julius II, Pope 36
Jürgens 342
Kalff, J. 268, 270, **271**, **273**, 274
Kent, William 120, 122, 146
Kieft, Willem 196
Knobelsdorff, Georg Wenzeslaus
    von 156
Koch, Edward 224
Koenig, P. **417**
Kowallek, Adolf 390, **391**
Kramer, Piet 276, **283**
Krupp, family 422
Landmann, Ludwig 364
Läuger, Max 342, **343**
Le Corbusier 21, 90
Lemercier, Jacques 66
Lenné, Peter Joseph 146, **147**, 148,
    158, 164, **167**, 168, 170, 172, **172**,
    173, 174, 176, **176**, 178, **181**, 330,
    382, 414
Leonidov, Ivan **326**
Lescot, Pierre 80
Leverton, Thomas 122, 124, **127**
Lichtwark, Alfred 338, 342, **343**
Ligorio, Pirro 48, 52
Linne, Otto **340**
Livia, wife of Augustus 42
Lobbrecht, Crijn Fredericksz 196
Louis Napoleon 260
Louis XIII 66, 80
Louis XIV 66, 76, 78, 86, 88
Lully, Jean Baptiste 66
Marcus Aurelius 42
Martí I 234
May, Ernst 356, 358, 364, **366**, 372,
    374, 376, 378
Meacham, George F. 300
Meath, Lord **415**
Medici, family De' 76
Médicis, Maria de 76, 80
Menzel, Otto 344
Meyer, Gustav 178
Michaël, Johann Georg 260
Michelangelo 42
Migge, Leberecht 330, 342, 350, **351**,
    352, 356, 358, **359**, 364, **366**, 368,
    372, **372**, 374, 376, 378, 404
Minuit, Peter 196
Miranda, Vicente **252**, 254
Möhring, Bruno 358, **359**
Molière 66
Mollet, Claude 66, 138
Montespan, Mme de 78
More, Thomas 413
Morgan, Jonathan 122

Mos, Egbert 284
Moses, Robert 224, 226
Mould, Jacob Wrey 204
Muthesius, Hermann 342
Napoleon 88
Napoleon III 50, 88, 94, 96, 98
Nash, John 106, 108, 118, 120, 122,
    124, 126, **126**, **127**, 128, 134, 136,
    138, 140, **141**, 194
Nash, Richard 'Beau' 114
Nassau-Siegen, Johann Moritz 156
Nelson, Horatio 138
Nero, Emperor 42
Neve, Felipe de 414
Nicholas I of Russia, Czar 170
Niftrik, J.G. van 268, **269**, 270, 274,
    275, **283**
Nolli, Giovanni Battista 38, **41**, **47**
Normans 74, 116
Nôtre, André le 66, 76, **79**, **80**, **81**, 82,
    83, 84, **84**, 86, 88, 90, 92, 94, 100,
    140, 154, 382
Nôtre, Jean le 66
Nôtre, Pierre le 66
Nussbaum, Theodor 398, 408, **409**, 410
Ochs, Jacob 330, 358
Olmsted Junior, Frederick 290
Olmsted, Frederick Law 21, 186, **187**,
    188, 194, 204, 210, 212, 214,
    216, 222, 224, 226, **291**, **293**, 304,
    306, 308, **309**, 310, **311**, 312, **312**,
    314, **315**, 316, 318, **318**, **319**, 322,
    324, 424
Olmsted, John Charles 290, **309**
Orléans, Duke of 66
Owen, Robert 413
Palma, Giardino della 50
Parisii (Celtic tribe) 74
Paulus III, Pope (= Alessandro
    Farnese) 28, 42
Paulus V, Pope 38
Paxton, Joseph 140, 188, 194, 212, 324
Pepler, George 413, **415**
Percier, Charles 88, 90
Peretti, Felice (= Pope Sixtus VI) 42
Perronet, Jean 88
Persius, Friedrich Ludwig 158, 160, 174
Peruzzi, Baldassare 28
Peterssen, Richard 358, **359**
Philippe Auguste 74, 80
Philippe d'Orléans 76
Phocion, general **16**
Pilat, Ignatz 204, 214
Pliny the Younger 158, 162
Porte, Giacomo della 42
Portland, Duke of 120, 122
Poussin, Nicolas **16**
Prince Regent (= George IV) 106, 120,
    122, 128, 130, 134, 138
Pückler-Muskau, Prince Hermann von
    168, 324
Putman, George Palmer 216
Rainaldi, Carlo 24
Rainaldi, Girolamo 28, 48
Redeker Bisdom, N. 274
Rehorst, Carl 392
Reiser, Jesse **425**, 426
Remus 36, 42
Rennie, Charles 130
Repton, Humphry 108, 118, 122, 128,
    146, 188, 324
Rhea Silvia, daughter of king Numitor
    36
Richelieu, Cardinal-Duc de 66
Romans 116
Romulus 36, 42, 54
Roosevelt, Franklin D. 226
Rovere (Il Terrible), Giuliano della (=
    Pope Julius II) 36
Royer, Louis 270, **277**, **283**
Sachsen-Weimar, Augusta von 168

Sangallo, Antonio da 28
Sargent Codman, Henry 324
Sargent, Charles Sprague 312, 314
Sargent, Ignatius 312
Sarphati, Samuel 270, 274
Scharoun, Hans 178
Schinkel, Karl Friedrich 146, 148, 158,
    160, 162,164, 168, 174, 178
Schumacher, Fritz 330, 332, 338,
    342, 344, 346, 350, 352, **353**,
    392, **393**, 394, **394**, **395**, 396, **397**,
    398, 404, 408, **408**, 410
Sello, Hermann 158
Septimius Severus, Emperor 44
Servien, Abel 78
Sforza, Francesco 17
Shaw, Henry 202
Sinck, Lucas 266
Sixtus IV, Pope 38
Sixtus V, Pope 36, 38, 42
Slade, James 300
Sperber, Ferdinand 342, **343**
Spreckelsen, J.O. 92, **92**, 94
Springer, Leonard 260, **283**
Stevin, Simon **18**, 19, 21
Stooss, A. 396
Stresemann, Gustav 356
Stübben, Josef 390, **391**
Stumpff, J. 270
Stuyvesant, Peter 196
Tacitus 116
Taut, Bruno 178, 356, 358, **359**
Taylor, Frederick Winslow 358
Taylor, Robert 106
Thijsse, Jac. P. 280, **282**
Thouin, André 146
Thouin, Gabriel 146
Tiberius, Emperor 42
Trajanus, Emperor 44
Tschumi, Bernard 418, **419**, 420
Ubii 388
Umemoto, Nanako **425**, 426
Unwin, Raymond 356, 413, **415**
Valadier, Giuseppe 42
Valckenburgh, Jan van 338
Vardy, John 122
Varro, Marcus Terrentius 56
Vau, Louis Le 82
Vaux, Calvert Bowyer 186, 188, 202,
    204, 212, 214, 216, 222
Vergilius 36, 42
Vermehren, Eduard 342, **343**
Viele, Egbert Ludovicus 202
Vignola, Giacomo (or Jacopo) Barozzi
    da 28, 48, 52, 54, 56, 60
Viollet-le-Duc, E. 274
Vitruvius 17, 19
Voigt, Georg 364
Voorhelm Schneevoogt, firm (at Sas-
    senheim) 270
Wagner, Martin 358, 382, **394**
Waring, George 204
Weide, Auke van der 428
White, John 122, 126, **126**
William I, Emperor (son of Frederick
    William III) 168
Witkamp, P.H. 270, **271**
Wood The Elder, John 114, 120, 122
Wood The Younger, John 114, 120,
    122, 128
Wren, Sir Christopher 118
Wright, Frank Lloyd 21, **22**
York, Duke of 196
Zocher Jr., Johan (Jan) David 258,
    260, 270, 280
Zocher Sr., Johann David 258, 260
Zocher, family 258, 260, 278, 280,
    283, 284
Zocher, L.P. 258, 260, 270, 272, **277**,
    280, **280**, **283**
Zola, Emile 21

Sources

Literature and Digital Sources

Acker, M. van, 'Infrastructurele landschappen met een publieke horizon. Vijf projecten van Michel Desvigne Paysagiste', in: *De Architect*, nr 44, June 2008.

Adams, W.H., *The French Garden 1500-1800* (New York 1979).

Alphand, A., *L'Art des Jardins* (Paris, nd).

Alphand, A., Hochereau, E., *Les Promenades de Paris* (Paris 1867-1873).

Argan, G.C., 'Sul concetto di tipologia architettonica', in: Argan, G.C., *Progetto e destino* (Milan 1965).

Bacon, E., *Design of Cities* (London 1967).

Bakker, B., et al., *Het landschap van Rembrandt. Wandelingen door Amsterdam* (Amsterdam 1998), p. 49.

Baltrusaitis, J., *Anamorphic art* (Cambridge 1976).

Banham, R., *Los Angeles:The architecture of four ecologies* (London 1990).

Barlow, E., *The Central Park Book* (New York 1977).

Barlow, E., William A., *Frederick Law Olmsted's New York* (New York 1972).

Barzilay, M., et al., *L'Invention du Parc. Parc de la Villette, Paris. Concours International/International Competition 1982-1983* (Tours 1984).

Beckett, P., Dempster, P., 'Birkenhead Park', in: *Landscape Design*, Nov. 1989.

Bekkers, G., et al., *Ode aan het Vondelpark* (Amsterdam 1997).

Bell, C. en R., *City Fathers. The Early History of Town Planning in Britain* (Harmondsworth 1972) (1969).

Belli Barsali, I., Branchetti, M.G., *Villa della Campagna Romana* (Milan 1981).

Belli Barsali, I., *Ville di Roma* (Milan 1983).

Benedetti, S., *Giacomo Del Duca e l'architettura del Cinquecento* (Rome 1972).

Benevolo, L., *The history of the city* (London 1980).

Benevolo, L., *The Origins of Modern Town Planning*. Vertaling van *Le origine dell'urbanistica moderna* (London 1967).

Berendsen, H.J.A., *Landschap in delen: overzicht van de geofactoren* (Assen 2005).

Bergman, E.E., Poll, T.W., *A Geography of the New York Metropolitan Region* (Dubuque 1975).

Betthausen, P., *Karl Friedrich Schinkel*: with fifteen colour plates and fifty-four black and white plates (Berlin 1986).

Beveridge, Ch.E. (ed), 'Slavery and the South, 1852-1857', in: *The Papers of Frederick Law Olmsted* Volume II (Baltimore 1981).

Beveridge, Ch.E., 'Frederick Law Olmsted's Theory of Landscape Design', in: *Nineteenth Century*,Vol. 3, no. 2 (Summer 1977), pp. 38-43.

Beveridge, Ch.E., Rocheleau, P., *Frederick Law Olmsted. Designing the American Landscape* (New York 1998).

Beveridge, Ch.E., Schuyler, D. (eds.), 'Creating Central Park 1857-1861', in: *The Papers of Frederick Law Olmsted* Volume III (Baltimore 1983).

Bohigas, O., *Barcelona entre el pla Cerdà i el barraquisme* (Barcelona 1963).

Bollerey, F., *De stad in de negentiende en twintigste eeuw. Sociogenese van de moderne stedebouw.* Lecture notes, Faculty of Architecture (at the Technical University Delft. (Delft 1981/1982).

Bone, K. (ed.), *The New York Waterfront. Evolution and Building Culture of the Port and Harbour* (New York 1997).

Bouma, J., 'Inleiding', in: Bouma, J. (red.), *De toekomst van het Nederlands landschap. Wetenschappelijke bijdragen aan de toekomstige landschapskwaliteit* (Amsterdam 2008).

Bournon, F., *Histoire de Paris* (Paris 1977).

Boyceau, J.,*Traité du jardinage selon les raisons de la nature et de l'art* (Paris 1638).

Boyer, Ch., *Manhattan Manners. Architecture and Style 1850-1900* (New York 1985).

Branch Melville, C., *Comparative Urban Design. Rare Engravings 1830-1843* (New York/Los Angeles 1978).

Braudel, F., *On History* (London 1980). Original title: *Écrit sur l'histoire* (Paris 1969).

Burckhardt, L., et al., *Leberecht Migge, 1881-1935. Gartenkultur des 20. Jahrhunderts.* Catalogue exhibition, Worpsweder Verlag (Berlin 1981).

Burns, R., Sanders, J., Ades, L., *New York: an illustrated history* (New York 2003).

Busquets, J., *Barcelona: The Urban Revolution of a Compact City* (Cambridge, Massachusetts 2005).

Buttlar, F. v. (Hrsg.), *Peter Joseph Lenné: Volkspark und Arkadien* (Berlin 1989).

Castex, J., *De architectuur van renaissance, barok en classicisme: een overzicht 1420-1720* (Nijmegen 1993).

Castex, J., Depaule, J.Ch., Panerai Ph., *De rationele stad. Van bouwblok tot wooneenheid* (Nijmegen 1984).

Castex, J., et al., *Lecture d'une ville. Versailles* (Paris 1980).

Caus, S. de, *La perspective avec la raison des ombres et miroirs* (London 1611).

Censer, J.T. (ed.), 'The Civil War and the U.S. Sanitary Commission 1861-1863', in: *The Papers of Frederick Law Olmsted* Volume IV (Baltimore 1986).

Cerdà, I.,*Teoría de la Construcción de las Ciudades. Aplicada al projecto de Reforma y Ensanche de Barcelona* (1859), reproduced in: Cerdà y Barcelona (vol. 1), Instituto Nacional de la Administración Pública i Ajuntament de Barcelona (Madrid 1991).

Cerdà, I.,*Teoría General de la Urbanización. Reforma y Ensanche de Barcelona* (1867), reprinted by the Instituto de Estudios Fiscales (Madrid 1968).

[Cerdà] Generalitat de Catalunya, Department de Política Territorial i Obres Públiques, *Cerdà, Urbs i Territori, Una visió de futur*, Cataleg de la MOSTRA CERDÀ. Urbs i territori (Barcelona 1994).

Chadwick, G.F., 'Paxton's Design Principles for Birkenhead Park', in: *Landscape Design*, maart 1990.

Chadwick, G.F., *The Park and the Town. Public Landscape in the 19th and 20th Centuries* (London 1961).

Chadwick, G.F., *The Works of Sir Joseph Paxton* (London 1961).

Charageat, M., 'André le Nôtre et l'optique de son temps', in: *Bulletin de la Société de l'Histoire de l'Art Français* (np 1955).

Chartier, R., et al., 'Histoire de la France urbaine', in: *La Ville Classique,* t. 3 (np 1981).

Christ, Y., *Le Louvre et les Tuileries* (Paris 1949).

[Cologne] Stadt Köln, *Köln* (Cologne 1979).

[Cologne] Stadt Köln, Stadskaart van Keulen (Cologne 1980).

Connolly, P., 'Embracing openness: Making landscape urbanism landscape architectural: Part 2', in: Raxworthy, J., Blood, J. (eds), *Mesh The Landscapes of Infrastructure* (Melbourne 2004), pp. 200-219.

Cook, C.C., *Description of the New York Central Park.* Reprint of the 1869 edition (New York 1979).

Corpechot, L., *Parcs et Jardins de France (les jardins de l'intelligence)* (Paris 1937).

Cremers, E., Kaaij, F., Steenbergen, C.M., *Bolwerken als stadsparken. Nederlandse stadswandelingen in de negentiende en twintigste eeuw* (Delft 1981).

Davis, T., *John Nash, the Prince Regent's Architect* (London 1966).

Davis, T., Summerson, J., *The Architecture of John Nash* (London 1960).

Descargues, P., *Perspective* (New York 1977).

Desvigne, M., Dalnoky, C., Delluc, M., Marot, S., *The Return of the Landscape* (New York 1997).

Devillers, P., *L'axe de Paris et André le Nôtr,* grand jardinier de France (Paris 1959).

Druon, M., *The History of Paris from Caesar to Saint Louis* (Paris 1963).

Eck, J. van, *De Amsterdamse Schans en de Buitensingel* (Amsterdam 1948).

Eisenman, P., *Diagram Diaries* (London 1999).

Eliot, Ch.W., *Charles Eliot, Landscape Architect.* Reprint of the 1901 edition, with an introduction by Keith N. Morgan. (Amherst 1999).

Emerald Necklace Conservancy, *A guide to the Parks of Boston's Emerald Necklace* (Boston 2011).

Emerson, G.B., *A Report on theTrees and Shrubs Growing Naturally in the Forests of Massachusetts* (Boston 1846).

Engel, H., Velzen, E. van (red.), *De architectuur van de stadsrand. Frankfurt am Main, 1925-1930* (Delft 1987).

Estienne, C., *Praedium Rusticum* (Lutetiae 1554), translated into French in 1564 as *L'Agriculture et maison rustique*, after 1572 with additions by J. Liebault (Paris 1572).

Evenson, N., *Paris, a Century of Change 1878-1978* (New Haven 1979).

Fabos, J.G., Milde, G.T., Weinmayr, V.M., *F.L. Olmsted, Sr.: Founder of Landscape Architecture in America* (Boston 1968).

Fassbinder, H., *Berliner Arbeiterviertel 1800-1918* (Hamburg 1975).

Fein, A. (ed.), *Landscape into Cityscape. Frederick Law Olmsted's Plans for a Greater New York City* (New York 1967).

Fein, A., *Frederick Law Olmsted and the American Environmental Tradition* (New York 1972).

Fischer, M.F., *Fritz Schumacher. Bauten und Planungen in Hamburg* (Hamburg 1994).

Fisher, I.D., *Frederick Law Olmsted and the City Planning Movement in the United States* (Ann Arbor 1976, 1986).

Fouquier, M., *De l'État des Jardins de XVe du XXe siècle* (Paris 1911).

Fox, H.M., *André Le Nôtre, Garden Architect to Kings* (London 1963).

Fraenkel, M., Kistemaker, R. (red.), *Brood, aardappelen en patat. Eeuwen eten in Amsterdam* (Amsterdam/Purmerend 1983), pp. 64-65.

Frecot, J., *Berlin und Potsdam, Architekturphotographien 1872-1875* (München 1980).

Frieling, D.H.,*Veranderende cultuurpatronen.* Lecture notes on the occasion of the 100-anniversary of the Amsterdamse Bureau voor Onderzoek en Statistiek (Amsterdam 1994).

Gaehtgens, T., *Napoleons Arc de Triomphe* (Göttingen 1974).

Galjaard, J., *Bath bijvoorbeeld.* Unpublished study, Faculty of Architecture at the Technical University Delft. (Delft 1983).

Galofaro, L., *Digital Eisenman. An Office of the Electronic Era* (Basel 1999).

Ganay, E. de, *André Le Nostre* (Paris 1962).

Ganay, E. de, *Les jardins de France et leur décor* (Paris 1949).

Gebser, J., 'Ursprung und Gegenwart', in: *Die Fundamente der aperspektivischen Welt*, Bd 1 (Stuttgart 1949).

Geuze, A., 'Accelerating Darwin', in: Smienk, G. (red.), *Nederlandse landschapsarchitectuur. Tussen traditie en experiment* (Amsterdam 1993), pp. 12-22.

Giedion, S., 'Het plan van Sixtus V', in: Brand, J. (red.), *Het idee van de stad* (Arnhem 1983).

Giedion, S., *Space, time and architecture. The growth of a new tradition* (Cambridge, Massachusetts 1941[1], 2008- 5th ed., rev. and enl).

Ginisty, P., *Les anciens boulevards* (Paris 1925).

Giovine, M. di (a cura di), *Guida al verde di Roma* (Rome 1999).

Goecke, M., *Stadtparkanlagen in Industriezeitalter. Das Beispiel Hamburg* (Hannover/(Berlin 1981).

Gotheim, M.L., *A History of Garden Art.* Vol. II (New York 1979).

Grub, H., Lejeune, P., *Grün zwischen Städten. Emscher Landschaftspark, Nordrhein Westfalen. Grüngürtel Frankfurt, Regionalpark RheinMain. Grüne Nachbarschaft Baden-Württemberg* (Munich/New York 1996).

Guidobaldi, P., *The Roman Forum* (Rome 1998).

Günter, H., Harksen, S. (Bearbeiter), Schönemann, H. (Hrsg.), *Peter Joseph Lenné – Katalog der Zeichnungen* (Tübingen/(Berlin 1993).

Güttler, P., *Berlin Brandenburg – Ein Architekturführer* (Berlin 1990).

Hall, P.,*The World Cities* (London 1966).

Hautecoeur, L., *Histoire du Louvre: le château, le palais, le musée des origines à nos jours 1200-1928* (Paris 1940).

Hautecoeur, L., Nolhac, P. de, Vanvest, G., *Histoire des châteaux du Louvre et des Tuileries tels qu'ils furent nouvellement construits* (Paris 1927).

Hazlehurst, F.H., *Gardens of Illusion: the genius of Andre le Nostre* (Nashville 1980).

Heckscher, M.H., *Creating Central Park* (New York 2008).

Heimans, E., Thijsse, J.P., *In het Vondelpark* (Amsterdam 1901).

Heinemeijer, W.F., Wagenaar, M.F., et al., *Amsterdam in kaarten. Veranderingen van de stad in vier eeuwen cartografie* (Ede/Antwerpen 1987).

Hennebo, D., Schmidt. E., *Entwicklung des Stadtgrüns in England.* Geschichte des Stadtgrüns Band III (Hannover, Berlin z.j.).

Hinz, G., *Peter Joseph Lenné – Landschaftsgestalter und Städteplaner.* Musterschmidt (Göttingen 1977).

Hinz, G., *Peter Joseph Lenné. Das Gesamtwerk des Gartenarchitekten und Städteplaners.* 2 dln. (Hildesheim/Zurich/New York 1989).

Hirschfeld, Ch.C.L., *Theorie der Gartenkunst.* 5 dln (Leipzig 1779-1785). Reprint (Hildesheim 1990).

Hogarth, W., *The Analysis of Beauty* (London 1753) (Reprint New Haven 1997).

Hoogewoud, G., Kuyt, J., Oxenaar, A., *P.J.H. Cuypers en Amsterdam, gebouwen en ontwerpen 1860-1898* (The Hague 1985), p. 20.

Howard, R.A., 'The Arnold Arboretum', in: *Plant Science Bulletin, A Publication of the Botanical Society of America, Inc.*, vol 21, nr 2, 1975.

Hulstijn, W., 'Het dagelyksch brood, 1855-1930'. Article in *De Nwe Courant* en de *Nwe Rotterdammer* (1930).

Humboldt, A. von, *Kosmos. Entwurf einer physischen Weltbeschreibung* 5 vol. (1845-1862).

Ibbeken, H., Blauert, E. (Hrsg.), *Karl Friedrich Schinkel: Das architektonische Werk heute = the architectural work today* (Stuttgart 2002).

IFCCA, Prize for the Design of Cities

vol. 1 no. 1. Newspaper (New York 1999).

Institut Français d'Architecture, *Tête Défense, Concours International d'Architecture.* Monographie (Paris 1983).

Jansen, H., (Hrsg.), *Der historische Atlas Köln. 2000 Jahre Stadtgeschichte in Karten und Bildern* (Cologne 2003).

Jellicoe, G., et al., *The Oxford companion to gardens* (Oxford/New York 1986).

Johnston, J., *Frederick Law Olmsted: Partner with Nature* (New York 1975).

Jong, E. de, Reh, W., 'De tuin en de Stad. De Amsterdamse grachtentuin in vogelvlucht', in: *Amsterdamse Grachtentuinen. Keizersgracht* (Amsterdam 1997), p. 29 e.v.

Karling, S., *The French Formal Garden* (Washington 1974).

Kask, T., *Symmetrie und Regelmäßigkeit, Französische Architektur im Grand Siècle* (Basel/Stuttgart 1971).

Kier, H., *Die Kölner Neustadt. Planung, Enstehung, Nutzung* (Düsseldorf 1978).

Kooij, E. van der, et al., *Buiten Plaats, (ont) spanningsveld* (Delft 2000).

Kooij, E. van der, Steenbergen, C.M., *Het Montagelandschap. Het stadspark als actuele ontwerpopgave* (Delft 1991).

Koolhaas, R., 'The Generic Citry', in: Koolhaas, R., Mau, B., Sigler, J., and Werlemann, H., *S, M, L, XL* (Rotterdam 1995).

Koolhaas, R., 'Toelichting bij een prijsvraagontwerp uit 1987 voor Melun-Sénart', in: *Archis*, nr 3, 1989, p. 34.

Kossak, E., 'Wohnquartiere in Hamburg. Zu Entwicklung, Struktur und Gestalt von Gebäudetypen und Quartierseinheiten des inneren Stadtgebietes', in: *Neue Heimat*, 9, 1981.

Kostof, S., *The City Shaped. Urban Patterns and Meanings through History* (London 1999).

Krause, K., 'Topografia antica nell'area della Domus Tiberiana', in: Cazzato, V. (red.), *Gli Orti Farnesiani sul Palatino* (Rome 1990).

Krause, K., et al., *Domus Tiberiana* (Zurich 1985).

Krieger, A., Cobb, D.A., Turner, A. & Bosse, D.C., *Mapping Boston* (Cambridge, Massachusetts 1999).

Lavedan, P., 'Histoire de l'urbanisme', in: *Renaissance et temps modernes*, vol. 2 (Paris 1952).

Lavedan, P., et al., *L'urbanisme à l'époque moderne* (Genève 1982).

Leeman, F., et al., *Anamorfosen* (Cologne 1975).

Leinders, J.J.M., et al., *Geologie rondom plaattektoniek* (Heerlen 1989).

Leupen, B., 'De stad van de jaren negentig, het fragment als strategie', in: *Werk, Bauen + Wohnen*, nr. 3 (Zurich 1990).

Leupen, B., et al., *Ontwerp en analyse* (Rotterdam 1993).

Ligorio, P., *L'Antiquità* (Rome ca. 1560).

Lynch, K., *The Image of the City* (Cambridge, Massachusetts 1960).

Mansbridge, M., *John Nash. A complete catalogue* (Oxford 1991).

Marceca, M.L., 'Reservoir, circulation, residue. J.C.A. Alphand, technological beauty and the green city', in: *30 Lotus International* (1981), pp. 57-79.

Mariage, T., 'L'Univers de Le Nostre et les origines de l'aménagement du territoire', in: *Monuments Historiques*, no. 143, Feb./March 1986.

Marie, A., *Jardins Français Classiques des XVIIe et XVIIIe siècle* (Paris 1949).

Marot, S., 'Het landschap als alternatief', in: Vandermarliere, K. (ed), *Het landschap, vier internationale landschapsontwerpers* (Antwerpen 1995).

May, E., 'Rationalisierung des Bauwesens', in: *Frankfurter Zeitung*, 14 april 1926.

May, E., 'Siedlungspläne – Der Besiedlungsplan für Industriestädte', in: *Schlesisches Heim*, no. 3 (1920).

May, E., 'Städtebau und Wohnungsfürsorge', in: *Süddeutsche Monatshefte*, 24ste jg, nr. 6, pp. 429-431.

May, E., 'Typ und Stil', in: *Schlesisches Heim*, nr. 5 (1924).

May, E., Boehm, H., 'Stadtweiterung mittels Trabanten', in: *Der Städtebau*, nr. 19 (1922).

McLaughlin, Ch.C. (ed.), 'The Formative Years 1822-1852', in: *The Papers of Frederick Law Olmsted* Volume I (Baltimore 1977).

Meijer, H., *De stad en de haven. Stedebouw als culturele opgave. Londen, Barcelona, New York, Rotterdam* (Rotterdam 1996).

Meynen, H., *Die Kölner Grünanlagen* (Düsseldorf 1979).

Migge, L. (mit Dr. Ing. Hahn), 'Bodenproduktive Abfallwirtschaft Wirtschaftliche Stadtsiedlung', in: *Zeitschrift für Kommunalwirtschaft*, 12de jg., nr. 9 (1922).

Migge, L., 'Das wachsende Haus der Stadt-Landsiedlung', in: Wagner, M., *Das wachsende Haus* (Berlin 1932).

Migge, L., 'Der kommende Garten', in: *Die Gartenschönheit*, Märzheft (1927).

Migge, L., 'Dezentralisierungsprobleme der Grosstadt', in: *Die Baugilde* (1927).

Migge, L., 'Die heutige Grünpolitik der Städte', in: *Zeitschrift für Kommunalwirtschaft*, Heft 16 (1925).

Migge, L., 'Essay über Gartengestaltung'. Undated essay found in his estate. In: *Garten und Landschaft*, 10,1982.

Migge, L., 'Grundsätzliches zur Kleingartenpolitik', in: *Der Städtebau*, Heft 10 (1929).

Migge, L., 'Grünpolitik der Stadt Frankfurt am Main', in: *Der Städtebau*, Heft 2 (1929).

Migge, L., 'Kleingarten- und Kleingartenpachtordnung', in: *Kommunale Praxis*, Heft 2/3 (1921).

Migge, L., 'Kritik am Landschaftlichen Park der Jahnhundertwende – heute noch aktuell?', in: *Der Hamburger Stadtpark und die Neuzeit* (1909).

Migge, L., 'Rationalisierung des Gartens', in: *Soziale Bauwirtschaft*, Heft 7 (1926/27).

Migge, L., 'Siedlungswirtschaft', in: *Mitteilungen der Internationalen Siedlerschule*, Heft 1-12, (Worpswede 1923, 1924, 1925, 1926, 1927, 1928, 1929).

Migge, L., 'Städtische Grüngürtel', in: *Die Gartenstadt*, nr. 1 (1925).

Migge, L., 'Stadtlandkultur im neuen Städtebaugesetz', in: *Die Gartenstadt Berlin*, nr. 11 (1925).

Migge, L., 'Versuch den Gartenbau zu industrialisieren', in: *Die Bauwelt*, Heft 12 (1927).

Migge, L., 'Weltstadtgrün – ein Aufruf zur rentablen Grünpolitik', in: *Wasmuths Monatshefte für Städtebau*, Heft 5 (1930), pp. 241 e.v.

Migge, L., *Der Ausbau eines Grüngürtels der Stadt Kiel.* Manuskript (Kiel 1922).

Migge, L., *Deutsche Binnenkolonisation – Sachgrundlagen des Siedlungswesens* (Berlin 1926).

Migge, L., *Die Gartenkunst des 20. Jahrhunderts* (Jena 1913).

Migge, L., *Die wachsende Siedlung nach biologischen Gesetzen* (Stuttgart 1932).

Migge, L., *Jedermann Selbstversorger – eine Lösung de Siedlungsfrage durch neuen Gartenbau* (Jena 1918).

[Migge] Fachbereich Stadt- und Landschaftsplanung der Gesamthochschule Kassel, *Leberecht Migge 1881-1935. Gartenkultur des 20. Jahrhunderts* (Bremen 1980).

Morganti, G., *Gli Orti farnesiani* (Milan 1999), pp. 30-31, 53-54, 58, 63 en 74.

Morini, M., *Atlante di storia dell' Urbanistica* (Milan 1963).

Mostafavi, M., Najle, C., et al., *Landscape Urbanism: A Manual for the Machinic Landscape* (London 2003).

Mumford, L., *The City in History* (New York 1961).

Nassuth, G.A., 'Schijnbare wanorde in de ontwikkeling van stedelijke systemen', in: *Schijnbare chaos.* Study Series Rijksplanologische Dienst (The Hague 1989).

Nehring, D., *Stadtparkanlagen in der erste Hälfte des 19. Jahrhunderts. Ein Beitrag zur Kulturgeschichte des Landschaftsgartens.* Geschichte des Stadtgrüns Band IV (Hannover, (Berlin 1979).

Neutelings, W.J., 'De Ringcultuur', in: *Vlees en Beton*, 10 (Gent 1988).

Neutelings, W.J., et al., 'De transformatie van de Haagse stadsrand. De Randstad als ruimtelijk-programmatisch tapijt', in: Geurtsen, R., *Stadsontwerp in 's-Gravenhage* (Delft 1989).

Newton, N.T., *Design on the Land. The Development of Landscape Architecture (*Cambridge, Massachusetts 1971).

[Nôtre] Societé Nationale d'Horticulture de France, '250 anniversaire de la mort d'André Le Nôtre', in: *Jardins de France*, no. Spécial (Paris 1951).

Nussbaum, Th., 'Der Ideenwettbewerb für die städtebauliche und architektonische Gestaltung eines Fest- und Aufmarschplatzes in Köln am Rhein', in: *Gartenkunst*, Jg. 49 (1936), pp. 59-64.

[Ohlsdorf] Baubehörde Hamburg, *Hauptfriedhof Ohlsdorf im Wandel der Zeit* (Hamburg 1977).

Oldenburger, C.S., 'Het Vondelpark van de Zochers', in: *Tuinjournaal*, Vol. 14, no 4; Revision of lecture of 22-5-1997 (1997).

Oldenburger-Ebbers, C.S., 'De tuinarchitectuur van de Zochers', in: *Groen*, no. 7, (1990), pp. 9-13.

Olmsted Jr., F.L., Kimball, T. (eds.), *Forty Years of Landscape Architecture. Central Park.* Reproduced from the 1928 edition (Cambridge, Massachusetts 1973).

Olmsted Jr., F.L., Kimball, T., *Frederick Law Olmsted: Landscape Architect 1822-1903* (New York 1970).

Olmsted Sr., F.L., *A Journey in the Back Country.* Reprinted from the 1860 edition (Williamstown 1972).

Olmsted Sr., F.L., *Walks and Talks of an American Farmer in England* (1852).

Olmsted, F.L., *A Traveler's Observations on Cotton and Slavery in the American Slave States* (1861).

Olsen, D.J., *Town Planning in London* (New Haven 1964).

Ons Amsterdam, Vol. 29, no. 9 (1977), pp. 251-252.

Pace, P., *Gli acquedotti di Roma e il de acquaeductu di Frontino* (Rome 1983).

[Parc de la Villette] Établissement Public Parc de la Villette, *Parc de la Villette, Concours International* (Paris 1982).

[Parijs] Atelier Parisien d'Urbanisme, *Les Espaces verts de Paris. Situation et Projects* (Paris 1981).

Paul-Lévy, F., *La Ville en Croix* (Paris 1984).

Pechère, R., *Jardins dessinés, grammaire des jardins* (Brussel 1987).

Pinon, P., *Les Plans de Paris* (Paris 2004).

Planungsverband Ballungsraum Frankfurt/Rhein-Main. *Regionalpark Rhein-Main. Der Landschaft einen Sinn, den Sinnen eine Landschaft* (Mainz 2004).

Pohl, N., *Der kommende Stadtpark. Über urbane Grundbefindlichkeiten und die Einmischung der Natur* (Delft 1995).

Préfecture de la région d'Île de France, *Project de Schéma Directeur d'Aménagement et d'Urbanisme de la Region d' Île de France* (Paris 1980).

Price, U., *Essays on the Picturesque.* 3 vols. (Farnborough 1971; reprint London 1810).

Prossek, A., Schneider, H., Wetterbau, B., Wessel, H.A., Wiktorin, D., *Atlas der Metropole Ruhr. Vielfalt und Wandel des Ruhrgebiets im Kartenbild* (Cologne 2009).

Rasmussen, S.E., *London, The Unique City* (London 1937; Cambridge, Mass./London 1982).

Read, S., and Pinilla, C. (ed.), *Visualizing the Invisible: Towards an Urban Space* (Amsterdam 2006).

Ree, P. van der, Smienk, G., Steenbergen, C.M., *Italian Villas and gardens. A corso di disegno* (Amsterdam/Munich/London 1991).

Reed Jr., H.H., Duckworth, S., *Central Park. History and a Guide* (New York 1967, 1972).

[Regent's Park] Architectural Review, The, *Regent's Park* Volume LXII (1927).

Reh, W., 'De derde ontginning', in: Reh, W., Frieling, D.H., Weeber, C., *Delta Darlings* (Delft 2003), pp. 10-39.

Reh, W., 'Het stedelijk landschap als tijd-ruimtestelsel. Naar een architectonisch management van ruimte en tijd', in: *Deltametropool. Tijd als instrument van ordening* (Delft 1999), pp. 90 e.v.

Reh, W., *Arcadia en Metropolis. Het landschapsexperiment van de Verlichting* (Delft 1996).

Reh, W., Steenbergen, C.M., 'Ontwerpend onderzoek en landschapsvorming. Methode, kritiek en perspectief', in: *Drie over Dertig. Ontwerpen aan de zandgronden van Noord- en Midden Limburg* (Maastricht 2003), pp. 138-154.

Reh, W., Steenbergen, C.M., Aten, D., *Zee van Land. De droogmakerij als atlas van de Hollandse landschapsarchitectuur* (Wormerveer 2005).

Reh, W., Steenbergen, C.M., De Zeeuw, P.H., *Landschaps-transformaties. Stedelijke transformaties van het Nederlandse landschap* (Delft 1995).

Reh, W., Steenbergen, C.M., *Stadsparken. De architectuur van het stedelijk landschap. Prototypen van het negentiende en twintigste eeuwse stadspark.* Dictaat Faculteit der Bouwkunde (Delft 1992).

Roever, M. de, 'Wonen buiten de grachtengordel', in: *Ons Amsterdam*, juni 2002, pp. 210-214.

[Rome] CROMA, 'Carta Nolli Digitalizzato', in: Boemi, M.F., Travaglini, C.M., *Roma dall'Alto* (Rome 2006).

Rooijen, M. van, *De wortels van het stedelijk groen* (Breda 1990).

Rosenau, H., *The Ideal City in its Architectural Evolution* (London 1959).

Rosenzweig, R., Blackmar, E., *The Park and the People. A History of Central Park* (Ithaca/London 1992).

Saunders, A., *Regent's Park. A study of the Development of the Area from 1086 to the Present Day* (London 1969).

[Schinkel] Bauakademie der DDR, *K.F. Schinkel – Sein Wirken als Architekt* (Munich 1981).

[Schinkel] *Karl Friedrich Schinkel (1781-1941)*, Catalogue exhibition Altes Museum Berlin 23 October 1980 – 29 March 1981 (Berlin 1981).

Schönemann, H., *Karl Friedrich Schinkel – Charlottenhof, Potsdam-Sanssouci* (Stuttgart/London 2001).

Schumacher, F., *Das Werden einer Wohnstadt.* Reprint of the edition of 1932 (Hamburg 1984).

Schumacher, F., *Ein Volkspark. Dargestellt am Hamburger Stadtpark* (Munich 1928).

Schumacher, F., *Hamburgs Wohnungspolitik von 1818-1919. Ein Beitrag zur Psychologie der Gross Stadt* (Hamburg 1919), p. 30.

Schumacher, F., *Köln – Entwicklungsfragen einer Groszstadt* (Cologne 1923).

Schwarze-Rodrian, M., Bauer, I., Scheuvens, R., Cüppers, J., Luchterhandt, D. (red.), *Masterplan Emscher Landschaftspark* 2010 (Essen 2005).

Sijmons, D., Feddes, F., et al., *Landkaartmos, en andere beschouwingen over het landschap* (Rotterdam 2002).

Slabbers, S., Bosch, J.W., Hamer, J.H., van den, Ulijn, J., *Grote bossen bij Europese steden. Onderzoek naar de landschappelijke kwaliteit van de* bossen Epping Forest, Grunewald en Forêt de Saint Germain (Wageningen 1993).

Sodin, M., Karl Friedrich Schinkel: A Universal Man (New Haven/London, 1991).

Speckter, H., Paris, Städtebau von der Renaissance bis zur Neuzeit (Munich 1964).

Spellman, C., Re-Envisioning Landscape Architecture (Barcelona 2003).

Spies, P., 'Cieraet deser stede. De grachtengordel bewonderd, bedreigd en beschermd', in: Spies, P., Kleijn, K., et al., Het Grachtenboek (Den Haag 1991), p. 20.

Stam, J., 'Het nieuwe Vondelpark zweeft', in: de Volkskrant, 31.03.2010.

Steenbergen C.M., 'Teatro Rustico. The formal strategy and grammar of landscape architecture', in: Modern Park Design. Recent Trends (Amsterdam 1993).

Steenbergen, C.M., Compositie en Strategie. De ontwerpgrammatica van de Nieuwe Hollandse Waterlinie (Delft 2004).

Steenbergen, C.M., De stap over de horizon. Een ontleding van het formele ontwerp in de landschapsarchitectuur (Delft 1990).

Steenbergen, C.M., Jong, E. de, Vlist, E. van der, Eene aangename publieke wandeling. Een schets van historische stads- en singelparken (Zutphen 1997).

Steenbergen, C.M., Kooij, E. van der, Aben, R., Buitenplaats, City-escape (Delft 2000).

Steenbergen, C.M., Kooij, E. van der, et al., Het Montagelandschap. Het stadspark als actuele ontwerpopgave (Delft 1991).

Steenbergen, C.M., Meenks, S., Nijhuis, S.: Ontwerpen met landschap. De

tekening als vorm van onderzoek (Bussum 2008).

Steenbergen, C.M., Reh, W., 'De buitenplaats als een kritisch model voor het metropolitaine landschap', in: Kooij, E. van der, Buiten Plaats (ont)spanningsveld (Delft, 2000), pp. 20-31.

Steenbergen, C.M., Reh, W., 'The composition of new landscapes', in: Steenbergen, C.M., Mihl, H., Reh, W., Aerts, F. (eds.), Architectural Design and Composition (Bussum 2002), pp. 192-207.

Steenbergen, C.M., Reh, W., Architecture and Landscape. The Design Experiment of the Great European Gardens and Landscapes (Basel/Berlin/Boston 2003).

Steenbergen, C.M., Reh, W., Bobbink, I., Parkstad Amsterdam. De voltooiing en transformatie van het moderne landschapsexperiment (Delft 2002).

Steenbergen, C.M., Reh, W., Nijhuis, S., Pouderoijen, M.T., The Polder Atlas of The Netherlands. Pantheon of the Low Lands (Bussum 2009).

Steenbergen, C.M., Zeeuw, P.H. de, Reh, W., m.m.v. Aben, R. (ed): Het montagelandschap. De landschapsarchitectuur van de stad (Delft 1996).

Stevenson, E., Park Maker. A Life of Frederick Law Olmsted (New York 1977).

Stooss, A., 'Die städtebauliche Entwicklung der Stadt Cöln', in: Die Stadt Cöln im ersten Jahrhundert unter Preußischer Herrschaft 1815-1915, heraus. v. der Stadt Cöln, 2. Band (Cologne 1915).

Stübben, J., Der Städtebau. Handbuch der Architektur Teil 4 (Darmstadt 1924).

Summerson, J., Georgian London (London 1988) (1978, 1969, 1962).

Summerson, J., John Nash, Architect to King George IV (London 1949).

Summerson, J., The Life and Works of John Nash, Architect (Cambridge Massachusetts 1980).

Sutton, S.B. (ed.), Civilizing American Cities: Frederick Law Olmsted's Writings on City Landscapes (Cambridge, Massachusetts 1971, 1979).

Tarragó Cid, S., 'Idelfons Cerdà, Teoría de la Construcción de Ciudades, Teoría de la Viabilidad Urbana, neologismos cerdianos', in: Arquitectura, Ciudad y Entorno, Vol 1 nr 3, 2007.

Tate, A., Great City Parks (London 2003).

Taverne, E., 'Amerikaanse Stadsparken oftewel het begin van de moderne stadsplanning', in: Wonen TA/BK, 12, 1973.

Taverne, E., 'Van Pont-Neuf tot Champs Elysées. Het straatbeeld van Parijs 1600-1914', in: De straat, vorm van samenleven (Eindhoven 1972).

Thomas, D., London's Green Belt (London 1970).

Todd, J.E., Frederick Law Olmsted (Boston 1972).

Tomei, M.A., The Palatine (Rome 1998).

[Urban Landscapes] European Community, Vital Urban Landscapes, the vital role of sustainable and accessible urban landscapes (London 2006).

Valentien, O., 'Die Erhaltung der alten Nidda', in: Gartengestaltung (1929).

Vandermarliere, K., et al., Het landschap/The Landscape. Vier internationale landschapsontwerpers/Four international Landscape Designers. Tentoonstellingscatalogus De Singel (Antwerp 1995).

Veldman, M., Dutch Cities. Amsterdam, Rotterdam, The Hague, Utrecht. Interne publicatie (Delft 2005).

[Versailles] Collectif Monum, Monumental 2005 - semestriel 2 -

Dossier Versailles (Paris 2005).

Vidler A., 'The third typology', in: Rational Architecture: the Reconstruction of the European City (Brussel 1978).

Vitruvius, The Ten Books on Architecture. Translation Morris H. Morgan (New York 1960).

[Vondelpark] Stadsdeel Amsterdam Oud Zuid, Vondelpark, renovatie en beheerplan. Naar een duurzaam beheer van een levend rijksmonument (Amsterdam 2001).

Wagner, M., Städtische Freiflächenpolitik (Berlin 1915).

Waldheim, C. (ed.), The Landscape Urbanism Reader (New York 2006).

Weide, A. van der, Steenbergen, C.M., Homan, A., Highrise Belvédère – transformatie van de villa urbana (Delft 2001).

Wennekens, E., Paleis voor Volksvlijt (1864-1929) (Den Haag 1999), p. 27.

West 8, Bureau, De periferie als centrum. Een case-studie naar bos- en landschapsbouw in het stadsgewest Utrecht (Utrecht 1989).

Wheatly, J.B., The Diary of Samuel Pepys 9 dln. (London 1893-1899).

Wigand, H., Entwicklung des Stadtgrüns in Deutschland, zwischen 1890 und 1925 am Beispiel der Arbeiten Fritz Enckes. Geschichte des Stadtgrüns, Band II (Berlin/Hannover 1975).

Willis, P., Charles Bridgeman and the English Landscape Garden (London 1977).

Wimmer, C.A., 'Sichtachsen des Barock in Berlin und Umgebung. Zeugnisse fürstlicher Weltanschauung, Kunst und Jägerlust', in: Berliner Hefte, 2 (Berlin 1985).

Wittkower, R., Architectural Principles in the Age of Humanism (London 1949).

Wolters, R., Stadtmitte Berlin (Tübingen 1978).

Woltjer, J., Steenbergen, C.M., 'Het case study house 22', in: Werkboek Architectuur en Landschap (Delft 1999), pp. 46-59.

Wörner, M., Mollenschott, D., Architekturführer Berlin (Berlin 1989).

Woud, A. van der, Het lege land. De ruimtelijke orde van Nederland 1798-1848 (Amsterdam/Antwerpen 1987), p. 350.

Wright, F.L. The Disappearing City (New York 1932).

Zaitzevsky, C., Frederick Law Olmsted and the Boston Park System (Cambridge, Massachusetts/London 1992).

Zandbelt&vandenBerg Bureau, Paris: L'histoire se répète (Rotterdam 2004).

Zandbelt, D., Rimmelzwaan, M., Atlas of big plans (Delft 2010).

Zeeuw, P.H. de, Reh, W., Steenbergen, C.M., Pantheon der Lage Landen. Grondvormen van het Hollandse landschap (Delft 1994).

http://penelope.uchicago.edu
http://www.archeologia.beniculturali.it/
http://www.cca.qc.ca/prize Website of the International Foundation for the Canadian Centre for Architecture (IFCCA) on the 1999 Design Competition for the Design of Cities.
http://www.historischetuinen.nl/oldenburger/pdf/zocher-online
http://www.iberianature.com
http://www.inghist.nl
http://www.romasegreta.it/acquedotti/acquedotti.htm
http://www.stadtentwicklung.berlin.de/umwelt/stadtgruen/geschichte/index.shtml

Maps and Digital Geographic Data

Corine Land Cover 2000 vector database, European Environment Agency, Copenhagen.
Medium and High resolution National Hydrography Dataset, U.S. Geological Survey.
National Land Cover Data 2001, U.S. Environmental Protection Agency http://www.epa.gov/mrlc/nlcd-2001.html
SRTM 3-arc-second elevation dataset, shaded relief and water mask, NGA/NASA.
U.S. Geological Survey 1/3 and 1 arc-second National Elevation Dataset, http://seamless.usgs.gov

----

http://www.openstreetmap.org
http://www.maps.google.com

Horti Farnesiani, Rome 1556
G.B. Falda, Pianta di Roma (1676).
G.B. Nolli, Nuova Carta di Roma (1768).

"Roma City Map", GeoTraveller, scale 1:13.000.
"ARCHEOMAP", Supplemento n.03 al periodico annuale "La citta' eterna", Registrazione presso il tribunale di Roma n.625/96, Lozzi Roma s.a.s.
IGM (Istituto Geografico Militare) Serie Topografica d'Italia serie 25/DB. Around 2000.
IGM (Istituto Geografico Militare) DTM (matrix data).
Comune di Roma, Carta Tecnica Regionale.
'Carta Topografica d'Italia, scala 1:25.000, Foglio nr. 374 SEZIONE III, Roma Sud-Ovest', Serie 25DB, Edizione 1, I.G.M. (1996-1999)

SIDRO (Sistema Interattivo Idrografico), Carta Idrografica Nazionale.
SIT (Sistema Informativo Geografico), cartografia on-line 2D: Agricoltura e vegetazione (Carta Agroforestale Camera di Commercio), Idrografia e acque interne, Mobilita' e trasporti, Beni culturali (Sistema storico).
http://www.it.wikipedia.org
http://www.romeartlover.it
http://www.archeoroma.com

Jardin des Tuileries, Paris 1664
Carte des Chasses du Roi des Environs de Versailles (1764-1773).

BDALTI 50m, IGN (Institut Géographique National), Paris.
Carte topographique TOP25. IGN (Institut Géographique National), Paris. Around 2000.

Service Géologique National, Orléans, Carte géologique de la France a l'échelle du millionième, 6e édition révisé, 2003.

Regent's Park, London 1811
William Lithgow A Plan of the City and Suburbs of LONDON as fortified by Order of PARLIAMENT in the Years 1642 & 1643.
Map of London 1746.
James Crew's Survey 1753.
Plan Regent's Street, Nash 1814.
Plan Charing Cross, Nash 1826.
Plan St. James's Park, Nash 1828.
Regent's Park, Nash 1828.

OS Explorer Map 1:25.000, Ordnance Survey, Southampton. Around 2000.
Land-Form PROFILE, Ordnance Survey, 2005.

The Gartenreich of Potsdam-Berlin 1826
Neuer geometrischer Stadtplan. J.C. Rhoden, 1772.
Großer Stadtplan von Feldmarschall Graf von Schmettau, 1748.
[Untitled]. Johann Friedrich von Balbi, 1748.
Verschönerungsplan der Umgebung von Potsdam; P.J. Lenné, 1833.
Berlin. Published under the superintendence of the Society for the Diffusion of Useful Knowledge. Drawn by W.B. Clarke, Archt. Engraved & printed by J. Henshall. Published by Baldwin & Cradock, 47 Paternoster Row, Augt. 1. 1833. (London: Chapman & Hall, 1844). David Rumsey Historical Map Collection, http://www.davidrumsey.com.
Projectirte Schmuck und Grenzzüge v. Berlin mit nächsten Umgegend bearbeitet von den Kon. Garten Director P.J.Lenné 1840.
Karte von der Halbinsel Potsdam, 1842 en 1869; P.J. Lenné.

Quadrat-Meilen um Berlin. C. Delius, around 1870.

Topographische Karte en Topographische Stadtkarte 1:25.000, Landesvermessungsamt Brandenburg. Around 2000.
GIS-data, Senatsverwaltung für Stadtentwicklung Berlin.
Bundeswasserstrassenkarte mit der Gliederung der Wasser- und Schifffartsverwaltung des Bundes (DBWK 1000) Bundesministerium für Verkehr, Bau und Stadtentwicklung, Regensburg 2009.
Digitale Bundeswasserstrassenkarte 1:500.000 (DBWK 500) Wasser- und Schifffartsverwaltung des Bundes / Wasser- und Schifffahrtsditektion Ost, Berlijn 2005.

----

http://www.spsg.de

Central Park, New York 1857
Commissioners' Plan of New York City, 1811.
Topographical Map Of The City and County Of New - York, and the adjacent Country: With Views in the border of the principal Buildings and interesting Scenery of the Island. Published By J.H. Colton & Co. No. 4 Spruce St. New-York. 1836. Engraved & Printed by S. Stiles & Company, New-York. 1836, by J.H. Colton & Co. New York. David Rumsey Historical Map Collection, http://www.davidrumsey.com
"New-York" from Tanner, H.S. The American Traveller; or Guide Through the United States. Eighth Edition. New York, 1842. www.lib.utexas.edu/maps/new_york.html
Map of the Hudson River Rail Road trom New York to Albany. N[ew] Y[ork], c1848. Library of Congress, Washington D.C. http://memory.loc.gov/ammem/index.html
Map of the City of New York Extending Northward to Fiftieth St. Surveyed and drawn by John F. Harrison C.E. Published by M. Dripps... 1852. David Rumsey Historical Map Collection, http://www.davidrumsey.com
Atlas of the entire city of New York. Complete in one volume. From actual surveys and official records by G.W. Bromley & Co., civil engineers. Published by Geo. W. Bromley & E. Robinson. 82 & 84 Nassau St., New York. 1879. Entered ... 1879, by G.W. Bromley & Co., ... Washington. Engraved by A.H. Mueller, Walnut St., Philadelphia. Printed by F. Bourquin, S. Sixth St., Philadelphia. David Rumsey Historical Map Collection, http://www.davidrumsey.com
Coast Chart No. 20 New York Bay And Harbor, New York. From a Trigonometric Survey under the direction of A.D. Bache Superintendent of the Survey Of The Coast Of The United States ... Published in 1866. Verified J.E. Hilgard Assist. Coast Survey In charge of Office. Electrotype Copy No. 3 by G. Mathiot U.S.C.S. Redd. Drng. by E. Hergesheimer, M.H. McClery and A. Balbach. Engd. by J. Enthoffer, J. Knight, H.S. Barnard

and J.C. Kondrup. David Rumsey Historical Map Collection, http://www.davidrumsey.com
"New York - 1880 Parks" From Report on the Social Statistics of Cities, Compiled by George E. Waring, Jr., United States. Census Office, Part I, 1886. www.lib.utexas.edu/maps/new_york.html
Atlas of the city of New York. Manhattan Island. From actual surveys and official plans by Geo. W. & Walter S. Bromley, civil engineers. Published by G.W. Bromley & Co., 120 Nth. Seventh St., Philadelphia. 1891. Engraved by Rudolph Spiel, 30 N. Fifth St., Phila. Printed by F. Bourquin, 31 S. Sixth St., Phila. David Rumsey Historical Map Collection, http://www.davidrumsey.com
Beers, F. W. (Frederick W.); Watson, Gaylord, Map of New York, Brooklyn, Jersey City &c. Published by Gaylord Watson, 278 Pearl Street, New York. 1891. David Rumsey Historical Map Collection, http://www.davidrumsey.com

----

U.S. Geological Survey 1:24.000 Digital Raster Quadrangles, New York State GIS Clearinghouse, http://www.nysgis.state.ny.us
U.S. Geological Survey 1:24.000 Digital Raster Quadrangles, New Jersey Geological Survey, http://www.state.nj.us/dep/njgs/geodata/
National Atlas, Streams and Waterbodies. http://www.nationalatlas.gov/

----

http://en.wikipedia.org/wiki/Frederick_Law_Olmsted

Eixample, Barcelona 1859
Plan of the city of Barcelona for Mr. Tindal's continuation of Mr. Rapin's History of England ; J. Basire sculp. 1745. Institut Cartogràfic de Catalunya.
I. Cerdà, Plano de los Alrededores de la ciudad de Barcelona levantado por orden del gobierno para la formacion del proyecto de ensanche, 1855.
Cerdà, Ildefons (1859) Plano de los alrededores de la ciudad de Barcelona - Proyecto de Reforma y Ensanche.

Montserrat Galera, Francesc Roca, Salvador Tarrago, Atlas de Barcelona (Siglos XVI-XX), Publicaciones del Colegio Oficial de Arquitectos de Cataluna y Baleares, 1972.
Institut Cartogràfic de Catalunya, Mapa topografia de Catalunya 1:10.000, first edition 1999–2000.
Institut Cartogràfic de Catalunya, Direcció General del Medi Natural, Mapa dels hàbitats a Catalunya 1:50.000.
Model d'elevacions del terreny 30x30m, Institut Cartogràfic de Catalunya 2000.
Design sketch of Daniel Freixes and Vicente Miranda for the Parque del Clot, Ajuntament de Barcelona.

----

www.tmb.cat (Transports Metropolitans de Barcelona)
http://www.proeixample.cat/1000/1400.html (ProEixample)
http://www.bcn.es/parcsijardins/cat/parcs/pa_mapa.html (Parcs i Jardins, Ajuntament de Barcelona).

Vondelpark, Amsterdam 1865
Topografische en Militaire Kaart van het Koningrijk der Nederlanden 1850-1864.
Kaart van Amsterdam | met Kadastrale indeeling der Perceelen | Zamengesteld en geteekend door | A.J. Van Der Stok senior, | gepens[ioneer] d Hoofd opzichter bij de Publieke Werken der Gemeente | uitgegeven door J.C. Loman Jr. en Scheltema en Holkema | Amsterdam. [1881]. Uitgave in 4 bladen, schaal 1:3.750. GAA Z 505-8 t/m 11, GAA Z 505-12 t/m 15.
Kaart van Amsterdam | Bewerkt door het 1e Hoofdbureau der Afdeeling Publieke Werken | ingevolge de Opdracht van burgemeester en Wethouders | dd 13 october 1896. | 1900 | schaal 1:3.750 | 12 bladen | Bewerkt door H.J. Scheltema. GAA Z 301-1 through 12, GAA Z 301-13 through 24 (on linen).

NWB (Nationaal Wegenbestand). Adviesdienst Verkeer en Vervoer, Rijkswaterstaat. Around 2000.
TOP10vector, Topografische Dienst, Emmen. Around 2000.
Digitale Grootschalige Basiskaart Amsterdam.
TOP25raster, Topografische Dienst, Emmen. Around 2000.
Omegam Geotechniek i.o.v. deelgemeneente Oud-Zuid, 1996.

----

http://www.amsterdam.nl.
http://www.gisdro.nl/groensite
http://www.dewoonomgeving.nl (Kadastrale Minuutbladen).

Emerald Necklace, Boston 1876
Reproduction of a 1775 map of Boston (32723, 12/7/92), courtesy of the Boston Public Library Print Department.
Boynton, George W., Plan of Boston With parts of the Adjacent Towns. Boston Bewick Company, 1835. http://www.flickr.com/photos/normanbleventhalmapcenter
Map of the Metropolitan District of Boston Massachusetts Showing the existing public reservations and such new Open Spaces as are proposed by Charles Eliot, Landscape Architect in his report to the Metropolitan Park Commission Dated January 2nd 1893. (Boston Public Library, Norman B. Leventhal Map Center, G3764.B6E63 1893.W3)

USGS Topographic Quadrangle Images - December 1995, June 2001, Office of Geographic and Environmental Information (MassGIS), Commonwealth of

Massachusetts Executive Office of Environmental Affairs.
Vector data layers, Office of Geographic and Environmental Information (MassGIS), Commonwealth of Massachusetts Executive Office of Environmental Affairs. Around 2000.

Stadtpark Hamburg 1902
Topographische Karte 1: 25 000. Landesbetrieb Geoinformation und Vermessung, Hamburg. Around 2000.
Digitales Geländemodell 25m (DGM25), Landesbetrieb Geoinformation und Vermessung, Hamburg 2009.
Digitales Geländemodell 25m (DGM25), Landesvermessungsamt Schleswig-Holstein, Kiel 2009.
Digitales Geländemodell 25m (DGM25), Landesvermessung und Geobasisinformation Niedersachsen, Hannover 2009.

----

http://fhh.hamburg.de/stadt/Aktuell/behoerden/stadtentwicklung-umwelt/stadtplanung/landschafts-planung/gruenes-netz/start.html

The Nidda Valley, Frankfurt 1925
Matthäus Merian, Frankfurt am Main, 1645.

Topographische Karte 1: 25 000. Hessische Verwaltung für Bodenmanagement und Geoinformation, Wiesbaden. Around 2000.
Digitales Geländemodell (DGM10). Hessische Verwaltung für Bodenmanagement und Geoinformation, Wiesbaden, 2010.

The Grüngürtel, Cologne 1925
Digitales Basis-Landschaftsmodell (Basis-DLM). Bundesamt für Kartographie und Geodäsie, Frankfurt am Main, 2006.
Digitales Geländemodell 50m (DGM50), Bezirksregierung Köln, 2006.

----

http://www.geoserver.nrw.de/

Metropolitan landscape architecture
Landsat 7 ETM+ false color satellite image, NASA
Inland Waters, Seas and Estuaries, and Census 2000 layers from California Spatial Information Library (CaSIL), http://www.atlas.ca.gov/
Digitales Basis-Landschaftsmodell (Basis-DLM). Bundesamt für Kartographie und Geodäsie, Frankfurt am Main. Around 2000.
Spörhase map of the Ruhr region on cd-rom. Bibliothek Regionalverband Ruhr, Essen.

----

http://www.elp2010.de (Masterplan Emscher Landschaftspark 2010)

About the authors

CLEMENS M. STEENBERGEN (b. 1946) is a landscape architect and was Professor of Landscape Architecture on the Faculty of Architecture at the Technical University Delft from 1993 to 2011. He has published extensively on architecture and landscape architecture. His dissertation *De stap over de horizon* (1990) comprises an analysis of the rational design of the Italian Renaissance villa and the formal design of the French Baroque garden.

WOUTER REH (b. 1938) is a landscape architect and was Senior University Lecturer at the Faculty of Architecture at the Technical University Delft from 1994 to 2003, and after that also continued to be active there as a researcher. He has written widely on landscape architecture, urban development and planning. His dissertation *Arcadia en Metropolis* (1996) discusses the anatomy of picturesque landscape design, as it took form in the development of the English landscape garden.

Since 1984 the two authors have been working together on research into the foundations, instruments and techniques of landscape architecture. In 2003 the results of their two decades of fundamental design research were published by THOTH Publishers as *Architecture and Landscape: The Design Experiment of the Great European Gardens and Landscapes,* in both a Dutch and English edition.

Other books, publications and design studies they have written involve the design of the Dutch country estate and the design of the water and polder landscapes and polder cities in the west of The Netherlands. Important milestones were *Sea of Land: The Polder as an Atlas of Dutch Landscape Architecture* and *The Polder Atlas of The Netherlands: Pantheon of the Low Lands*, which appeared in 2005 and 2009, respectively, in both Dutch and English editions. A separate study on the role of the drawing as a research instrument in landscape architecture appeared in book form in 2008 under the title *Composing Landscapes: Analysis, Typology and Experiments for Design.* This also appeared in simultaneous Dutch and English editions.

METROPOLITAN LANDSCAPE ARCHITECTURE – Urban Parks and Landscapes is the pinnacle of a long series of studies on urban landscape architecture and the final piece in the studies deepening the understanding of landscape architecture as a design discipline which the two authors have produced.

METROPOLITAN LANDSCAPE ARCHITECTURE is a research project of the Chair of
Landscape Architecture in the Faculty of Architecture at the Technical University Delft.

Delft University of Technology

The publication was made possible in part by financial support from
the Netherlands Architecture Fund

CONCEPT, RESEARCH AND TEXT
Clemens M. Steenbergen, PhD
Wouter Reh, PhD

RESEARCH CONTRIBUTIONS AND DRAWINGS
Eelco Dekker (Boston)
Lonneke van den Elshout (London)
Susanne Hoekstra (Barcelona)
Stephanie Holtappels (Amsterdam, Berlin, Hamburg, Frankfurt, Cologne, Duisburg)
Bastiaan Kwast (Vondelpark, spatial models of Paris, London, Potsdam, Central Park,
    the Boston Park System, Stadtpark Hamburg and the Nidda Valley, Frankfurt)
Michiel T. Pouderoijen (Amsterdam, Randstad Holland, Boston, Los Angeles, all maps of
    the geomorphology and the urban domain)
Hans Stotijn (Paris)
Fabiana Toni (Rome: Horti Farnesiani, Barcelona: Parque del Clot)
Mark Veldman (Tokyo)
Cindy Wouters (New York, Central Park)
Danielle Wijnen (Manhattan, Central Park)

FINAL EDITING OF DRAWN MAPS Michiel T. Pouderoijen

MAP AND PICTURE RESEARCH Michiel T. Pouderoijen

DESK EDITING Wim Platvoet (THOTH Publishers)

TRANSLATION Words & Pictures, Rotterdam

GRAPHIC DESIGN Studio Hans Lemmens, Amsterdam

PRINTING Bema-Graphics, Wommelgem

BINDING Boekbinderij Van Waarden, Zaandam

ISBN 978 90 6868 591 6